DYING TO BE MEN

The Routledge Series on Counseling and Psychotherapy with Boys and Men

SERIES EDITOR

Mark S. Kiselica

The College of New Jersey

ADVISORY BOARD

VOLUMES IN THIS SERIES

DYING TO BE MEN

Psychosocial, Environmental, and Biobehavioral Directions in Promoting the Health of Men and Boys

Will H. Courtenay

Routledge
Taylor & Francis Group
New York   London

Routledge
Taylor & Francis Group
270 Madison Avenue
New York, NY 10016

Routledge
Taylor & Francis Group
27 Church Road
Hove, East Sussex BN3 2FA

Printed in the United States of America on acid-free paper
10 9 8 7 6 5 4 3 2 1

International Standard Book Number: 978-0-415-87875-3 (Hardback) 978-0-415-87876-0 (Paperback)

Library of Congress Cataloging-in-Publication Data

Courtenay, William.
 Dying to be men : psychosocial, environmental, and biobehavioral directions in promoting the health of men and boys / William Courtenay.
     p. ; cm.
 Includes bibliographical references and index.
 Summary: "Men have specific gender-related influences that can affect their health and psychological well-being, and it is thus necessary for mental health practitioners to be knowledgeable in effective interventions for working with them. The purpose of this book is to provide a thorough foundation for understanding men health and risks and the differences between men. It will discuss effective, evidence-based strategies for practitioners to improve the health and well being of boys and men by drawing from a wealth of literature and research in a diverse array of disciplines, as well as from the authors original research designed specifically to examine gender and men's health"--Provided by publisher.
   ISBN 978-0-415-87875-3 (hardcover : alk. paper) -- ISBN 978-0-415-87876-0 (pbk. : alk. paper)
   1. Men--Health and hygiene. 2. Health behavior. I. Title.
   [DNLM: 1. Men's Health--United States. 2. Health Behavior--United States. 3. Health Promotion--methods--United States. 4. Health Status--United States. 5. Masculinity--United States. WA 306]
 RA564.83.C68 2010
 613'.04234--dc22   2010037177

Visit the Taylor & Francis Web site at
http://www.taylorandfrancis.com

and the Routledge Web site at
http://www.routledgementalhealth.com

To my kids, Justine and Tate
I love you more than words can express.
I hope the world continues to open its
gendered borders, so you can live and
work and play as freely as you like.

Contents

Series Editor's Foreword

Although traditional men are socialized to be providers for and protectors of others, they tend to be poor guardians of their own health. Compared to women, men are less likely to get routine physicals, and when they feel sick or are injured, men are more likely to ignore their symptoms and less likely to seek medical care (Arias, Anderson, Kung, Murphy, & Kochanek, 2003; Sandman, Simantov, & An, 2000). Similarly, when faced with emotional distress, men are less likely than women to seek professional assistance with their mental health concerns (Addis & Mahalik, 2003). Men are also more likely than women to engage in a host of health risk behaviors (e.g., smoking, substance abuse, drinking and driving, and poor diets) that are associated with a variety of diseases, injuries, and death (Courtenay, 2001).

Health experts consider the propensity of men to ignore their health needs, take risks, and have unhealthy lifestyles to play a key role in some adverse health outcomes in men. Consider just a few, related, alarming statistics. Rates of heart disease, cancer, stroke, and HIV/AIDS are higher for men than women (Men's Health Network, 2010). Men are more likely than women to suffer accidental injuries, work-related and fireworks-related injuries and deaths, unintentional drowning, motor-vehicle deaths, death by homicide, and suicide (Centers for Disease Control and Prevention, 2010). Moreover, life expectancy is 5.1 years shorter for men than women (Centers for Disease Control and Prevention, 2010). Many of these injuries, illnesses, and deaths could be prevented and the life span of males could be extended if men changed their attitudes about their lifestyles and about seeking help and talking with health care professionals.

Over the past 20 years, my attempts to study and understand health-related difficulties of men consistently took me to the work of Dr. Will Courtenay, a dedicated and passionate advocate for men and their health needs. Recognizing that Dr. Courtenay is also an accomplished scholar of men's health issues, I reached out to him, hoping that he would contribute his impressive expertise on the topic to *The Routledge Series on Counseling and Psychotherapy with Boys and Men.* Eager to synthesize his wide body of work on the subject, Dr. Courtenay enthusiastically agreed to compose *Dying to Be Men: Psychosocial, Environmental, and Biobehavioral Directions in Promoting the Health of Men and Boys* for this series. I am so glad that he did!

In *Dying to Be Men,* Dr. Courtenay takes us into the world of boys and men, alerting us to the troubling fact that too many males are killing themselves, sometimes slowly over the course of a lifetime through a series of poor lifestyle choices contributing to the development of life-threatening illnesses, and at other times, abruptly through impulsive risk taking, violent encounters, and suicide. Dr. Courtenay summarizes what is known about gender differences in diseases, accidents, and mortality, and he discusses the attitudes and behaviors that place males at risk for injury, illness, and death, including the role of masculine ideology in men's health. He provides a comprehensive analysis of the medical and psychological problems experienced by boys and men across the life span, and he offers gender-sensitive interventions for addressing these problems. No doubt, the wealth of information provided in this book can help all health care providers to enhance their efforts to promote the well-being of boys and men. I am deeply grateful for this information, and I am pleased and honored to have Dr. Courtenay's fine work as a volume in this series.

REFERENCES

Addis, M. E., & Mahalik, J. R. (2003). Men, masculinity, and the contexts of help-seeking. *American Psychologist, 58,* 5–14.

Arias, E., Anderson, R. N., Kung, H. C., Murphy, S. L., & Kochanek, K. D. (2003). Deaths: Final data for 2001. *National Vital Statistics Reports, 52*(3). Hyattsville, MD: National Center for Health Statistics.

Centers for Disease Control and Prevention. (2010). *Men's health at CDC.* Retrieved November 7, 2010, from http://www.cdc.gov/Features/MensHealthatCDC

Courtenay, W. H. (2001). Counseling men in medical settings: The six-point HEALTH plan. In G. R. Brooks & G. E. Good (Eds.), *The new handbook of psychotherapy and counseling with men: A comprehensive guide to settings, problems, and treatment approaches* (pp. 59–91). San Francisco, CA: Jossey-Bass.

Men's Health Network. (2010). *Men's health facts.* Retrieved November 7, 2010, from http://www.menshealthnetwork.org/library/menshealthfacts.pdf

Sandman, D., Simantov, E., & An, C. (2000). *Out of touch: American men and the health care system.* New York: Commonwealth Fund.

Mark S. Kiselica, Series Editor
The Routledge Series on Counseling and Psychotherapy
with Boys and Men
The College of New Jersey

Acknowledgments

This book and the ideas it contains have developed over many years. Consequently, its creation is the result of input and assistance from innumerable people. As much as I would like to recognize the contributions of everyone, most of these people must necessarily remain unnamed: They approached me after a talk I gave and shared incisive thoughts; they commented anonymously on a manuscript under peer review and offered me critical feedback; and they attended my trainings and proffered thoughtful reflections about their own hands-on experiences working with men. The fact is, a book of this scope could not be written without the contributions—in all their various forms—of countless people to whom I feel indebted. I will take this opportunity to express my gratitude to a small number of these people, many of whom supported my work long before the topic of men's health sold magazines.

First, I want to recognize those who—most tangibly—made this book possible. I am much indebted to Mark S. Kiselica, the book series editor, who graciously invited me to join a long list of esteemed scholars and authors who have contributed to *The Routledge Series on Counseling and Psychotherapy with Boys and Men*. His warmth and grace, and diligence, was welcomed and deeply reassuring throughout the process of authoring this work. I'm also indebted to my editors at Taylor and Francis, Dana Bliss and Christopher Tominich, for their guidance in shepherding this project from its earliest stages all the way through to its completion.

I am especially grateful to those friends and colleagues who have coauthored chapters of this book: Don Sabo, Don McCreary, Michael Addis, Abigail Mansfield, Joseph Merighi, and Deborah Saucier. I am grateful not only for their contributions to this book but also for their intellects, energy, enthusiasm, time, and friendship. Each of these coauthors has deeply influenced my thinking and my work in their own unique and personal way. I am particularly grateful to Don and Don, who are both long-term friends and collaborators. An enormous debt of gratitude goes to Don Sabo, who has been my strongest—and fiercest—mentor, and who is also a great guy. When I was a young researcher, Don was the first seasoned scholar to take me under his wing, and like a great mentor, "Sabo" always seemed to be more concerned about my work than his own. His unwavering support and collaboration throughout the years have been an incredible boon to both my spirit and my work. I am also deeply indebted to Don McCreary. Apart from being the consummate statistician for most of the quantitative research and analysis my work has required and continues to require—which is enormously valuable in its own right—he also has been an incredibly important and patient teacher, an absolutely dedicated and delightful colleague, and a great buddy. In terms of friends and colleagues, they simply don't get any better than Don and Don.

I am also deeply grateful to my former colleagues at Harvard Medical School, McLean Hospital, particularly William Pollack. His encouragement throughout the years, as well as his support in the endeavor we share helping men, has been—and remains—invaluable. I am especially thankful for his continued collaboration with me through the Center for Men and Young Men at McLean Hospital, where he is Director. I am similarly grateful to my former colleagues at the University of California, San Francisco, especially Bill Shore in the Department of Family and Community Medicine, who has demonstrated steadfast support for addressing the health needs of men and boys.

I want to extend my warmest thanks to the members of the Society for the Psychological Study of Men and Masculinity (Division 51 of the American Psychological Association), including Ron Levant, past president of the American Psychological Association, Mark S. Kiselica, Bill Pollack, Joe Pleck, Glenn Good, Gary Brooks, Jim O'Neil, Michael Addis, Jim Mahalik, Don McCreary, Chris Kilmartin, Aaron Rochlin, Dan Quinn, and many others. These men have supported my work and me personally for over a decade, and are a constant source of intellectual inspiration.

Like so many other scholars who have studied and written about masculinity, men, fathers, and boys over the past several decades, I am deeply indebted to Jim Doyle at Men's Studies Press, who since 1992 has been independently publishing, disseminating, and promoting our work (besides being a published scholar on this subject himself). It was Jim who, in 1999, had the prescience to conceive of the first professional journal of men's health and approached me to serve as its first editor. In his own quiet, determined way, Jim—and his tireless dedication to men's studies—has truly transformed the way social scientists and other professionals understand, study, and help men and boys.

I also want to offer my deepest gratitude to those who enabled me to develop and apply my work throughout the years; to all the clinicians, researchers, scholars, and health professionals who have always encouraged me and believed in my research on a subject relatively few scholars examine, particularly at a time when men's health was not yet considered a legitimate field of specialization, and when there was little cultural or social support for studying the subject. I am especially grateful to the professionals in the fields of higher education, family planning, and public health throughout the United States who had the foresight to see the value of addressing men's health. Although there are far too many health professionals to thank personally, I do want to extend special thanks to Richard Keeling and Gar Kellom, who have both provided extensive support to me in reaching other health professionals in higher education. I also want to express similar gratitude to Susan Moskosky, Director for the Federal Office of Family Planning, who invited me to provide numerous trainings on men's sexual and reproductive health to providers nationally, and to Marsha Gelt at the Center for Health Training in Oakland, who has enlisted me to do similar trainings in California. In the field of public health, I want to extend my thanks to Irvienne Goldson at Action for Boston Community Development; John Rich at the Drexel University School of Public Health; Owen Borda, who served the New York Public Health Department for decades; and Larry Cohen at Prevention Institute in Oakland. Each of these individuals has been a staunch supporter of me throughout the years and has given me strength in my pursuits. Irvienne Goldson, in particular, enabled me to put many of my ideas and intervention strategies into action in serving men of color in Boston for nearly a decade. Irvienne's undaunted dedication to her community is extraordinary and I am convinced the men in Boston are living longer and healthier lives as a result of her efforts.

I want to extend deep and heartfelt thanks to Irene Elmer, who for nearly 20 years has been and remains my copyeditor. Besides being a lovely person, she has quite diligently made certain that my modifiers are never misplaced and that my participles have not been left dangling. I am deeply indebted to Irene for her conscientious attention to—quite literally—my every word. I must also express my deep gratitude to Sally Douglas Arce, my publicist, who for nearly 20 years has very effectively helped me to get my messages about men's health out to the public, while also being a wonderful person to work with. I also want to extend special thanks to Kathryn Day, who gratefully appeared during the last year at the 11th hour to help out as my research assistant. Although she was finalizing her dissertation at the time, she enthusiastically embraced the work of this book as if it were her own. Her assistance during this time was invaluable.

Because much of this book has been previously published in various forms, I would also like to extend my thanks to the countless social scientists, colleagues from various disciplines, reviewers, journal editors, and book publishers who have provided critical feedback to me on earlier versions of this work. Over the years, they have all contributed to strengthening my critical thinking, my research, and my writing. Similarly, I wish to acknowledge my tremendous debt to the many researchers and scholars who preceded me in the field of women's health. Their work was truly foundational for me and also crucial to the development of my feminist perspectives on men's health.

Of course, no book can be written without the strong support of family and friends, and this one is no exception. The list of friends who have supported me and my work throughout the years is—gratefully— quite extraordinary. I wish I could include every one of you here, but I trust you know how important you are to me and how I value both your friendship and the support you have provided to me.

Lucian Burg and Mark Swanson are the best friends a guy could ever have; they have had my back for decades and I love them both deeply. Their wives, my dearest friends Marie Pollard and Claudia Sieber, are family to me and their enduring support and love—and especially their frank opinions over many years—have been invaluable to me. I am also deeply indebted and grateful to Lucian, in particular, for his labor of love in designing the evocative (we might say "haunting") cover for this book.

Deep and heartfelt thanks also go to my kids Tate and Justine, who, for the most part, good-naturedly endured my all-too-frequent recent absences while I was completing this book, and to my wife and partner of 20 years, Amy Huang, whose love has been a constant in my life. Amy always keeps me honest, and thankfully never hesitates to point out when I'm being a "men's health hypocrite!"

I also want to express deep gratitude to my father and late mother. I am especially grateful for their enduring unconditional love and steadfast commitment to me, despite my innumerable gender transgressions throughout my life. The foundation they provided for me has remained my bedrock.

Introduction

Twenty years ago, when I began researching and writing about men's health at the University of California at Berkeley, men in the United States were dying more than 7 years younger than women. It was a time when "men's health" was really nothing more than an oxymoron. The gender gap in longevity, however, was not new; it had been steadily widening since 1920, when women and men in the United States lived lives that were equal in length. But when I conducted training sessions about improving men's health, physicians and other health professionals were consistently shocked to learn of this gap in the life spans of women and men, as well as other gender differences in health and health-related attitudes and behaviors. With few exceptions, these gender differences were also largely unknown to—or ignored by—other health scientists.

The gender gap in longevity has finally begun to narrow. Today men die 5 years younger than women. And today *Men's Health* magazine is the top-selling magazine in the United States—and the largest men's magazine in the world, with 10 million readers in 39 countries. The subject of men's health has also finally captured the attention of medical communities and health scientists—as well as policy makers and governments around the world, including in Australia, the United Kingdom, Austria, and Switzerland. Most of these changes have occurred during the past decade. In 2000, I served as guest editor for a special issue of the *Journal of American College Health* (Courtenay & Keeling, 2000b). This was the first time a professional or medical journal devoted an entire issue to the subject of men's health. Since then, special issues on men's health have appeared in journals of other organizations and disciplines, including public health (Treadwell, 2003) and sociology (Annandale & Riska, 2009). Similarly, when I became the founding editor of the *International Journal of Men's Health* in 2001, it was the only professional or academic journal on the subject. Today there are three such professional journals of men's health internationally. Men's sexual and reproductive health is also increasingly being addressed—and acknowledged as a necessary step in improving the sexual and reproductive health of women. For several years during the past decade, I served as consultant to the federal government's Office of Family Planning in its first attempts to train health educators nationally in providing sexual and reproductive health and family planning services to men. Similar efforts are now being made in Africa, Central America, South America, and parts of Asia.

As a result of these efforts and cultural shifts, men are increasingly adopting healthy lifestyles and living longer lives. However, gender differences in health-related behavior, chronic illness, severe disease, and death persist, so that women still outpace men in health and longevity. Consequently, I continue to ask myself the same question that first motivated my work 20 years ago: "*Why* do men and boys suffer more disease and disability, and die younger, than women and girls?"

In this book, I propose gender-specific approaches for answering that question, and for improving the physical and mental health of men and boys, which incorporate sociocultural, psychological, biological, environmental, behavioral, and structural factors. These approaches are consistent with the national health promotion and disease prevention initiative in the United States, referred to as *Healthy People 2010* (Department of Health and Human Services [DHHS], 2000c). One of its primary goals is to eliminate health disparities. The National Institutes of Health defines populations with health disparities as "a population where there is a significant disparity in the overall rate of disease incidence, prevalence, morbidity, mortality, or survival rates in the population as compared to the health status of the general population" (DHHS, 2002a, p. 7). As I make abundantly clear in this book, men and boys constitute one such population.

As the title suggests, a central point that I discuss throughout this book is the powerful impact that masculinity has on the health of men and boys. There is a large body of both quantitative and qualitative research—which I review—showing that masculinity, measured in a variety of ways, is associated with men's health risks. The evidence I provide includes my own longitudinal research of young men nationally. As I demonstrate, many of the behaviors men use to "be men" are the same behaviors that increase their risk of disease, injury, and death. However, these enactments of masculinity are not simply a matter of personal choice. On the contrary, they are fostered and reinforced by families, communities, institutions, and cultures, as well as by individual men. But there are also new and developing healthy aspects of masculinity—which is a complex, dynamic, and ever-changing concept enacted differently in different contexts. One of the most promising contemporary approaches to improving men's health—which I discuss—is tapping into these new notions of masculinity and correcting men's misperceptions that other men hold traditionally unhealthy beliefs about masculinity and that they are unconcerned about their health.

In Section I of the book, I identify why men and boys get sick and die young. Chapter 1 is a broad multidisciplinary overview, in which I provide a summary of key determinants of the health and well-being of men and boys in the United States. I identify 31 key determinants of physical and mental health from an extensive review of literature. The findings reported in this review indicate that men's greatest health risks are the result of modifiable factors, and that efforts to address these factors through practice, policy, and research would contribute to enhanced health conditions for men and boys, as well as to healthier families and communities.

In Chapter 2, I provide an extensive review of research regarding both gender differences in health-related behaviors and the health consequences of these differences. This is a major update of a previous review I wrote, which was published in 2000. At that time, it was the first such review to examine a wide range of health-related behaviors previously unexamined by health scientists, and available data were relatively limited. In the ensuing years, epidemiological and medical research seems to have increased exponentially. An immense amount of sophisticated research is now available, including data from large prospective studies, population-based research, meta-analyses, and national surveillance systems. Consequently, this review is dense in terms of data; it is both exhaustive and—admittedly—at times exhausting. But these data provide powerful information for understanding men's health, as well as differences between men and women. They also provide overwhelming evidence that men's behaviors are the primary reasons for their increased risks relative to women. This chapter systematically demonstrates that males of all ages are more likely than females to engage in more than 30 behaviors that increase the risk of disease, injury, and death. These findings compellingly show that the greatest disparities in men's health are preventable.

In 2000, I was invited by the American Psychological Association to discuss the research of a panel of scholars at the association's annual meeting, which was held in Washington, DC. The title of the panel was "Men's Health in the New Millennium: Emerging Research, Theory, and Practice." My comments serve as the introduction to Section II of this book. I provide a critique of previous models for understanding men's health and propose a new model, as well as new directions for research, based on emerging approaches to both understanding and addressing men's health in the 21st century. In the following two chapters, I provide my own comprehensive approaches for understanding and conceptualizing men's health.

I make clear in Section I of the book that men are at greater risk than women for nearly all key indicators of health, and that men's attitudes and behaviors are the biggest contributors to their increased risk for disease, injury, and death. But this is not to suggest that the problem is simply a matter of men "behaving badly." In fact, it is a simplistic and incorrect reading of my work to suggest that "men are victims of their own behavior" (Smith, Braunack-Mayer, & Wittert, 2007, p. 81). As I illustrate in Section II, there are powerful social, environmental, institutional, and cultural influences that both foster men's adoption of unhealthy behaviors and constrain their adoption of healthier ones.

During the past 2 decades, I have frequently voiced the need to examine and understand the environments and social contexts within which health behaviors occur. In recent years, other health scientists and organizations have increasingly joined in this effort, including the American Cancer Society (Kushi et al., 2006). To help explain why women and men adopt the health beliefs and behaviors that they do, Chapter 3 reviews research examining gender differences in social experiences, cultural representations of gender, and additional social and institutional structures, such as the media and the health care system. This review reveals that North Americans collectively work diligently to reinforce stereotypically feminine or masculine behavior in themselves and others, and that the beliefs and behaviors fostered in men and boys, the resources available to demonstrate masculinity, and the resources boys and men use to enact gender are largely unhealthy. It illuminates how cultural dictates, everyday interactions, and social and institutional structures help to sustain and reproduce men's risks.

In Chapter 4, I further explain gender differences in health-related attitudes and behaviors. In doing so, I propose a relational theory of men's health from a social constructionist and feminist perspective. In this theoretical model, I suggest that health-related beliefs and behaviors, like other social practices that women and men engage in, are a means for demonstrating various forms of femininity and masculinity. In examining constructions of masculinity and health within a relational context, this theory proposes that health behaviors are used in daily interactions in the social structuring of gender and power. It further proposes that the social practices that undermine men's health are often signifiers of masculinity and instruments that men use in the negotiation of social power and status. In this chapter, I explore how factors such as ethnicity, economic status, educational level, sexual orientation, and social context influence the kind of masculinity that men construct and contribute to differential health risks among men in the United States. I also examine how masculinity and health are constructed in relation to femininities and to institutional structures—such as the health care system—and how social and institutional structures help to sustain and reproduce men's health risks and the social construction of men as "the stronger sex."

Throughout the book, I use the term *men's health*. This is for the sake of convenience and not intended to "homogenize" men's experiences related to their health. Although I discuss differences *among* men in other chapters, in Section III, I more closely examine the health needs of specific populations of men. It opens with "Ethnicity Matters." Indeed, ethnicity—along with socioeconomic status—is strongly linked with health disparities among men. African American men, for example, die 6 years younger than European American men (DHHS, 2009a). There are a number of additional factors that influence health and that differ among men, which I discuss in the introduction to Section III and in the following chapters of that section. Chapter 5 focuses on rural men. Using a social constructionist approach, I examine differences in health behaviors and risks by comparing rural men and women, as well as rural men and other populations of men. I explore how rural men's health beliefs and behavior are used as a form of gendered practice, and provide a conceptual and theoretical framework that suggests the very practices that undermine rural men's health are often used to negotiate social power in relation to rural women and also within hierarchies of men.

In Chapter 6, I examine the health of college men, who are in the age group with the greatest gender disparities in injury and death. They are also more likely than college women to engage in unhealthy behaviors, which research shows frequently continue into adulthood. In this multidisciplinary overview, I discuss the health risks of college men, college men's failure to adopt health-promoting behaviors, their propensity to engage in risky behaviors, their beliefs about manhood, their attitudes concerning their own vulnerability, and their limited knowledge about health. I discuss men's socialization as boys to provide a framework for understanding why so many college men have adopted unhealthy lifestyles. I also briefly outline how masculinity and stereotypes about manhood influence the health services that are provided to college men, and stress the importance of providing gender-specific interventions and programs to these men.

As Don Sabo and I explain in Chapter 7, there is a dire need for preventive health strategies in prisons. However, developing such strategies within the prison context is a complex matter. In this chapter, we present the insights, observations, and conclusions that were developed from the experiences of 22 students who participated in a college-level seminar in the sociology of health and medicine conducted at a northeastern U.S. maximum-security prison. To do this, we use standpoint theory. This theory holds that disadvantaged and less powerful members of a society can provide unique and useful knowledge to others. In this chapter, the male students identify health risks of prisoners, the effects of masculinity on health, realistic prevention strategies for prisoners, and potential obstacles to implementing these strategies.

In 1999, the Columbine High School massacre shook the United States. Sadly, this was neither the first—nor the last—such incident on a school campus. However, as disturbing as it is to read or hear news accounts of these incidents, it is more disturbing to me that these accounts consistently remain genderless; the fact that it is always *boys* who commit these heinous acts is rarely mentioned. After the shootings at Columbine, I wrote a short opinion piece that was published in the *Journal of American College Health* (Courtenay, 1999b), which provides the introduction to Section IV. In it, I contend that until we as a society fully recognize that it is boys who kill—and acknowledge the effects of the conflicting messages we give to boys—we will not be able to prevent these shootings. I argue, in essence, the need for examining and more deeply understanding masculinity, which is the focus of this section of the book.

Section IV presents four empirical studies that were conducted by several of my colleagues and me. In these chapters, we examine associations between masculinity and various factors related to men's health, specifically, health beliefs and practices, high-risk behavior, help seeking, and the desire to be muscular. In Chapter 8, my colleagues Donald R. McCreary, Joseph R. Merighi, and I explore the extent to which college men and women of various racial and ethnic groups differ in their health beliefs and behaviors. Exploratory factor analyses of survey responses from a diverse sample of more than 1,800 undergraduate students reveal 21 items in six cohesive domains: diet, anger and stress, preventive care, medical compliance, substance use, and beliefs about masculinity. Applying analyses of variance, we explore group differences across these domains. Our findings demonstrate consistent gender differences, with men engaging in riskier behaviors and holding riskier beliefs than women. Main effects for ethnicity are also reported. In conclusion, we discuss the implications of this research for establishing gender- and ethnicity-based health promotion and disease prevention interventions.

In the following chapter, Donald R. McCreary and I go on to examine the relationships between specific aspects of masculinity and young men's likelihood of engaging in multiple high-risk behaviors. Self-reported health risks (i.e., alcohol use, sexual activity, safety belt use) are used to identify low-risk and high-risk men. We carried out a binary logistic regression analysis to determine the degree to which beliefs about masculinity and masculine gender role conflict uniquely predict the likelihood of engaging in multiple risk behaviors. Our findings reveal that while beliefs about masculinity and gender role conflict are both associated with multiple high-risk behaviors at the bivariate level, two aspects of gender role conflict more than double the probability of men engaging in multiple high-risk behaviors when the data are analyzed using multiple regression. We demonstrate in this chapter that men who place emphasis on achievement and status, as well as on gaining authority and control over others, and men who are uncomfortable disclosing their feelings to others—especially to other men—are at increased risk for involvement in multiple high-risk behaviors.

Chapter 10 describes the development and psychometric evaluation of the Barriers to Help Seeking Scale, which was developed by my colleagues Abigail K. Mansfield, Michael E. Addis, and me. The measure is designed to assess reasons that men identify for not seeking professional help for mental and physical health problems. Exploratory factor analyses in a sample of 537 undergraduate men reveal a 5-factor solution of internally consistent subscales. An additional study of 58 undergraduate men included in this chapter confirms the reliability of the scale and provides evidence of convergent and criterion validity between the scale and measures of masculine gender role conflict and attitudes toward seeking professional help. In this chapter, we demonstrate that men's help seeking is influenced not only by norms of masculinity but also by social psychological processes, as well as practical constraints. A threat to their sense of autonomy is a primary reason why these men avoid health care. They also tend to minimize the seriousness of their problems to avoid care. Practical constraints, such as those related to time and money, are also cited by these men as important barriers to care.

In the final chapter of Section IV, Donald R. McCreary, Deborah M. Saucier, and I examine masculinity and men's body image. Previous qualitative research suggests that people assume muscular men are more masculine. This assumption was tested quantitatively in two studies in this chapter. In the first study, men and women completed measures of gender role traits and behaviors; in the second, men completed measures of gender role conflict and traditional attitudes about men. We discuss how the first study reveals a correlation between self-rated male-typed traits and behaviors, with a need to be more muscular for both men and women. In the second study, men with more traditional attitudes about men also wanted to be more muscular. Furthermore, men who wanted to be more muscular experienced conflict with regard to society's expectations that they be successful, powerful, and competitive, and they reported that finding a balance between work and leisure is difficult.

Some additional research that I conducted with Donald R. McCreary also revealed surprising and interesting results: Men are more concerned about their health than they think other men are concerned about their health. This may not seem like a particularly important finding, but it is. In fact, it is very important. This is because social norms research shows that our perceptions of others' behavior influence our own behavior. These perceptions—and *mis*perceptions—of normative group behavior often influence our behavior by providing information about what is "normal" (for example, how we should—and should not—act as a man). In the introduction to Section V, I briefly discuss this kind of research and its implications for men's health and interventions with men—which is the focus of this section of the book.

In the first chapter of Section V, I outline a practice guideline for working with men in clinical settings. The recommendations for this guideline are based on an extensive review of biopsychosocial research related to men's gender and health. It identifies behavioral and psychosocial factors that affect the onset, progression, and management of men's health problems; reviews evidence demonstrating the effectiveness of various interventions; and outlines specific recommendations for addressing these factors when working with men in clinical practice. It is organized into six sections—each of which represents one type of intervention discussed in the guideline—forming an acronym that spells HEALTH: *h*umanize, *e*ducate, *a*ssume the worst, *l*ocate supports, *t*ailor plan, and *h*arness strengths. In Chapter 13, I go on to provide an example of applying this guideline—as well as identifying other evidence-based, gender-specific strategies—in working with a particular population, specifically college men.

The final section of this book, Section VI, looks to the future of men's health. In doing so, I begin by taking a step back. In 1999, the Philadelphia Department of Public Health sponsored the first national conference on men's health, and I was invited to give an opening address (Courtenay, 2000e). That address provides the introduction to Section VI, which explores the health concerns of two men viewed from diverse professional and disciplinary perspectives. How men's health is understood, in fact, depends on the lens through which it is examined. Although it has historically been viewed from biomedical perspectives, social scientists such as myself have also identified countless cultural, psychosocial, and behavioral factors that influence men's health. I highlight the strengths and limitations of each disciplinary perspective as I examine the complexity of these men's lives and well-being. I conclude by proposing an interdisciplinary biopsychosocial and behavioral approach to the study of men's health that unites these complementary perspectives.

In the final chapter of the book, I provide a global perspective on the field of men's health. In doing so, I recommend a variety of precepts for developing new theoretical paradigms and research models for men's health, and offer some direction for social scientists and practitioners in this nascent field. In particular, I advocate interdisciplinary approaches that explore how biological, sociocultural, psychological, and behavioral factors interact to mediate the physical and mental health of men and boys. I recommend that these approaches apply social structural analyses, examine geographic and cultural contexts, integrate recent theory and research on masculinity, and develop relational paradigms that recognize dynamic intersections of various social factors. I also suggest that new global community health models that can address the convergence of micro and macro health determinants at international, national, community, and individual levels are necessary, given the multinational nature of men's health.

Much of what is written in this book was previously published and was read—or heard—in a variety of places designed for health professionals from diverse disciplines. Consequently, the research I review derives from a broad array of disciplines, and my style of writing varies throughout the book. Some chapters are written in a style that is sociological, whereas others are epidemiological. Other chapters are written for practitioners and provide hands-on advice, and the introductions to several sections of the book are conversational. All of it, however, is intended for a large readership. My intention and hope is that a broad range of readers will find the book easily accessible and readable, and that you as a reader will be stimulated by and engaged in the perspectives from other disciplines.

Why Men and Boys Get Sick and Die Young

1

Key Determinants of the Health and Well-Being of Men and Boys

An Overview[*]

Men in the United States have greater socioeconomic advantages than women. These advantages, which include higher social status and higher-paid jobs, provide men with better access to health-related resources (Bird & Rieker, 1999; Doyal, 2000). Despite these advantages, men—on average—are at greater risk of serious chronic disease, injury, and death than women. Men in the United States typically die more than 5 years earlier than women (Department of Health and Human Services [DHHS], 2009a). The current life expectancy is 80 years for women and 75 years for men (DHHS, 2009a). For nearly all 15 leading causes of death, men and boys have higher age-adjusted death rates[†] than women and girls (DHHS, 2009a; see Table 1.1). This remains true in every age group and throughout the life span (DHHS, 2009a). These 15 leading killers account for more than 80% of all deaths in the United States (DHHS, 2009a).

---

[*] An earlier version of this chapter appeared in the *International Journal of Men's Health*, *2*(1), 2003, 1–30, and is used by permission in modified/revised form.

[†] Women outlive men, so the female population as a whole is older than the male population as a whole. To account for this difference when comparing female and male deaths, health scientists use data that have been age adjusted. These age-adjusted figures are referred to as *death rates*.

TABLE 1.1   The 15 Leading Causes of Death and Gender
Differences (Ratios) in Age-Adjusted Death Rates

Cause	Ratio
1. Heart disease	1.5
2. Cancer	1.4
3. Stroke	1.0
4. Lower respiratory diseases	1.3
5. Accidents	2.2
6. Diabetes	1.4
7. Alzheimer's disease	0.7
8. Influenza and pneumonia	1.4
9. Kidney disease	1.4
10. Septicemia	1.2
11. Suicide	4.0
12. Liver disease and cirrhosis	2.1
13. Hypertension	1.0
14. Parkinson's disease	2.2
15. Homicide	3.9

Source: Department of Health and Human Services, Deaths:
Final Data for 2006 (DHHS Publication No. [PHS]
2009–1120), *National Vital Statistics Reports,* 57,
National Center for Health Statistics, Hyattsville,
MD, 2009.

The greatest gender disparity is in the death rates for suicide
and homicide, which are 4 times greater for men than they are for
women. Men are also more than twice as likely as women to die from
Parkinson's disease, unintentional injuries, and chronic liver disease
and cirrhosis (DHHS, 2009a).* Men's age-adjusted death rates for
heart disease and cancer—the two leading causes of death, which
account for almost half of all deaths—are 50 and 80% higher, respectively, than women's rates (DHHS, 2009a; Jamal et al., 2008), and
one in two men—compared with one in three women—will develop
cancer in his lifetime (American Cancer Society [ACS], 2008). The
only cause of death for which women are at greater risk is Alzheimer's
disease. This is because Alzheimer's disease is most likely to occur
late in life, when only the healthiest men remain alive. The death
rate for stroke is the same for men and women. But like Alzheimer's
disease, stroke—which is the third leading killer—occurs late in life

---

* The terms *unintentional injuries* and automobile *crashes*—rather than *accidents*—are
used throughout this book to emphasize the fact that these events are preventable; see
Cramer, 1998.

(Ingall, 2004). However, the incidence of stroke is consistently higher among men than women (Ingall, 2004) and is 25% higher among men aged 55 to 64 years and 50% higher among those aged 65 to 74 years (American Heart Association [AHA], 2009a). The incidence rates for the most common infectious diseases are also higher among men in the United States than among women (Centers for Disease Control and Prevention [CDC], 1997a; Kruszon-Morin & McQuillan, 2005; Whitfield, Weidner, Clark, & Anderson, 2002). For example, men are nearly twice as likely as women to become infected with tuberculosis (Khan et al., 2008). Not only do men contract more diseases than women, but they also tend to suffer more seriously from those diseases and to recover more slowly (Restif & Amos, in press).

Men are also more likely than women to suffer severe chronic conditions and fatal diseases (Restif & Amos, in press; Verbrugge & Wingard, 1987), such as heart disease (CDC, 2007a; Dick et al., 2005; Mendelson & Karas, 1999; National Institutes of Health, 2006)—which kills one person in the United States every 37 seconds (AHA, 2009a); cancer (Cepeda & Gammack, 2006; Kevorkian & Cepeda, 2007); diabetes (CDC, 2008a; DHHS, 2009a); and hypertension (AHA, 2009a). Cardiovascular disease is the underlying cause of one of every three deaths in the United States (Rosamond et al., 2007), and the lifetime risk of developing heart disease after age 40 is 49% for men and 32% for women (AHA, 2009b). After middle age, more men than women live with heart disease: 20% more among 45- to 64-year-olds; 50% more among 65- to 74-year-olds; and 20% more among those aged 75 years and older (DHHS, 2007a). One in every eight men suffers sudden cardiac death, 3 times the number of women who do so (Lloyd-Jones, Berry, Ning, Cai, & Goldberger, 2009). Men also suffer from severe chronic and fatal diseases at an earlier age. Until late in life, rates of major cardiovascular events among women lag 10 years behind those of men (AHA, 2009a), and nearly three of four persons under age 65 who die from heart attacks are men (AHA, 1994).

At any age, males are far more likely than females to be injured or to die violent deaths (specifically, deaths from unintentional injuries, suicide, or homicide). Among men and boys under age 45, unintentional injuries are the leading cause of death (DHHS, 2009b), and nearly three of four people who die from unintentional injuries are male (DHHS, 2007b). While unintentional injuries are the sixth leading cause of death for women, they are the third leading cause of death for men (DHHS, 2007b), and although death rates for unintentional injuries reached a 26-year low in 1992, they have been increasing since then (DHHS, 2008a). Violent deaths in general are far more common among men. Among those under age 45, men and boys account for three of four violent deaths, and these violent deaths account for more than one third (35%) of all deaths that occur among those under age 45 (DHHS, 2007b). Each day, 166 men under age 45 die violent deaths in the United States (DHHS, 2009b). Nonfatal injuries are also much more common among men and boys, who suffer up to 1.5 times more of these injuries than women (CDC, 2004a). Males of all ages account for nearly three quarters of the 1.4 million people who sustain a traumatic brain injury each year (CDC, 2006a). Men's suicide rates are staggering. As I mentioned previously, the suicide death rate is 4 times higher among males than females overall. Suicide rates for males range from 2 times higher among children aged 10 to 14 years to 18 times higher among adults aged 85 years or older (see Table 1.2). Suicide is the eighth leading cause of death for men but is not ranked among the 10 leading causes of death for females (DHHS, 2007b).

National data also consistently indicate that, during their lifetimes, either equal numbers of men and women or more men meet criteria for psychiatric diagnoses (DHHS, 1995; Kessler, 1998; Kessler et al., 2005; Robins, Locke, & Regier, 1991). Antisocial, narcissistic, obsessive-compulsive, paranoid, schizoid, and schizotypal personality disorders are all more common among men (American Psychiatric Association [APA], 1994, 2000; Golomb, Fava, Abraham, & Rosenbaum, 1995). Recent international data also show that personality disorders are significantly more common in men than women and are associated with a wide range of functional role impairments (Huang et al., 2009). Obstructive

TABLE 1.2   Male and Female Suicide Death Rates[a] and Gender Differences (Ratios), by Age Group

Age Group	Male Rate	Female Rate	Ratio
10–14	1.4	0.8	1.8
15–19	10.9	2.7	4.0
20–24	21.4	4.0	5.4
25–29	19.5	4.7	4.2
30–34	18.3	5.2	3.5
35–44	23.9	6.8	3.5
45–54	25.8	8.8	2.9
55–64	21.4	7.0	3.1
65–74	21.5	3.4	6.3
75–84	27.3	3.9	7.0
85 or older	38.6	2.2	17.5
All ages[b]	17.8	4.6	3.9

Source: Centers for Disease Control and Prevention, *Morbidity and Mortality Weekly Report, 58,* 1, 2009.

[a] Per 100,000 U.S. population.

[b] *Source:* Department of Health and Human Services, Deaths: Final Data for 2006 (DHHS Publication No. [PHS] 2009–1120), *National Vital Statistics Reports, 57,* National Center for Health Statistics, Hyattsville, MD, 2009.

sleep apnea syndrome, adult sleepwalking, gender identity disorder, alcohol- and other substance-related disorders, pyromania, intermittent explosive disorder, and pathological gambling also occur much more frequently among men, as do most sexual disorders—such as exhibitionism, pedophilia, and voyeurism (APA, 1994, 2000; Gomez, 1991). Men are also at greater risk for schizophrenia and experience earlier onset, less complete remissions, and more severe exacerbations, and they have poorer prognoses—based on rehospitalizations, length of hospital stay, duration of illness, time to relapse, response to medication, and social or work functioning (APA, 1994, 2000; Gomez, 1991). Boys are also at greater risk than girls for a number of mental health problems first diagnosed in infancy, childhood, or adolescence. These include mental retardation; attention deficit hyperactivity disorder (ADHD), which is diagnosed up to 9 times more often in boys than in girls; dyslexia; conduct disorder; Tourette's disorder; stuttering; and autism and Asperger's disorder—which are both diagnosed up to 5 times more often in boys (APA, 1994, 2000). Autism spectrum disorders are 5 to 8 times more common in boys than in girls (CDC, 2009a). Nearly twice as many boys as girls aged 5 to 17 years—more than one in five—have functional difficulties (sensory, movement, cognitive, emotional, or behavioral) (DHHS, 2009c). These psychiatric problems also increase men's physical health risks. Indeed, mental disorders are a leading cause of premature death (CDC, 2005a).

GENDER-SPECIFIC HEALTH CARE AND MEN

Although gender-based medicine and health care are receiving increasing attention among health professionals (see Legato, 2009; Lent & Bishop, 1998), most of this attention has focused on women's health concerns (e.g., Legato, 2003). The gender-specific health care needs of men and boys have only recently begun to be examined (e.g., Broom & Tovey, 2009; Courtenay, 2000a, 2009; Courtenay & Keeling, 2000a, 2000b; Furman, 2010; Lee & Owens, 2002; Sandman, Simantov, & An, 2000). In addition to having different reproductive health needs (Forrest, 2001), men and women have different risks for specific diseases and disabilities, and they differ in their perceptions of health. Gender-based health care addresses these differences, as well as other biological, psychological, social, economic, environmental, and behavioral factors that influence the health of men and women.

In writing this book, I had two primary goals. The first was to provide readers with a solid foundation for understanding men's health and men's risks, including understanding differences among men and how masculinity influences men's health. The second was to provide direction to researchers, academics, and practitioners, including effective, evidence-based strategies for clinicians, community health workers, public health officials, psychologists, and other health care professionals to improve the health and well-being of men and boys. To accomplish this, I drew from a wealth of literature and research in a diverse array of disciplines—as well as from original research specifically designed to study gender and men's health. This first chapter examines the main influences on the health of men and boys in the United States. It does so by identifying and discussing 31 key determinants of physical and mental health and well-being (see Table 1.3). It summarizes these factors under the following four categories: behaviors of men and boys, health-related beliefs and the expression of emotions and physical distress, underlying factors that influence the health and health-related behaviors and beliefs of men and boys, and health care.

BEHAVIORS AND HEALTH PRACTICES OF MEN AND BOYS

Men's and boys' behaviors and health practices are a major determinant of their excess mortality and premature deaths. An estimated one half of all men's deaths each year in the United States could be prevented through changes in personal health habits (U.S. Preventive Services Task Force, 1996). Chapter 2 provides an extensive review of large, population-based studies, national data, and meta-analyses systematically demonstrating that men and boys are more likely than women and girls to engage in more than 30 behaviors that increase the risk of disease, injury, and death. This section summarizes some of these findings in regard to six aspects of men's behaviors: health-promoting behavior, risk-taking behavior, physical abuse and violence, social support, behavioral responses to stress, and health care use.

Health-Promoting Behavior

Men and boys, in general, have less healthy lifestyles than women and girls, and they engage in far fewer health-promoting behaviors (CDC, 2003a; Courtenay, 2000b). This gender difference remains true across a variety of racial and ethnic groups (Courtenay, McCreary, & Merighi, 2002). For example, men are more often overweight than women, and they have less healthy dietary habits. They eat more meat, fat, and salt and less fiber, fruits, and vegetables than women. Men are less likely to conduct self-examinations; have higher cholesterol and blood pressure, and do less to reduce them; use less sun protection; wear safety belts less often; and use fewer medications, vitamins, and dietary supplements. Men also sleep less, and less well, and they stay in bed to recover from illness for less time than women do.

Risk-Taking Behavior

As I discuss in Chapter 2, men and boys further compound the risks associated with not adopting health-promoting behaviors by engaging

TABLE 1.3   Thirty-One Key Determinants of the Health and
Well-Being of U.S. Men and Boys

Behaviors of men and boys

 1. Health-promoting behavior
 2. Risk-taking behavior
 3. Physical abuse and violence
 4. Social support
 5. Behavioral responses to stress
 6. Health care use

Health-related beliefs and the expression of emotions and physical distress

 7. Self-rated health status
 8. Perceived susceptibility to risk
 9. Body image
10. Personal control
11. Readiness to change unhealthy behaviors
12. Masculinity
13. Expression of emotions and physical distress

Underlying factors that influence the health and health-related
 behaviors and beliefs of men and boys

14. Biology and genetics
15. Psychophysiology
16. Ethnicity
17. Socioeconomic status
18. Age group
19. Marital status
20. Sexual orientation
21. Occupational hazards
22. Unemployment
23. Imprisonment
24. Societal beliefs about masculinity and the social treatment of
    boys and men
25. Media and advertisements
26. Health knowledge

Health care

27. Insurance coverage and health care costs
28. Health care access
29. Institutional influences and research methodology
30. Clinician–patient interaction and communication
31. Clinicians' gender biases

in risk-taking behaviors. Compared with women, men use more alcohol and other drugs. More men than women use tobacco products and have more dangerous patterns of tobacco use. Men and adolescent males engage in more reckless and illegal driving, and drive drunk more frequently than women and adolescent females. They also have more sexual partners than women, and engage in significantly more high-risk physical activities—such as dangerous sports and leisure-time activities— and physical fights. They are also more likely than women and girls to carry guns or other weapons, and engage in more criminal activity. Gender differences in risk taking remain true across a variety of racial and ethnic groups.

These risk-taking behaviors undermine not only the health of men who engage in these behaviors but also the health and well-being of other men, women, and children. For example, men are at fault for most automobile accidents, including most injury crashes. Similarly, men's high-risk sexual practices are largely responsible for the continued spread of sexually transmitted diseases (STDs), which have a seriously damaging impact on the lives of both men and women.

Physical Abuse and Violence

There is extensive empirical evidence (reviewed in Chapter 2) indicating that men and boys are more likely than women and girls to be the victims of physical abuse and violence. For example, nearly one half of men nationally have been punched or beaten by a person, who in most cases is another man. The violent victimization rate among those aged 12 to 19 years is 50% higher for boys than for girls (DHHS, 2000a). Among high school students nationally, boys are nearly 70% more likely than girls to have been in a physical fight and more than twice as likely to be injured in a physical fight (CDC, 2008b, 2008c). Among adolescent boys nationally in grades 5 through 12, more than 1 in 10 (12%) report that they have been physically abused (Schoen, Davis, DesRoches, & Shekhdar, 1998). Although half as many boys (5%) as girls (10%) nationally report having been sexually abused, sexual victimization increases the health risks of both girls and boys (Schoen et al., 1998; Silverman, Raj, Mucci, & Hathaway, 2001). Among adolescent boys nationally, those who have been sexually abused are more likely than those who were not abused to report poor mental health and are twice as likely to smoke or drink frequently or to have used drugs (Schoen et al., 1998; Wolf, Crooks, Lee, McIntyre-Smith, & Jaffe, 2003). Violent deaths from suicide and homicide are a leading cause of premature death. The suicide rate is 2 to 18 times higher for men and boys than for women and girls (see Table 1.2), and the homicide death rate is 4 times higher (DHHS, 2009b). The gender disparity in homicide is greatest among those aged 16 to 29 years; death rates of males are 5 to 7 times higher than those of females (DHHS, 2008b). Each day, 15 children and young adults aged 10 to

24 years are murdered, and nearly 85% of them are boys or young men (DHHS, 2007b).

Social Support

As we will see in Chapter 2, research consistently indicates that men have much smaller social networks than women do. Men and boys also have fewer, less intimate friendships, and they are less likely to have a close confidant, particularly someone other than a spouse. Men's restricted social networks limit their levels of social support. In times of stress, for example, men mobilize less varied social supports than women do. Among adolescents nationally in grades 5 through 12, boys are more likely than girls to have no one to turn to for support at times when they feel stressed, overwhelmed, or depressed (Schoen et al., 1998). This is more likely still if the boy adheres to traditional masculine norms (Lindsey et al., 2006; Sears, Graham, & Campbell, 2009). Furthermore, there is consistent evidence that the lack of social support constitutes a risk factor for mortality—especially for men. Men with the lowest levels of social support are 2 to 3 times more likely to die than men with the highest levels of social support, even after controlling for health and a variety of other possible confounding factors. Men's social isolation significantly decreases their chance of survival after heart disease, cancer, and stroke. Men with higher levels of social support also maintain more positive health practices. They are more likely to modify unhealthy behavior and to adhere to medical treatment.

Behavioral Responses to Stress

Men respond to stress in less healthy ways than women do (see Chapter 2). They are more likely than women to use avoidant coping strategies—such as denial, distraction, and increased alcohol consumption—and are less likely to use healthy, vigilant coping strategies and to acknowledge that they need help. Furthermore, men have been found to respond to stress by engaging in more risk-taking behaviors, whereas women respond to stress by engaging in fewer such behaviors (Lighthall, Mather, & Gorlick, 2009). Similarly, job strain appears to be associated with increases in health risk behaviors among men, but not among women, who report more effective coping strategies (Frankenhaeuser, 1996); these behaviors include cigarette smoking, excessive alcohol and coffee consumption, and lack of exercise (Hellerstedt & Jeffery, 1997; Landsbergis et al., 1998). Increased alcohol consumption—as well as depression—after exposure to a disaster has been found among men but not among women.

Compared with women, men are more likely to deny their physical or emotional distress (Lee & Owens, 2002), or attempt to conceal their illnesses or disabilities (Charmaz, 1995; Courtenay, 1998a, 2001a; Stanton & Courtenay, 2003; Sutkin & Good, 1987)—responses that have been linked with the emergence of psychological disorders (Silver, Holman, McIntosh, Poulin, & Gil-Rivas, 2002). Among people with depression, for example, men are more likely than women to rely only on themselves, to withdraw socially, and to try to talk themselves out of feeling depressed. These behavioral responses contribute to the poor outcomes associated with stressful events that men and boys experience (see Chapter 2). For example, boys are more severely affected than girls by the death of a parent, and men are more negatively affected than women by the death of a spouse—and at higher risk of death, including suicide. Similarly, there is evidence that more men than women may commit suicide in response to stress. Exposure to stress can also lead to enhanced cardiovascular arousal or reactivity, which has been shown to predict heart disease, particularly in men (I discuss this later in the chapter, under Psychophysiology).

Health Care Use

Epidemiological data consistently indicate that men use fewer health care services than women do and visit physicians less often. Twice as many men (20%) as women (11%) have no regular source of health care; furthermore, even among those with a usual source of health care, more than 1.5 times more men than women consider a hospital emergency room or outpatient department to be their usual source of health care (DHHS, 2009d). Given the lack of a regular source of health care, it is not surprising that twice as many men (23%) as women (12%) have not seen a doctor in the past year (DHHS, 2009e). Indeed, among adults aged 18 to 64 years, women make more than 1.5 times more physician visits than men (DHHS, 2009e); women between the ages of 18 and 44 make twice as many visits (DHHS, 2006a). More than half (53%) of men aged 18 to 29 years do not have a regular physician compared with one third (33%) of women in this age group; among 30- to 44-year-olds, two of five men (38%) and one of five women (22%) lack a regular physician (DHHS, 2010a; Sandman et al., 2000). More than twice as many men as women have not visited a physician in 2 to 5 years, and men represent 75% of those who have not done so in more than 5 years (DHHS, 2009d). These gender differences in health care use remain even when reproductive and other sex-specific conditions are excluded (Koopmans & Lamers, 2007; Merzel, 2000). Indeed, among adults over the ages at which most women bear children, men are still less likely to have a regular physician. Twenty-four percent of men aged 45 to 64 years have no regular doctor—compared with 13% of women in this age group (Sandman et al., 2000). These differences also remain true for mental health care. As noted earlier, more men than women meet criteria for psychiatric diagnoses. Despite this increased risk, half as many men as women seek psychological services (DHHS, 2004a). Research has consistently shown for decades that men are less likely than women to receive help for mental health problems (DHHS, 2004a;

Good, Dell, & Mintz, 1989; Kessler, Brown, & Boman, 1981; Padesky & Hammen, 1981; Weissman & Klerman, 1977) or for substance abuse (McKay, Rutherford, Cacciola, & Kabaskalian-McKay, 1996; Thom, 1986). Men's relative reluctance to seek psychiatric care may help to explain why their mental health conditions are more serious when they finally do seek care (Fabrega, Mezzich, Ulrich, & Benjamin, 1990; World Health Organization, 2001a).

Although gender differences in seeking care often begin to disappear when a health problem is serious, there is consistent evidence that men are generally less willing and have less *intention* than women to seek help when they need it (Chandra & Minkovitz, 2006; Courtenay, 1998a, 2000b, 2001a; Fischer & Turner, 1970; Good et al., 1989; Tudiver & Talbot, 1999; Wills & DePaulo, 1991), and that men delay seeking care when they are ill (Galdas, Cheater, & Marshall, 2005). It has been suggested that men are least likely to ask for help when they are most in need of it (Rappaport, 1984). One in four men nationally says he would wait as long as possible before consulting a physician if he felt sick or experienced pain, or if he was concerned about his health (Sandman et al., 2000). Indeed, among people *with* health problems, men are significantly more likely than women to have had no recent physician contacts regardless of income or ethnicity (DHHS, 1998a). Delays in obtaining timely health care can have profound consequences for men's health; early detection is often critical for preventing disease and premature death (see Chapter 2).

HEALTH-RELATED BELIEFS AND THE EXPRESSION OF EMOTIONS AND PHYSICAL DISTRESS

The attitudes and beliefs that one adopts can have powerful influences on both one's health and one's health behavior. In the United States, men and boys are more likely than women and girls to adopt attitudes and beliefs that undermine their health and well-being (Courtenay, 1998a, 2000c, 2003). This section will discuss the following six attitudes and beliefs: self-rated health status, perceived susceptibility to risk, body image, personal control, readiness to change unhealthy behaviors, and masculinity. This section will also examine the relationship between the expression of emotions and physical distress and men's health.

Self-Rated Health Status

Despite their greater risk of death and serious chronic health problems, the majority of American men believe that their health is "excellent" or "very good" and rate their health as better than women do (DHHS, 1998b, 2007a; Goldberg, 2009; Merighi, Courtenay, & McCreary, 2000; Ross & Bird, 1994). Even among African Americans—who are least likely to report that their health is excellent or very good—men are still significantly more likely to do so (DHHS, 2007a). Similarly, men in Europe generally see themselves as having better health than women (White & Cash, 2003). A large study of European and U.S. adolescents also found that boys from the age of 11 report better health than girls (Torsheim et al., 2006).

Men are also more likely than women to rate their health behavior as better than the health behavior of their peers (Rakowski, 1986). Similarly, men report significantly fewer symptoms of physical and mental illness than women do (Hibbard & Pope, 1986; Koopmans & Lamers, 2007; Verbrugge, 1988; Wyke, Hunt, & Ford, 1998). Self-reports of symptoms and health behaviors are generally assumed to be accurate determinants of men's risks, but often they are not. Men may be less likely than women to notice signs of illness when they are ill (Verbrugge, 1985). Even when measured physiological responses to a stressful event are greater among men than women, men still report less distress (Frankenhaeuser et al., 1978; Rauste-von Wright & Frankenhaeuser, 1989). Self-reported risk is also confounded by what appears to be the underestimation of health needs among men. For example, although men get far less sleep than women—which increases their risk of death—far more men than women report that they get more sleep than they need (46 and 35%, respectively); alternatively, more women than men report getting less sleep than they need (24 and 19%, respectively) (Sleep Foundation, 2005).

Furthermore, men are frequently found to misrepresent their health behavior. One large study of safety belt use that compared self-reports with actual use showed that among drivers who had been observed not wearing safety belts—more than three of four of whom were men—one third had reported that they always wore safety belts (Preusser, Williams, & Lund, 1991). The validity of self-reported hypertension or high blood pressure has also been found to be lower among men than women nationally (Vargas, Burt, Gillum, & Pamuk, 1997). Similarly, men—but not women—have been found to report more colorectal cancer screening than they actually receive (Griffin et al., 2009). People who think they are healthy despite being ill, and who underreport symptoms or risk behaviors, may be less likely to seek health care or to be counseled or diagnosed correctly when they do.

Perceived Susceptibility to Risk

Men are consistently found to be less likely than women to perceive themselves as being at risk for illness, injury, and a variety of health problems (Boehm et al., 1993; Cutter, Tiefenbacher, & Solecki, 1992; Davidson & Freudenberg, 1996; DeJoy, 1992; Dosman, Adamowicz, & Hrudey, 2001; Finucane, Slovic, Mertz, Flynn, & Satterfield, 2000; Gustafson, 1998; Savage, 1993; Slovic, 1999; Weissfeld, Kirscht, & Brock, 1990). This consistent gender difference is found in a variety of countries (e.g., Antoñanzas et al., 2000a, 2000b; Brown & Cotton, 2003; Liu & Hsieh, 1995; Lundborg & Lindgren, 2002). Despite being at greater risk from drug and alcohol use, for example, males of all ages perceive significantly less risk associated with the use of cigarettes, alcohol, and other drugs than females do (DHHS, 2009f; Flynn, Slovic, & Mertz, 1994; Kauffman, Silver, & Poulin, 1997; Lundborg & Lindgren, 2002; Pascale & Evans, 1993; Spigner, Hawkins, & Loren, 1993; Thomas, 1995). The most common substances abused by adolescents are tobacco products, alcohol, and marijuana, and for all three substances, males are significantly less likely than females to accurately perceive the risks associated with their use (DHHS, 2009f). Similarly, men and boys perceive themselves as less susceptible to skin cancer than women and girls do and underestimate the risks associated with sun exposure (Banks, Silverman, Schwartz, & Tunnessen, 1992; Flynn et al., 1994; Mermelstein & Riesenberg, 1992). About three of four men nationally report that they are not worried about becoming infected with HIV or getting an STD, even when their sexual experiences put them at high risk (EDK Associates, 1995). Although they represent three of four of those infected with HIV (CDC, 2009b), men perceive less risk from HIV disease than women do (Flynn et al., 1994). Men are also more likely than women to underestimate the risks associated with involvement in physically dangerous activities (Zuckerman, 1983, 1984, 1994), including risks associated with dangerous driving (DeJoy, 1992; Flynn et al., 1994; Savage, 1993). Similarly, they perceive less risk than women for being the victim of violent crime or of dying from any cause (Department of Justice [DOJ], 2009a; Lerner, Gonzales, Small, & Fischhoff, 2003), although men are at significantly greater risk for both. For example, 1.5 times more women than men worry about being murdered (DOJ, 2009a), despite the fact that four of five people murdered are men (DHHS, 2009a).

With rare exceptions, people who think they are invulnerable take fewer precautions with their health—and thus have greater health risks—than people who recognize their vulnerability (Courtenay, 1998a, 2000c, 2003). Perceptions of risk are often associated with health-related behaviors, and this association is consistently a negative one (DHHS, 2009f). In terms of alcohol, tobacco, or other substances, for example, as risk perception decreases, substance use increases. This negative relation between perceived risks and risk taking is consistently found for risks related to smoking, with nonsmokers having stronger perceptions of the risks associated with cigarettes than smokers (e.g., Antoñanzas et al., 2000a, 2000b; Viscusi, 1990, 1992); driving (e.g., Brown & Cotton, 2003; Parker, Manstead, Stradling, & Reason, 1992; Ryb, Dischinger, Kufera, & Read, 2006; Stasson & Fishbein, 1990; Svenson, Fischhoff, & MacGregor, 1985); and drug and alcohol use (DHHS, 2009f). Men's perceived invulnerability can prevent them from practicing preventive care or changing unhealthy behavior, thus increasing their health risks (Janz & Becker, 1984; Kreuter & Strecher,

1995; Mermelstein & Riesenberg, 1992; Reno, 1988; Rosenstock, 1990; Taylor, 1986; Weinstein, 1987). In contrast, there is evidence that risk perception influences health screenings in a positive fashion. African American men with a higher than average perceived risk of prostate cancer have been found to be more likely than others to have had a recent prostate-specific antigen test (Bloom, Stewart, Oakley-Girvans, Banks, & Chang, 2006). A review of research has also shown that perceived susceptibility to severe acute respiratory syndrome during the 2003 outbreak was positively associated with hand washing (Fung & Cairncross, 2007), which can significantly reduce the risk of disease and death (see Chapter 2).

Body Image

Men's and boys' perceptions of their muscularity and weight influence their physical and mental health. Researchers studying eating disorders have focused primarily on the desire to be thin, which is most common among women and girls (see McCreary, 2009). Only recently have researchers begun to study the health effects of the desire to be physically big, which is most common among men and boys (McCreary & Sadava, 2001; McCreary & Sasse, 2000; Pope, Olivardia, Gruber, & Borowiecki, 1999). Most of these researchers have focused on the drive for muscularity. Boys with a stronger desire to be muscular tend to have poorer self-esteem and more depressive symptoms than other boys (McCreary & Sasse, 2000). A preoccupation with muscularity has also been found to be associated with psychological distress, impaired social functioning, and substance abuse, including abuse of anabolic steroids (see Pope, Gruber, Choi, Olivardia, & Phillips, 1997). However, men also misperceive their weight. Whereas women tend to perceive themselves as heavier than they really are, men tend to perceive themselves as smaller than they are (Chang & Christakis, 2003; McCreary, 2002; McCreary & Sadava, 2001; Yan, Zhang, Wang, Stoesen, & Harris, 2009). Men who do not accurately perceive themselves as overweight will be unlikely to attempt to reduce or control their weight.

Personal Control

Men believe less strongly than women that they have control over their future health or that personal actions contribute to good health (Furnham & Kirkcaldy, 1997; Verbrugge, 1990; Wilson & Elinson, 1981). Although research findings are not entirely consistent and have been challenged (Ratner, Bottorff, Johnson, & Hayduk, 1994), the perception of health as internally controlled rather than controlled by luck or chance has been found to be associated with reduced risk of heart disease (Friedman & Booth-Kewley, 1987). It has also been found to be associated with such health-promoting behaviors as abstaining from smoking, maintaining healthy drinking habits, wearing safety belts, controlling one's weight, maintaining a healthy diet (Hayes & Ross, 1987; Palank, 1991), and practicing monthly self-testicular examinations (Neef, Scutchfield, Elder, & Bender, 1991)—and with a health-promoting lifestyle in general (e.g., Courtenay, 1998a, 2003; Pender, Walker, Sechrist, & Frank-Stromborg, 1990; Rakowski, 1986; Weiss & Larson, 1990).

Readiness to Change Unhealthy Behaviors

Extensive research has examined people's readiness to change unhealthy behaviors and has identified discrete stages that people move through in changing those behaviors (i.e., Stages of Change or Transtheoretical Model; see Prochaska, Norcross, & DiClemente, 1994). When gender is analyzed in this research, a consistent finding is that women are more likely than men to contemplate changing unhealthy habits, or to already maintain healthy habits (Auld et al., 1998; Glanz et al., 1994; Weinstock, Rossi, Redding, Maddock, & Cottrill, 2000). Men, however, are more likely than women not to consider changing unhealthy behaviors, and to deny that these behaviors are problematic; they are also more likely than women not to maintain healthy behaviors (e.g., Laforge, Greene, & Prochaska, 1994; Laforge, Velicer, Richmond, & Owen, 1999; Rossi, 1992). For example, among inactive adults in a recent large population-based study, men were less likely than women to have little or no intention of increasing physical activity (Garber, Allsworth, Marcus, Hesser, & Lapane, 2008).

Masculinity

There are various forms of masculinity, and these masculinities are adopted by various populations of men—both in the United States and around the world. Masculinities derive from cultural and subjective meanings that shift and vary over time and place (Kimmel, 1995; Rotundo, 1993). As I discuss in Chapter 3, there is currently high agreement among people in the United States about what are considered to be typically feminine and typically masculine characteristics, and men and boys in particular experience a great deal of social pressure to conform to these stereotypic characteristics. These dominant norms of masculinity dictate, for example, that men should be self-reliant, strong, robust, and tough; that men should welcome danger; and that men should never reveal vulnerability, back down, or do anything "feminine." These norms represent an idealized form of gender—often referred to as "traditional masculinity"—that is a particularly damaging form of masculinity for men.

With few exceptions (Levant et al., 2003; Levant, Wimer, Williams, Smalley, & Noronha, 2009; Wade, 2008a), a large body of empirical research reveals that men who endorse these traditional beliefs or dominant norms of masculinity engage in poorer health-related behaviors and have greater health risks than men who hold less traditional beliefs (Courtenay, 1998b; Granié, 2010; Hamilton & Mahalik, 2009; Huselid & Cooper, 1992; Locke & Mahalik, 2005; Mahalik, Burns, & Syzdek, 2007; Mahalik et al., 2003; Mahalik, Lagan, & Morrison, 2006; Mahalik, Levi-Minzi, & Walker, 2007; Marcell, Ford, Pleck, & Sonenstein, 2007; McCreary, Newcomb, & Sadava, 1999; McCreary & Sadava, 2009; Morman, 2000; Neff, Prihoda, & Hoppe, 1991; Pleck, Sonenstein, & Ku, 1994; Powell, 2005; Springer & Mouzon, 2009). Poor health practices and greater risks have also been found among men and adolescent males who experience high levels of masculine gender role stress (Copenhaver & Eisler, 1996; Eisler, 1995; Eisler & Blalock, 1991; Eisler, Skidmore, & Ward, 1988) and gender role conflict (Berger, Levant, McMillan, Kelleher, & Sellers, 2005; Blazina & Watkins, 1996; Fragoso & Kashubeck, 2000; Good et al., 1989; Good & Mintz, 1990; Lane & Addis, 2005; Mansfield, Addis, & Courtenay, 2005; McCreary & Courtenay, 2003; Monk & Ricciardelli, 2003; O'Neil, 2008; O'Neil, Good, & Holmes, 1995; Robertson & Fitzgerald, 1992). Two prospective studies have shown that traditional beliefs about manhood predict both involvement in a variety of high-risk behaviors over time among a large, nationally representative sample of young men (Courtenay, 1998b) and a greater risk of death (Lippa, Martin, & Friedman, 2000). In contrast, androgynous (Baffi, Redican, Sefchick, & Impara, 1991; Shifren, Bauserman, & Carter, 1993) or feminine gender identity (Kaplan & Marks, 1995) and nontraditional masculinity (Wade, 2008b) have been found to be associated with positive health behaviors in men. Additionally, a recent, large community-based general population study found that higher femininity scores in men were associated with a decreased risk of death from coronary heart disease, and femininity remained a significant predictor of lower risk when controlling for a variety of known risk factors for heart disease (Hunt, Lewars, Emslie, & Batty, 2007). A growing body of qualitative research has also linked traditional or dominant beliefs about masculinity with poor health behavior and increased health risks in men (Bottorff, Oliffe, Kalaw, Carey, & Mroz, 2006; Canaan, 1996; Chapple, Ziebland, & McPherson, 2004; Eisler, 1995; Emslie & Hunt, 2009; George & Fleming, 2004; McCreary et al., 1999; Nasir & Rosenthal, 2009; Neff et al., 1991; Nobis & Sandén, 2008; O'Brien, Hunt, & Hart, 2005; Pleck et al., 1994; Robertson, 2007; Singleton, 2008; Smith, Braunack-Mayer, & Warin, 2007). This research has also elucidated the variations in men's experiences of masculinity and in the experiences that influence their health (O'Brien et al., 2005; Robertson, 2007).

The endorsement of traditional masculinity or dominant norms of masculinity has been linked with low levels of health-promoting practices (Chapple et al., 2004; George & Fleming, 2004; Mahalik, Burns, et al., 2007; Mahalik et al., 2006; Mahalik, Levi-Minzi, et al., 2007; Morman, 2000; Powell, 2005; Singleton, 2008) and a variety of specific, unhealthy behaviors—including smoking; alcohol and drug use; and behaviors related to safety, diet, sleep, sexual practices, and driving (Baffi et al., 1991; Blazina & Watkins, 1996; Eisler et al., 1988;

Hamilton & Mahalik, 2009; Huselid & Cooper, 1992; Korcuska & Thombs, 2003; Locke & Mahalik, 2005; Mahalik, Burns, et al., 2007; Mahalik et al., 2003, 2006; McCreary et al., 1999; McCreary & Sadava, 2009; Monk & Ricciardelli, 2003; Shifren et al., 1993). One of the studies revealed that alcohol use and problem drinking are strongly associated with traditional masculinity; this association is even stronger than the link between problem drinking and being male (Huselid & Cooper, 1992). Men with high gender role conflict are also more likely to engage in multiple health risk behaviors (McCreary & Courtenay, 2003; see also Chapter 9). Men who adopt traditional beliefs about manhood also experience higher levels of depression and are more vulnerable to psychological stress and maladaptive coping patterns (Eisler & Blalock, 1991; Fragoso & Kashubeck, 2000; Good et al., 1989; Good & Mintz, 1990; Liu & Iwamoto, 2006; Oliver & Toner, 1990; O'Neil, 2008; Sharpe & Heppner, 1991). Indeed, in O'Neil's (2008) review of 27 studies that examined gender role conflict specifically, only three studies found no significant relationship between gender role conflict and depression. Masculine gender role stress has also been linked with higher levels of depression in men, as well as psychological stress and maladaptive coping patterns (Eisler et al., 1988; Good et al., 1989; Sharpe, Heppner, & Dixon, 1995); it is also associated with heightened cardiovascular reactivity in situations of stress, including situations that potentially threaten traditional masculinity (Cosenzo, Franchina, Eisler, & Krebs, 2004; Eisler, 1995; Eisler, Franchina, Moore, Honeycutt, & Rhatigan, 2000; Franchina, Eisler, & Moore, 2001; Lash, Eisler, & Schulman, 1990; Lash, Gillespie, Eisler, & Southard, 1991; Moore & Stuart, 2004; Thompson & Pleck, 1995).

Compounding these health risks, the endorsement of traditional or dominant norms of masculinity is consistently found to have a negative influence on a man's willingness to seek help or to use health services when he needs them (Addis & Mahalik, 2003; Berger et al., 2005; Blazina & Watkins, 1996; Burda & Vaux, 1987; Chapple et al., 2004; Galdas et al., 2005; George & Fleming, 2004; Good et al., 1989; Lane & Addis, 2005; Levant et al., 2009; Mahalik et al., 2006; Mansfield, Addis, & Mahalik, 2003; Mansfield et al., 2005; Marcell et al., 2007; Moller-Leimkuhler, 2002; O'Brien et al., 2005; O'Neil et al., 1995; Powell-Hammond, Matthews, & Corbie-Smith, 2010; Robertson & Fitzgerald, 1992; Singleton, 2008; Springer & Mouzon, 2009). Nineteen studies have examined the relationship between help seeking and masculine gender role conflict specifically, and only one reported no significant relationship (O'Neil, 2008). There is increasing evidence that men delay seeking care when they are ill (for a review of this research, see Galdas et al., 2005). Dominant norms of masculinity are consistently implicated in these delays (Galdas et al., 2005), including delays in seeking care for cancer (Chapple et al., 2004; George & Fleming, 2004; Singleton, 2008)—which increases the risk of not detecting the cancer until it is advanced, and often incurable. In the only empirical, population-based study examining masculinity and preventive health care screening in a large sample of middle-aged men, those men who endorsed traditional norms of masculinity were nearly 50% less likely than other men to seek preventive health care services—including physical examinations; these findings remained true even after controlling for socioeconomic status, marital status, and previous health status (Springer & Mouzon, 2009). Similarly, among men with heart disease, one study found that those who held traditional beliefs were less likely to follow their physician's orders and made fewer healthy lifestyle changes after hospital discharge than their less traditional peers (Helgeson, 1994).

Not all aspects of traditional masculinity are unhealthy. Indeed, some aspects of traditional masculinity have been found to be positively associated with men's health and health-promoting practices (Eisler, 1995; O'Brien et al., 2005; Robertson, 2007; Sabo & Gordon, 1995; Wade, 2008a). Among men in rehabilitation for spinal cord injuries, researchers have found a positive association between recovery and restrictive emotionality (Schopp, Good, Mazurek, Barker, & Stucky, 2007). Similarly, certain masculine-identified characteristics have been found to be highly adaptive for both men and women. These characteristics include the ability to act independently, to be assertive, and to be decisive (e.g., see Eisler, 1995; Nezu & Nezu, 1987; Sharpe et al., 1995). Reliance on masculine-identified characteristics such as these has been found to help enable men to cope with cancer (Gordon, 1995) and chronic illness (Charmaz, 1995). Among African American men, Wade (2008a) found that traditional masculine attitudes of self-reliance and aggression were associated with personal wellness. Self-reliance, for example, was associated with being aware of and thinking about one's health, being motivated to avoid poor health and to keep in excellent health, and believing that one can exert an influence—whether positive or negative—on one's health. These studies show that certain aspects of traditional masculinity are associated with good health in men. However, the weight of the evidence suggests that—for the most part—the endorsement of these traditional or dominant norms of masculinity increases men's risks. Furthermore, as I discuss in Chapter 3, the vast majority of the gender resources men have at their disposal to demonstrate masculinity, or to be masculine, are unhealthy.

Expression of Emotions and Physical Distress

In general, women are more emotionally expressive than men—except when it comes to expressing anger, which men do more frequently; men also report less fear or emotional distress than women do, and are less likely than women to cry (Allen-Burge, Storandt, Kinscherf, & Rubin, 1994; Balswick, 1982; Belle, Burr, & Cooney, 1987; Brody, 1999; Chino & Funabiki, 1984; Courtenay, 2001a, 2003; Croake, Myers, & Singh, 1987; Grigsby & Weatherley, 1983; Hyde, 1986; Kraemer & Hastrup, 1986; Lee & Owens, 2002; Liddell, Locker, & Burman, 1991;

Lombardo, Crester, Lombardo, & Mathis, 1983; Stapley & Haviland, 1989; Tannen, 1990; Williams, 1985). Men's inexpressiveness can have both direct and indirect effects on their health and well-being. Self-disclosure, for example, has been found to be associated with improvements in immune functioning and physical health (Pennebaker, 1997; Smyth, 1998). Men are also more likely than women to exhibit emotionally inexpressive Type A behavior and to experience or express hostility, both of which are strongly linked with increased health risks—particularly for cardiovascular disease (Booth-Kewley & Friedman, 1987; Chida & Steptoe, 2009; Friedman, 1991; Strube, 1991; Weidner, Kopp, & Kristenson, 2002; Whitfield et al., 2002), which is the leading killer of men. Furthermore, the findings from a recent meta-analysis of 729 studies (Chida & Hamer, 2008) indicate that anger and hostility are more strongly linked with cardiovascular responses to psychological stressors in men than they are in women; this finding from more than 30 years of research suggests that the accumulation of stress responses in daily life may have greater pathophysiological significance for heart disease among men than among women.

Research also suggests that men are disinclined to discuss experiences of pain or physical distress. Compared with women, men report less pain for the same pathology, less severe pain, greater tolerance of pain, higher pain thresholds, and shorter duration of pain (Gijsbers van Wijk & Kolk, 1997; Miaskowski, 1999; Unruh, Ritchie, & Merskey, 1999; Wiesenfeld-Hallin, 2005). Although hormones may play some role in mediating the experience of pain (Miaskowski, 1999; Wiesenfeld-Hallin, 2005), research indicates that psychosocial factors are certainly a contributor. Men have been found to report less pain in front of female experimenters than male experimenters (Aslaksen, Myrbakk, Høifødt, & Flaten, 2007; Kallai, Barke, & Voss, 2004), and to female health professionals than to male health professionals (Levine & DeSimone, 1991; Puntillo & Weiss, 1994). Traditional masculinity has also been found to be associated with emotional inexpressiveness in general (e.g., Eisler, 1995; Moller-Leimkuhler, 2002; Thompson, Grisanti, & Pleck, 1985) and with higher thresholds of pain specifically (Otto & Dougher, 1985; Wise, Price, Myers, Heft, & Robinson, 2002). The reluctance to acknowledge or report physical or emotional distress can have far-reaching implications for men's health; it can influence help-seeking decisions, delay intervention, and undermine diagnosis and treatment planning.

UNDERLYING FACTORS THAT INFLUENCE THE HEALTH AND HEALTH-RELATED BEHAVIORS AND BELIEFS OF MEN AND BOYS

A variety of additional factors contribute to men's health risks both directly and indirectly through their influence on men's health behaviors and beliefs. This section examines the health influences of biology and genetics, psychophysiology, ethnicity, socioeconomic status, age, marital status, occupational status, unemployment, imprisonment, societal beliefs about masculinity and the social treatment of boys and men, media and advertisements, and men's health knowledge.

Biology and Genetics

Biology contributes to men's and boys' greater risk of death, which begins in utero (Kraemer, 2000). Although an estimated 120 to 160 males are conceived for every 100 females, by birth the sex ratio drops to approximately 106:100 (Stillion, 1995). Boys are also more likely than girls to die from congenital cardiovascular defects, which are the most common cause of infant death (AHA, 2009b), and males are at greater risk of mortality as a result of congenital anomalies throughout the life span (DHHS, 1991, 2009b; Kraemer, 2000). Biological sex differences in mitochondria (intracellular organelles responsible for oxidative metabolism) and oxidative damage to mitochondria DNA are believed to contribute to gender differences in life expectancy (Kevorkian & Cepeda, 2007). Consistent differences are found in the immune functioning of women and men—including higher antibody levels in women—which probably contribute to the gender difference in longevity (Kevorkian & Cepeda, 2007; Whitfield et al., 2002). Biology also contributes to a variety of sex-specific reproductive health problems. For example, erectile dysfunction—which can result in significant emotional and interpersonal distress—occurs in at least one in four U.S. men (Goldberg, 1993), and this risk increases with age. In a survey of more than 3,000 health professionals, the frequency of erectile dysfunction was 4% in men under age 50, 26% in those aged 50 to 59 years, and 40% in those aged 60 to 69 years (Bacon et al., 2003). More than half of all men over 70 experience erectile dysfunction (Melman & Gingell, 1999).

Hormonal differences also contribute to gender differences in longevity (Kevorkian & Cepeda, 2007). Although some studies have cast doubt on the protective role of estrogen in heart disease (Barrett-Connor, 1997; Rossouw, 1999), it is generally believed that men's lack of estrogen increases their risk of heart disease by lowering their levels of "good" cholesterol relative to women (Kevorkian & Cepeda, 2007; Mendelson & Karas, 1999; Rosano & Panina, 1999). In addition, there is extensive research suggesting that estrogen contributes to the lower levels of atherosclerosis—or hardening of the arteries—found in women compared with men, which provide women with significant protection from stroke, heart attack, and death (AHA, 2009a; Iemolo, Martiniuk, Steinman, & Spence, 2004; Reis et al., 2000; Williams, Adams, Herrington, & Clarkson, 1992; Williams, Adams, & Klopfenstein, 1990). Similarly, estrogen affects levels of cellular oxidation and the length of telomeres.* Both of these are believed to influence gender differences in longevity (Kevorkian & Cepeda, 2007).

The enzyme monoamine oxidase (MAO), a neuroregulator, and hormones in the brain, such as androgens and cortisol, are associated with a desire for varied and intense sensations and experiences. Decades of research have consistently linked this desire—which is significantly more common among men than women—with risky driving, high-risk sexual activity, alcohol use, drug use, and cigarette smoking, as well as involvement in high-risk sports and criminal activity (Struber, Luck, & Roth, 2008; Zuckerman, 1983, 1984, 1994). Low serotonin levels in the male brain may also contribute to men's greater displays of physical aggression (Volavka, 1999; Wallner & Machatschke, 2009). Stress hormones—and the balance between cortisol and rapid adrenocorticotropin (ACTH)—are also believed to influence longevity (Kevorkian & Cepeda, 2007). In addition, biology may mediate the health effects of substances such as nicotine and alcohol. For example, there is some evidence that men metabolize nicotine faster than women do, and that the protective effects of moderate alcohol consumption—through its influence on levels of "good" cholesterol—occur at higher doses of alcohol in men than in women (Whitfield et al., 2002).

Although findings are controversial, there is some evidence of possible biological differences among men. Recent research suggests, for example, that biology might explain the prostate cancer death rate for African American men, which is nearly 2.5 times greater than that for European American men and more than 5 times greater than that for Asian and Pacific Islander men (DHHS, 2009a). Findings from studies specifically designed to examine the contributions of socioeconomic, clinical, and pathologic factors have led researchers to conclude that biology might play a role in explaining African American men's greater risk (Hoffman et al., 2001; Lunn, Bell, Mohler, & Taylor, 1999; Makridakis et al., 1999; Sartor, Zheng, & Eastham, 1999; Thompson et al., 2001). (For further discussion regarding ethnicity, race, genetics, and disease, see Cooper, 2003; Frank, 2007; Karter, 2003.)

Although a variety of biological factors do contribute to men's risks, research indicates that the explanatory power of biological factors in predicting gender differences in morbidity and mortality is comparatively small (Kandrack, Grant, & Segall, 1991; Krantz, Grunberg, & Baum, 1985; Ory & Warner, 1990; Verbrugge, 1985, 1990; Waldron, 1997, 2008; Whitfield et al., 2002). Biological influences on health and longevity are best understood within the complex interaction among biology, environment, and behavior (Foley et al., 2004; Kevorkian & Cepeda, 2007). One line of research suggests that certain diseases, including asthma and diabetes, are linked with gender-based susceptibilities caused by the interplay of sex steroid hormones or sex chromosomes

---

* Telomeres are structures at the ends of the chromosomes that protect them from damage and that shorten with age.

with environmental risk factors at particular developmental windows, which would explain why these diseases are more common among males (Gabory, Attig, & Junien, 2009). Indeed, behavioral and other modifiable factors associated with men's poor health can further compound men's biological risks. In the study of erectile dysfunction among 3,000 health professionals cited previously, for example, the frequency was significantly higher in men who were hypertensive, diabetic, obese, or smokers (Bacon et al., 2003).

Genetic factors can also increase men's risk. Men with a family history of heart disease (Lloyd-Jones et al., 2004; Murabito et al., 2005), prostate cancer (Chung, Isaacs, & Simons, 2007; Grönberg, 2003; Isaacs & Xu, 2007), or colorectal cancer (Kushi et al., 2006) are at much greater risk for these diseases. Indeed, life expectancy itself has a strong genetic basis (Kevorkian & Cepeda, 2007). Hereditary influences similarly contribute to men's risk of ADHD (Elia & Devoto, 2007) and depression (Kendler & Prescott, 1999). However, genetic factors—like biological ones—are mediated by a variety of additional factors. An analysis of international trends in prostate cancer incidence and mortality throughout the world, for example, suggests that the large disparities that exist between countries are the result of the interaction of genetic and environmental factors (Hsing, Tsao, & Devesa, 2000). Similarly, although MAO has a strong genetic determination (Zuckerman, 1994), research examining antisocial behavior in boys has demonstrated that the influence of MAO is mediated by the environment (Foley et al., 2004).

Psychophysiology

Psychophysiological responses to emotional stress—such as increased catecholamine and cortisol excretion, ACTH responses, heart rate, and blood pressure—are hypothesized to be related to the risk of death in general (Kevorkian & Cepeda, 2007). Studies consistently report that men exhibit greater psychophysiological responses during acute behavioral stress, and that men are slower to recover from stress—which may help to explain men's greater risk of death in general, and of coronary heart disease mortality in particular (Allen, Stoney, Owens, & Matthews, 1993; Chaplin, Hong, Bergquist, & Sinha, 2008; Cosenzo et al., 2004; Dorn et al., 1996; Glynn, Christenfeld, & Gerin, 2002; Kajantie, 2008; Kirschbaum, Wust, & Hellhammer, 1992; Kudielka, Hellhammer, & Kirschbaum, 2000, 2007; Kudielka & Kirschbaum, 2005; Lash et al., 1990, 1991; Otte et al., 2005; Polefrone & Manuck, 1987; Stone, Dembroski, Costa, & MacDougall, 1990; Stoney, Davis, & Matthew, 1987; Weidner & Messina, 1998). Similarly, systolic and diastolic blood pressure reactivity is also greater among men and boys than it is among women and girls (Earle, Linden, & Weinberg, 1999; Girdler, Turner, Sherwood, & Light, 1990; Glynn et al., 2002; Jackson, Treiber, Turner, Davis, & Strong, 1999; Lash et al., 1990;

Murphy, Stoney, Alpert, & Walker, 1995; Polefrone & Manuck, 1987; Stoney et al., 1987; Traustadottir, Bosch, & Matt, 2003). Heightened cardiovascular reactivity has also been found among men with gender role stress in situations that threaten traditional masculinity (Cosenzo et al., 2004; Eisler et al., 2000; Franchina et al., 2001; Lash et al., 1990; Moore & Stuart, 2004). The activation of the autonomic nervous system and the subsequent response of the cardiovascular system are generally considered to be the common pathway by which stress compromises physical health (Kevorkian & Cepeda, 2007; Matthews et al., 1986). In addition, strong and consistent associations between stress and decreased levels of human immune system functioning, as well as stress and chronic disease—such as heart disease—are consistently found (Carver, 2007; Cohen, Janicki-Deverts, & Miller, 2007; Gouin, Hantsoo, & Kiecolt-Glaser, 2008; Herbert & Cohen, 1993). Although it is difficult to directly control or alter psychophysiological responses to emotional stress, it is relatively easy to modify the behavioral and situational factors that stimulate these responses.

Ethnicity

There are important differences in mortality and in the leading causes of death among men and boys of various ethnicities (Courtenay, 2001b, 2002, 2003). The difference between the life spans of African American men and European American men is greater than the difference between the life spans of men and women in general: African American men die 6 years younger than European American men, whereas—on average—men die 5 years younger than women (DHHS, 2009a). African American men experience earlier onset of disease, more severe disease, higher rates of complications, and more limited access to medical care than European American men (Barnett et al., 2001). Among American Indian and Alaska Native men, unintentional injuries are the second leading cause of death (Rhoades, 2003), surpassing cancer, which is the second leading cause of death among all other ethnic groups of men (CDC, 2006b). The death rate for motor vehicle–related deaths among American Indians and Alaska Natives is nearly twice as high as the rate for European Americans and African Americans (CDC, 2009c). HIV disease is among the five leading causes of death for African American and Latino men (DHHS, 2009a), but it is not even among the top 10 leading causes for any other ethnic group of men (CDC, 2006b). African American men are 8 times more likely than European American men and 24 times more likely than Asian and Pacific Islander men to die from HIV disease (DHHS, 2009a). Similarly, homicide ranks among the five leading causes of death only for African American men (DHHS, 2009a)—not for men of other ethnic groups. Stroke ranks as the third leading cause of death among Asian American men but not among men of any other ethnic group, for whom injuries are a greater risk (DHHS, 2009a). Compared with European American men, African American men experience earlier onset of heart disease, more severe heart disease, and higher rates of complications resulting from heart disease (Barnett et al., 2001). Gender differences in mortality, however, persist regardless of ethnicity. For example, within all ethnic groups, nearly 1.5 times more men than women die from cardiovascular diseases (DHHS, 2006b, 2009a) (see Table 1.4). The largest gender gap in death from all causes occurs among 15- to 24-year-old Latinos; four of every five deaths are males (DHHS, 2000b, 2007b).

Ethnicity is also linked with risk factors for disease. Among adults aged 55 years or older, for example, risk factors for chronic disease are much more common among American Indians and Alaska Natives than European Americans (Denny, Holtzman, Turner-Goins, & Croft, 2005). Similarly, ethnicity is associated with health care use (CDC, 2004b; Courtenay, 2001b, 2002, 2003). Latino Americans, for example, are less likely to have health care coverage or providers, or to have a regular place of care; they are also less likely to be screened for blood cholesterol and colorectal cancers (CDC, 2004b). Almost twice as many Latino men (33%) as European American men (17%) or African American men (18%) do not have a usual source of health care (DHHS, 2009d). Despite their high risks, Latino and African American men are significantly less likely than European American men to see a physician regularly; 55% of Latino men and 45% of African American men do not have a doctor who they see regularly compared with 33% of European American men (Sandman et al., 2000). These findings probably help to explain why, for example, African and Latino Americans are significantly more likely

TABLE 1.4 Gender Differences in Heart Disease Death Rates by Ethnicity

	Heart Disease Death Rates[a]		
	Males	Females	Ratio[b]
European American	305	214	1.4
African American	420	296	1.4
American Indian or Alaskan Native	207	156	1.3
Latino American	225	162	1.4
Asian or Pacific Islander	189	132	1.4

Source: Department of Health and Human Services, Deaths: Final Data for 2006 (DHHS Publication No. [PHS] 2009–1120), *National Vital Statistics Reports*, 57, National Center for Health Statistics, Hyattsville, MD, 2009.

[a] Per 100,000 U.S. population.

[b] These ratios indicate that the death rates for men are nearly 1.5 times greater for men than women, or 40% higher for men (except in the case of American Indians and Alaskan Natives, for whom heart disease death rates are 30% higher for men).

than European Americans to be first diagnosed with an advanced-stage cancer (Halpern et al., 2008; Wu et al., 2001). Among adolescent boys nationally in grades 5 through 12, more Asian (30%), Latino (27%), and African Americans (25%) than European Americans (17%) report not having a usual source of health care (Schoen et al., 1998). Among young men aged 20 to 29 years, young European American men make more than 1.5 times more doctor visits than young African American men and nearly twice as many visits as young Latino men (Fortuna, Robbins, & Halterman, 2009). Young African and Latino men also receive only half as much care for chronic conditions compared with European American men (Fortuna et al., 2009). The patient's ethnicity also influences both the clinician's treatment and the patient's satisfaction with health care. Mental health clinicians, for example, are less likely to correctly diagnose mental health problems among African Americans and Latinos than among European Americans (Borowsky et al., 2000). Not surprisingly, African Americans—including African American men—report being more dissatisfied with their care by doctors and in hospitals than European Americans (Blendon, Aiken, Freeman, & Corey, 1989; Cooper-Patrick et al., 1999; LaVeist, Nickerson, & Bowie, 2000; Powell-Hammond et al., 2010).

Ethnicity, however, does not explain gender differences in health care utilization; the gender-specific patterns of use reported previously can be found in most ethnic groups (Dunlop et al., 2002; Neighbors & Howard, 1987; Williams, 2003). Women in every ethnic group, for example, are more likely than men to have a usual source of care (DHHS, 2007a). Among African Americans, women make more than 1.5 times more physician visits than men (DHHS, 1990), and men are significantly less likely to visit physicians regardless of the type or severity of their health problem (Neighbors & Howard, 1987). One study was specifically designed to examine health care utilization and interactions between gender and ethnicity; this research, based on national data from a probability sample of more than 6,000 community-dwelling adults aged 65 years or older, reveals that African American and Latino American men are twice as likely as women of any race or ethnicity not to have seen a physician in the past 2 years (Dunlop, Manheim, Song, & Chang, 2002). National data indicate that among persons with health problems, men are significantly more likely than women to have had no recent physician contacts regardless of ethnicity (see Chapter 2). Among Latinos, more men than women have not had a physical examination within the past 5 years, and these differences persist regardless of acculturation (Marks, Garcia, & Solis, 1990). Twice as many Mexican American men as Mexican American women report having no routine place to get health care, and 1.5 times more women than men report having had a routine physical examination within the previous 2 years (Solis, Marks, Garcia, & Shelton, 1990). Similarly, both outpatient and inpatient health services are used far less often by American Indian and Alaska Native men than women, despite much greater risk of illness and death among these men compared with women (Rhoades, 2003).

Socioeconomic Status

A large body of research indicates a clear and strong association between poor health and low socioeconomic status (SES), both in the United States (Courtenay, 2002, 2003; DHHS, 1998a; Dunn, 2010; Hayward, Pienta, & McLaughlin, 1997; Phelan & Link, 2005; Rich & Ro, 2002; Sorlie, Backlund, & Keller, 1995; Whitfield et al., 2002) and in other countries (Kunst, Feikje, Mackenbach, & EU Working Group on Socioeconomic Inequalities in Health, 1998; Mackenbach et al., 2008). SES is typically based on income, education, and occupation. Of these three proxies, income is most strongly associated with health (Whitfield et al., 2002). Economically disadvantaged men are more likely to live in crowded, substandard housing and in areas with high levels of crime; to be exposed to dangerous and toxic environments; to lack access to health information; and to experience greater overall life stress (Rich & Ro, 2002). However, the association between SES and health is not limited to a comparison between poor and wealthy populations. Among most ethnic groups in the United States, there is a continuous gradient in this association between SES and health, so that the health of persons of middle SES is worse than the health of those of slightly higher SES (DHHS, 1998a). As people's SES rises, their health improves (Adler et al., 1994; Phelan & Link, 2005; Sandman et al., 2000).

Although differences and disparities in SES are the result of many factors—including differences in accessing a variety of resources (Berkman & Epstein, 2008)—one way SES influences people's health is by influencing their access to medical care (Rich & Ro, 2002). Men with the lowest income are also the most likely to report not having a regular doctor and to report that it is somewhat, very, or extremely difficult for them to get the medical care they need (Sandman et al., 2000). Among adolescent boys nationally in grades 5 through 12, those from lower-income families are 50% more likely than boys from higher-income families not to have received medical care (Schoen et al., 1998). One in five boys nationally has not received medical care when he needed it (Schoen et al., 1998), and among urban middle and high school students, males are significantly more likely than females to believe that it is difficult to obtain health care (Aten, Siegel, & Roghmann, 1996).

SES, however, does not explain gender differences in mortality any more than does ethnicity. As Williams (2003) explains, men's greater health risks and increased mortality persist at all levels of SES. Similarly, despite its relevance to access and care, SES does not account for gender differences in health care utilization (Neighbors & Howard, 1987). Even among a variety of income groups in the United States, men are still less likely to use health care than women. Among those who are poor, men are twice as likely as women to have had no recent contact with a health care provider (DHHS, 1998a). Even when health services are provided without cost, men use them less than women (Stockwell, Madhavan, Cohen, Gibson, & Alderman, 1994; Wells, Manning, Duan, Newhouse, & Ware, 1986). Similarly, high-income men are 2.5 times more likely than high-income women to have had no recent contact with a health care provider. Even among persons with health problems, men are significantly more likely than women to have had no recent physician contact regardless of income (DHHS, 1998a). Indeed, it appears as though health-related behaviors such as these are the cause of men's greater risks. A sophisticated, 25-year prospective cohort study of nearly 10,000 people revealed that the strong association between SES and the risk of early death largely disappears when differences in health behaviors are taken into account (Stringhini et al., 2010).

Age Group

The age group with the greatest gender disparity in mortality is 15- to 24-year-olds (DHHS, 2000b). Three of every four deaths in this age group are males (DHHS, 2007b). Male adolescents experience 174% more injuries (Rivara, Bergman, LoGerfo, & Weiss, 1982) and are significantly more likely to be hospitalized for serious injuries than female adolescents (Slap, Chaudhuri, & Vorters, 1991). The incidence of traumatic brain injury is highest among 16- to 24-year-old males, whose injury rates are 3 to 4 times higher than those for females in this age group (Bruns & Hauser, 2003; Winslade, 1998). Among adolescents, males are also significantly more likely than females to be exposed to a variety of work hazards (Dunn, Runyan, Cohen, & Schulman, 1998). Violent deaths (unintentional injuries, homicide, and suicide) account for 80% of all deaths among 15- to 24-year-olds, and four of five of these deaths are males (DHHS, 2007b). Each day, 15 young men aged 15 to 24 years die violent deaths (DHHS, 2007b). Most of these diseases, injuries, and deaths are preventable; they result from young men's lack of healthy habits and their propensity to engage in high-risk behaviors. Motor vehicle crashes are the leading cause of death in this age group (DHHS, 2009b), which has higher motor vehicle death rates than any other age group (CDC, 2009c), and young men represent three of four people killed (DHHS, 2007b, 2009b). Among high school students nationally, males are more likely than females to engage in 39 of 59 specific health risk behaviors (CDC, 2008c), and among California college students, males are more likely than females to engage in 20 of 26 specific high-risk behaviors (Patrick, Covin, Fulop, Calfas, & Lovato, 1997). Young men of this age are also at far greater risk than women for STDs (see Chapter 2). Boys are significantly more likely than girls to smoke cigarettes or marijuana and to drink alcohol for the first time before age 13 years (CDC, 2008b, 2008c). Among both high school and college students nationally, the use of marijuana, cocaine or crack cocaine, inhalants, and injection drugs is greater among males than females (see Chapter 2). Indeed, according to the CDC, the leading causes of disease, injury, and death among children and adolescents are significantly related to six categories of modifiable behaviors: behaviors that contribute to unintentional injuries and violence; tobacco use; alcohol and other drug use; sexual behaviors that contribute to unintended pregnancy and STDs, including HIV infection; unhealthy dietary behaviors; and physical inactivity (CDC, 2008b). With the one exception of physical activity, significantly more male than female children and adolescents engage in these behaviors. Furthermore, once established in childhood or adolescence, these behaviors frequently continue into adulthood (CDC, 2008b) and are frequently associated with disease, injury, and death in adulthood (DHHS, 2000a).

Marital Status

As I discuss in Chapter 2, marriage is an important health-related factor. Whether single, separated, widowed, or divorced, unmarried men have more serious health risks than married men, and they engage in poorer health behavior (Ben-Shlomo, Smith, Shipley, & Marmot, 1993; Courtenay, 2000b). For example, unmarried men drink and smoke more; they eat fewer fruits and vegetables; they are at greater risk of contracting STDs; they use medical services less often; they are less likely to have had a blood pressure test in the past year or ever; and they are likelier to commit suicide. Not surprisingly, marriage is consistently found to be positively associated with longevity (Kaplan & Kronick, 2006). Furthermore, all the current evidence indicates that this correlation with mortality—and the other health risks associated with being unmarried—are greater for men than for women (see Courtenay, 2000b and Chapter 2).

Sexual Orientation

Men who have sex with men (MSM)—gay and bisexual men, or other MSM—and transsexuals are at increased risk for disease and death relative to other men. They are more likely to participate in high-risk behaviors such as substance abuse, smoking, drinking before sexual activity, and having multiple sexual partners (Blake et al., 2001). STDs are more common in MSM, particularly among those who engage in unsafe sex practices (Gay and Lesbian Medical Association [GLMA], 2001). Consequently, MSM are 44 to 86 times more likely than non-MSM men to be diagnosed with HIV, and unlike other high-risk groups, their rate of infection is increasing (Division of HIV Prevention, 2010). They also suffer more frequently from hepatitis, pneumonia, and some cancers, and there is further evidence suggesting that the high prevalence of smoking among MSM additionally increases their risk for hypertension and heart disease (ACS, 2010; Division of Viral Hepatitis, 2010). There is also substantial research suggesting that their experience of stigmatization, social exclusion, and violence puts MSM and transgender people at risk for mental disorders, including substance abuse, eating disorders, depressive disorders, and suicide (Cochran, 2001; Feldman & Meyer, 2007; GLMA, 2001; Gruskin et al., 2007; Meyer, 2003).

When seeking health care, MSM and transsexuals are often faced with unique challenges that can compound their risks (GLMA, 2001; Johnson, Mimiaga, & Bradford, 2008). Out of fear of stigmatization, these men often hesitate to disclose their sexual identity, which can result in unhealthy delays in seeking care (GLMA, 2001). They also often encounter a lack of cultural competence, as well as discrimination, on the part of health care providers. Transgender persons, in particular, have unique needs that are little understood by providers (Dean et al., 2000; Green, 2000; Tewksbury & Gagne, 1996). Access to care may also be limited because male partners in committed relationships are often denied health insurance provided to heterosexual spouses (Benditt, Engel, Gavin, & Stransky, 2009). Because MSM are "invisible" and do not always identify themselves as MSM, health research with this population is difficult; data are often limited and unreliable, particularly at a national level (Benditt, Engel, Gavin & Stransky, 2009; Boehmer, 2002). These health care dynamics only further compound the particular vulnerabilities of these populations of men.

Occupational Hazards

Jobs held by men are the most dangerous jobs, as I explain in Chapter 2 (see also Courtenay, 2000b). Although men constitute only half (53%) of the workforce (National Institute for Occupational Safety and Health [NIOSH], 2004), they account for nearly all (92%) fatal injuries on the job (Bureau of Labor Statistics [BLS], 2008; CDC, 2001, 2007b; National Safety Council, 2010). Mining, construction, timber cutting, and fishing have the highest injury death rates, and the largest number of total injury deaths occurs in production, craft and repair, transportation, labor, farming, foresting, and fishing—all of which are jobs held primarily by men (BLS, 1993, 2008; CDC, 1998a, 2010a; NIOSH, 1993, 2006). Among law enforcement officers, 95% of those killed in the line of duty are male (Federal Bureau of Investigation, 2009), and 97% of all firefighters killed are male (U.S. Fire Administration, 2009). Young men aged 25 to 34 years account for the largest number of occupational injury deaths (CDC, 2001).

Injuries, however, are only one cause of occupational morbidity and mortality. Approximately 32 million workers are exposed to one or more chemical hazards (Winawer & Shike, 1995). The five occupations with the greatest percentage of workers exposed to hazardous chemicals are, in descending order, construction, agriculture, oil and gas extraction, water transportation, and forestry—all jobs held primarily by men.

Unemployment

Unemployment is consistently linked with a variety of negative health effects, and there is evidence that these negative effects are greater for men than for women (Artazcoz, Benach, Borrell, & Cortès, 2004; Courtenay, 2000b; Mathers & Schofield, 1998) (see also Chapter 2). Associations between unemployment and psychological problems are stronger among men, and rates of suicide are linked with unemployment and times of economic depression for men, but not for women (Bambra, 2010; Courtenay, 2000b; see also Chapter 2). One prospective study among youth found that unemployment is also a risk factor for increased alcohol consumption, increased tobacco use, illicit drug use, suicide, and unintentional injuries, particularly for males (Hammarstrom, 1994).

Imprisonment

Nearly 1.5 million men are incarcerated in U.S. state and federal prisons (DOJ, 2008a). Prisoners are among those at highest risk for tuberculosis, hepatitis, and HIV (Courtenay & Sabo, 2001; Polych & Sabo, 2001; see also Chapter 7). The incidence of HIV disease in prison is 14 times greater than the incidence of HIV disease in the general population (Smyer, Gragert, & LaMere, 1997). It is estimated that 41% of prisoners in California are infected with hepatitis C (see Polych & Sabo, 2001). Of those, it is estimated that chronic infection will develop in 85%, and that within 20 years, cirrhosis will develop in 20% (Spaulding, Greene, Davidson, Schneidermann, & Rich, 1999). In American jails and prisons, suicide is the third leading cause of death; suicide rates for prisoners are up to over four times higher than the rates for individuals in the general population, and nearly all these deaths are male (CDC, 2010b; Mumola, 2005). Other factors that increase the health risks of prisoners include violence, prison health care, poor health knowledge, and poor diet and nutrition (Courtenay & Sabo, 2001). Finally, newly released prisoners face an increased risk of death 13 times higher than that of the general population; causes include drug overdose, cardiovascular disease, homicide, and suicide (Binswanger et al., 2007).

Societal Beliefs About Masculinity and the Social Treatment of Boys and Men

North Americans strongly endorse the cultural—and health-related—beliefs that men are independent, self-reliant, strong, robust, and tough (Courtenay, 2000c). As I explain in Chapter 3, men and boys experience enormous social pressure to adopt these beliefs, and in general experience comparatively greater social pressure than women and girls to endorse societal prescriptions about gender. Boys experience more ridicule and are punished more severely than girls—by both peers and adults—for engaging in nontraditional or nonstereotypical "boy" behavior (e.g., expressing hurt or asking for help). As I explain in Chapter 3, the contexts in which men and boys live, work, and play often foster unhealthy forms of masculinity. In many of men's sports, for example, the use of aggression, the acceptance of health risks, and the denial of pain are both rationalized and glorified.

From birth through adolescence and early adulthood, parents and other adults treat girls and boys differently in ways that can profoundly influence their health. One study demonstrated that, even in preschool, the degree to which boys conform to masculine norms predicts their injury risk behaviors (Granié, 2010). But even at this age they are expected to conform to gender norms more than girls are (Kane, 2006). Despite the fact that boys are at relatively greater risk, parents are less concerned about the safety of their sons than they are about the safety of their daughters, and boys are also less likely to receive warmth and nurturance, which may both contribute to the development of boys' risks and further compound their risks (Beyers, Bates, Pettit, & Dodge, 2003; Schwartz et al., 2009). Boys are talked to less about sadness and more about anger (Dunn, Bretherton, & Munn, 1987); are perceived as being physically stronger and less vulnerable—despite being more vulnerable; are handled more roughly; engage in more intense and competitive play; and are physically punished more. They are exposed to more violence both inside and outside the home. Boys are also more likely than girls to be encouraged in activities that distance them from their parents, to be discouraged from seeking help, and to be punished when they do seek help. Once at school and among peers, masculinity—toughness and athletic ability—is often associated with high status (Adler, Kleiss, & Adler, 1992), and peer pressure, bullying, or *gay baiting* (calling a boy gay when he demonstrates behavior that is not stereotypically boy behavior) of boys to conform to sex-typical behavior aggressively promote traditional gender norms. This pressure to conform is typically exerted by children who link their own masculine behavior with self-esteem (Gini & Pozzoli, 2006; Lamb, 2009).

This differential treatment by parents and social pressure by peers has both short- and long-term effects on the health of men and boys. As noted earlier, compared with women and girls, men and boys have greater difficulty identifying and expressing their emotions, are more likely to perceive themselves as invulnerable to risks commonly associated with unhealthy behavior and to engage in violent behavior, and are less likely to ask others for help.

Media and Advertisements

My review of research, both in this book (see Chapter 3) and elsewhere (Courtenay, 2000c), indicates that clear distinctions are drawn in the media between the health and health behavior of women and girls and that of men and boys. For example, in prime-time television, 3 times more male than female characters are obese. On television and in films, men are shown smoking 3 to 7 times more often than women. Two thirds of all characters who drink in prime-time television programs are men, and in the various media, alcohol, masculinity, and high-risk behaviors are consistently linked. Boys are 60% more likely than girls to be portrayed using physical aggression on television, and men and boys on television are more likely than women and girls to initiate violence—which typically is rewarded and without negative consequences. In general, women and girls are portrayed in the media as having the greatest health risks and being the most likely to die, whereas men and boys are portrayed as engaging in unhealthy or high-risk behaviors—and as being healthy and invulnerable to the risks that their high-risk behaviors pose. These media representations of gender and health have been found to contribute to negative health effects. For example, there is an association between the viewing of television or video violence and subsequent violent and aggressive behavior, which may be causal (e.g., Anderson & Bushman, 2002; Bushman & Anderson, 2001; Sege & Dietz, 1994; Signorielli, 1993). Similarly, exposure to alcohol consumption on television has been found to be associated with more favorable attitudes toward drinking (Engels, Hermans, van Baaren, Hollenstein, & Bot, 2009; Signorielli, 1993).

Research indicates that advertisements reinforce unhealthy and stereotypical gender behavior among boys and men, which I discuss in Chapter 3. Toy commercials, for example, are more likely to portray boys demonstrating aggressive behavior than girls. Alcohol advertisements are strategically placed in magazines and television programs with predominantly male audiences. For example, *Sports Illustrated*, a magazine most often read by men, has more tobacco and alcohol advertisements than any other magazine (Klein et al., 1993). Advertisers also often portray men in high-risk activities to sell their products. Beer commercials, for example, have been found to link men's drinking with taking risks and facing danger without fear (Signorielli, 1993; Strate, 1992). Tobacco companies link the use of smokeless tobacco with virility and athletic performance in marketing to men (Connolly, Orleans, & Blum, 1992).

Health Knowledge

Research shows that men and boys are less knowledgeable than women and girls are about health in general (American School Health Association, 1989; Chandra & Minkovitz, 2006; Courtenay, 1998a; Mills, 2000), about mental health in particular (Chandra & Minkovitz, 2006), and about specific diseases, such as cancer (Beier & Ackerman, 2003; Bostick, Sprafka, Virnig, & Potter, 1993; Mermelstein & Riesenberg, 1992; Polednak, 1990), heart disease (Ford & Jones, 1991; White & Klimis-Tavantzis, 1992), stroke (CDC, 2008d), STDs (Allen, Fantasia, Fontenot, Flaherty, & Santana, 2009; EDK Associates, 1995), and influenza (Bethel & Waterman, 2009). For example, far more men than women are unaware of the correct symptoms of a stroke—which needs to be treated within the first 3 hours of the first signs of symptoms for the treatment to be effective (CDC, 2008d). Researchers have consistently reported that women and girls know significantly more about skin cancer, sunscreen protection, and the harmful effects of sun exposure than men and boys do (American Academy of Dermatology, 2005; Bostick et al., 1993; Mermelstein & Riesenberg, 1992; Vail-Smith & Felts, 1993). Young men know significantly less about self-examinations for testicular cancer than young women know about self-examinations for breast cancer (Katz, Meyers, & Walls, 1995). Men even have limited knowledge of prostate cancer (Demark-Wahnefried et al., 1995; Steele, Miller, Maylahn, Uhler, & Baker, 2000). Less than half (40%) of men in the United States and Europe identify prostate cancer when asked to identify cancers that they have heard about (Schulman, Kirby, & Fitzpatrick, 2003). Many studies of young adults' knowledge have examined risk factors for HIV and HIV disease. Although gender differences were not found consistently in those studies, when differences are found, young men were less knowledgeable than women (Carroll, 1991; CDC, 2008b; Dekin, 1996; Jadack, Hyde, & Keller, 1995; Johnson et al., 1992; Lollis, Johnson, Antoni, & Hinkle, 1996). The Department of Agriculture (2003) found that men in the United States score significantly lower than women regarding their knowledge of diet, including knowledge of the sources and nutrients in foods, the relationship of specific dietary components to specific diseases, and the number of servings of various food groups in a healthy diet.

This lack of knowledge has a significant impact on men's health. The consistent research finding that men have poorer knowledge of warning signs for cancer than women is believed to explain men's frequent failure to conduct self-examinations for cancer, as well as to explain men's delays in seeking medical help for symptoms of cancer (Evans, Brotherstone, Miles, & Wardle, 2005; Love, 1991). For example, a population-based, case-control study found that people with the least knowledge about skin cancer were at greater risk of death from melanoma (Berwick et al., 2005). Knowledge about prostate cancer has been found to be associated with attending cancer screening (Nijs, Essink-Bot, DeKoning, Kirkels, & Schroder, 2000), and increased knowledge of testicular cancer is associated with positive attitudes toward testicular self-examination, stronger intentions to conduct testicular self-examinations, and higher levels of actual practice of testicular self-examination (Best, Davis, Vaz, & Kaiser, 1996; Murphy & Brubaker, 1990; Steffen, Sternberg, Teegarden, & Shepherd, 1994). A national study (EDK Associates, 1995) found that those people who were least knowledgeable about STDs—and most of them were men—were nearly half as likely as those with more knowledge to look for signs and symptoms. Among those people at highest risk, the least knowledgeable were also the least likely to practice safer sex consistently. The men with less knowledge were less likely to feel comfortable telling their doctors they had an STD, or to have discussed risk assessment, testing, or prevention with a health professional. Indeed, health knowledge is frequently found to be an important determinant of reductions in risky sexual behaviors related to HIV disease (Carmel, 1990; Carroll, 1991; Lollis, Johnson, Antoni, & Hinkle, 1996; Thomas, Gilliam, & Iwrey, 1989). Similarly, most men lack basic knowledge about foods and nutritional risk factors (Altekruse, Cohen, & Swerdlow, 1997). This knowledge is considered essential to improving dietary practices and reducing health risks. Men's lack of knowledge about health matters is caused, in part, by the failure of the health care institutions to educate men, a topic that is discussed in the following section.

HEALTH CARE

The health care system and its allied health fields represent important influences on men's health. This section will discuss the following aspects of health care: insurance coverage and health care costs, health care access, institutional influences and research methodology, clinician–patient interaction and communication, and clinicians' gender biases.

Insurance Coverage and Health Care Costs

Having health insurance coverage is one of the most important predictors of receiving preventive and diagnostic clinical services—such as periodic health examinations and blood and cholesterol screenings (Faulkner & Schauffler, 1997; Hadley, 2003; Urban Institute, 2008). Nearly 5 times more people under age 65 who are uninsured (48%) have no usual place of health care compared with people with private health care coverage (10%) (DHHS, 2009d). Adults under age 65 who are uninsured are also significantly less likely than insured adults to have last contacted a doctor or other health professional within the past 6 months (DHHS, 2009d), and are less likely than those with insurance to seek preventive care (DHHS, 2007a). People without insurance are also at significantly greater risk of being first diagnosed with cancers that are advanced stages (Halpern et al., 2008). Among young adults aged 20 to 29 years, those who are insured make nearly 4 times more doctor visits per year than those who are not insured; among young men specifically, those without insurance are seen for preventive care once every 25 years compared with roughly once every 9 years among young men in general (Fortuna et al., 2009). Consequently, people without health insurance coverage experience greater morbidity, tend to be more severely ill when they are finally diagnosed, and receive less therapeutic care (Hadley, 2003; Urban Institute, 2008). More significantly, people without insurance are at increased risk of death, regardless of whether they are employed (Sorlie, Johnson, Backlund, & Bradham, 1994; Urban Institute, 2008).

In the United States, more men (19%) than women (15%) under age 65* lack health insurance coverage; nearly one in three (29%) unmarried men have no coverage (DHHS, 2009e). Four million more men than women aged 18 to 64 years lack health insurance, and more men than women are uninsured at every age (Institute for Women's Policy Research, 2010). Women represent 7 of 10 adults enrolled in Medicare, the national health insurance program for people aged 65 and older in the United States (DHHS, 2006c). Seventy percent of working-aged men who are uninsured have no regular physician compared with only 27% of those who are insured (Sandman et al., 2000). Nearly one half (48%) of uninsured men recently surveyed did not visit a doctor in the previous year compared with one fifth (21%) of men who were continuously insured (Sandman et al., 2000). These uninsured men were also 3 times more likely to have gone without needed care and not to have had a prescription filled because they could not afford it (Sandman et al., 2000). Men with full coverage are nearly 2 to 3 times more likely to receive recommended preventive services—such as periodic health examinations and blood and cholesterol screenings—than men whose plans do not cover these services (Faulkner & Schauffler, 1997). Adolescents without health insurance are more than twice as likely not to have visited a physician or other health professional in the past year as adolescents with health insurance (DHHS, 2000a). Nearly 3 in 10 (29%) uninsured adolescent boys nationally in grades 5 through 12 report a time when they did not receive needed medical care (Schoen et al., 1998).

Cost (and perceived cost) of medical care are also barriers to health care utilization, particularly for people with low incomes and people without a job or health insurance (Nelson, Thompson, Bland, & Rubinson, 1999). Among adolescent boys nationally, one quarter report that they did not receive medical care because it cost too much or because they lacked health insurance (Schoen et al., 1998). Among male college students, cost was also recently found to be a leading barrier to obtaining health care (Davies et al., 2000). Cost and insurance coverage, however, do not account for gender differences in health care utilization. Even when there is no fee for those services—or when care is paid for through insured health plans—men still use fewer health services than women (Stockwell et al., 1994; Wells et al., 1986). One study showed that women used significantly more primary care medical services than men, even though their mean incomes were lower and the mean cost of their care was higher (Bertakis, Rahman-Azari, Helms, Callahan, & Robbins, 2000).

---

* Persons over 65 years of age in the United States are eligible for government-sponsored Medicare and Medicaid services.

Health Care Access

One in five adolescent boys nationally has not received medical care when he needed it (Schoen et al., 1998), and among urban middle and high school students, males are significantly more likely than females to believe that it is difficult to obtain health care (Aten et al., 1996). One in three men has no regular physician (Sandman et al., 2000). Factors such as geography and time contribute to differences in health care access between men and women, and among men. The unavailability of health services during nonwork hours may further limit access to health care for many working men. People living in rural U.S. communities find it more difficult to obtain care than people in metropolitan areas (Mueller, Ortega, Parker, Patil, & Askenazi, 1999). Rurality, however, does not explain gender differences in access to care. Among rural populations, men and boys in general are less likely than women and girls to visit a physician or to seek help from a mental health clinician (Cook & Tyler, 1989; Dansky, Brannon, Shea, Vasey, & Dirani, 1998; Hoyt, Conger, Valde, & Weihs, 1997).

Institutional Influences and Research Methodology

The health care system, public health departments, and other health-related institutions—as well as medical researchers—have contributed to cultural portrayals of men as healthy and to the invisibility of men's poor health status (Courtenay, 2000a, 2000c, 2002). Historically, women but not men in the United States have been encouraged to pay attention to their health. For example, cancer education during the 20th century was directed primarily at women (Reagan, 1997). Despite their greater risk for the disease, significantly fewer high school men than women in the United States have been taught about AIDS and HIV infection (CDC, 2008b). A variety of scientific methodological factors and research methods also contribute to misperceptions about men's health status. For example, the use of behavioral indices of health—such as bed rest and health care utilization—to determine health status underestimates the significance of men's health problems and confounds our understanding of morbidity. These indices represent how men and women *cope* with illness rather than representing true health status (for further discussion on this topic, see Chapter 4).

Clinician–Patient Interaction and Communication

Men receive significantly less physician time in their health visits than women do, and they generally receive fewer services and dispositions than women (Courtenay, 2000a, 2000c; 2001a). As I discuss in Chapters 3 and 12, men are also provided with fewer and briefer explanations—both simple and technical—in medical encounters. Men also receive less information overall from physicians. In fact, no study has ever found that women receive less information from physicians than men do. Although they are more likely to engage in high-risk behaviors and less likely to adopt health-promoting behaviors, men receive less advice from physicians about changing risk factors for disease during checkups than women do (Friedman, Brownson, Peterson, & Wilkerson, 1994). For example, only 30% of men nationally are counseled by their physicians about the health risks associated with smoking, 22% are counseled about drinking, and only 14% are counseled about STDs (Sandman et al., 2000). They are also less likely than women to be taught how to perform self-examinations (Faigel, 1983; Misener & Fuller, 1995). Only 29% of physicians routinely provide age-appropriate instruction on performing self-examinations for testicular cancer compared with 86% who provide age-appropriate instruction to women on performing breast self-examinations (Misener & Fuller, 1995).

Clinicians' Gender Bias

Gender biases about men and boys (as well as women and girls) influence the counseling and diagnostic decisions of clinicians (Adler, Drake, & Teague, 1990; Fernbach, Winstead, & Derlega, 1989; Ford & Widiger, 1989; Waisberg & Page, 1988). For example, men and boys are under-diagnosed for those mental health disorders that are more commonly diagnosed among women and girls. Perhaps because major depression is diagnosed more often in women than in men (APA, 2000), mental health clinicians are less likely to correctly diagnose depression in men; this remains true even when they have similar scores on standardized measures of depression or present identical symptoms to clinicians (Borowsky et al., 2000; Callahan et al., 1997; Potts, Burnam, & Wells, 1991; Stoppe, Sandholzer, Huppertz, Duwe, & Staedt, 1999). One large and well-constructed study found that clinicians were less likely to identify the presence of depression in men than in women, and that they failed to diagnose nearly two thirds of the depressed men (Potts et al., 1991). This gender bias in the diagnosis of depression contributes to a suicide rate that is up to 18 times higher for men than it is for women (see Table 1.2). Similarly, more women than men are diagnosed with eating disorders; however, some populations of men—notably men involved in athletics and gay or bisexual men—appear to be at increased risk for such disorders (Andersen, 1999; Gomez, 1991; Hausenblas & Carron, 1999). Gender biases may also influence the medicines that one is prescribed. Men are less likely than women to be prescribed any kind of medication (Simoni-Wastila, Ritter, & Strickler, 2004), including psychotropic drugs (Simoni-Wastila, 2000), which further compounds their health risks. (I discuss this further in Chapter 2.) Women in the United States are prescribed nearly 1.5 times more medications than men (DHHS, 2009e). For example, 30% more women than men receive prescriptions for medication to control their high blood pressure (DHHS, 2009e). In contrast, boys may be overprescribed some psychotropic medications. For example, the use of stimulants to treat ADHD among 5- to 14-year-olds has increased significantly during the past 15 years, and methylphenidate medication—which accounts for 90% of the stimulant treatment—is prescribed to 3 to 4 times more boys than girls (Zito et al., 2000).

CONCLUSION

The preceding review provides an overview and brief summaries of key determinants of the health and well-being of U.S. men and boys. Thirty-one key determinants of physical and mental health were identified from a review of literature and were discussed under the following four categories: behaviors of men and boys, health-related beliefs and the expression of emotions and physical distress, underlying factors that influence the health and health-related behaviors and beliefs of men and boys, and health care. This review has important implications for public and private organizations or institutions and health care providers who provide services to men and boys, as well for future policy and research.

Culturally appropriate, gender-specific health promotion and disease prevention interventions are needed for men and boys. Although many counseling and psychological interventions with men have been recommended in the past 2 decades (Courtenay, 2000d), rarely are these interventions designed to reduce men's health risks. Even more rarely are health interventions designed to address the unique needs of various populations of men, such as gay and bisexual men (Ramirez-Valles, 2007; Scarce, 1999), men in prison (Courtenay & Sabo, 2001), African American men (Davis, 1999; Rich, 2001), Native American men (Joe, 2001), rural men (Courtenay, 2006b), men with cancer (Nicholas, 2000), or other populations of men at risk for physical and mental health problems (Furman, 2010). Furthermore, this review suggests that new intervention strategies must go beyond addressing the physiology of individual men to address the environmental, sociocultural, psychological, and behavioral determinants identified here that influence the health of various communities of men and boys, as well as the ways in which these factors mediate men's biological and genetic risks. It is important to note that the social, environmental, psychological, behavioral, biological, and genetic determinants discussed here do not occur in isolation; they are interrelated, and often these determinants compound one another. The multifactorial nature of the risks to the health and well-being of men and boys, as well as the complex interrelationships among these factors, suggests that multidisciplinary and interdisciplinary interventions designed to address the dynamic intersection of these various health determinants are especially needed (Bird & Rieker, 2008; Courtenay, 2000e, 2002; Courtenay & Keeling, 2000a; Rieker & Bird, 2005).

Multidisciplinary and interdisciplinary research, which would inform the development of intervention strategies, is also needed. Although the past decade has witnessed a dramatic increase in the level of interest in men's health among scholars and health scientists internationally, relatively little is known about the subject. Both basic and applied research is necessary, as well as interdisciplinary collaboration to develop interactive models and new gender-specific perspectives on human behavior, health, and illness. The development of interdisciplinary approaches to investigate men's health will require addressing a variety of methodological challenges, including the numerous and varied health determinants involved, and disciplinary differences in outcome measures, populations studied, methodologies applied, and rigor of intervention evaluations.

Most of the key determinants identified here represent factors that are modifiable. Consequently, the resulting adverse health effects of these determinants are preventable. Efforts to address these factors through practice, policy, and research could contribute to enhanced health conditions for men and boys. Furthermore, as the preceding data suggest, many of the health concerns of men and boys—including their injuries and premature mortality as well as their risk behaviors—affect not just themselves but everyone in the community. Therefore, efforts to address these concerns and improve men's health not only will lead to enhanced health conditions for men and boys, but also will contribute to building healthier families and communities.

2

Behavioral Factors Associated With Disease, Injury, and Death Among Men

Evidence and Implications for Prevention*

A variety of factors have been found to influence health. Among these factors are access to care, economic status, and ethnicity (Adler et al., 1994; Angell, 1993; Department of Health and Human Services [DHHS], 1998a; Gibbs, 1988; Laveist, 1993; Pappas, Queen, Hadden, & Fisher, 1993). Gender, however, consistently emerges as the strongest predictor of health and longevity (see Chapter 1). A variety of explanations for the gender disparities in health and longevity have been advanced in the past several decades (Kandrack, Grant, & Segall, 1991; Ory & Warner, 1990; Verbrugge, 1985, 1990; Verbrugge & Wingard, 1987; Wingard, 1984; Wingard, Cohn, Kaplan, Cirillo, & Cohen, 1989). The explanatory power of biological factors in predicting gender differences in morbidity and mortality is compara-tively small (Kandrack et al., 1991; Krantz, Grunberg, & Baum, 1985;

---

* An earlier version of this chapter appeared in the *Journal of Men's Studies*, 9(1), 2000, 81–142, and is used by permission in modified/revised form.

Neel, 1990; Ory & Warner, 1990; Verbrugge, 1985, 1990; Waldron, 1997, 2008). The possibility that poor health behavior on the part of men might account for the disparity was raised as early as the mid-1970s (Goldberg, 1976; Harrison, 1978; Lewis & Lewis, 1977; Waldron, 1976; Waldron & Johnston, 1976). Many of these reviews remain the most frequently cited works on the topic. However, all of them lack the robust evidence provided by national surveillance systems and a large number of more recently published prospective studies and meta-analyses. In addition, these reviews focus principally on smoking, on the use of alcohol and other drugs, and to some extent on risk-taking behavior and occupational hazards. They are limited in their examinations of many other relevant health behaviors. One previous and more extensive review of mine suggested that the more than 5-year difference in the life expectancies of men and women is primarily the result of men's less healthy lifestyle habits (Courtenay, 2000b). There are, however, no recent or thorough reviews that support this belief.

In light of substantial evidence on disease prevention and health promotion derived from research conducted since the mid-1980s, many health scientists contend that health behaviors are one of the most important factors influencing health (Lloyd-Jones, Adams, et al., 2009) and that modifying health behaviors is "probably the most effective way" to prevent disease (Woolf, Jonas, & Lawrence, 1996, p. xxxvii). Although not all health professionals and scholars might agree, the evidence is compelling. According to one former U.S. surgeon general, a wealth of scientific data have "confirmed the importance … of health behaviors in preventing disease" and "suggest that efforts directed at improving these behaviors are more likely to reduce morbidity and mortality in the United States than anything else we do" (Koop, 1996, p. viii). An independent scientific panel established by the U.S. government that has evaluated thousands of research studies during the 1990s estimated that half of all U.S. deaths each year could be prevented through changes in personal health practices (Agency for Healthcare Research and Quality [AHRQ], 2009; U.S. Preventive Services Task Force [USPSTF], 1996). Other health experts reviewing hundreds of studies reached similar conclusions (Woolf et al., 1996).

During the past 10 years, additional analyses of sophisticated and large-scale studies have likewise concluded that half of all deaths are the result of modifiable behaviors (McGinnis & Foege, 2004; Mokdad, Marks, Stroup, & Gerberding, 2004; Stringhini et al., 2010). For example, a recent analysis of national data that examined the decrease in U.S. deaths from heart disease between 1980 and 2000 (Ford et al., 2007) suggests that approximately half of this decrease is the result of changes that people made in four risk factors: cholesterol, hypertension, smoking, and physical inactivity. The risk for diabetes could also be reduced by half through changes in behavior (Tuomilehto & Lindström, 2003). A large case-control study of 52 countries has shown that improvements in nine modifiable risk factors can reduce the risk for a first heart attack by 90% (Yusuf et al., 2004). Consequently, the American Heart Association (AHA) contends that improving such lifestyle factors as diet, weight, cholesterol, blood pressure, physical activity, and tobacco use is "critical" to reducing the risk for heart disease (Lichtenstein et al., 2006, p. 82). A national committee, made up of a coalition of 39 major professional, public, and voluntary organizations and seven federal agencies, has concluded that the "adoption of healthy lifestyles … is critical for the prevention of high blood pressure and is an indispensable part of the management of those with hypertension" (Chobanian et al., 2003, p. 1216). The American Cancer Society (ACS) has also acknowledged that, although genetic factors can play a part in the development of cancer in some individuals, noninherited, modifiable factors have the largest effect on cancer risk (ACS, 2009).

The present review summarizes evidence of gender differences in behaviors that significantly influence the health and longevity of men and women in the United States. Findings from national surveillance systems, population-based studies, and meta-analyses are included whenever possible. The health-related behaviors examined here include those related to health care utilization, preventive care, diet, weight, physical activity, substance use, risk taking, violence, social support, and employment. These behaviors represent risk factors that are modifiable lifestyle habits. Consequently, the adverse health effects of these behaviors are preventable.

HEALTH CARE UTILIZATION

Regular medical examinations are critical to the early detection of many potentially fatal diseases. There are substantial gender differences in health care utilization. Twice as many men (20%) as women (11%) in the United States have no regular source of health care (DHHS, 2009e). Even among those with a usual source of health care, that source is a hospital emergency room or outpatient department for more than 1.5 more men than women (DHHS, 2009d). Men also use fewer health care services than women do and visit physicians less often (DHHS, 2009d). This has been true for decades (e.g., DHHS, 1998a; Hulka & Wheat, 1985; Solis, Marks, Garcia, & Shelton, 1990), and it remains true even when reproductive and other sex-specific conditions are excluded (Centers for Disease Control and Prevention [CDC], 1993a; Green & Pope, 1999; Kandrack et al., 1991; Mansfield, Addis, & Mahalik, 2003; Verbrugge, 1985; Wingard, 1984). Indeed, among adults past the age of childbearing, men are still less likely to have a regular physician. One in four men (24%) aged 45 to 64 years lacks a regular doctor compared with 13% of women (Sandman, Simantov, & An, 2000). Even among persons *with* health problems (e.g., those who report poor health or a limitation in activity resulting from a chronic condition), men are significantly less likely than women to have seen a physician in the past year (DHHS, 1998a).

Having a regular source of medical care (i.e., a regular provider or site) is one of the strongest predictors of access to health care services, which is associated with greater use of preventive health services (Bindman, Grumbach, Osmond, Vranizan, & Stewart, 1996; CDC, 1998b; Lambrew, DeFriese, Carey, Ricketts, & Biddle, 1996). Consequently, men visit doctors less frequently than women. The most recent national data show that more than one in four U.S. men (27%)—almost twice the number of women (14%)—have not seen a physician or other health care professional in more than 1 year (DHHS, 2009d). More than twice as many men as women last saw a physician or other health care professional more than 2 but less than 5 years ago, and the vast majority (75%) of people who have not seen a doctor in more than 5 years are men (DHHS, 2009d). More than twice as many men as women have *never* consulted with a physician or other health care professional (DHHS, 2009d). Men also receive less preventive care. Among adults in the United States, women make 1.5 times as many visits for preventive care as men—22% compared with only 15%, respectively (DHHS, 2003).

These gender differences persist in most age groups. More than half (53%) of men aged 18 to 29 years do not have a regular physician compared with one third (33%) of women in this age group; among 30- to 44-year-olds, two of five men (38%) and one of five women (22%) lack a regular physician (Sandman et al., 2000). Among adults aged 18 to 64 years, women make 1.5 times as many physician visits as men; women between the ages of 18 and 44 make twice as many visits (DHHS, 2009e). Among young adults aged 20 to 29 years, women make more than 4 times as many physician visits as men; in fact, on average, young men see a doctor less than once in 9 years (Fortuna, Robbins, & Halterman, 2009).

These gender differences also remain true for mental health care. As we saw in Chapter 1, men and women are equally likely to meet the criteria for mental health problems and psychiatric diagnoses. Despite this risk, only one third of people who receive psychological services are men (Substance Abuse and Mental Health Services Administration [SAMHSA], 2009, Table G.38). Although more men in the United States have received mental health care or counseling during the past decade, consistently higher numbers of women have done so—17% versus 9% for men (SAMHSA, 2009, Table G.38). Studies for the past 2 decades have found that men are less likely to receive help for interpersonal concerns, substance abuse, or psychological distress—even when their symptoms are similar to those of women (Chino & Funabiki, 1984; Corney, 1990; DHHS, 1993; Good, Dell, & Mintz, 1989; Kessler, Brown, & Boman, 1981; McKay, Rutherford, Cacciola, & Kabaskalian-McKay, 1996; O'Neil, Lancee, & Freeman, 1985; Padesky & Hammen, 1981; Rhodes & Goering, 1994; Rogler & Cortes, 2008; Thom, 1986; Vessey & Howard, 1993; Weissman & Klerman, 1977; Wells, Manning,

Duan, Newhouse, & Ware, 1986; Wills & DePaulo, 1991). Boys are also less likely to receive the care they need. For example, among children and adolescents aged 9 to 17 years who are depressed, boys are less likely than girls to receive professional help (Wu, Hoven, et al., 2001). Similarly, although the prevalence of drug and alcohol dependence or abuse is significantly higher among men than women, nearly twice as many men (11%) as women (6%) do not receive the treatment that they need (SAMHSA, 2009, Table G.34).

Physician visits are especially important for the early detection of disease, particularly for those diseases generally detected through screening (Eyre, Kahn, Robertson, & the ACS/ADA/AHA Collaborative Writing Committee, 2004). Diabetes provides one example. The fact that men see doctors less often helps to explain why, according to the AHA (2009a), twice as many men as women have diabetes that remains undiagnosed. More men than women have diabetes (CDC, 2008a; DHHS, 2009e), which is the sixth leading cause of death in the United States; death rates are nearly 1.5 times higher for men than for women (DHHS, 2009a). Men are 32% more likely than women to be hospitalized for long-term complications of diabetes; they are also more than twice as likely as women to have a leg or foot amputated as a result of complications related to the disease (DHHS, 2010b, 2010c). In addition, the risk for cardiovascular death is 2 to 4 times higher for people with diabetes (Triplitt & Alvarez, 2008). During a 12-year period, people with diabetes are 3 times more likely to suffer an incident of cardiovascular disease than people without diabetes and who have normal blood pressure (Zhang et al., 2006). As noted in Chapter 1, heart disease kills 1.5 times more men than women. Diabetes is also a risk factor for sudden cardiac death, which strikes 3 times more men than women (Lloyd-Jones, Berry, Ning, Cai, & Goldberger, 2009). People with diabetes are at 2 to 6 times more risk for death from stroke (Ingall, 2004; National Institute of Neurological Disorders and Stroke [NINDS], 2004; Triplitt & Alvarez, 2008). Recent research also suggests a link between diabetes and cancer (Giovannucci et al., 2010).

The fact that men see doctors less often also reduces the chance that they will adopt other health-promoting behaviors. For example, people who see a doctor regularly are more likely both to stop smoking and to successfully quit smoking (Kottke, Battista, DeFriese, & Brekke, 1988; Silagy & Stead, 2001). Smoking is the single most preventable cause of illness and death in the United States, as I explain below. Annual medical checkups are also one of the most consistent predictors of ever having a variety of cancer screening tests, or of having had a recent cancer screening test (Bostick, Sprafka, Virnig, & Potter, 1993; Evans, Brotherstone, Miles, & Wardle, 2005; Polednak, 1990). Because men do not receive timely or regular care, their disease is often advanced when they finally do seek help (Dunlop, Manheim, Song, & Chang, 2002). This reduces their life expectancy. Infrequent doctor visits help to explain why more men than women in the United States are first diagnosed with advanced forms of colorectal cancer (Wu, Chen, et al., 2001), skin cancer (Geller, Koh, Miller, Mercer, & Lew, 1992), and kidney cancer (Aron, Nguyen, Stein, & Gill, 2008). The probability of surviving for 5 years among men who are first diagnosed with advanced-stage prostate cancer is only 34% compared with nearly 99% for men who are diagnosed with either localized or regional-stage disease (Stanford et al., 1999). Nearly one in three men (30%) with testicular cancer is not first diagnosed when the disease is localized; consequently, only 72% of these men survive their cancers (Sokoloff, Joyce, & Wise, 2007). Similarly, men's under-utilization of mental health services may help to explain why their mental health problems are more serious than those of women when they do receive psychiatric care (Fabrega, Mezzich, Ulrich, & Benjamin, 1990). It may also help to explain why only 7% of men compared with 14% of women are prescribed medication for a mental health problem each year (SAMHSA, 2009). The underutilization of mental health services and psychotropic medication among males probably contributes to their extraordinarily high suicide rate, which is 2 to 18 times higher than the rate for females (see Chapter 1).

Men and women also differ in their use of other forms of health care. Fewer men (54%) than women (69%) use complementary or alternative forms of medicine to improve their health (CDC, 2005b). Fewer men than women have regular dental checkups (DHHS, 2007c, 2009e; Marks, Garcia, & Solis, 1990; Prohaska, Leventhal, Leventhal, & Keller, 1985; Ronis, Lang, Farghaly, & Passow, 1993)—a fact that contributes to poor oral health among men. Nearly one in three men (28%) compared with one in five women (22%) has not been to a dentist in the past year (American Dental Association [ADA], 2008). This failure to see a dentist regularly further compounds the problems associated with men's poor oral care. I discuss oral care at greater length in the Dental Care section of this chapter.

As I discussed in Chapter 1, these differences cannot be explained by ethnicity; in each ethnic group, men are less likely than women to access health care. For example, in every ethnic group, men are less likely than women to have a usual source of care (DHHS, 2007a). Nor can these differences be explained by socioeconomic status; at each socioeconomic level, men are less likely to access health care. Given that men are at greater risk for heart disease, cancer, and all 10 leading causes of death, these data provide overwhelming evidence that men are underusing health care services. Indisputably, this increases their risk for disease and death. Physician visits are consistently found to be associated with a variety of positive outcomes; in addition, they serve as an occasion to receive "opportunistic" preventive care (Eyre et al., 2004). For example, having a regular source of medical care and seeing a physician in the past year are strongly associated with taking action to control high blood pressure (CDC, 1994a). Consequently, fewer men than women have had their blood pressure checked in the past 2 years, and they are significantly less likely than women to know that they have hypertension, to have it treated, or to have in under control (Burt et al., 1995; CDC, 2005c; Chobanian et al., 2003; Cutler et al., 2008; Egan, Zhao, & Axon, 2010; Ong, Cheung, Man, Lau, & Lam, 2007). Thirty percent more women than men receive prescriptions for medication to control their high blood pressure (DHHS, 2009e). Consequently, 5 to 20% fewer men are treated with medication for hypertension, and 30 to 50% more women than men have their hypertension under control (Burt et al., 1995; CDC, 2005d, 2007c; Chobanian et al., 2003; DHHS, 1998a; Klungel, de Boer, Paes, Seidell, & Bakker, 1997). In fact, during the past 20 years, the treatment of hypertension among women has increased, which has contributed to decreases in the prevalence of high blood pressure among women; however, the prevalence of hypertension has increased among men during the same period (Egan et al., 2010). The fact that women see a doctor more often may also explain why more women than men receive a prescription for *any* kind of medication. In fact, as I noted in Chapter 1, women in the United States are prescribed nearly 1.5 times more medications than men. For example, a recent study showed that individuals needing cholesterol-lowering drug treatment who did not have a regular source of medical care—which, as I have explained, results in fewer doctor visits—were nearly 4 times less likely to receive this needed treatment (Spatz, Canavan, Krumholz, & Desai, 2009).

PREVENTIVE CARE AND SELF-CARE

Preventive care and self-care can significantly reduce the risk for disease and death. Men are less likely than women to engage in a variety of preventive and self-care practices, which contributes to men's increased health risks. For example, fewer men than women with hypertension attempt to control it by changing their eating habits, reducing or eliminating the use of salt or alcohol, losing weight, exercising, or taking medication (CDC, 1994a, 2005c, 2007c), which contributes to men's higher risk for heart disease death. Men are also less likely than women to restrict their activities or stay in bed for both acute and chronic conditions, and they are less likely to persist in caring for a major health problem (DHHS, 1998a; Kandrack et al., 1991; Verbrugge, 1985, 1990). Fewer U.S. men (46%) than women (51%) aged 50 years or older get a flu vaccination, or—among those aged 65 years and older—a vaccination for pneumonia (55 vs. 60%, respectively) (DHHS, 2010d). The failure to receive vaccinations contributes to why men are 24% more likely to be hospitalized for pneumonia that could have been prevented (DHHS, 2010b, 2010c) and why nearly 1.5 times more men than women die of flu and pneumonia every year (DHHS, 2009a). Men are also more likely than women to engage in high-risk food-handling and preparation behaviors that increase their risk for contracting foodborne diseases; these behaviors lead to an estimated 76 million illnesses, 325,000 hospitalizations, and 5,000 to 9,000 deaths in the United States each year—for which men are at significantly greater risk (CDC, 2004c; Mead et al., 1999; Yang et al., 1998). Eight additional preventive and self-care practices are examined below: screening tests, self-examinations, sun protection, dental care, sleep, handwashing, the use of medicines and vitamin supplements, and behavioral responses to stress.

Screening Tests

Screening tests are designed to detect disease before the patient experiences symptoms, at an early stage, when successful treatment is most likely. Although a variety of screening tests are known to be effective in detecting disease early and in reducing the risk for death (Eyre et al., 2004; Lloyd-Jones, Adams, et al., 2009), men are less likely than women to get screened. Men are less likely than women to have had their cholesterol levels checked or checked recently (AHA, 2009a; Powell-Griner, Anderson, & Murphy, 1997; Rossi, 1992), which significantly increases men's risk for cardiovascular disease and diabetes. (Cholesterol is discussed at greater length in the Cholesterol section of this chapter.) The following two sections examine the importance of screening for heart disease and stroke, and screening for other diseases.

Screening for Heart Disease and Stroke

The early detection and treatment of hypertension greatly reduce the risk for death from both heart disease and stroke (Eyre et al., 2004; Ford et al., 2007; Lloyd-Jones, Adams, et al., 2009; National Stroke Association [NSA], 1994; Ong et al., 2007). Recent research indicates that interventions to reduce hypertension should begin in early adulthood (AHA, 2009a). In a study of nearly 10,000 men, researchers in Britain found that hypertension in early adulthood is associated with the risk for death from heart disease and stroke in later life (McCarron, Smith, Okasha, & McEwen, 2000). Reducing the prevalence of men's hypertension by middle age could significantly improve their health and longevity (Terry et al., 2005).

Tragically, these reductions in high blood pressure are not occurring. On the contrary, hypertension is steadily increasing among adults in the United States (Cutler et al., 2008; Fields et al., 2004). Research consistently shows that men have higher rates of hypertension than women (Burt et al., 1995; DHHS, 2009e; Dustan, 1996; Stewart & Silverstein, 2002; Weidner, 2000), although this gender difference begins to reverse after age 55, when women are postmenopausal and the least healthy men have already died. One in three men nationally has hypertension (DHHS, 2009e), up from the one in five that I reported in 2000 (Courtenay, 2000b). An estimated 42 million men in the United States—1.5 times the number of women—have prehypertension, the precursor to high blood pressure (Qureshi, Suri, Kirmani, & Divani, 2005).

As noted previously, fewer men than women have had their blood pressure checked in the past 2 years, and men are less likely than women to be aware of their hypertension, to have it treated, or to have in under control. This greater likelihood of having undiagnosed and untreated high blood pressure is a major contributor to men's greater risk for serious chronic diseases and death. Research, including data from large prospective studies, consistently shows that hypertension significantly increases the risk for heart disease and is also the top controllable risk factor for stroke, which are the first and third leading causes of death in the United States, respectively (AHA, 1996, 2009b; Burt et al., 1995; Chobanian et al., 2003; DHHS, 1991, 2009a; Eyre et al., 2004; Gorelick et al., 1999; Ingall, 2004; Keil et al., 1993; Lichtenstein et al., 2006; Lloyd-Jones, Adams, et al., 2009; Lloyd-Jones, Dyer, Wang, Daviglus, & Greenland, 2007; Lloyd-Jones et al., 2006; Mensah, Brown, Croft, & Greenlund, 2005; NINDS, 2004; NSA, 1995; Stamler et al., 1999; Terry et al., 2005). As I discussed previously, the death rate from heart disease is 1.5 times greater for men than women. Hypertension also increases the risk for sudden cardiac death specifically, which 3 times more men than women die from (Lloyd-Jones, Berry, et al., 2009). Stroke accounts for approximately 1 of every 17 deaths in the United States, and on average every 40 seconds someone has a stroke and every 3 to 4 minutes someone dies from it (AHA, 2009b). Depending on the severity of hypertension, the risk for stroke is 3 to 8 times greater as a result of high blood pressure (Ingall, 2004). Although there is no gender difference in the death rate for stroke, the incidence of stroke is greater among men than women in every age group—except after age 85, when the average man has been dead 10 years (AHA, 2009b).

Screenings are also important to identify atherosclerosis (AHA, 2009a). Evidence from large prospective studies shows that men have worse atherosclerosis than women and that this significantly increases men's risk for heart attack, stroke, and other cardiovascular disease (Dick et al., 2005; Iemolo, Martiniuk, Steinman, & Spence, 2004; Mullenix et al., 2006; NINDS, 2004). Similarly, there is strong evidence to support the value of regular screening to detect diabetes (Eyre et al., 2004), particularly for men; the prevalence of undiagnosed diabetes is significantly higher in men than in women (Cowie et al., 2006). There is also sufficient evidence to recommend regular screening for prediabetes (Eyre et al., 2004). (Before people develop type 2 diabetes, they almost always have prediabetes—blood glucose levels that are higher than normal but not yet high enough to be diagnosed as diabetes.) Screening for prediabetes is especially important because most people with this condition experience no symptoms. According to one large prospective study, prediabetes (specifically defined as impaired fasting glucose levels) increases the 5-year risk for death from heart disease by 250% (Barr et al., 2007). Based on the National Health and Nutrition Examination Survey (NHANES), which examines biological samples of respondents, 26% of adults in the United States aged 20 years or older have prediabetes, and the prevalence is higher among men (Cowie et al., 2006). The prevalence of prediabetes is also higher among boys than girls, and it is increasing for adolescents of both sexes 12 to 19 years old. Between the 1999–2000 and 2005–2006 survey years, impaired fasting glucose levels increased from 7% to 13% for this age group (Li, Ford, Zhao, & Mokdad, 2009; Williams et al., 2005). In 2009, the prevalence of prediabetes for this age group was 16%, and it was nearly 2.5 times greater for boys than for girls (Li et al., 2009).

Screening for Other Diseases

Screening tests are also critical for the early detection of cancer. Half of all new cancer cases can be detected by screening, and the 5-year survival rate is 95% when—through regular screening—these cancers are diagnosed at a localized stage (Eyre et al., 2004; Winawer & Shike, 1995). However, because men see a doctor less often—particularly for preventive care—studies often show that men are less likely than women to be screened for cancer (Bostick et al., 1993; Evans et al., 2005). Although findings regarding gender and screening for some cancers may not be entirely consistent (Evans et al., 2005), men are consistently found to be less likely to get screened for skin cancer—despite their greater risk for melanoma (Berwick, Fine, & Bolognia, 1992; Evans et al., 2005; Geller et al., 2003; Janda et al., 2004; Koh et al., 1991, 1996). Significantly fewer men are screened for prostate cancer than women are screened for cervical and breast cancer (Evans et al., 2005).

Although there is insufficient evidence to recommend routine prostate cancer screening (Smith, Cokkinides, & Brawley, 2009), there is substantial evidence to show that screening significantly reduces the risk for colorectal cancer, the third leading cause of cancer deaths (ACS, 2008; Eyre et al., 2004; Pignone, Rich, Teutsch, Berg, & Lohr, 2002). Typically, early-stage colorectal cancer has no symptoms. Therefore, screening is necessary to detect this cancer in its earliest stages, when it is most curable (ACS, 2008). Ninety percent of people who are diagnosed with colorectal cancer at an early, localized stage survive at least 5 years. However, only 39% of colorectal cancers are diagnosed at this stage (ACS, 2009). With more advanced colorectal cancer, the chance of surviving for 5 years decreases to 10% (ACS, 2009). Consequently, research consistently shows that screening tests substantially decrease the risk for death from colorectal cancer (AHRQ, 2009; Mandel et al., 1993; Newcomb, Norfleet, Storer, Surawicz, & Marcus, 1992; USPSTF, 1996; Winawer, 1993). It is estimated that 50 to 60% of colorectal cancer deaths could be prevented if everyone aged more than 50 were screened routinely (Pignone et al., 2002). Screening for colon cancer is done with a fecal occult blood test (home stool-testing kit) or with a lower endoscopy test (sigmoidoscopy, colonoscopy, or proctoscopy). Beginning at age 50, the former is recommended annually and the latter is recommended every 5 to 10 years (ACS, 2008). Approximately half of U.S. men aged 55 years or older have never received an endoscopy test (CDC, 1999a). Fewer men than women have taken the fecal occult blood test (CDC, 1999a; Evans et al., 2005), which can reduce the risk for cancer by 33% (CDC, 1999a). National data based on a telephone survey indicate that men and women aged 50 years or older are nearly equally likely to have undergone some type of colorectal screening (61 and 60%, respectively) (CDC, 2008e; see also Coups, Manne, Meropol, & Weinberg, 2007). However, the only study to compare medical records with self-reports of colorectal cancer screening found that men—but not women—*reported* undergoing screening more than they actually underwent screening (Griffin et al., 2009). Overreporting of colorectal cancer screening among men in national surveys would help to explain why men's colorectal cancer death rate is 1.5 times higher than the rate for women (ACS, 2008), and why between the early 1970s and the late 1990s the colorectal death rate decreased 25% for women and only 12% for men (ACS, 1997).

Screening is also important for identifying HIV. In fact, the CDC recently recommended that HIV screening be included as part of routine medical care for everyone aged 13 to 64 years (CDC, 2006c). Early diagnosis enables infected people to obtain medical care that can prolong and improve the quality of their lives, and to adopt behaviors to prevent the further transmission of HIV (CDC, 2008f). Indeed, after becoming aware that they are HIV positive, most infected people reduce their high-risk sexual behavior (Marks, Crepaz, Senterfitt, & Janssen, 2005). However, approximately one of four of the estimated 1 million persons living with HIV is unaware that he or she is infected (CDC, 2008f). Three of four of all those infected with HIV are men, and from 2004–2007, newly diagnosed HIV and AIDS cases increased approximately 18% among men and only 8% among women (CDC, 2009b). Despite their substantially greater risk, far fewer men than women are tested for HIV in every age group, from 18 through 45 years (CDC, 2009d). Adolescents and young adults aged 13 to 24 years represent 4% of all those living with HIV, but comprise an estimated 10% of undiagnosed cases (CDC, 2009e). Among high school students, nearly 1.5 times more girls (15%) than boys (11%) have been tested for HIV (CDC, 2009e).

Self-Examinations

Like screenings, self-examinations help to promote health and to detect the early signs and symptoms of disease, particularly for men who see physicians infrequently. Research consistently reveals that, at any age, males are less likely than females to practice self-examinations. Although the majority of men are at medium to high risk for getting a sexually transmitted disease (STD), most men never look for signs and symptoms of STDs (EDK Associates, 1995). Men are also significantly less likely to practice testicular self-examinations than women are likely to practice self-examinations for breast cancer (Katz, Meyers, & Walls, 1995). Between 18 and 40% of women practice breast self-examination, whereas just over 1 to 22% of men practice testicular self-examination (Evans et al., 2005). This remains true even among survivors of cancer, for whom the risk for developing second cancers is high. Only 17% of men in this group perform regular self-examinations for testicular cancer compared with 27% of women who perform breast self-examinations regularly (Yeazel et al., 2004). The failure among men to practice self-examinations contributes to preventable deaths from testicular cancer, which is on the rise. Between the mid-1970s and the late 1990s, the incidence of testicular cancer increased 51% (McKiernan, Goluboff, Liberson, & Fisch, 1999), and it continues to increase (Sokoloff et al., 2007).

Studies suggest that regular self-examinations play a critical role in the prevention of skin cancer (Berwick et al., 2005; Koh, Geller, Miller, & Lew, 1995; Poo-Hwu et al., 1999; Weinstock, 2006), which is the most common and most rapidly increasing cancer in the United States (ACS, 2007; CDC, 1995a, 2003b; Linden, 2004; Rager, Bridgeford, & Ollila, 2005), and according to one study, has now reached epidemic proportions (Rogers et al., 2010). Melanoma is 95% curable when discovered early (CDC, 1995a, 1995b). A population-based, case-control study found that self-examinations may reduce mortality from melanoma by as much as 63% (Berwick, Begg, Fine, Roush, & Barnhill, 1996). However, although men are at greater risk for melanoma, studies consistently show that they are far less likely than women to perform self-examinations for skin cancer (Balanda, Lowe, Stanton, & Gillespie, 1994; Coups, Manne, & Heckman, 2008; Del Mar, Stanton, Gillespie, Lowe, & Balanda, 1996; Girgis, Campbell, Redman, & Sanson-Fisher, 1991; Hill, White, Borland, & Cockburn, 1991; Janda et al., 2004; Kasparian, McLoone, & Meiser, 2009; Miller et al., 1996; Robinson, Rigel, & Amonette, 1998; Weinstock et al., 1999). In one community sample, women were more than 8 times more likely than men to examine their skin thoroughly for signs of cancer (Weinstock et al., 1999). Consequently, studies show that 66 to 69% of women discovered their own skin cancer lesions compared with only 42 to 47% of men (Brady et al., 2000; Koh et al., 1992). A recent population-based study has shown that, even among people *with* melanoma, women are nearly 3 times more likely than men to examine their skin for new lesions (Mujumdar et al., 2009).

Inadequate self-examination—along with insufficient screening by doctors, which I discussed previously—contributes to men's greater risk for melanoma. Although rates of skin cancer continue to increase dramatically (CDC, 2003b; Linden, 2004; Rogers et al., 2010), death rates for melanoma are increasing among men but not women (Jemal et al., 2009). Between 1969 and 1999, the incidence of melanoma among European Americans increased 300% in middle-aged men (aged 45 to 64 years) and 500% in older men (aged 65 years or older); during the same period, mortality rates increased 66% in middle-aged men and 157% in older men compared with 19 and 49% among women in these two age groups, respectively (Geller et al., 2002). Currently, the incidence of melanoma is nearly 60% higher among men than women in the United States (Jemal et al., 2008), and the death rate for men is nearly double that for women (DHHS, 2009a). Inadequate self-examination and screening also help to explain why men are more likely than women to be first diagnosed with thick or advanced-stage melanomas, which significantly increase the risk for death (Berwick et al., 2005; Desmond & Soong, 2003; Geller et al., 1992). Although it is well established that men are also significantly less likely than women to survive a diagnosis of melanoma, it remains unclear whether there is an underlying biological determinant for women's survival advantage or whether this is simply the result of men's tendency to delay postpone seeing a physician (Galdas, Cheater, & Marshall, 2005; Scoggins et al., 2006) or to their failure to examine their skin.

Sun Protection

As noted previously, skin cancer is the most commonly diagnosed and most rapidly increasing cancer in the United States. Melanoma causes approximately three fourths of all skin cancer-associated deaths (CDC, 1995a, 1995b), and males account for two of every three melanoma deaths (DHHS, 2009a). Avoiding direct sunlight and wearing sunscreen, hats, and protective clothing reduce the incidence of many skin cancers (American Academy of Dermatology [AAD], 2005; ACS, 1997). In fact, the most modifiable risk factor for skin cancer is unprotected ultraviolet exposure (Armstrong, 2004; CDC, 2003b). People are exposed to ultraviolet light in a variety of ways, the most intentional of which is through sunbathing. Although more European American women (27%) than men (23%) sunbathe "frequently" (Koh et al., 1997), significantly fewer men than women stay in the shade to avoid the sun (Hall, Miller, Rogers, & Bewerse, 1999) or are careful to protect their skin from sun exposure (AAD, 2005). More women (35%) than men (21%) say that they try to stay in the shade when they are outdoors for a long period (AAD, 2005). In fact, despite greater exposure to the sun and greater risk for melanoma among males, both national data (AAD, 2005; Hall, May, Lew, Koh, & Nadel, 1997; Koh et al., 1997; Santmyire, Feldman, & Fleischer, 2001) and studies of specific populations (Banks, Silverman, Schwartz, & Tunnessen, 1992; Berwick et al., 1992; Hall & Rogers, 1999; Mermelstein & Riesenberg, 1992; Robinson, Rademaker, Sylvester, & Cook, 1997; Weinstock, Rossi, Redding, Maddock, & Cottrill, 2000) consistently show that females of all ages are 1.5 to 4 times more likely than males to engage in a variety of specific sun-protective behaviors—including the use of sunscreen, shade, and protective clothing, and avoiding the sun during midday. Because they fail to protect themselves, more men than women in the

United States experience sunburn (CDC, 2007d; Hall et al., 2003; Saraiya, Hall, & Uhler, 2002), which—according to a meta-analysis of 57 studies—doubles the risk for melanoma (Gandini et al., 2005).

Reviews of research suggest that using sunscreen can reduce the risk for skin cancer, although this finding is not without controversy (Gasparro, Mitchnick, & Nash, 1998; Naylor & Farmer, 1997). It is estimated that sunscreen with a solar protection factor (SPF) of at least 15 blocks 93% of the burning rays (Preston & Stern, 1992). Sunscreen used in young adulthood was estimated in one study to lower the risk for skin cancer by as much as 80% (Stern, Weinstein, & Baker, 1986). More than twice as many women (34%) as men (16%) apply sunscreen when they are going to be out in the sun (AAD, 2005), and studies have consistently found that males are less likely than females to wear sunscreen with an SPF of 15 or higher and to reapply sunscreen after swimming (Banks et al., 1992; Koh et al., 1997, Mermelstein & Riesenberg, 1992; Weinstock et al., 2000). Among high school students nationally, half as many males (7%) as females (14%) use sunscreen most of the time or always when they are outside for more than 1 hour on a sunny day (CDC, 2008b). However, there is scant evidence that using sunscreen prevents cancer (Dadlani & Orlow, 2008). More important than the use of sunscreen—or any single form of sun protection—is the use of multiple protective strategies, which is less common among men than women. In fact, national data indicate that men are more likely than women to engage in multiple skin cancer risk behaviors (Hall et al., 1997), including infrequent use of sun-protective clothing, staying out in the sun on a sunny day, infrequent use of sunscreen with an SPF of at least 15, use of indoor tanning devices, and getting sunburns (Coups et al., 2008). This contributes to men's disproportionate risk for dying from skin cancer, which is double that of women.

Dental Care

Twelve percent fewer men (74%) than women (86%) in the United States believe that taking good care of mouth, teeth, and gums is absolutely necessary for good health (ADA, 2008). It is not surprising, then, that men have poorer dental care habits than do women. National data consistently reveal that men are significantly less likely than women to brush or floss their teeth (ADA, 2004a, 2004b, 2008, 2009; Ronis et al., 1993; Swank, Vernon, & Lairson, 1986). Only 66% of men, compared with 86% of women, brush their teeth at least twice a day (ADA, 2008, 2009), and only one in five men, compared with nearly one in three women, brush their teeth after every meal (ADA, 2004b). Although dentist visits are a critical part of preventive dental care, fewer men (75%) than women (89%) have a dentist (ADA, 2004b), and men have consistently fewer visits than women (DHHS, 2007c; Marks et al., 1990; Prohaska et al., 1985; Ronis et al., 1993). In every age group, far fewer U.S. males than females have been to a dentist in the past year (DHHS, 2009e). Among those aged 18 to 64 years, only 57% of men, compared with 67% of women, have seen a dentist in the past year (DHHS, 2009e). Nearly 1.5 times more men than women have not been to a dentist for more than 5 years; twice as many men as women have never been to a dentist (DHHS, 2009d).

As a result of men's poor dental habits, the prevalence of root caries, or tooth decay, is higher among men than women (DHHS, 2007c). The prevalence of untreated tooth decay is higher among adult men (28%) than women (23%), and the prevalence of destructive periodontal disease is nearly twice as high in men (20%) as in women (12%) (DHHS, 2007c). Poor oral hygiene, periodontal disease, and tooth loss can cause bacteria to enter the bloodstream—causing inflammation and contributing to atherosclerosis (I discuss atherosclerosis at greater length in the Diet, Weight, and Physical Activity section of this chapter); they have also been found to be independent risk factors for heart disease (De Oliveira, Watt, & Hamer, 2010; for reviews, see Humphrey, Fu, Buckley, Freeman, & Helfand, 2008; Mustapha, Debrey, Oladubu, & Ugarte, 2007) and a variety of cancers, including oral, lung, and pancreatic cancer (for reviews, see Fitzpatrick & Katz, 2010; Meyer, Joshipura, Giovannucci, & Michaud, 2008). As noted previously, the risk for both heart disease and cancer is significantly higher among men than women. The death rate for both oral and lung cancer is nearly 300% higher for men than women, and the death rate for pancreatic cancer is 30% higher (Jemal et al., 2008).

Sleep

Getting sufficient sleep is another form of self-care. People who sleep fewer than 6 hours per night, in particular, are at increased risk for disease and death. Only 71% of men compared with 80% of women believe that getting a good night's sleep is absolutely necessary for good health (ADA, 2008). Not surprisingly, men get significantly less sleep than women (CDC, 2008g; Rediahs, Reis, & Creason, 1990; Reyner & Horne, 1995; Sleep Foundation, 2002, 2005; Van den Berg et al., 2009; Verbrugge, 1988). Far more women (35%) than men (26%) report getting more than 8 hours of sleep on workdays and on the weekends (54 and 51%, respectively) (Sleep Foundation, 2002). On the other hand, more men than women report sleeping 6 hours or less per night (CDC, 2008g; Sleep Foundation, 2005). Even among a national sample of 11,000 health-conscious respondents, the men reported sleeping 6 hours to the women's 8 hours (Results of National Stress Survey, 1995). Furthermore, although both men and women get less sleep than they report (Lauderdale, Knutson, Yan, & Rathouz, 2008), women are more accurate in their reporting than men, who significantly overestimate the time they sleep (Van den Berg et al., 2009).

People who sleep fewer than 6 hours per night significantly increase their risk for hypertension (Gangwisch et al., 2006; Gottlieb et al.,

2006), diabetes (Gangwisch et al., 2007), and cardiovascular disease or death from any cause (Ferrie et al., 2007; Kripke, Garfinkel, Wingard, Klauber, & Marler, 2002). Sleep influences health in a variety of ways. Insufficient sleep or chronic partial sleep loss can increase the risk for obesity and diabetes by causing changes in appetite and other physiological changes (Knutson, Spiegel, Penev, & Van Cauter, 2007; Patel & Hu, 2008). Sleep also influences health behavior. Compared with people who are well rested, people who get insufficient sleep are far less likely to exercise (28% vs. 8%), eat healthy foods (23% vs. 7%), or engage in leisure activities (30% vs. 7%); they are also more likely to smoke cigarettes or use other forms of tobacco (18% vs. 10%) (Sleep Foundation, 2009). Compared with men who sleep 7 to 8 hours per night, men who sleep fewer than 6 hours are more likely to smoke, drink five or more drinks in 1 day, engage in less physical activity, and be obese (Schoenborn & Adams, 2008). There is also growing evidence that immune function decreases with even modest sleep deprivation (Imeri & Opp, 2009; Irwin et al., 1994; Lashley, 2003; Moldofsky, Lue, Davidson, & Gorczynski, 1989).

The quality of men's sleep is also poorer than that of women (Kripke et al., 1997; Rediahs et al., 1990; Redline, Kump, Tishler, Browner, & Ferrette, 1994; Reynolds, Mesiano, Houck, & Kupfer, 1993; Van den Berg et al., 2009; Wauquier, Van Sweden, Lagaay, Kemp, & Kamphuisen, 1992). Men's sleep is more fragmented (Van den Berg et al., 2009); one in four middle-aged and older men experience sleep-disordered breathing at night, which often remains undiagnosed (Mehra et al., 2007; Young et al., 1993). Sleep apnea is the most serious of the sleep disorders; undiagnosed sleep apnea is a major public health problem (Phillipson, 1993; Punjabi, 2008; Young et al., 1993). Research from both clinic-based and epidemiological studies indicates that sleep apnea is 3 to 8 times more prevalent in men than women (Hla et al., 1994; Punjabi, 2008; Redline et al., 1994; Young et al., 1993). The most comprehensive assessment of mortality risks associated with sleep-disordered breathing to date found that people with severe sleep-disordered breathing were 3 times more likely to die from any cause during the course of the study than people without sleep-disordered breathing (Young et al., 2008). The risk for death was even greater for those whose condition remained untreated. People with untreated, severe sleep-disordered breathing were 4 times more likely to die from any cause and 5 times more likely to die from cardiovascular disease (Young et al., 2008). Previous studies have linked sleep-disordered breathing and sleep apnea with an increased risk for hypertension, heart attack, cardiovascular disease, and death (Gami, Howard, Olson, & Somers, 2005; Hung, Whitford, Parsons, & Hillman, 1990; Marin, Carrizo, Vicente, & Agusti, 2005; Marshall et al., 2008; Mehra et al., 2007; Nieto et al., 2000; Punjabi, 2008; Yaggi et al., 2005). Sleep-disordered breathing is also associated with poorer driving performance (CDC, 2009f; Findley, Levinson, & Bonnie, 1992; Vorona & Ware, 2002). One study found that people with mild to moderate sleep-disordered breathing performed worse on reaction time tests than people whose blood alcohol levels were sufficiently high to be illegal for driving a commercial motor vehicle (Powell et al., 1999).

Gender differences in sleep probably also contribute to men's significantly higher injury rates. (Rates of injuries caused by risk taking are discussed in the Risk Taking and Reckless Behavior section of this chapter.) Each year, sleepiness is believed to cause 17,000 nighttime injury deaths, 3,500 unintentional injury deaths at home, and more than half of all work-related injury deaths (Leger, 1994). Men account for 93% of the 16 work-related deaths that occur each day (CDC, 2001, 2007b), and although gender-specific nighttime injury death rates are not available, males of all ages account for nearly 7 of every 10 unintentional injury deaths (NSC, 1994, 2010). Driving while drowsy also contributes to an estimated 200,000 automobile crashes, thousands of deaths each year (National Highway Traffic Safety Administration cited in National Sleep Foundation, 1995), and as many as one in four single-vehicle crashes (Brown, 1994; Summala & Mikkola, 1994). Men are at far greater risk than women for crashes that are caused by sleepiness (CDC, 2009f).

Hand Washing

Washing one's hands with soap can significantly reduce the spread of viral infections, including norovirus (Heijne et al., 2009), rotavirus (Lieberman, 1994), and influenza (Grayson et al., 2009; Moyad & Robinson, 2008). Research based on observations or electronic surveillance of public washrooms consistently shows that men are significantly less likely than women to wash their hands, or to wash them effectively with soap (Anderson et al., 2006; Fung & Cairncross, 2007; Judah et al., 2009; Kinnison, Cottrell, & King, 2004). Men's failure to wash their hands contributes to their increased risk for viral infections, including flu—which is among the 10 leading causes of death and kills nearly 1.5 times more men than women (DHHS, 2009a). The failure to wash one's hands can also increase the risk for contracting foodborne illnesses (CDC, 2004c; Mead et al., 1999). As noted previously, people in the United States contract an estimated 76 million foodborne illnesses a year, resulting in 325,000 hospitalizations and 5,000 to 9,000 deaths. The incidence of foodborne illness is significantly higher among males than females of all ages (CDC, 2006d). The most common foodborne illness is campylobacteriosis, which is linked to—among other things—the improper handling, preparation, or consumption of poultry products (Altekruse, Cohen, & Swerdlow, 1997; CDC, 2006d; Friedman et al., 2004). The incidence of campylobacteriosis is substantially higher among males than females (CDC, 2006d; Friedman et al., 2004).

Use of Medicines and Vitamin Supplements

Men take significantly fewer medicines than women do (Cafferata, Kasper, & Berstein, 1983; Helling et al., 1987; Lassila et al., 1996;

Rossitter, 1983; Verbrugge, 1982, 1985, 1990). This applies to many different classes of drugs, both prescription and nonprescription (Simoni-Wastila, Ritter, & Strickler, 2004), as well as psychotropic drugs (Simoni-Wastila, 2000). This also remains true even for medical conditions that are more likely to occur among males (Rossitter, 1983), such as hypertension (Burt et al., 1995; CDC, 2005c, 2007c; Cutler et al., 2008; DHHS, 1998a, 2009d; Klungel et al., 1997). Men are also at highest risk for not taking their hypertension medication (Costa, 1996), which increases their risk for heart disease. Among older adults, men are less likely than women ever to have been vaccinated against pneumonia (CDC, 2008h; Powell-Griner et al., 1997); this may help to explain why the death rate for pneumonia is nearly 1.5 times higher for men (DHHS, 2009a). Women have also been found to be 48% more likely than men to use any psychotropic medication, after controlling for health status, economic status, diagnosis, and other demographics (Simoni-Wastila, 2000).

As I explain in the Diet section of this chapter, men's diets are less nutritious and consequently provide insufficient vitamins and minerals. For example, 23% of men, compared with 15% of women, have diets that provide inadequate levels of vitamin E (Murphy, Subar, & Block, 1990). Despite this deficit in their diets, men are less likely than women to take vitamin and mineral supplements (Balluz, Kieszak, Philen, & Mulinare, 2000; Block et al., 1988; Dickinson, Block, & Russek-Cohen, 1994; Evatt, Terry, Ziegler, & Oakley, 2009; Rakowski, 1986; Schleicher, Carroll, Ford, & Lacher, 2009; Slesinski, Subar, & Kahle, 1995; Subar & Block, 1990). A majority of women (57%), compared with a minority of men (43%), use supplements, and more women than men use supplements in every age and ethnic group (Balluz et al., 2000). In a large study of college students, men were less likely than women to have positive attitudes toward vitamin-fortified foods and to believe that these foods provided health benefits (Kolodinsky et al., 2008). In one study of elderly subjects, women were significantly more willing than men to take calcium and vitamin D supplements to help prevent fractures; men over 85 were the most resistant to supplement therapy (Larsen, Mosekilde, & Foldspang, 2001). Yet according to one global study, elderly men may be more at risk for deficiency than women (Wilkins, Shelin, Roe, Birge, & Morris, 2006).

Although there is increasingly strong evidence of the health-protective effects of vitamins from natural sources, findings regarding the protective effects of vitamin supplements are equivocal. There is increasing evidence, however, that vitamin E and C supplements can improve immunity in healthy individuals and reduce the risk for heart disease, cancer, and overall mortality (Enstrom, Kanim, & Klein, 1992; Gridley et al., 1992; Kristal, Stanford, Cohen, Wicklund, & Patterson, 1999; Losonczy, Harris, & Havlik, 1996; Meydani et al., 1997; Rimm et al., 1993; Stephens et al., 1996; Suzukawa et al., 1998). There is also evidence linking vitamin D supplements with the prevention of osteoporosis and bone fractures, as well as healthy immune and cognitive functioning, and positive mood among older adults (Wilkins et al., 2006).

Behavioral Responses to Stress

Self-care in response to stress is an important factor in minimizing the potentially negative effects of stress. Men, however, tend to respond to stress in less healthy ways than women do—ways that not only fail to reduce men's stress but also often further compound the negative effects of that stress (Stanton & Courtenay, 2003). They are more likely than women to use avoidant coping strategies—such as denial, distraction, and increased alcohol consumption—and are less likely to use healthy, vigilant coping strategies and to acknowledge that they need help (Addis & Mahalik, 2003; Biener, 1987; Chaplin, Hong, Bergquist, & Sinha, 2008; Friedman, 1991; Hellerstedt & Jeffery, 1997; Kopp, Skrabski, & Szedmak, 1998; Landsbergis et al., 1998; Mansfield et al., 2003; Stanton & Courtenay, 2003; Weidner, 2000; Weidner, Boughal, Connor, Pieper, & Mendell, 1997; Weidner & Collins, 1993; Whitfield, Weidner, Clark, & Anderson, 2002). Furthermore, recent research suggests that, in response to stress, men engage in more risk-taking behaviors, whereas women become more avoidant of risk (Lighthall, Mather, & Gorlick, 2009). Men—but not women—respond to job strain by increasing such unhealthy behaviors as cigarette smoking, excessive alcohol and coffee consumption, and failure to exercise (Weidner et al., 1997). Similarly, men—but not women—who are exposed to a disaster often respond by increasing their alcohol consumption (Solomon, 2002).

Men have also been found to deny their physical or emotional distress, or to attempt to conceal their illnesses or disabilities (Charmaz, 1995; Courtenay, 1998a, 2001a, 2003; Stanton & Courtenay, 2003; Sutkin & Good, 1987). Among people with depression, men are more likely than women to rely only on themselves, to withdraw socially, to try to talk themselves out of feeling depressed, and to drink alcohol or use drugs, intending to distract themselves or to alleviate their depression (Chino & Funabiki, 1984; Courtenay, 1998a, 2003; Nolen-Hoeksema, 1987; O'Neil et al., 1985; Stanton & Courtenay, 2003; Warren, 1983). These behavioral responses compound the problems associated with depression. Furthermore, they contribute to the poor outcomes associated with stressful events among men, and boys as well. The consequences of not receiving needed mental health care can be dire. For example, although boys are more negatively affected than girls by the death of a parent, and men are more negatively affected than women by the death of a spouse (Gomez, 1991; Miller & Wortman, 2002; Stroebe, Stroebe, & Schut, 2001), men and boys are less likely to be treated for these emotional crises. This contributes to the high rate of suicide among men and boys, which I discussed in Chapter 1. Unhealthy behavioral responses can also compound the problems associated with heightened cardiovascular arousal or reactivity to stress, which is more common in men than in women, and which has been shown to predict heart disease—particularly in men. I discuss this subject at greater length below.

DIET, WEIGHT, AND PHYSICAL ACTIVITY

For the past 20 years, more and more people have been eating a poor diet and getting insufficient exercise—factors that may soon surpass tobacco as the leading risk factor associated with death (Mokdad et al., 2004). Today one in three cancer deaths is attributed to poor diet and physical inactivity (ACS, 2009). Whereas deaths resulting from other causes decreased since 1990, deaths attributable to poor diet—along with a sedentary lifestyle—increased significantly during this same period (Mokdad et al., 2004). Indeed, after tobacco use, poor diet and physical inactivity account for the most disease that leads to death (Mokdad et al., 2004). In this section, I discuss gender differences in diet, weight, and physical activity, and the health effects of these differences.

Diet

Eating a healthy diet significantly reduces the risk for death from any cause (Knoops et al., 2004), including heart disease (Dauchet, Amouyel, Hercberg, & Dallongeville, 2006) and cancer (Byers et al., 2002; Kushi et al., 2006); it appears to even help prevent cancer in people whose diet was poor in the past (Winawer & Shike, 1995). A decreased risk for a variety of chronic diseases and causes of death is associated with dietary patterns that emphasize whole-grain foods, legumes, vegetables, and fruits and that limit red meat, full-fat dairy products, and foods and beverages high in added sugars (Eyre et al., 2004; Hu & Willet, 2002; Kushi et al., 2006). A healthy diet can improve several of the known risk factors for heart disease (Eyre et al., 2004; Hu & Willet, 2002; Lichtenstein et al., 2006), and—in conjunction with physical activity—can reduce the risk for diabetes even more effectively than medication (Diabetes Prevention Program Research Group, 2009). An estimated one third of all cancer deaths are attributable to diet, regardless of body weight or level of physical activity (Eyre et al., 2004).

The diets and dietary habits of women differ considerably from those of men. Research consistently suggests that women attach greater importance to healthy eating and to choosing foods that are high in nutrients (Fagerli & Wandel, 1999; Levi, Chan, & Pence, 2006; Melanson, 2008; Wardle et al., 2004). Only 74% of men believe that eating well is absolutely necessary for good health, compared with 86% of women (ADA, 2008), and women are more likely to read food labels or be aware of which foods are healthy (Levi et al., 2006; Wardle et al., 2004). It is not surprising, then, that men's diets are consistently found to be less healthy and less nutritious than women's diets (Melanson, 2008; Oleckno & Blacconiere, 1990a; Renner et al., 2008; Shi, 1998; Walker, Volkan, Sechrist, & Pender, 1988; Wardle et al., 2004; Weissfeld, Kirscht, & Brock, 1990). Men are significantly less likely than women to eat fruit and vegetables, or to eat foods that are high in fiber and low in fat or sodium (Baker & Wardle, 2003; Melanson, 2008; Serdula et al., 2004; Stables et al., 2002; Wardle et al., 2004). Only one in five men (20%), compared with nearly one in three women (29%), eats fruits and vegetables five or more times a day (Serdula et al., 2004). Research also consistently shows that men eat much more red meat than women (Center for Nutrition Policy and Promotion, 2000; Gossard & York, 2003; Kann et al., 1998; Prattala et al., 2006; Williamson, Foster, Stanner, & Buttriss, 2004) and are less likely than women to limit red meat in their diets (Kann et al., 1998; Rakowski, 1986). National data indicate that this difference amounts to 74 grams a day (Gossard & York, 2003), or nearly 1.5 times more servings of meat a day than women eat (Center for Nutrition Policy and Promotion, 2000). In addition, 70% more men than women get their dietary calories from alcohol rather than food (DHHS, 2002b). Based on extensive research linking poor health with poor diet—including high red meat consumption and low fruit and vegetable intake—gender differences in diet and dietary habits are clearly a major contributor to men's disproportionately high risk for heart disease and cancer, the leading killers in the United States (ACS, 1997; AHA, 1996; Denke, Sempos, & Grundy, 1993; Emmons et al., 2005; National Cancer Institute [NCI], 1996; Oppenheim, 1994); these factors are also a major contributor to men's risk for the precursor to heart disease: metabolic syndrome. This syndrome consists of a cluster of risk factors linked to heart disease, including high glucose levels, abnormal cholesterol levels, excess weight, and hypertension. Among adults in the United States, where differences in the prevalence of metabolic syndrome exist, men are at greater risk (Ford, 2005). This gender disparity in risk is seen as early as adolescence. As a result of their poorer diet (along with their lack of sufficient exercise), metabolic syndrome is 2.5 to 3 times more common among 12- to 19-year-old males than among females of the same age (Cook, Auinger, Li, & Ford, 2008; Pan & Pratt, 2008).

Poor dietary habits also contribute significantly to men's and boys' increased risk for being overweight. Compared with nonoverweight youth, overweight adolescent boys consume a greater proportion of their daily energy (nearly 10%) from soft drinks (Troiano, Briefel, Carroll, & Bialostosky, 2000). (I discuss obesity and overweight at greater length in the Weight section of this chapter.) Among high school students nationally, 10% more males (39%) than females (29%) drink a can, bottle, or glass of soda at least once a day (CDC, 2008b). Adolescents who do not drink soft drinks consume fewer overall calories per day than those who drink more than 26 ounces of soft drinks per day (Harnack, Stang, & Story, 1999). A recent large study provides preliminary findings of a link between the consumption of two or more soft drinks per week and a nearly doubled risk for pancreatic cancer (Mueller et al., 2010)—which, as noted previously, kills 30% more men than women. The AHA recommends limiting the consumption of beverages with added sugars to help reduce the risk for heart disease (Lichtenstein et al., 2006). Indeed, a recent study has linked a high intake of fructose—which is found in soft drinks—with higher levels of blood pressure (Jalal, Smits, Johnson, & Chonchol, in press).

Meats and Dietary Fat

High levels of dietary fat, particularly saturated fat, have been associated with increased risk for heart disease (Ascherio, 2002; Eyre et al., 2004; Kuller, 2006)—the leading cause of death—and cancer (ACS, 2009; Byers et al., 2002; Eyre et al., 2004; Mayne et al., 2001). Limiting dietary fat is considered a primary means to improve health, reduce weight, and prevent these diseases, as well as stroke and diabetes (AHA, 1996; Eyre et al., 2004; Winawer & Shike, 1995). Most saturated fat comes from animal sources—especially from meat.

As noted previously, men eat more meat that women do. They are also less likely than women to limit fat in their diets (Kann et al., 1998; Rakowski, 1986), and more likely than women to eat meals away from home or in restaurants, and to eat convenience foods, which are all high in fat (Department of Agriculture, 2003; Foerster & Hudes, 1994). Consequently, males of all ages consume more saturated fat than females do, even when sex differences are adjusted for body size (American School Health Association [ASHA], 1989; Block, Rosenberger, & Patterson, 1988; CDC, 1995c, 1997a, 2010c; Kann et al., 1998; Rossi, 1992; Shi, 1998; Van Horn et al., 1991). Total fat intake in grams is 1.5 times higher for males than females of all ages (DHHS, 2002b).

Saturated fat is a significant risk factor for heart disease and stroke (AHA, 2009a; Eyre et al., 2004; Hu, Manson, & Willett, 2001; Hu & Willet, 2002). Dietary fat—and animal fat in particular—is directly related to the risk for advanced prostate cancer (ACS, 2009; Byers et al., 2002; Franceschi, 1994; Gann et al., 1994; Giovannucci et al., 1993; Hayes et al., 1999; LeMarchand, Kolonel, Wilkens, Myers, & Hirohata, 1994; Meyer, Bairati, Shadmani, Fradet, & Moore, 1999; Pienta & Esper, 1993a, 1993b; Whittemore et al., 1995). Population-based, prospective data indicate that a high intake of red meat is linked with a greater risk for rectal cancer, and that long-term consumption of both red and processed meats is associated with colon cancer—particularly when compared with consumption of poultry and fish (Byers et al., 2002; Chao et al., 2005; Cross et al., 2007; Larsson & Wolk, 2006). A high intake of red meat and processed meats has also been linked with a greater risk for lung cancer, and a high intake of red meat has been linked with cancers of the esophagus and liver (Cross et al., 2007). In contrast, a diet high in fresh vegetables and fruits—particularly citrus fruits—has been linked with a reduced risk for cancer of the esophagus (De Stafani, Deneo-Pellegrini, Ronco, Boffetta, & Barrios, 2006). As noted previously, the death rate for lung cancer is nearly 3 times higher for men than for women. In addition, the death rate for esophageal cancer is nearly 5 times higher for men than for women, and the death rate for liver cancer is 3 times higher (Jemal et al., 2008). Finally, there is evidence that a low-fat diet decreases the incidence of skin tumors in those with a history of skin cancer (Black et al., 1994); as noted previously, men are far more likely than women to have skin cancer.

Cholesterol

Dietary cholesterol increases levels of total cholesterol and low-density lipoprotein (LDL or "bad") cholesterol in the blood (Hu, Manson, & Willett, 2001), which significantly increases the risk for heart disease (AHA, 2009a; Lichtenstein et al., 2006; Lloyd-Jones et al., 2006). Furthermore, dietary cholesterol intake has been shown to have an independent influence on the risk for heart disease, apart from its role in increasing blood cholesterol levels (National Academies Press, 2005; Stamler, Neaton, Garside, & Daviglus, 2005). The primary sources of dietary cholesterol are eggs, dairy, and meat. Whereas the dietary cholesterol intake of girls and women of all ages is generally within the recommended range, the cholesterol intake of boys and men is much higher (Block et al., 1988; Briefel & Johnson, 2004; CDC, 2010c; Lloyd-Jones, Adams, et al., 2009; White & Klimis-Tavantzis, 1992). As a result, national surveys have consistently found that men and boys have lower high-density lipoprotein (HDL or "good") cholesterol levels than women and girls, even when gender differences are adjusted for body size (Block et al., 1988; Carroll et al., 2005; Van Horn et al., 1991; Weidner, 2000). At the same time, significantly more men than women have higher levels of LDL cholesterol (AHA, 2009b; Carroll et al., 2005; Lichtenstein et al., 2006). Only after age 70 (when only the healthiest men are still alive) do women's LDL levels exceed those of men (Carroll et al., 2005). Men under age 50 are at especially high risk for having elevated total cholesterol levels (Carroll et al., 2005; Stewart & Silverstein, 2002; Williams, Winkleby, & Fortmann, 1993). Disturbingly, abnormal cholesterol levels are now found in one in five youth aged 12 to 19 years (CDC, 2010c). Of these, 1.5 times more males (24%) than females (16%) have levels that are abnormal; furthermore, nearly 3 times more male (11%) than female (4%) youth have low HDL levels (CDC, 2010c). Up to twice as many men as women under age 55 have cholesterol levels high enough to require clinical intervention (Sempos et al., 1993). Consequently, a large national population-based study found that dyslipidemia—that is, abnormal blood cholesterol levels, including LDL, HDL, and total cholesterol levels—is significantly more common in men than in women (Goff et al., 2006).

This study also found that dyslipidemia is treated and controlled less often in men than in women.

Research, including large prospective studies, consistently shows that high blood cholesterol significantly increases the risk for diabetes (Sattar et al., 2008), and death from heart disease (Eyre et al., 2004; Keil et al., 1993; Lewington et al., 2007; Lloyd-Jones et al., 2006; Lloyd-Jones, Adams, et al., 2009; Mensah et al., 2005; Stamler et al., 1999, 2005; Stamler & Neaton, 2008; Terry et al., 2005)—including the risk for sudden cardiac death specifically (Lloyd-Jones, Berry, et al., 2009). One study estimated that every 1% reduction in cholesterol leads to a 2% reduction in heart disease risk (Roth & Streicher-Lankin, 1995). A recent analysis of national data concluded that between 1980 and 2000, 24% of potential deaths from heart disease were prevented by reductions in cholesterol (Ford et al., 2007).

One in three men, compared with 1 in 10 women, will develop a major cardiovascular disease before age 60 (AHA, 2000). Therefore, reducing cholesterol levels is especially important for men. Indeed, there is some evidence that reducing cholesterol levels may be even more important for men than for women in lowering the risk for heart disease (Walsh & Grady, 1995). One large study involving 360,000 men found that for every 38 mg/dl decrease in cholesterol, there is a 50% decrease in death from cardiovascular causes (Stamler, Vaccaro, Neaton, & Wentworth, 1993). Lowering men's cholesterol early in adulthood also appears to be important. A strong correlation has been found between men's serum cholesterol level measured early in adult life and the incidence of cardiovascular disease in midlife (Klag et al., 1993). Furthermore, a large prospective study has shown that lower levels of blood cholesterol in middle age predict morbidity-free survival to age 85, including the freedom from heart disease and cancer (Terry et al., 2005).

Blood cholesterol levels have been shown to predict levels of atherosclerosis (Stensland-Bugge, Bonaa, & Joakimsen, 2001). Atherosclerosis—or hardening of the arteries—is the buildup of plaque within the walls of the arteries. This plaque, which is prone to calcification, consists of fatty deposits, inflammation, cells, and scar tissue. The buildup of plaque is caused primarily by consuming animal fat and dietary cholesterol; it is the underlying cause of most cardiovascular disease (AHA, 2009a), including heart attacks, which are caused by an interruption of, or an inadequate supply of, blood and oxygen to the heart. Evidence from large prospective studies shows that men have more atherosclerosis than women do, which contributes to men's increased risk for heart attack and other cardiovascular diseases (Dick et al., 2005; Iemolo et al., 2004; Mullenix et al., 2006). One recent large population-based study has shown that nearly three of four men aged 45 to 84 years have coronary artery calcification, 1.5 times the number of women in this age group (Bild et al., 2005). This gender difference is also apparent at younger ages. A large study in a diverse population has shown that 3 times more men (15%) than women (5%) aged 33 to 45 years already

had calcification (Loria et al., 2007). Atherosclerosis and high cholesterol also contribute, specifically, to carotid stenosis—the narrowing of
the carotid arteries, which supply blood to the brain; carotid stenosis
is a major risk factor for stroke and other cardiovascular diseases (Dick
et al., 2005; Iemolo et al., 2004; Mullenix et al., 2006; Stensland-Bugge
et al., 2001). Recent studies indicate that men are significantly more
likely than women to have more atherosclerosis and calcification in
their carotid arteries (Dick et al., 2005; Iemolo et al., 2004; Mullenix
et al., 2006). These gender differences in blood cholesterol levels and
atherosclerosis contribute to men's greater risk for heart disease, stroke,
and other cardiovascular diseases.

Fiber, Fruits, and Vegetables

There is robust evidence that the consumption of fiber, fruits, and veg-
etables reduces the overall risk for death (Ascherio & Willett, 1995;
Eyre et al., 2004; Franchesci et al., 1994; Giovannucci et al., 1995;
Hu & Willet, 2002; Winawer & Shike, 1995), and specifically death
from heart disease (Ascherio & Willett, 1995; Eyre et al., 2004; Ness &
Fowles, 1997), cancer (ACS, 2009; Block, Patterson, & Subar, 1992;
Byers et al., 2002; Ekman, 1999; Eyre et al., 2004; Liebman, 1995;
Mayne et al., 2001; NCI, 1996; Winawer & Shike, 1995), and stroke—
even after controlling for other risk factors (Gillman et al., 1995). Men
consume significantly less fiber and fruit and fewer vegetables than
women (CDC, 2007e, 2007f; Foerster & Hudes, 1994; Leigh & Fries,
1993; McClelland, Demark-Wahnefried, Mustian, Cowan, & Campbell,
1998; Prohaska et al., 1985; Rossi, 1992; Serdula et al., 1995, 2004;
Stables et al., 2002; Subar et al., 1995; Van Horn et al., 1991). The
most recent national data show that only 20% of men, compared with
29% of women, consume the recommended five or more fruits and vegetables per day (Serdula et al., 2004; Stables et al., 2002). Only 29% of
men, compared with 36% of women, eat fruit two or more times a day;
22% of men and 32% of women eat vegetables three or more times per
day (CDC, 2007e, 2007f). Among adults nationally, men are less likely
than women to consume carotenoid-rich foods, such as carrots, spin-
ach, broccoli, and other greens (Nebeling, Forman, Graubard, & Snyder,
1997). Findings are similar for boys and girls. A recent and extensive
review of research of youth aged 6 to 18 years found that girls tend
to eat more fruits and vegetables than boys (Rasmussen et al., 2006).
These researchers note studies show that eating habits such as these
established in adolescence tend to be maintained in adulthood.

These gender differences in fiber, fruit, and vegetable consumption
contribute to men's increased risks. Low consumption of fruits and vegetables is often associated with a significant risk for cancer (ACS, 2009;
Block et al., 1992; Byers et al., 2002; Ekman, 1999; Eyre et al., 2004;
Liebman, 1995; NCI, 1996; Winawer & Shike, 1995). Although not all
studies indicate that fruit and vegetable consumption lowers the risk for

cancer, the weight of the evidence suggests that they lower the risk for most of the cancers studied (Riboli & Norat, 2003). This is particularly true for cancer of the lungs, esophagus, stomach, and colon or rectum (Kushi et al., 2006)—especially among people who follow a strict diet, one low in fat and high in fiber, fruit, and vegetables (Sansbury et al., 2009). People who consume at least five servings of fruits and vegetables daily significantly reduce their risk for lung cancer; this is true even for smokers (Blot & Fraumeni, 1992; Byers et al., 2002; Kushi et al., 2006). Lung cancer is the second leading cause of cancer death among men, and the death rate for men is 3 times higher than the rate for women (Jemal et al., 2008). Several large studies suggest that a diet high in fruits and vegetables may also reduce the risk for prostate cancer (ACS, 2009; Kushi et al., 2006).

Salt Consumption

Salt consumption in the United States appears to have increased during the past 20 years (Loria, Obarzanek, & Ernst, 2001). Men's high consumption of salt contributes to their increased health risks. The DHHS recommends consuming not more than 2,300 mg of sodium per day—which amounts to 1 teaspoon of salt—and not more than 1,500 mg of sodium for high-risk groups, including people with hypertension and everyone aged 40 years and older (CDC, 2009g). One review of research suggests that even these recommendations may not be low enough to prevent hypertension (Kaplan, 2000).

Studies consistently show that men and boys consume more salt than women and girls, and significantly more than the recommended levels (Loria et al., 2001; Prohaska et al., 1985; White & Klimis-Tavantzis, 1992). National data indicate that, on average, men consume 10.4 g of salt per day and women consume 7.3 g (Department of Agriculture, 2009). Salt intake is higher for men and boys than for women and girls in every age group by at least 1,000 mg per day (Loria et al., 2001). Among those under age 60, only 1 to 13% of men and boys—compared with 30 to 45% of women and girls—consume less than the recommended daily levels (Loria et al., 2001).

A recent, extensive meta-analysis examining salt intake among more than 170,000 participants (Strazzullo, D'Elia, Kandala, & Cappuccio, 2009) confirmed previous findings that high salt consumption is associated with significantly increased risk for high blood pressure, stroke, and other cardiovascular diseases—and that reducing dietary salt intake reduces the risk for these diseases (Cappuccio & MacGregor, 1997; CDC, 2009g; Chobanian & Hill, 2000; Institute of Medicine, 2004; Kaplan, 2000; Khaw et al., 2004; Lichtenstein et al., 2006; Loria et al., 2001; MacGregor, 1997; Nothwehr, Elmer, & Hannan, 1994; NSA, 1994). It was recently estimated that if daily consumption of salt were reduced by only 3 g, new cases of a number of diseases would likewise be reduced. Heart disease would be reduced by 60,000 to 120,000 new cases annually, stroke by 32,000 to 66,000 new cases, and heart attacks by 54,000 to 99,000 new cases. In addition, the number of deaths from any cause would be reduced by 44,000 to 92,000 annually (Bibbins-Domingo et al., 2010). It is widely accepted that to lower high blood pressure it is necessary to limit sodium consumption (Chobanian et al., 2003; Kaplan, 2000; Loria et al., 2001). Sodium consumption has also been linked to cancer of the esophagus (Chang-Claude et al., 1995; Correa & Chen, 1994; De Stafani et al., 2006; Enzinger & Mayer, 2003). Cancer of the esophagus is one of only three cancers that have continued to increase during the past 30 years; however, since 1990, this increase has occurred only among men (Jemal et al., 2009). Currently, the death rate for esophageal cancer is 5 times higher for men than women (Jemal et al., 2008). It has been estimated that substituting fresh fruits and vegetables for poorly preserved, high-salt foods may reduce the risk for esophageal cancer by as much as half (Enzinger & Mayer, 2003). Salt intake is also associated with cancer of the stomach (Joossens et al., 1996; Kneller et al., 1992; Mayne et al., 2001; Tsugane & Sasazuki, 2007; Wang, Terry, & Yan, 2009), and the death rate for cancer of the stomach is twice as high in men as it is in women (Jemal et al., 2008).

Weight

Maintaining desirable weight is unequivocally associated with better health and lower mortality rates (ACS, 2009; Andres, Muller, & Sorkin, 1993; Belloc, 1973; Belloc & Breslow, 1972; Berkman, Breslow, & Wingard, 1983; Breslow & Enstrom, 1980; Byers et al., 2002; CDC, 2008i; Dixon, 2010; Enstrom, Kanim, & Breslow, 1986; Eyre et al., 2004; Flegal, Graubard, Williamson, & Gail, 2007; Jenkins, 2005; Kaplan, Seeman, Cohen, Knudsen, & Guralnik, 1987; Lloyd-Jones, Adams, et al., 2009; Pi-Sunyer, 1993). However, rates of overweight and obesity have continually increased during the past 2 decades (CDC, 2008i; Jenkins, 2005). Even among youth, a recent study suggests that childhood obesity is much worse than was previously believed (Koebnick et al., 2010).

Overweight and obesity have increased especially among men (Galuska, Serdula, Pamuk, Siegel, & Byers, 1996; Ogen et al., 2006). National data consistently indicate that more men (67%) than women (50%) are overweight (CDC, 2003a). Men are also more likely to be obese (CDC, 2008i), and the percentage of men who are obese continues to increase. From 1991 to 1998, obesity increased 52% among men and 47% among women (Mokdad et al., 1999). An analysis of trends from 1999 to 2004—the most recent time frame for which data on trends are available—shows that whereas the prevalence of obesity in men increased significantly in 1999 and 2000, and again in 2003 and 2004, the prevalence of obesity in women remained steady (Ogen et al., 2006). It is estimated that in the next several years, nearly one in three men aged 30 to 59 years will become overweight—more than

1.5 times the number of women who will—and those who do become overweight will be at greater risk for becoming obese (Ramachandran, Pencina, Cobain, Freiberg, & D'Agostino, 2005). Among people aged 20 to 74 years, 73% of men—compared with 61% of women—are either overweight or obese (DHHS, 2009e), and the prevalence of overweight and obesity is consistently higher for adult men in all age groups up to age 80 (National Institutes of Health [NIH], 1998). More boys than girls are also overweight (CDC, 2008b, 2008c; DHHS, 2009e) or obese (Koebnick et al., 2010; Ogden et al., 2006; Popkin & Udry, 1998), and this remains true for college students aged 18 to 24 years (CDC, 1997b). Overweight adolescents have a 70% chance of being overweight or obese in adulthood (DHHS, 2007d). Finally, despite men's greater risk for being overweight, national surveys consistently show that approximately 1.5 times more women than men attempt to lose weight (Bish et al., 2005; CDC, 1996; Kruger, Galuska, Serdula, & Jones, 2004; Serdula et al., 1993).

Obesity accounts for an estimated 112,000 to 325,000 adult deaths per year (Allison, Fontaine, Manson, Stevens, & VanItallie, 1999; Flegal, Graubard, Williamson, & Gail, 2005). A recent analysis suggests that if current trends continue, the negative health effects of obesity will completely offset the positive health effects of the reductions in smoking that have taken place during the past 30 years (Stewart, Cutler, & Rosen, 2009). A 40-year-old, nonsmoking man who is overweight can expect to die 3 years earlier than he would have if he had not been overweight; if he is obese, he can expect to die 6 years earlier (Peeters et al., 2003). People who are even a few pounds overweight are at risk for developing serious chronic conditions (Chobanian et al., 2003). Overweight and obesity are associated with a variety of chronic conditions—including heart disease, diabetes, dyslipidemia, hypertension, stroke, arthritis, high serum cholesterol, and erectile dysfunction—as well as with premature death (AHA, 1996, 2009a; Bacon et al., 2003; CDC, 2008i; Chobanian et al., 2003; DHHS, 2009e; Dixon, 2010; Eyre et al., 2004; Field et al., 2001; Flegal et al., 2007; Gortmaker, Dietz, & Cheung, 1990; Jenkins, 2005; Lloyd-Jones, Adams, et al., 2009; Mokdad et al., 2003; Nothwehr et al., 1994; NSA, 1994; Pi-Sunyer, 1993; Sowers, 2003; Suk et al., 2003). In one large prospective study, men with waists measuring at least 40 inches were nearly 3 times as likely to develop heart disease as men with 34-inch waists (Rimm et al., 1995).

Obese people without any other risk factors are at increased risk for cardiovascular disease (Dixon, 2010; Lichtenstein et al., 2006; Lloyd-Jones et al., 2006; Lloyd-Jones, Adams, et al., 2009); this is especially true for men (Chobanian et al., 2003; Field et al., 2001). The finding of greater risk among overweight men is not uncommon. For example, overweight men, but not overweight women, are at increased risk for stroke; similarly, the risk for diabetes is greater for overweight men (Chobanian et al., 2003). This finding regarding diabetes is especially relevant for adolescent boys. As noted previously, the risk for prediabetes is nearly

2.5 times greater for adolescent boys than it is for adolescent girls, and it is nearly double for adolescents who are overweight (Li et al., 2009). Prediabetes is reversible through lifestyle changes related to weight, physical activity, and diet, as well as pharmacological intervention (Gillies et al., 2007; Li et al., 2009).

Excess weight is also a primary contributor to hypertension (Cutler et al., 2008; Fields et al., 2004; Kotchen, Kotchen, & Boegehold, 1991; Nothwehr et al., 1994), which is a major risk factor for heart disease and stroke. One study found that the increase in overweight and obesity accounts for nearly all the increase in hypertension that occurred in men between 1988 and 2004 (Cutler et al., 2008). Two thirds of the hypertension among men aged 25 to 44 years is potentially attributable to excess weight (Kotchen et al., 1991). Excess weight has also been shown to predict the degree of atherosclerosis (Stensland-Bugge et al., 2001), which is a risk factor for cardiovascular disease, as I explained previously.

National and prospective data also show that excess weight is associated with a variety of cancers and cancer death (ACS, 2009; Byers et al., 2002; Calle, Rodriguez, Walker-Thurmond, & Thun, 2003; De Stafani et al., 2006; Dixon, 2010; Eyre et al., 2004; Flegal et al., 2007; Kushi et al., 2006). Overweight and obesity contribute to as many as one of five cancer deaths (ACS, 2009). The risk for cancer among overweight men is more than 1.5 times greater than the risk for cancer among men who are not overweight (Calle et al., 2003). A man who is 40% more than his ideal weight increases his risk for cancer by 30% (Winawer & Shike, 1995). People who are overweight increase their risk for colon cancer by 86%; people who are obese triple their risk (Ford, 1999).

Excess weight is also a major risk factor for sleep apnea (Peppard, Young, Palta, Dempsey, & Skatrud, 2000; Phillipson, 1993; Punjabi, 2008; Young et al., 1993). As we have seen, sleep apnea is more common among men, and it significantly increases the risk for disease, injury, and death. A 10% increase in weight increases the risk for developing severe sleep apnea by 600% (Peppard et al., 2000). As I discussed previously, sleep disorders increase the risk for car crashes. One study that examined both excess weight and sleep disorders found that overweight truckers were more than twice as likely to be in crashes as truckers with sleep disorders who were not overweight; truckers with sleep-disordered breathing also doubled their risk for crashes compared with those with no sleep disorders (Stoohs, Guilleminault, Itoi, & Dement, 1994).

Physical Activity

There is overwhelming and consistent evidence that physical activity significantly reduces the risk for major chronic diseases and premature death (AHA, 2009a; Berlin & Coditz, 1990; Bouchard, Shephard, Stephens, Sutton, & McPherson, 1990; Byers et al., 2002; DHHS, 1996a, 2008c,

2009e; Enstrom, Kanim, & Breslow, 1986; Eyre et al., 2004; Kaplan et al., 1987; Kushi et al., 2006; Lee, Hsieh, & Paffenbarger, 1995; Nocon et al., 2008; Paffenbarger et al., 1993; Powell, Caspersen, Koplan, & Ford, 1989; Warburton, Nicol, & Bredin, 2006; Wei et al., 1999; Wendel-Vos et al., 2004). This remains true even after controlling for genetic factors (Kujala, Kaprio, Sarna, & Koskenvuo, 1998), and the link appears to be causal (Carlsson, Andersson, Lichtenstein, Michaelsson, & Ahlbom, 2007; DHHS, 2008c; Livengood, Caspersen, & Koplan, 1993). Aerobic activity, for example, reduces blood pressure and improves cholesterol levels (Hagberg, 1990; King, Haskell, Young, Oka, & Stefanick, 1995; Oppenheim, 1994). Studies show that people who are physically active or aerobically fit reduce their risk for developing heart disease by 25 to 50% compared with people who are sedentary or have low aerobic fitness (Haskell et al., 2007). Physical activity also reduces the risk for some cancers (ACS, 2009; Blair et al., 1989; Byers et al., 2002; DHHS, 2008c; Eyre et al., 2004; Kushi et al., 2006; Lee, Paffenbarger, & Hsieh, 1991; Warburton et al., 2006; Winawer & Shike, 1995); the risk for colon cancer specifically is reduced significantly (DHHS, 2008c; Giovannucci et al., 1995; Samad, Taylor, Marshall, & Chapman, 2005; Thune & Furberg, 2001; Warburton et al., 2006; Winawer & Shike, 1995). Simply not being sedentary can substantially reduce the risk for some cancers (Byers et al., 2002). One in three cancer deaths can be attributed to physical inactivity, along with poor diet (ACS, 2009). In 1995, the CDC reported that 12% of all deaths are attributable to physical inactivity (Pate et al., 1995). More recently, they reported that 17% of all deaths are attributable to physical inactivity, along with poor diet (Mokdad et al., 2004).

Physical activity is the primary health-related behavior for which men's actions, relative to women's, would appear to give men a health advantage. However, a close examination of the data leads to more complicated and less clear conclusions (Courtenay, 2000b; Livingstone, Robson, Wallace & McKinley, 2003). Indeed, physical activity is one of the most difficult—and problematic—health-related behaviors to examine (Livingstone et al., 2003), especially in terms of gender. This is partly because of the way in which physical activity is measured.

Physical activity is a complex behavior, and there are more than 30 techniques for measuring it (Livingstone et al., 2003). In addition, many different aspects of physical activity are associated with health and longevity. Examples include energy expenditure, aerobic intensity, weight-bearing activity, resistance and endurance activity, and high-range movement (Livingstone et al., 2003). In this section, I review research related to self-reported physical activity, self-reported physical inactivity, objectively measured physical activity, type and intensity of physical activity, age and physical activity, trends in physical activity, and additional factors influencing our understanding of physical activity. I examine each of these topics in relation to gender, and discuss the implications of gender differences for men's health.

Self-Reported Physical Activity

The DHHS defines physical activity as at least 30 minutes of moderate-intensity activity 5 days per week, or 20 minutes of vigorous-intensity activity 3 days per week (DHHS, 2000c). However, this is but one definition. Three national surveillance systems track physical activity among adults. The prevalence of physical activity can vary considerably, depending on how it is defined and assessed in these three surveys (Carlson, Densmore, Fulton, Yore, & Kohl, 2009). Differences in survey format and period of recall may also contribute to differences found in survey results (CDC, 2008j). Current national surveillance systems indicate that roughly similar percentages of men and women in the United States are physically active, with slightly more men reporting being active. Overall, only 30 to 48% of adults report being physically active (Carlson et al., 2009). The age-adjusted percentages for physical activity based on gender in the three national surveys are 32, 34, and 50% for men compared with 29, 33, and 47% for women, respectively (Carlson et al., 2009). The findings on various levels of physical activity are also similar. For low-level activity, they are 16% for men and 16.5% for women; for medium-level activity, 34 and 32%; for medium-high-level activity, 24 and 23%; and for high-level activity, 17 and 16%, respectively (DHHS, 2007e).

In survey research involving youth, boys typically report more physical activity than girls (CDC, 2008b; Sallis, Prochaska, & Taylor, 2000; Singh, Kogan, Siahpush, & van Dyck, 2008), although this finding is not entirely consistent. An analysis of reported physical activity among 9- to 13-year-olds found that although more boys (81%) than girls (74%) participate in free-time physical activity, more girls (39%) than boys (38%) report participating in organized physical activity with a coach, instructor, or leader (CDC, 2003c). More recently, a survey of nearly 13,000 10- to 18-year-olds found that boys and girls spend an almost identical amount of time engaging in physical activity, but that boys report the least amount of time. Mean hours of physical activity ranged from 7.3 to 11.6 hours per week reported by boys and from 8.0 to 11.2 hours per week reported by girls (Kahn et al., 2008). Among high school students, far more males (44%) than females (26%) report being physically active (CDC, 2008b). This gender difference appears smaller among urban youth. In a study of the 100 largest cities in the United States, approximately 40% of girls and 57% of boys aged 14 to 17 years report being physically active (Butcher, Sallis, Mayer, & Woodruff, 2008).

Self-Reported Physical Inactivity

Another indicator of health risk is physical inactivity—or a sedentary lifestyle. Physical inactivity is defined by the DHHS as no, or less than 10 minutes of, moderate- or vigorous-intensity physical activity per day (DHHS, 2000c). Physical inactivity increases the risk for death, particularly from heart disease (AHA, 2009a; DHHS, 2008c; Eyre et al., 2004; Haskell et al., 2007; Warburton et al., 2006; Warren et al., 2010). In fact, physical inactivity increases the risk for heart disease up to nearly 2.5 times—a risk that is comparable with the risks associated with high blood cholesterol, high blood pressure, or cigarette smoking (AHA, 2009b). Physical inactivity has been shown to be an independent predictor of atherosclerosis (Stensland-Bugge et al., 2001) and to nearly double the risk for metabolic syndrome (Ford et al., 2005), which—as noted previously—both increase the risk for developing heart disease.

Nearly equal numbers of men and women report being physically inactive. The age-adjusted percentages for physical inactivity based on gender from the three national surveillance systems are 39, 31, and 13% for men compared with 42, 33, and 14% for women, respectively (Carlson et al., 2009). Similarly, nearly equal numbers of women (41%) and men (39%) report that they spend most of the day sitting down (DHHS, 2007e). No national surveys have been conducted on sedentary behavior per se among youth, but among high school students nationally, 32% of young women, compared with only 18% of young men, report not having participated in at least 1 hour of physical activity in the past week (CDC, 2008b). However, in the survey of nearly 13,000 youth cited previously, I noted that boys reported engaging in nearly 1 hour less of physical activity per day than girls. Television viewing, computer use, and video games are major contributors to physical inactivity in this age group (DHHS, 2001), especially for boys. Significantly more boys than girls in high school use computers for 3 or more hours on an average school day, and watch television for 3 or more hours (CDC, 2008b). Boys aged 8 to 18 years use entertainment media nearly 1 hour more per day than do girls; they spend 4 times as much sedentary time playing console video games as girls do (Rideout, Foehr, & Roberts, 2010).

As I explained previously, physical inactivity—along with poor diet—increases the risk for metabolic syndrome among both men and boys and results in a greater risk for death among men. A low level of physical activity in men has also been shown to be an independent predictor of atherosclerosis, another risk factor for heart disease and death (Stensland-Bugge et al., 2001). Indeed, inactive men have been found to be 2 to 3 times more likely to die from any cause than their more active peers (Berkman et al., 1983; Powell et al., 1987). Men with low fitness levels who are also overweight are especially at risk for death (Koster et al., 2009; Ming et al., 1999; Sui et al., 2007). Although findings are not consistent, inactive men may also be at increased risk for prostate cancer—especially for aggressive cancer (Clarke & Whittemore, 2000; Patel et al., 2005).

Objectively Measured Physical Activity

NHANES—one of the three national surveillance systems I mentioned previously—objectively measured physical activity through the use of accelerometers in the 2003–2004 survey cycle. This is the first time that objective physical activity has ever been monitored and measured in a nationally representative sample of youth and adults. Several studies have used data from this survey to analyze various aspects and levels of physical activity.

In general, these studies report greater physical activity among males than females of all ages (Hawkins et al., 2009; Metzger et al., 2008; Nader, Bradley, Houts, McRitchie, & O'Brien, 2008; Troiano et al., 2008; Whitt-Glover et al., 2009). However, there are important differences, based on level of intensity, ethnicity, and age group. For example, boys and girls aged 6 to 19 years spend an equal number of hours per day in sedentary behaviors (Whitt-Glover et al., 2009). By age 30, however, these objectively measured data indicate that men start to become more sedentary than women (Matthews et al., 2008). In middle age, when ethnicity is examined, Latina women aged 40 to 59 years are just as physically active as men of all ethnicities in the same age group (Hawkins et al., 2009). By age 60—which is when the risk for death, particularly from heart disease, increases—men are significantly more sedentary than women (Matthews et al., 2008). Indeed, over age 60, men are no more likely than women to engage in physical activity (Troiano et al., 2008).

Although physical activity was "objectively measured" in these studies, bias resulting from an intervention effect is still possible. This is because participants' awareness that their activity levels are being monitored can lead to significant modifications in physical activity. In one study (Van Sluijs et al., 2006), researchers concluded that performing measurements—which included the use of accelerometers—resulted in a heightened awareness of the subjects' physical activity levels and increased their levels of activity. To date, no study has examined whether bias resulting from intervention differs by gender, and if so, to what extent. However, the significant findings from all these studies indicate that both men and women engage in far less physical activity than they report and that the vast majority of people are either inactive or engaging in much less physical activity than is considered healthy. One study found that less than 10% of the population aged 12 years or older engaged in recommended levels of physical activity; these percentages steadily decreased with age to less than 3% among adults aged 60 or older (Troiano et al., 2008). Another study (Metzger et al., 2008) found that the least active people represented 79% of the population, and that less than 1% of the population meets the DHHS's recommendation of vigorous physical activity 3 or more days per week for 20 or more minutes per occasion (DHHS, 2000c).

Type and Intensity of Physical Activity

During the past 20 years, health scientists have increasingly specified the amount and intensity of physical activity that is necessary for good health (Haskell et al., 2007; USPSTF, 1996). Research has consistently shown that light to moderate exercise provides the most health benefits (Blair et al., 1989; Giovannucci et al., 1995; Livingstone et al., 2003; Pate et al., 1995; Schneck et al., 1995). As I will explain, women are more likely to engage in this type of exercise than men. Light to moderate exercise—which can include walking, gardening, aerobics, dancing, housework, and playing with children (DHHS, 1993, 1996b, 2006c; Ransdell, Vener, & Sell, 2004; Simpson et al., 2003)—provides substantial health benefits even when done in short bouts and has been found to reduce the risk for death by more than 40% (Livingstone et al., 2003; Paffenbarger et al., 1993). Consequently, the DHHS recommends that to reduce the risk for chronic disease, adults should engage in "at least 30 minutes of *moderate-intensity physical activity*, above usual activity, at work or home on most days of the week" (DHHS, 2005, p. viii; emphasis added). This is the consistent, central message of most public health recommendations (Livingstone et al., 2003). This level of intensity is generally equivalent to a brisk walk (Haskell et al., 2007), and, in fact, walking is the most frequently reported activity among adults who meet this recommendation (Simpson et al., 2003). A recent meta-analysis of 18 prospective studies and nearly 460,000 people found that walking was associated with lower risks of both heart disease and death from any cause in both men and women, thus supporting current physical activity recommendations that emphasize moderate-intensity activity (Hamer & Chida, 2008).

Type and intensity of physical activity differ by gender. Women tend to engage in more moderate, and less vigorous, physical activity than men (Ransdell, Vener, & Sell, 2004; Salmon, Owen, Crawford, Bauman, & Sallis, 2003). This often includes walking. Between 1987 and 2000, the number of women who reported walking regularly increased nearly twice as much as the number of men (Simpson et al., 2003); 70% more women than men walk regularly as a form of exercise (DHHS, 2006c). Women place greater value on exercising for health (Weissfeld et al., 1990), and they adhere to more regular exercise patterns (Walker et al., 1988). These patterns focus on various forms of moderate physical activity, as described previously. Twice as many women as men garden, and 3 times more women engage in aerobics (DHHS, 2006c). Similarly, more women (69%) than men (54%) use techniques such as yoga, tai chi, and qi gong to improve their health, and more women (14%) than men (8%) do deep-breathing exercises (CDC, 2005b).

Men are more likely than women to engage in strengthening exercises (such as weightlifting) and team sports (Kann et al., 1998; Simpson et al., 2003; Stevens, Jacobs, & White, 1985). Significantly more men than women play football, basketball, and baseball, and engage in bicycling and running (CDC, 1992a; DHHS, 1996a, 2006c). More than 3 times more men than women run, for example, and nearly 6 times more men play basketball (DHHS, 2006c). Although engaging in these physical activities provides numerous health benefits to men, it also contributes to their increased risk for injury and death (which I discuss in the Sports and Recreation section in this chapter). This is true even when they engage regularly in physical activities. It is even more true when they engage in strenuous activities on an infrequent basis.

Men are more likely than women to engage in infrequent, strenuous activity, which is a well-known risk factor for heart attacks (Franklin, Bonzheim, Gordon, & Timmis, 1996; Kloner, 2006; Nguyen et al., 2007), as well as sudden death from heart attacks (DHHS, 2008c). People who engage in infrequent but strenuous physical activity—such as jogging, playing tennis, shoveling snow, moving furniture, or mowing the lawn less than once or twice a week—significantly increase their risk for heart attack and death (Franklin et al., 1996; Giri et al., 1999; Hallqvist et al., 2000; Kloner, 2006; Nguyen et al., 2007; Thompson et al., 2007; Tofler & Muller, 2006; Willich et al., 1993). People who engage in this type of activity are sometimes called "weekend warriors."

In a study of objective national data cited previously (Metzger et al., 2008), researchers identified a segment of the population who engaged in moderate levels of physical activity Monday through Friday but in much higher levels of physical activity on the weekend. These weekend warriors were more likely to be men (J. Metzger, personal communication, February 25, 2010). Whether they are playing racquetball or shoveling snow, these men increase their risks substantially. In one study, for example, they increased their risk for heart attack more than 100 times (Mittleman et al., 1993). Another study found that the risk for heart attack while jogging is 56 times greater among men who exercise infrequently, but only 5 times greater among men who exercise frequently (Siscovick, Weiss, Fletcher, & Lasky, 1984). In a study of more than 8,000 men, researchers compared the risk for death among weekend warriors with that of men who engage in a similar amount of activity over a longer period, and with that of men who are either relatively inactive or sedentary (Lee, Sesso, Oguma, & Paffenbarger, 2004). They found that being a weekend warrior does not increase a man's risk when he is very healthy, but it does increase his risk when he is not. Weekend warriors who had just one risk factor for heart disease (specifically, those who either smoked, were overweight, had a history of hypertension, or had high cholesterol) significantly increased their risk for death. Among men with any risk factor for heart disease, only those who were physically active on a regular basis decreased their risk for death. As a result of research with findings such as these, the AHA and the American College of Sports Medicine now recommend that physical activity include vigorous-intensity aerobic activity for a *minimum* of 20 minutes *3 days* a week (Haskell et al., 2007).

Age and Trends in Physical Activity

Research consistently shows that physical activity decreases with age, beginning in early adolescence and continuing into older adulthood (Allison, Adlaf, Dwyer, & Irving, 2007; Hawkins et al., 2009; Jones et al., 1998; Kahn et al., 2008; Marshall et al., 2007; Matthews et al., 2008; Whitt Glover et al., 2009). Ninety percent of 9- to 11-year-olds exercise 1 hour a day compared with only 30% of 15-year-olds; the rate of decrease in physical activity during adolescence is the same for both sexes (Nader et al., 2008). Adults aged 65 or more are approximately 5 times more likely than adults aged 18 to 24 to report never being physically active (DHHS, 2007e). However, among older adults, women have been found to maintain their levels of physical activity over time, whereas levels among men decrease significantly (Stanley & Freysinger, 1995). In addition, as noted previously, once past age 60, men are no more likely than women to achieve recommended levels of physical activity and are—in fact—more likely to be inactive.

There are gender differences in trends of physical activity over time. Although adults in the United States do not appear to have been engaging in less "leisure-time" physical activity over the past 30 years (Livingstone et al., 2003), overall physical activity has decreased significantly. An analysis of long-term trends during the past 50 years found decreasing levels of physical activity related to work, home life, and getting from one place to another, as well as increasing levels of sedentary activity (Brownson, Boehmer, & Luke, 2004). An analysis of recent trends in physical activity among adults in the United States found that where these trends have changed, they have changed for the worse (DHHS, 2007e). However, these decreases are seen only among men. The number of men who engaged in the two lowest levels of leisure-time physical activity (no activity and some, but irregular, activity) increased. At the same time, the number of men who engaged in regular leisure-time physical activity decreased; the numbers for women in all categories remained constant over time (DHHS, 2007e).

During the past several decades, analyses of physical activity patterns based on national data indicate that women are making more beneficial changes than are men (Caspersen & Merritt, 1995; CDC, 2006e, 2008k; Simpson et al., 2003). Consistent with this trend, recent research shows that between 2001 and 2005 the prevalence of regular physical activity increased 9% among women and only 4% among men (CDC, 2008j). Not surprisingly, a recent large population-based study found that among inactive adults, men were more likely than women to have little or no intention of increasing physical activity (Garber, Allsworth, Marcus, Hesser, & Lapane, 2008). Similar gender differences in these trends are seen among adolescents. An analysis of data from six large, representative samples of boys and girls aged 14 to 18 during a recent 10-year period found small but significant overall trends of both decreased physical activity and increased inactivity over time among boys. No changes were found among girls (Adams, 2006).

Additional Factors

Physical activity—and inactivity—have historically been measured among U.S. residents by surveying random representative samples of the population over the telephone and asking them about the physical activities they engage in. Typically, these surveys—which I reviewed previously—have found that men report greater physical activity, particularly leisure-time physical activity, than women. However, as others have argued (Livingstone et al., 2003), there are a number of reasons to believe that women are more active than these surveys report. Not the least of these reasons is the failure of these surveys to assess household activities—which women are significantly more likely to engage in than men. Instead, these surveys have historically emphasized sports and recreational activities—activities that men, but not women, tend to engage in—while ignoring the physical activities that women tend to engage in (Livingstone et al., 2003). As others have pointed out (Livingstone et al., 2003; Wareham & Rennie, 1998), this emphasis is not proportionate to the amount of time that men and women spend in these respective physical activities. Light- to moderate-intensity activities— such as household tasks, playing at home, getting to and from places, and so forth—are no less relevant to health outcomes, but they are difficult both to define and to recall accurately (Ainsworth, 2000; Hopkins, Wilson, & Russell, 1991; Livingstone et al., 2003; Sallis et al. 1985). In a fascinating quantitative analysis, researchers calculated the energy expenditure for 87 different, specific physical activities in a representative sample of more than 7,000 U.S. adults (Dong, Block, & Mandel, 2004). Their results indicate that when both high- and low-intensity physical activities are included in the determination of estimated total energy expenditure—which is what affects health, for better or for worse—the energy expended is *equal* in men and women. A failure in most surveys to accurately measure women's levels of activity may help to explain why physical activity has historically been a relatively poor predictor of mortality among women (Livingstone et al., 2003).

Further complicating these survey findings are inaccuracies in self-reports. In a study that compared national survey data with objectively measured levels of activity, self-reports of physical activity were significantly higher than objectively measured levels (Troiano et al., 2008). Although gender was not assessed in this particular study, as I pointed out previously, studies that assess both gender and self-reporting have found that men—but not women—report health behaviors that are more favorable than they actually are. It is also worth noting that physical activity levels vary by season (Matthews et al., 2001; Pivarnik, Reeves, & Rafferty, 2003), and that these seasonal differences are different for men and women (McCormack, Friedenreich, Shiell, Giles-Corti, & Doyle-Baker, in press; Plasqui & Westerterp, 2004; Uitenbroek, 1993). None of the studies of physical activity in the United States has taken these seasonal gender differences into account.

Summary

Although more boys than girls in the United States are physically active, roughly the same number of adult women and men report being physically active, or inactive. Where there are differences in reporting, men generally report more activity than women. When physical activity is objectively measured, men, in general, are more active. However, equal numbers of boys and girls under age 20 are inactive; by age 30, men begin to become less active than women; by age 60, they have become more inactive. Men are also more likely than women to engage in infrequent, strenuous physical activity, which significantly increases men's risk for heart attack. In contrast, women are far more likely than men to engage in moderate physical activity—which research suggests provides the greatest health benefits. Finally, when it comes to trends, all the available research indicates that more and more women are making healthy changes in physical activity, whereas more and more men are making unhealthy changes. Although these gender differences in physical exercise may appear small or inconsequential, they are significant contributors to men's disproportionate risk for high blood pressure, elevated cholesterol levels, heart disease, cancer, and all-cause mortality.

SUBSTANCE USE

The use of tobacco, alcohol, anabolic steroids, and other drugs or substances is significantly greater among men and boys than it is among women and girls (CDC, 2008b; SAMHSA, 1997, 2009). Substance abuse and dependence is also consistently found to be much greater among men than women (Kessler et al., 1994; Robins et al., 1984). Currently, the prevalence of drug and alcohol dependence or abuse is twice as high among men (12%) as it is among women (6%) (SAMHSA, 2009). These gender differences are consistent for all substances. Gender differences are also consistent across ethnic groups (Rigotti, Lee, & Wechsler, 2000; SAMHSA, 1998, 2009). Males in each of 11 ethnic subgroups are more likely than females in the same subgroup to use substances, to be dependent on alcohol, and to need treatment for abuse of illicit drugs (SAMHSA, 1998). These gender differences are apparent at an early age. Among high school students nationally, 30% of males use some form of tobacco compared with 21% of females (CDC, 2008b). The use of marijuana, cocaine, crack cocaine, and injection drugs is also greater among high school males than females (CDC, 1995c, 2008b; Kann et al., 1998). Among high school students nationally, 42% of males, compared with 35% of females, have ever tried marijuana; more than twice as many high school males (11%) as females (5%) tried marijuana for the first time before they were 13 years old (CDC, 2008b). Among college students nationally, significantly more men (38%) than women (30%) currently use tobacco (Rigotti et al., 2000).

Tobacco, alcohol, anabolic steroids, and other drugs and substances are implicated in a variety of health problems. The death rate for drug-induced deaths—which excludes unintentional injuries, homicides, and other indirect causes related to use—is twice as high for men as it is for women (DHHS, 2009a). Even more distressing is the fact that the men's death rate for drug-induced mortality has been steadily increasing and has nearly doubled since 1999 (DHHS, 2009a). Users of marijuana or cocaine, for example, are at significantly greater risk for fatal (as well as nonfatal) injuries and car crashes (Macdonald et al., 2003; Mokdad et al., 2004). Illicit drug use is also associated with suicide, homicide, HIV infection, pneumonia, violence, mental illness, and hepatitis (Mokdad et al., 2004)—all of which are more common among men than women, as I noted previously. Men account for two of three of the nearly 2 million emergency department visits that are associated with illicit drug use or abuse (SAMHSA, 2008a). Frequent and heavy use of alcohol and other drugs is strongly associated with high-risk sexual activity and risk for STDs, including HIV disease (Cooper & Orcutt, 1997; Cooper, Pierce, & Huselid, 1994; Ericksen & Trocki, 1992, 1994; National Institute on Alcohol Abuse and Alcoholism [NIAAA], 2004/2005; O'Leary, Goodhart, Jemmott, & Boccher-Lattimore, 1992; Randolph, Torres, Gore-Felton, Lloyd, & McGarvey, 2009; Shafer et al., 1993). Persons under the influence of alcohol or drugs—including those who are not necessarily problem users—are at increased risk for suicidal thoughts and unplanned suicide attempts (Borges, Walters, & Kessler, 2000). As noted previously, the suicide rate for men far exceeds the suicide rate for women. In this section, I will examine gender differences in the use of tobacco, alcohol, and anabolic steroids.

Tobacco Use

Cigarette, Pipe, and Cigar Smoking

Smoking is considered the single most preventable cause of illness and death in the United States, even after controlling for potentially confounding factors, such as other health practices and health status at the time of survey (Berkman et al., 1983; Camacho & Wiley, 1983; CDC, 2009h; DHHS, 1998a, 2004b; Enstrom et al., 1986; Eyre et al., 2004; Kaplan et al., 1987; McGinnis & Foege, 1993; Mokdad et al., 2004). A recent study of more than 12,000 smokers, former smokers, and nonsmokers found that current smokers more than doubled their risk for death from any cause over a 3-year period compared with those who had never smoked; current smokers had a 3.5 times greater risk for dying from cancer and a 2.5 times greater risk for dying from any cause during the course of the 3 years (Berger et al., 2009). Tobacco use accounts for roughly one in five deaths overall and one in four deaths among those aged 35 to 64 years (ACS, 2008; Bartecchi, MacKenzie, & Schrier, 1995; McGinnis & Foege, 1993; Winawer & Shike, 1995); it also causes nearly 30% of cancer deaths, the vast majority (87%) of lung cancer deaths, and nearly 20% of deaths from heart disease (ACS, 2008, 2009; Eyre et al., 2004; Hecht, 2008). Although many people believe that smoking pipes and cigars is safer than smoking cigarettes, the evidence contradicts this belief (DHHS, 2009g; Jacobs, Thun, & Apicella, 1999; NCI, 1998; Shapiro, Jacobs, & Thun, 2000). A recent, large population-based study has shown that pipe and cigar smokers have nicotine-related toxins in their bodies that result from smoking, and that they experience airway obstruction twice as often as non-smokers (Rodriguez et al., 2010).

National data from the late 1990s showed that significantly more men than women smoked—26% compared with 21% (CDC, 1998c; Courtenay, 2000b). (One analysis of these data indicated that the percentages were underestimated for men and overestimated for women; Arday et al., 1997.) Although the number of smokers decreased slightly during the 1990s and the first decade of this century (CDC, 2009i), the significantly higher rate of smoking among men persists; 23% compared with 18% for women (CDC, 2009h). Furthermore, the decreases in smoking during the 1990s were not seen among those aged 18 to 24 years (CDC, 2002a), particularly among college students, whose smoking increased dramatically during that time (Rigotti et al., 2000; Wechsler, Rigotti, Gledhill-Hoyt, & Lee, 1998). Currently, significantly more college men than women are smokers (Rigotti et al., 2000; Thompson et al., 2007). Although 28% of both college men and women smoke, 4 times more men than women smoke cigars (16 and 4%, respectively) and more than 6 times more men than women smoke pipes (3% and 0.4%) (Rigotti et al., 2000). Furthermore, college men are more likely than college women to transition from occasional smokers to regular smokers over time (Wetter et al., 2004). Among adults and youth, in general, cigars and pipes are smoked primarily by men. (Cigar smoking is discussed below.) Of the 2 million pipe smokers in the United States, three of four are male (SAMHSA, 2009). There is some research to suggest that these national data underestimate the prevalence of smoking among men. A recent analysis specifically designed to examine smoking among Asian Americans—including non-English-speaking Asian Americans, who are often excluded from national studies and whose rates of smoking are much higher than those for any other ethnic group—suggest that the prevalence of smoking among men in the United States is even higher than the nearly one in four currently reported (Chae, Gavin, & Takeuchi, 2006). Furthermore, significantly more men than women have ever smoked or are current smokers (52 and 41%, respectively), and fewer men than women have never smoked (48 and 59%, respectively) (Mokdad et al., 2004). These facts contribute significantly to men's disproportionate health risks. Despite these risks, men are significantly less likely than women to attempt to quit smoking or to plan to quit (DHHS, 2007a; Mokdad et al., 2004). The same holds true for male high school and college students compared with female students (CDC, 1997b, 1998d, 2009j; Harris, Schwartz, & Thompson, 2008).

Men's smoking habits are also more dangerous than women's—a significant, yet frequently overlooked, fact. Previously, I reported that more men than women smoke a pack or more of cigarettes a day. Men also inhale more deeply than women, smoke cigarettes that are higher in tar and nicotine, and smoke cigarettes without filter tips (Courtenay, 2000b). Men constitute approximately 60% of *hard-core smokers*—a term that is typically defined as established daily smokers who consume 15 or more cigarettes per day and who have never attempted to quit (Augustson & Marcus, 2004; Emery, Gilpin, Ake, Farkas, & Pierce, 2000). Furthermore, more than 4 times as many men as women report using other forms of tobacco—including smokeless tobacco, cigars, pipes, or other tobacco products—in addition to smoking cigarettes (CDC, 2010d).

More dangerous smoking habits are also more common among male than female youth and young adults (Courtenay, 1998a, 2000b). Among 19- to 30-year-olds, 19% of men compared with 15% of women smoke daily, and more than 40% more men (13%) than women (9%) smoke more than half a pack of cigarettes a day. Among college students nationally, daily smoking and the use of multiple forms of tobacco (e.g., smoking both cigarettes and cigars) is far more common among men (Presley, Meilman, & Cashin, 1996; Rigotti et al., 2000). Twice as many college men (58%) as women (28%) have used more than one form of tobacco in the past year, and more than 3 times as many men (38%) as women (11%) have done so in the past month (Rigotti et al., 2000). Among high school students nationally, more males than females are likely to smoke frequently (CDC, 1998e, 2008b; Kann et al., 1998). High school males are also more likely than females to be at risk for a variety of tobacco-smoking behaviors: lifetime cigarette use, current cigarette use, smoking cigarettes on 20 or more days during the past month, not trying to quit smoking cigarettes, smoking a whole cigarette for the first time before age 13, and smoking cigars, cigarillos, or little cigars on at least 1 day during the past month (CDC, 2008b). High school males are also more likely than females to smoke bidis—sweet-smelling cigarettes that contain more nicotine than standard cigarettes (CDC, 2000a). Smoking during adolescence is particularly harmful because hard-core smokers are more likely than other smokers to have started smoking at an early age (Augustson & Marcus, 2004).

It is not surprising, then, that at least twice as many male as female deaths are attributed to smoking (ACS, 2008; CDC, 1994b, 1997c, 2009k; Nelson et al., 1994). The greater prevalence of smoking among men largely accounts for men's higher rates of cardiovascular disease and stroke, which account for more than 40% of all deaths (AHA, 1994, 2009a; Gorelick et al., 1999; Lloyd-Jones et al., 2006; Lloyd-Jones, Adams, et al., 2009; Mensah et al., 2005; NINDS, 2004; Stamler et al., 1999; Terry et al., 2005). The risk for heart attack among smokers is more than double the risk for nonsmokers, and the risk for sudden cardiac death is up to four times greater (AHA, 1996, 2009b; Lloyd-Jones, Berry, et al., 2009; NSA, 1994). As I have explained, men are at greater risk for these health problems. Smoking also accounts for 45% of cancer deaths among men compared with 22% among women (Shopland,

Eyre, & Pechacek, 1991); of the nearly one-half million people who die from tobacco-related cancer deaths each year, the majority are men (ACS, 1997; NCI, 1996). The lung cancer death rate for men is nearly twice as high as the rate for women, and nearly 90% of these deaths can be directly attributed to cigarette smoking (ACS, 2009). Smoking is an independent predictor of the level of atherosclerosis, a risk factor for cardiovascular disease and death (Stensland-Bugge et al., 2001). The risk for diabetes is also up to 4 times higher for heavy smokers than it is for nonsmokers (Ingall, 2004; Willi, Bodenmann, Ghali, Faris, & Cornuz, 2007). As noted previously, the risks of death from both atherosclerosis and diabetes are higher for men than they are for women. Men who smoke die—on average—13 years younger than men who do not smoke (DHHS, 2004b). A 55-year-old man who smokes has about the same 10-year risk for death from any cause as a 65-year-old man who has never smoked (Woloshin, Schwartz, & Welch, 2008). A 50-year-old man who smokes and has one other risk factor for heart disease—such as high cholesterol or hypertension—can expect to die 10 years sooner than he would have otherwise (Lloyd-Jones et al., 2006). The risk for lung cancer is more than 2,000% higher for men who smoke than it is for men who do not smoke (NCI, 1996). Men who smoke double their risk for prostate cancer (Daniell, 1995; Hiatt, Armstrong, Klatsky, & Sidney, 1994). Smoking also appears to increase the risk for erectile dysfunction (Bacon et al., 2003).

More than 8 of 10 (82%) cigar smokers are men (Burns, Hoffman, Cummings, & Amacher, 1998; CDC, 1998e; SAMHSA, 2009). Almost 11 million men smoke cigars; nearly 2 million have smoked cigars in the past year, and nearly 10% have smoked cigars in the past month (SAMHSA, 2009). Currently, 38% of college men have smoked cigars in the past year, and 16% are current smokers, compared with only 4% of women (Rigotti et al., 2000). Even among middle school and high school boys, 8 and 20%, respectively, smoke cigars (CDC, 2000a, 2008b); they are 3 times more likely to do so than middle and high school girls (DHHS, 2009g). During the 1990s, the consumption of cigars increased dramatically among young and middle-aged men, especially (200%) among men aged 18 to 24 (Burns et al., 1998). Between 1993 and 2006, the sale of cigars in general also increased dramatically—from 32% for cigarillos to as much as 148% for large cigars (ACS, 2008; Kozlowski, Dollar, & Giovino, 2008). Smoking cigars increases the risk for a variety of diseases, including several types of cancer, and the health consequences are similar to those of cigarette smoking (DHHS, 2009g; NCI, 1998). The risk for dying from oral, esophageal, or laryngeal cancer is 4 to 10 times higher for regular cigar smokers than it is for nonsmokers (DHHS, 2009g). Regularly smoking cigars doubles a man's risk for lung cancer and increases his risk for oral cancer by 800 to 1,600%; cigar smokers who inhale deeply increase their risk for oral cancer by 27,000% (NCI, 1998). A prospective study of male smokers—excluding men who had ever smoked cigarettes or pipes—found that cigar smoking increases the risk for lung cancer by 500%, the risk for cancer of the larynx by 1,000%, the risk for cancer of the oral cavity and pharynx by 400%, and the risk for esophageal cancer by nearly 200% (Shapiro et al., 2000; see also DHHS, 2009g). Additional research suggests that cigar smoking also increases the risk for coronary heart disease, particularly among younger men (Jacobs et al., 1999). The risk for death from any cause is significantly greater among cigar smokers than it is among people who have never smoked (NCI, 1998).

Smokeless Tobacco

Smokeless tobacco products—which include chewing tobacco, moist snuff, and dry snuff—are also used primarily by men. The use of these products tripled from the early 1970s to the early 1990s (CDC, 1993b), although since then it has declined among most populations (Mumford, Levy, Gitchell, & Blackman, 2006; Nelson et al., 2006). Since 2002, however, the use of smokeless tobacco has increased significantly among males aged 12 to 17 years (DHHS, 2009h) and among 10th and 12th graders (University of Michigan, 2009). Currently, 8.7 million people aged 12 years or older use smokeless tobacco, and 95% of these people are male (SAMHSA, 2009). Nearly one in three men (32%) has used smokeless tobacco during his lifetime (SAMHSA, 2009). Use rates among males of all ages and for all patterns of use range from 7 to more than 40 times higher than the rates among females (SAMHSA, 1997). Among college students nationally, 14 times more men (14%) than women (1%) have used smokeless tobacco in the past year, and 21 times more men (8.7%) than women (0.4%) are current users (Rigotti et al., 2000). Among high school students nationally, 13% of males report current use of smokeless tobacco compared with only 2% of females (CDC, 2008b). Among middle school students nationally, 4 times more boys (4%) than girls (1%) use smokeless tobacco (CDC, 2000a).

Although some health scientists have suggested that smokeless tobacco should be actively promoted as a safer alternative to cigarette smoking (Kozlowski, 2002; Rodu, 1994), others disagree (Hatsukami, Lemmonds, & Tomar, 2004; Institute of Medicine, 2001). Smokeless tobacco is a known carcinogen in humans (International Agency for Research on Cancer, 2008; NCI, 2003). There is considerable evidence that smokeless tobacco causes oral, pharyngeal, and pancreatic cancers, as well as precancerous lesions of the mouth, gum recession, bone loss around the teeth, and nicotine addiction (ACS, 2008; Ferrence, Slade, Room, & Pope, 2000; Hatsukami et al., 2004; Hatsukami & Severson, 1999; NCI, 1986, 1992, 2003; NIH, 1986; Tomar & Winn, 1999). The use of smokeless tobacco increases the risk for developing oral cancer by nearly 50,000% (ACS, 1997, 2008; CDC, 1993b; NCI, 1986, 2003; Shopland et al., 1991), and although most cancers occur late in life, oral cancers are increasingly diagnosed in younger persons (NCI, 1991). Men's greater use of smokeless tobacco contributes to an incidence of oral cancer that is more than twice as high as the incidence among women, and a death rate that is nearly 3 times as high (ACS, 1997). One recent and sophisticated study found similar levels of tobacco-specific carcinogens in cigarette smokers and in users of smokeless tobacco (Hecht, 2008). According to a recent meta-analysis, smokeless tobacco use also increases the risk for death from heart attack and stroke among nonsmokers (Boffetta & Straif, 2009). Another large study found that the risk for both fatal and nonfatal heart attack associated with smokeless tobacco use was nearly equal to the risk associated with cigarette use (Teo et al., 2006). Finally, there is some evidence that use of smokeless tobacco may lead to cigarette smoking (Tomar, 2003).

Alcohol Use

Although alcohol use in the United States leveled off during the 1990s, recent analyses of trends among adults nationally suggest that it may be increasing, especially among young adults aged 18 to 25 years (Naimi et al., 2003; Serdula, Brewer, Gillespie, Denny, & Mokdad, 2004). Men drink more alcohol, and they drink alcohol more often, than women (Chan, Neighbors, Gilson, Larimer, & Marlatt, 2007; Hasin, Grant, & Weinflash, 1988; McCreary, Newcomb, & Sadava, 1999; Russell, Light, & Gruenewald, 2004; SAMHSA, 2009; Wilsnack, Kristjanson, Wilsnack, & Crosby, 2006). Although there has been some recent public concern about increased drinking among women (Grucza, Norberg, & Bierut, 2009), there appears to be little evidence to support this concern (Chan et al., 2007; Wilsnack et al., 2006). Research consistently reveals greater problem drinking and heavy drinking among men, and a higher prevalence of alcohol abuse and dependence (Hasin et al., 1988; Huselid & Cooper, 1992; Kann et al., 1998; Kessler et al., 1994; Lex, 1991; Robins et al., 1984; Russell et al., 2004; SAMHSA, 2009; Thomas, 1995). Among adults nationally, men are 7 times more likely to be chronic drinkers (CDC, 2009l; Powell-Griner et al., 1997; SAMHSA, 2008b). *Chronic drinkers* are defined as those who have had five or more drinks in 1 day on at least 12 days in the past year. In every age group, significantly more adult men than women meet this definition. Among 25- to 44-year-olds, 4 times more men (19%) than women (5%) are chronic drinkers; among 45- to 64-year-olds, nearly 6 times more men (11%) than women (2%) are chronic drinkers; and among 65- to 74-year-olds, 5 times more men (5%) than women (1%) are chronic drinkers (DHHS, 2009e).

Binge drinking is defined as consuming five or more drinks at one sitting. Although the prevalence of binge drinking specifically appears to be increasing among both sexes, it remains much greater among males. National data from 1993–2001 indicated that men were 3 times more likely than women to binge drink; men account for 81% of all binge drinking episodes (Naimi et al., 2003). These findings are consistent with those of another study, which found that nearly 24% of all men are binge drinkers compared with 8% of all women (CDC, 2009l). According to the most recent survey data available from the Substance Abuse and Mental Health Services Administration National Survey on Drug Use and Health, more than twice as many men (32%) as women (15%) are binge drinkers (SAMHSA, 2008b). In one study that analyzed 20 metropolitan areas with the highest levels of binge drinking, gender was consistently found to be strongly and independently associated with binge drinking; it was up to 4.5 times more prevalent among men than it was among women (Nelson, Naimi, Brewer, Bolen, & Wells, 2004). *Heavy drinking* is defined as drinking five or more drinks on the same occasion on each of 5 or more days in the past 30 days. Heavy drinking is also more prevalent among men; more than 3 times as many men (11%) as women (3%) engage in heavy drinking (SAMHSA, 2008b).

Similar gender differences are found among youth and young adults; both heavy drinking and binge drinking are consistently found to be more prevalent among males than among females in these two groups (CDC, 1995c, 2000; Guthrie, Loveland-Cherry, Frey, & Dielman, 1994; Kann et al., 1998; Patrick, Covin, Fulop, Calfas, & Lovato, 1997; Perkins, 1992; Prendergast, 1994; Presley et al., 1996; SAMHSA, 2009; Thomas, 1995; Wechsler, Davenport, Dowdall, Moyekens, & Castillo, 1994; Wesley, 1992). Among 12- to 20-year-olds, more males (19%) than females (15%) are binge drinkers, and nearly twice as many males (7%) as females (4%) are heavy drinkers (SAMHSA, 2009). Among high school students nationally, young men are significantly more likely to be heavy drinkers (CDC, 2008b). Among college students nationally, men are significantly more likely than women to be binge drinkers (Wechsler, Lee, Kuo, & Lee, 2000). Among 18- to 24-year-olds, nearly 3 times more men (25%) than women (9%) engaged in binge drinking on at least 12 days in the past year (DHHS, 2009e). Furthermore, nearly 1.5 times more males (27%) than females (20%) had their first drink before age 13 years (CDC, 2008b). Starting to drink in early adolescence increases the risk for addiction and other alcohol-related problems in adulthood (Gonzalez, 1989; King & Chassin, 2007; McGue, Iacono, Legrand, Malone, & Elkins, 2001; Robins, 1978; SAMHSA, 2010).

Excessive drinking is associated with a variety of serious health problems (CDC, 2004d; Naimi, Town, Mokdad, & Brewer, 2006). Even when controlling for potentially confounding variables, it is strongly correlated with hypertension and stroke, and it is considered one of the strongest contributors to men's excess morbidity and mortality from cardiovascular disease (Flegal & Cauley, 1985; Kotchen et al., 1991; Nothwehr et al., 1994; NSA, 1994; Verbrugge, 1985; Wallace, Lynch, Pomehn, Criqui, & Heiss, 1981). It can induce both cancer (ACS, 2009; Byers et al., 2002; Gong et al., 2009; NCI, 1996; Winawer & Shike, 1995) and cirrhosis, which kill 1.5 and more than 2 times more men than women, respectively (DHHS, 2009a). Heavy drinking increases the risk for diabetes by up to 400% (Ingall, 2004), which contributes to men's disproportionate risk for diabetes. People who drink are also significantly more likely to smoke cigarettes (SAMHSA, 2009) and to not have had a medical checkup within 2 years (Town, Naimi, Mokdad, & Brewer, 2006), which further compound their risks. The health risks associated with drinking also apply to adolescents and young adults (NIAAA, 2004/2005). They include unintentional injuries and motor vehicle crashes (Hingson, Heeren, Winter, & Wechsler, 2005; National Highway Traffic Safety Administration [NHTSA], 2003a; NIAAA, 2004/2005; Smith, Branas, & Miller, 1999); violence, physical assault, and rape (Hingson et al., 2005; Wells, Graham, Speechley, & Koval, 2005); risky sexual behavior (Cooper & Orcutt, 1997; Cooper et al., 1994; NIAAA, 2004/2005); and impairments in brain functioning (Brown & Tapert, 2004; Brown, Tapert, Granholm, & Delis, 2000; Sher, 2006).

Binge drinking specifically typically causes severe impairment in functioning and is associated with a wide range of serious health risks, including unintentional injuries, motor vehicle crashes, assaults, domestic violence, rape, vandalism, alcohol poisoning, and alcohol dependence (Babor et al., 2003; CDC, 2004d; DHHS, 2000d; Naimi et al., 2003; Randolph, Torres, Gore-Felton, Lloyd, & McGarvey, 2009; Wechsler et al., 1994, 2002; Wechsler, Lee, Kuo, & Lee, 2000; Wechsler, Lee, Nelson, & Kuo, 2002, 2003). Among college students nationally, frequent binge drinkers are more than 10 times more likely than their nonbinging peers to get hurt or injured (Hingson et al., 2005; Wechsler et al., 1994). Among 12- to 20-year-olds, alcohol use increases the risk for the three leading causes of death in this age group—unintentional injury, homicide, and suicide (SAMHSA, 2010)—and the vast majority of these deaths occur among males. As noted previously, alcohol use also increases men's risks of STDs and HIV disease. Among college students nationally, binge drinkers are 7 times more likely than their nonbinging peers to have unprotected sex (Wechsler et al., 1994), and frequent binge drinkers are 7 times more likely to engage in unplanned sexual activities (Wechsler, Lee, et al., 2000). Heavy drinking specifically has been found to be a predictor of STDs in men only (Ericksen & Trocki, 1994).

The death rate for alcohol-induced causes (excluding unintentional injuries, homicides, and other indirect causes related to use) is more than 3.5 times higher for men than it is for women (DHHS, 2009a). Men account for three of four deaths attributed to excessive alcohol use, which kills 150 men each day (CDC, 2004d). Men are 3 times more likely than women to die from motor vehicle crashes, homicides, and suicides that are attributed to the use of alcohol (CDC, 2004d). Approximately half of all violent acts—most of which are committed by men—occur under the influence of alcohol (Brewer & Swahn, 2005). Men's alcohol consumption also contributes heavily to their higher rates of both nonfatal and fatal injuries, particularly from motor vehicle crashes (DHHS, 1990; NHTSA, 2009a). Men account for most of the nearly 10 million hospital emergency room visits that are alcohol or drug related (McDonald, Wang, & Camargo, 2004; SAMHSA, 2008a). A meta-analysis of 65 medical examiner studies found that 47% of people who died by homicide, 31% of those who died of injuries, and 29% of those who died by suicide tested positive for alcohol (Smith et al., 1999). Far more men than women die from all these causes. Among pedestrians killed nationally, two of three are men, and more than 40% of those men tested positive for alcohol compared with only 20% of women (CDC, 1994c; NHTSA, 2003a, 2009a). One of four fatally injured bicyclists had been drinking, and more than 90% of them were male (Rodgers, 1995).

Alcohol is considered the "ubiquitous catalyst" for drowning (Modell, 1993, p. 256); up to 50% of persons who drown have consumed alcohol near the time of death (CDC, 1993c; Warner, Smith, & Langley, 2008), and up to 70% of these people were involved in recreational activities (Driscoll, Harrison, & Steenkamp, 2004). Drowning is the leading cause of gender differences in fatal injuries, and the drowning death rate is 4 to 5 times higher for males than for females (NSC, 1998, 2010). Males of all ages account for nearly 8 of 10 drowning deaths; in the 15- to 24-year-old age group, the ratio is as high as 10:1 (NSC, 1998, 2010). Half of men compared with one third of women use alcohol during aquatic activities (CDC, 1993c; Warner et al., 2008). One in three college men nationally, aged 18 to 24 years, has drunk alcohol while boating or swimming compared with one in four college women (CDC, 1997b). More than half of boating-related deaths involve alcohol (Smith et al., 2001; U.S. Coast Guard, 2006), which is the leading contributing factor in fatal boating accidents (U.S. Coast Guard, 2009). According to the U.S. Coast Guard, 9 of 10 recreational boaters who die each year are men (S. Tomczuk, personal communication, April 19, 2010). Recreational boaters with a blood alcohol level of .10%—which is .02% more than the legal limit—are estimated to be 10 times as likely to die as nondrinking boaters (Driscoll et al., 2004). Half of all people who injure their spinal cords in swimming pools had been drinking, and nearly 90% of those injured are men (DeVivo & Sekar, 1997).

It is important to note that women's more moderate drinking contributes to their health and longevity. A recent large meta-analysis of 34 prospective studies and more than 1 million individuals provides strong evidence of the reduced risk for death among people who drink moderate amounts of alcohol (typically defined as one to two drinks per day for women and two to four drinks per day for men) (Di Castelnuovo et al., 2006). There is consistent and conclusive evidence that light or moderate drinkers are in better health and have lower mortality rates than both heavy drinkers and people who do not drink at all (Camacho, Kaplan, & Cohen, 1987; DHHS, 2005; Hulley & Gordon, 1981; Peele, 1993; Steinberg, Pearson, & Kuller, 1991; Wiley & Camacho, 1980; Wolf, Kannel, & Verter, 1983). In particular, moderate drinking protects against heart disease and stroke and increases levels of HDL, the "good" cholesterol (Bagnardi, Zatonski, Scotti, La Vecchia, & Corrao, 2008; Berger et al., 1999; Colditz et al., 1985; Corrao, Bagnardi, Zambon, & La Vecchia, 2004; Friedman & Kimball, 1986; Frimpong & Lapp, 1989; Gaziano et al., 1993, 2000; Hulley & Gordon, 1981; Kannel & Ellison, 1996; Koppes, Dekker, Hendriks, Bouter, & Heine, 2006; Linn et al., 1993; Maclure, 1993; Moore & Pearson, 1986; Reynolds et al., 2003; Rimm & Moats, 2007; Sacco et al., 1999; Steinberg et al., 1991).

Anabolic Steroid Use

The illicit use and abuse of anabolic (specifically, anabolic–androgenic) steroids is a predominantly male phenomenon (National Institute on Drug Abuse [NIDA], 2009a) and is associated with a variety of health risks (NIDA, 2009b; Yesalis & Bahrke, 2005). Anabolic steroids, which are synthetically produced variants of the naturally occurring male sex hormone testosterone, are taken either orally or by intramuscular injection (NIDA, 2009b; Yesalis & Bahrke, 2005). Although during the 1990s it was believed that steroids were used primarily by athletes (see Courtenay, 2000b; DHHS, 1991), most current research challenges this belief. With the exception of college students nationally (McCabe, Brower, West, Nelson, & Wechsler, 2007), most studies (Cohen, Collins, Darkes, & Gwartney, 2007; Parkinson & Evans, 2006)—including a study of a nationally representative sample of more than 16,000 high school students (Miller et al., 2005)—indicate that the vast majority of users are not athletes. Indeed, among adults, most use steroids for cosmetic reasons, including increased muscle mass and enhanced physical appearance (Cohen et al., 2007; Parkinson & Evans, 2006).

Fortunately, there has been a decrease in steroid use since 2001, after increases during the 1990s. The exception is the percentage of high school seniors who have recently used steroids, which has remained stable (NIDA, 2009b, 2009c). Currently, 2.5% of male high school seniors say that they have used steroids in the past year (NIDA, 2009c), and 6% say that they have ever used steroids (CDC, 2008b). Although these percentages are not large, they represent 100,000 and 240,000 male high school seniors, respectively (Transportation Research Board, 2003). Younger male students also use steroids. A little more than 1% of boys in the 8th and 10th grades have used steroids in the past year (NIDA, 2009c), and among male high school students in all grades, 5% have used steroids (CDC, 2008b). Approximately 2% of college men report the nonmedical use of anabolic steroids (McCabe et al., 2007). By age 30, 4% of adults have used steroids (NIDA, 2009c); based on 2009 U.S. Census Bureau population estimates, this number represents approximately 177,487 men. The use of anabolic steroids is consistently much higher among males than females; it is 4 times higher among 19- to 30-year-olds, 6 times higher among high school seniors

(NIDA, 2009c), and 10 times higher among college students (McCabe et al., 2007). Furthermore, there is evidence that self-reported use is much lower than actual use (Beel, Maycock, & McLean, 1998; Yesalis & Bahrke, 2005).

There is increasing evidence that steroid use can cause significant physical and mental damage—damage that can be life threatening (SAMHSA, 2006). Long-term steroid use can lead to serious—and some-times irreversible—health problems, including damage to liver, heart, and reproductive systems (Brower, 1998; NIDA, 2009b; SAMHSA, 2006; Street, Antonio, & Cudlipp, 1996). In addition to liver damage and jaundice, the most dangerous problems include high blood pres-sure, increases in LDL cholesterol, and decreases in HDL cholesterol, which increase men's already disproportionately high risk for heart disease (Brower, 1998; NIDA, 2009b; Street et al., 1996). There is also some evidence of an increased risk for prostate cancer associated with steroid use (NIDA, 2009b). In addition, people who inject ste-roids risk contracting bloodborne diseases passed by needle sharing, including HIV/AIDS and hepatitis—which causes serious damage to the liver (NIDA, 2009b; SAMHSA, 2006). As I have explained, men are at greater risk for all these health problems. Some studies have also identified steroids as a gateway drug, the use of which leads to the use of other substances, including opioids (Arvary & Pope, 2000; Pope & Kanayama, 2005). People who have abused steroids and who then stop using them can experience a variety of withdrawal symptoms; one of the most dangerous is depression, which can sometimes lead to suicide (NIDA, 2009b).

Steroid use can also increase the risk for injury, homicide, and suicide—particularly through its effects on mental functioning. It has been linked to severe mental disorders, including mania, depression, suicidal behavior, and psychoses (SAMHSA, 2006); as I said previously, males are at greater risk for these disorders. Research also shows that abuse of steroids can lead to uncontrolled anger or combative behavior ("roid rage") (NIDA, 2009b; SAMHSA, 2006). Extreme mood swings can also occur with use, including manic-like symptoms, paranoid jeal-ousy, extreme irritability, and impaired judgment stemming from feel-ings of invincibility (NIDA, 2009b). All these can increase the risk for violence, suicide, or homicide, as well as other risky health behaviors in general (Beaver, Vaughn, DeLisi, & Wright, 2008; Brower, 1998; McCabe et al., 2007; Street et al., 1996). College men who use steroids are also more likely to use other drugs (McCabe et al., 2007), includ-ing marijuana, cocaine, tobacco, and alcohol; nearly three of four users report arguments or fights as a consequence of using steroids, and nearly half report being hurt or injured (Meilman, Crace, Presley, & Lyeria, 1995). Nearly three of four long-term steroid users meet criteria for an alcohol use disorder (McCabe et al., 2007). Multiple and simultaneous drug use may further increase the risks associated with anabolic steroids (Brower, 1998).

RISK TAKING AND RECKLESS BEHAVIOR

At every age, death from injuries is far more common among men than women (DHHS, 2008b). Males of all ages represent nearly 7 of every 10 unintentional injury deaths (NSC, 1994, 2010). Among adults in their 20s, injury death rates are 4 times higher among men; in all other age groups, they are 2 to 3 times higher (DHHS, 2008b). Injury is the leading cause of death for everyone under the age of 45 and the primary reason for the large gender differences in mortality at these ages (CDC, 1994d; DHHS, 2009b; NSC, 1998); in this age group, males account for nearly 3 of 4 deaths resulting from unintentional injuries (DHHS, 2007b). Among those aged 15 to 24 years, three of every four deaths from any cause are male, and unintentional injuries are the leading killer, claiming nearly 3 times more lives than homicide, the next-leading cause of death (DHHS, 2007b). The death rate for falls is twice as high for men as for women (DHHS, 2000).

Risk taking and reckless behavior by men and boys is a major contributor to their injury deaths. The common everyday practice of crossing the street provides a surprisingly striking example. Most pedestrians are injured or killed because they were crossing roads or intersections improperly, or running into streets (NSC, 2010). Males are more likely than females to cross streets improperly or to jaywalk (ASHA, 1989; NHTSA, 1997, 2008a). Indeed, nearly 80% of pedestrians killed are killed by unsafe or reckless behavior, and the vast majority of these are males. These behaviors include crossing streets improperly (27%); walking, playing, or working in the street (25%); failure to yield the right-of-way (14%); and jaywalking (12%) (NHTSA, 2008a). From 1997 to 2006, a total of 49,128 pedestrians were killed, and more than two thirds of them were male (NHTSA, 2008a). The following sections further examine gender differences in some specific risk-taking behaviors: reckless driving, drinking and driving, safety belt use, sexual activity, and sports and recreation.

Reckless Driving

Motor vehicle crashes are the fifth leading cause of death in the U.S. population as a whole (DHHS, 2009a). However, for those up to age 35, they are the number one cause of death (CDC, 2005e; NHTSA, 2009b). Among young adults, car crashes cause 70% of all fatalities, and young men are 3 times more likely to die in a crash than young women (NHTSA, 2008b; Park et al., 2006). Motor vehicle-related fatalities account for more than half of all unintentional injury deaths (NSC, 1998), and nearly three of four people (70%) killed in car crashes are male (NHTSA, 2008b). The death rate for car crashes is more than twice as high for men as it is for women; each day car crashes kill nearly 100 men in the United States (CDC, 2009c). Since 1996, the number of men killed in car crashes has increased, whereas the number of women killed in car crashes has decreased (NHTSA, 2007a). These crashes also contribute to men's greater risk for nonfatal injury; they are the cause, for example, of the vast majority of men's hospitalizations for traumatic brain injuries (CDC, 2006a). The number of miles driven does not account for the gender difference in motor vehicle injury and death; per mile driven, men are at consistently greater risk than women for being in a car crash—regardless of whether the crash is fatal (Massie, Green, & Campbell, 1997; NSC, 1992). What accounts for this difference is men's reckless and risky driving behavior.

Males of all ages are consistently found to be more likely than females to drive dangerously—for example, by tailgating, driving while distracted, speeding, driving aggressively, and running red lights or stop signs (DeJoy, 1992; Farrow & Brissing, 1990; NHTSA, 2007a, 2007b; Preusser, Williams, & Lund, 1991; Retting, Ulmer, & Williams, 1999; Schlundt, Warren, & Miller, 2004; Zuckerman, 1983, 1984, 1994). Three of four people who run red lights are men (Hu & Young, 1999)—and running a red light leads to the most common type of car crash (Retting, Williams, & Greene, 1998). These crashes are also the likeliest to cause injuries; 45% of crashes related to red light running involve injury compared with 30% of all other crashes (Retting et al., 1998).

Excessive speed contributes to one third of all traffic fatalities (NSC, 2010), and significantly fewer men than women obey speed limits (CDC, 1994e; DeJoy, 1992; NHTSA, 2008c; Pinch, Heck, & Vinal, 1986). Males are 1.5 times more likely than females to be speeding when a fatal car crash occurs, and this holds true for males in every age group (NHTSA, 2008c). Men are also more likely than women to have committed moving violations and to have had their driver's license suspended or revoked, and they are twice as likely as women to drive with an invalid license; 14% of men, compared with 7% of women, drive with an invalid license (DeJoy, 1992; NHTSA, 2009c).

More men (80%) than women (71%) admit to talking on a cell phone or texting (66 and 63%, respectively) while driving (Pew Research Center, 2010). Among high school students nationally, males are more likely than females to engage in a variety of other behaviors that contribute to motor vehicle injuries (CDC, 2008b). Nearly one third of young men report taking risks for fun while driving—more than 4 times the number of young women who do so (Jessor, 1987). One study found that significantly more male than female high school students drive 20 mph over the speed limit, pass a car in a no-passing zone, pass two cars at a time on a two-lane road, or take risks while driving because it makes driving more fun (CDC, 1994e).

As a result of their reckless driving, males are 1.5 times more likely than females to be the driver in injury crashes, and 3 times more likely to be the driver in fatal crashes (NHTSA, 2008b). Furthermore, between 1997 and 2007 the percentage of female drivers in fatal crashes decreased, whereas the percentage of male drivers remained the same (NHTSA, 2008d). In fact, despite public perception to the contrary, there is no evidence of women's increased involvement in fatal car crashes since 1975 (Mayhew, Ferfuson, Desmond, & Simpson, 2003). Nearly three of four drivers (72%) who kill pedestrians are men (when the gender of the driver is known), and reckless driving accounts for nearly all these deaths (NHTSA, 2003b). Approximately 40% of motor vehicle crashes occur at intersections (Retting et al., 1999), and men are responsible for the majority of these crashes (NHTSA, 2007b)—they are responsible for most crashes that result from running red lights, as I discussed previously, and 69% of crashes that result from running stop signs. In California, men are at fault in nearly 8 of 10 fatal crashes, and are responsible for twice as many injury crashes as women (California Highway Patrol [CHP], 1994). Speed is a primary cause of injury crashes and the second leading cause of fatal crashes in California (CHP, 1994). Male drivers are also more likely than female drivers to be killed in crashes that result from improperly following too close to another vehicle (Kostyniuk, Streff, & Zakrajsek, 2002).

Drinking and Driving

Every year, drunk driving causes as many deaths as homicide (Schwartz, 2008), and even a small amount of alcohol significantly increases the risk for a fatal crash (Zador, Krawchuk, & Voas, 2000). Among 16- to 20-year-old male drivers, a blood alcohol level of only .02%—one quarter the legal limit—more than doubles that risk; at .09%, the risk is more than 50 times greater (Zador et al., 2000). Alcohol-related motor vehicle crashes account for one third of all traffic fatalities (NHTSA, 2008b); for those aged less than 25, driving while impaired by alcohol or other drugs is the leading cause of death (CDC, 1994f). Men are responsible for three of four alcohol-related motor vehicle fatalities (CDC, 2004d). Men (7%) are also far more likely than women (3%) to drive under the influence of alcohol or drugs (Department of Justice [DOJ], 2005).

Alcohol-impaired driving has increased significantly since the 1990s, when it had decreased (Quinlan et al., 2005). Men are approximately 3 times more likely than women to drive while drinking, drive after having had too much to drink, ride with a drinking driver, or ride as a passenger while drinking (Chou et al., 2005, 2006). However, the rate of alcohol-impaired driving has been found to be as much as 5 times higher among men than among women nationally (Simin et al., 1997). According to self-reports, 12% of people report having driven under the influence of alcohol at least once in the past year, and males (16%) are nearly twice as likely as females (9%) to have done so (SAMHSA, 2009). The rate of alcohol-impaired driving is highest among men aged 18 to 34 years (Simin et al., 1997). Twenty-six percent of young adults aged 21 to 25 report having driven under the influence of alcohol in the past year (SAMHSA, 2009), and twice as many young men as women have done so (Chou, et al., 2005). Young men in both high school and college are significantly more likely than young women to drive after drinking (CDC, 1997b, 2008b; Kann et al., 1998; Lewis, Goodhart, & Burns, 1996; Patrick et al., 1997). Among high school students nationally, 13% of males report having driven after drinking alcohol at least once in the past month—more than 1.5 times the number of females (8%) (CDC, 2008b). Among college students nationally, two in five men (41%) have driven after drinking compared with fewer than one in three women (31%) (Wechsler et al., 2003).

The vast majority of drunk drivers are binge drinkers—most of whom are men (Flowers et al., 2008; Naimi et al., 2003). One study found that more than 1 in 10 binge drinkers nationally drove during or within 2 hours of engaging in binge drinking, and men were nearly twice as likely as women to do so (Naimi, Nelson, & Brewer, 2009). Among college students nationally, 19% of men, compared with 9% of women, report having driven after consuming five or more drinks (Wechsler et al., 2003); among men who are frequent binge drinkers, 62% report having driven after drinking (Wechsler et al., 1994).

More than four in five people arrested for drunk driving are men (Schwartz, 2008). Although arrests of female drunk drivers have increased during the past 2 decades, extensive analyses of data indicate that this is not because of increased drunk driving among women. Rather, it is the result of changes in arrest patterns. Gender differences in drunk driving have not changed, and there is no evidence that more women are driving drunk (Mayhew et al., 2003; Schwartz, 2008; Schwartz & Rookey, 2008). Furthermore, men have higher blood alcohol levels when they are arrested for drunk driving, and they are 4 times more likely than women to drive drunk *repeatedly* (CDC, 1994g; Mayhew et al., 2003; Schwartz, 2008; Zador et al., 2000).

It is not surprising, then, that men are responsible for most alcohol-related motor vehicle crashes—including fatal crashes—and are also more likely than women to die in these crashes. Males represent 84% of all drivers with a blood alcohol level of .08 or more involved in a fatal crash, which is considered an alcohol-impaired crash (NSC, 2010). One in four male drivers in fatal car crashes had a blood alcohol level of .08 or more at the time of the crash, compared with one in eight female drivers (NHTSA, 2009a). These figures hold true for motorcycle operators as well (NHTSA, 2006). Nearly half of fatally injured drivers aged 21 to 30 were legally intoxicated; for fatally injured drivers aged 16 to 20, the figures are one in four (DHHS, 2008b). People who are arrested for drunk driving—most of whom are men—are substantially more likely than other people to die in an alcohol-related motor vehicle crash (CDC, 1994g). Finally, one sophisticated study found that men who drive after drinking are significantly less likely to wear safety belts, which further compounds their risk for injury and death (Foss, Beirness, & Sprattler, 1994).

Safety Belt Use

Wearing safety belts, particularly in combination with air bags, is the most effective method for preventing injuries from motor vehicle crashes (CDC, 1993d, 2009c; NHTSA, 2008e). Men of all ages, and younger men in particular, are less likely than women to report wearing safety belts or be observed wearing them, either as drivers or as passengers (CDC, 1992b, 1992c, 1995c, 1997a, 2008b; Dinh-Zarr et al., 2001; Eby, Molnar, & Olk, 2000; Foss et al., 1994; Hunter, Stutts, Stewart, & Rodgman, 1990; Kann et al., 1998; Leigh & Fries, 1993; Lewis et al., 1996; Mayrose & Jehle, 2002; Oleckno & Blacconiere, 1990b; Patrick et al., 1997; Pinch et al., 1986; Powell-Griner et al., 1997; Preusser et al., 1991; Rossi, 1992). Although the use of safety belts has increased during the past 20 years, it has increased more among women than among men (Zaza, Briss, Harris, & Task Force on Community Preventive Services, 2005). Depending on the state and its seat belt laws, fewer men (69 to 81%) than women (80 to 90%) say that they *always* wear safety belts (Beck, Shults, Mack, & Ryan, 2007). Among students in grades 9 through 12, more than 1.5 times more males than females never or rarely wear a safety belt (CDC, 2008b). In one study where drivers were both observed and questioned, more than three of four of those who were observed not wearing a safety belt were male; one third of these unbelted male drivers had reported that they always wore safety belts (Preusser et al., 1991). Among occupants in motor vehicle crashes, men are more likely than women to be unbelted at the time of collision (Hargarten & Karlson, 1994).

The failure to wear safety belts significantly increases men's risks. Wearing safety belts reduces the risk for fatal injury to anyone in the front seat of a passenger car by 45%, and the risk for moderate to critical injury by 50% (CDC, 2009c). For anyone occupying the front seat of a light truck, safety belts reduce the risk for fatal injury by 60% and the risk for moderate to critical injury by 65% (NHTSA, 2008e). In 2007, the use of safety belts in motor vehicles saved an estimated 15,147 lives and could have saved an additional 5,024 lives if everyone in these vehicles had been wearing them (NHTSA, 2008e). More than half of the people who were killed in motor vehicles crashes had not been wearing safety belts (CDC, 2009c; NHTSA, 2008e). A recent study found that nearly one in three people killed in car crashes during a 20-year period—most of whom were male—would not have been killed if he or she had been wearing a safety belt (Cummings, Rivara, Olson, & Smith, 2006). A study on the impact of safety belt use on nearly 1,000 people injured in car accidents found that unbelted occupants were more likely to be male, to have been in a head-on or rollover crash, to have had more severe injuries, to have been permanently disabled, or to have died in the hospital (CDC, 1993d). Not surprisingly, wearing safety belts also substantially reduces the risk for traumatic brain injury. Approximately 46% of those who sustain traumatic brain injury—who, as I have discussed previously, are mostly men—are not wearing a safety belt at the time that they are injured (CDC, 2003d).

Helmet Use

Bicycle Helmets

Bicycle helmets are known to prevent head injuries (CDC, 1995d, 2003d). They reduce the risk for head injuries in general by 85% and the risk for brain injury specifically by as much as 88% (CDC, 1992b, 1998f). Yet only 43% of bicyclists wear a helmet all or most of the time (Rodgers, 2000). The most recent national data available show that only slightly fewer males than females say they always or almost always wear a bicycle helmet; slightly more males say they never or almost never wear one (Rodgers, 2000). However, more recent data are available for high school students nationally, and here the differences are greater. The vast majority (85%) of these bicyclists say that they rarely or never wear a helmet, and more young men (87%) than women (82%) say this (CDC, 2008b).

Men's greater incidence of bicycle injuries suggests that they take more risks—apart from not wearing a helmet—than women do when they ride a bicycle. This makes the failure to wear a helmet even more dangerous than it would be otherwise. The injury rate for bicyclists is more than 5 times higher for males than it is for females, and the death rate is 8 times higher (NHTSA, 2008f). Eighty-three percent of bicyclists injured are males, and 88% of bicyclists killed are males (NHTSA, 2008f). A recent review shows that most injured mountain bikers are also men, and that these injuries tend to be caused by riding too fast downhill and losing control (Carmont, 2008). Apart from possible riskier riding patterns such as these—which are rarely studied—this increased risk among males is probably explained by the fact that males do not wear helmets as often as they say they do. (The same principle applies to safety belt use, as noted previously.) In fact, nearly all bicyclists (96%) killed were not wearing helmets when they sustained their fatal injuries (CDC, 1998f). Both fatal and nonfatal bicycle-related head injuries are higher for males than females in all age groups (CDC, 1995d). An estimated 41% of bicyclists were not wearing helmets at the time of their traumatic brain injury (CDC, 2003d), which—as noted previously—are primarily sustained by males.

Motorcycle Helmets

Helmet use reduces the risk for death from motorcycle crashes by 28 to 73% (CDC, 1992b, 2003d; NHTSA, 2008g). Although scarce, available data regarding motorcycle helmet use do reveal gender differences. Among adolescent motorcyclists, only 40% always wear a helmet, and more males than females rarely or never use them (ASHA, 1989;

CDC, 1995c). Among high school students nationally, more males (38%) than females (27%) rarely or never wear a helmet (CDC, 2008b). This has important health implications for adolescent males because they are nearly twice as likely as adolescent females to ride motorcycles or minibikes (ASHA, 1989; CDC, 1992c). Among California college students, men are significantly less likely to wear a helmet always when riding a motorcycle (Patrick et al., 1997). More than half (53%) of motorcyclists nationwide were not wearing a helmet at the time they sustained a traumatic brain injury, which—as noted previously—is an injury that is sustained primarily by men (CDC, 2003d).

Sexual Activity

Each day, 52,000 Americans become infected with STDs, including chlamydia, gonorrhea, syphilis, genital herpes, and human papillomavirus (HPV) (CDC, 2009m). High-risk sexual behavior accounts for an estimated 20,000 to 30,000 deaths annually (McGinnis & Foege, 1993; Mokdad et al., 2004). Twice as many men as women engage in high-risk sexual activities (Bastani et al., 1996; EDK Associates, 1995). There is consistent evidence that males are more likely to be sexually active, to have more sexual partners, to have sex while under the influence of alcohol or other drugs, to have had large numbers of sexual partners overall, and to be nonmonogamous in adulthood (Bastani et al., 1996; CDC, 1992d, 1997a; EDK Associates, 1995; Ericksen & Trocki, 1992, 1994; Kann et al., 1998; Laumann, Gagnon, Michael, & Michaels, 1994; Leigh, Temple, & Trocki, 1993; Oliver & Hyde, 1993; Patrick et al., 1997; Poppen, 1995; Seal & Agostinelli, 1996; Wiley et al., 1996; Zuckerman, 1994). Males have their first experiences of sexual intercourse earlier than females (Zimmer-Gembeck & Helfand, 2008), and among men, those who had sexual intercourse at an earlier age are more sexually active, have greater numbers of sexual partners, and have greater numbers of casual sexual partners (DHHS, 2006d). More than 50% of all men have had six or more partners during their lifetimes, compared with 25% of women (EDK Associates, 1995). More than 1 in 10 men nationally (11%) had concurrent sexual partnerships in a recent year; these men are also twice as likely to report drug or alcohol intoxication during sexual intercourse, and they are 6 times more likely to have nonmonogamous female sexual partners compared with men without concurrent partnerships; all these sexual behaviors increase men's health risks (Adimora, Schoenbach, & Doherty, 2007). Similarly, only one in four men always uses a condom, and fewer than one in three men at high risk for STDs always does so (EDK Associates, 1995).

These findings hold true for adolescents and young adults. Greater sexual risk behaviors among males than females are consistently reported in large, nationally representative samples of adolescents (Halpern et al., 2004; Santelli et al., 2004; Santelli, Lowry, Brener, & Robin, 2000). Even among U.S. students in grades 9 through 12, up to twice as many males as females have had sexual intercourse with four or more persons during their lifetimes. In addition, nearly twice as many 11th- and 12th-grade males (28 and 29%, respectively) as females (15 and 17%, respectively) drank alcohol or used drugs before their last sexual intercourse, which further increases their sexual health risks (CDC, 2009n). In fact, among high school students nationally, males are more likely than females to engage in six of eight sexual behaviors that increase the risk for STDs, including HIV infection (CDC, 2008b). Among 15- to 19-year-old sexually active males nationally, 33% did not use a condom at last intercourse, 27% had at least one experience of unprotected sex in the year before being surveyed, and 10% never use a condom (Sonenstein, Ku, Lindberg, Turner, & Pleck, 1998). Among college students, 22% of men, compared with 13% of women, had drunk alcohol or used drugs at last sexual intercourse (CDC, 1997b). These problems show no sign of diminishing; as a result, the CDC recently recommended the need for public health efforts to address young men's sexual risk behaviors (CDC, 2008l).

As a result of these risky sexual behaviors, men are much more likely than women to be in the highest-risk group for HIV disease and other STDs (CDC, 2008b, 2009d; EDK Associates, 1995; Ericksen & Trocki, 1992, 1994; Leigh et al., 1993; Shafer et al., 1993). The percentage of men at high risk for STDs is estimated to be double that of women (Bastani et al., 1996; EDK Associates, 1995). Eighty-six percent of all STDs occur among those under age 30 (CDC, 1992e), and 48% occur among those aged 15 to 24 (Weinstock, Berman, & Cates, 2004); 60% of men under age 30 are estimated to be at medium to high risk for STDs compared with 24% of women (EDK Associates, 1995). The most lethal STD is HIV. Currently, three of four of those infected with HIV are men (CDC, 2009b), and the death rate for HIV is 3 times higher for men than it is for women (DHHS, 2009a). The annual rate of AIDS diagnoses among males aged 15 to 19 years nearly doubled between 1997 and 2006 (CDC, 2009n). Apart from HIV, more than 25 diseases are spread primarily through sexual activity; the most common are chlamydia, gonorrhea, syphilis, genital herpes, HPV, and hepatitis (CDC, 2000b). Although the prevalence of chlamydia among adolescents aged 14 to 19 is somewhat greater among females than males, among young adults aged 20 to 29, the prevalence is greater among males (CDC, 2009n). The rates of syphilis and hepatitis are also higher for men (CDC, 2009m; Dunne, Nielson, Stone, Markowitz, & Giuliano, 2006); the rate of syphilis is 6 times higher (CDC, 2009m). Cases of viral hepatitis (A, B, and C)—which is characterized by inflammation of the liver—have decreased during the past several decades; however, they remain common, particularly among men (CDC, 2009m). The rate of hepatitis A in males is almost twice that in females (CDC, 2009m). Hepatitis B, which can be transmitted through body fluids such as saliva and semen exchanged during sex, increases the risk for liver cancer (Winawer & Shike, 1995). Men are 1.5 times more likely than women to become infected with hepatitis B (CDC, 1995e). Infection with HPV is also common in men; as many as three of four men are infected (Dunne et al., 2006), and there is strong, consistent evidence linking HPV with penile cancer (Bleeker et al., 2009; Fackelman, 1992; Maden et al., 1995; Zazove, Caruthers, & Reed, 1991). Because the majority of STDs remain undiagnosed (CDC, 2009m), and because men have fewer contacts with health professionals who can diagnose them, it is likely that current estimates understate the prevalence of many STDs in men (Dariotis, Pleck, Sonenstein, Astone, & Sifakis, 2009). Furthermore, research has shown a failure among physicians to diagnose STDs in men (Phillips et al., in press).

Sports and Recreation

It has been suggested that sports injuries pose a greater public health risk than many reportable infectious diseases (Kraus & Conroy, 1984). Indeed, in a recent year, Americans made more than 14 million visits for medical care because of injuries related to sports and leisure activities (NSC, 2010). An estimated 4.3 million nonfatal sports- and recreation-related injuries are treated annually in hospital emergency departments nationally, and males account for nearly three of four (68 to 70%) of these injuries (CDC, 2002b; Flores, Haileyesus, & Greenspan, 2008). Furthermore, injury rates are significantly higher among males than among females in every age group (CDC, 2002b). Snowboarding and sledding are associated with the greatest number of injuries requiring emergency department visits (Flores et al., 2008). Head injuries account for nearly 4 of 10 (39%) of all skiing, snowboarding, and sledding injuries, and more than half (55%) of sledding injuries specifically; 80% of these injuries are sustained by males (Federiuk, Schlueter, & Adams, 2002). Traumatic brain injuries account for more than 1.5 million to nearly 4 million sports- and recreation-related injuries, and most often result from activities involving bicycling, football, playground activities, basketball, and riding all-terrain vehicles (CDC, 2007g). Males of all ages account for nearly three of four (70%) of these injuries, which can result in long-term impairment (CDC, 2007g). Similarly, nearly 1 in 10 (9%) spinal cord injuries are sports-related (Boden & Jarvis, 2009), and four of five people who experience traumatic spinal cord injuries are male (Jackson, Dijkers, DeVivo, & Poczatek, 2004). Given these figures, sports- and recreation-related injuries clearly constitute a substantial health risk for males.

Contributing to these injuries is the fact that men and boys are more likely than women and girls to participate in risky sports and recreational activities. For example, men are significantly more likely than women to engage in "extreme sports," such as skydiving, hang gliding, auto racing, scuba diving, mountain climbing, and whitewater kayaking (Zuckerman, 1983, 1984, 1994; Zuckerman & Kuhlman, 2000). Almost three in four adolescent males, compared with fewer than half of adolescent females, drive or ride go-carts, snowmobiles, or all-terrain vehicles, and they do so more frequently (ASHA, 1989). Sports and recreation contribute heavily to injuries sustained by those under age 18 (Scheidt et al., 1995), and boys under age 18 have much higher sports and recreation injury rates than girls (CDC, 2002b, 2007g; Rivara, Bergman, LoGerfo, & Weiss, 1982). Sports that are almost exclusively male are responsible for a large number of injuries and deaths. For example, an estimated 517,726 high school football-related injuries occur annually in the United States (Shankar, Fields, Collins, Dick, & Comstock, 2007). Indeed, the highest injury rates among high school athletes nationally are for all-male sports: football, wrestling, and boys' soccer (CDC, 2006f). Furthermore, male football and wrestling injuries account for the most *severe* injuries sustained by high school athletes in the United States (Darrow, Collins, Yard, & Comstock, 2009). Football accounts for the most injuries among high school athletes; the injury rate for football is almost twice that for basketball, the second-most popular sport (Shankar et al., 2007).

Higher rates of sports injuries among males are also a consistent finding in most studies examining sports in which nonathletes of both sexes frequently participate, such as skiing and bicycle riding. For example, males account for 83% of all nonfatal bicycle injuries (NHTSA, 2008c), 82% of basketball injuries (CDC, 2002b), 60% of skiing- and snowboarding-related injuries (Xiang, Kelleher, Shields, Brown, & Smith, 2005), and 59% of all exercise-related injuries treated in hospital emergency departments (CDC, 2002b). One explanation for these higher rates of injury is that men and boys take greater physical risks than women and girls while engaged in sports and recreation activities (Kontos, 2004; Morrongiello & Lasenby-Lessard, 2007; Morrongiello & Rennie 1998; Zuckerman, 1984, 1994; Zuckerman & Kuhlman, 2000). Among adolescent bike riders, for example, only one third as many males as females use a bicycle light and always wear reflective clothing when riding at night (ASHA, 1989). As noted previously, males account for 80 to 90% of all bicycle injuries and deaths.

Water sports also contribute heavily to men's higher injury and death rates. Water skiing, wakeboarding, and inner tubing result in an nearly 12,000 estimated injuries annually, and injury rates are significantly higher for males than females—more than 2 times higher for wakeboarding, 3 times higher for water skiing, and nearly 1.5 times higher for inner tubing (Baker, Griffin, Brauneis, Rue, & McGwin, 2010). As noted previously, males account for nearly 8 of 10 drowning deaths. Risky swimming, diving, and boating habits increase the risk for drowning and spinal cord injury among men and boys. National data indicate that men are significantly more likely than women to swim in a natural body of water (as compared with a swimming pool), swim alone, drink alcohol while swimming alone, and drink alcohol while boating without a life jacket (Howland, Hingson, Mangione, Bell, & Bak, 1996). Similarly, more boys than girls nationally swim and ice skate in unsupervised areas, or swim alone and dive into water of unknown depth (ASHA, 1989). Diving causes three of four recreation-related spinal cord injuries, and most of these are sustained by men (DeVivo, Rutt, Black, Go, & Stover, 1992; DeVivo & Sekar, 1997; Kraus, Franti, Riggins, Richards, & Borhani, 1975; Perrine, Mundt, & Weiner, 1994). Nine of 10 of these diving injuries occur in 6 feet of water or less, and approximately half occur in rivers, lakes, and oceans; males account for more than 8 of 10 (82%) diving-related injuries that occur in swimming pools, and more than 9 of 10 (92%) that occur in the natural environment (Gabrielsen, McElhaney, & O'Brien, 2001). Although the risk for diving-related injuries is higher for young females than for older ones (Gabrielsen et al., 2001), it remains highest for young males; among those under age 20, males account for two thirds (63%) of all diving-related injuries (Day, Stolz, Mehan, Smith, & McKenzie, 2008). Furthermore, boys are twice as likely as girls to suffer diving-related head or head and neck injuries, which can result in severe spinal cord damage and paralysis (Day et al., 2008).

As noted previously, men's alcohol use while boating also represents a substantial health risk. It contributes to a death rate for boating-related drowning that is 14 times higher for men than for women (CDC, 1993c). Among recreational boaters of all ages nationally, males are less likely than females to wear personal flotation devices or life jackets—which reduce the risk for drowning (U.S. Coast Guard, 2003, 2008). More than two thirds of all fatal boating accident victims drown, and of these, 90% were not wearing a life jacket (U.S. Coast Guard, 2009). One and half times more females (63%) than males (42%) wear life jackets either always or most of the time, whereas 1.5 times more males (40%) than females (26%) rarely or never use them (U.S. Coast Guard, 2003). One observational study of boaters in two states found that females were 1.5 times more likely than males to wear life jackets (Quan, Bennett, Cummings, Trusty, & Treser, 1998). Although the U.S. Coast Guard does not report gender differences in boating-related injuries and deaths, the state of Florida does. In Florida, the vast majority of those injured (62 to 65%) or killed (84 to 90%) in boating accidents are men (Florida Fish and Wildlife Conservation Commission, 2006). The boat operators were at fault in most of these accidents. Indeed, careless or reckless operation is the leading cause of recreational boat accidents nationally (U.S. Coast Guard, 2009). In accidents involving fatalities in Florida, nearly all (93%) of the operators were males, and the top five leading causes of accidents (in order) were no one serving as lookout, alcohol use, overloading, operator inexperience, and carelessness or inattention (Florida Fish and Wildlife Conservation Commission, 2006).

VIOLENCE

There is consistent evidence that American men express significantly more aggression than American women—particularly physical aggression (Archer, 2004; Benenson, Carder, & Geib-Cole, 2008; Cohn,

1991; Côté, 2007; DOJ, 1994a, 2005; Eagly & Steffen, 1986; Knight, Guthrie, Page, & Fabes, 2002; Maccoby, 1988), which they associate with controlling others (Campbell & Muncer, 2008; Sijtsema, Veenstra, Lindenberg, & Salmivalli, 2009) and with what it means to be male (Krug et al., 2002). Males are much more likely than females to be both the perpetrators and the victims of violence (DOJ, 1995, 2005; Loeber et al., 2005), which remains true among youth (Courtenay, 1999b). In fact, according to an extensive review of research on adolescent violence, male gender is the *only* risk factor consistently associated with the perpetration of violence (AHRQ, 2004). Men's willingness to engage in overt physical aggression and violence contributes to their health risks and premature deaths. In the United States, violent deaths from suicide and homicide are the third leading cause of premature death (defined by years of potential life lost) before age 65 (Anderson, 2001; CDC, 1994h, 2010b). One recent study, examining data from a nationally representative sample of adults, estimated gender differences in years of potential life lost during a lifetime and found that traumatic deaths accounted for a large proportion of these differences; men lost 415 more years of potential life per 1,000 individuals than women as a result of homicide and suicide, which combined account for 20% of the gender disparity in years of potential life lost before age 75 (Wong et al., 2006). As I discussed in Chapter 1, both homicide and suicide death rates are 4 times greater for men than they are for women—and are as much as 7 times higher for homicide and 18 times higher for suicide in certain age groups.

Physical Fighting

Nearly one half of men nationally have been punched or beaten by another person compared with one quarter of women (DOJ, 1994a). Each year, one in four men is physically assaulted, nearly 1.5 times the number of women (DOJ, 2005); similarly, the rate of aggravated assault victimization is nearly twice as high for men as it is for women (DOJ, 2007a). Among adolescents, national data have consistently shown that approximately half of all male students are in a physical fight during the course of 1 year, and the incidence of fighting is nearly 2 to 4 times greater for males than for females (ASHA, 1989; CDC, 1992c, 1992f, 2008b; Kann et al., 1998). The most recent data indicate that among high school students nationally, almost half (44%) of young men have been in a physical fight one or more times in the past year compared with a little more than one in four (27%) young women (Borowsky & Ireland, 2004; CDC, 2008b). In addition, 5 times more male than female high school seniors nationally have hit an instructor or supervisor (5% compared with 1%), twice as many have gotten into a serious fight at work or school (19% compared with 9%), and 4 times more have hurt someone badly enough to need bandages or a doctor (19% compared with 5%) (DOJ, 2005). Similarly, college men are twice as likely as college women to have been in a physical fight (CDC, 1997b; Lewis et al., 1996; Patrick et al., 1997).

Regardless of the provocation, more adolescent males than females nationally have been found to consider physical fighting to be an appropriate response (ASHA, 1989). For example, 3.5 times more male than female students believe that fighting is appropriate when someone cuts into the front of a line (ASHA, 1989). Fighting among men and boys contributes to both their injury and their homicide rates, which, as noted previously, are far greater among males than females of all ages. Among high school students nationally, twice as many males (10%) as females (5%) have been threatened or injured with a weapon on school property in the past year, and twice as many males (6%) as females (3%) have been in a physical fight in the past year that resulted in an injury requiring care by a physician or nurse (CDC, 2008b). One of every 30 adolescents reports that he or she has received medical care for injuries related to physical fighting (Lowry, Powell, Kann, Collins, & Kolbe, 1998). Among adolescents, 11% of boys and 6% of girls were involved in alcohol-related fighting (Bonomo et al., 2001). Fighting is the most immediate antecedent behavior for a great proportion of homicides and is often considered a necessary, if not a sufficient, cause (CDC, 1992f; DHHS, 1991; Gelles & Straus, 1988); it is also predictive of suicide attempts in adolescent males (Nickerson & Slater, 2009).

Although females are more likely than males to report adverse childhood experiences—such as chronic drug and alcohol abuse in the home and physical or sexual abuse—high school boys are significantly more likely than high school girls to respond to these experiences with violent behavior. This behavior includes bullying, weapon carrying, dating violence, and suicide attempts (Duke, Pettingell, Morris, & Borowsky, 2010). Many activities associated with violence, such as binge drinking and illicit drug use, are engaged in more frequently by men (World Health Organization [WHO], 2006). Large meta-analyses have shown that the chronic effects of violence in the community and in the home have lasting ill effects on the mental health of both male and female children and adolescents (Fowler, Tompsett, Braciszewski, Jacques-Tiura, & Baltes, 2009; Wolfe, Crooks, Lee, McIntyre-Smith, & Jaffe, 2003).

Weapon Ownership and Use

Between 2000 and 2007, more than 8 million years of potential life were lost through the use of firearms, which accounts for 5% of all deaths in the United States (CDC, 2010e). In the United States, nearly 3 times more men (17%) than women (6%) carry a gun for defense, and almost twice as many men carry a knife for defense (16 and 9%, respectively) (DOJ, 2007c). Firearms, specifically, are owned and used primarily by males (Wyant & Taylor, 2007). Far more men (49%) than women (31%) have a gun in their home (DOJ, 2009b), and more than twice as many men live in households with loaded firearms (Powell, Jacklin, Nelson, & Bland, 1998). More men (56%) than women (39%) believe that having a gun in the home makes it safer; more women (49%) than men (36%) think that having a gun in the home makes it more dangerous (DOJ, 2006). Furthermore, men have larger firearm collections than women (Wyant & Taylor, 2007) and are more likely than women to own automatic or semiautomatic guns (Hemenway & Richardson, 1997). More than 1.5 times as many adolescent males as females have access to guns (ASHA, 1989). Not surprisingly, among students nationally, young men in both high school and college are significantly more likely than young women to carry a weapon (CDC, 2008b; DOJ, 2005; Lewis et al., 1996; Patrick et al., 1997). Among high school students nationally, nearly one in three males (29%)— nearly 4 times the number of females (8%)—has carried a weapon in a recent month, and nearly 1 in 10 males (9%)—9 times the number of females (1%), has carried a gun (CDC, 2008b). Among high school seniors specifically, 7 times more males (7%) than females (1%) have used a knife, gun, or other weapon to get something from a person (DOJ, 2005). More than 1 of 10 college men nationally carries a gun, knife, or other weapon, nearly 3 times the number of women who do (CDC, 1997b; Presley, Meilman, & Cashin, 1997). In children under 14, four of five firearm-related injuries are sustained by boys, and in three of four firearm deaths, the victim is a boy; the majority of these injuries (80%) are caused by male relatives (Eber, Annest, Mercy, & Ryan, 2004).

Owning and carrying weapons increases men's risks (Loeber et al., 2005). Firearm-related injuries are 7 times greater among males than females (Annest, Mercy, Gibson, & Ryan, 1995). More than 30,000 persons die from firearm-related injuries each year, and 87% of these are male (NSC, 2010). More than half of all firearm-related deaths are suicides, and more than 40% are homicides (NSC, 1998, 2010). Firearm-related homicide deaths have been steadily increasing nearly every year since the turn of the 21st century (NSC, 2010). A survey of 52 countries found that firearms were used in approximately two thirds of all homicides (WHO, 2001b). Among the seven juveniles murdered each day, nearly three of four are male and 61% are killed with a firearm (Sickmund, Snyder, & Poe-Yamagata, 1997). Nearly 90% of the homicides among those aged 15 to 19 are firearm related, and nearly four of five victims are male (CDC, 1994i, 2010e; DHHS, 1996b). One study found that homicide offenders were 3 times more likely to carry a gun than nonoffenders (Loeber et al., 2005). Gun use has been implicated in a recent surge in homicides, especially among young African American males—including juveniles—who are disproportionately both victims and perpetrators (Fox & Swatt, 2008). Gun ownership also significantly increases the risk for suicide (Nickerson & Slater, 2009; Wintemute, Parham, Beaumont, Wright, & Drake, 1999). Findings from two population-based, case-control studies indicate that gun ownership is independently associated with a higher risk for both suicide and homicide, nearly tripling the risk for homicide (Kellermann et al., 1993) and increasing the risk for suicide almost 5 times (Kellermann et al., 1992).

As I discussed previously, death rates for suicide and homicide are—on average—4 times greater among males than females. National data also indicate that gun ownership is associated with an even greater risk for suicide than for homicide (Kaplan & Geling, 1998). More than half of all firearm-related deaths are suicides (CDC, 2010e; NSC, 1998).

Criminal Activity

Men account for the vast majority of felons convicted in state courts, and 9 of 10 of those convicted for violent offenses (DOJ, 2004). In U.S. district courts, men account for nearly 9 of 10 (87%) people convicted of any crime, and most people sentenced for violent crimes, including murder (88%), manslaughter (82%), kidnapping or hostage taking (92%), sexual abuse (98%), robbery (90%), assault (90%), and arson (90%) (DOJ, 2007b). More males than females use many kinds of illicit drugs, including inhalants, heroin, and cocaine (NIDA, 2009c). Like other unhealthy male habits, criminal behavior is often first apparent in boyhood (e.g., see Klein et al., 1993). An examination of 15 high-risk delinquent activities among high school seniors nationally reveals consistently greater male involvement for each activity (DOJ, 2005). For example, 3 times more males than females have stolen something worth more than $50 (18%, compared with 6%); more than twice as many have stolen a car (7%, compared with 3%); 7 times more have set fire to property on purpose (7%, compared with 1%); 3 times more have damaged school property on purpose (20%, compared with 6%); 4 times more have damaged property at work on purpose (11%, compared with less than 3%); and 3 times more have been arrested and taken to a police station (12%, compared with 4%) (DOJ, 2005). Boys are also far more likely than girls to be arrested for criminal behavior; 11 times more boys are arrested for robbery, 6 times more for burglary, and nearly 4 times more for aggravated assault (Finley, 2007). Boys represent nearly 9 of 10 (86%) youth under the age of 18 arrested for murder (Finley, 2007).

Crime is a dangerous activity, and men's greater involvement in crime contributes significantly to their injuries and deaths—as well as to their greater risk for being a victim of violence compared with women (DOJ, 2005). For example, the death rate resulting from interventions by law enforcement officials is 4 times greater for men than for women (DHHS, 1996b). In U.S. jails, suicide was the leading cause of death during the 1980s (DHHS, 1991; Salive, Smith, & Brewer, 1989). Although these rates have decreased, suicide remains the cause of death in one third (32%) of the prison population, which is 12 times the suicide rate for the general population, and nearly all these deaths are male (CDC,

2010b; Mumola, 2005). Of those sentenced to death, 98% are male (DOJ, 2008a).

SOCIAL SUPPORT AND MARRIAGE

Social Support

Social relationships and social support are strongly associated with longevity (e.g., Berkman & Breslow, 1983; House, Landis, & Umberson, 1988; Kiecolt-Glaser & Newton, 2001; Shye, Mullooly, Feeborn, & Pope, 1995; Umberson, 1992; Weidner, 2000). Research consistently indicates, however, that men have much smaller social networks than women do (Belle, 1987; Broadhead et al., 1983; Burda, Vaux, & Schill, 1984; Fischer & Oliker, 1983; Kandrack, Grant, & Segall, 1991; Knox et al., 1998; Muhlenkamp & Sayles, 1986; Orth-Gomer, 1994; Verbrugge, 1985; Weidner, 2000). Men have fewer, less intimate friendships than women (McGill, 1985; Rubin, 1983; Sherrod, 1987), and they are less likely to have a close confidant, particularly someone other than a spouse (Antonucci & Akiyama, 1987; Corney, 1990; O'Neil et al., 1985; Umberson, Wortman, & Kessler, 1992; Whitfield et al., 2002; Williams, 1985). Some researchers have even concluded that most men have no close friends (Levinson, 1978; McGill, 1985). Men's social networks are also less multifaceted and supportive than women's (Antonucci & Akiyama, 1987), and in times of stress men mobilize less-varied social supports than women do (Belle, 1987; Taylor 2007). Even among adolescents and young adults, males are less likely than females to seek social support when they need help (Ashton & Fuehrer, 1993; Frydenberg & Lewis, 1991). Older men's support networks also tend to be smaller than those for women (Kiecolt-Glaser, Glaser, Cacioppo, & Malarkey, 1998).

There is consistent evidence that the lack of social relationships constitutes a risk factor for mortality—especially for men (Berkman, 1984; Berkman & Breslow, 1983; Blazer, 1982; Coyne & DeLongis, 1986; House et al., 1988; House, Robbins, & Metzner, 1982; Schoenbach, Kaplan, Fredman, & Kleinbaum, 1986; Seeman, Kaplan, Knudsen, Cohen, & Guralnik, 1987; Shye, Mullooly, Feeborn, & Pope, 1995; Umberson, 1992). Men with the lowest levels of social relationships are 2 to 3 times more likely to die than men with the highest levels of social relationships, even after controlling for health and a variety of other possible confounding factors (Berkman, 1984; Berkman & Breslow, 1983; House et al., 1982; Schoenbach et al., 1986). Men's social isolation significantly decreases their chance of survival after heart disease, cancer, and stroke (Berkman, Leo-Summers, & Horwitz, 1992; Friedman & Booth-Kewley, 1987; Kaplan, 1985; Oxman, Freeman, & Manheimer, 1995; Reynolds & Kaplan, 1990; Ruberman, Weinblat, Goldberg, & Chaudhary, 1984; Vogt, Mullooly, Ernst, Pope, & Hollis,

1992). In one study of heart disease patients, 50% of those without a confidant were dead after 5 years compared with only 17% of those with a spouse or confidant (Williams et al., 1992). People with higher levels of social support also maintain more positive health practices (Bovbjerg et al., 1995; Cwikel, Dielman, Kirsch, & Israel, 1988; Lonnquist, Weiss, & Larsen, 1992; Muhlenkamp & Sayles, 1986). They are likelier to modify unhealthy behavior (Gruninger, 1995) and to adhere to medical treatment (Meichenbaum & Turk, 1987; O'Brien, Petrie, & Raeburn, 1992). Their immune systems function better (Kaplan, 1991; Winawer & Shike, 1995), and they have lower psychophysiological responses to stress (Fleming, Baum, Gisriel, & Gatchel, 1982; Kirschbaum, Klauer, Filipp, & Hellhammer, 1995; Lepore, Allen, & Evans, 1993).

Marriage

Marriage is an important health factor. Being married predicts survival, and all the current scientific evidence indicates that this correlation—and unhealthy behaviors and other health risks associated with being unmarried—are greater for men than for women (DiMatteo, 2004; Dupre, Beck, & Meadows, 2009; Helakorpi, Uutela, Prättälä, & Puska, 2005; House et al., 1988; Johnson, Backlund, Sorlie, & Loveless, 2000; Koskinen, Martelin, & Rissanen, 1999; Pietinen, 2006; Sandman et al., 2000; Schoenbach et al., 1986; Schone & Weinick, 1998; Shye et al., 1995; Whitfield et al., 2002; Willcox et al., 2006). There is even evidence that the beneficial physiological responses to stress (specifically, reduced levels of stress hormones) that result from having a partner or spouse are greater for men than for women (Kirschbaum et al., 1995; Orth-Gomer & Chesney, 1997; Whitfield et al., 2002). In contrast, widowhood has a particularly negative impact on men. Research consistently shows that, compared with married people, widowed men are more likely than widowed women to become depressed and to experience greater morbidity and mortality (Miller & Wortman, 2002; Stroebe et al., 2001). Men who were widowed have a death rate that is more than double that of men who were married at the time of death (DHHS, 2008a).

There is evidence, however, that marriage itself can pose health challenges. Overall, marital stress is an important psychosocial risk factor (Smith & Ruiz, 2002)—one that appears to be more detrimental for men than for women (Burman & Margolin, 1992; House et al., 1988). A marriage characterized by hostile and negative behaviors may constitute a major source of repeated and chronic stressors that can damage the cardiovascular system and the immune system (Kiecolt-Glaser & Newton, 2001; Robles & Kiecolt-Glaser, 2003; Robles, Shaffer, Malarkey, & Kiecolt-Glaser, 2006). Marital discord has been found to lead to higher blood pressure and heart rate (Broadwell & Light, 1999; Thomsen & Gilbert, 1998). Health problems—including colds, influenza, rheumatoid arthritis, and dental caries—that reflect the functioning of the immune system, are more prevalent and more severe in those who report that their marriages are unhappy (Cohen et al., 1998; Marcenes & Sheiham, 1996; Zautra, Burleson, Matt, Roth, & Burrows, 1994). In contrast, high marital satisfaction has been found to be associated with better health outcomes for both husbands and wives (Ganong & Coleman, 1991; Ren, 1997).

Whether single, separated, widowed, or divorced, unmarried men have more serious health risks than married men, and they engage in poorer health behavior (Sandman et al., 2000; Umberson, 1992). For example, they drink and smoke more (DHHS, 1993; Umberson, 1992); they eat fewer fruits and vegetables (Serdula et al., 1995); they are at greater risk for contracting STDs (EDK Associates, 1995); they use medical services less often (Wingard, 1984); they are less likely to have had a blood pressure test in the past year or ever (DHHS, 1993), or to take prescribed medication (Pietinen, 2006; Trevino, Young, Groff, & Jono, 1990); and they are likelier to die in car crashes (Kposowa & Breault, 2009) or to commit suicide (Smith, Mercy, & Conn, 1988). Men who are not married account for 62% of all male suicides (CDC, 2009o). Similarly, men who live alone are less likely than men who live with spouses or partners to see a physician, receive preventive care, or come into contact with the health care system (Sandman et al., 2000). Three of 10 (28%) men who live alone report having not seen a physician in the past year compared with one in five (21%) men who are married or living with a partner; and two of five (42%) men who live alone lack a regular physician compared with one of four (27%) who are married or living with a partner (Sandman et al., 2000). Alternatively, married men are more likely to engage in positive health behaviors, such as drinking and smoking less, eating a healthier diet, and receiving health services. Spouses, in particular, play an important role in fostering these behaviors. For example, married men are significantly more likely to examine their skin for melanoma—an especially deadly form of cancer for men—and they do so typically with the assistance of their spouses (Brady et al., 2000; Weinstock et al., 2004). As discussed previously, melanoma is almost completely curable when discovered early, and monthly self-examinations play a critical role in its prevention. Similarly, as I discussed previously, the early detection of colorectal cancer through screening significantly reduces the risk for cancer death. Men who are married have been found to be more likely to get screened regularly for colorectal cancer (Coups et al., 2007). Recent studies in Ireland (George & Fleming, 2004) and Germany (Uwe & Sieverding, 2008) have also found that wives play a significant role in encouraging men to be screened. Consequently, national data indicate that the death rate for men in the United States who have never been married is 70% greater than that for men who have ever been married, and more than 2 times higher than that for men who are currently married (DHHS, 2009a).

EMPLOYMENT

Most jobs in America are neatly demarcated by sex. The vast majority of secretaries, receptionists, child care professionals, nurses, and salespeople are women (Bureau of Labor Statistics [BLS], 2010). Work in timber cutting, fishing, mining, construction, truck driving, farming, and foresting is done almost exclusively by men (BLS, 2010). Nearly 9 of 10 (88%) of all local and state police officers are male (DOJ, 2008b), as are 95% of firefighters (National Fire Protection Association, 2010).

As I discussed in Chapter 1, jobs held by men are the most dangerous jobs. Although males constitute only a little more than half (53%) of the workforce, they account for nearly all (92%) fatal injuries on the job. Mining, construction, timber cutting, and fishing have the highest injury death rates, and the largest number of total injury deaths occurs in production, craft and repair, transportation, labor, farming, foresting, and fishing—all of which are jobs held primarily by men. Men are involved in more accidents, including falls, fires, and equipment-related injuries (BLS, 2008). Each day, 13 men are killed at work (NSC, 2010). Men represent 95% of law enforcement officers killed in the line of duty, as well as 97% of all firefighters killed. Young men aged 25 to 34 years account for the largest number of occupational injury deaths (CDC, 2001). Younger males are also at greater risk. Among adolescents, studies consistently show that rate of occupational injuries is 2 to more than 4 times higher for males than for females (Breslin, Koehoorn, Smith, & Manno, 2003; Breslin, Smith, & Dunn, 2007; Brooks & Davis, 1996; Horwitz & McCall, 2005; Miller & Kaufman, 1998; Simoyi et al., 1998). For example, the highest rates among young workers aged 16 to 19 years in West Virginia are in construction and manufacturing, which are 2.5 and 4.5 times higher among males, respectively (Simoyi et al., 1998). In one study examining a variety of occupational risks among adolescents, which used a population-based sample of North Carolina youth, males were significantly more likely than females to be exposed to all nine work hazards examined (Dunn, Runyan, Cohen, & Schulman, 1998). Loss of productivity resulting from injuries in 2000 was estimated at $283 billion for males, more than twice that for females (Sattin & Corso, 2007).

Injuries are only one cause of occupational morbidity and mortality. Approximately 32 million workers are exposed to one or more chemical hazards (Winawer & Shike, 1995). According to the Occupational Safety and Health Administration, the five occupations with the greatest percentage of workers exposed to hazardous chemicals are, in descending order, construction, agriculture, oil and gas extraction, water transportation, and forestry (cited in Winawer & Shike, 1995, p. 185)—all jobs held primarily by men. Occupational diseases that result from chemical exposure account for approximately 350,000 new cases of illness and up to 70,000 deaths each year (Landrigan & Baker, 1991). Based on the most conservative estimates, 137 workers die each day from occupational diseases (NIOSH, 1994a), and an estimated 130 of these are male (derived from data in NIOSH, 1994a). Men exposed to solvents such as cleaning fluids, degreasers, gasoline, kerosene, and jet fuel for 1 year or more are 6 times more likely to develop Alzheimer's disease than men with no exposure (Kukull et al., 1995). Men also account for 95% of occupational deaths resulting from work-related lung diseases (NIOSH, 1994b).

U.S. industry uses approximately 160 proven carcinogens and 2,000 more potential carcinogens (Winawer & Shike, 1995), and an estimated 3 to 9 million workers are exposed to them (NIOSH, cited in Landrigan & Baker, 1991), with an estimated 125,000 to 350,000 new cases every year (Newman, 1995). There is sufficient evidence to indicate a causal association between cancer in humans and a large variety of chemicals—including asbestos, benzene, chromium, and vinyl chloride—as well as a variety of industrial processes—such as furniture manufacturing, iron and steel founding, and nickel refining (NCI, 1996). A recent meta-analysis provides further evidence that the chemical benzene causes non-Hodgkin's lymphoma (Weed, 2010). Workers exposed to asbestos alone experience a 50% risk for dying from cancer, nearly 3 times greater than the cancer risk for the average population (Winawer & Shike, 1995). Occupational exposure accounts for up to 35% of male lung cancer deaths (Vineis et al., 1988; Vineis & Simonato, 1991), or nearly 35,000 new cases of male lung cancer every year (ACS, 1997). Bladder cancer is also strongly linked to occupational exposure (Devesa, Grauman, & Blot, 1994), and the death rate for bladder cancer is nearly 3.5 times greater for men than women (ACS, 1997). Occupational exposure has also been implicated in the development of kidney cancer, which kills more than two men for every woman (ACS, 1997; NCI, 1989, 1996), and prostate cancer (Oppenheim, 1994). Workplace exposure may help to explain why one in two men, compared with one in three women, will develop cancer in his lifetime (ACS, 1997, 2008).

A variety of chemical and nonchemical workplace factors have been implicated in the development of cardiovascular disease (Harrington, 1991), which is the leading killer of men. However, cardiovascular disease has been examined in only one workplace study, which found that an estimated one half of the deaths could have been avoided if the occupational risk factors had not occurred, and that 3 times more males than females died prematurely from cardiovascular disease (Olsen & Kristensen, 1991).

Job-related stress also has a significant impact on men. A large population-based study found that high job strain more than doubled the risk for depression among men but was not associated with depression among women (Blackmore et al., 2007). Unemployment is also consistently linked with a variety of negative health effects (Abraham & Krowchuk, 1986; Hammarstrom, 1994), and there is similar evidence that these negative effects are greater for men than for women (Elder & Liker, 1982; United Nations, cited in Edwards, 1994). For example, associations between unemployment and psychological problems are stronger among men than women (Catalano, Dooley, & Jackson, 1981; Frank, 1981; Horwitz, 1982; Marshall & Funch, 1979; Warr & Parry, 1982). Similarly, rates of suicide have been linked with unemployment and economic depression for men but not for women (Boor, 1980; Holinger, 1979; Vigderhous & Fishman, 1978). One prospective study found that unemployment is also a risk factor for increased alcohol consumption among youth, particularly for males, as well as for increased tobacco use, illicit drug use, suicide, and unintentional injuries (Hammarstrom, 1994; see also Mortensen, 2000)—all of which are behaviors that are more common among males.

CONCLUSION

Men in the United States suffer a greater number of chronic conditions than women; they die more than 5 years younger; and they have higher death rates for nearly all the 15 leading causes of death. The research and other data reviewed in this chapter provide irrefutable evidence that men's behavior is a major—if not the primary—determinant of their excess mortality and premature deaths. Furthermore, this evidence shows that the leading causes of disease and death among men are clearly linked to more than 30 behaviors and health-related lifestyle habits that are controllable and that can all be modified (see Table 2.1).

It is important to point out that many men *do* practice health-promoting behaviors. For example, many men do, in fact, go to the doctor. Indeed, among adults in the United States, an identical percentage of women and men—representing nearly half (47%) of all adults—visit a doctor one to three times a year (DHHS, 2009e). However—as is true of most health-related behaviors—where differences do exist, those differences consistently indicate a greater health risk for men. In the case of doctor visits, as I noted previously, more than one in four men report no health care visits in the past year—compared with only almost one in nine women. The conclusions drawn here find support in studies conducted during the past several decades examining overall health-promoting behavior patterns; this research provides strong evidence that U.S. men have significantly less healthy lifestyles than women (e.g., Brener & Collins, 1998; Kandrack et al., 1991; Lloyd-Jones et al., 2006; Lonnquist et al., 1992; Merighi, Courtenay, & McCreary, 2000; Oleckno & Blacconiere, 1990a; Prohaska et al., 1985; Rakowski, 1986; Rossi, 1992; Shi, 1998; Walker et al., 1988; Weiss, Larson, & Baker, 1996; Weissfeld et al., 1990; Whitfield et al., 2002), and that being a woman may, in fact, be the strongest predictor of health-promoting behavior (Brown & McCreedy, 1986; Ratner, Bottorff, Johnson, & Hayduk, 1994). Similar findings of unhealthy lifestyles and

TABLE 2.1   Controllable Behaviors and Health-Related Lifestyle Habits That Increase Men's Risk for Disease, Injury, and Death

Health care utilization
Preventive care and self-care
   Screening tests
   Self-examinations
   Sun protection
   Dental care
   Sleep
   Hand washing
   Use of medicines and vitamin supplements
   Behavioral responses to stress
Diet
   Meats and dietary fat
   Cholesterol
   Fiber, fruits, and vegetables
   Salt consumption
Weight
Physical activity
Substance use
   Tobacco use
   Alcohol use
   Anabolic steroid use
Risk taking and reckless behavior
   Reckless driving
   Drinking and driving
   Safety belt use
   Helmet use
   Sexual activity
   Sports and recreation
Violence
   Physical fighting
   Weapon ownership and use
   Criminal activity
Social support and marriage
   Social support
   Marriage
Employment

limited health-promoting behaviors have been identified in men in eastern Europe (Weidner & Cain, 2003), Ireland (South Eastern Health Board, 2004), Australia (Mahalik, Walker, & Levi-Minzi, 2007), and Canada (Dawson, Schneider, Fletcher, & Bryden, 2007).

Although it is not always the case (see Chapter 8), the behaviors examined here frequently co-occur in healthy or unhealthy clusters (e.g., Brener & Collins, 1998; Donovan, Jessor, & Costa, 1993; Emmons, Marcus, Linnan, Rossi, & Abrams, 1994; Leigh & Fries, 1993; Merighi et al., 2000; Oleckno & Blacconiere, 1990; Schoenborn, 1993; Schoenborn & Benson, 1988). For example, men who engage in infrequent, strenuous activity are also more likely than regularly active men to eat red meat and to be overweight, and less likely to eat vegetables or to take vitamins or mineral supplements (Lee et al., 2004). Research—including large, population-based studies and national data—consistently shows that men are more likely than women to have unfavorable cardiovascular disease risk profiles based on a cluster of controllable risk factors for these leading causes of death (Ford, Li, Zhao, Pearson, & Capewell, 2009; Lloyd-Jones et al., 2006; Lloyd-Jones, Dyer, Wang, Daviglus, & Greenland, 2007; Mensah, Brown, Croft, & Greenlund, 2005; Stamler et al., 1999; Terry et al., 2005). Indeed, far more men than women have known major risk factors for heart disease and stroke (CDC, 2004e). An analysis of data from 24 countries reveals that 40% of men's greater risk for heart disease can be explained by gender differences in five potentially modifiable risk factors: blood pressure, total cholesterol, HDL cholesterol, cigarette smoking, and obesity (Jackson et al., 1997). Similarly, men with metabolic syndrome are at 4 times greater risk for death from heart disease and 2 times greater risk for death from any other cause of death, even when other factors, such as age, smoking, and family history of heart disease, are taken into account (Lakka et al., 2002). These findings are similar for youth. As I noted in Chapter 1, the CDC contends that the leading causes of disease, injury, and death among children and adolescents are significantly associated with six interrelated categories of modifiable behaviors, five of which are more common among male than female children and adolescents. Similarly, as noted previously, 2.5 to 3 times more adolescent boys than girls have metabolic syndrome—which describes a cluster of risk factors linked to heart disease—and, once established in childhood or adolescence, these unhealthy behaviors typically extend into adulthood.

Research also shows that while the presence of a single major risk factor is associated with substantially increased lifetime risk, these risks are cumulative (Lloyd-Jones et al., 2006, 2007; Mensah et al., 2005). For example, a man aged 50 years who has elevated levels for just two risk factors for heart disease—such as high cholesterol and high blood pressure—can expect to live 10 years less than a man who has optimal levels (Lloyd-Jones et al., 2006). Similarly, men are more likely than women to have multiple behavioral risk factors for colon cancer (Emmons et al., 2005) and skin cancer (Coups et al., 2008). Furthermore, the interaction of various behaviors can compound men's health risks. For example, when combined with alcohol use, tobacco use activates cell division and tumor growth, increasing the already high risk for cancer from the use of either substance independently up to 15 times (Kushi et al., 2006; Winawer & Shike, 1995). Similarly, unbelted drivers also drive dangerously, which compounds the risk for injury (CDC, 1993d; Hunter et al., 1990; Preusser et al., 1991). Rather than representing a collection of discrete and isolated activities, these behaviors may represent constellations of behavior or a risk behavior syndrome (Jessor, Donovan, & Costa, 1991; Schulte, Ramo, & Brown, 2009). This review suggests that such a syndrome would be far more common among men than among women.

The findings presented here are consistent with earlier research that has found that women engage in far more health-promoting behaviors than men and have more healthy lifestyle patterns (Kandrack et al., 1991; Lonnquist et al., 1992; Rossi, 1992; Walker et al., 1988). They are also consistent with the conclusion reached by previous researchers that being a woman is likely the strongest predictor of preventive and health-promoting behavior (Brown and McCreedy, 1986; Mechanic and Cleary, 1980; Ratner et al., 1994). The central question raised by these findings is *why* men are more likely than women to engage in behaviors that put them at greater risks for disease, injury, and death. Rarely is this question posed. Instead, health scientists and health educators too often accept men's shorter lives as inevitable. For example, the AHA and the NSA have both suggested that male "gender" and "being male" are "uncontrollable" risk factors that "can't be changed" (AHA, 1996, p. 20; NSA, 1994, p. 15). Similarly, researchers at the CDC recently contended that "*intrinsic* factors ... such as age and gender, cannot be readily altered ... to reduce injury risk" (Gilchrist, Saluja, & Marshall, 2007, p. 118; emphasis added). The underlying assumption is that men's greater risks for sports injuries and for developing heart disease and stroke are strictly inherent or biological. There is, however, limited scientific evidence to support this assumption.

Several implications for future study can be drawn from this review. Although researchers have long examined relationships between biological sex and health practices, few attempts have been made to move beyond the use of biological sex as an independent or control variable and to explain "what about gender, exactly, is at work" (Kunkel, 1996, p. 294). Why do men behave more self-destructively than women, and why do they do less to promote their own health? For example, even though it was established long ago that men drink far more alcohol and drink more often than women, *why* men drink more still remains largely unexplained (Holmila & Raitasalo, 2005). Similar questions remain regarding men's greater use of tobacco and other substances. The lack of research examining this issue appears to reflect the cultural assumption that using tobacco, alcohol, and other drugs is simply what men do (McCreary et al., 1999); the topic appears too obvious or irrelevant to warrant scientific scrutiny. In the following two chapters, I demonstrate that U.S. life links drinking and drug use with normal male behavior, both fostering this behavior among men and contributing to the cultural resignation in addressing the subject.

Similarly, although injury and death resulting from recreation, risk taking, and violence are consistently associated with being male, epidemiological data are consistently presented as if gender were of no particular relevance. Few researchers even identify male biological sex as a risk factor, and even fewer have attempted to explain what it is exactly about men that leads them to engage in activities that seriously threaten their health. As I have argued previously (Courtenay, 1998a, 1998b, 1999a, 2000a, 2000c, 2006a), the failure to identify and examine men's risk taking as problematic perpetuates the false, yet widespread, cultural assumption that these behaviors are "natural" or inherent. Indeed, the failure to question men's risk-taking behavior and violence reflects an underlying social assumption that it is normal—that men just are violent or are risk takers. The data presented here suggest that there is something specific to men that makes them more likely than women to engage in behaviors that are apt to harm them.

The fact that unhealthy behaviors cluster suggests that there may be an underlying "cause" of men's unhealthy lifestyles. Masculinity may be an important mediating factor in the co-occurrence of multiple health risk behaviors. Indeed, as I contend in Chapter 4, men's risk-taking behavior and disregard for their health are among the resources that men use to define themselves as "masculine" or "manly." My own work, and that of others, indicates that boys are encouraged to adopt a variety of behaviors that increase their health risks (Courtenay, 2000c; Morrongiello & Dayler, 1996). Furthermore, as I discussed in Chapter 1, a substantial body of research provides evidence that men who adopt traditional beliefs about masculinity are at increased risk for a variety of health problems. Masculinity may, in fact, be the missing cofactor—the "secret, powerful social factor" (Verbrugge, 1990, p. 183)—in analyses of gender and health where men's greater risks persist and remain unexplained despite adjustment for numerous variables. However, as I illustrate in Chapter 4, men's individual gender identities and their health behaviors are not simply personal choices; there are innumerable social forces and environmental factors that foster these identities and behaviors.

More rigorous examinations of gender differences in physical activity and dieting are also needed. Less-than-thorough analyses are misleading. Unsupported assumptions accompanying many studies that report gender differences in exercise typically suggest that "strenuous" exercise is healthy and that dieting is unhealthy. In fact, as the data presented here suggest, women's more numerous attempts to control their diet may contribute to their reduced risk for mortality. Furthermore, most discussions of diet and body image focus on weight loss and the culturally feminine ideal of slimness. Relatively little is known about weight gain and the culturally masculine ideal of muscularity. One study has demonstrated that the standard of bodily attractiveness for men is bigger and bulkier than that for women, that between 28 and 68% of all normal-weight adolescent boys want to gain weight, and that this desire is associated with dieting to increase weight (McCreary & Sasse, 2000). The evidence from another study of college students (see Raudenbush & Zellner, 1997) is consistent with these findings. Given these findings, as well as the higher prevalence of overweight among men, epidemiological data are warranted to further examine gender and intended weight gain. Similarly, although the evidence regarding the health benefits associated with physical activity is irrefutable, much remains unclear about subtle gender differences in the health effects of various types and levels of physical activity. Troubling inconsistencies lie in the fact that although men, particularly younger men, seem to engage in more physical exercise than women, they are likely to die earlier. This review of the research suggests that men's tendency to engage in infrequent but strenuous physical activity—and activities that increase the risk for physical injury and premature death—and to engage in less activity as they grow older may help to explain these inconsistencies.

This review also has important implications for health care providers who work with men. I address these implications in Chapters 12 and 13. Although many counseling and psychological interventions with men have been recommended in the past 2 decades (Courtenay, 2000d), rarely are these interventions designed to reduce men's health risks. Given this lack of clinical guidance, it is not surprising that men receive significantly less physician time in medical encounters than women, and that men are provided with fewer and briefer explanations—both simple and technical (see Chapters 12 and 13). As I explained previously, despite men's greater involvement in high-risk behaviors, they receive less advice from physicians about changing risk factors for disease than women do during checkups.

If men are to live as long as women do—and the evidence presented here suggests that they can—they will need to change their unhealthy behavior. However, they are unlikely to do so until the underlying motivations for their behavior—as well as the social, cultural, environmental, and institutional factors that influence these behaviors—are identified. Only then will men reclaim the more than 5 years that their own behavior has stolen from them.

Why Men and Boys Do the Things That Make Them Sick and Kill Them

INTRODUCTION

In 2000, I was invited by the American Psychological Association to discuss the research of a panel of scholars at the association's annual meeting, which was held in Washington, DC. The title of the panel was *Men's Health in the New Millennium: Emerging Research, Theory, and Practice*. My comments at that meeting serve as the introduction to Section II. I provide a critique of previous models for understanding men's health and propose a new model, as well as new directions for research, based on emerging approaches to both understanding and addressing men's health in the 21st century. In the following two chapters, I provide comprehensive frameworks for understanding and conceptualizing men's health.

WHO ARE THE "MEN" IN "MEN'S HEALTH"?[*]

I am going to begin my comments today by confronting an old colleague in our midst. This fellow has been revered for decades, and perhaps for that reason, his authority is rarely challenged. But despite his power and influence, he has seriously undermined our work. His continued influence in our field represents a major barrier to the advancement of our true understanding of masculinity and men's health.

Who is this fellow I'm referring to? He is "The Male Gender Role"—a conceptual construction that has been around far too long.

---

[*] An earlier version of this article appeared in *The Society for the Psychological Study of Men and Masculinity Bulletin*, 6(3), 2001, 10–13, and is used by permission.

Now, it would be against my principles to do violence to this fellow. I would, however, like to see him laid to rest. But despite being very old and basically on life support, we keep breathing new life into him every day.

Let me tell you five problems I have with this old guy.

The first problem is that The Male Gender Role would have us believe that masculinity resides solely in each man's individual psychology. With a sleight of hand, he blinds us to the social systems—such as school and workplaces—that are powerful influences in shaping masculinity.

The second problem is that The Male Gender Role normalizes masculinity and implies that manhood is some kind of universal experience. He's rather narcissistic that way. He thinks every man in the world is just like him—White, middle class, heterosexual, and in college.

The third problem I have with this guy is that to keep his feeble identity propped up, he leans heavily on unfounded biologic assumptions. He thinks it's just "natural"—and inevitable—that men and women differ.

The fourth problem with this fellow—perhaps due to his senility—is that he does not seem to have any memory of the past. It would seem he has no history.

The fifth problem with The Male Gender Role? He never seems to change. He would have us believe that masculinity is fixed and constant.

You may be asking yourself, "Why all this concern about The Male Gender Role in a symposium on men's health?" It's because The Male Gender Role limits the ways that we understand men and conceptualize men's psychology—and, consequently, how we understand and think about men's health. It keeps us from asking the most important question: "Who are the *men* in 'men's health'?"

So, what might emerging psychologies—or disciplines—of men's health look like when we finally give up our fight to keep The Male Gender Role alive? Well, to begin with, new paradigms would address the five points that I have just mentioned.

First, they would look beyond individuals. As people interested in psychology, we tend to think that everything begins and ends with individuals. But our lives and the world are never simply a matter of individual people—or what we think, what we feel, and what we do. We are always participating in social systems that are larger than us—families, schools, and larger social systems, such as the American Psychological Association.

We live in dynamic relationship with these social systems. They shape our sense of who we are, our relationships, our place in the world, our gender, and our health behavior.

So with new paradigms, we wouldn't simply think of men's health as something about individual people—our personalities or our biology. We would think about how men's health gets shaped by social systems—like dangerous worksites, poor communities, and the health care system.

New paradigms would also acknowledge the biologic systems that influence men's health and psychologies—like our brains. Every month, there are new findings about sex differences in brain functioning—such as women moving more quickly than men between the left and right hemispheres of the brain.

This research may help to explain long-reported gender differences in emotional expression. Putting words to emotions requires both hemispheres of the brain—the right side to experience emotions and the left side to articulate them.

Now this is not to say that men's brains are simply hard wired to be inexpressive and that this gender difference is immutable. On the contrary, we are also learning how the environment shapes brain development—as do social systems. Men and boys *learn* that they gain greater social advantages when they remain stoic.

New paradigms would enable us to better understand the complex interplay between these social and biologic influences on men's health. And to do this will require interdisciplinary methods—not simply multidisciplinary ones.

The second problem I mentioned in regard to The Male Gender Role is that it universalizes masculinity. Note the term's very language: *the* male gender role—as if men have only one gender role.

Take Brannon and David's influential and enduring model of masculinity (Brannon & David, 1976). One of their four constructs is for a man to be "a sturdy oak." But we never distinguish between the "sturdy oaks" that grow in wealthy, White suburbs and the "sturdy oaks" that grow in poor, Black, urban neighborhoods.

We are hearing more these days about the disturbing 5-year difference in the life spans of women and men. But new paradigms must recognize that there is a greater difference in the life spans of Black and White men than there is between women and men. African American men die 6 years younger than European American men. In fact, men of color account for much of the gender difference in mortality.

So, these new models would acknowledge differences among men. They would recognize that there is not one masculinity; there are many masculinities—and many gender roles.

Not all men endorse traditional beliefs about manhood. Men with less education and lower family income are more likely to endorse them—as are African Americans. But even among Black men there are differences; younger, nonprofessional men hold more traditional beliefs than older, professional men.

And what about gay men—what is *their* masculinity? We rarely stop to ask ourselves that question because The Male Gender Role marginalizes these men. What is the masculinity of *Latino* gay men? Or, the masculinity of Chicano men in Albuquerque who have sex with men? Does it differ from the masculinity of queer, activist Latino men in San Francisco? And how do these masculinities, contexts, cultures, and communities influence the sexual risks and other health behaviors of these men? New, emerging models of masculinity and men's health could explore these questions.

They could also challenge biologic-based assumptions about men and women—the third problem. The Male Gender Role is based on the belief that we *are* our biologies—that there must be essential differences between men and women simply because male and female reproductive organs differ.

But new paradigms would recognize that maintaining this notion of gender as difference has required that we disregard decades of research indicating that—at least psychologically—men and women are more similar than dissimilar. They would remind us that findings of gender difference often result from small statistical differences between a minority of the population—and that they rarely represent categorical differences between all men and all women.

The fourth problem I mentioned is a lack of historical perspective. We forget or simply do not acknowledge the fact that in the first half of the 19th century, there was little concern among men about physical strength. It was not physical strength, but strength of character that was valued among men.

When it comes to men's bodies, the last several decades have witnessed significant changes. Donald McCreary (2002, 2009) has previously demonstrated that the cultural standard for men's bodies has become increasingly large and muscular. Through better understanding the history, evolution, and vicissitudes of masculinity, we will better understand the full range of its potential.

And, finally, the new paradigm would recognize that masculinity is not fixed or static. The same man demonstrates masculinity differently in different contexts. He may believe that it is not OK to cry at work or in front of peers, but that it is OK to cry at home or with his wife. A man's psychology is one way when he is with his street gang and another way when he is with his children.

And men's beliefs about manhood can and do change over time. Some men reinforce and reproduce traditional masculinity. But other men redefine and transform it. Still other men resist traditional standards and create their own standards of manhood. Other men simply reject any relevance of masculinity at all.

So to truly understand masculinity and men's health—whether we are practitioners or researchers—we need to consider them within the contexts in which they occur and at what age, time, and place they occur.

I will now turn to the excellent and timely work of my colleagues on this panel. I want to take a look at some of the important questions their findings raise—questions that researchers and theorists of a new, emerging discipline of men's health might address.

As a result of Donald McCreary's research, we finally understand something about how men think about their weight, and how their perceptions of their bodies might contribute to their being overweight. He and his colleague Stanley Sadava explored the interaction between gender, weight, and self-perception in a large community-based sample of adults (McCreary & Sadava, 2000).

The results of their study indicate that although men are more likely than women to be overweight, men think they weigh less than they really do—and, in comparison to overweight women, men who are overweight rate themselves as more attractive, healthier, and higher in life satisfaction. Furthermore, among underweight adults, women rate themselves as more attractive, healthier, and higher in life satisfaction than men.

Now the women and men in this study are from eastern Canada. Although more U.S. men than women are also overweight, will the findings of men's perceptions hold true for men in the United States? Geography certainly plays a role in men's health. Being overweight is strongly linked with cardiovascular disease—which is the leading killer of men. But the death rate for cardiovascular disease is highest in the southern United States. What accounts for this? Is it the Southern diet? Or is it something about Southern men's views about manhood?

National data indicate that Southern men hold the most traditional views about gender (see Chapter 5). But the geography is even more specific. *Rural* Southern men have the most traditional views—and data indicate these men also have more health problems.

And how does the media—as a social system—influence these perceptions, and men's weight and dietary habits? Donald McCreary's prior research indicates that watching television can foster inaccurate weight perceptions. But how exactly does this happen? And what about movies and magazines?

In the study by Matt Loscalzo and his colleagues (Loscalzo, Hooker, Zabora, & Bucher, 2000), over 5,729 patients with cancer completed the Brief Symptom Inventory, a 53-item self-report

symptom scale. Among the results presented were the findings that more men than women with cancer reported practical
problems—such as parking and insurance—and that more women
reported pain and psychosocial problems—such as problems with
emotions and communication with children. However, they also
found no gender differences in the experience of anxiety or depression, and—in the case of lung cancer—they found that more men
reported somatic complaints.

Why is it that 1.5 times more women than men in this study
experienced pain with cancer? There is evidence that hormones
likely play some role in mediating pain. But we also know that
psychosocial factors do, too. In front of a female clinician—for
example—men are less likely to report pain. So how do hormones
and the gender of clinicians—or researchers—influence the reporting of pain among cancer patients?

Now their finding of no difference in depression between men
and women—though not statistically significant—is, nonetheless,
a significant finding. This result—which challenges the popular
myth that men simply don't get depressed—is consistent with
findings among other populations as well, like college students.

But let's assume that the people in this study are somewhat
representative of the population and that more women than men
were depressed to begin with. Does this finding suggest that men
are more likely than women to experience depression in response
to cancer? And, if so, why?

Are there gender differences in the way people with cancer cope
with depression? Among people—in general—with depression, men
are more likely than women to rely on themselves, withdraw socially,
and to try to talk themselves out of depression. Do these differences
disappear when a man gets cancer? Or, do they intensify?

Michael Diefenbach (2000) presented findings from a study
designed to explore treatment expectations, distress, and treatment decision making among more than 300 men diagnosed with
early-stage prostate cancer. Compared with men who chose surgery, those who chose radiation or seed therapy did so because
they expected it to have fewer side effects, to be more convenient,
and to be less painful and invasive—even though they were less
convinced that these treatments would provide the best chance
of a cure. Patients who chose radiation also reported significantly
less distress about their treatment choice, lower levels of distress
during the decision-making process, and greater satisfaction with
ongoing treatment.

Now, in this study, 90% of the men were European American—
and we don't know their socioeconomic status or sexual orientation. And research indicates that economically disadvantaged

people, sexual minorities, and people of color have very different health care experiences than do White, middle-class heterosexuals. Future researchers might explore whether the treatment expectations and decisions—and levels of distress—differ among men based on their ethnicity, class, and sexual orientation.

Roughly half of the men in Michael Diefenbach's study chose surgery. How might class, ethnicity, and sexual orientation influence these decisions? Black patients rate their doctors—and their doctors' decision-making styles—as less participatory than Whites do. Black men also trust doctors less. It would seem that these factors would influence surgery decisions—which do differ among groups. A study this year found that the rate of glaucoma surgery among Blacks is nearly 50% below what it should be compared with Whites (Devgan, Yu, Kim, & Coleman, 2000).

And how would distrust and less participation by clinicians influence Black men's satisfaction with radiation? Would their satisfaction be as high as it is for White men? And how does the relative social power and privilege of clinicians and patients influence both decision making and satisfaction?

Dana Mills (2000) reported the results of a study designed to assess health knowledge and skills among 11,691 students from all 172 Rhode Island elementary schools. The findings indicated that being White, upper class, and female were all significant predictors of greater health knowledge and skills.

These findings are consistent with many other studies of both adolescents and adults that show that men are less knowledgeable about health in general and about specific diseases, and skills for risk reduction. Future researchers might explore what it is exactly about gender that contributes to these differences. Is it due to the fact that men and boys are less likely than women and girls to perceive themselves at risk for health problems? Is it that men and boys consider health knowledge and skill acquisition to be feminine endeavors?

And what about socioeconomic status? One of the strengths of Dana Mills' work is that it examines the interaction of socioeconomic status and ethnicity with gender. And, indeed, it was not gender, but socioeconomic status, that was the strongest predictor of knowledge. But *how* exactly does socioeconomic status interact with gender and ethnicity? We have much to learn about these kinds of intensely complex interactions.

Now, simply because men and boys are less knowledgeable about health does not mean that they can't learn about it. Indeed, the findings from Ashok Shankar and Irvienne Goldson's study (2000) of the Men's Preventive Health Counseling Program in Boston suggest otherwise.

The program—administered by Action for Boston Community Development—is designed to provide comprehensive family planning and reproductive and sexual health care services for lower-income African American and Latino men. The preliminary results from this study suggest that the program has been successful in increasing men's level of knowledge of—and their involvement in—family planning, reproductive health, and sexual health care. They also suggest that the program has positively influenced men's beliefs about manhood, men's behavior, and men's readiness to adopt healthy habits.

The findings from this study also raise important questions about differences among men based on their age. Younger men in their program endorsed several beliefs that increase the chances of unwanted pregnancies. What accounts for these age-based differences? The truth is, we know very little about developmental differences in men's and boys' health beliefs—and the effects of these beliefs on their well-being.

Family planning clinics are increasingly addressing the needs of men. It seems most men would support this change. Research shows that men generally believe that preventing pregnancy is a shared responsibility—which is consistent with the findings of Ashok Shankar and Irvienne Goldson.

Research also shows that programs that involve men do result in positive outcomes for men and their partners. But in order for these programs to be most effective, we need to learn what it is exactly that makes them successful. In the Boston program, all of the counselors are men. What significance, if any, does this have on men's knowledge, beliefs, and behaviors over time?

Emerging paradigms offer new promise for understanding the pathways through which social relationships among men influence men's health. New research indicates that some men are reluctant to address their health needs for fear that they will be perceived by other men to be unmanly or gay. Research also shows that men can positively influence each other through group discussions about health.

Well, as for our own group discussion here, I hope the practitioners and researchers on this panel have influenced you—and inspired you—as much as they have inspired me. There are many yet-unanswered questions about men's health.

During the last century, we were enormously successful in addressing the *health* part of "men's health." But as we think about men's health and search for answers in the new millennium—and as we guide emerging research, theory, and practice—we need also to ask ourselves, "Who are the *men* in 'men's health'?"

3

Engendering Health

*The Social Construction of Gendered Health Beliefs and Behaviors**

A variety of factors contribute to gender differences in health and longevity, such as biology, economic status, and ethnicity. As we have seen in the preceding chapter, health behavior is among the most important of these factors—if not *the* most important one. And although many sociocultural factors are associated with health behavior, gender is the most important. Men have significantly less healthy lifestyles than women, and being a woman may, in fact, be the strongest predictor of health-promoting behavior. Few contemporary researchers or theorists have offered explanations for these gender differences and their implications for men's health (Lee & Owens, 2002; Sabo & Gordon, 1995).

Feminist scholars were among the first to engender health, noting, for example, the absence of women as participants in health research and the use of men as the standard for health (e.g., see Boston Women's Health Book Collective, 1973; Mastroianni, Faden, & Federman, 1994; Ruzek, 1978; Ruzek & Becker, 1999). The result, however, is that "gender and health" have now become synonymous with "women's health" (e.g., Bayne-Smith, 1995; Dugan & Prather, 2007; Legato, 2003). Although health science of the past century frequently used males as

---

* An earlier version of this chapter appeared in *Psychology of Men and Masculinity*, *1*(1), 2000, 4–15, and is used by permission in modified/revised form.

study participants, the health risks associated with men's gender—or masculinity—have remained largely unproblematic and taken for granted. Little is understood about *why* men engage in less healthy life-styles and adopt fewer health-promoting beliefs and behaviors, and the social practices and institutional structures that influence these beliefs and behaviors have not been studied. The consistent, underlying pre-sumption in medical literature is that what it means to be a man in the United States has no bearing on how men work, drink, drive, fight, or take risks. Even in studies that address health risks more common to men than women, the discussion of men's greater risks and of the influence of men's gender is often conspicuously absent. Instead, the "gender" that is associated with greater risk remains unnamed (e.g., Donnermeyer & Park, 1995, p. 474). Left unquestioned, men's shorter life span is often presumed to be natural and inevitable. In this chapter, I use a social constructionist framework to examine these topics and to explain gen-der differences in health-related behavior.

MAKING A DIFFERENCE: THE SOCIAL CONSTRUCTION OF GENDERED HEALTH BEHAVIOR

According to social constructionist theory, women and men think and act in the ways they do based on concepts about femininity and mascu-linity that they adopt from their culture. (I discuss social construction-ism and gender at length in Chapter 4.) In the following sections, I review evidence of gender differences in social experiences, cultural representa-tions of gender, and social structural influences on gender. The review is limited to evidence that has implications for the health of women and men. Many of the studies reviewed examined gender stereotypes, that is, characteristics that are generally believed to be "typical" either of women or of men. The theoretical bases for the studies vary widely and include research based on sex role theories that ignore agency or construct gender as one type. Nonetheless, this research offers a rich source of data that provides a basis for better understanding how women and men come to construct their beliefs about health, what resources are available to them for "the doing of health" (Saltonstall, 1993, p. 12), and how they learn to use health beliefs and behaviors to demonstrate gender.

These findings must be interpreted with caution. It is frequently claimed or implied that sex causes certain beliefs or behaviors simply because an association—which may be explained by other factors—has been found. Furthermore, contrasting two categorical notions of gender can reinforce binary distinctions of gender and can obscure the fact that women and men are more similar than dissimilar (Hyde, 2005). It can also obscure the many differences among men. Despite these possible limitations, examination of gender differences in social experiences is a potentially valuable constructionist strategy (Crawford, 1995). It illu-minates a process in which biological sex is transformed into gender.

Differential Treatment of Girls and Boys: The Early Makings of Gendered Health Behavior

Because there is high agreement in U.S. society about what are considered to be typically feminine and typically masculine characteristics (Bergen & Williams, 1991; Hosoda & Stone, 2000; Lueptow, Garovich, & Lueptow, 1995; Lueptow, Garovich-Szabo, & Lueptow, 2001; Williams & Best, 1990), it is not surprising that parents and other adults treat girls and boys differently from the first day of life (Brophy-Herb et al., 2009). In fact, regardless of an infant's gender, parents and other adults interact with the infant based on what they believe to be the infant's gender. If adults believe that an infant is a boy, for example, they will perceive it as stronger, firmer, and less fragile than an infant who they believe is a girl (Golombok & Fivush, 1994).

Research indicates that parents provide less warmth and nurturance to their sons than to their daughters, although warmth promotes emotional regulation and social development, such as the ability to form and maintain friendships (Bocknek, Brophy-Herb, & Banerjee, 2009; Brophy-Herb et al., 2009; Denham, Mitchell-Copeland, Strandberg, Auerbach, & Blair, 1997; Lytton & Romney, 1991), and boys' development of emotional understanding is more influenced by their parents' contribution than is that of girls (Denham et al., 1997). From infancy to adolescence, parents and other adults interact differently with girls than with boys (Klimes-Dougan et al., 2007), they talk more about interpersonal emotions to girls (Fivush, Brotman, Buckner, & Goodman, 2000), and they interpret the same emotional response as fear in girls but as anger in boys (Carli, 1997; Golombok & Fivush, 1994; Plant, Hyde, Keltner, & Devine, 2000); fathers in particular tend to inhibit the expression of sadness in boys but to encourage the expression of anger (Cassano, Perry-Parrish, & Zeman, 2007; Fabes & Martin, 1991). Similarly, girls are encouraged to look inside themselves and notice their feelings, whereas boys are not (Block, 1984; Cervantes & Callanan, 1998). Parental interactions predict children's understanding of others' feelings, and girls have been found to understand others' feelings more consistently than boys (Dunn, Brown, Slomkowski, & Tesla, 1991). Research indicates that parents promote gender stereotypes through their preferences with respect to games, toys, and children's activities, and this is a consistent finding (Carli, 1997; Lytton & Romney, 1991; Raag, 1999). Male infants and boys are also played with and handled more roughly than girls (Golombok & Fivush, 1994; Jacklin, DiPietro, & Maccoby, 1984; Maccoby & Jacklin, 1974). Parents physically distance themselves more from boys than from girls, encourage boys in activities that limit proximity to others, encourage boys to be less dependent than girls, and express less concern about danger to their sons than to their daughters (Aries & Olver, 1985; Burbach, 2003; Golombok & Fivush, 1994; Lytton & Romney, 1991; Morrongiello & Dawber, 1998, 2000; Morrongiello & Hogg, 2004; Pomerantz & Ruble, 1998). Furthermore, one study showed that boys were actively discouraged from seeking the help of their parents or other adults and were even punished when they did (Fagot, 1984). It is also well established that boys receive significantly more physical punishment than girls—both from adults and from their peers (Golombok & Fivush, 1994; Kerr, Lopez, Olson, & Sameroff, 2004; Lytton & Romney, 1991; Maccoby & Jacklin, 1974; Pepler et al., 2006; Wauchope & Strauss, 1990). Moreover, boys are encouraged to fight. In fact, three of four people in the United States believe that it is important for a boy to have a few fistfights while he is growing up (Gelles & Straus, 1988).

From a social constructionist perspective, girls and boys are not blank slates that are written on or "socialized"; rather, they are active participants—along with the world around them—in the construction and reconstruction of gender. Peers provide boys and girls with important information about the responses they can expect for demonstrating behaviors considered appropriate or inappropriate for their gender. Girls and boys punish peers whose behavior crosses gender-stereotypic boundaries (Adler, Kless, & Adler, 1992; Carter & McCloskey, 1984; Hekner, 1995; Thorne, 1993). Not surprisingly, how girls and boys think their peers will act and respond to them greatly influences their gender-related preferences (Katz & Boswell, 1986; Katz & Ksansnak, 1994).

Despite a popular assumption that gender stereotypes are loosening, research shows no evidence of any trend among parents to treat their daughters and sons in less sex-differentiated ways (Lytton & Romney, 1991). In fact, parents, teachers, other adults, and peers do everything they can through approval, ridicule, and exclusion—as well as bullying from peers—to encourage gender-stereotypic behavior in boys and girls (Adler et al., 1992; Golombok & Fivush, 1994; Maccoby, 2002; McCreary, 1994). Research consistently indicates, however, that more stringent demands to conform to gender-stereotypic behavior are placed on boys than on girls and that boys become subject to these demands at an earlier age (Golombok & Fivush, 1994; Granié, 2010; Kane, 2006; Martin, 1990; McCreary, 1994). Boys have far less latitude in choosing what they can wear, what they can play, and whom they can play with, and they are seen far more negatively than girls when they engage in nonstereotypic behavior (Alfieri, Ruble, & Higgins, 1996; Bartini, 2006; Maccoby & Jacklin, 1974; McCreary, 1994). Girls and boys themselves react more negatively toward male than toward female peers who display behaviors or preferences that cross gender stereotypes, and these reactions become increasingly negative as they grow older; for example, boys are hit and ridiculed, whereas girls are ignored (Carter & McCloskey, 1984; Gini & Pozzoli, 2006; Golombok & Fivush, 1994; Lamb, 2009; Zucker, Wilson-Smith, Kurita, & Stern, 1995).

These gender differences in the early social experiences of girls and boys each have important implications for men's health (see Sidebar 3.1). They may help to explain why, for example, boys take greater risks in sports and recreation, and why men perceive themselves to be less vulnerable to physical harm than women do (see Chapters 1 and 2). These implications are addressed in greater detail subsequently.

SIDEBAR 3.1   Lessons About Health That Boys Learn

It is tempting to think that men just "naturally" adopt the behaviors and beliefs that undermine their health, but that is not the case. It takes years of training and enforcement by peers, parents, coaches, and other adults for men to learn these risky habits. Here are just a few examples of the lessons about health that boys learn growing up.

Compared with girls, boys are:

- Seen as stronger and less fragile
- Discouraged from and punished for seeking help
- Encouraged to take risks

The long-term health effects of these kinds of lessons become apparent as early as young adulthood.

Compared with women, men are more likely to:

- Think they are invulnerable to disease and injury
- Seek health care infrequently
- Take risks in recreation and sports

Additional Social Transactions and Institutional Influences

Gender is not static; it is something that people construct and reconstruct. This dynamic process occurs in ongoing interaction with social and institutional structures. As noted by Connell (1993), *"masculinity is an aspect of institutions*, and is produced in institutional life, *as much as it is an aspect of personality"* (p. 602). Institutional structures provide both limits and opportunities to learn and display gender and can either foster or undermine people's attempts to adopt healthy habits. Therefore, health beliefs and behaviors are best understood when they are situated in the social transactions and structures that contribute to sustaining and reproducing them. This section focuses primarily on media and the health care system.

Engendered Media and Health

Clear distinctions are drawn in the media between the health behavior of women and that of men. In top-grossing U.S. films, smoking is done primarily by men, who are represented smoking up to 4 times more often than women (Hazan, Lipton, & Glantz, 1994; Worth, Dal Cin, & Sargent, 2006). On prime-time television, up to 6.5 times more male than female characters smoke, and these characters rarely demonstrate the negative consequences of smoking (Byrd-Bredbenner, Finckenor, & Grasso, 2003; Gerbner, Gross, Morgan, & Signorielli, 1981; Signorielli, 1993). Even when controlling for potentially confounding factors, one third to one half of those who began to smoke did so because they saw characters smoking in the movies (Dalton et al., 2003; Titus-Ernstoff, Dalton, Adachi-Mejia, Longacre, & Beach, 2008). Linking the use of smokeless tobacco with virility and athletic performance is a common marketing strategy of tobacco companies, which target young men in particular (Connolly, Orleans, & Blum, 1992; National Cancer Institute, 2008). *Sports Illustrated*, the magazine most often read by men and adolescent boys, has been found to have more tobacco—as well as alcohol—advertisements than any other magazine (Cordry, 2001; Klein et al., 1993). It is no coincidence that the most popular Madison Avenue icons of smoking—Joe Camel and the Marlboro Man—are male. Documents released by R.J. Reynolds Tobacco Company reveal that the "Joe Camel" advertising campaign was "designed to lure teenagers … especially boys" ("Joe Camel," 1998, p. A1). Not surprisingly, research of college students' attitudes reveals that smoking makes females look slutty and out of control, whereas males who smoke are described as looking manly, relaxed, and in control; this research also reveals such comments as stating it is "just not as cool for a girl to smoke as a guy" (Nichter et al., 2006, p. 224). As others suggest (Bunton, Crawshaw, & Green, 2004), for college males, engaging in risk behavior—such as smoking—can serve to reaffirm their identity as men.

Gendered media portrayals of alcohol consumption are similar. At least one character drinks alcohol in 60% of all prime-time television programs, and the vast majority of these characters are men (Byrd-Bredbenner et al., 2003; Wallack, Breed, & Cruz, 1987). Research consistently reveals an unmistakable link between alcohol and masculinity in the various media, an association that is further strengthened by advertisers who "[interjoin] their products with athletic events" and who "strategically [place] ads in magazines and television programs with predominantly male audiences" (Lemle & Mishkind, 1989, p. 215; see also Slater et al., 1996; Wenner & Jackson, 2009). Beer commercials further link men's drinking with taking risks and facing danger without fear (Signorielli, 1993; Strate, 1992; Wenner & Jackson, 2009). There is also some evidence that exposure to alcohol consumption on television is associated with more favorable attitudes toward drinking (Signorielli, 1993; Slater et al., 1996), and also that in late adolescence the increase in the use of alcohol by young men—which is not paralleled by a similar increase in young women—is driven by their growing adherence to norms of masculinity, fostered by the media.

Body image and the relevance of diet are also gendered in the media. Women and girls are consistently portrayed as slimmer than men and boys in television, movies, and magazines (Greenberg, Eastin, Hofschire, Lachlan, & Brownell, 2003; Signorielli, 1993; Silverstein, Peterson, & Kelley, 1986). In prime-time television, 3 times more male than female characters are obese (Gerbner et al., 1981). Women's magazines have far more messages about staying healthy and fit than men's magazines, which promote alcohol consumption almost exclusively (Signorielli, 1993). In newspaper articles, hearty meals and poor diets have been found to be portrayed as masculine, whereas dieting has been linked with femininity (Gough, 2007).

Men and boys on television are also more likely than women and girls both to initiate violence and to get away with it (e.g., Glascock, 2008; Larson, 2001; McGhee & Frueh, 1980; Signorielli, 1993). Violent and antisocial behaviors are often portrayed as effective means for male characters to meet their objectives; typically, these behaviors are rewarded and have no negative consequences (Heintz-Knowles, 1995; Sege & Dietz, 1994; Signorielli, 1993). Boys are 60% more likely than girls to be portrayed using physical aggression (Heintz-Knowles, 1995). Toy commercials demonstrate similar gender differences in aggressive behavior (Sobieraj, 1998; Zuckerman, Singer, & Singer, 1980).

Content analyses of children's television programs show that the frequency of injury–risk behaviors on the part of characters far exceeds the modeling of safety behaviors, and most of the risk behaviors portrayed do not result in injuries that have substantive negative or sustained consequences for the victim (Greenberg, 1982; Pelletier et al, 2000; Potts, Doppler, & Hernandez, 1994; Potts & Henderson, 1991; Potts, Runyan, Zerger, & Marchetti, 1996; Potts & Swisher, 1998). Research examining the effect of television on children's behavior shows that exposure to programs that portray high risk taking results in children taking greater physical risks in hypothetical situations (Morrongiello & Lasenby-Lessard, 2007). Significantly more boys than girls in high school watch television for 3 or more hours a day (CDC, 2008b) and are therefore exposed to more modeling of risk taking. Indeed, engagement with all kinds of entertainment media—including watching television, listening to music, using computers, and playing video games—has increased among youth since the beginning of the century, and boys are engaged with these media almost 1 hour more per day than girls; they spend 4 times as much time playing console video games as girls do (Rideout, Foehr, & Roberts, 2010).

Despite unhealthy behavior by men as portrayed in the media, it is women who are twice as likely to receive advice from physicians on television; it is also women who are most likely to die in daytime serials (Gerbner et al., 1981; Signorielli, 1993). For example, they are 4 times more likely than men to die from heart disease (Signorielli, 1993). Men represent three of four of those infected with HIV (CDC, 2009b); on television, however, women and children account for 75% of characters suffering from the disease (Signorielli, 1993). This evidence suggests that, in the world of television, men and boys are invulnerable to the risks that their unhealthy behaviors pose. Indeed, invincible superheroes are characterized primarily as men (Baker & Raney, 2007; Fitzpatrick & McPherson, 2010; Pecora, 1992).

These media representations of gender have been found to contribute significantly to negative health effects (e.g., Hazan et al., 1994; Heintz-Knowles, 1995; Wallack et al., 1987). Research consistently reveals an association between the viewing of television violence and subsequent violent and aggressive behavior; there is also some evidence that this association is causal (Anderson & Bushman, 2002; Bushman & Anderson, 2001; Glymour, Glymour, & Glymour, 2008; Sege & Dietz, 1994; Signorielli, 1993). Boys who watch television 25 hours or more per week—as most do—are more likely than those who do not to adopt the unhealthy, "manly" behavior that is demonstrated (McGhee & Frueh, 1980; Smith & Donnerstein, 1998). There is also some evidence that exposure to alcohol consumption on television is associated with increased favorable drinking attitudes (Signorielli, 1993; Slater et al., 1996).

Other Social Transactions and Structural Influences

One of the most important structural influences on gendered health behavior is work, which I demonstrate in Chapters 1 and 2. "Women's work"—work in which the vast majority of employees are female—includes such positions as secretary, receptionist, child care professional, nurse, and salesperson. Timber cutting, fishing, mining, construction, truck driving, and farming are carried out almost exclusively by males and are considered "men's work." The work that men do is the most dangerous work, and consequently—although they constitute only half (53%) of the workforce—men account for nearly all (93%) of the 16 fatal injuries that occur on the job each day.

Cooking and nutrition are socially constructed as feminine (Gough, 2007). On television, far more women than men are homemakers and cooks (Peirce, 1989; Swenson, 2009), and men's magazines suggest that food choices are irrelevant to men (Signorielli, 1993). In the minds of both girls and boys, the enjoyment of cooking is associated with feminine behaviors (Golombok & Fivush, 1994). Not surprisingly, fewer than one third of men report that they like to cook ("Health Bulletin," 1995); one large-scale study indicates that although there was a significant shift from 1965 to 1998 toward sharing household chores, women in 1998 spent more than twice as much time cooking as did men (Sayer, 2005). As I discussed in Chapter 1, most men lack basic knowledge about foods and nutritional risk factors, which are considered essential in improving dietary practices and reducing health risks.

Playing sports is a major element in defining traditional masculinity (Connell, 1995; Kidd, 1987). On television, for example, male characters are more often portrayed as playing sports than are female characters (Peirce, 1989). Sport has long been a male preserve and has been consciously designed to make men out of males (Kidd, 1987). In many of men's sports, use of aggression and acceptance of health risks are rationalized and idealized (Messner et al., 1999; Messner & Sabo, 1994; White, Young, & McTeer, 1995); not surprisingly, men are more likely than women to engage in dangerous sports, and men account for three of four of the more than 4 million sport injuries that occur each year (see Chapter 2).

Cultural explanations may also play a role in the observed sex differences in concussion rates. Traditionally, as a society, the United States has tended to be more protective of female than of male athletes (Vertinsky, 1994). This may lead coaches, athletic trainers, and parents to treat head injuries in female athletes more seriously or to delay their return to play. Similar cultural tendencies may encourage male athletes to play despite any injuries or to avoid reporting injuries, particularly in certain sports. Thus, some boys suffering from head injuries may not report their symptoms for fear of being removed from play (Lovell et al., 2002). A reluctance to report head injury was demonstrated in high school football players. Fewer than half (47%) of players claiming to have suffered a concussion reported their injury. Underestimating the seriousness of the injury, not wanting to be withdrawn from competition, and not being aware of having suffered a concussion have been cited as reasons for underreporting concussion injury (McCrea, Hammeke, Olsen, Leo, & Guskiewicz, 2004).

As Don Sabo and I discuss in Chapter 7, the institutional structure of prisons also contributes to constructions of masculinity, particularly violent and unhealthy forms of masculinity. More than 9 in 10 prisoners are men; nearly 1.5 million men are incarcerated in U.S. jails and prisons (Department of Justice, 2008c, 2009c). Similarly, the military is both gendered and gender defining. Combat soldiers are almost exclusively men. In defending this standard, the U.S. military has argued that the country is not culturally prepared to witness the things happening to women that happen to combat soldiers and prisoners of war (Lieutenant Colonel Robert Maginnis, cited in Suarez, 1995). Consequently, in the Vietnam War, 58,000 U.S. men and 8 U.S. women were killed (Brende & Parson, 1985); as of June 2010, 4,143 U.S. men and 102 U.S. women had been killed in the war in Iraq (Congressional Research Service, 2009).

Health Care and the Social Construction of Gendered Risk

The health care system and its allied health fields represent a particularly important structural influence in the construction of gendered health behavior. In the case of cardiovascular disease, for example, it is often noted that the fact that women are less likely than men to be routinely tested or treated for symptoms can foster unrealistic perceptions of risk among women (Steingart et al., 1991; Wenger, 1994). Rarely, however, have the ways in which health care contributes to social constructions of men's health been examined. It has been argued that sociologists, medical researchers, and other health professionals have all contributed to cultural portrayals of men as healthy and women as the "sicker" gender (Gijsbers van Wijk et al., 1991, p. 104), to strongly held beliefs that men's bodies are structurally more efficient than and superior to women's bodies (Courtenay, 2000a), and to the "invisibility" of men's poor health status (Annandale & Clark, 1996, p. 30).

Gendered Health Messages

As Nathanson (1977) noted more than 3 decades ago, sex differences in health and health-related behavior arise "out of a medical model that has singled out women for special professional attention.... Women are encouraged and trained to define their life problems in medical terms and to seek professional help for them" (pp. 148–149). Historically, women but not men in the United States have been encouraged to pay attention to their health (Annandale & Clark, 1996; Lonnquist, Weiss, & Larsen, 1992; Nathanson, 1977; Oakley, 1994; Reagan, 1997; Signorielli, 1993; Vertinsky, 1994). As I discussed in Chapter 1, despite their greater risk for HIV, significantly fewer young U.S. men than women in high school have been taught about AIDS or HIV infection (CDC, 2008b). According to Reagan (1997), who analyzed decades of cancer education in the United States, these educational efforts have been directed primarily at women. As I discussed previously, many counseling and psychological interventions with men have been recommended in the past 2 decades; however, rarely are these interventions designed to reduce men's health risks (Courtenay, 2001a, 2004a). Men also receive significantly less physician time in their health visits than women do (Blanchard et al., 1983; Hall, Roter, & Katz, 1988; Roter & Hall, 1997, 2004; Waitzkin, 1984; Weisman & Teitelbaum, 1989) and generally receive fewer services and dispositions than women (Verbrugge & Steiner, 1985). Men are provided with fewer and briefer explanations—both simple and technical—in medical encounters (Bertakis & Azari, 2007; Hall et al., 1988; Roter & Hall, 1997, 2004; Waitzkin, 1984; Weisman & Teitelbaum, 1989). During checkups, they receive less advice from physicians about changing risk factors for disease than women do (Bertakis & Azari, 2007; Friedman et al., 1994). Studies show that men receive less information about self-examination for cancer than women do (Faigel, 1983; Misener & Fuller, 1995); one (Misener & Fuller, 1995) found that only 29% of physicians routinely provide age-appropriate instruction on performing self-examinations for testicular cancer, compared with the 86% who provide instruction to women on performing breast examinations. One study suggests that the greater support given to the prevention of breast cancer may affect efforts to promote early detection of testicular cancers (Clarke, 2004). One review by leading researchers on clinical communication revealed that no study has ever found that women received less information from physicians than men, which led the authors to conclude that the findings "may reflect sexism in medical encounters, but this may act to the advantage of female patients, who have a more informative and positive experience than is typical for male patients" (Roter & Hall, 1997, p. 44).

Gendered Illness: The Social Construction of Morbidity

It is popularly assumed that women are at a greater risk of illness—or morbidity—than men. This assumption has been contested, along with data from two large studies that revealed few differences between the physical health of women and that of men (Macintyre, Hunt, & Sweeting, 1996). Less-than-thorough analyses of morbidity data, along with uncritical reiterations of "women's excess illness" in the literature, contribute to medicine's neglect of men's poor health. As was noted by Macintyre et al. (1996), "The predominance of the 'women's higher morbidity' paradigm … has tended to persist … taking on the characteristics of a dominant scientific paradigm with anomalous or inconsistent findings not being noticed or seriously discussed" (p. 623). This paradigm serves to define, construct, and reinforce strongly held cultural beliefs about gender and health.

Self-reported health status fosters assumptions of women's greater morbidity. However, as I demonstrated in Chapter 1, self-reports are not an accurate indicator of gendered risks. Morbidity statistics, often based on similarly unreliable self-reports, have greatly contributed to the cultural belief that women have poorer health than men. Although the evidence is not entirely consistent, reviews of research typically conclude that men report fewer physical or psychological symptoms and report illness less readily than women (Verbrugge, 1988). These findings may simply reflect the ability of women to perceive and report symptoms at a lower threshold than men rather than documenting real gender differences in the incidence of symptoms and disease (Gijsbers van Wijk et al., 1991).

Social Construction of Healthy and Unhealthy Bodies

A variety of scientific methodological factors and research methods—developed and conducted primarily by men—have also contributed to the model of deficient women's bodies, and to the social construction that men are healthy and women are not (Courtenay, 2006a). For example, the use of behavioral indices of health—such as bed rest and health care utilization—both pathologizes women's health and underestimates the significance of men's health problems. These indices confound our understanding of morbidity because they represent how men and women *cope* with illness rather than representing their true health status (Gijsbers van Wijk et al., 1991); thus, they obscure what may be greater illness among men (Kandrack et al., 1991; Verbrugge, 1988). The assumption underlying these and other indices of health is that male behavior is the normative or hidden referent; consequently, researchers and theorists alike presume that women are in poorer health because women get more bed rest than men do and see physicians more often. The terms applied to these behaviors—behaviors that can be considered health promoting—further pathologize women's health: women's *excess* bed rest and women's *over*utilization of health services. These terms simultaneously transform curative actions into indicators of illness, make women's health problematic, and reinforce men's position in providing the standard of health or health behavior.

Given that women are unquestionably less susceptible to serious illness and live longer than men, it would seem that women should provide the standard against which men's health and men's health behavior are measured. If this were the case, we would be compelled instead to confront men's *inadequate* bed rest and men's *under*utilization of health care. However, the social forces that maintain women's health as problematic are strong. When morbidity statistics and women's greater propensity for illness are challenged as an artifact of research, for example, the conventional reading of this challenge as noted by Oakley (1994) further pathologizes women's health by suggesting that women "aren't really ill at all, they're only inventing it" (p. 431). In contrast, the interpretation that men really *are* ill and they are simply denying it is rarely proposed. It has been argued that a cultural perception of men's health problems as nonexistent is required both to construct women's bodies as deficient and to reinforce women's disadvantaged social position (Annandale & Clark, 1996; Vertinsky, 1994). To maintain this construction, "women 'cannot' be well and … men cannot be ill; they are 'needed' to be well to construe women as sick" (Annandale & Clark, 1996, p. 32). By dismissing their health needs and taking physical risks, men are legitimizing themselves as the "stronger" sex. As I discuss in the following chapter, medical and epidemiological research further reinforces stereotypes by consistently failing to take into account gender, apart from biological sex. Men's risk taking and violence, for example, are simply taken for granted.

MANHOOD AND HEALTH

The preceding review demonstrates how U.S. life is distinctly divided by gender. The social practices required to enact gender differ categorically for women and men. Individuals are not required, per se, to adhere to these gender stereotypes. However, most individuals do so. From a constructionist perspective, differing social experiences and transactions do not cause demonstrated gender differences between women and men; rather, women and men learn to adopt different behaviors to enact or demonstrate gender as socially prescribed. Based on the evidence presented thus far, what health-related beliefs and behaviors would one expect to be demonstrated by a man?

A man who enacts gender as socially prescribed would be relatively unconcerned about his health and well-being in general and would place little value on health knowledge. He would see himself as stronger, both physically and emotionally, than most women. He would think of himself as independent, not needing to be nurtured by others. He would not develop close friendships, and his social networks would be small. He would be unlikely to ask others for help. Work and employment would be central to his sense of self and essential for maintaining his self-esteem. The intense and active stimulation of his senses would be something he would come to depend on. He would face danger fearlessly, disregard his risks, and have little concern for his own safety. He would see himself as invulnerable to the risks commonly associated with unhealthy behavior. He would lack the vocabulary to describe physical sensations and would have difficulty identifying and expressing most of his emotions. However, he would consider anger to be acceptable, particularly when expressed physically. He would view physical violence as a sometimes necessary part of life. He would not be interested in learning about health, nutrition, or cooking, and he would be unconcerned about his weight, diet, or hygiene. Finally, he would adamantly reject doing anything that he or anyone else would consider feminine.

This gendered profile does not simply represent hypotheses about men's health beliefs and behaviors. There is abundant evidence that this is indeed how men typically think and behave and that the adoption of these beliefs and behaviors significantly influences men's health and longevity (see Chapter 2). It should be noted that some men do defy these social prescriptions of masculinity and adopt healthy behaviors, such as getting annual physicals and eating healthy foods. But although these men are constructing a form of masculinity, it is not among the dominant forms that are encouraged in men, nor is it among the forms adopted by most men. It should also be noted that women can and do adopt unhealthy beliefs and behaviors to demonstrate femininities, as in the case of unhealthy dieting to attain a culturally defined body ideal of slimness. However, as the preceding review indicates, the striving for cultural standards of femininity leads women to engage primarily in healthy, not unhealthy, behaviors.

Each embodied health practice that a man demonstrates simultaneously reinforces and reproduces gender (and gender as difference). Unhealthy behaviors often serve as cultural signifiers of "true" masculinity. Indeed, men often boast to others of these behaviors: "I haven't missed a day of work in my life!" or "I can drink *and* drive!" In these ways, many men and boys define their masculinity against healthy behaviors and beliefs that are socially constructed as feminine.

CONCLUSION

Research consistently demonstrates that women in the United States adopt healthier beliefs and behaviors than men. A wealth of scientific data suggest that this distinction accounts in no small part for the fact that women suffer less severe chronic conditions and live more than 5 years longer than men. From a social constructionist perspective, this distinction can be understood as being among the many differences that women and men are expected to demonstrate. If men want to enact dominant ideals of manhood as defined in U.S. society, they must adhere to cultural definitions of masculine beliefs and behaviors and actively reject what is feminine. The use of health beliefs and behaviors to define oneself as a woman or a man—unlike the presumably innocent effects of wearing lipstick or wearing a tie—has a profound impact on one's health and longevity.

The preceding analysis and review of research demonstrates that the resources available in the United States for constructing masculinities—and the signifiers of "true" masculinity—are largely unhealthy. Men and boys indeed use these resources and adopt unhealthy beliefs and behaviors to construct gender and signify manhood. Although nothing strictly prohibits a man from demonstrating masculinities differently, to do so would require that he cross over socially constructed gender boundaries, and risk reproach and sometimes physical danger for failing to demonstrate gender correctly. The preceding analysis further demonstrates that social and institutional structures compound men's health risks by fostering unhealthy behavior and constraining health-promoting practices, which I will explore further in Chapter 4.

4

Constructions of Masculinity and Their Influence on Men's Well-Being

*A Theory of Gender and Health**

As I explained in the previous chapters, a variety of factors influence and are associated with health and longevity, including economic status, ethnicity, and access to care. However, these factors cannot explain gender differences in health and longevity. For example, as I discussed in the preceding chapters, although lack of adequate health care, poor nutrition, and substandard housing all contribute to the health problems of African Americans, they cannot account for cancer death rates that are nearly 2 times higher among African American men than among African American women (Jemal et al., 2008). However, as I demonstrated in Chapter 2, health-related behaviors do help to explain gender differences in health and longevity; and although many biogenetic and sociocultural factors are associated with and influence health-related behavior, gender is the most important of these factors.

This chapter expands on Chapter 3 and proposes a relational theory of men's health from a social constructionist and feminist perspective. It provides an introduction to social constructionist perspectives on

---

* An earlier version of this chapter appeared in *Social Science & Medicine*, 50(10), 2000, 1385–1401, and is used by permission in modified/revised form

gender and a brief critique of gender role theory before illustrating how
health beliefs and behavior are used in constructing gender in North
America, and how masculinity and health are constructed within a relational context. It further examines how men construct various forms
of masculinity—or masculinities—and how these different enactments
of gender, as well as differing social structural influences, contribute to
differential health risks among men in the United States.

HEALTH AND THE SOCIAL
CONSTRUCTION OF GENDER

Constructionism and Theories of Gender

The first explanations of masculinity and men's health focused primarily on the hazardous influences of "*the* male sex role" (Goldberg, 1976;
Harrison, 1978; Harrison et al., 1992; Nathanson, 1977; Verbrugge,
1985). These explanations relied on theories of gender socialization
that have since been widely criticized (Connell, 1995; Deaux, 1984;
Epstein, 1988; Gerson & Peiss, 1985; Kimmel, 1986; Messerschmidt,
1993; Pleck, 1987; West & Zimmerman 1987). The sex role theory of
socialization, still used in analyses of gender, has been criticized for
implying that gender represents "two fixed, static, and mutually exclu-
sive role containers" (Kimmel, 1986, p. 521) and for assuming that
women and men have innate psychological needs for gender-stereotypic
traits (Pleck, 1987). Sex role theory also fosters the notion of a singular female or male personality, a notion that has been effectively dis-
puted, and obscures the various forms of femininity and masculinity
that women and men can and do demonstrate (Connell, 1995).

   From a constructionist perspective, women and men think and act in
the ways that they do not because of their role identities or psychological
traits, but rather because of concepts about femininity and masculinity
that they adopt from their culture (Pleck et al., 1994a). Gender is not
two static categories, but rather "a set of socially constructed relationships
which are produced and reproduced through people's actions" (Gerson &
Peiss, 1985, p. 327); it is constructed by dynamic, dialectic relationships
(Connell, 1995). Gender is "something that one does, and *does* recurrently, in interaction with others" (West & Zimmerman, 1987, p. 140;
italics theirs); it is achieved or demonstrated and is better understood as
a verb than as a noun (Bohan, 1993; Crawford, 1995; Kaschak, 1992).
Most importantly, gender does not reside in the person, but rather in
social transactions defined as gendered (Bohan, 1993; Crawford, 1995).
From this perspective, gender is viewed as a dynamic, social structure.

Gender Stereotypes

   Gender is constructed from cultural and subjective meanings that
constantly shift and vary, depending on the time and place (Kimmel,

1995). Gender stereotypes are among the meanings used by society in the construction of gender, and are characteristics that are generally believed to be typical either of women or of men. There is high agreement in our society about what are considered to be typically feminine and typically masculine characteristics (Golombok & Fivush, 1994; Street, Kimmel, & Kromrey, 1995; Williams & Best, 1990). These stereotypes provide collective, organized—and dichotomous—meanings of gender and often become widely shared beliefs about who women and men innately *are* (Pleck, 1987). People are encouraged to conform to stereotypic beliefs and behaviors, and commonly do conform to and adopt dominant norms of femininity and masculinity (Bohan, 1993; Deaux, 1984; Eagly, 1983). Conforming to what is expected of them further reinforces self-fulfilling prophecies of such behavior (Crawford, 1995; Geis, 1993).

Research indicates that men and boys experience comparatively greater social pressure than women and girls to endorse gendered societal prescriptions—such as the strongly endorsed *health-related* beliefs that men are independent, self-reliant, strong, robust, and tough (Golombok & Fivush, 1994; Martin, 1995; McCreary, 1994; Williams & Best, 1990). Therefore, it is not surprising that their behavior and their beliefs about gender are more stereotypic than those of women and girls (Katz & Ksansnak, 1994; Levant & Majors, 1998; Rice & Coates, 1995; Street et al., 1995). From a social constructionist perspective, however, men and boys are not passive victims of a socially prescribed role, nor are they simply conditioned or socialized by their cultures. Men and boys are active agents in constructing and reconstructing dominant norms of masculinity. This concept of agency—the part individuals play in exerting power and producing effects in their lives—is central to constructionism.

Health Beliefs and Behaviors: Resources for Constructing Gender

The activities that men and women engage in, and their gendered cognitions, are a form of currency in transactions that are continually enacted in the demonstration of gender. Previous authors have examined how a variety of activities are used as resources in constructing and reconstructing gender; these activities include language (Crawford, 1995; Perry et al., 1992), work (Connell, 1995), sports (Connell, 1992; Messner & Sabo, 1994), crime (Messerschmidt, 1993), and sex (Vance, 1995). The manner in which women and men do these activities contributes both to the defining of one's self as gendered and to social conventions of gender.

Health-related beliefs and behaviors can similarly be understood as a means of constructing or demonstrating gender. In this way, the health behaviors and beliefs that people adopt simultaneously define and enact representations of gender. Health beliefs and behaviors, like language, can be understood as "a set of strategies for negotiating the social land-scape" (Crawford, 1995, p. 17), or tools for constructing gender. Like crime, health behavior "may be invoked as a practice through which masculinities (and men and women) are differentiated from one another" (Messerschmidt, 1993, p. 85). The findings from one small study exam-ining gender differences and health led the author to conclude that "the doing of health is a form of doing gender" (Saltonstall, 1993, p. 12). In this regard, "health actions are social acts" and "can be seen as a form of practice which constructs … 'the person' in the same way that other social and cultural activities do" (Saltonstall, 1993, p. 12).

The social experiences of women and men provide a template that guides their beliefs and behavior (Kimmel, 1995). The various social transactions, institutional structures, and contexts that women and men encounter elicit different demonstrations of health beliefs and behaviors, and provide different opportunities to conduct this particular form of demonstrating gender. If these social experiences and demonstrated beliefs or behaviors had no bearing on the health of women and men, they would be of no relevance here. This, however, is not the case. The social practices required for demonstrating femininity and masculinity are associated with different health advantages and risks. As I discussed in Chapter 3, unlike the presumably innocent effects of wearing lipstick or wearing a tie, the use of health-related beliefs and behaviors to define oneself as a woman or a man has a profound impact on one's health and longevity.

THEORIZING MASCULINITY IN THE CONTEXT OF HEALTH

As Messerschmidt (1993) notes in regard to the study of gender and crime, a comprehensive feminist theory of health must similarly include men "not by treating men as the normal subjects, but by articulating the gendered content of men's behavior" (p. 62). The following sections provide a relational analysis of men's gendered health behavior based on constructionist and feminist theories, and examine how cultural dic-tates, everyday interactions, and social and institutional structures help to sustain and reproduce men's health risks.

Gender, Power, and the Social Construction of the "Stronger" Sex

A discussion of power and social inequality is necessary to understand the broader context of men's adoption of unhealthy behavior—as well as to address the social structures that both foster unhealthy behavior among men and undermine men's attempts to adopt healthier habits. Gender is negotiated in part through relationships of power. Microlevel power practices (Pyke, 1996) contribute to structuring the social trans-actions of everyday life, transactions that help to sustain and reproduce broader structures of power and inequality. These power relationships are located in and constituted in, among other practices, the practice of health behavior. The systematic subordination of women and lower-status men—or patriarchy—is made possible, in part, through these gendered demonstrations of health and health behavior. In this way, males use health beliefs and behaviors to demonstrate dominant— and hegemonic—masculine ideals that clearly establish them as men. Hegemonic masculinity is the idealized form of masculinity at a given place and time (Connell, 1995; Connell & Messerschmidt, 2005). It is the socially dominant gender construction that subordinates femininities and other forms of masculinity, and reflects and shapes men's social relationships with women and other men; it represents power and authority. Today in the United States, hegemonic masculinity is embodied in heterosexual, highly educated, European American men of upper-class economic status.

The fact that there are a variety of health risks associated with being a man in no way implies that men do not hold power. Indeed, it is in the pursuit of power and privilege that men are often led to harm themselves (Clatterbaugh, 1997).The social practices that undermine men's health are often the instruments men use in the structuring and acquisition of power. Men's acquisition of power requires, for example, that men suppress their needs and refuse to admit to or acknowledge their pain (Kaufman, 1994). Additional health-related beliefs and behaviors that can be used in the demonstration of hegemonic masculinity include the denial of weakness or vulnerability, emotional and physical control, the appearance of being strong and robust, dismissal of any need for help, a ceaseless interest in sex, the display of aggressive behavior, and physical dominance. These health-related demonstrations of gender and power represent forms of microlevel power practices, practices that are "part of a system that affirms and (re)constitutes broader relations of inequality" (Pyke, 1996, p. 546). In exhibiting or enacting hegemonic ideals with health behaviors, men reinforce strongly held cultural beliefs that men are more powerful and less vulnerable than women, that men's bodies are structurally more efficient than and superior to women's bodies, that asking for help and caring for one's health are feminine, and that the most powerful men among men are those for whom health and safety are irrelevant.

Recent research demonstrates that some men, under certain circumstances, can and do resist enacting a hegemonic masculinity that undermines their health (Emslie, Ridge, Ziebland, & Hunt, 2006; O'Brien, Hunt, & Hart, 2005; Robertson, 2007). However, as I demonstrated in Chapter 3, the resources available in the United States for constructing masculinities are largely unhealthy. Men and boys often use these resources and reject healthy beliefs and behaviors to demonstrate and achieve manhood. By dismissing their health care needs, men are constructing gender. When a man brags, "I haven't been to a doctor in years," he is simultaneously describing a health practice and situating himself in a masculine arena. Similarly, men are demonstrating dominant norms of masculinity when they refuse to take sick leave from work, when they insist that they need little sleep, and when they boast that drinking does not impair their driving. Men also construct masculinities by embracing risk. A man may define the degree of his masculinity, for example, by driving dangerously or performing risky sports—and displaying these behaviors like badges of honor or achievements of manhood. In these ways, masculinities are defined *against* positive health behaviors and beliefs.

To carry out any one positive health behavior, a man may need to reject multiple constructions of masculinity. For example, the application of sunscreen to prevent skin cancer—the most rapidly increasing cancer in the United States (see Chapter 2)—may require the rejection of a variety of social constructions: masculine men are unconcerned about health matters; masculine men are invulnerable to disease; the application of lotions to the body is a feminine pastime; masculine men don't "pamper" or "fuss" over their bodies; and "rugged good looks" are produced with a tan. In *not* applying sunscreen, a man may be simultaneously demonstrating gender and an unhealthy practice. The facts that significantly more men than women nationally believe that one looks better with a tan (American Academy of Dermatology, 2005), that men are far less likely to use sunscreen, and that the skin cancer death rate is twice as high for men as for women (see Chapter 2) may be testaments to the level of support among men for endorsing these constructions.

When a man does experience an illness or disability, the gender ramifications are often great. Illness "can reduce a man's status in masculine hierarchies, shift his power relations with women, and raise his self-doubts about masculinity" (Charmaz, 1995, p. 268). The friend of a U.S. senator cautioned him against publicly discussing his diagnosis of prostate cancer, contending that "some men might see [his] willingness to go public with his private struggle as a sign of weakness" (Jaffe, 1997, p. 134). In efforts to preserve their masculinity, one researcher found that men with chronic illnesses often worked diligently to hide their disabilities: A man with diabetes, unable to maneuver both his wheelchair and a cafeteria tray, would skip lunch and risk a coma rather than request assistance; a middle-aged man declined offers of easier jobs to prove that he was still capable of strenuous work; and an executive concealed dialysis treatments by telling others that he was away attending meetings (Charmaz, 1995).

Feminities and Men's Health

It is not only the endorsement of hegemonic ideals but also the rejection of feminine ideals that contributes to the construction of masculinities and to the systematic oppression of women and less powerful men. Rejecting what is constructed as feminine is essential for demonstrating hegemonic masculinity in a sexist and gender-dichotomous society.

Men and boys who attempt to engage in social action that demonstrates feminine norms of gender risk being relegated to the subordinated masculinity of "wimp" or "sissy." A gay man who grew up on Indiana farms said he would have been ridiculed as a "sissy" had he done the (risk-free) tasks of cooking, baking, and sewing that he preferred: "My uncle would have started it and it would have spread out from there. Even my grandfather would say, 'Oh, you don't want to do that. That's girl stuff.'" (Fellows, 1996, p. 12). Health care utilization and positive health beliefs or behaviors are also socially constructed as forms of idealized femininity (Courtenay, 1998a, 2000c; see also Chapter 3). Therefore, they are potentially feminizing influences that men must oppose with varying degrees of force, depending on what other resources are accessible or are being used in the construction of masculinities. Forgoing health care is a means of rejecting "sissy stuff."

Men's denial and disregard of physical discomfort, risk, and health care needs are all means of demonstrating difference from women, who are presumed to embody these "feminine" characteristics. These behaviors serve both as proof of men's superiority over women and as proof of their ranking among "real" men. A man's success in adopting (socially feminized) health-promoting behavior, like his failure to engage in (socially masculinized) physically risky behavior, can undermine his ranking among men and relegate him to a subordinated status. That men and boys construct masculinities in opposition to the healthy beliefs and behaviors of women—and less masculine (i.e., "feminized") men and boys—is clearly apparent in their discourse, as evidenced by the remarks of one firefighter: "When you go out to fires, you will work yourself into the ground. Just so nobody else thinks you're a puss" (Delsohn, 1996, p. 95). Similarly, one author, the chief editor of a major publishing company, revealed his concern about disclosing his pain to others after a radical prostatectomy: "I was reluctant to complain further [to hospital staff], for fear of being thought a sissy" (Korda, 1996, p. 148). In prison, men criticize fellow prisoners who "complain too much" about sickness or pain or make frequent health care visits as displaying signs of "softness" (see Chapter 7).

Differences Among Men

Contemporary feminist theorists are as concerned about differences among men (and among women) as they are about differences between women and men. As Messerschmidt (1993, p. 87) notes, "'Boys will be boys' differently, depending upon their position in social structures and, therefore, upon their access to power and resources." Although men may endorse similar masculine ideals, different men may enact these ideals in different ways. For example, although most young men in the United States may agree that a man should be "tough" (Courtenay, 1998b), *how* each man demonstrates being tough—and how demonstrating toughness affects him physically—will be influenced by his age, ethnicity, social class, and sexuality. Depending on these factors, a man may use a gun, his fists, his sexuality, a mountain bike, physical labor, a car, or the relentless pursuit of financial strength to construct this particular aspect of masculinity.

Social class positioning "both constrains and enables certain forms of gendered social action" (Messerschmidt, 1993, p. 94) and influences which unhealthy behaviors are used to demonstrate masculinity. Demonstrating masculinities with fearless, high-risk behaviors may entail skydiving for an upper-class man, mountain climbing for a middle-class man, racing hot rods for a working-class man, and street fighting for a poor urban man. Many working-class masculinities that are constructed as exemplary—as in the case of firemen—require the dismissal of fear, as well as feats of physical endurance and strength, that often put these men at risk for injury and death. The avoidance of health care is another form of social action that allows some men to maintain their status and to avoid being relegated to a subordinated position in relation to physicians and health professionals, as well as other men. For an upper middle-class business executive, refusing to see a physician can be a means of maintaining his position of power. Prisoners can similarly maintain their status by disregarding their health care needs: "When you got stabbed you usually bandaged yourself up…. To go to the doctor would appear that you are soft" (Courtenay & Sabo, 2001, p. 165).

It is important to point out that demonstrating masculinity, for some men, does require the maintenance of good health. Among populations of Mexican American men, for example, masculinity—or *machismo*—requires that they both seek health care and remain healthy, so they can be good fathers, husbands, brothers, sons, workers, and community members (Sobralske, 2006). Similarly, demonstrating masculinity for some men requires not only the successful performance of their jobs but also the successful maintenance of their health to do so. One qualitative study found, for example, that some firefighters were willing to see a doctor to enable them to remain healthy and keep their jobs (O'Brien et al., 2005). There is also quantitative evidence consistent with this finding. In a large population-based study of masculinity and health-care seeking among U.S. middle-aged men, those with blue-collar jobs (e.g., machine operators, truck drivers, construction workers, and farm workers)—including those with strong beliefs about masculinity—were more likely to obtain care; these findings led the authors to conclude that, for these men, any threat to masculinity associated with seeking health care was less concerning than the threat of being unable to perform their jobs (Springer & Mouzon, 2009). It is also important to note, however, that these men's occupational roles provide powerful resources for constructing hegemonic masculinity, which can protect them—when seeking health care—from being relegated to a subordinated masculinity.

The construction of health and gender does not occur in isolation from other forms of social action that demonstrate differences among men. Health practices may be used simultaneously to enact multiple social constructions, such as ethnicity, class, and sexuality. The use of health beliefs and behaviors to construct the interacting social structures of masculinity and ethnicity is illustrated in this passage by a Chicano novelist:

> A macho doesn't show weakness. Grit your teeth, take the pain, bear it alone. Be tough. You feel like letting it out? Well, then let's get drunk with our *compadres*.... Drinking buddies who have a contest to see who can consume the most beer, or the most shots of tequila, are trying to prove their maleness. (Anaya, 1996, p. 63)

Too often, factors such as ethnicity, class, and sexuality are simply treated by health scientists as variables to be controlled for in statistical analyses. However, the social structuring of ethnicity, sexuality, and class is intimately and systematically related to the social structuring of gender and power. These various social structures are constructed concurrently and are intertwined. When European American working-class boys speed recklessly through a poor African American neighborhood, not wearing safety belts and yelling epithets out their windows, they are using health risk behaviors—among other behaviors—in the simultaneous construction of gender, power, class, and ethnicity; when they continue these behaviors in a nearby gay neighborhood, they are further reproducing gender, power, and normative heterosexuality. Similarly, poor health beliefs and behaviors are used by men and boys to construct masculinities in conjunction with the use of other behaviors such as crime (Messerschmidt, 1993), work (Pyke, 1996), and being "cool" (Majors & Billson, 1992). Committing criminal acts may be insufficient to win a young man inclusion in a street gang; he may also be required to prove his manhood by demonstrating his willingness to ignore pain or to engage in physical fighting.

Masculinities and the Negotiation of Power and Status

Just as men exercise varying degrees of power over women, so they exercise varying degrees of power among themselves. "Masculinities are configurations of social practices produced not only in relation to femininities but also in relation to one another" (Pyke, 1996, p. 531). Dominant masculinities subordinate lower-status, marginalized masculinities—such as those of gay, rural, or lower-class men. As Connell (1995, p. 76) notes, "To recognize more than one kind of masculinity is only a first step"; "we must also recognize the relations between the different kinds of masculinity: relations of alliance, dominance and subordination. These relationships are constructed through practices that exclude and include, that intimidate, exploit, and so on" (Connell, 1995, p. 37). For example, some men denigrate and physically attack other men perceived to be gay as a means of establishing membership among groups of higher-status, heterosexual men (Parrott, 2008). In negotiating this perilous landscape of masculinities, the male body is often used as a vehicle. The comments of one man in prison illustrate how the male body can be used in structuring gender and power:

> I have been shot and stabbed. Each time I wore bandages like a badge of honor.… Each situation made me feel a little more tougher than the next guy.… Being that I had survived, these things made me feel bigger because I could imagine that the average person couldn't go through a shoot out or a knife fight, survive and get right back into the action like it was nothing. The perception that I had constructed in my mind was that most people were discouraged after almost facing death, but the really bad ones could look death in the eye with little or no compunction. (Courtenay & Sabo, 2001, p. 165)

Physical dominance and violence are easily accessible resources for structuring, negotiating, and sustaining masculinities, particularly among men who because of their social positioning lack less dangerous means.

The health risks associated with any form of masculinity will differ depending on whether a man is enacting a hegemonic, subordinated, marginalized, complicit, or resistant form. When men and boys are denied access to the social power and resources necessary for constructing hegemonic masculinity, they must seek other resources for constructing gender that validate their masculinity (Messerschmidt, 1993). Disadvantages resulting from such factors as ethnicity, class, educational level, and sexual orientation marginalize certain men and augment the relevance of enacting other forms of masculinity. Rejecting health behaviors that are socially constructed as feminine, embracing risk, and demonstrating fearlessness are readily accessible means of enacting masculinity. Messerschmidt (1993) notes that "participation in street violence, a more frequent practice when other hegemonic masculine ideals are unavailable (e.g., a job in the paid-labor market), demonstrates to closest friends that one is 'a man'" (p. 110)—or as one young man reported, "If somebody picks on you or something, and you don't fight back, they'll call you a chicken. But … if you fight back … you're cool" (Majors & Billson, 1992, p. 26). Among some African American men and boys, "toughness, violence, and disregard of death and danger become the hallmark of survival in a world that does not respond to reasonable efforts to belong and achieve" (Majors & Billson, 1992, p. 34). The results of one small study suggest that toughness and aggression are indeed means for young inner-city African American men to gain status in communities where few other means of doing so are available: "If a young man is a 'tough guy,' peers respect him.… The highest value is placed on individuals who defend themselves swiftly, even if by doing so they place themselves in danger" (Rich & Stone, 1996, p. 81). Gay and bisexual men or boys may also attempt to compensate by endangering themselves or by adopting physically dominant behaviors rather than being relegated to a lower-status position. As one man put it, "I really hated football, but I tried to play because it would make me more of a man" (Fellows, 1996, p. 40). Gay men may also refuse to engage in behavior that reduces the risk of contracting HIV disease when that behavior contradicts dominant norms of masculinity: "Real men ignore precautions for HIV disease risk reduction, seek many sexual partners, and reject depleasuring the penis. Abstinence, safer sex, and safer drug use compromise manhood" (Levine, 1998; pp. 146–147). Among gay men and other men who have sex with men, a large body of research shows that African Americans—who are already consigned to a subordinated status based on their ethnicity—are less likely than other men who have sex with men to identify as gay (Millett, Peterson, Wolitski, & Stall, 2006), which would only serve to further reduce their status among men. However, there is also some evidence that the nondisclosure of sexual identity among African American men may increase their health risks associated with HIV (Millett et al., 2006).

Marginalized men may also attempt to compensate for their subordinated status by defying hegemonic masculinity and constructing alternative forms of masculinity. As Pyke (1996) explains, men "with their masculine identity and self-esteem undermined by their subordinate order-taking position in relation to higher-status males" can and do use other resources to "reconstruct their position as embodying *true* masculinity" (p. 531; emphasis added). Other authors have variously referred to these alternative enactments of gender as *oppositional* (Messerschmidt, 1993), *compulsive* (Majors & Billson, 1992), *compensatory* (Pyke, 1996), or *protest* (Connell, 1995) masculinities. These "hypermasculine" constructions are frequently dangerous or self-destructive (Meinecke, 1981). Majors and Billson (1992) suggest that compulsive masculinity can "lead toward smoking, drug and alcohol abuse, fighting, sexual conquests, dominance, and crime" (p. 34). Pyke (1996) describes lower-class men who "ostentatiously pursued drugs, alcohol, and sexual carousing … [to compensate] for their subordinated status in the hierarchy of their everyday work worlds" (p. 538). Similarly, working-class men can and do "use the physical endurance and tolerance of discomfort required of their manual labor as signifying true masculinity, [as] an alternative to the hegemonic form" (Pyke, 1996, p. 531). When the demonstration of the (dominant) heterosexist ideal is not an option—as among gay men—dismissing the risks associated with high numbers of sexual partners or unprotected anal intercourse can serve for some men as a means of demonstrating a protest masculinity. In describing coming out gay, one young man said, "Rage, rage, rage! Let's do everything you've denied yourself for 25 years. Let's get into it and have a good time sexually" (Connell, 1995, p. 153). Research of gay and bisexual men reveals that those men who endorse traditional notions of masculinity (e.g., "sexual performance is an important part of masculinity," "a masculine man has lots of sex," and "sex is a celebration of masculinity") are more likely than men who do not to engage in intentional unprotected anal sex—or "barebacking" (Halkitis & Parsons, 2003; Halkitis, Parsons, & Wilton, 2003). It is important to note that although these hypermasculinities may aspire to or be complicit in the reconstruction of an idealized form of masculinity, they are not hegemonic. The fact that some inner-city African American men are successful in being "tough" or "cool," and that some gay men refuse to have protected sex, does not mean that these men are enacting hegemonic masculinity. On the contrary, for marginalized men, "the claim to power that is central in hegemonic masculinity is constantly negated" (Connell, 1995, p. 116).

Like unhealthy behaviors, dominant or idealized beliefs about manhood also provide the means for demonstrating gender. These signifiers of "true" masculinity are readily accessible to men who may otherwise have limited social resources for constructing masculinity. In fact, among young men nationally, lower educational level, lower family income, and African American ethnicity are all associated with traditional, dominant norms of masculinity (Courtenay, 1998b). The stronger endorsement of traditional masculine ideology among African American men than among non–African American men is a consistent finding (Levant & Majors, 1998; Levant, Majors, & Kelley, 1998; Pleck et al., 1994b). Among African American men, the endorsement of dominant norms of masculinity has been found to be stronger for both younger, less educated, nonprofessional men than it is for older, better-educated, professional men (Harris, Torres, & Allender, 1994; Hunter & Davis, 1992).

Gay and bisexual men may also adopt culturally sanctioned beliefs about masculinity to compensate for their subordinated and less privileged social position. National data indicate that young men in the United States who are not exclusively heterosexual hold more traditional or dominant beliefs about masculinity than young men who are exclusively heterosexual (Courtenay, 1998b). Although this finding may at first glance appear counterintuitive, it is consistent with a constructionist theory of men's health. The endorsement of hypermasculine beliefs can be understood as a means for gay and bisexual men to prove to others that, despite their sexual preferences, they are still "real" men. Diaz (1998) also maintains that gay Latino men are more compelled to demonstrate dominant norms of masculinity than nongay Latino men.

A large body of research provides evidence that men who endorse dominant norms of masculinity engage in poorer health behaviors and have greater health risks than their peers with less traditional beliefs (see Chapter 1). One longitudinal study of 1,676 young men in the United States, aged 15 to 23 years, is among the few nationally representative studies to examine the influence of masculinity on health behavior over time (Courtenay, 1998b). When a variety of psychosocial factors were controlled for, beliefs about masculinity emerged as the strongest predictor of risk-taking behavior 2.5 years later. Dominant norms of masculinity—the most traditional beliefs about manhood adopted by young men—predicted the highest level of risk taking and of involvement in behaviors such as cigarette smoking, high-risk sexual activity, and use of alcohol and other drugs.

This feminist structural framework for understanding men's health may help to explain the many health differences found among men based on their ethnicity, socioeconomic status, and education (see Chapter 1 and Section III). It may help to explain, for example, why U.S. men with the least education have been found to be twice as likely to smoke cigarettes as the most highly educated men, and nearly 3 times more likely to report frequent heavy alcohol use, as well as why their death rate for injuries is nearly 3.5 times higher and (among those 25 to 44 years of age) their death rate for homicide is 7 times higher (Department of Health and Human Services [DHHS], 1998a).

Rethinking Compulsive, Oppositional, Compensatory, and Protest Masculinities

The terms *compulsive, oppositional, compensatory,* and *protest* masculinities can be somewhat misleading. *Most* men are compulsive in demonstrating masculinity, which, as Connell (1995) notes, is continually contested. Furthermore, *most* masculinities that men demonstrate in the United States are oppositional or compensatory; relatively few men construct the hegemonic masculine ideal. This is not to suggest, however, that hegemonic masculinity is not profoundly influential. On the contrary, hegemonic masculinity is a ubiquitous aspect of U.S. life. Most men necessarily demonstrate alternative masculinities in relation to hegemonic masculinity that variously aspire to, conspire with, or attempt to resist, diminish, or otherwise undermine hegemonic masculinity. They do this not only in relation to other men perceived to embody hegemonic ideals, but also in relation to institutionalized, hegemonic social structures—including the government and media, the judicial system, corporate and technological industries, and academia. However, to suggest that only certain men are compulsive in demonstrating dominant norms of masculinity is to risk further marginalizing the subordinated masculinities of lower-class, non–European American, nonheterosexual men. Masculinity *requires* compulsive practice because it can be contested and undermined at any moment.

Whichever term one chooses to use to describe masculinities that resist (or undermine) hegemonic masculinity, it is critical to distinguish among various forms of resistant masculinity. In terms of men's health, the risks associated with enacting gender can differ greatly among different forms of resistant masculinity. Gay men who identify as *radical fairies* (Rose, 1997) and pacifists provide two examples of men who actively undermine hegemonic masculinity. These men are enacting very different resistant masculinities than those enacted by inner-city gang members, who are constructing an alternate *yet still authoritative and dominant* form of masculinity. Indeed, when lower-class men who lack access to cultural or economic resources attempt to demonstrate power and authority through the use of physical violence, it could be argued that they are not enacting a "compensatory" form of masculinity, but rather a form of *situational or interpersonal hegemony*. Furthermore, the resistant masculinities demonstrated by pacifists, radical fairies, and inner-city gang members lead to very different levels and categories of health risk; the masculinities enacted by radical fairies and pacifists may in fact reduce their risks, unlike those forms requiring the use of physical dominance or violence.

Further Contextualizing Men's Health

As Messerschmidt (1993) notes, "Although men attempt to express hegemonic masculinity through speech, dress, physical appearance, activities, and relations with others, these social signs of masculinity are associated with the specific context of one's actions and are self-regulated within that context" (p. 83). Because masculinity is continually contested, it must renegotiated in each context that a man encounters. A man or boy will enact gender and health differently in different contexts. On the football field, a college student may use exposure to injury and denial of pain to demonstrate masculinity, whereas at parties he may use excessive drinking to achieve the same end. A man may consider the expression of emotional or physical pain to be unacceptable with other men but acceptable with a spouse or girlfriend. In some contexts, such as a prison setting (see Chapter 7), the hierarchies of masculinities are unique to that particular context.

Farm life provides a context within which to examine the negotiation of one form of rural masculinity. Growing up on a farm, much of what boys learn to do to demonstrate hegemonic masculinity requires them to adopt risky or unhealthy behaviors, such as operating heavy equipment before they are old enough to do so safely. As two rural men said, "If you're over ten, you'd better be out doing men's work, driving a tractor and that kind of thing" (Fellows, 1996, p. 173); and, "My brother Tony and I started driving the pickup on the farm at age six, as soon as we could reach the pedals. We also learned how to drive a tractor" (Fellows, 1996, p. 305). Another rural man describes similar expectations: "If you were a guy ... you were born to be a total, typical, straight male—to play sports, to hunt, to do everything a guy was supposed to do" (Fellows, 1996, p. 307). The ways to enact masculinity are dictated in part by cultural norms, such as the belief held by most Pennsylvanians that "farmers *embody* the virtues of independence and self-sufficiency" (Willits, Bealer, & Timbers, 1990, p. 572; emphasis added). Farmers who attempt to demonstrate this cultural ideal of masculinity undermine their health—and there are many such farmers. Among Wisconsin residents who had suffered agricultural injuries—most of whom were men—farmers were the most likely to delay seeking health care; half of them waited for more than 2 hours, and one in four waited 24 hours (Stueland et al., 1995). Long (1993) described a farmer who caught his finger in equipment while harvesting his wheat field; he pulled his finger out—severing it—wrapped his hand in a handkerchief, and finished his work for the day before seeking medical care.

It has been emphasized elsewhere (Courtenay & Sabo, 2001; Rich & Stone, 1996) that the negotiation of masculinity in certain contexts can present men with unique health paradoxes, particularly in regard to physical dominance and the use of violence. The perception both among some men in prison (see Chapter 7) and some inner-city African American men (Rich & Stone, 1996) is that failing to fight back makes a man vulnerable to even more extreme victimization than does retaliating. This health paradox is reflected in the "protective, though violent, posture" described by Rich and Stone (1996): "If you appear weak, others will try to victimize you ... if you show yourself to be strong (by retaliating), then you are perceived as strong and you will be safe" (pp. 80–81). Although these men neither actively resist nor demonstrate hegemonic masculinity, they are complicit in its reconstruction.

Institutional Structures, Masculinities, and Men's Health

The institutionalized social structures that men encounter elicit different demonstrations of health-related beliefs and behaviors, and provide different opportunities to conduct this particular means of enacting gender. These structures—including the government and the military, corporations, the technological and health care industries, the judicial system, academia, health care, and the media—help to sustain gendered health risks by cultivating stereotypic forms of gender enactments and by providing different resources for demonstrating gender to women than they provide to men. Institutional structures, by and large, foster unhealthy beliefs and behaviors among men, and undermine men's attempts to adopt healthier habits (Courtenay, 2000c, 2002).

The workforce is one such structure. It has been previously noted that the traditional "provider" role of men puts them at greater risk than women for premature death that results from accidents and exposure to occupational hazards (Doyal, 2000; Waldron, 1983). The work that men do is the most dangerous work. As I discuss in Chapters 1 and 2, mining, construction, timber cutting, and fishing have the highest injury death rates in the United States, and the largest number of total injury deaths occur in production, craft and repair, transportation, labor, farming, foresting, and fishing—all of which are jobs held primarily by men. Consequently—although they comprise only half (53%) of the U.S. workforce—men account for nearly all (93%) fatal injuries on the job. Furthermore, as one small study found, positive health-related activities often conflict with the work activities expected of men—and work is typically given precedence, as evidenced by one man's comments: "I'd do more [to be healthy], but I can't with my job hours. My boss at the lab would kill me" (Saltonstall, 1993, p. 11). When a corporate law firm requires its employees to work 12- to 14-hour days, it is limiting access to health care for its (primarily male) attorneys.

Although they have a profound influence on men's health, institutional structures are not simply imposed on men any more than a prescribed male sex role is simply imposed on men. "Social structures do not exist autonomously from humans; rather ... as we engage in social action, we simultaneously help create the social structures that facilitate/limit social practice" (Messerschmidt, 1993, p. 62). Men are agents of social practice. When men demonstrate gender "correctly," in the ways that are socially prescribed, they "simultaneously sustain, reproduce, and render legitimate the institutional arrangements that are based on sex category" (West & Zimmerman, 1987, p. 146). In a continuous cycle, definitions of gender influence social structures, which guide human interactions and social action, which in turn reinforce gendered social structures. This ongoing process results in a gender division and a differential exposure that inhibits both women and men from learning behaviors, skills, and capacities considered characteristic of the "opposite" gender (Epstein, 1988; West & Zimmerman, 1987). Men sustain and reproduce institutional structures in part for the privileges that they derive from preserving existing power structures. The businessman who works tirelessly, denies his stress, and dismisses his physical needs for sleep and a healthy diet often does so because he expects to be rewarded with money, power, position, and prestige. Thus, although they are increasing their health risks, men who achieve these hegemonic ideals are compensated with social acceptance, with diminished anxiety about their manhood, and with the rewards that such normative, masculine demonstrations provide in a patriarchal society.

In these regards, men also contribute to the construction of a health care system that ignores their gendered health concerns. Indeed, they are often the very researchers and scientists who have ignored men's gendered health risks. As Assistant Surgeon General Susan Blumenthal, who directs the Office on Women's Health at the U.S. Public Health Service, noted, "Men need to become advocates and speak passionately about their health, but they may be concerned that speaking out will reveal weakness, not strength" (Jaffe, 1997, p. 136). As Coward (1984) notes, men have kept their bodies from being the subjects of analysis: "Men's bodies and sexuality are taken for granted, exempted from scrutiny, whereas women's are extensively defined and overexposed. Sexual and social meanings are imposed on women's bodies, not men's ... men have left themselves out of the picture because a body defined is a body controlled" (p. 229).

The Medical Institution and Its Constructions of Gender and Health

In Chapter 3, I demonstrate that the health care system and its allied health fields represent a particularly important structural influence in the construction of men's and women's health behavior. Whereas the personal practice of participating in health care is constructed as feminine, the institutional practice of conducting, researching, and providing health care is constructed as masculine and defined as a domain of masculine power. Physicians, who are primarily men, maintain power and control over the bodies of men who are not physicians and the bodies of women—as well as over male and female health professionals in lesser positions of power, such as nurses and orderlies. In these ways, the health care system does not simply adapt to men's "natural" masculinity; rather, it actively constructs gendered health behavior and negotiates among various forms of masculinity. Medical, sociological, and feminist approaches to addressing gender and health have all contributed to the devaluing of women's bodies and to the privileging of men's bodies, as two feminist authors have noted (Annandale & Clark, 1996).

Despite countless examples in research, literature, and daily life, the poor health beliefs and behaviors that men use to demonstrate gender remain largely invisible—a testament to the potency of the social construction of men's resiliency and health. Medical and epidemiological examinations of health and health behavior consistently fail to take into account gender, apart from biological sex. For example, although men's greater use of substances is well known, the reasons *why* men are more likely to use substances are poorly understood and rarely addressed. Similarly, although injury and death resulting from recreation, risk taking, and violence are always associated with being male, epidemiological and medical findings are consistently presented as though *gender* were of no particular relevance. Few health scientists, sociologists, and theorists identify masculinities—and rarely even male sex—as a risk factor; fewer still have attempted to identify what it is about men, exactly, that leads them to engage in behaviors that seriously threaten their health. Instead, men's risk taking and violence are taken for granted.

The failure of medical and epidemiological researchers to study and explain men's risk taking and violence perpetuates the false, yet widespread, cultural assumption that risk taking and violent behaviors are natural to, or inherent in, men. Similarly, cultural assumptions that men simply do not (read, inherently) seek help prevent society from defining men's underutilization of health services as a problem. Although it too is taken for granted, there is nothing natural about the fact that men make fewer health visits than women. Early in their lives, most adolescent girls in the United States are *taught* the importance of regular physical examinations and are introduced to them as a part of being a woman; adolescent boys are not taught that physical examinations are part of being a man. Furthermore, for many men, it is their wives, girlfriends, and mothers who monitor their health and schedule any medical appointments that they have. Men who want to take greater responsibility for their health will need not only to cross gendered boundaries but also to learn new skills. Gendered health perspectives that address social structural issues and masculinity are similarly absent from health science research and literature. Such perspectives could, for example, use a gendered approach to examining men's work and their far greater exposure to industrial carcinogens as a possible explanation for their greater risk of cancer compared with women.

The Social Construction of Disease

Depression provides one example of how the health care system contributes to the social construction of disease. Despite suicide rates that are 2 to 18 times higher for men than for women in the United States (see Chapter 1, Table 1.2), according to Warren (1983), early documentation on the prevalence of depression among women based on self-reporting has resulted in an emphasis on treating women for depression and suggested an immunity to depression among men. Although young men account for five of six suicides among those 15 to 24 years old (DHHS, 2009b)—an age group in which suicide is the third leading cause of death—one large study based exclusively on self-report data concluded that depression is a "more critical" health problem for college women than for college men (Sax, 1997, p. 261). This study fails to take into account men's suicides in this age group. It also disregards decades of research that have consistently found a lack of significant sex differences in *diagnosable* depression among college students (Courtenay, 1998a; Nolen-Hoeksema, 1987; see also Chapter 6).

Treatment rates are also used as indicators of morbidity. However, because depressed men have been found to be more likely than depressed women to not seek help (see Chapter 2), treatment rates are likewise an inaccurate measure of depression. Gender-biased diagnostic decisions of mental health clinicians also contribute to inaccuracies in morbidity statistics (see Chapter 1). Research consistently shows that clinicians are less likely to correctly diagnose depression in men than in women, even when men have similar depression scores and symptoms.

Although the failure among clinicians to diagnose depression in men contributes to men's low treatment rates, men's own unwillingness to seek help contributes to the social construction of their invulnerability to depression. Indeed, in response to depression, men are more likely than women to rely on themselves, to withdraw socially, to try to talk themselves out of depression, or to convince themselves that depression is "stupid" (see Chapter 2). Nearly half of men over age 49 nationally who reported experiencing an extended depression did not discuss it with anyone (American Medical Association, 1991b). Instead, men tend to engage in private activities, including drinking and drug use, designed to distract themselves or to alleviate their depression (see Chapter 2). Denial of depression is one of the means men use to demonstrate masculinities and to avoid assignment to a lower-status position relative to women and other men. As Warren (1983) notes, "The linkage between depression and femininity may provide men with the strongest motivation to hide their depression from others," and, "Because depression is frequently accompanied by feelings of powerlessness and diminished control, men may construe depression as a sign of failure" (p. 151).

CONCLUSION

If men want to enact dominant ideals of manhood, they must adhere to cultural definitions of masculine beliefs and behaviors and actively reject what is feminine. The resources available for constructing masculinity as defined in U.S. society are largely unhealthy, and men and boys do indeed use these resources to construct gender and signify manhood. By successfully using unhealthy beliefs and behaviors to demonstrate idealized forms of masculinity, men are able to assume positions of power—relative to women and less powerful men—in a patriarchal society that rewards this accomplishment. By dismissing their health needs and taking risks, men legitimize themselves as the "stronger" sex. In this way, men's use of unhealthy beliefs and behaviors helps to sustain and reproduce social inequality and the social structures that, in turn, reinforce and reward men's poor health habits. As I discussed in the preceding chapter, some men do defy these social prescriptions of masculinity and adopt healthy behaviors. However, these men are not demonstrating the dominant forms of masculinity that are encouraged in men, nor are they the forms most men strive to attain.

This theory of gender and men's health will undoubtedly meet with resistance from some quarters. As a society, we all work diligently at maintaining constructions of women's health as deficient, of the female body as inferior, of men's health as ideal, and of the male body as structurally efficient and superior. From a feminist perspective, these constructions can be viewed as preserving existing power structures and the many privileges enjoyed by men in the United States. Naming and confronting men's poor health status and unhealthy beliefs and behaviors may well improve their physical well-being, but it will necessarily undermine men's privileged position and threaten their power and authority in relation to women.

Specific Populations

INTRODUCTION

In this section of the book, I more closely examine the health needs of specific populations of men. I open with an article titled "Ethnicity Matters." Indeed, ethnicity—along with socioeconomic status—is strongly linked with health disparities among men, as I discussed in Chapters 1 and 2. African American men, for example, die 6 years younger than European American men. There are a number of additional factors that influence health and that differ among men. I examine these factors in this introduction and in the next three chapters.

ETHNICITY MATTERS[*]

Just as there are enormous health disparities between men and women, there are also enormous health disparities among men (Rich & Ro, 2002; Ro, Casares, Treadwell, & Thomas, 2004; White & Cash, 2003). Men are a heterogeneous group; their life experiences and health can vary dramatically based on ethnicity (e.g., Barnett et al., 2001). While men of color are exposed to many of the same underlying factors that contribute to poor health among men in general, their risks are often compounded by additional social, economic, and political factors (Bobak & Marmot, 1996; Gornick, 2003; Rich & Ro, 2002; Ro et al., 2004; Smith, 2003; Waldron, 2008). Health needs, coping styles, barriers to care, and care received also vary among diverse populations of men (e.g., Borowsky et al., 2000; Canto et al., 2000; Devgan, Yu, Kim, & Coleman, 2000; Giles et al., 1995; Gornick, 2003; Lew & Tanjasiri, 2003; Lowe et al., 2001; Peterson, Folkman, & Bakeman, 1996; Rhoades, 2003; Vaccarino et al., 2005 Whitfield, Weidner, Clark, & Anderson, 2002). In

---

[*] An earlier version of this article appeared in *Social Work Today*, 1(8), 2000, 20–22, and is used by permission.

this introduction to Section III, I discuss some of the important differences among men.

ETHNIC DIFFERENCES IN DEATH RATES AND LEADING CAUSES OF DEATH

The deaths of men of color account for much of the gender difference in mortality. In the United States, the difference between the life expectancies of African American men and European American men exceeds the difference between the life expectancies of women and men; on average, African American men die 6 years younger than European American men (Department of Health and Human Services [DHHS], 2009a). Similarly, American Indians and Alaska Natives have higher age-adjusted death rates than European Americans for 5 of the 15 leading causes of death. The largest disparities are for chronic liver disease and cirrhosis, homicide, diabetes, and unintentional injuries; for these causes, the death rates for American Indian and Alaska Native men are 1.5 to 2 times higher than the death rates for European American men (DHHS, 2009a).

There are other important differences in mortality and in the leading causes of death among men of various ethnicities. The biggest difference with respect to life span is that between African Americans and Asians or Pacific Islanders; the risk of death for African American men is nearly 2.5 times greater than Asian and Pacific Islander men (DHHS, 2009a). The death rate for unintentional injuries among American Indian and Alaska Native men is higher than it is for any other ethnic group—ranging from nearly 1.5 times higher than that for European American men to 3.5 times higher than that for Asian and Pacific Islander men (DHHS, 2009a). The death rate for motor vehicle–related deaths among American Indian and Alaska Native men is nearly twice as high as the rate for European American and African American men (Centers for Disease Control and Prevention [CDC], 2009c). HIV disease is among the five leading causes of death for African American and Latino men (DHHS, 2009a), but it is not even among the top 10 leading causes for any other ethnic group of men (CDC, 2006b). African American men are 8 times more likely than European American men to die from HIV disease, and 24 times more likely to die than Asian and Pacific Islander men (DHHS, 2009a). Similarly, homicide ranks among the five leading causes of death only for African American men (DHHS, 2009a)—not for men of other ethnic groups. Stroke ranks as the third leading cause of death among Asian American men but not among men of any other ethnic group, for whom injuries are a greater risk (DHHS, 2009a).

There are also important differences between men of various ethnic groups based on their age. Among men aged 65 years or older, diabetes is the fourth leading killer in all ethnic groups except for European American men, for whom diabetes is not even among the five leading killers (DHHS, 2007b). Among men aged 15 to 34 years, accidents are the leading cause of death with the exception of African American men, for whom homicide is the leading killer (DHHS, 2007b). Homicide is the second leading killer for Latino men in this age group but not for men of any other ethnic group (DHHS, 2007b). Among 25- to 34-year-old men, heart disease is the third leading killer only for African Americans and Asians or Pacific Islanders, homicide is the third leading killer for American Indian and Alaska Native men, and suicide is the third leading killer for Latino men. However, the heart disease death rate for African American men is nearly 4 times higher than the heart disease death rate for Asian and Pacific Islander men (DHHS, 2007b).

UTILIZATION OF HEALTH CARE

Ethnicity is also associated with the utilization of health care. Although one of three men—on average—has no regular physician, more Latinos (55%) and African Americans (45%) than European Americans (33%) report having no regular doctor (Sandman, Simantov, & An, 2000). Asian American men use significantly fewer health care services, and use these services less frequently, than European American men and U.S. men of other ethnic groups (Myers, Kagawa-Singer, Kumanyika, Lex, & Markides, 1995; Ray-Mazumder, 2001). Despite their high risks, Latino and African American men are less likely than European American men to have a usual source of health care; only 62% of Latino men and 78% of African American men have one compared with 92% of European American men (DHHS, 2007a). They are also less likely to see a physician regularly; 55% of Latino men and 45% of African American men do not do so compared with 33% of European American men. Among adolescent boys nationally in grades 5 through 12, more Asian (30%), Latino (27%), and African Americans (25%) than European Americans (17%) report having no regular source of health care (Schoen et al., 1998). Among men aged 65 years or older, African Americans and Latino Americans are twice as likely as European Americans to report not having seen a physician in the past 2 years, regardless of economic factors that can influence access (Dunlop, Manheim, Song, & Chang, 2002).

QUALITY OF HEALTH CARE

When a man does receive health care, the quality of care that he receives also differs based on his ethnicity. Ethnicity influences the type of medical treatments a man receives (e.g., Bach, Pham, Schrag, Tate, & Hargraves, 2004; Canto et al., 2000; Devgan et al., 2000; Felix-Aaron et al., 2005; Giles et al., 1995; Vaccarino et al., 2005) and his satisfaction with health care (e.g., Cooper-Patrick et al., 1999; Ray-Mazumder, 2001). Asian Americans—particularly Chinese and Korean Americans—express the least satisfaction, citing unresponsiveness and cultural insensitivity on the part of clinicians as the primary problem (Commonwealth Fund, 1995; Ray-Mazumder, 2001). Men also have different experiences within various systems of health care—such as emergency room care (e.g., Lowe et al., 2001) or U.S. Medicare services (Canto et al., 2000; Devgan et al., 2000)—based on their ethnicity. In the United States, African American men are less likely than European American men to receive certain specific treatments or clinical procedures for coronary heart disease (Canto et al., 2000; Giles et al., 1995; Vaccarino et al., 2005), to be prescribed a potentially life-saving medication for ischemic stroke (Johnston et al., 2001), to receive surgery for glaucoma (Devgan et al., 2000), or to receive quality end-stage renal disease care (Felix-Aaron et al., 2005). They are also more likely to be denied insurance authorization for emergency treatment than are European American men (Lowe et al., 2001). In terms of mental health care, clinicians are less likely to diagnose mental health problems correctly among both African Americans and Latino Americans than among European Americans (Borowsky et al., 2000).

Not surprisingly, African American men report being more dissatisfied with their care by doctors and hospitals than European Americans (Blendon, Aiken, Freeman, & Corey, 1989; Cooper-Patrick et al., 1999; LaVeist, Nickerson, & Bowie, 2000; Musa, Schulz, Harris, Silverman, & Thomas, 2009; Powell-Hammond, Matthews, & Corbie-Smith, 2010). They also rate their doctors and their doctors' decision-making styles as less participatory than do European American men (Cooper-Patrick et al., 1999). Nor is it surprising that fewer African American men—and Latino men—say they trust doctors compared with European American men (Boulware, Cooper, Ratner, LaVeist, & Powe, 2003; Corbie-Smith, Thomas, & St. George, 2002; Gamble, 1997; Hall, Dugan,

Zheng, & Mishra, 2001; LaVeist et al., 2000; Lillie-Blanton, Brodie, Rowland, Altman, & McIntosh, 2000; Petersen, 2002; Powell-Hamond, Matthews, & Corbie-Smith, 2010).

HEALTH-RELATED BEHAVIORS
AND PREVENTIVE CARE

Men of color are less likely than White men to practice self-examination or to attend health screenings for a variety of diseases that frequently kill men (Solis, Marks, Garcia, & Shelton, 1990). Among men in the United States, Latino Americans are significantly less likely than European Americans to have had their blood pressure measured in the past 2 years or cholesterol measured in the past 5 years (Stewart & Silverstein, 2002); they are also less likely than other ethnic groups of men to be screened for colorectal cancer (with either the fecal occult blood test, colonoscopy, or sigmoidoscopy), prostate cancer (with the prostate-specific antigen [PSA] test) (Babey et al., 2003; CDC, 2004b; Felix-Aaron et al., 2005; Huerta, 2003; O'Brien et al., 2003), or cardiovascular disease (Felix-Aaron et al., 2005). Along with Latinos, Asians and Pacific Islanders are the least likely groups of men to be screened for prostate cancer (with the PSA test) and cholesterol (Babey et al., 2003; CDC, 2005f). Asian American and African American men are also significantly less likely to have received a variety of preventive services and screenings (Felix-Aaron et al., 2005). For example, compared with European Americans, Asian American and Pacific Islander men are less likely to have had their blood pressure measured recently (Stewart & Silverstein, 2002), and— among men over age 65—African Americans are less likely to undergo prostate cancer screening (Fowke, Schlundt, Signorello, Ukoli, & Blot, 2005; Gilligan, Wang, Levin, Kantoff, & Avorn, 2004). There are also differences among various ethnic subgroups within broader categories of men of color. Among "Black" men, for example, prostate cancer screening has been found to be lower among Haitian men than Caribbean, Dominican, Puerto Rican, or African American men (Consedine, Morgenstern, Kudadjie-Gyamfi, Magai, & Neugut, 2006). These screenings are critical for identifying prostate cancer early, when it can be more effectively treated.

Men of color are also less likely to practice self-examinations. Among adolescent boys, for example, African Americans are less likely than European Americans to practice testicular self-examination (Ward, Vander Weg, Read, Sell, & Beech, 2005). Consequently, African Americans are significantly less likely than

European Americans to be diagnosed with testicular cancer when the cancer is localized, and, conversely, they are more likely to have malignant tumors that have spread (Sokoloff, Joyce, & Wise, 2007). Similarly, Latino Americans are less likely than European Americans to practice self-examinations for skin cancer (Friedman et al., 1994; Oliveria et al., 1999; Rouhani, Hu, & Kirsner, 2008). Self-examinations are particularly important for men. Because they seldom visit physicians, self-examination is the only way most men will detect a variety of diseases while those diseases are still curable. The failure among Latino men to practice skin examinations helps to explain why melanoma in Latino men is diagnosed so late that it is often fatal (Rouhani et al., 2008).

RACIAL OR ETHNIC DISCRIMINATION

Discrimination and cultural stereotypes or misperceptions about various ethnic groups can undermine the health of members of these groups in a variety of ways. Both interpersonal discrimination (e.g., Williams, 1999) and societal or structural discrimination (e.g., Bach et al., 2004; Epstein, 2004) have been shown to contribute to the large disparities in the health of African Americans and European Americans. Even presumably "positive" misperceptions can be detrimental. For example, the stereotype that Asian Americans are the "model minority" can blind health professionals and society at large to the health risks of Asian Americans (Chen & Hawks, 1995; Constantine, Kindaichi, Okazaki, Gainor, & Baden, 2005). Indeed, there is a tendency among both policy makers and researchers to assume that Asian Americans are healthier than other racial or ethnic groups (Myers et al., 1995). This assumption—based also on the fact that Asian Americans use fewer health care services (Myers et al., 1995)—is not completely unfounded; Asian Americans have the lowest death rates of any racial or ethnic group in the United States (Collins et al., 1999; DHHS, 2009a). However, there can be large differences among various groups of Asian Americans—differences that get lost in aggregated data (Lew & Tanjasiri, 2003).

The Asian American and Pacific Islander population comprises the fastest-growing ethnic group in the United States (U.S. Bureau of the Census, 2001, 2002). It is also a complex ethnic group, made up of more than 40 diverse ethnic and language subgroups. These diverse groups can have quite different diets and quite different health practices. Among Asian American youth, substance use can also vary among subgroups, with greater use among Pacific Islanders, Filipinos, and Southeast Asians than among Chinese,

Japanese, and Korean Americans (Harachi, Catalano, Kim, & Choi, 2001). A large study of ethnically diverse students in public universities, conducted by my colleagues and myself, revealed that Asian Americans were significantly less likely than every other ethnic group to engage in preventive health behaviors (see Chapter 8). Furthermore, Asian Americans were at greater risk than European Americans and Latino Americans for unhealthy behaviors related to anger and stress, and held riskier health-related beliefs than either Latinos or respondents of mixed heritage. However, there were differences among Asians as well; Filipino Americans had significantly healthier beliefs and behaviors than either Chinese or Vietnamese Americans. These data suggest that if the health beliefs and behaviors of Asian Americans do not change— particularly among men—their current mortality advantage is likely to decrease in the future. Similarly, if the current trends in high rates of smoking among various groups of Asian Americans continue, mortality rates from lung and heart diseases—particularly for Southeast Asian American men—will likely surpass those for other racial and ethnic groups (Chae, Gavin, & Takeuchi, 2006; Chen, 1993; Lew & Tanjasiri, 2003). Nearly 3 times more Asian American men (42%) than women (15%) have ever smoked (Chae et al., 2006), and nearly three of four Laotian men in the United States smoke cigarettes, compared with one in four men in general (Lew & Tanjasiri, 2003; Moeschberger et al., 1997).

MASCULINITIES

As I discussed in the preceding chapters, men demonstrate a variety of masculinities. These masculinities derive from cultural, ethnic, and subjective meanings that shift and vary over time and geography (Kimmel, 1995; Lazur & Majors, 1995; Rotundo, 1993). There is tremendous variation, in general, within what appear to be monolithic ethnic groups. As I noted above, "Asian" men in the United States represent more than 40 subgroups, and these men originate from countries and cultures as diverse as China, Korea, Japan, Taiwan, Thailand, the Philippines, Vietnam, Laos, and Cambodia. Similarly, Hispanic and Latino men can originate from Cuba, Puerto Rico, the Dominican Republic, Mexico, and a variety of countries in South America. These Latino cultures can vary widely, and men from these cultures can often hold very different ideas about manhood.

Latino masculinity—or *machismo*—for example, is often defined by characteristics such as strength, male dominance, and being a successful provider and protector of the family (Sue &

Sue, 2003), as well as by exaggerated, hypermasculine behaviors, such as heavy drinking, toughness, aggressiveness, and risk taking (Boulding, 1990; Mosher, 1991). However, far more nuanced and complex descriptions of the qualities or attributes associated with *machismo* have also been found (Mirandé, 1997; Torres, 1998). Among Chicano and Latino American men, these include emotionally responsive, collaborative, and flexible forms of *machismo* (Torres, Solberg, Scott, & Carlstrom, 2002), which incorporate such characteristics as *respeto* (respect), *dignidad* (dignity), *personalismo* (relating to others), *afecto* (affection), and *marianismo* (which means the opposite of *machismo*, specifically, femininity in Latinas) (Torres, 1998); culturally desirable and valued ideals of masculinity that include courage, honor, physical strength, and authority (Abreu, Goodyear, Campos, & Newcomb, 2000; Lazur & Majors, 1995; Mirandé, 1997); and *caballerismo*, which represents nurturance, family centeredness, and chivalrousness (Arciniega, Anderson, Tovar-Blank, & Tracey, 2008). Latino masculinity is further mediated by other sociocultural factors, such as sexual orientation; gay Latino men appear to endorse traditional masculinity more strongly than do nongay Latino men (Diaz, 1998).

TRADITIONAL OR DOMINANT NORMS OF MASCULINITY

Despite the sometimes broad range of differences in masculinities among men of various ethnic groups, there is strong support for dominant norms of masculinity among all groups of men. The support of these norms appears to be strongest among Latino men compared with African American and European American men (Abreu et al., 2000). Indeed, the strong endorsement of traditional masculinity—and even hypermasculinity—is a consistent finding among various populations of Latino and Chicano men (Abreu et al., 2000; Mirandé, 1997; Saez, Casado, & Wade, 2009; Torres et al., 2002), particularly Latino men with strong ethnic identities (Abreu et al., 2000; Saez et al., 2009). African American men also strongly endorse traditional masculine ideology—more strongly than European American men, according to many studies (Courtenay, 1998b; Levant, Richmond, et al., 2003; Levant & Majors, 1998; Levant, Majors, & Kelley, 1998; Pleck et al., 1994b), and, in one study, more strongly than Latino American men (Levant, Richmond, et al., 2003). However, among African American men—as well as Latino American men (Mirandé, 1997)—the endorsement of dominant norms of masculinity has been found to be stronger for younger, less educated, nonprofessional men than it is for older, better educated, professional men (Harris et al., 1994; Hunter & Davis, 1992). Regarding Asian American men, one study has shown that Chinese American men are less likely than men from China to endorse traditional masculinity (Levant, Wu, & Fisher, 1996). In addition, there is evidence that Chinese and Japanese American men differ from European American men in endorsing less dominant and more flexible forms of masculinity—forms that include, for example, willingness to do nurturing and domestic tasks (Chua & Fujino, 1999). Given the association between traditional masculinity and health risks, it is likely that these differences in masculinity help to explain why Asian American men live longer than men of other ethnic groups.

As I discussed in Chapter 1, dominant norms of masculinity are associated with risk-taking behavior, failure to engage in health-promoting practices, poor health, and death. One way that this occurs is that masculinity mediates other significant influences on men's health. The health advantages usually associated with higher socioeconomic status, for example, can be lost with men's endorsement of traditional masculinity. Therefore, any attempt to understand or to improve men's health must take masculinity into account, as well as the complex interactions among masculinity, ethnicity, and the various other factors that influence men's health.

5

Rural Men's Health

Situating Men's Risk
in the Negotiation
of Masculinity*

Rural men have greater health risks than both rural women and non-rural men. In this chapter, I use a social constructionist framework to examine the previously unexplored territory of rural men's health and to achieve two primary aims. First, I review available research regarding the health behaviors and risks of rural men and women and of various specific populations of men. Examining gender differences in social activities and experiences—as well as differences among men (Courtenay, 2000a)—can be a valuable social constructionist strategy. It illuminates the process by which biological sex is transformed into gender and demonstrates how power is negotiated and structured through everyday social actions (Crawford, 1995). Second, I discuss rural men's health beliefs and behavior as a form of gendered practice. I provide a conceptual and theoretical framework that shows how the social practices that undermine rural men's health are often signifiers of masculinity and the instruments men use in negotiating social power—not only in relation to women but also within hierarchies of men.

---

* An earlier version of this chapter appeared in H. Campbell, M. Mayerfeld-Bell, & M. Finney (Eds.). (2006). *Country boys: Masculinity and rural life* (pp. 139–158). University Park, PA: Pennsylvania State University Press, and is used by permission in modified/revised form.

MEN'S HEALTH

As I discussed in Chapter 1, in the United States[*] men die more than 5 years younger than women and are more likely to die from nearly all 15 leading causes of death. According to a recent study conducted by the U.S. Department of Agriculture (USDA, 2009), people who live in rural, nonmetropolitan areas have higher death rates, as well as more disability and chronic disease, than people who live in urban or metropolitan areas. Furthermore, the study reveals that these disparities have been steadily increasing since 1990. People who live in rural or nonmetropolitan areas, for example, are at greatest risk for heart disease—which is the leading killer (Barnett et al., 2001; Gillum, 1994; Mensah, Mokdad, Ford, Greenlund, & Croft, 2005; Pearson & Lewis, 1998). Similarly, death rates from stroke—the third leading cause of death for men—are also highest in the South (Glymour, Kosheleva, & Boden-Albala, 2009). Cancer is the second leading killer, and farmers are among those at greatest risk for developing certain types of cancer, such as leukemia, non-Hodgkin's lymphoma, melanoma, and cancer of the brain (Blair & Zahm, 1991; USDA, 2009). Rural men also have more health problems, in general, than urban men (Hayward, Pienta, & McLaughlin, 1997). As I identify in this chapter, these problems include risks associated with tobacco use and heavy drinking, as well as problems resulting from injuries. Most importantly, in regards to gender, rural men have higher death rates than rural women for all leading causes of death (Hessler, Jia, Madsen, & Pazaki, 1995; Smith, Anderson, Bradham, & Longino, 1995). But why?

The health and longevity of rural populations are both strongly influenced by social factors, such as access to care, economic status, and ethnicity (USDA, 2009). But, as I discussed in Chapter 1, neither these factors nor genetic and biological circumstances can explain gender differences in longevity. We can, however, explain some of the gender difference in mortality among rural populations in terms of health practices. There is substantial and compelling evidence that individual health practices are the most important factors influencing longevity, and that there are significant and consistent gender differences in health-related behavior. Indeed, as I demonstrated in Chapter 2, men and boys are more likely than women and girls to engage in more than 30 controllable behaviors conclusively linked to a greater risk for disease, injury, and death—a gender difference that remains true across a variety of ethnic groups (Courtenay, McCreary, & Merighi, 2002). Despite these findings, however, men's poor health practices are rarely addressed by health scientists. Consequently, we know little about *why* men—including rural men—adopt these unhealthy attitudes and behaviors.

---

[*] Unless otherwise noted, all studies and statistics refer to people in the United States.

RURAL MEN'S BEHAVIORS AND HEALTH BELIEFS, AND THE ASSOCIATED RISKS

In this chapter, I use both empirical and epidemiological studies from the health sciences to investigate rural men's health and health behavior as a form of gendered practice. This section reviews these studies, focusing on evidence of rural men's behaviors and health beliefs related to tobacco use, diet and physical activity, unintentional injuries, alcohol use, health care utilization and help seeking, social support, perceived susceptibility to risk, and beliefs about manhood, as well as the health risks associated with these behaviors and beliefs. Because research examining gender and the health behavior of rural populations is limited, this review incorporates data on a wide range of often diverse rural populations—such as nonmetropolitan and farm populations. Whenever possible, I make comparisons both with rural women and with men nationally because constructionist theorists are as concerned with differences among men (and among women) as they are with differences between women and men.

Tobacco Use

Men are more likely than women to smoke cigarettes and to smoke heavily, which are leading causes of heart disease and cancer (see Chapter 2). The greatest number of smokers live in nonmetropolitan areas (Department of Health and Human Services [DHHS], 1997; Gfroerer, Larson, & Colliver, 2007; Substance Abuse and Mental Health Services Administration [SAMHSA], 2009); 29% of people living in rural areas (aged 12 years or older) smoke cigarettes compared with 23% of those who live in large metropolitan areas (SAMHSA, 2009). The highest percentage of smokers is found in Kentucky (American Heart Association [AHA], 2009b). Among youth, rural European American males smoke more often than any other group (Sarvela, Cronk, & Isberner, 1997). Not surprisingly, among men, those who live in the rural South have the highest death rates for heart disease (Barnett et al., 2001).

As I discussed in Chapter 2, the use of smokeless tobacco has increased significantly since 2002 among males aged 12 to 17 years and among 10th and 12th graders. Smokeless tobacco is used almost exclusively by men, most heavily by young, nonmetropolitan, and rural men (DHHS, 1997; Gfroerer et al., 2007; McKnight, Koetke, & Mays, 1995; Nelson, Tomar, Mowery, & Siegel, 1996; Salehi & Elder, 1995; SAMHSA, 2009). However, unlike cigarettes, many men also begin using smokeless tobacco in adulthood (Howard-Pitney & Winkleby, 2002). People living in rural areas are more than 3 times more likely to use smokeless tobacco than people living in metropolitan areas (7% compared with 2%) (SAMHSA, 2009). Despite popular perceptions, a recent study—which included urine analyses—shows that using smokeless tobacco products is not safer than smoking cigarettes; it also found similar levels of tobacco-specific carcinogens in users of either tobacco product (Hecht, 2008). Although most cancers occur late in life, oral cancers are increasingly diagnosed in younger persons, and they kill nearly 3 times as many men as women (see Chapter 2).

Diet

Research consistently shows that men have less healthy diets than women and that this increases their risk for heart disease, cancer, and many chronic diseases. Men eat less fiber and fewer fruits and vegetables than women, and more cholesterol and saturated fat (see Chapter 2). Among rural African Americans in North Carolina, being a woman is one of the two strongest predictors of fruit and vegetable consumption (McClelland, Demark-Wahnefried, Mustian, Cowan, & Campbell, 1998). One large study of both rural and urban older adults in six New England states showed that dietary cholesterol intake was considerably higher than recommended levels, particularly among men (Posner, Jette, Smigelski, Miller, & Mitchell, 1994). Among rural African Americans in Virginia, low levels of high-density lipoproteins—"good" cholesterol— were found in one in four men compared with only 1 in 20 women (Willems, Saunders, Hunt, & Schorling, 1997). In the New England study, men were also less likely than women to have diets that provided adequate levels of vitamins.

Physical Activity and Inactivity

Physical inactivity also increases the risk for the leading killers—heart disease and cancer—as well as other chronic diseases, which I discussed in Chapter 2. By age 30, men begin to become less active than women, and by age 60, they have become more inactive. Physical inactivity increases the risk for sudden cardiac death, for example, which is suffered by one in eight men—3 times the number of women (Lloyd-Jones, Berry, Ning, Cai, & Goldberger, 2009). Among rural men in Iowa, it has been found to be a risk factor for prostate cancer (Cerhan et al., 1997). Among men in the United States, Southerners are the least physically active; for example, compared with men from the Northeast, Southern men are 31% less likely to be irregularly active and 25% less likely to be regularly active (Ahmed et al., 2005). Not surprisingly, as a consequence of both physical inactivity and a relatively poor diet, the prevalence of obesity is highest in the South (Centers for Disease Control and Prevention [CDC], 2008i, 2009p).

Gender differences in physical activity among rural adults are also found. Among rural Kansas couples, although men are more physically active overall than women, they are 2.5 times more likely to be sedentary between the ages of 45 and 64 years (Holcomb, 1992). As noted previously, this is the age bracket in which men are at much greater risk than women for experiencing a deadly heart attack. Physical activity can differ greatly between various ethnic groups. Among African Americans in rural Virginia, for example, far more women than men are sedentary—although both women and men are less sedentary than African Americans nationally (Willems et al., 1997). The type and intensity of physical activity among adults also influence health. Contrary to popular belief, as I demonstrated in Chapter 2, women have made the most beneficial changes in their levels of physical activity in recent years. One large study of residents in rural counties of New York found that although women and men did not differ in their level of physical activity, the women—like women nationally—were more likely than men to engage in light to moderate and aerobic exercise (Eaton, Nafziger, Strogatz, & Pearson, 1994). These are the types of exercise that health scientists now agree are the best for maintaining good health.

Unintentional Injuries

Unintentional injuries claim the lives of nearly 3 times more men than women and are the leading cause of death for men under age 45 (DHHS, 2009b). Among 15- to 24-year-olds, young men account for three of every four deaths—nearly half of which are caused by unintentional injuries (DHHS, 2007b). Among farm residents, men suffer the most injuries. Approximately 2,400 of these injuries result in death each year, whereas another 400,000 are disabling (National Safety Council [NSC], 1994). Each year, approximately 100 children and youth under age 20 are killed on farms, and another 32,800 are injured; 40% of those injured are left with permanent disabilities (Department of Labor, 1999). Among rural adolescents, boys are far more likely than girls to suffer unintentional injuries, primarily from their work or their reckless driving (Alexander, Somerfield, Ensminger, Kim, & Johnson, 1995). Compared with rural girls, rural boys also suffer 1.5 times more injuries that result from sports and recreational activities, and nearly 2.5 times more rural men than women suffer these injuries (Kurszewski et al., 2006).

Occupational Injuries and Deaths

In terms of occupational injuries, the industries of agriculture, mining, construction, timber cutting, and fishing have the highest injury death rates, and transportation, forestry, and fishing account for the largest number of total deaths from injury (see Chapters 1 and 2). Farming has one of the highest death rates (USDA, 2009). These jobs are all typically performed by rural men. In one study, 83% of Wisconsin residents who suffered agricultural injuries were men (Stueland et al., 1995). In New Mexico, the occupational injury death rate for farm workers is 4 times higher than that for nonfarm workers, and among farm workers the death rate is 4 times higher for men than for women (Crandall, Fullerton, Olson, Sklar, & Zumwalt, 1997). Most occupational injury deaths are motor vehicle related (NSC, 1994).

Motor Vehicle Injuries and Deaths

Motor vehicle–related fatalities account for more than half of all unintentional injury deaths, and males represent nearly three of four people who die in motor vehicle crashes (see Chapter 2). Most of these deaths occur in the South (CDC, 2009c) and in rural areas (NSC, 1994). Indeed, although only 23% of people in the United States live in rural areas, rural fatalities account for 57% of all traffic fatalities (National Highway Traffic Safety Administration [NHTSA], 2007c). Rural drivers in Michigan have a 96% higher risk for dying in a motor vehicle crash than nonrural drivers (Maio, Green, Becker, Burney, & Compton, 1992). Among adults over age 64 in rural Iowa, the risk for a motor vehicle crash is 60% higher for men than for women (Foley, Wallace, & Eberhard, 1995). Among adolescents in the United States, those living in rural counties have the highest rates of motor vehicle-related fatalities (DHHS, 2000a). In Colorado, for example, death rates for motor vehicle crashes—as well as for other unintentional injuries—are higher among rural than urban youth (Hwang, Stallones, & Keefe, 1997). Among rural youth aged 5 to 14 years, motor vehicle death rates are from 1.5 to 2 times higher for boys than for girls, and death rates for other unintentional injuries are 13 to 28 times higher for boys (Hwang et al., 1997).

As I demonstrated in Chapter 2, gender differences in the number of miles driven do not explain gender differences in motor vehicle–related deaths, but poor driving habits do. For example, men are less likely than women to wear safety belts, and the vast majority of all those charged with drunk driving are men. Similarly, when miles driven are taken into account, fatal motor vehicle–related crashes are 2.5 times higher in rural areas compared with urban ones (Baeseman, 2009; NHTSA, 2001). Of all fatalities resulting from alcohol-impaired driving in the United States, the majority (57%) occur in rural areas (NHTSA, 2007c). In Wisconsin, deaths involving alcohol are more than twice as likely in rural than urban counties; however, motor vehicle–related deaths that do not involve alcohol still remain more than 1.5 times higher in rural counties (Baeseman, 2009). Compared with drivers in all other rural crashes, operators of farm vehicles—who are mostly men—have a greater proportion of convictions for driving while intoxicated (Gerberich, Robertson, Gibson, & Renier, 1996). Similarly, national data show that rural youth are significantly more likely than urban youth to drive under the influence of alcohol or other drugs (Lambert, Gale, & Hartley, 2008). Compounding their risks, compared with urban teenagers, rural Iowan teenagers are less likely to use front seat safety belts or helmets, and young men are less likely than women to wear back seat safety belts or moped helmets (Schootman, Fuortes, Zwerling, Albanese, & Watson, 1993). In fact, national data also show that compared with drivers in urban areas, those in rural areas are less likely to wear safety belts (NHTSA,

2007c). These geographic differences remain true among American Indians and Alaska Natives (Garcia, Kushang, Patel, & Guralnik, 2007). Among rural Iowans, in general, male farmers are the least likely to wear safety belts (Zwerling et al., 2001). In Mississippi, rural adolescent males are less likely than females to use safety belts (Pope, Smith, Wayne, & Kelleher, 1994). Not surprisingly, more rural people (56%) than urban people (51%) killed in car crashes had been unbelted at the time of the crash (NHTSA, 2007c). One rural trauma center in West Virginia reported that 80% of the patients who required hospitalization from motor vehicle accidents had not used safety belts (Sokolosky, Prescott, Collins, & Timberlake, 1993). Consequently, the severity of injuries was 34% higher for unbelted than for belted drivers, and their need for extended care after leaving the center was 97% higher.

Alcohol and Other Substance Use

Both the quantity and the frequency of alcohol consumption are higher among men than among women, as I outline in Chapter 2. Although alcohol use is generally less common among nonmetropolitan adults than it is among adults nationally, this is not true for those under age 26 (DHHS, 1997). In fact, national data show that among youth and young adults aged 12 to 25 years, both alcohol and methamphetamine use are significantly higher in rural than urban areas, and the more rural the area, the higher the use (Gfroerer et al., 2007; Lambert et al., 2008). Furthermore, both heavy drinking and binge drinking have been increasing in rural areas nationally since the 1990s, with a greater increase in heavy drinking in rural than in metropolitan areas; currently, heavy drinking—5.5 times more common among men than women—is nearly equal in rural and metropolitan areas (Jackson, Doescher, & Hart, 2006). Among rural Kansas couples, women are more likely than men to drink moderately or not at all (Holcomb, 1992). Among rural adolescents, findings are equally consistent: Boys are far more likely than girls to drink alcohol, to drink more often, to experience problems related to drinking, and to start drinking at a young age (DHHS, 1997; Donnermeyer & Park, 1995; Felton et al., 1996; Gibbons, Wylie, Echterling, & French, 1986; Pope et al., 1994; Sarvela & McClendon, 1988). Researchers of one large Mississippi study found that gender differences in problem drinking among rural adolescents were particularly pronounced in ethnic minority groups (Pope et al., 1994). Compared with girls, problem drinking was 1.5 times higher for European American boys, nearly 3 times higher for African American boys, and 5 times higher for boys of "other" ethnicities.

Men's alcohol use contributes significantly to their risk for disease, injury, and death. Findings from one rural trauma center revealed that nearly twice as many male as female trauma patients had been drinking (52% compared with 29%) (Ankney et al., 1998). Most injuries suffered by eighth graders in another rural Maryland study were associated with both risky behavior and alcohol use, and most of the injured students were boys (Alexander et al., 1995). Furthermore, one Illinois study found that among rural adolescents who drank (predominantly young men), those who drank while driving also drank more often (Donnermeyer & Park, 1995).

Health Care Utilization and Help Seeking

Men use fewer health care services than women, a gender difference not explained by health status, access to care, income, or health insurance coverage. This discrepancy can be explained, however, by looking at men's attitudes toward seeking help (see Chapters 1 and 2). Men are less willing and have less intention than women to seek help when they need it. Although rural populations face many obstacles to accessing health care (Gamm, Hutchinson, Dabney, & Dorsey, 2003; USDA, 2009), these factors do not explain gender differences in the use of rural health care services. Among rural people, men and boys are less likely than women and girls to be receptive to help, to seek support, or to visit a physician (Cook & Tyler, 1989; Dansky, Brannon, Shea, Vasey, & Dirani, 1998; Hoyt, Conger, Valde, & Weihs, 1997; Sorensen, 1994). Farmers may be even less inclined than other rural men to seek help. For example, in any given year, farm and nonfarm rural women are equally likely to have had a medical checkup, whereas farm men are less likely than nonfarm rural men to have had one (Muldoon, Schootman, & Morton, 1996). Farmers are also less likely than other nonmetropolitan men to have had a health care checkup or a prostate cancer screening in the past year (National Institute for Occupational Safety and Health [NIOSH], 2006). In one study of Wisconsin residents who had suffered agricultural injuries—most of whom were men—farm residents were the most likely to delay seeking health care. Half of them waited for more than 2 hours. One in four of these farm residents waited more than 24 hours—twice the number of nonfarm residents who did so (Stueland et al., 1995). Similar findings are reported for mental health care utilization. In Tennessee, more than half of farmers (compared with one third of nonfarmers) reported waiting for emotional problems to go away rather than seeking support (Linn & Husaini, 1987). However, often these problems do not simply disappear. Suicide among rural men is extraordinarily high, ranging from 3 to 5 times higher than national averages (Stamm, 2003). Although suicide rates have decreased or remained unchanged for most groups during the past several decades, they have increased significantly for rural men (Singh & Siahpush, 2002).

Social Support

Research, which I review in Chapter 2, consistently shows that men have smaller social networks than women, and that lacking social relationships is a risk factor for death—especially for men. These findings remain true among rural residents. A 20-year longitudinal study of rural older adults in Missouri showed that levels of social support predicted longevity and simultaneously revealed that men had less extensive networks and less frequent contact with friends than women (Hessler et al., 1995). Rural men who have never married have a 50% greater risk for death than married rural men (Smith et al., 1995). Researchers have also found that depression is more common among farmers who have small families (Belyea & Lobao, 1990) and few friends nearby (Linn & Hasaini, 1987).

Perceived Susceptibility to Risk

Although men are more susceptible than women to a variety of health problems, they are also more likely than women to believe they are not at risk for these problems (see Chapter 1). With rare exceptions, people who think they are invulnerable take fewer precautions with their health—and thus have greater health risks—than people who recognize their vulnerability. Young rural men and boys have been found to express significantly fewer concerns or fears than young rural women and girls about a variety of health problems (Davidson, White, Smith, & Poppen, 1989; Weiler, 1997). Rural men are also less likely than women to report fearing crime (Krannich, Berry, & Greider, 1989), even though rural men are most likely to experience all forms of crime (except rape) (Bachman, 1992). One study that examined perceived risk for skin cancer among male farmers and their spouses found that 53% of men, compared with 45% of women, thought that they were at risk for developing skin cancer in the future (Rosenman, Gardiner, Swanson, Mullan, & Zhu, 1995). Although this suggests that many farmers are aware of their increased risk for skin cancer, these percentages do not reflect that men are twice as likely as women to develop this disease.

Beliefs About Manhood

As I demonstrated in Chapter 1, empirical research provides compelling evidence that men who endorse dominant norms of masculinity—such as the belief that "a man should be physically tough even if he's not big"—adopt fewer health-promoting behaviors and have greater health risks than men who do not hold such beliefs. Unfortunately, there is only one similar type of study of rural men: Among male Canadian farmers, several dominant norms of masculinity have been found to have strong, if indirect, effects on farming-related accidents. Farmers who endorsed these norms, moreover, were more likely to minimize the likelihood of a farming accident resulting in injuries (Harrell, 1986). However, a study of national data examining gender indicated that Southerners—particularly men and rural dwellers—held the most traditional views about gender (Rice & Coates, 1995). We can extrap-olate from these findings that rural men—at least those in Southern states—have greater health risks because they endorse these beliefs. In fact, the leading killer, heart disease, is indeed most common among people in the nonmetropolitan South (Barnett et al., 2001; Gillum, 1994; Mensah et al., 2005; Pearson & Lewis, 1998). Among middle-aged European Americans, men in the nonmetropolitan South are nearly twice as likely to suffer from heart disease as men in the metro-politan Northeast (Gillum, 1994).

SUMMARY

This review provides us with a preliminary profile of rural men's health behavior. Although limited, these data suggest that, like men in general, rural men have less healthy lifestyles than rural women. In some cases, rural men are also at greater risk than nonrural men. Overall, three behavioral risk factors are more common in rural men than in either rural women or nonrural men: tobacco use, behaviors that lead to unin-tentional injuries (such as reckless driving), and reluctance to seek help or use health care. These three factors alone have an enormous influ-ence on the health and well-being of rural men. Smoking is the single most preventable cause of illness and death, and car crashes—which kill nearly 3 times as many men as women each day—are the leading cause of death from unintentional injury (see Chapter 2). Similarly, underuse of health services and delays in obtaining timely health care can have profoundly negative consequences for men's health. In terms of their health-related beliefs, compared with either rural women or nonrural men, rural men hold the most traditional attitudes about gender and masculinity—attitudes that have been linked with increased health risks. Four additional behavioral risk factors are more common among rural men than rural women: poor diet, heavy drinking, limited social support, and perceived insusceptibility to risk.

MASCULINITY AND RURAL MEN'S HEALTH

Clearly, rural men are at increased risk relative to rural women and some nonrural men because of their unhealthy practices. What remains unclear is why rural men adopt beliefs and behaviors that undermine their health. To explore this question, this section examines four criti-cal topics: health practices as gendered social action, the association between masculinity and the individual health practices of rural men, the cultural dictates and everyday interactions that shape gendered health practices used in the structuring of social power, and the inter-action between masculinity and other social structures influencing men's health.

Health Practices as Gendered Social Action

From a social constructionist perspective, gender is not something that individuals possess. Although it is often experienced as something deeply personal, masculinity is a social system or structure—or, more specifically, multiple structures. Masculinity organizes daily life and social relations, and shapes institutions such as rural governance (Little & Jones, 2000), agricultural industries (Liepins, 2000), and rural health care systems. Gendered social structures facilitate some men's access to positions of power and dominance (e.g., physicians and farm managers) and frequently relegate women to subordinate roles (e.g., nurses and housewives). Masculinity is also a way of structuring social practices—both the practices of individual men and the practices of groups of men. Many of these social practices significantly influence the health and well-being of men and boys, whether these are health care practices or the practices of sport, farming, and other forms of labor.

Previous explanations of the damaging health effects of masculinity have focused primarily on the hazardous influences of "*the* male sex role" (see Chapter 4). But men and boys are not passive victims of a singular, socially prescribed gender role, nor are they simply conditioned by their cultures. Rather, they are actors—active agents—in their own socialization, generating a *variety* of male "roles" that variously influence their health. Similarly, masculinity traditionally has been seen as originating in each man's individual psychology. For social constructionists, however, gender does not reside in the person, but rather in social transactions defined as gendered: It is a dynamic "set of socially constructed relationships, which are produced and reproduced through people's actions" (Gerson & Peiss, 1985, p. 327).

The activities in which men and women engage, and their gendered ideas and beliefs, operate as "currency" in the continual transactions that construct and demonstrate gender. Gender is "something that one does, and does recurrently, in interaction with others" (West & Zimmerman, 1987, p. 140). It is achieved through "sustained social performances" (Butler, 1999, p. 180). Health practices—like language (Crawford, 1995; Perry, Turner, & Sterk, 1992), work (Connell, 1995), sports (Messner & Sabo, 1994), sex (Vance, 1995), and crime (Messerschmidt, 1993)—become resources in negotiating and reconstructing gender. The ways in which women and men think about health, and the social practices in which they engage that affect their physical well-being, are signifiers of gender that simultaneously reinforce and reproduce gender differences. By either rejecting or embracing healthy practices, women and men are constructing gender.

As I discussed in Chapters 3 and 4, the use of health practices to define oneself as a woman or a man has a profound effect on one's health and longevity. Many men and boys define masculinity *against* positive health behaviors and beliefs. When a man brags, "I haven't been to a doctor in years," or "I can drink and drive!" he is simultaneously describing a health practice and situating himself in a masculine arena. In this way, men's health risks are both a function of, and a means of securing, socially dominant forms of masculinity.

Health Practices and Rural Masculinities

Growing up on a farm, many rural boys learn that to demonstrate masculinity successfully they must adopt risky or unhealthy behaviors, such as operating heavy equipment before they are old enough to do so safely. As one rural man said, "If you're over 10, you'd better be out doing men's work, driving a tractor and that kind of thing"; another said, "My brother Tony and I started driving the pickup on the farm at age six, as soon as we could reach the pedals. We also learned how to drive a tractor" (Fellows, 1996, p. 173). These gendered practices help to explain the extraordinarily high rate of motor vehicle injuries and deaths among rural adolescent boys. Other gendered practices of rural men are closely associated with risk. According to one rural man, "If you were a guy … you were born to be a total, typical, straight male—to play sports, to hunt, to do everything a guy was supposed to do" (Fellows, 1996, p. 305). In performing these particular gendered social practices, men sustain most of the estimated 4 million to 14 million annual sports injuries and the 1,132 nonfatal and 139 fatal hunting injuries that occur each year (see Chapter 2).

Social norms of rural masculinity—or "the rural masculine" (Campbell & Bell, 2000)—dictate how rural men should perform gender. Imagery of the rural masculine, for example, "has implications for the concrete practices of the masculine rural, by providing widely recognized cultural categories of appropriate masculinity" (Campbell & Bell, 2000, p. 540–541). Much of this imagery also has implications for rural men's health, such as the influence of the Marlboro cowboy on the high rates of smoking among rural men. The media consistently portray farmers as rugged, strong, and tough (Liepins, 2000). Not surprisingly, the vast majority of Pennsylvania residents believe that farmers "*embody* the virtues of independence and self-sufficiency" (Willits, Bealer, & Timbers, 1990, p. 572; emphasis added). As we have seen, many male farmers construct this idealized masculinity and consequently undermine their health by not seeking the social support or health care they need. Unquestioned social norms—such as notions about men's invulnerability—can have powerful indirect influences on men's health (Courtenay, 2004b, 2007). For example, although rural young men have a higher risk for injury and death as a result of heavy drinking than nonrural men and young rural women, rural parents are more likely to disapprove of their adolescent daughters' drinking than that of their sons (Pope et al., 1994).

Performing gendered health practices inextricably involves men's bodies, which are used as vehicles in negotiating the landscape of rural masculinities. Social norms—such as the rural masculine depicted in the media—dictate how the body should be used. Typically, the rugged, tough bodies of male farmers are portrayed with tensed muscles, accentuated veins, clenched fists, and flexed biceps (Liepins, 2000). Gender is signified through embodied enactments of these muscular portrayals and through the ways in which gender is inscribed on the body. In Chapter 4, I described a farmer who severed his finger in farm equipment and finished harvesting his field before seeking medical care at the end of the day.

Rural men construct a variety of masculinities—ethnic, professional, and farm masculinities, to name a few—that variously influence their health. The specific ways in which the body is used and the specific health practices used by rural men in constructing masculinity are patterned by a variety of social structures and available resources. For a rural college baseball player, smokeless tobacco is a readily accessible and socially normative signifier of athletic masculinity. Likewise, for many hunters, alcohol is a ubiquitous prop in performing rural masculinity. Alternatively, a rural businessman may eat mostly high-fat restaurant food and engage in excessive drinking and smoking, and a rural farmer may drive recklessly and fail to "pamper" his body by getting sufficient sleep. However, because neither masculinity nor a man's demonstration of manhood is static, the same man may enact gender differently in different contexts—prohibiting himself from displaying pain at work or in front of drinking buddies, perhaps, but permitting himself to do so at home or with his wife.

In defining and operationalizing the health of "rural men," we run the chance of normalizing rural men's experiences and universalizing their risks. With increasing diversity in rural settings, however, it is apparent that rural men do not represent a homogeneous group (Hoyt et al., 1997). There are often enormous health disparities among populations of men, which vary depending on their ethnic identity, marital status, social class, education, income, age, participation in the labor force, sexual orientation, and religious affiliation (Courtenay, 2001b, 2002). The health and health practices of rural men who are economically, socially, and politically disadvantaged can differ greatly from those of other rural men. To understand the basis for these disparities and the broader contexts in which men's health practices are displayed, we need to examine power and social inequality.

Gender, Power, and Health Practices

As I discussed in Chapter 4, gender is negotiated through relationships of power. Microlevel power practices contribute to structuring the social transactions of everyday life—transactions that help to sustain and reproduce broader social structures of power and inequality. Among other social practices, power relationships are located and constituted in the demonstration of health practices. Gendered health practices are used in patterning these social relationships—and are used by men in negotiating their status and establishing their ranking in the hierarchy of men.

Among rural men, dominant masculinities subordinate lower-status, marginalized masculinities, such as those of gay men and "hillbillies." The male body is central to this structuring of gender and power. Rather than allow themselves to be relegated to a lower-status position, for example, rural gay men may negotiate their status by engaging their bodies in physically dominant or aggressive behaviors; as one rural gay man put it, "I really hated football, but I tried to play because it would make me more of a man" (Fellows, 1996, p. 40). Researchers examining injuries among rural adolescent youth found that physically underdeveloped boys were among those at greater risk and concluded that these boys may take unnecessary risks or pick fights to prove their manhood because they feel defensive about their size (Alexander et al., 1995). Playing fields, local bars, country roads, farms, hunting and recreational areas, and rodeo stadiums are all sites where the male body is enlisted to legitimize dominant forms of masculinity.

Disadvantages resulting from such factors as ethnicity, class, geography, educational level, and sexual orientation marginalize certain men. These men may attempt to compensate for their subordinated status by adopting hypermasculine beliefs and behaviors, or oppositional (Messerschmidt, 1993) or compensatory (Pyke, 1996) forms of masculinity. Risk taking, physical dominance, minimization of risk, and rejection of health-protective behaviors are readily accessible resources and forms of social action for men who may otherwise have limited ways in which to construct masculinity. Dominant beliefs about masculinity are another readily accessible resource. In fact, men's endorsement of these beliefs is associated with lower educational levels, nonprofessional occupational status, lower income, African American ethnicity, and sexual orientation that is not exclusively heterosexual (see Chapter 4).

Men also use other health beliefs, such as the minimization of and perceived insusceptibility to risk, as means of successfully performing and securing hegemonic masculinity. In a study of rural men's pub drinking in New Zealand, Hugh Campbell found that the successful performance of masculinity required men to retain fine motor coordination after drinking a lot, and that "highly disciplined and controlled men derided inept drinkers for 'drinking like girls'" (Campbell, 2000, p. 152). Like the Canadian farmers in the study I discussed previously, it is likely that these "controlled" rural drinkers misperceive their actual risk (Harrell, 1986). In a unique study of drinking and diving, researchers found progressive and significant impairment of diving performance when divers' blood alcohol level reached just .04%—the level that the average man would have after drinking only two cans of beer in 1 hour (Perrine, Mundt, & Weiner, 1994). The male divers themselves, however, were not aware of either their progressive impairment in diving performance or their increased risk for injury (Perrine et al., 1994). "Controlled drinkers" dismiss the high risks associated with their heavy drinking and ridicule "inept" drinkers as a means of situating themselves in positions of dominance in the hierarchy of men. This kind of gender performance not only reifies normative masculinity but also simultaneously fosters the continuous reproduction of the marginalized or lower-status masculinities necessary to support the dominant norm.

Adopting healthy practices requires men to cross gendered boundaries. The demonstration of even one healthy behavior—such as using sunscreen—can contradict, and require a man to dismiss, multiple constructions of masculinity that would relegate him to the status of feminized masculinities. Farmers, who are heavily exposed to the sun, are at increased risk for skin cancers of all kinds (Blair & Zahm, 1991; USDA, 2009), which—as I discussed previously—represent the most rapidly increasing form of cancer. Men's lack of sun protection is a major contributor to their high risk for melanoma, which kills twice as many men as women. Despite their risk, most Wisconsin dairy farmers do not use sun protection (Marlenga, 1995). Among rural Michigan farmers, only 40% of men, compared with 65% of women, protect themselves from the sun (Rosenman et al., 1995). The application of sunscreen as one form of sun protection requires farmers to reject a variety of social constructions of gender: Men are unconcerned about health matters, men are invulnerable to disease, the application of lotions to the body is feminine, men do not "pamper" or "fuss" over their bodies, and "rugged good looks" are achieved by getting a tan. In fact, significantly more men than women nationally believe that people look better with tans (American Academy of Dermatology, 2005). By not using sunscreen, a farmer is using a poor health practice to demonstrate endorsement of numerous social constructions of gender.

As several of these examples illustrate, it is not only the endorsement of masculine ideals but also the rejection, or negation (Campbell, 2000), of feminine signifiers of gender that contributes to the construction of masculinities and to the structuring of power. Rural men and boys who attempt to engage in social practices demonstrating feminine norms of gender risk being relegated to the subordinated masculinity of "wimp" or "sissy." In Chapter 4, I discussed a gay man who grew up on a farm and who described being ridiculed as a "sissy" for wanting to cook, bake, and sew, which the men in the family referred to as "girl stuff." I demonstrate in preceding chapters that positive health practices are signifiers of idealized femininity. They are, therefore, potentially subordinating influences that men must oppose with varying degrees of force, depending on which other resources are accessible—or are already being used—in the construction of their masculinity. Disregarding risk and dismissing health care needs are means of rejecting "girl stuff." A man's visit to a bar instead of a rural health clinic, therefore, becomes a mode of signification through which gender is enacted.

Denial of physical or emotional discomfort is another means of demonstrating difference from women and from "weaker" men, who are believed to embody this "feminine" characteristic. Emotional stoicism is a performative signifier of masculinity. In the words of one rural man, "Geared toward being strong, silent and tough, I accumulated lots of layers as I went along. I didn't *feel* tough at all, but I certainly created a veneer for myself" (Fellows, 1996, p. 13). This and other public displays of robust masculine health and vitality serve to conceal—in the sense that Butler (1993) uses this term—the contradiction that men are at greater risk than women for chronic disease, injury, and death. Such performances render invisible the fact—based on most health indices—that men are the more vulnerable, if not the weaker, sex. These sleights of hand reinforce the social constructions that men are more powerful and less vulnerable than women, that men's bodies are structurally more efficient than and superior to women's bodies, that asking for help and caring for one's health are feminine, and that the most powerful men are those to whom health and safety are irrelevant.

Interaction Between Masculinity and Other Social Structures

The social structures that women and men encounter elicit different demonstrations of health practices and provide different opportunities to conduct this particular form of gendered practice. Rural men and boys are constantly participating in dynamic relationships with social systems such as families, schools, churches, bars, and agricultural agencies, where their lives are structured by a broad range of material, political, religious, institutional, ideological, and cultural factors. These systems and social structures either foster or restrict the adoption of particular beliefs and behaviors that influence health.

By and large, social and institutional structures foster poor health practices among men and undermine men's attempts to adopt healthier habits—a rural health care system that largely ignores men's gendered health care needs is but one example. Men and boys in the few countries where state or national rural men's health policies have been adopted, such as Australia (Blackwell, 2001), may develop different health perceptions, beliefs, and practices than rural men in countries (such as the United States) that lack such policies.

Economic structures also profoundly influence health and shape rural men's health and health practices. As I have demonstrated in the preceding chapters, economically disadvantaged men have the worst health of any population. Class systems and the structure of economic markets expose those working-class men involved in manual labor to a range of occupational health and safety hazards—one explanation for why men constitute 53% of the workforce yet account for 92% of fatal injuries on the job. Rural working-class men labor in jobs that require the use of dangerous equipment, such as heavy machinery, and jobs that expose them to hazardous chemicals—construction, agriculture, oil and gas extraction, water transportation, and forestry.

Relationships among various institutionalized social structures—such as governments, the military, corporations, the media, judicial systems, and health care systems—further mediate the health of men. The dynamic interplay of these institutional structures and other social structures (such as those related to ethnicity, economics, and gender) results in different opportunities for, and constraints on, realizing optimal health. The risks of rural working-class men, for example, are compounded by the interaction of various structural factors, such as limited or poorly implemented occupational health and safety policies, lack of health insurance coverage, limited financial resources for health care, substandard living conditions, and limited geographic access to health services.

In closing, it is important to note that these social and institutional structures are not simply imposed on men, any more than a prescribed male sex role is imposed on men: "Social structures do not exist autonomously from humans; rather ... as we engage in social action, we simultaneously help create the social structures that facilitate/limit social practice" (Messerschmidt, 1993, p. 62). Definitions of gender influence social structures, which guide human interactions and social practices, which in turn reinforce gendered social structures and the notion of gender as difference. Men and masculinity are complicit in shaping rural health care systems, as well as reinscribing rural health policy, in ways that ignore men's gendered health concerns. Indeed, men are often the very researchers and scientists who have ignored the subject of rural men's health. Such masculine-gendered patterning of social structures is what Campbell and Bell (2000) term *the masculine rural.*

Men sustain and reproduce social structures—and the masculine rural—in part for the privileges they derive from preserving them. Similarly, rural men who work tirelessly, deny their stress, and dismiss their physical needs for health care also do so, in part, because they expect to be rewarded with money, power, respect in their communities, and reassurance that they are rugged, self-sufficient, "self-made" men. Men who achieve hegemonic ideals by engaging in poor health practices are often compensated with social acceptance, with diminished anxiety about their manhood, and with the rewards that such normative demonstrations of masculinity provide in their rural communities. In constructing these exemplary rural masculinities, however, men simultaneously recreate the social structures that limit the forms of social action necessary for good health.

6

College Men's Health[*]

Information on the health and well-being of young adults in college is extremely limited (Park, Mulye, Adams, Brindis, & Irwin, 2006). Disease, injury, and death rates specifically for college students, for example, are unavailable. A general profile of college men's health can only be inferred from the risks for this approximate age group. As I discussed in Chapter 1, among 15- to 24-year-olds nationally, three of every four deaths each year are men. Fatal injuries and violent deaths (unintentional injuries, homicides, and suicides) account for 80% of all deaths among 15- to 24-year-olds, and four of five people in this age group who die violent deaths are young men. Three young men die from unintentional injuries for every woman who dies. Among adolescents, boys are also more likely than girls to be hospitalized for injuries (see Chapter 2). Young men of this age are also at a greater risk than women for sexually transmitted diseases (STDs). Nearly all the deaths, diseases, and injuries in this age group are preventable.

As I discussed in the preceding chapters, despite the tremendous losses that these statistics represent, policy makers and health professionals alike have paid little attention to men's health risks or to their greater risk for premature death. Although health science of this century has frequently used *males* as study subjects (Mastroianni, Faden, & Federman, 1994), research typically neglects to examine *men* and the health risks associated with their gender. Regarding the health concerns of college men, in particular, little has been written other than a few articles addressing specific health issues, such as STDs (Sawyer & Moss, 1993), testicular cancer (Neef, Scutchfield, Elder, & Bender, 1991), and mental health (Whitaker, 1987).

---

[*] An earlier version of this chapter appeared in the *Journal of American College Health*, 46(6), 1998, 279–290 and is used by permission in modified/revised form.

Furthermore, young adulthood—from 18 to 24 years of age—constitutes a unique stage of development, one that poses health risks distinct from those of adolescence. Independence, the desire to have different experiences before settling down to the responsibilities of employment and married life can influence risk-taking behaviors for many young adults, particularly men (Park et al., 2006). Although White, middle-class, and affluent men are disproportionately represented in the male college population compared with men who are Latino, African American, and lower class (Department of Education, 2006), men from all backgrounds share many common characteristics and risks as they move into young adulthood. These factors may account, in part, for higher rates of risk behavior in college students (Park et al., 2006; see also Chapter 2). As I discussed in Chapter 1, health-related behaviors established in adolescence and young adulthood frequently continue throughout life and are often associated with disease, injury, and death in adulthood.

Even in studies that address risks more common to college men than to college women, the discussion of men's greater risks (Wiley et al., 1996) and of the influence of men's gender is often conspicuously absent (Presley, Meilman, & Cashin, 1997). Despite this dearth of literature, men's health has been ranked by American College Health Association (ACHA) members as the fifth top priority for their continuing education (Snope, 1994).

In this chapter, I provide an overview of college men's health, identify the health risks of college men, explore various explanations for men's poor health status, and recommend interventions to improve their health. Wherever possible, I refer to data from college samples. Where no such data exist, I use research on adolescent males and men in general to identify health concerns that call for further examination.

MAJOR CONTRIBUTORS TO COLLEGE MEN'S HEALTH RISKS

Failure to Adopt Health-Promoting Behavior

The gender gap in longevity has widened steadily since 1920, when women and men lived lives of equal length (Department of Health and Human Services [DHHS], 1994). This suggests that there is nothing natural, inevitable, or biological about men's shorter life span. Although a number of genetic and biological factors may contribute to the difference, they do not explain it (see Chapter 1). Additional factors, such as access to care, economic status, and race or ethnicity, also influence health and longevity (Pappas, Queen, Hadden, & Fisher, 1993). Many health scientists contend that personal health behaviors are the most important of these factors—a belief supported by a wealth of data (Woolf, Jonas, & Lawrence, 1996). As I discussed in Chapter 2, there is substantial evidence indicating that half of all deaths in the United States could be prevented through changes in modifiable, health-related behaviors (Agency for Healthcare Research and Quality [AHRQ], 2009; McGinnis & Foege, 2004; Mokdad, Marks, Stroup, & Gerberding, 2004; U.S. Preventive Services Task Force [USPSTF], 1996; Woolf et al., 1996).

Gender is one of the most important determinants of health behavior (see Chapter 2). Research consistently shows that men engage in fewer health-promoting behaviors and have less healthy lifestyles than women. Indeed, as I demonstrated in Chapter 2, men of all ages are more likely than women to engage in more than 30 controllable behaviors that are conclusively linked with a greater risk for disease, injury, and death: Men eat more fat and less fiber, they sleep less, and they are more often overweight than women, to cite just a few examples. College men, specifically, engage in far fewer health-promoting behaviors than college women do. They consistently score lower on an index of health-protective behaviors that includes safety belt use, sleep, health information, eating habits, and exercise. College men are also significantly less likely to practice self-examinations for testicular cancer than college women are to practice self-examinations for breast cancer. Furthermore, college men's health-promoting behaviors have been found to decrease over time, whereas those of college women increase.

Fewer college men than women have received dietary and nutritional information from their college or university (Centers for Disease Control and Prevention [CDC], 1997b), or from their family or magazines. Consistent with this better-informed outlook, more women than men report that they have tried low-fat or low-carbohydrate diets, agree that they consume too much sugar, or agree that they need to control their weight. Far fewer college men than women eat fruits and vegetables, and those who do, eat less than women do (ACHA, 2008). In one recent study of college students, men were found to be significantly more overweight than women (Davy, Benes, & Driskell, 2006), which is consistent with national findings (see Chapter 2). More college women (67%) than men (58%) are at a healthy weight, and far more men (29%) than women (18%) are overweight (ACHA, 2008). As I demonstrated earlier, the failure among young men—in general—to adopt health-promoting behaviors increases their risks. Although teenage males get more exposure to the sun, more than twice as many female teenagers use sunscreen regularly. Young men also reapply sunscreen less frequently and use lower solar protection factor protection and fewer other forms of sun protection. There is no evidence that these findings differ for college students. Young men's failure to protect themselves from exposure to the sun contributes to their greater risk for skin cancer, and an increase in this cancer among men that is higher than that from any other cancer. Two of every three people who die of melanoma are men, yet use of sun protection in young adulthood can lower the risk for skin cancer significantly.

As I discussed in Chapter 2, college men are also significantly less likely than college women to use safety belts as either drivers or passengers. Wearing safety belts is potentially the single most effective method for preventing injuries in a motor vehicle crash; they reduce the risk for fatal injury to anyone in the front seat of a passenger car by 45%, and the risk for moderate-to-critical injury by 50%. The failure to wear safety belts contributes to the fact that nearly 3 times more men than women aged 16 to 24 years die in car crashes each year (National Highway Traffic Safety Administration [NHTSA], 2008b) and that young men in this age group are at the greatest risk for traumatic brain injuries (Joly, McDermott, & Westhoff, 2000).

Risk Behavior

As I made clear in previous chapters, young men also take greater risks than women do. Both age and gender have been found to be related to safety beliefs and behaviors among college undergraduates in the Midwest, for example, and both safety beliefs and behaviors decreased from 1993 to 2002 (Blair, Seo, & Torabi, 2004). As I discussed previously, car crashes cause 70% of fatalities in young adults, and young men are 3 times more likely to die in a crash than young women. Men drive more dangerously and are more likely to tailgate and run red lights, drive 20 mph above the posted speed limit, pass in no-passing zones, or pass two cars at a time on a two-lane road (see Chapter 2). Nearly one third of adolescent males take risks "for fun" while driving, more than 4 times the number of women who do so. Similar findings have been reported for college men (Zuckerman, 1994). Among college students nationally, young men are significantly more likely than young women to drive after drinking (see Chapter 2). Two in five college men (41%) have driven after drinking, compared with fewer than one in three college women (31%); 19% of men, compared with 9% of women, report having driven after consuming five or more drinks (Wechsler, Lee, Nelson, & Lee, 2003). Among college men who are frequent binge drinkers, 62% report having driven after drinking (Wechsler, Davenport, Dowdall, Moyekens, & Castillo, 1994). In a thorough analysis of gender and driving risks among college students, the men received significantly higher scores than the women did for problem driving, including speeding or reckless driving, moving violations, arrests for driving under the influence, and license suspensions or revocations (DeJoy, 1992).

Research also consistently shows that men engage in riskier sexual practices (see Chapter 2). Among college students, men have more sexual partners; are more likely to acquire human papillomavirus (HPV) infections, putting them at risk for penile cancer (ACHA, 1995, 2008; Kiviat & Koutsky, 2007); and are more likely than women to have sex while under the influence of alcohol or other drugs (Jadack, Hyde, & Keller, 1995; O'Leary, Goodhart, Jemmott, & Boccher-Lattimore, 1992; Patrick, Covin, Fulop, Calfas, & Lovato, 1997; Wiley et al., 1996;

Zuckerman, 1994). In 1999, an estimated 400,000 college students had unprotected sex after drinking (Hingson, Heeren, Zakocs, Kopstein, & Wechsler, 2002). College men, for example, are 2.5 times more likely than women to have more than 10 sexual partners (Kotloff et al., 1991) and to have more casual partners (Poppen, 1995). Members of fraternities have been found to engage in more sex under the influence of alcohol or drugs, and to have more sexual partners, than nonfraternity students (Scott-Sheldon, Carey, & Carey, 2008). Studies of African American college students have also found riskier sexual practices among men than among women (Lollis, Johnson, Antoni, & Hinkle, 1996; Taylor, Dilorio, Stephens, & Soet, 1997).

In fact, gender differences among college students have been found for most health risk behaviors (CDC, 1997b). Results from research have consistently indicated, for example, that college men are much more likely than college women to engage in risky sports, work, and travel (Zuckerman, 1983, 1994). Young men are more than 3 times as likely as young women to die of accidental causes (DHHS, 2009e). One study of California college students revealed that men were more likely than women to engage in 20 of 26 specific high-risk behaviors, including smoking, drug use, carrying weapons, and fighting (Patrick et al., 1997). Among college students in New Jersey, men are more likely than women to engage in 12 of 14 high-risk behaviors (Lewis, Goodhart, & Burns, 1996). Nationwide, college men are more likely than college women to report the use of marijuana or other drugs, or to combine the use of illegal drugs and alcohol (CDC, 1997b). At more competitive colleges, men are more likely than women to use opioid analgesics nonmedically, and this behavior is linked both with other drug use and with driving after drinking (McCabe et al., 2005). Illicit drug use on college campuses has increased from being found in 29% of students in 1991 to 35% in 2008; drugs included marijuana, hallucinogens, cocaine, and narcotics such as hydrocodone/acetaminophen (Vicodin) (Johnston, O'Malley, Bachman, & Schulenberg, 2009). Male college students are far more likely than female college students to drink alcohol, and they are much more likely to drink heavily (see Chapter 2 and The Health Effects of College Men's Socialization section of this chapter). National data show that more than 1 in 10 college men carries a gun, knife, or other weapon, nearly 3 times the number of women who carry weapons. Students who carry weapons are more likely to drink and are more likely to fight if they are binge drinkers (Presley et al., 1997).

College men's risk taking compounds the health hazards associated with their failure to adopt the health-promoting behaviors. Their dangerous driving habits compound the risks associated with their not wearing safety belts. Failure to use condoms is another example of compounded risk. Only one third to one half of sexually active college men use condoms (Patrick et al., 1997; Weiss & Larson, 1990). Even among those at high risk for STDs, three of four never or only occasionally use condoms (Sawyer & Moss, 1993). Another study found that one in four young gay or bisexual men was having unprotected anal intercourse; although the college men in that study were somewhat less likely than their noncollegiate peers to have unprotected sex, the difference was not statistically significant (Seage et al., 1997). Failure to use condoms compounds the risks associated with college men's unsafe sexual practices.

Masculinity

Simply being male is linked to poor health behaviors and increased health risks, but so are gender and men's beliefs about "being a man." A large body of compelling research, which I review in Chapter 1, indicates that men who adopt traditional attitudes about manhood have greater health risks than men with less traditional attitudes. One of the studies among 13- to 19-year-olds revealed that alcohol use and problem drinking are strongly associated with "traditional" masculinity; this association is even stronger than the link between drinking and being male (Huselid & Cooper, 1992).

Findings from a national study of nearly 2,000 young men aged 15 to 19 years, including college men, indicated that traditional beliefs about manhood are associated with a variety of poor health behaviors, including drinking, drug use, and high-risk sexual activity (Pleck, Sonenstein, & Ku, 1994). For example, young men who hold traditional beliefs (e.g., "a guy" should be "sure of himself" and not "act like a girl") have more sexual partners and are more likely *not* to use condoms consistently, associations that hold true regardless of education level, race, and ethnicity. In a longitudinal, national study of young men—including college men—traditional beliefs about manhood emerged as the strongest predictor of risk behaviors over time (Courtenay, 1998b). Another national study of young men, including 18- and 19-year-olds, also found that these beliefs are associated with decreased health care use (Marcell, Ford, Pleck, & Sonenstein, 2007).

Among college students, traditional attitudes about masculinity have been linked to such poor health behaviors as smoking, using alcohol and other drugs, and behaviors related to safety, diet, sleep, and sexual practices (Baffi, Redican, Sefchick, & Impara, 1991; Korcuska & Thombs, 2003; Locke & Mahalik, 2005; Mahalik, Lagan, & Morrison, 2006; McCreary & Courtenay, 2003; O'Neil, 2008; see also Chapter 9). College men who rigidly adhere to traditional notions of masculinity—or who experience greater gender role stress or gender role conflict—have more anxiety and poorer health habits than their less traditionally minded peers (Eisler, Skidmore, & Ward, 1988; see also Chapter 9), and they have greater cardiovascular reactivity in stressful situations (Cosenzo, Franchina, Eisler, & Krebs, 2004; Eisler, Franchina, Moore, Honeycutt, & Rhatigan, 2000; Franchina, Eisler, & Moore, 2001; Lash, Eisler, & Schulman, 1990; Lash, Gillespie, Eisler, & Southard, 1991; Moore & Stuart, 2004; Thompson & Pleck, 1995). College men who adopt traditional attitudes about manhood also experience higher levels of depression and are more vulnerable to psychological stress and maladaptive coping patterns (Eisler & Blalock, 1991; Good, Dell, & Mintz, 1989; Good & Mintz, 1990; Oliver & Toner, 1990). Furthermore, these men compound their risks because they tend not to seek help from others and to underuse campus professional services (Good et al., 1989; Good & Mintz, 1990; Mansfield, Addis, & Courtenay, 2005; see also Chapter 10).

Concealing Vulnerability

Men further increase their risks by concealing pain and illness. Suicide provides the most extreme example. Throughout the life span, suicide rates for men are 2 to 18 times higher than for women (see Chapter 1). For young men, suicide rates are staggering. Although suicide rates among young adults decreased during the 1990s, rates have been increasing significantly since 2003 among young men aged 15 to 19 years (CDC, 2007h). The rate of suicide for college students has been found to be half that of the general population (Silverman, Meyer, Sloane, Raffel, & Pratt, 1997). However, it is still a significant concern for college men. For this approximate age group (aged 15 to 24 years), suicide is the third leading cause of death, and more than five of six people who commit suicide are men (DHHS, 2009b). Each day, 10 young men aged 15 to 24 years kill themselves (DHHS, 2007b).

In the college population, 1 of 1,000 men commits suicide, more than twice the rate of women who do so; in undergraduates aged 17 and 19, the ratio of men to women is more than 4 times higher (Applebaum, 2006). Despite this high risk, friends and family consistently speak of their "complete shock" when college men commit suicide ("Student dies of self-inflicted gunshot wound," 1994, p. 1). The mother of one college junior who shot himself said she had "no reason to believe" her son would do such a thing ("Student dies of gunshot wound," 1993, p. 1). One explanation for people's shock at young men's suicides is that college men successfully conceal their vulnerabilities. They are less likely than college women to confide in close friends, express vulnerability, or disclose their problems to others (Johnson, 1988; Williams, 1985). Consequently, others are often unaware when these men are in pain. A psychiatrist interviewing friends and family of a well-liked, successful student athlete who committed suicide reported that "no one really knew what [his] feelings were … he seemed to hide them" ("Athlete dies young," 1995, p. S1, S7).

The desire to conceal their vulnerability can influence college men's decisions not to seek care and can affect clinicians' assessments and diagnoses when men do seek help. College men are significantly less willing than college women to seek support in situations where help is needed (Ashton & Fuehrer, 1993; Johnson, 1988; Rule & Gandy, 1994). In a large study of Midwestern students, researchers found that college men were less willing than college women to seek help for physical illnesses (Boehm et al., 1993). Consequently, among first-year college students in one state, more women than men had made recent medical visits, and twice as many men as women had made no medical visits in more than 1 year (Foote, Harris, & Gilles, 1996).

College men's reluctance to seek help can result in serious delays in treatment. Nearly three of four college men in one study had delayed getting help for STDs from 2 months to more than 6 months after they developed symptoms (Sawyer & Moss, 1993). College men in another study were more likely than college women to delay seeking psychological help (Prosser-Gelwick & Garni, 1988). Findings in two studies of depressed college students revealed that the men were more likely than the women to rely on themselves, to withdraw socially, and to try to talk themselves out of depression (Chino & Funabiki, 1984; O'Neil et al., 1985).

College men's self-reliance and denial of pain can also contribute to others' inattention to men's health needs. One example is mental illness. Although psychiatric disorders affect fully half of the college population, fewer than one in four students seek treatment (Blanco et al., 2008). Men's responses to depression, for example, foster the widespread belief that college men do not get depressed. In fact, studies of college students based on the results of psychological testing have consistently found no significant differences between men and women in *diagnosable* depression (Lester, 1990; Nolen-Hoeksema, 1987; Oliver & Toner, 1990; O'Neil et al., 1985; Stangler & Printz, 1980). Despite this strong evidence, survey research based on students' self-reports rather than on psychological tests typically leads to the false conclusion that depression is a "more critical" health problem for college women than for men (Sax, 1997, p. 261).

Perceived Invulnerability

As I discussed in Chapter 1, the vast majority of American men believe that their health is "excellent" or "very good." Despite their higher risks, men report better health than women do. Men are also less likely than women to perceive themselves as being at risk for illness or injury. In one national study, researchers reported that more men than women perceived less risk for each of the 25 health problems examined; men's gender remained a significant predictor of low perceived risk when controlling for level of education (Flynn, Slovic, & Mertz, 1994). In other studies, men, including young men, perceived themselves as less susceptible to skin cancer than women did and underestimated the risks associated with sun exposure. The one study that examined perceived skin cancer risk specifically among college students also found that men perceived less risk than women did (Vail-Smith & Felts, 1993).

Similarly, college men in a large study perceived significantly less risk associated with the use of cigarettes, alcohol, and other drugs than college women did (Spigner, Hawkins, & Loren, 1993). Other studies have consistently found that college men are more likely than college women to underestimate the risks associated with involvement in physically dangerous activities (Zuckerman, 1983, 1994). In fact, college men have been found to perceive less risk than college women for a variety of health threats (Boehm et al., 1993; Cutter, Tiefenbacher, & Solecki, 1992; DeJoy, 1992).

The same kinds of gender differences in perceptions have been found for driving risks and for automobile accidents (Flynn et al., 1994; Savage, 1993). Young men are more likely than women to expect that no consequences, such as a citation, crash, or injury, will result from their more frequent reckless driving (Farrow & Brissing, 1990). Among college students in one well-constructed study that examined 15 risky driving behaviors, men scored significantly lower than women in their perceptions of risk (DeJoy, 1992). The men believed that drinking and driving, not using a safety belt, and not making a full stop at a stop sign were much less serious risks than women did. In fact, the author of that study concluded that college men possess a particularly lethal combination of perceptions that compound their risks—an exaggerated sense of their own driving skill and the perception of less risk associated with a variety of dangerous driving habits. These beliefs are inconsistent with the finding that men are at fault in the vast majority of automobile accidents and most injury crashes (see Chapter 2). Although comparisons are not available, I see no reason to believe that college men are any less at fault than noncollege men, particularly given the ample evidence of college men's risky driving habits.

Men also differ from women in their perceptions of sexual health risks. Based on their involvement in various sexual behaviors, including sex under the influence of drugs and numbers of sexual partners, men of all ages nationally are much more likely than women to be at high risk for STDs and HIV (see Chapter 2). Currently, the largest proportion of new HIV infections occurs among persons under the age of 30 years (CDC, 2009b). Based on their sexual histories, 60% of men under the age of 30 are at medium to high risk for sexual infections, a percentage that is 2.5 times the percentage for women. According to the most recent data, 73% of adults and adolescents living with HIV/AIDS are male (CDC, 2009b), and men represent three of four deaths attributable to HIV (DHHS, 2009a).

Of particular relevance is the finding that higher education has been positively associated with greater STD risk (Tanfer, Cubbins, & Billy, 1995). The most recent data also show that 13- to 29-year-olds are the group at highest risk for new HIV infection (CDC, 2009b). Among college students, men who have sex with men have the highest rates of infection—from 1.3% (Seage et al., 1997) to 2.6% (Kotloff et al., 1991). However, it has been noted that many heterosexual college men may also be at risk for STDs and HIV because of their high-risk sexual practices (Kotloff et al., 1991; Seage et al., 1997). New cases of HIV/AIDS resulting from high-risk heterosexual contact increased among men during each of the 3 years from 2005 to 2007; the most recent data show that 13% of newly infected men were infected through high-risk heterosexual contact (CDC, 2009b). Between 2005 and 2007, the estimated numbers of HIV/AIDS diagnoses increased among both adolescents and adults with HIV infection attributed to high-risk heterosexual contact (CDC, 2009b).

Despite those statistics, many researchers have found that college men perceive less risk for HIV than college women do (Hansen, Hahn, & Wolkenstein, 1990; Johnson et al., 1992; Lollis et al., 1996), although some researchers have found either no gender differences between men and women (Dekin, 1996) or have reported mixed results (Goldman & Harlow, 1993). However, college men have been found to report little concern, even when their actual risks for STDs and HIV are high (Jadack et al., 1995; Sawyer & Moss, 1993). In one study, three of four college men involved in high-risk sexual behavior believed that their risk for HIV was either low or extremely low (Sawyer & Moss, 1993). Their belief in their own invulnerability prevents college men from changing their behavior. With rare exceptions (DiIorio, Parsons, Lehr, Adame, & Carlone, 1993), perceived susceptibility among college students has been linked with positive changes in risk behaviors (DiIorio et al., 1993; Gray & Saracino, 1989; Thurman & Franklin, 1990). Unrealistic perceptions of risk, including the beliefs that only intravenous drug users, prostitutes, and men who have sex with men contract STDs and HIV, may explain why otherwise knowledgeable college students continue to engage in high-risk sexual behaviors (Johnson et al., 1992).

Men's perceptions of invulnerability, in addition to being associated with sexual health risks, are associated with risks of many other kinds (Rosenstock, 1990; Weinstein, 1987). In one thorough study, perceived susceptibility to skin cancer and sun damage emerged as the strongest predictor of teenagers' use of sunscreen (Mermelstein & Riesenberg, 1992). Similar studies have yet to be conducted with college students.

Perceived invulnerability is also associated with men's failure to adopt such positive health behaviors as testicular self-examinations (Blesch, 1986). Detected early, testicular cancer is highly curable. Nearly one in three men (30%) with testicular cancer are not diagnosed when the cancer is localized (Sokoloff, Joyce, & Wise, 2007), when it is least likely to be fatal or disabling (Prout & Griffin, 1984). Although college men are among those at highest risk for testicular cancer, only 41% performed a self-examination in the last month (ACHA, 2008). Because testicular tumors grow quickly, monthly examinations have been recommended (Einhorn, Richie, & Shipley, 1993); without self-examinations or medical visits, early detection is unlikely. Perceived invulnerability can undermine college men's practice of self-examination. Fear of developing cancer, according to one study of college students, was among the best predictors of men practicing testicular self-examinations (Katz, Meyers, & Walls, 1995).

Health Knowledge

As I discussed in Chapter 1, research consistently shows that men—including college men—are less knowledgeable than women are about health in general, and about specific diseases, such as cancer, STDs, and heart disease. College women, for example, know significantly more about skin cancer, sunscreen protection, and the harmful effects of sun exposure than college men do. College men also know significantly less about self-examinations for testicular cancer than college women know about self-examinations for breast cancer (Katz et al., 1995).

College men are also usually found to be less knowledgeable than the college women about HIV. One review of research concluded that knowledge is also an important determinant of positive changes in risky sexual behaviors related to HIV disease (Carmel, 1990), but that finding is not consistent for college students. Several studies have linked knowledge with decreased HIV risk among college students (Carroll, 1991; Lollis et al., 1996; Thomas, Gilliam, & Iwrey, 1989). Knowledge *alone*, however, is not necessarily sufficient to promote safer sex practices (DiIorio et al., 1993; Gray & Saracino, 1989; O'Leary et al., 1992; Thurman & Franklin, 1990).

College men have had relatively little experience with the health care system and may lack even basic health information, such as how to make an appointment. In a study at a Midwestern university, more than one of five men had a health problem that he needed to discuss with a clinician but did not know with whom to discuss it (Pinch, Heck, & Vinal, 1986). Men's ignorance about health matters can increase their risks. A lack of knowledge, for example, is a major contributor to delays in seeking care for cancer symptoms (Love, 1991), and health knowledge is associated with health-promoting behaviors, such as limiting exposure to sunlight and doing testicular self-examination.

THE HEALTH EFFECTS OF COLLEGE MEN'S SOCIALIZATION

Men's unhealthy attitudes and behaviors are not surprising in light of their socialization. Young men and boys receive many contradictory messages about health as they are growing up. A health professional might encourage a young man to seek help when he needs it; however, analysis of research findings repeatedly show that parents, other adults, and peers all discourage boys from seeking help—and often ridicule and punish boys when they seek help (see Chapter 3).

Health education campaigns attempt to teach young men that it is wrong to be violent, yet boys and men are encouraged to use aggressive force in sports, the military, and business. Television programs are 60% more likely to portray boys rather than girls using violence, and analyses of such programs reveal that violence is most often portrayed as an *effective* means for men and boys to attain their goals (see Chapter 3). Boys are also encouraged to fight; three of four Americans believe that it is important for boys to have a few fist fights while they are growing up. Not surprisingly, nearly one in seven college men in California surveyed in a study published in 1997 had been in a physical fight in the past year (Patrick et al., 1997).

Young men also receive mixed messages about drinking. Health professionals encourage abstinence, yet young men grow up in a society that consistently conveys the message that drinking is part of being a man (Courtenay, 2000c; see also Chapter 3). Lemle and Mishkind (1989) examined representations of alcohol in various media and found that the material conveyed an unmistakable link between drinking and masculinity. These investigators also provided compelling evidence that "advertisers further the association between alcohol and masculinity by interjoining their products with athletic events and by strategically placing ads in magazines and television programs with predominantly male audiences" (Lemle & Mishkind, 1989, p. 215). In fact, *Sports Illustrated*, the magazine most read by young men, has more alcohol and tobacco advertisements than any other magazine, according to one study (Klein et al., 1993). These advertisements, like television beer commercials, conspicuously equate drinking with being a man, taking risks, and facing danger without fear (Strate, 1992).

Given these findings, it is no wonder that recent analyses of national trends suggest that alcohol use is increasing among young adults aged 18 to 25 years (see Chapter 2). Among college students, problem drinking is much more common in men than in women (Patrick et al., 1997; Perkins, 1992; Wechsler, Kuo, & Lee, 2000; see also Chapter 2). Data from the Core Alcohol and Drug Survey have revealed that, on average, college men consume nearly seven drinks per week, 2.5 times the number of drinks that women consume (Presley, Meilman, & Cashin, 1996). College men are also 2.5 times more likely to consume 10 or more drinks per week and 6 times more likely to consume 21 drinks. College men are more likely to be heavier drinkers, and to binge more frequently, than younger adolescents, young adults who are not in college, and older adults (ACHA, 2008; Johnston, O'Malley, & Bachman, 2002; O'Malley & Johnston, 2002; Park et al., 2006; Serdula, Brewer, Gillespie, Denny, & Mokdad, 2004). These findings reflect consistent trends demonstrating that college men are more likely than college women to drink alcohol, to drink more, and to drink more often (Capraro, 2000; Perkins, 1992; Prendergast, 1994). Consequently, college men meet criteria for alcohol abuse and dependence more frequently than do college women (Presley, Leichliter, & Meilman, 1998).

College men are also more likely to be binge drinkers. Among 18- to 24-year-olds, in general, nearly 3 times more men (25%) than women (9%) engaged in binge drinking on at least 12 days in the past year (DHHS, 2009e). Among college students nationally, men are significantly more likely than women to be binge drinkers; nearly half of college men, compared with less than one third of college women, binge drink during a 2-week period (see Chapter 2). Furthermore, nearly twice as many college men (16%) as women (9%) have binged 3 to 5 times in the last 2 weeks and more than twice as many men (5%) as women (2%) have binged 6 or more times (ACHA, 2008). Even when a gender-specific definition of binge drinking is used, with fewer drinks required for women to meet the binging definition, half of college men nationally, compared with 39% of college women, are binge drinkers; 23% of men and 17% of women are frequent binge drinkers (Wechsler et al., 1994). Although younger college students drink less frequently than their older peers, they binge drink more than older ones; 58% of men under 21 binge when they drink and do so with the intention of getting drunk (Wechsler, Lee, Nelson, & Kuo, 2002).

College men's alcohol use can be devastating to their well-being. Compared with college women, college men are invariably found to experience more negative consequences of drinking, including impaired driving and physical injury (Perkins, 1992). Alcohol is the leading contributor to unintentional injury deaths in the 18- to 24-year-old age group; it is a factor in more than 5,000 deaths per year (Hingson, Zha, & Weitzman, 2009). As I discussed in Chapter 2, motor vehicle crashes are the leading cause of death in this age group; for those under age 25, driving while impaired by alcohol or other drugs is the leading cause of death, and the vast majority of those who die are young men. Although there were significant decreases in drinking and driving among college students from 1999 to 2005, between 1998 and 2001, the number of students who reported driving while under the influence of alcohol increased from 2.3 million to 2.8 million; from 1998 to 2005, the number of alcohol-related accidental deaths in the college population increased from 1,442 to 1,825, with alcohol-related traffic deaths in 2005 conservatively estimated at 468 (Hingson et al., 2009). Drinking can also increase the risk for drowning. Of the 77% of students who report boating or swimming, more than one third of young men report drinking beforehand, whereas only one quarter of young women do so (CDC, 1997b). Among young adults aged 15 to 24 years generally, 10 times more men than women die from drowning (National Safety Council [NSC], 1994, 1998, 2010); as many as half of those men had been drinking shortly before they drowned (CDC, 1993c; Warner, Smith, & Langley, 2008). More than half a million students reported unintentional injuries sustained while drinking (Hingson, Heeren, Winter, & Wechsler, 2005), and men are 8 times more likely than women to visit their college health service for alcohol-related injuries (Meilman, Yanofsky, Gaylor, & Turco, 1989). Underage men are at greater risk for many of these alcohol-related negative consequences than men aged more than 21 years (Wechsler, Lee, Nelson, & Kuo, 2002).

Binge drinkers, in particular, are more than 21 times as likely as non-binge drinkers to report alcohol-related problems (Hingson et al., 2002). More than half of the students who report frequent binge drinking also report five or more alcohol-related problems during the school year (Wechsler, Lee, & Nelson, 2003). College binge drinkers are also over 10 times more likely than their nonbinging peers to get hurt or injured and 7 times more likely to engage in unplanned sexual activities or have unprotected sex (see Chapter 2). Research also shows that problems associated with college binge drinking have been increasing (Wechsler, Lee, Kuo, Seibring, Nelson, & Lee, 2002). One study reports that interventions have so far proved ineffective on a national level, especially with men: "No reduction in binge drinking has been realized for 18- to 20-year-old college men" (Grucza et al., 2009, p. 700). Finally, students on campuses with a high rate of binge drinking are more likely to suffer the secondhand consequences of binge drinking, such as assault and property damage (Wechsler et al., 2002). In 1998, more than 600,000 students reported being assaulted by a drunken student, and 70,000 students reported date rape perpetrated by a student who had been drinking (Hingson et al., 2005). In 2001, these numbers increased to 696,000 assaults and 97,000 date rapes (Hingson et al., 2009).

Young men also receive mixed messages about the use of tobacco. Although public health campaigns attempt to convince young men not to use tobacco, other influences attempt to convince them differently. The popular *Sports Illustrated* is also the magazine with the most tobacco advertisements. Men are far more likely than women to receive tobacco industry promotional items (Gilpin, Pierce, & Rosbrook, 1997). Documents released by the R.J. Reynolds Tobacco Company revealed that the "Joe Camel" advertising campaign "was designed to lure teenagers as young as 12, especially boys" ("Joe Camel," 1998, p. A1). It is not surprising, therefore, that significantly more men than women currently smoke—23% compared with 18%—and that the decreases in smoking that are occurring are among women but not among men (see Chapter 2). The decrease in smoking since 1980 among older teenagers is also greater for females than for males (Nelson et al., 1995).

Statistics on tobacco use among college students are not entirely consistent. Furthermore, the decreases in smoking during the 1990s were not seen among college students, whose smoking increased dramatically during that time (Rigotti, Lee, & Wechsler, 2000; Wechsler, Rigotti, Gledhill-Hoyt, & Lee, 1998). Currently, significantly more college men than women are smokers (Rigotti et al., 2000; Thompson et al., 2007). National data from the Core Alcohol and Drug Survey show more tobacco use among college men than among women at all levels of frequency of use during the previous 30 days, including daily use (Presley et al., 1996). Currently, 19% of college men and 14% of college women have smoked during the last month (ACHA, 2008). Among differing colleges and regions, findings have varied. Some investigators found that more women than men smoked, but the differences were never significant (Lewis et al., 1996; Foote et al., 1996; Sax, 1997); others reported that significantly more men smoke (CDC, 1997b; Fiore et al., 1993; Johnston, O'Malley, & Bachman, 1996; Patrick et al., 1997).

In 30 colleges in the Pacific Northwest, researchers found that men were significantly more likely to smoke than women (Thompson et al., 2007); another study found that although college students tended to be light smokers, college men were more likely than women to transition from light to regular smoking habits over time (Wetter et al., 2004). Smoking was also linked with using alcohol and other substances, and with a lower sense of psychological well-being; although many college students have attempted to quit, only a minority actually do so (Patterson, Lerman, Kaufmann, Neuner, & Audrain-McGovern, 2004). However, college men are significantly less likely than college women to attempt to quit smoking or to plan to quit (Harris, Schwartz, & Thompson, 2008).

Researchers rarely examine specific smoking habits, which are more dangerous among men. Men, in general, smoke more cigarettes per day, inhale more deeply, and are more likely to smoke cigarettes without filter tips and cigarettes that are high in tar and nicotine (see Chapter 2). Among students in one state, 43% of the men who smoked consumed two or more packs per day, compared with only 20% of women who smoked that amount (Foote et al., 1996).

Research findings have shown that a common marketing strategy of tobacco companies is to link the use of tobacco products—particularly smokeless tobacco—with virility and athletic performance and to target young men in particular (Connolly, Orleans, & Blum, 1992). Smokeless tobacco consumption has, in fact, nearly tripled since the 1970s (CDC, 1993b; Glover, Laflin, Flannery, & Albritton, 1989) and continues to steadily increase today (Hecht, 2008); among young men, use has increased between 250 and 300% (National Cancer Institute [NCI], 1991). Most smokeless tobacco use is initiated in the teenage years, particularly during college (Glover et al., 1989; Levenson-Gingiss, Morrow, & Dratt, 1989). Fourteen percent of college men, compared with 1% of women, have used smokeless tobacco in the past year, and 21 times more men (8.7%) than women (0.4%) are current users (Rigotti, Lee, & Wechsler, 2000); male college athletes have been found to be more likely than nonathletes to use chewing tobacco (Glover et al., 1989; Wechsler, Davenport, Dowdall, Grossman, & Zanakos, 1997). Consequently, although most cancers occur later in life, oral cancers, which kill nearly twice as many men as women (NSC, 1994), are increasingly diagnosed in younger persons (NCI, 1991). Among 12- to 17-year-olds, nationally, smokeless tobacco lesions have been found in 3% of males compared with 0.1% of females (Tomar, Winn, Swango, Giovino, & Kleinman, 1997).

Men and boys receive contradictory messages about physical activities and sports. Despite public health efforts to foster caution, my review of the research literature shows that at home, at school, and on television boys learn to take more physical risks than girls (see Chapter 3). Therefore, it is not surprising that college men are more likely than college women to engage in sports that are physically dangerous—mountain climbing, scuba diving, parachuting, hang gliding, and body-contact sports (Zuckerman, 1983, 1994). Men, including college men, also take greater risks in sports than women do, even in sports such as skiing; consequently, injuries among skiers are significantly higher for men than for women (see Chapter 3).

Men also take greater risks on their bicycles. Males of all ages account for 83% of all nonfatal bicycle injuries, and 88% of all bicycle-related deaths each year (NHTSA, 2008c). Persons between 18 and 24 years of age use bicycles more than any other adult age group but report the lowest rates of helmet use (Bolen, Kresnow, & Sacks, 1998). Among college students nationally, more than 1 in 5 (23%) never wears a helmet when riding a bicycle and more than 1 in 10 (12%) wears one only rarely or sometimes (ACHA, 2008). Nine of 10 of bicyclists killed in California were not wearing helmets (California Highway Patrol [CHP], 1994), although helmets can reduce the risk for head injuries from crashes by 85% (CDC, 1992b). The amount of bicycle riding that men do does not explain these differences; taking into account use patterns and exposure, the risk for fatal bicycle injuries for men is 5.5 times greater than that for women (Rodgers, 1995).

The eating habits of men and women also differ. College women are more likely than college men to adopt healthy dietary habits, such as choosing baked, broiled, boiled, or stewed foods rather than fried foods; eating chicken, fish, or beans instead of red meat; and limiting their consumption of fat, salt, and sugar (Courtenay, McCreary, & Merighi, 2002). Women perceive healthy food choices to be more personal and relevant than do men. It has been suggested that food choices are closely associated with ideas about what it means to be a man or woman in the United States, and that to combat obesity, it is essential to address these intervening ideas about gender—particularly regarding men and masculinity (Levi et al., 2006).

Compared with women, men also engage in less healthy forms of physical activity (see Chapter 2). Women are more likely than men to engage in light-to-moderate exercise, the type that research indicates is optimal for physical well-being. Women place greater value on exercising for health, they adhere to more regular exercise patterns, and they engage primarily in aerobic exercises or walking. By contrast, men are more likely to participate in body-contact sports that can lead to injuries, such as football and basketball. Football accounts for more than half a million high school injuries annually and on an average year is responsible for approximately 13 high school and college student deaths (NSC, 1994; Shankar, Fields, Collins, Dick, & Comstock, 2007).

Some young men use anabolic steroids in an attempt to attain cultural ideals of the muscular male physique. The unprescribed use and abuse of steroids occur most often among men between the ages of 18 and 30 years (see Chapter 2). Among college students, approximately 2% of men report the nonmedical use of anabolic steroids, which is 10 times higher than the percentage of women who report using steroids (McCabe, Brower, West, Nelson, & Wechsler, 2007). Among adolescents, steroid use has been found to be associated with changes in physiology, behaviors, and perceptions that are consistent with psychological dependence (DHHS, 1991). College men who use steroids are also more likely to use other drugs, including marijuana, cocaine, tobacco, and alcohol (McCabe et al., 2007; Meilman, Crace, Presley, & Lyerla, 1995). Nearly three of four users report arguments or fights as a consequence of using steroids, and nearly half report being hurt or injured (Meilman et al., 1995). Similarly, nearly three of four long-term steroid users meet criteria for an alcohol use disorder (McCabe et al., 2007). As I discussed in Chapter 2, multiple and simultaneous drug use may further increase the risks associated with anabolic steroids.

HOW GENDER AND STEREOTYPES INFLUENCE SERVICE PROVISION

Stereotypes about men and boys are deeply ingrained in society. These stereotypes contribute to the invisibility of men's health risks and to men's poor health behaviors (see Chapter 4). The very attitudes and behaviors that increase men's risks are often considered normal and to be expected. "Boys," people say, "will be boys." Stereotypes contribute to strongly held societal beliefs that men and boys are stronger, tougher, and more robust than women and girls, beliefs that are consistent with men's own perceptions of themselves as being invulnerable (see Chapter 3).

As I discussed in Chapter 3, boys are exposed to these stereotypes from infancy. When people are told that an infant is a boy, they are more likely to believe that it is "firmer" and "less fragile" than when they are told that the same infant is a girl. Health professionals are not immune to these stereotypic perceptions. Gender role stereotypes influence the diagnostic decisions of mental health clinicians, for example, who often make diagnoses based on whether patients conform to traditional gender roles.

The consequences of these stereotypes can be damaging to men's health. In one large and well-constructed study, the researchers found that mental health clinicians are significantly less likely to diagnose depression in men than in women; in fact, the clinicians failed to diagnose nearly two thirds of the depressed men (Potts et al., 1991). As a result, more women than men are treated for depression, and women's higher treatment rates, along with studies relying on self-reports, have contributed to a cultural perception of men's immunity to depression (Nolen-Hoeksema, 1987; Warren, 1983). This perception endures despite suicide rates, which are indexes of depression, that are as much as 18 times higher for men.

The finding that depression is undiagnosed in many men is particularly relevant for college health professionals. As I have already noted, there are no significant gender differences in diagnosable depression among college students; therefore, undiagnosed depression in young men may contribute to their extraordinarily high rates of suicide. Mental health problems among college men are on the increase, with reported rates of depression increasing from 6.2% in 2000 to 10.8% in 2005 (ACHA, 2006b). Risks associated with untreated mental health issues such as depression include substance abuse, poor academic motivation and achievement, poor social relationships, and poor vocational outcomes, as well as suicide (Cook, 2007; Goldsmith, Pellmar, Kleinman, & Bunney, 2002). Indeed, suicide is the second-leading cause of death among college students; 1,100 students commit suicide each year, and most of them are men (Hunt & Eisenberg, 2010; National Mental Health Association & The Jed Foundation, 2002). Suicide rates in this age group are 4 to 5 times higher for men than women (see Chapter 2).

Gender can influence the quality of care that college men receive from health care providers in other ways. Despite their high health risks, men in general receive less information and fewer, briefer explanations in medical encounters than women receive (Hall, Roter, & Katz, 1988; Roter & Hall, 1997, 2004). As I discussed at the beginning of this chapter, significantly fewer college men than women report having received dietary and nutritional information from their college or university (CDC, 1997b). Similarly, among college students, men are less likely to be questioned about tobacco use during medical visits (Foote et al., 1996). Consistent findings of gender differences in physician–patient communication have led to the conclusion by some leading health communication researchers that those findings "may reflect sexism in medical encounters, but this may act to the advantage of female patients, who have a more informative and positive experience than is typical for male patients" (Roter & Hall, 1997, p. 44). Nationally, young women are more likely to visit doctors, dentists, and mental health providers than young men (see Chapter 2). It is unclear whether this fact is the cause, or the effect, of gender stereotypes associated with health care provision.

CONCLUSION

The statistics I have reviewed in this chapter indicate that college men's greatest health risks are preventable and are the result of controllable behaviors. Interventions should be designed to help college men change modifiable behaviors that increase their health risks. That women typically visit college health services more often than men is not simply "natural." Early in their lives, young women are taught the importance of regular physical examinations. Men need to be taught the importance of receiving periodic evaluations and taking personal responsibility for their health. College men's lack of routine health care makes any health care provider's contact with a male student an important opportunity for education, assessment, and intervention. These interventions can effectively reduce risk, as demonstrated by a recent randomized controlled study of 14- to 18-year-olds seen in an urban emergency department; those at risk for future injury who received brief interventions to reduce harm reported a decrease in negative consequences related to aggression and alcohol use 3 to 6 months later (Walton et al., 2010). Similar results should be expected in acute care in particular because students rate campus health educators and medical staff to be the most believable source of health information (Leino & Kisch, 2005). Furthermore, an acute care visit or campus outreach may well be the only encounter a college man will have with *any* health professional for a long time. Unfortunately, too few strategies for making the most of these contacts have been developed, and few strategies have been developed for addressing college men's health in general. In particular, college health service providers need to address gender stereotypes that can influence their interventions with college men. I have developed a practice guideline for health professionals who work with men in general, and with college men in particular—which I outline in Chapters 12 and 13. In Chapter 13, I identify a variety of additional gender-specific interventions for college men specifically, including educational campaigns, marketing, and outreach.

Although researchers have long examined relationships between sex and health practices, few attempts have been made to move beyond biological sex as an independent or control variable and to explain which aspects of gender influence health. *Why* do college men engage in more health risk behaviors than college women? Research is needed to examine this question. Research is also needed to understand whether increasing perceptions of skin cancer risk, for example, will result in college men's reducing their exposure to sunlight. Other critical areas for research are investigations of how race or ethnicity, socioeconomic status, and sexual orientation influence the health of college men and how their health risks compare with those of noncollege men. Contrary to popular assumptions, education level, socioeconomic status, and race or ethnicity are not necessarily indicators of young men's health behavior (Pleck et al., 1994), and college students' health behaviors can be significantly worse than the behaviors of their nonacademic peers (Clark, 1993; Tanfer et al., 1995).

Ultimately, a national system for tracking injuries and deaths among students in U.S. colleges and universities must be developed for accurate epidemiological comparisons of students and nonstudents, as well as for identifying gender differences in health-related college attrition. Many unexplained paradoxes of gender and health remain. Why are suicide rates in this age group 5 times higher for young men, even though college women are far more likely to report considering suicide? Why are college men less likely to be questioned about health risks in medical visits? Research addressing these questions is warranted—and long overdue.

7

Preventive Health Strategies for Men in Prison*

WILL H. COURTENAY AND DON SABO

This chapter explores the health risks of men in prison and identifies preventive strategies that prisoners can use to improve their health. As discussed in preceding chapters, there is compelling evidence that the practice of preventive health behaviors favorably influences health and longevity in the larger population. Little is known, however, about its effects among men in prison. Furthermore, as is well established in this book, preventive health behavior is a gendered practice. Women are more likely than men to adopt health-promoting beliefs, behaviors, and lifestyles. Although the underlying assumption in much of the medical literature is that what it means to be a man has no bearing on men's health, emerging theories and research are examining and identifying health risks associated with masculinity and the daily practice of being a man. The gendered aspects of health among prisoners have only begun to be investigated (Polych & Sabo, 1995; Sabo & London, 1992).

Although there is a need to address prevention in prisons (Weisbuch, 1991), applying a preventive health model within the prison context is a complex matter. There is significant variation in prison conditions

* An earlier version of this chapter appeared in D. Sabo, T. A. Kupers, & W. London (Eds.). (2001). *Prison masculinities* (pp. 157–172). Philadelphia: Temple University Press, and is used by permission in modified/revised form.

(e.g., from maximum-security institutions to "country clubs") and among prisoners (e.g., in personality, health beliefs, intelligence, and educational background). Moreover, the concepts of *health promotion* and *preventive health* often contradict the institutional mandate of prisons to surveil and to punish their inhabitants. The overall philosophy and day-to-day operations of many prisons revolve around hurting prisoners, not coddling them. Preventive health proponents urge individuals to take personal responsibility for making decisions and developing habits that decrease their risk for disease. However, prisons are total institutions that limit personal autonomy, regiment behavior, and discourage individual initiative. Simply put, prisons are generally not about wellness, and health care delivery in prisons is designed primarily to treat illness after—not before—it occurs.

The institutional limits imposed by the prison on men's health are further compounded by external factors (Marquart, Merianos, Cuvelier, & Carroll, 1996). A majority of prisoners come from poor and working-class communities where educational opportunities and high-quality health care are not readily available, and where people are apt to be more concerned with day-to-day survival than with planning a healthy future. Furthermore, the proportion of young men in the prison population has grown in recent years, and these men are unlikely to be emotionally or educationally prepared to practice preventive health behaviors or be responsible for their own health.

The observations and conclusions presented in this chapter grew out of a college-level seminar in sociology of health and medicine conducted at a northeastern U.S. maximum-security prison. The 22 student-prisoners agreed to work collectively with the instructor to study the concept of health risk, to identify the health risks of prisoners, to articulate realistic prevention strategies for prisoners, and to explore the influence of masculinity on health. This endeavor was facilitated by the self-administered health risk assessment for men (Courtenay, 1996a). The assessment tool consists of 54 items that assess 10 areas of risk, such as diet, drug use, safety, sexual health, social support, and attitudes about manhood. Each student completed the assessment and determined his level of risk in each category and his overall risk. Then, the term papers of students were systematically analyzed. In these term papers, each student discussed his individual health history, identified health risks that he faced in prison, and specified preventive strategies that he found effective to summarize the students' health-related experiences.

This study draws on standpoint epistemology, which holds that disadvantaged and less powerful members of a society have unique and useful knowledge to offer others (Nielsen, 1990). It is exploratory and speculative. The insights and interpretations that are presented were developed from the perceptions and voices of the students who participated in the seminar. The seminar participants, as a group, were probably unrepresentative of the larger prison population. They were racially and ethnically diverse, and their social and educational backgrounds were varied. Approximately two thirds came from impoverished inner-city or rural backgrounds, whereas approximately one third grew up in working- or middle-class communities. Two men held college degrees, but for the rest, the prison college program was the first higher education they had received.

MEN'S HEALTH RISKS IN PRISON

The student's identified many factors that are commonly known to increase the health risks of prisoners and nonprisoners alike. These included the use of tobacco, drugs, and alcohol; sexual health risks; being overweight; biological influences and genetic predispositions; and physical inactivity. Health risks identified by students that are relevant to the prison context are examined in the following sections.

Violence

Violence was the most frequently cited health risk. Stabbings and cuttings by fellow inmates and beatings by guards were described as common occurrences. Risk factors for violence among prisoners include gambling, involvement in the drug trade, stealing, reneging on debts, "snitching," and "not showing respect." Prisoners use razors, can tops, polymethyl methacrylate (Plexiglas), and bedsprings to "slash," "rip," "stab," and "touch" fellow inmates. Two students implicated guards' harassment of prisoners in the violence among prisoners, suggesting that inmates "displace their anger toward one another."

Environment

The students expressed concern about high levels of noise, second-hand smoke, inadequate fire safety precautions, and a general lack of sanitary conditions, especially with respect to food safety. They cited unsterilized utensils, poor hygiene among food handlers, and birds and bats in food areas. The environmental risks most often cited, however, were overcrowding and close quarters. These factors, students argued, increased the risk for infectious and communicable diseases, including HIV disease, tuberculosis, hepatitis, colds, and flu. These diseases were one of their primary health concerns. Prisoners are, in fact, among those at highest risk for tuberculosis, hepatitis, and HIV (Centers for Disease Control and Prevention [CDC], 1992g; Hammett, Harrold, Gross, & Epstein, 1994; MacIntyre, Kendig, Kummer, Birago, & Graham, 1997; Polych & Sabo, 2001; Wilper et al., 2009).

Health Care

Half the students considered the prison health care system itself to be a risk factor, citing "inadequate," "substandard," inconsistent, and noncomprehensive care. They described delays in treatment, infrequent examinations, inadequate staffing, and inferior medications. They spoke of treatment being withheld as punishment and prescribed medication being denied. They also cited inadequate access, such as the inability to receive emergency care at night. Similar criticisms were leveled against prison dental care. Distrust of prison medical care was also said to make some prisoners reluctant to seek help or to sustain treatment. However, a Federal Bureau of Prisons study seems to contradict these claims. According to this study, 89% of inmates experienced no change in their overall health status during incarceration, 4% improved, and 7% deteriorated (Wallace, Klein-Saffran, Gaes, & Moritsugu, 1991).

Health Knowledge

Many students identified their own limited health knowledge and lack of health information among inmates as key risk factors. A study of the health knowledge of prisoners in a maximum-security prison in the state of Washington found that most did not know the causes of common health problems or how to prevent them (Kruzich, Levy, Ellis, & Olson, 1984). Men in prison are not alone in their lack of knowledge about health matters. A consistent finding among civilian populations is that men in the United States are far less knowledgeable than women about health in general and about risk factors for specific diseases, such as heart disease, cancer, and sexually transmitted diseases (STDs) (see Chapter 1).

Diet and Nutrition

Most students cited inadequate diet and poor nutrition as potential health risks. Specific risks included limited nutritional choices, poor food quality, and improper preparation—such as overcooked vegetables and undercooked meats. The prison diet was also criticized for offering inadequate portions and insufficient servings of fresh fruits and vegetables, for being high in cholesterol and sodium, and for using spoiled or "deliberately tampered with" foods. The lack of money to purchase healthy dietary supplements through the commissary was also cited as a risk.

Mental Health

Psychological problems, such as chronic stress and depression, were considered by some students to be a daily health risk. Indeed, mental health problems are considered a "ubiquitous" aspect of prison life (Wilper et al., 2009, p. 669). One indirect index of depression that substantiates these claims is the risk for suicide among prisoners. Suicide is the third leading cause of death in the prison population, and the suicide death rate for prisoners is up to over four times higher than the rate for the general population; and nearly all these deaths are male (CDC, 2010e;

Mumola, 2005). According to the students, depression undermines prisoners' ability to practice preventive care. Sources of stress and depression that they cited included a lack of close contact or communication with family and friends, tension and conflict with guards, and violence.

Prison Culture

Several students identified negative health effects of the prison culture. The general lack of social support in prison, the prevalence of "type A" coronary-prone behavior, and men demonstrating aggressive forms of masculinity were considered health risks. For example, wearing scars—especially facial scars from fighting or attacks—was described as "almost stylish," particularly among young prisoners who have grown up in urban gang subcultures. Students often lamented the lack of social support from family, society, or fellow inmates. As one man put it:

> Here in prison I have yet to recognize anyone whom I can go to for real support. Sure I have a few fellow inmates I can depend on for help, but there is a limit to how much. Most inmates have their own problems and they surely are not too interested in helping others. And…the employees here, from what I've observed and experienced, have no concern for inmates' well-being.

PREVENTIVE HEALTH STRATEGIES FOR PRISONERS

The students were challenged by the assignment to identify preventive health strategies for men in prison. Some had initially negative reactions to the health risk assessment, saying that it was designed primarily for "men on the street." Many of the lifestyle factors that were covered, they argued, simply did not pertain to prisoners. Some scoffed at dietary items such as "eating fresh fruits and vegetables," which they said were scarce in prison. Items that pertained to social support and help seeking were criticized for failing to recognize that self-disclosure and socializing with others in prison can be both impractical and dangerous. Some laughed at the items assessing safer sex practices because they had not been sexually active with women for years.

These initial claims were eventually rebutted by other prisoners in the seminar. Counterarguments were spelled out and defended: Even if the prison diet was generally unhealthy, there were healthier options on the menu; fresh fruit could be purchased from the commissary in lieu of potato chips; it was possible to make friends in prison and to be more diligent at maintaining family ties; and inmates do have sex with women through the visitation programs, and some have sex with other inmates. A consensus emerged around the conclusion that even though prison conditions create unique obstacles to well-being, preventive health choices can still be made. Students also recognized that, despite some marked differences, there are similarities between the health options of prisoners and those of men on the street. Both, for example, can choose to abstain from tobacco, alcohol, and drugs. The preventive health strategies later identified by students in their papers are summarized in the following sections.

Practice Self-Care

Students recommended that prisoners practice self-care and take personal responsibility for their health. However, they viewed this largely as a way to compensate for the perceived inadequacies of prison health care. This perspective is reflected in comments like these:

> Prisoners are given the bare minimum when it comes to adequate health care. Basically the only real care is self-care.

> In here, it's up to me to take responsibility for my own state of health and expedite an organized plan of self-maintenance.

> Prevention is difficult but is of paramount importance because cures are a rarity with the limited efforts put forth by the Department of Corrections.

That these students, as well as other inmates, take personal responsibility for health matters out of necessity does not make the practice any less valuable. Research among civilians indicates that an individual's active involvement with health care is associated with a variety of positive outcomes (Deber, 1994; Meichenbaum & Turk, 1987; O'Brien, Petrie, & Raeburn, 1992). However, it is unlikely that most men in prison are provided with the information, basic skills training, and institutional support that make self-care feasible.

Reduce Violence

The students identified a variety of ways to address anger and to reduce violence. Many believed that individual inmates should take responsibility for their own safety rather than rely on the prison system for protection. Strategies included being vigilant to potential violence, "resisting harmful influences," and avoiding dangerous activities—such as gambling and drug use—that could instigate aggressive reprisals. Meditation and breathing exercises were also suggested as techniques for reducing frustration. One student suggested that prisoners "confront the danger they pose to each other" and recognize that safety from violence is a "reciprocal right" that is granted to those who give it to others. Students recommended a variety of interpersonal techniques that were consistent with this notion. These techniques included "practicing good social habits," being "prudent" in developing relationships, keeping anger to one's self, being "polite to everyone even if they are abrasive," and never

responding to guards or prisoners who are offensive or trying to instigate conflict. Participation in prison programs was also recommended
to reduce violence and foster positive feelings. In fact, one prison study
found that anger management training reduced inmates' vengeful and
hostile feelings, suggesting that the incidence of aggressive acts among
prisoners can be reduced (Holbrook, 1997).

Lower Environmental Risk Exposure

Students suggested a variety of strategies for decreasing the risk for communicable and infectious diseases. These strategies included washing
hands with soap before eating or handling food, and encouraging others
to do so; not sharing eating utensils and not drinking out of another's
cup; greeting others by touching closed fists, rather than by shaking
hands; not getting tattooed; keeping windows open and fans operating
for ventilation; and spending time outdoors when weather and routine
permit. One student suggested staying away from smokers to decrease
one's exposure to secondhand smoke.

Reduce Sexual Risks

Several strategies for reducing sexual risks in prison were put forth. Most
students recommended complete abstinence from sexual contact with
other prisoners. Additional strategies included having only protected sex,
promoting safer sex, and participating in prison HIV disease educational
programs. One man cautioned against participation in the conjugal visitation program to avoid risks associated with "unfaithful wives." Finally,
masturbation was seen as a safe and viable sexual outlet for prisoners.

Increase Health Knowledge

Education was frequently cited as a means of reducing risks and improving health. One student said that prisoners have "a willingness to gain
good knowledge and information about how to maintain one's health,"
adding that in so doing they "avoid the unnecessary worry and stress
that comes with rumor, myth and falsehood." Students suggested that
prisoners need to learn more about disease and also gather information about their family health history to identify potential health risks.
This "learn more" strategy appears warranted in light of research findings that health knowledge is positively associated with seeking care
for cancer symptoms, practicing safe sex, and avoiding risky behaviors
associated with HIV disease (see Chapter 1). According to one student, "Education has played a major role in my adopting these new
life habits." Another student said, "As I become more knowledgeable
about my health and the various factors that affect it, I am taking
steps to improve my overall physical, mental, emotional, and spiritual
condition."

Improve Diet and Nutrition

Most students described strategies for improving diet and nutrition. This is particularly relevant because rates of hypertension and diabetes are high among prisoners (Wilper et al., 2009). A primary goal was to be selective at meals whenever possible, and to choose foods that were low in saturated fat and high in fiber, protein, and complex carbohydrates. Additional recommendations were to supplement the prison diet with fresh fruits and vegetables; to request healthy foods from home; to purchase healthy foods and vitamin supplements from the commissary; to consume protein drinks; to limit consumption of "junk food," salt, and processed sugars; and to drink 8 to 10 cups of water each day.

Reduce Stress and Emotional Conflict

Some students recommended reducing stress through mental, physical, and breathing exercises. One man described how he reduced his stress by reading magazines and books. Others suggested channeling stress through the use of humor and activities that increase positive feelings. Involvement in enjoyable activities—such as sports, reading, watching television, and listening to the radio—was also recommended as a means of reducing boredom. Some students cited religion, spiritual practice, and meditation as strategies for reducing stress and improving health. One prisoner described how his spiritual practice enabled him to contend with everyday stress: "Active involvement in church activities … [has] led to a more stable emotional state, which in turn has led me to a healthier physical state."

Increase Social Support

Several students suggested that prisoners could improve their health by increasing their social support. Specific strategies for creating stronger social bonds included forming support groups, getting married, getting involved in religious organizations, maintaining family ties, and attending school. These recommendations are well advised in the context of research that shows that men have much smaller social networks than women do, and that the lack of social relationships can be a risk factor for mortality—especially for men (see Chapters 1 and 2). We know of no research that examines the relationship between social support and health or health behavior among prisoners, although some of the students' remarks suggest that there is an association. "I am quite able to pull myself out of the blues using my immediate family as support and one or two close associations with fellow inmates," one man said. "Social support from fellow inmates … allows you to cope with daily strains," another student remarked.

Adopt Healthy Attitudes and Beliefs

Many men approach health matters intellectually, using their cognitive skills (Courtenay, 1996b, 1998c, 2001a; see also Chapter 12). Incarceration fosters self-reflection, and men in prison spend much of their time thinking. It is not surprising, then, that half of the men identified cognitions that would favorably influence their health. One student recommended being "mindful" of personal health, making healthy decisions, and remaining "consciously aware of the environment and its negative aspects at all times." The importance of "thinking through" the consequences of one's behavior before taking action was also recommended. Strategies for managing one's cognitions were also discussed; these included "restructuring" the meaning of imprisonment to reduce the effects of its emphasis on deprivation. In one man's words, "Mental thoughts…and how I cope with them, is a prerequisite for achieving and maintaining proper physical and mental health."

Several students emphasized the importance of clinging to hope and thoughts about life after release from prison. These cognitions may foster positive health behaviors in some prisoners. As one man stated, "The strong desire to not only survive my prison term, but to also live my remaining years in a good state of health, drove me to reevaluate my health and examine what I could do to reduce my health risks." Some studies of civilian populations indicate that future-oriented people are more likely than present-oriented people to adopt positive health behaviors (Mahon & Yarcheski, 1994; Mahon, Yarcheski, & Yarcheski, 1997), to engage in safer sex practices (Rothspan & Read, 1996), and to avoid intravenous drug use (Alvos, Gregson, & Ross, 1993). Future orientation has also been associated with reduced risk for depression and suicide among nonprisoners (Breier-Williford & Bramlett, 1995). We know of no similar research among prisoners, but students' comments suggest that their health behaviors are linked to a future time perspective. "It is in my best interest to guard against sickness and disease so that when I am released I will not be debilitated physically and will thus be able to enjoy my remaining years in a productive and fulfilling manner," one student said. Another one said, "If I had no hope for the future, why bother to watch what I eat? Why not extract all the pleasure I possibly could by eating all the junk food I desire?"

PRISON MASCULINITIES AND PREVENTIVE HEALTH

Women and men use health-related beliefs and behaviors as resources in demonstrating femininity and masculinity (see Chapters 3 and 4). In many North American cultural settings, positive health beliefs and behaviors are constructed as forms of idealized femininity. Therefore, when a man brags, "I haven't been to a doctor in years," he is simultaneously describing a health practice and situating himself in a masculine arena. Men can also use unhealthy or risky behaviors to negotiate their status in relation to women and other men. A man who adopts a "tough guy," "I don't care if I work myself to death" persona—or who dismisses pain or symptoms as "sissy stuff"—may be positioning himself within the hierarchy of men and distancing himself both from "feminine" characteristics and from women. Therefore, the constructions of masculinity and some health behaviors can be linked to relationships of power and to identity construction (Courtenay, 2006a; Kaufman, 1994; Pyke, 1996; Sabo, 1995). In this way, the social actions that individuals demonstrate when they enact gender and health simultaneously sustain and reproduce broader structures of power and inequality.

Prison Masculinities and Health Behaviors

On entering a maximum-security prison, a man is stripped of much of his identity. Subsequently, as one student explained, he "constructs an identity that is consistent with his new hardcore environment." The institutional structures of prison life dramatically restrict the variety of resources and social actions available to men to "do" gender (West & Zimmerman, 1987). As Newton (1994) points out, "The prisoner's masculinity is in fact besieged from every side: through loss of autonomy and independence, enforced submission to authority, lack of access to material goods, all of which are central to his status as a 'man'" (p. 197).

The narrowing of prisoners' options for constructing masculinity can foster the adoption of hegemonic forms of masculinity that pervade prison cultures—that is, the acceptance of hierarchy, toughness and stoicism, physical dominance, aggressiveness, heterosexism, and homophobia. The forms of hegemonic masculinity that some prisoners adopt differ from the forms of masculinity they practiced on the outside as loving fathers, supportive spouses, or workers. For other prisoners, however, the pursuit of hegemonic masculinity is consistent with their former identities as gangsters, abusive husbands, street fighters, or con men. Newton (1994) has concluded that prisoners generally adopt "a tough, hypermasculine ideal, an abhorrence of femininity and aggressive homophobia" that are more extreme than the hypermasculinity adopted by subordinated men outside of prison (p. 198).

We speculate that pursuit of hegemonic masculinity undermines the health of many men in prison. As one student put it, inmates learn to adopt prison values that "actually go against the message of preventive health." Many codes of "manly" conduct require stoic denial of pain, physical dominance, and personal risk. One middle-aged student said, "When you got stabbed you usually bandaged yourself up and dealt with the guy when you saw him. To go to the doctor would appear that you are soft." Others observed, "'Real' prisoners are tough, stand-up guys," or, "Prisoners conceive of themselves as tough, fearless, and hard and they have a 'don't take any shit' attitude and are always ready to prove their 'manliness.'" Violence and physical dominance are central to the structuring and sustaining of hierarchic relationships in prison (Sim, 1994), as illustrated by the comments of one student:

> I have been shot and stabbed. Each time I wore bandages like a badge of honor.... Each situation made me feel a little more tougher than the next guy.... Being that I had survived, these things made me feel bigger because I could imagine that the average person couldn't go through a shoot out or a knife fight, survive and get right back into the action like it was nothing. The perception that I had constructed in my mind was that most people were discouraged after almost facing death, but the really bad ones could look death in the eye with little or no compunction.

For some men, incarceration itself was a means of negotiating masculinity and status in the hierarchy of men. As one student explained, "Jail was seen as a rite of passage for young Black boys into manhood. If we could survive prison … then we would have greater standing among our peers and be harder and tougher men."

Like the failure to engage in physically risky behavior, the adoption of health-promoting behavior can undermine a man's ranking among prisoners and relegate him to a subordinated status. "If you told the officer that you had been stabbed, then you were a punk and possibly a snitch, so you had to handle it." Students described prisoners as openly criticizing fellow inmates who "complained too much" about sickness or pain. Excessive complaining was seen as a sign of personal inadequacy or "softness." Some prisoners who made frequent visits to the health clinic were considered by fellow inmates to be malingerers or were suspected of hustling medications to "handle their bid." Students' comments suggested that similar attitudes were held by prison personnel and health care providers.

At least one third of the students debunked "macho" definitions of manhood as naive and dangerous. Some reminisced about how, as boys and younger men, they had considered themselves to be "invincible," or "invulnerable to serious injury," or "immune to physical harm." Now older and wiser, they saw that these "Superman" images were unrealistic. As the semester progressed, they discussed their personal experiences with aches and pains, surgery, prostate problems, hypertension, impotence, and other illnesses as a means of conveying their dawning awareness of their vulnerability to aging, illness, and death. These classroom discussions were sometimes startlingly frank and compassionate, and to some extent, they expressed changes in the ways the men perceived their bodies, their health options, and their identities of manhood.

It is relevant that the students could critically assess the links between masculinity and their health risks. A large body of research indicates that men who adopt traditional beliefs about manhood have greater health risks than men with less traditional beliefs (see Chapter 1). Men who rigidly adhere to traditional notions of masculinity   or who experience gender role stress—have more anxiety and poorer health habits than their less traditionally minded peers, and they have greater cardiovascular reactivity in stressful situations. Men who adopt traditional beliefs about manhood also experience higher levels of depression and are more vulnerable to psychological stress and maladaptive coping patterns.

Finally, although the topic of homosexuality came up during the seminar, detailed discussions about risks such as rape and man-on-man sex did not occur. We can only speculate about the experiences and health beliefs of men who have sex with men in prison, gay and bisexual prisoners, and those men who have been "enslaved" through prison rape. Their perceptions of and approaches to both health risk and prevention are no doubt different from those of other prisoners.

OBSTACLES TO PREVENTIVE HEALTH IN PRISON

Official and public indifference to prisoners' health, along with harsh conditions and long sentences, makes many prisons desolate places in which to live and work—and especially difficult places to practice preventive health. We have identified four specific obstacles prisoners face in their attempts to take personal responsibility for their health and to adopt preventive health behaviors.

First, they must overcome the sense of powerlessness and the lack of self-efficacy that many prisoners experience. Among civilians, a perceived lack of control over one's life and health has been associated with risk-taking behaviors and poor preventive health practices (Courtenay, 1998b). Among prisoners, there are a number of factors that undermine one's sense of control and self-efficacy. Many prisoners come from poor and underclass backgrounds, where fatalism is often a way of life. Poverty and harsh, unhealthy social conditions breed this fatalism and foster the belief that much of what happens in life is beyond one's control. In a wealthy economy and status-driven class system, poor people do not exert as much control over their lives as middle-class or professional people do. For many of the poor men who make up the majority of the prison population, fatalism is, in fact, realism.

Institutionalized powerlessness and stigmatization may further undermine prisoners' self-efficacy in practicing preventive health strategies. Goffman (1961) described the prison as a "total institution" in which individuals are systematically stripped of autonomy and efficacy by routinization, surveillance mechanisms, and depersonalization. The inculcation of obedience, subservience, and conformity is unlikely to foster self-efficacy among prisoners. Indeed, many of the students were reluctant to recognize that they had an investment in, or a responsibility for, their own health. After being institutionalized, prisoners often construct identities as victims of the economy or the criminal justice system. Consequently, they internalize both the stigma and the powerlessness associated with prisoner status. A prisoner's identity as victim and his real powerlessness in relation to guards, the prison bureaucracy, and the health care system do not promote the motivations and ambitions necessary for practicing preventive health.

Second, if men in prison are to adopt preventive health measures, they must embrace social practices and self-care strategies that have been in some ways culturally constructed as "feminine." Because prison life tends to promote hegemonic masculinity and to devalue forms of femininity that are associated with self-care, a prisoner's pursuit of preventive health practices and philosophies may present personal and social contradictions. Furthermore, even if prisoners are willing to risk undermining their demonstrations of hegemonic masculinity, they may be unfamiliar with specific self-care practices. Whereas girls often learn self-care during adolescence through regular physical and reproductive health examinations, this is not something that boys are typically taught. For most prisoners, it was probably their wives, girlfriends, and mothers who monitored their health and scheduled any medical appointments that they had. Prisoners who want to take greater responsibility for their health will need not only to cross gendered boundaries but also to learn new skills. As one student pointed out, "It is up to the inmate to take initiative and take advantage of available resources and to keep track of annual exams or check-ups."

Third, social support represents something of a health paradox for prisoners. One strategy for reducing health risks in prison that a few students suggested was to "stay to yourself." This recommendation contradicts the decades of research among civilians cited previously, which conclusively links social relationships with health and longevity. Other students, however, described the importance of social support, and the benefits they gained from group, gang, or organizational affiliations. The potential health rewards of these affiliations are evident in the remarks of one student who described his group's goals:

> To enhance Latino pride; a group bent on self-improvement; the main goal was to give its members a direction to change the negative traits that got us in prison and to become better and productive members of society; to be a positive role model for the younger generation to look up to.

However, this student also acknowledged the potential risks associated with this affiliation, noting that it could lead to involuntary participation in gang violence:

> The problem of one member is the problem of all the members. I don't go around looking for trouble, but many of my so-called brothers do.... As it stands, I am at a very large risk of losing my life because of someone else's bad judgment.

Social support is further complicated and made contradictory as a health strategy by what inmates learn through their social relationships in prison. One student described the influence of these associations on his construction of masculinity: "As a result of my incarceration, those peers, many who I've accepted as role models, I've developed the same masculine identity traits in myself, and they represented a major [unhealthy] influence in my life and my health." How prisoners can overcome these particular obstacles in negotiating gender and preventive health remained unclear to students.

Finally, for some men, incarceration itself can represent a health paradox. Several students described prison as a protective and healthy environment compared with their lives on the outside:

> I'm almost certain that had I not been arrested all the times I ended up in prison, I would have been dead a long time ago from a drug overdose, a deadly STD such as AIDS, or someone preventing me from stealing their property could have killed me.

> In prison I got healthier than I had been in years. I ate regularly three meals that are not nearly as high in fat, calories, and cholesterol as the fast foods I lived on.

Indeed, some men have greater access to health care in prison than they have in their communities outside of prison. The study of Federal Bureau of Prisons cited previously found that the health of some inmates improves during their incarceration, and the health of most prisoners at least does not worsen (Wallace et al., 1991). Furthermore, recent research shows that former inmates face an increased risk for death 13 times higher than that of the general population (Binswanger et al., 2007). This suggests that transitional, supportive services for living healthy lifestyles are needed for men who are released from prison.

CONCLUSION

Men in prison are among those populations at highest risk for disease, injury, and death (Polych & Sabo, 2001; Wilper et al., 2009). Despite these high risks, little is understood about their health. The preventive health practices of prisoners have never before been examined. In this chapter, we provided an analysis and summary of the term papers of 22 prisoners who were students in a college-level sociology of health seminar. By examining preventive health from the perspectives of these students, we were able to identify risks and preventive practices that are particular to men within the prison context. More importantly, when given the opportunity to explore their own health concerns, the students produced insights and preventive agendas that are unique to men in prison.

The seminar provided a structure that enabled the student-prisoners to take the first steps toward improving their health. They developed a working understanding of how basic preventive measures can decrease their risk for illness and death. They learned that health is not something that just happens to men's bodies, but rather something that men can often control and influence. During the semester, they also came to view health not simply as the absence of disease, but also more holistically, as a state of being intimately related to emotions, attitudes, personal relationships, institutional conditions, and changing social and historical patterns.

The students identified seven general areas of risk. They recommended ways for prisoners to address these risks, offering specific strategies for practicing self-care, reducing violence and environmental or sexual risks, increasing health knowledge, improving diet and nutrition, reducing emotional problems, increasing social support, and adopting healthier attitudes and beliefs. These strategies are in many cases supported by research that demonstrates their effectiveness among civilian populations. Future research is needed to substantiate the risks identified by these prisoners and to assess the effectiveness of the recommended strategies.

Although we have briefly addressed the influence of masculinity on men's health, we would like to conclude by emphasizing the complexity of its influence on the health of prisoners in particular. Negotiating masculinity presents prisoners with a unique health paradox. Although the students acknowledged that endorsing hegemonic masculinity increased their risks, they also suggested that the failure to enact a degree of manliness in the prison hierarchy would invite trouble. Although most agreed that belligerent or confrontational behavior was dangerous, they were also willing to resort to aggression "if necessary." Therefore, the student-prisoners faced a challenge: They must renegotiate masculinity in ways that protected their health but at the same time reinforced some of the exploitative and violence-prone power structures in the prison hierarchy. Thus, they continually grappled with tensions and contradictions between the definitions of manliness that pervaded the institution itself and their personal feelings and thoughts as men. Additional research is needed to better understand how prison masculinities influence the health risks of prisoners.

Although we have focused on prisoners' personal health practices, it is important to reiterate that structural influences can either facilitate those practices or inhibit them. To the extent to which the prison system erodes men's ability to embrace preventive health values and practices, their collective prognosis remains poor. The continuing institutional failure to give millions of U.S. prisoners the educational tools and support they need to practice preventive health will only increase the future burden on the public health system.

SECTION

IV

Emerging Research on Men, Masculinity, and Health

INTRODUCTION

In 1999, the Columbine High School massacre shook the United States. Sadly, this was not the first—nor was it the last—such incident on a school campus. But disturbing as it is to read or hear news accounts of these incidents, it is more disturbing to me that these accounts consistently remain genderless; the fact that it is always *boys* who commit these heinous acts is rarely mentioned. After the shootings at Columbine, I wrote a short opinion piece that was published in the *Journal of American College Health*, which provides the introduction to this section of the book. In it, I contend that until we as a society fully recognize that it is boys who kill—and acknowledge the effects of the conflicting messages we give to boys—we will not be able to prevent these shootings. I argue, in essence, the need to examine and more deeply understand masculinity. The empirical research presented in the following four chapters attempts to contribute to meeting this need.

YOUTH VIOLENCE? LET'S CALL IT WHAT IT IS[*]

The headline reads, "School Yard Assassins Gun Down 13 in Littleton, Colorado." And everyone asks, "What turns kids into killers?" This is a compelling question. But it is the wrong question.

Who are these kids? A "14-Year-Old Shooter" in Paducah. Two "Middle-School Youth" in Jonesboro. An "Expelled Student" in Springfield. An "Honor Student" in Fayetteville. A "Sophomore" in Pearl. These "kids" all have one thing in common. They are all boys.

---

[*] An earlier version of this article appeared in the *Journal of American College Health*, *48*(3), 1999, 141–142, and is used by permission.

Why are they never referred to as boys? Instead, the media use euphemisms—"student," "youth," "killer." Perhaps it is too painful for us as a society to acknowledge that we have allowed so many of our sons to grow up killing and maiming under our watch. But much as we may hate to admit it, the truth is undeniable. Girls and women seldom kill and maim. Boys and men do. They commit 9 of 10 violent criminal acts in the United States (Department of Justice, 2004), and all of school shootings (Finley, 2007). Indeed, according to an extensive review of research on adolescent violence, male gender is the *only* risk factor consistently associated with the perpetration of violence (Agency for Healthcare Research and Quality, 2004).

School shootings get headlines. Yet the truth is that school shootings account for less than 1% of all homicides among school-age children (Kachur et al., 1996). Each day, 17 children and young adults under age 25 are murdered, and more than 8 of 10 of them are boys or young men (Department of Health and Human Services [DHHS], 2009b). According to the Office of Juvenile Justice and Delinquency Prevention, boys account for 94% of all known juvenile killers (Poe-Yamagata, 1997). In one 10-year period ending in the late 1990s, the number of children known to have committed murder increased 211% among boys and 34% among girls (Poe-Yamagata, 1997).

The common denominator in teen homicides is boys killing boys with guns (Courtenay, 2000a). More than half again as many boys as girls in the United States have access to guns (American School Health Association, 1989). One in 10 high school boys carries guns to school—compared with only about 1 in 70 girls (Centers for Disease Control and Prevention [CDC], 1998g). Among college students nationally, more than 1 in 10 men carries a gun or other weapon, nearly 3 times the number of women who do (Presley, Meilman, & Cashin, 1997); 6% of college men have a working firearm at school, 4 times the number of college women (Miller, Hemenway, & Wechsler, 1999). Among 15- to 19-year-olds, nearly 90% of homicides are firearm related and nearly four of five victims are boys (CDC, 1994e; DHHS, 1994).

As a society, we talk about stricter gun control laws. We talk about banning assault weapons. But if the problem is simply guns, why is it that girls so seldom carry them? And why do more boys than girls have access to guns?

The truth is, we never ask these questions. We take it for granted that boys, not girls, use guns. As long as we take this fact for granted, we will never stop to ask, "Why *boys*?"

Officially, we tell boys not to fight. And for good reason. Fighting precedes most teenage homicides and is often a necessary, if not a sufficient, cause (DHHS, 1991). Yet on television, boys are 60% more likely than girls to be shown using violence—and to be shown that violence is an effective means for male characters to meet their objectives without consequence (Heintz-Knowles, 1995). Three of four Americans believe that a boy *should* have a few fistfights while he is growing up (Gelles & Straus, 1988). Not surprisingly, half of all boys in high school get into a fight each year (CDC, 1998g), and nearly one in seven college men in California gets into a physical fight each year (Patrick, Covin, Fulop, Calfas, & Lovato, 1997).

The suicide mission at Columbine High School in Littleton was carried out by boys who were in pain. But in America we do not teach boys how to talk about their pain. Instead, we teach them to manage their feelings through anger and aggression. It is acceptable for young men to feel angry; it is not acceptable for them to feel sad.

When boys *do* need help, research shows that we discourage them from getting it (Courtenay, 2000c). It is no wonder, then, that when they are depressed, boys and young men are more likely than girls and young women to withdraw from their friends and families (Courtenay, 1998b, 2001a; Pollack, 1998). Eric Harris and Dylan Klebold, the two Columbine High School assassins, were withdrawn. It was a warning sign that went unnoticed.

We ask ourselves why we fail to see the warning signs. But it is warning signs in boys specifically that we do not see. From the day they are born, adults perceive boys as being stronger and less vulnerable than girls (see Chapter 3). When a boy shows signs of sadness we interpret them, instead, as signs of anger. The fact is that boys and young men are emotionally fragile. They account for five of six suicides among children and young adults. However, it is difficult for us to see weakness and vulnerability in our boys.

What, then, is the answer? There is no simple answer. But one thing is clear: We can no longer afford to overlook the violence of young men and boys (Keeling, 1999). Perhaps we can start by recognizing that boys are not *naturally* violent and aggressive. Although male hormones may be associated with violence, boys are also taught to be violent, and causation goes in both directions: The violence and aggression boys learn to demonstrate elevate their testosterone levels (Cohen, Nisbett, Bowdle, & Schwarz, 1996).

We need to acknowledge, as a society, that we are giving boys conflicting messages and that these conflicting messages are leaving boys confused, angry, and scared (Pollack, 1998). We also need to rethink how we teach boys to be boys. Fortunately, there are strategies and new research that can help us to do this (Courtenay, 2000d)—research indicating, for example, that violence is often used to prove or defend one's manliness (Courtenay, 2000a; Nisbett & Cohen, 1996) and that beliefs about masculinity can predict whether a man or boy is prone to get angry (Eisler, 1995).

Most important, any answer to the question of violence must begin with a question about gender. Only then will we begin to understand why it is that *boys* kill.

Gender and Ethnic Differences in Health Beliefs and Behaviors*

WILL H. COURTENAY, DONALD R. McCREARY,
AND JOSEPH R. MERIGHI

Gender differences in mortality found among the general population persist among various racial and ethnic groups in the United States. Among African Americans, for example, men die 7 years younger than women (Department of Health and Human Services [DHHS], 2009a). In every ethnic group, the age-adjusted death rate has been found to be at least 50% higher for men than for women: 80% higher for Hispanics, 70% higher for African Americans and Asian Americans, 60% higher for European Americans, and 50% higher for Native Americans (Collins, Hall, & Neuhaus, 1999). Health disparities also exist among men of various racial and ethnic backgrounds. Indeed, the difference between the life spans of African American men and European American men is greater than the difference between the life spans of women and men in general; African American men die 6 years younger than European American men (DHHS, 2009a). There are important distinctions in the leading causes of death between men of various racial and ethnic groups. The death rate for HIV is highest for African Americans and

---

* An earlier version of this chapter appeared in the *Journal of Health Psychology*, 7(3), 2002, 219–231, and is used by permission in modified/revised form.

Latinos; it is among the five leading causes of death for African American and Latino men (DHHS, 2009a), but it is not among the top 10 leading causes for any other ethnic group of men (Centers for Disease Control and Prevention [CDC], 2006b). African American men are nearly 8 times more likely than European American men to die from homicide or HIV disease (DHHS, 2009a).

As demonstrated in the preceding chapters, there is strong evidence that men and boys in the United States are more likely than women and girls to adopt a variety of attitudes, beliefs, and behaviors that undermine their health and well-being and contribute to their increased risk for serious chronic disease, injury, and death. However, as Neighbors and Howard (1987) note in their discussion of help seeking, little is known about the influence of any interactions between gender and race or ethnicity on health behavior because studies often neglect gender when examining race and neglect race when examining gender. Their large study of African Americans found that men were significantly less likely than women to seek professional help, contact a doctor, or use social services regardless of the type or severity of distressing personal problem that they experienced. Studies examining ethnicity and gender separately, however, suggest that gender differences in health risk behaviors are consistent across several racial and ethnic groups. For example, the prevalence of smoking among Southeast Asian immigrants has been found to be nearly 10 times higher for men than for women (CDC, 1992h), and rates for Southeast Asian American men range from 29% for Hmong to 55% for Cambodians and up to 72% for Laotians (Chen, 1993; Lew & Tanjasiri, 2003; Moeschberger et al., 1997).

Although there is consistent evidence that college men are more likely than college women to adopt unhealthy behaviors (see Chapters 2 and 6), no previous study of college students' health behaviors has been designed to examine possible interactions between gender and ethnicity. It remains unclear whether this gender difference is larger or smaller in certain groups. Similarly, little is known about whether college men from various racial and ethnic groups are equally likely to adopt specific high-risk behaviors and beliefs. Furthermore, previous surveys of college students (e.g., Douglas et al., 1997; Lewis, Goodhart, & Burns, 1996; Patrick, Covin, Fulop, Calfas, & Lovato, 1997)—as well as surveys of adolescents and young adults nationally (Kann et al., 1998)—have failed to examine many of the key indicators of health and well-being relevant to this population. These key indicators include breast and testicular self-examinations, sun protection, social support, help seeking, adherence to traffic regulations, anger and stress, and beliefs related to gender.

To learn more about the influence of gender and ethnicity on a broad range of health risks, the present study assessed young men's and women's involvement in 48 health risk behaviors and health-related beliefs in the following 10 domains: diet, exercise and fitness, substance use, preventive care, social support, safety, anger and stress, beliefs about masculinity, perceived invulnerability, and personal control over health. We addressed the following three research questions: Do women and men differ in their level of involvement in a broad variety of specific health risk behaviors, and in their adoption of health-related beliefs? Do ethnic groups differ in their level of involvement in these behaviors and beliefs? Does gender interact with ethnicity in determining level of involvement in health behaviors and beliefs?

METHOD

Participants

A convenience sample of 1,816 undergraduate students, ranging in age from 18 to 72 years ($M = 22$ years, $SD = 6$ years), was recruited from three 4-year, English-language, California public universities. The sample was composed of 60% women. Thirty-seven percent of the sample was Asian American, 28% European American, 18% Hispanic, 6% African American, and 12% reported their ethnicity as Other (e.g., Middle Eastern) or Mixed Heritage (e.g., Mexican/Irish). The gender and ethnic breakdown of this sample was similar to that of the overall undergraduate student population at 4-year California public colleges in 1999: 56% women, 27% Asian American, 43% European American, 20% Hispanic, 6% African American, and 4% Other/Mixed Heritage (California Postsecondary Education Commission, n.d.a, n.d.b). Twenty-three percent were freshmen, 18% were sophomores, 25% were juniors, and 34% were seniors. The participants represented a wide variety of academic majors, with business (26%), applied arts and sciences (21%), engineering (14%), and social sciences (12%) accounting for the majority. Sixty-nine percent of the sample were single or never married, 22% were in a long-term relationship with a domestic partner, and 8% were married. Most of the respondents lived off campus, either with family (55%), friends (21%) or alone (8%). Eighty-five percent of the participants rated their health as either "excellent" or "good," and 68% reported the same rating for their overall health behavior (i.e., things they did that could improve their health). The majority of respondents believed they had either a "low risk" or "very low risk" of serious illness (80%) and serious injury or accident (81%).

Measure

To assess health risk behaviors, a series of seven behavioral and three attitudinal/belief domains were identified from the extant literature (Courtenay, 2000b). A list of behaviors or beliefs was then generated for each domain. Forty-eight items were produced in total. The seven behavioral domains were *diet* (7 items: e.g., "I avoid chips and fried foods by choosing foods that are baked, broiled, boiled, poached, or stewed");

exercise and fitness (2 items: e.g., "At least three times each week I engage in physical activity that lasts at least 20 minutes and makes me breathe deeply and my heart beat faster"); *substance use* (4 items: e.g., "I smoke cigarettes"); *preventive care* (11 items: e.g., "I have physical and dental exams every year"); *social support* (5 items: e.g., "I have a close friend or family member that I talk to about things that are bothering me"); *safety* (4 items: e.g., "I buckle my safety belt when driving in a motor vehicle"); and *anger and stress* (4 items: e.g., "Things build up inside until I lose my temper"). The three health belief domains were *beliefs about masculinity* (5 items: e.g., "I believe a person should always try to control his or her emotions"); *perceived invulnerability* (3 items: e.g., "I believe it is unlikely I will have a health problem in the near future"); and *personal control over health* (3 items: e.g., "I believe I have control over my future health"). Items were written in the form of statements and worded in the first person. Respondents were asked to rate the extent to which each item was self-descriptive, using a scale from 1 (*always*) to 5 (*never*). Items were written so that they reflected both health risk behaviors or beliefs and health-promoting behaviors or beliefs. These latter items were reverse coded so that high scores on all items indicated a greater degree of health risk.

Procedure

After Institutional Review Board approval was obtained, study participants were recruited by contacting course instructors of all large, general education classes at the participating universities. Identical instructions, along with a detailed statement concerning the voluntary and anonymous nature of the study, were provided to participants to ensure consistency in the completion of the survey instrument. Students were asked to complete the surveys either in class or at home and return them to the investigator. There was an 85% return rate.

Data Analysis

Because we believed it was important to tap a broader range of health risk behaviors and beliefs, we created our own list of health risk items in each of 10 categories. Although we selected each behavior or belief because it was representative of a specific type of health risk (i.e., each item was face valid based on a review of the literature by the senior author; see Courtenay, 2000b), we could not be certain that the items formed psychometrically reliable and valid scales. Therefore, the sample was randomly split into two separate groups (each $N = 908$), and an exploratory factor analysis (EFA; principal components analysis with varimax rotation) was conducted separately for each subsample. Items that paired together on both EFAs were retained for the Gender × Race/Ethnicity ANOVAs that examined the main hypotheses being studied here. These ANOVAs were conducted on the entire sample.

RESULTS

Data Reduction: Forming Health Risk Domains

The Kaiser–Meyer–Olkin (KMO) measure of sampling adequacy was computed separately for both groups to determine whether the correlation matrix for each data set was suitable for EFA. Both KMO statistics (.783 and .784) were above the recommended cutoff of .600, which suggested that the EFAs should proceed. The health risk items were then subjected to EFA using a principal components extraction procedure and a varimax rotation. Because we had no a priori assumptions about the orthogonality of the health risk domains, we also performed the same analyses with an oblique rotation; the analyses with the oblique rotation, however, failed to converge, so only the orthogonal analyses were retained. Three criteria were used to determine how many factors to retain: (1) Kaiser's eigenvalues greater than 1.0 criterion, (2) analysis of the scree plot, and (3) factor interpretability. Within each factor, only items with rotated factor loadings greater than or equal to .40 were retained.

The EFA for the first random subsample produced 16 factors with eigenvalues greater than 1.0. The scree plot showed a discernable elbow at the seventh factor, but the seventh factor was not interpretable. Thus, we decided to retain the first six factors, which accounted for 34.54% of the variance. There were 25 items with rotated factor loadings greater than or equal to .40.

The EFA for the second group revealed 15 factors with eigenvalues greater than 1.0. Again, the scree plot showed an elbow at the seventh factor. As with the first group, that last factor was not interpretable, and only the first six factors were retained. The six factors combined to account for 33.98% of the variance. There were 24 items with rotated factor loadings greater than or equal to .40.

The 21 items that paired together on both EFAs were retained for future analysis. Table 8.1 shows those items and provides rotated factor loadings (per subsample) and descriptive information (based on the whole sample) for each item. In most cases, the items loaded on the same factors for which they were written (i.e., all Diet, Anger and Stress, Preventive Care, Substance Use, and Beliefs About Masculinity items in Table 8.1 were written for those domains). However, two items written for the Preventive Care domain ("I take prescription medicine only as directed by a physician," and "I fill my medical prescriptions immediately") loaded onto a separate, 2-item factor that we labeled Medical Compliance. It should be noted that, although some items from each domain were dropped as a result of the EFA, none of the Exercise and Fitness, Safety, Perceived Invulnerability, or Personal Control Over Health items fitted into the results from the EFAs.

Next, averages were calculated for each of the six health risk domains, or subscales, identified in Table 8.1. The overall domains are presented in terms of descending alpha reliability estimates. Pearson correlation

TABLE 8.1 Descriptive Information for the 21 Health Risk Items Retained After Exploratory Factor Analyses ($N = 1816$)

Scale and Item	RFL[a]	M[b]	SD
Diet ($\alpha \approx = .78$)			
I avoid chips and fried foods by choosing foods that are baked, broiled, boiled, poached, or stewed.	.673/.689	3.14	0.95
I limit the amount of red meat I eat by eating more chicken and fish or grains and beans.	.676/.636	2.66	1.15
I limit the amount of fat I eat by choosing low-fat milk and cheeses, and by reducing the amounts of butter, margarine, and salad dressing I eat.	.754/.771	2.85	1.22
I limit the amount of salt I eat by not adding salt to my food, avoiding salty food, and checking labels for sodium content.	.742/.706	3.21	1.23
I avoid eating large amounts of sugar by limiting candy, desserts, and soft drinks in my diet.	.718/.632	3.16	1.08
Anger and Stress ($\alpha \approx = .72$)			
I get angry and annoyed when I am caught in traffic.	.810/.826	3.17	0.89
I get irritated and mad when waiting in lines.	.846/.853	2.96	0.83
Things build up inside until I lose my temper.	.694/.638	2.67	0.95
Prevention ($\alpha \approx = .71$)			
I conduct a breast or testicular self-exam every month and check my skin for unusual spots or coloring every few months.	.433/.531	3.74	1.11
I have physical and dental exams every year.	.730/.725	2.28	1.19
I get my blood pressure checked every year.	.704/.743	2.97	1.44
I go to all my scheduled physical and mental health appointments.	.515/.533	1.87	0.92
I consult a physician or health care provider right away when I have unfamiliar physical symptoms.	.542/.600	2.57	1.09
Medical Compliance ($\alpha \approx = .70$)			
I take prescription medicine only as directed by a physician.	.841/.822	1.99	1.31
I fill my medicine prescriptions immediately.	.824/.790	2.42	1.24
Substance Use ($\alpha \approx = .57$)			
I smoke cigarettes.	.603/.550	1.55	1.01
I chew tobacco or smoke a pipe.	.518/.468	1.07	0.34
I drink more than two alcoholic drinks a day.	.715/.736	1.48	0.73
I use recreational drugs or steroids.	.727/.761	1.32	0.72

TABLE 8.1 Descriptive Information for the 21 Health Risk Items Retained After Exploratory Factor Analyses ($N = 1816$) (Continued)

Scale and Item	RFL[a]	M[b]	SD
Beliefs About Masculinity ($\alpha \times = .53$)			
I believe it is important for a person to be physically strong.	.564/.671	3.51	0.96
I believe a person should always try to control his or her emotions.	.678/.643	3.57	0.90

[a] RFL = rotated factor loadings (subsample 1/subsample 2).
[b] Range = 1 to 5.

coefficients were computed to assess the degree to which the scales were interrelated. As Table 8.2 shows, there was little overlap.

Gender × Race/Ethnicity

To determine the influence of gender and race or ethnicity on the six domains of health risk that emerged from the EFAs (i.e., Diet, Anger and Stress, Preventive Care, Medical Compliance, Substance Use, and Beliefs About Masculinity), which are outlined in Table 8.1, a series of 2 (Gender) × 5 (Race/Ethnicity) ANOVAs were performed on the entire sample, using domain means as the dependent variables. To control for the increased probability of making a Type I error that results from performing six ANOVAs, an adjusted p value of .008 (i.e., .05/6) was adopted.

Diet

When Diet was the dependent variable, the ANOVA revealed main effects for both Gender, $F(1, 1792) = 20.23$, $p < .0001$ ($\eta^2 = .01$), and

TABLE 8.2 Intercorrelations Among Six Health Risk Scales ($N = 1816$)

Scales	Diet	Anger and Stress	Prevention	Medical Compliance	Substance Use
Anger and Stress	.12**				
Prevention	.27**	.06**			
Medical Compliance	.11**	.03	.32**		
Substance Use	.05*	.12**	.01	.03	
Beliefs About Masculinity	−.04	.06*	.02	.03	−.06*

*$p < .05$; **$p < .01$.

Race/Ethnicity, $F(4, 1792) = 8.63$, $p < .0001$ ($\eta^2 = .02$). While the main effects showed that men engaged in a greater degree of risky dieting behavior than women, and that European Americans had the least risky dieting practices of all the Race/Ethnicity groups, there was a significant Gender × Race/Ethnicity interaction, $F(4, 1792) = 4.29$, $p < .0001$ ($\eta^2 = .01$). Tukey's HSD post hoc tests explored the presence of gender differences within each Race/Ethnicity category and showed that men had significantly poorer dieting practices ($p < .05$) in all Race/Ethnicity groups except Hispanics, where men's and women's dieting behaviors did not differ significantly (see Table 8.3).

Anger and Stress

This analysis revealed only a significant main effect for Race/Ethnicity, $F(4, 1792) = 4.45$, $p < .001$ ($\eta^2 = .01$). Tukey's post hoc tests explored differences in Anger and Stress scores among Race/Ethnicity categories. Findings revealed that Asian American participants reported significantly poorer levels of anger and stress than both European American ($p < .05$) and Hispanic ($p < .05$) participants (see Table 8.3).

Preventive Care

This ANOVA revealed main effects for both Gender, $F(1, 1792) = 49.20$, $p < .0001$ ($\eta^2 = .03$), and Race/Ethnicity, $F(4, 1792) = 24.90$, $p < .0001$ ($\eta^2 = .05$). The main effect for Gender revealed that men

TABLE 8.3   Means for Six Health Risk Domains, by Race and Ethnicity

	African American	Asian American	European American	Hispanic	Other
Diet[a]					
Men	3.25	3.25	3.10	3.06	3.10
Women	3.10	3.01	2.63	3.07	2.84
Anger and Stress[b]	2.91	3.02	2.88	2.85	2.93
Prevention	2.52	2.89	2.42	2.75	2.66
Medical Compliance	2.28	2.32	1.97	2.36	2.08
Substance Use	1.25	1.31	1.47	1.30	1.36
Beliefs About Masculinity	3.63	3.70	3.35	3.52	3.48

[a] The only significant Gender × Race/Ethnicity interaction occurred when the Diet domain was the dependent variable; post hoc tests explored gender differences within Race/Ethnicity groups; matching superscripts indicate a significant gender difference.

[b] All other dependent variables are main effects for Race/Ethnicity only.

reported engaging in fewer preventive behaviors than women (2.89 vs. 2.54, respectively). Post hoc tests exploring the Race/Ethnicity main effect showed that Asian Americans reported significantly more risky practices in the Preventive Care domain than all other Race/Ethnicity groups and that European Americans reported significantly better preventive behaviors (as evidenced by their lower risk scores) than Asian Americans, Hispanics, and those classified as Other (all $ps < .05$; see Table 8.3). The interaction was not significant.

Medical Compliance

When the medical compliance domain was the dependent variable, both the Gender, $F(1, 1792) = 15.84$, $p < .0001$ ($\eta^2 = .01$), and Race/Ethnicity, $F(4, 1792) = 8.17$, $p < .0001$ ($\eta^2 = .02$) main effects were significant. The Gender main effect showed that men reported a poorer degree of medical compliance than women (2.35 vs. 2.09, respectively). Post hoc tests exploring the Race/Ethnicity main effect showed that European Americans reported significantly better medical compliance (as evidenced by their lower risk scores) than the Asian American and Hispanic groups (both $ps < .05$; see Table 8.3). Those classified as Other or Mixed Heritage reported significantly better medical compliance than both Asian Americans and Hispanics (both $ps < .05$; see Table 8.3). The Gender × Race/Ethnicity interaction was not significant.

Substance Use

The ANOVA for Substance Use revealed main effects for both Gender, $F(1, 1792) = 8.01$, $p < .005$ ($\eta^2 = .01$), and Race/Ethnicity, $F(4, 1792) = 11.96$, $p < .0001$ ($\eta^2 = .03$). The main effect for Gender revealed that men reported engaging in riskier substance use practices than women (1.42 vs. 1.31, respectively). Post hoc tests exploring the Race/Ethnicity main effect showed that European Americans reported significantly healthier substance use practices (as evidenced by their lower risk scores) than all other Race/Ethnicity groups (all $ps < .05$; see Table 8.3). The Gender × Race/Ethnicity interaction was not significant.

Beliefs About Masculinity

This ANOVA revealed main effects for both Gender, $F(1, 1792) = 34.79$, $p < .0001$ ($\eta^2 = .02$), and Race/Ethnicity, $F(4, 1792) = 14.71$, $p < .0001$ ($\eta^2 = .03$). The main effect for Gender revealed that men reported riskier health-related beliefs than women (3.68 vs. 3.45, respectively). Post hoc tests exploring the Race/Ethnicity main effect showed that European Americans reported significantly healthier beliefs than Asian Americans, African Americans, and Hispanics (all $ps < .05$; see Table 8.3). In addition, Asian Americans reporter riskier beliefs about masculinity than Hispanics and those classified as Other or Mixed Heritage (both $ps < .05$; see Table 8.3). The Gender × Race/ Ethnicity interaction was not significant.

DISCUSSION

This study first examined whether women and men differed in their level of involvement in a variety of specific health risk behaviors and in their adoption of health-related beliefs. Exploratory factor analysis produced six health risk domains consisting of 21 items. Main effects were found for gender on five of the six domains, with men engaging in significantly riskier behaviors and possessing significantly riskier beliefs in every domain except for Anger and Stress. The finding of riskier behaviors among men than women is consistent with previous studies of college students (e.g., Douglas et al., 1997; Lewis et al., 1996; Patrick et al., 1997). The present study further extends the empirical base to include a range of behaviors and beliefs that is broader than those previously studied; that is, men were more likely than women to report poorer medical compliance and preventive health behaviors—such as self-examinations—as well as beliefs that indicated a greater level of risk.

The finding of no gender difference in risks associated with anger and stress was unanticipated because large and consistent gender differences for these characteristics have been found in previous research (Eagly & Steffen, 1986). The items in the Anger and Stress domain are worded similarly to those designed to assess hostility; men score significantly higher than women on hostility—which is associated with increased health risks, particularly for coronary heart disease (Friedman, 1991; Weidner, Kopp, & Kristenson, 2002; Whitfield, Weidner, Clark, & Anderson, 2002). One possible explanation for this finding is the relatively high percentage of students who commute to campus (84%) in a densely populated region that has experienced increased traffic congestion as a result of a rapidly growing local economy. These factors and their social contexts may have mediated the experience of anger or stress and minimized typical gender differences (Friedman, 1991).

Significant differences in risk based on race and ethnicity emerged in several domains. Asian Americans reported riskier habits than all other ethnic groups for behaviors related to preventive health. Additionally, Asian Americans were at greater risk than European Americans and Hispanics for behaviors related to anger and stress, and held riskier health-related beliefs than either Hispanics or respondents of Mixed Heritage. As discussed elsewhere (Myers, Kagawa-Singer, Kumanyika, Lex, & Markides, 1995), there is a tendency among both policy makers and researchers to assume that Asian Americans are healthier than other racial or ethnic groups. This assumption—which Myers et al. (1995) suggest is largely based on the low utilization of health services among Asian Americans—is not completely unfounded; Asian Americans have the lowest death rates of any racial or ethnic group in the United States (Collins et al., 1999). However, our data suggest that if the health beliefs and behaviors of Asian Americans do not change—particularly among men—their current mortality advantage is likely to decrease in the future. If current smoking trends among Asian Americans continue, for example, it is believed that the mortality rates from lung and heart diseases among Southeast Asian American men will surpass those among other racial and ethnic groups (Chen, 1993).

European Americans reported the least risky dieting practices of any racial or ethnic group. This finding appears consistent with one other study of college students' health behavior, which reported that European Americans—as well as Hispanics—had better dietary habits than African Americans (Douglas et al., 1997). European Americans in the present study also reported the least risky substance use behaviors, which is inconsistent with findings reported by Douglas et al. (1997). In their study of college students nationally, European Americans were more likely than either African Americans or Hispanics to use alcohol frequently, to be current episodic heavy drinkers, or to be current cigarette smokers. European Americans in the present study also reported significantly better medical compliance than Asian Americans and Hispanics, as well as healthier beliefs than Asian Americans, African Americans, and Hispanics.

The principal finding to emerge from this study of multicultural college students is that in nearly every racial and ethnic group, men remained more likely than women to engage in behaviors and adopt beliefs that were detrimental to their health. The one exception was that no gender differences were found among Hispanics for dietary risk factors. This finding is inconsistent with the results from one study of Hispanic adults, aged 20 to 74 years, which reported that fat intake was significantly higher among men than women (Polednak, 1997). Findings from the present study also indicate that Hispanics are at greater risk than European Americans for poor dietary habits. This has important implications for health among Hispanics, particularly given that national data indicate that Hispanics are among those populations whose risk for obesity increased the most during the 1990s (Mokdad et al., 1999). Currently, 21% more Hispanics than Whites are obese (CDC, 2009q). The finding of no interaction for nearly every domain in the present study extends previous research showing greater risk among college men than college women, indicating that this finding holds true regardless of race or ethnicity.

A secondary finding of interest in this study is that many of the health risk behaviors examined were intercorrelated. For example, Diet was positively correlated with Anger and Stress, Preventive Care, Medical Compliance, and Substance Use; the Anger and Stress domain was also correlated with both Preventive Care and Substance Use. However, the magnitude of the correlations was small. Therefore, the knowledge of a person's medical compliance tells us little about the degree to which the person engages in healthy dieting and tells us even less about her or his substance use. These findings suggest that researchers interested in health risk behavior should use a multidimensional approach and not simply assume that unhealthy behaviors correlate. Although some research has found that certain risk behaviors do correlate strongly (e.g., Brener & Collins, 1998), additional research is needed to explore the interrelation among health risk behaviors.

Even though the sample size was large, the findings in this study must be interpreted with caution because a nonrandom sample was used. Furthermore, respondents were residents of northern California, and their responses may not reflect the experiences of young adults in other regions of the United States. Another limitation of this study is that, although the response rate was high (85%), 15% of the surveys were not returned. These factors may have contributed to a selection bias. Additionally, the sample was made up of college students, a social group whose health habits and practices may differ from those of their peers who do not attend postsecondary institutions. College students may benefit from access to health-related services on campus, health education materials in their classes, and university-sponsored health campaigns. They may also benefit from easily accessible recreational facilities and fitness centers. Alternatively, the time restraints associated with attending classes, completing course work, and being employed either part-time or full-time may hamper students' effort to engage in positive health practices. A final limitation concerns the wording of one item in the Preventive Care domain. The item "I conduct a breast or testicular exam every month and check my skin for unusual spots or coloring every few months" is overinclusive and should be separated into two questions: one about breast or testicular cancer and one about skin cancer and melanoma. Although this item did load significantly onto the Preventive Care factor, it is unknown which part of the question the respondents were addressing.

Several implications can be drawn from this study. Most importantly, the findings suggest that gender-specific, culturally appropriate health promotion and disease prevention interventions are needed. Educational interventions appear particularly warranted for men. This is especially true because more men than women in this study reported that their overall health behavior was either "good" or "excellent," despite their obviously greater risk. Although many counseling and psychological interventions with men have been recommended in the past several decades (Courtenay, 2000d), rarely do these interventions address men's physical health. Even less frequently do these interventions address the specific health needs of men of various racial and ethnic backgrounds. Given that a link is consistently found between health risk and masculinity—as well as other psychosocial and behavioral factors—interdisciplinary approaches to fostering health and well-being are especially important. Outcome research is needed to measure the effectiveness of gender-specific interventions, such as those outlined in Chapter 12.

9

Masculinity and Gender Role Conflict

How They Influence the Likelihood That Men Will Engage in Multiple High-Risk Behaviors

WILL H. COURTENAY AND DONALD R. McCREARY

Men are more likely than women to adopt behaviors and beliefs that undermine their health, so they are at greater risk for preventable death. This gender difference remains true across a variety of racial and ethnic groups, and among adolescents and young adults, as we have seen in the preceding chapters. The age group with the greatest gender disparity in mortality is young adults aged 15 to 24 years, and three of every four deaths annually in this age group are male (see Chapter 1). Young adults are at serious risk for disease, injury, and death that result from driving, drinking alcohol, and being sexually active. The leading cause of death for 15- to 24-year-olds is injuries resulting from motor vehicle crashes. Wearing a safety belt reduces the risk for serious injury by up to 65% and reduces the risk for death by 45% (see Chapter 2). Men of all ages, and younger men in particular, are less likely than women to wear safety belts, either as drivers or as passengers. Men also drive more dangerously, and this, combined with their failure to wear safety belts, contributes to the fact that, among 15- to 24-year-olds, three of four of those killed in motor vehicle crashes are men.

Alcohol use is also strongly associated with men's health risks. As we have already seen, research consistently indicates that men drink more alcohol—and drink more frequently—than women, and that more men than women are alcohol dependent. These gender differences are also consistently reported for young adults. Among college students nationally, men are also significantly more likely than women to binge drink, which is associated with disease, injury, and death. College binge drinkers are more than 21 times more likely than their nonbinging peers to experience alcohol-related problems, 10 times more likely to get hurt or injured, and 7 times more likely to have unprotected sex (see Chapters 2 and 6). Men's alcohol consumption contributes to their higher rates of both nonfatal and fatal injuries, as well as to their greater risk for death as pedestrians and from motor vehicle crashes, homicide, suicide, drowning, and bicycling. Among young adults, men constitute the vast majority of those who drive drunk. Driving drunk is the leading cause of death for people under 25 years old, and most of those who die are young men.

Men—including young men—are more likely than women to be sexually active, to engage in high-risk sexual activities, to have more sexual partners, to have sex while under the influence of alcohol or other drugs, and to be nonmonogamous in adulthood. Consequently, the percentage of men at high risk for sexually transmitted diseases (STDs) is double that of women. Nearly half of all STDs occur among people aged 15 to 24 years. Among college students specifically, men begin sexual activity earlier in their lives, have more sexual partners, and are more likely than women to have sex under the influence of alcohol or other drugs. Compounding these risks, only one third to one half of sexually active college men use condoms; even among those at high risk for STDs, three of four use condoms occasionally or never. Thus, just being sexually active appears to be a significant risk factor for young adult males.

These risk behaviors do not typically appear in isolation. Indeed, as we have seen in preceding chapters, people's health-related behaviors frequently co-occur in healthy or unhealthy clusters. Therefore, it is not always a single behavior that places men's overall health at risk, but rather an interaction of multiple risk behaviors, such as driving while intoxicated and not wearing safety belts, or having unprotected sex while intoxicated. In short, it may be engaging in multiple health risk behaviors that places men's overall health at the greatest risk.

But why do men behave more self-destructively (e.g., by engaging in multiple high-risk behaviors) than women, and why do they do less to promote their health? As we saw in the preceding chapters, one possibility is that men's gender or masculinity influences men's health attitudes and behaviors. Social scientists have begun to examine the relationships between men's beliefs about how men should be (i.e., masculinity ideology [MI]; Thompson, Pleck, & Ferrera, 1992) and men's health behavior. As discussed in Chapter 1, these studies provide preliminary evidence that men and adolescent males who adopt traditional or stereotypic beliefs about masculinity (e.g., believing that a man should be "sure of himself," should not "act like a girl," and should be "physically tough") are more likely to engage in unhealthy behaviors—such as drinking and unprotected sex—and to have greater health risks than their peers with less traditional beliefs. These findings are consistent with a social constructionist perspective that risk taking and disregard for their health are among the resources that men use to define themselves as "masculine" or "manly" (see Chapters 3 and 4).

Masculinity, however, is a multidimensional construct (McCreary, 1990a), and MI is but one approach to conceptualizing and studying men's gender (see Chapter 4 for a critique of the concept of a single gender role and discussions regarding the plurality of masculinity—or masculinities). Other approaches include assessing the degree to which men have internalized male-stereotyped personality traits (e.g., Spence & Helmreich, 1978) or the extent to which they act in male-stereotypic ways (e.g., McCreary & Rhodes, 2001; Orlofsky, 1981). Another approach is to assess how men experience their gender and the stress they encounter in their attempts to adhere to perceived social norms of masculinity (Eisler, 1995; O'Neil, Good, & Holmes, 1995). One construct used to evaluate this masculinity-related stress is gender role conflict (GRC; O'Neil, Helms, Gable, David, & Wrightsman, 1986). GRC is defined as a psychological state that occurs when rigid, sexist, or restrictive gender roles result in personal restrictions, devaluation, or negative consequences for oneself or for others (O'Neil et al., 1995).

It has been hypothesized that men who experience GRC are at greater risk for health problems than other men (O'Neil et al., 1995). Stress and related psychological conflict have been found to be associated with several risk behaviors, including increased alcohol use (Cappell & Greely, 1987), smoking, and poor dietary habits (Ng & Jeffery, 2003). However, only two studies exploring the relationship between GRC and health behavior have been published (Blazina & Watkins, 1996; Monk & Ricciardelli, 2003). These studies both showed that higher levels of GRC were associated with increased alcohol and cannabis use. However, as we mentioned earlier, men are more likely than women to engage in multiple risky behaviors. No study has yet explored the relationship between various dimensions of masculinity and involvement in multiple high-risk behaviors. Thus, the primary purpose of the present study is to extend previous research by examining the relationships among MI, GRC, and the likelihood of engaging (vs. not engaging) in three age-related risk behaviors: alcohol use, inconsistent or no safety belt use, and sexual activity

METHOD

Participants

One hundred fifty-three young men from a small private liberal arts college in the Midwest volunteered to participate in this study. Participants' ages ranged from 17 to 25 years ($M = 19.54$, $SD = 1.34$). Participants represented all academic years: 40% were in their first year, 29% were sophomores, 17% were juniors, 14% were seniors, and 1% had already graduated. Eighty-nine percent reported their ethnic background as European American or White, with the remaining participants being mostly of Asian, Native American, or Hispanic origin. The majority of participants (88%) lived on campus.

Measures

All participants completed an intranet-based survey that assessed various demographic factors, health behaviors, and aspects of male gender role socialization.

Masculine Ideology

Traditional versus liberal attitudes about masculinity were assessed using five items: (1) Do you believe that taking risks that are sometimes dangerous is part of what it means to be a man and part of what distinguishes men from women? (2) As a man, how important is it for you to be self-sufficient and always to try to handle problems on your own? (3) As a man, how important is it for you to be physically strong and tough? (4) As a man, how important is it for you to control your emotions and never to reveal sadness or vulnerability? and (5) As a man, how important is it for you not to engage in activities that you think others might consider feminine? Each item was scored on a 4-point interval scale. All items were averaged, and higher scores indicate a more traditional view of how men should be. The alpha reliability estimate for the masculine ideology measure was .75. These items are similar to those used on preexisting, albeit larger, measures of MI (e.g., Male Role Norms Scale; Thompson & Pleck, 1995).

Gender Role Conflict Scale

Men's GRC was measured using the Gender Role Conflict Scale (GRCS) (O'Neil et al., 1986). The GRCS is a psychometrically validated questionnaire (Good et al., 1995) that contains 37 items grouped into four subscales. The first subscale—Success, Power, and Competition (SPC; 13 items)—measures concerns about personal achievement, as well as about gaining dominance and superiority over others. The second subscale—Restrictive Emotionality (RE; 10 items)—assesses difficulty and fears about emotional self-disclosure and the verbal expression of feelings. The third subscale—Restrictive Affectionate Behavior Between Men (RABBM; 8 items)—examines discomfort associated with verbal and physical expressions of caring toward other men. The fourth subscale—Conflicts Between Work and Family Relations (CBWFR; 6 items)—measures difficulty and dissatisfaction with the balancing of school or work and family relations, which results in health problems or other negative consequences. Each item is scored on a 6-point interval scale. All items were averaged, and higher scores indicate a higher degree of conflict in each area. Alpha reliability estimates in this sample were high: .91 (SPC), .90 (RE), .87 (RABBM), and .87 (CBWFR).

Health Risk Category

Responses to questions about three health-related behaviors were used to determine the participant's risk category as either low or high. The three behaviors were related to alcohol use, sexual activity, and safety belt use. Alcohol use was assessed by asking participants to indicate the number of alcoholic beverages they had consumed on a typical weekend night during the past month. Sexual activity was assessed by asking participants whether they had had sexual intercourse during the past year (Yes/No). Safety belt use was assessed by asking participants how frequently they had used safety belts during the past year. For this last question, responses were scored on a 5-point interval scale, ranging from *never* to *always*. Participants in the low Health Risk Category reported zero alcohol use during the past 30 days, no sexual intercourse during the past year, and consistent safety belt use during the past year. Participants in the high Health Risk Category reported greater than zero alcohol use during the past 30 days, sexual intercourse during the past year, and lack of consistent use of safety belts.

Procedure

Health officials at the university placed the survey on their intranet site and sent an e-mail to all students explaining the goals of the survey and encouraging them to participate. All participants were informed that, if they chose to participate, their responses would be confidential, that they did not have to answer any question they felt uncomfortable answering, and that they could withdraw their participation at any time. At the end of the survey, participants were given the option of completing a separate page with their name and contact information to win a prize or a store voucher. The data and identification information went to separate servers and were not combined. Of the 1,850 students enrolled at the college at that time, 527 (29%) completed usable surveys.

RESULTS

Of the 527 responses to the intranet survey, 79 low-risk and 74 high-risk individuals were identified. Analyses were conducted only on this high-versus low-risk subsample.

Descriptive Statistics

Means, standard deviations, and bivariate correlations are presented in Table 9.1. The means for all the gender role scales fall above the mid-point, suggesting that the average respondent holds a more traditional (vs. liberal) view of men and masculinity, and that he experiences a fairly high degree of GRC. The significant correlations among MI and the four GRCS subscales were moderate, with approximately 22% of their variances being shared. The correlations among GRCS subscales were slightly higher than those observed in other studies (e.g., Fisher & Good, 1998), but suggested that between only 9 and 35% of their content overlaps.

Univariate differences between low- and high-risk participants in the responses to the four GRCS subscales and the MI were explored using independent samples *t* tests. As Table 9.2 indicates, high-risk participants rated themselves significantly higher than the low-risk participants in both MI and the GRCS's SPC and RE subscales. However, it should be noted that these are only main effects. Because the GRCS and MI scales are somewhat intercorrelated (as shown in Table 9.1), a multiple regression analysis is needed to determine the unique associations between each of these predictors and Health Risk Category.

Regression Analyses

To determine the degree to which each of the masculinity measures uniquely predicted Health Risk Category membership, a binary logistic

TABLE 9.1   Descriptive Statistics for Male Gender Role Variables

Scale	*Range*	*M*	*SD*	MI	SPC	RE	RABBM
					Correlations		
MI	1–4	2.35	0.59				
SPC	1–6	3.67	0.96	.47***			
RE	1–6	3.11	1.00	.47***	.53***		
RABBM	1–6	3.16	1.01	.46***	.46***	.59***	
CBWFR	1–6	3.48	1.08	.07	.39***	.30***	.31***

Note: MI = Masculinity Ideology; SPC = Success, Power, and Control; RE = Restrictive Emotionality; RABBM = Restrictive Affectionate Behavior Between Men; CBWFR = Conflicts Between Work and Family Relations.
*$p < .05$; **$p < .01$; ***$p < .001$.

TABLE 9.2 Independent Samples *t*-Tests Exploring Differences in GRCS and MI as a Function of Health Risk Category

Scale	Low-Risk Category		High-Risk Category		*t*	95% CI for *t*-test
	M	*SD*	*M*	*SD*		
MI	2.25	0.58	2.46	0.59	−2.18*	−0.40 to −0.02
SPC	3.42	0.90	3.94	0.95	−3.49***	−0.82 to −0.52
RE	2.89	0.90	3.35	1.05	−2.90**	−0.77 to −0.15
RABBM	3.19	1.05	3.13	0.98	0.36	−0.27 to 0.39
CBWFR	3.46	1.05	3.50	1.12	−0.25	−0.39 to 0.30

Note: MI = Masculinity Ideology; SPC = Success, Power, and Control; RE = Restrictive Emotionality; RABBM = Restrictive Affectionate Behavior Between Men; CBWFR = Conflicts Between Work and Family Relations.
*p < .05; **p < .01; ***p < .001.

regression analysis was performed. For this analysis, low risk was coded as 0 and high risk was coded as 1. The MI scale and the four GRCS subscales were entered into the regression equation simultaneously.

The regression equation was statistically reliable, $\chi^2(5, n = 153) = 27.72$, $p < .0001$. This finding indicates that the masculinity variables can significantly differentiate low- and high-risk participants. The equation's ability to predict category membership correctly was high, with 76% of the low-risk and 63% of the high-risk group predicted correctly. The amount of variance explained by the equation was moderate, with the Nagelkerke $R^2 = .22$.

Table 9.3 contains the regression coefficients for each of the masculinity predictors. The Wald statistic reveals that only three of the five

TABLE 9.3 Regression Coefficients, Odds Ratios, and 95% CI for Odds Ratios for Model Predicting Health Risk Category From Five Measures of Masculinity

Variables	B	S.E.	Wald	Odds Ratio	95% CI for Odds Ratio
MI	.30	.37	0.65	1.35	0.66–2.76
SPC	.77	.27	8.16**	2.16	1.27–3.65
RE	.72	.27	7.16**	2.05	1.21–3.46
RABBM	−.90	.28	10.24***	0.41	0.24–0.71
CBWFR	−.17	.19	0.76	0.85	0.58–1.23

Note: MI = Masculinity Ideology; SPC = Success, Power, and Control; RE = Restrictive Emotionality; RABBM = Restrictive Affectionate Behavior Between Men; CBWFR = Conflicts Between Work and Family Relations.
*p < .05; **p < .01; ***p < .001.

variables were unique predictors of Health Risk Category. Higher levels of SPC and RE, as well as lower levels of RABBM, were all associated with a greater probability of being in the high-risk category. The odds ratios show the changes in the probabilities associated with being in the high-risk category, as a function of increases or decreases in scores on the gender role measures. A single-unit increase in either SPC or RE is associated with a doubling of the likelihood of being in the high-risk category. A single-unit decrease in RABBM is associated with a 60% decrease in the likelihood of being in the high-risk category.

DISCUSSION

Building on previous research linking MI with high-risk behavior (e.g., Courtenay, 1998a; McCreary, Newcomb, & Sadava, 1999), this study found that men who adopt traditional beliefs about masculinity are more likely than men whose beliefs are less traditional to engage in multiple high-risk behaviors. Not previously reported in the literature is the finding that men who experience GRC (related to SPC and RE) also engage in multiple high-risk behaviors. This suggests that men who place emphasis on achievement and status, as well as on gaining authority and control over others (i.e., SPC), or those who experience discomfort in disclosing their feelings to others—especially to other men (i.e., RE)—are at greater risk for physical harm associated with these behaviors than men who do not experience GRC. However, these are bivariate analyses only; they are confounded by moderate correlations among the masculinity measures.

When a regression analysis is used, and the unique associations between the predictors and the likelihood of engaging in multiple high-risk behaviors are assessed, two findings emerge. First, the associations between both SPC and RE and the two health risk categories remain significant. The odds ratios show the magnitude of the association: GRC in these two areas more than doubles the probability of being in the high-risk category. This finding is consistent with a variety of studies linking GRC with mental health problems, as well as with the decreased likelihood of seeking help for those problems (O'Neil, 2008; O'Neil et al., 1995). It is also consistent with one previous study that reported a slight positive correlation between alcohol dependence and the SPC subscale (Blazina & Watkins, 1996). However, the present study extends these findings. It indicates that GRC is associated with the likelihood of engaging in multiple health risk behaviors, specifically three potentially seriously harmful high-risk behaviors: alcohol use, sexual activity, and inconsistent safety belt use.

The second finding that emerged from the regression analysis was that the association between MI and the likelihood of engaging in multiple high-risk behaviors disappeared and was replaced by a negative association between RABBM and risky behavior. This indicates that the bivariate associations between MI and the GRC subscales (see Table 9.1) may have been suppressing the true association between RABBM and the likelihood of engaging in multiple high-risk behaviors.

The finding that greater conflict related to RABBM is associated with a decreased probability of engaging in multiple high-risk behaviors was unexpected and, we believe, reflects the complexity of masculinity. The high percentage of students involved in college sports on this particular campus leads us to speculate that athletic involvement might be a moderating factor in this association. Certain physical displays of affection (e.g., hugging) appear frequent and culturally acceptable among athletes, particularly among those involved in contact sports. New empirical research is needed to explore this possibility.

The finding that, among young men, GRC is associated with a greater risk for engaging in multiple high-risk behaviors is an important first step in exploring why men in general engage in riskier behavior. It has been suggested that GRC contributes to a fragile sense of masculinity, which men then attempt to bolster by rejecting that which is stereotypically feminine and embracing that which is hypermasculine (Blazina & Watkins, 2000). As discussed elsewhere (Courtenay, 2000b, 2000c), the health-related behaviors that people engage in—like the clothes they wear and the work they do—are tools for defining and enacting representations of gender. In many contemporary, westernized societies, adopting positive health behaviors is socially constructed as feminine, whereas dismissing preventive health practices and taking risks are considered means of demonstrating "real" manhood. From this perspective, one explanation for our findings is that men experiencing SPC- and RE-related GRC reject the adoption of safe drinking and driving, and sexual abstinence, and instead engage in riskier behaviors as a means of reducing GRC and demonstrating or proving their masculinity. However, given the quasi-experimental design of this study, cause and effect cannot be definitively determined.

Another explanation for our results is that men who engage in high-risk behaviors are exposed to a culture of hypermasculinity in which they experience increased conflict regarding their feared inability to live up to the rigid standards of that culture's social norms of masculinity (Courtenay, 2004b, 2007). Alternatively, high-risk behaviors may represent maladaptive responses to gender conflict and psychological stress. This explanation would be consistent with one study, which found that the well-documented link between stress and poor health outcomes is explained in part by unhealthy behaviors stimulated by stress (Ng & Jeffery, 2003). Furthermore, as discussed in Chapter 1, previous research indicates that men—particularly stereotypically traditional men—use less healthy or adaptive responses in coping with stress than women do. It is also conceivable that more than one of these explanations is true, and that there is a reciprocal relationship between these factors in mediating risk. Further research is needed to clarify the causes of men's involvement in multiple high-risk behaviors. However, the present study suggests that masculinity may be an important missing cofactor—one of the "secret, powerful social factors" (Verbrugge, 1990, p. 183)—in analyses of gender and health where men's greater risks persist and remain unexplained after adjusting for numerous variables (Wingard, 1984).

There are three limitations to our findings. First, this was an opt-in sample from the entire population of students at an all-male college. Only 29% of the students completed the survey, which may represent a sample bias. However, this sample size is consistent with the sample size for other types of opt-in procedures, such as mail-in surveys (Krosnick, 1999). Krosnick notes that the bias against small sample sizes is often unwarranted, and that higher response rates do not necessarily translate into increased representativeness and sample heterogeneity.

A second limitation to these findings is the ethnic and racial homogeneity of the sample. Almost 90% of the respondents were European Americans. This leads to questions about the generalizability of our findings to other racial and ethnic groups. Our previous research, reported in Chapter 8, has shown that college men are more likely than college women to adopt behaviors that undermine their health, and that this finding persists across racial and ethnic groups; however, it does not necessarily follow that the associations between these five dimensions of masculinity and the likelihood of engaging in multiple high-risk behaviors will be the same.

A final limitation is our categorization procedure. Our low-risk group was extremely low risk, in that they had never consumed any alcohol, were not sexually active, and consistently used safety belts. On the other hand, our high-risk group might more accurately have been called a higher-risk group, in that, although they reported risk behavior in all three areas, the degree to which they engaged in each behavior was not factored into the categorization. Thus, there may be gradations in the associations among our predictors and our criteria, as a function of degree of multiple high-risk behaviors. Unfortunately, sample size limitations prevented us from examining this question.

10

Measurement of Men's Help Seeking

*Development and Evaluation of the Barriers to Help Seeking Scale**

ABIGAIL K. MANSFIELD, MICHAEL E. ADDIS, AND WILL H. COURTENAY

Research has consistently documented that men seek help less often than women for a variety of problems in living, including substance abuse, mental illness, and physical problems (see Chapter 1). With regard to physical health, men are more likely than women to have gone at least 2 years since their last contact with a physician, but suffer higher rates of heart disease, cancer, suicide, and substance abuse than do women. Thus, overwhelming evidence suggests that men underuse health services. In a similar vein, men endorse more negative attitudes toward help seeking than do women and are generally less inclined than are women to seek help when they need it. As discussed in previous chapters, men's disinclination to seek help puts them at increased risk

* An earlier version of this chapter appeared in *Psychology of Men and Masculinity*, 6(2), 2005, 95–108, and is used by permission in modified/revised form

for physical and emotional problems, as well as for more severe problems when they do receive help.

Although lack of health insurance and the cost of health care create barriers to health care, especially among marginalized groups, these factors do not by themselves explain gender differences in health care utilization (see Chapters 1 and 2). Among both the poor and the rich, men are more likely than women to have had no recent contact with a health care provider. For example, African American men have been found to be less likely than African American women to visit physicians, even when income is held constant (Neighbors & Howard, 1987). Even when health services are provided without cost, men use them less than women.

ORGANIZING FRAMEWORKS OF THE BARRIERS TO HELP SEEKING SCALE

Because men's relatively low rates of help seeking and service utilization have only recently come to be considered problematic, what we currently know about why men do or do not seek help is limited (Addis & Mahalik, 2003). The present study describes the development and evaluation of the Barriers to Help Seeking Scale (BHSS), a measure designed to assess variables men identify as obstacles to seeking help for physical or mental health problems. Since 1970, most studies of help seeking have relied on Fischer and Turner's (1970) scale of attitudes toward help seeking, but there is currently no measure that targets *specific* barriers to help seeking for either mental health or physical problems. Indeed, Fischer and Turner's scale measures attitudes toward seeking professional psychological help; it does not measure specific barriers to help seeking, and it treats attitudes as stable, rather than contextually bound. We believe that a measure of contextually specific barriers to help seeking would make an important contribution to the study of help seeking. By first identifying specific obstacles to men's use of mental and physical health services, it may be possible to develop interventions that facilitate help seeking. Below we briefly describe two bodies of theory and research used as organizing frameworks for developing and evaluating the BHSS. They are derived from a theoretical integration of gender role socialization and social psychological analyses of help seeking (Addis & Mahalik, 2003).

Gender role socialization theories hold that men and women acquire gendered behaviors and attitudes from the cultures in which they live. Norms (prescriptions for how men and women should behave) and stereotypes (generalizations about what men and women are like) guide attitudes and behavior related to gender (Pleck, 1981, 1995). The constructs of gender role conflict (GRC; O'Neil, Helms, Gable, David, & Wrightsman, 1986), gender role strain (Pleck, 1981, 1995), and gender role stress (Eisler, 1995; Eisler & Skidmore, 1987) refer to specific consequences of masculine role socialization that may affect men's willingness and ability to seek help for problems in living. For example, O'Neil et al. (1986) have identified four categories of gender role conflict, including an orientation toward success, power, and competition; restrictive emotionality; restrictive affectionate behavior between men; and conflicts between work and family. Specific components of gender role conflict have been shown to be related both to negative attitudes toward help seeking and increased symptoms of depression (O'Neil, 2008). Thus, gender role theory and research suggest that there are individual differences in the degree to which men are affected by and endorse particular masculinity "messages," and that many of these messages militate against seeking help.

Existing measures of masculine gender roles and norms are geared toward the assessment of general and cross-situationally stable individual differences (Brannon & Juni, 1984; Eisler & Skidmore, 1987; O'Neil et al., 1986; Snell, 1986; Thompson & Pleck, 1986). These measures place limitations on the study of men's help seeking because they cannot account for within-person or cross-situational variability in men's behavior; some men may seek help for some problems but not others, under some conditions and not others (Addis & Mahalik, 2003). We took two steps toward addressing this possibility in designing the BHSS. First, in constructing items we incorporated specific masculinity norms and roles not as general personality characteristics (e.g., I don't like to show other people my feelings) but rather as context-specific barriers to seeking help for a particular problem (e.g., I would not seek help for this problem because I wouldn't want to get too emotional). Second, to identify processes that may distinguish barriers from situation to situation, we included items derived from basic social psychological research on help-seeking behavior.

The social psychology of help seeking draws attention to processes that mediate whether a person will seek help in a particular situation. Four such principles were instrumental to the development of the BHSS: the ego-centrality of a problem, or the degree to which a problem is perceived to reflect an important quality about oneself (Nadler, 1990); the normativeness of a problem, or the degree to which a problem is considered normal or common (Nadler & Maysless, 1983); *reactance*, which refers to the tendency to take steps to restore autonomy when one perceives that autonomy has been threatened (Brehm, 1966); and *reciprocity*, which refers to the extent to which a person receiving help will have the opportunity to return the help at some point in the future. Each of these variables has been shown to affect help-seeking behavior in experimental or correlational research on help seeking (Wills & DePaulo, 1991). For example, people are less likely to seek help for problems that are presented as highly ego-central and non-normative (Nadler, 1990; Nadler & Maysless, 1983). This principle is reflected in items such as "I would think less of myself for needing help" and "I would feel stupid for not knowing how to figure this problem out." Similarly, people are less likely to seek help when their autonomy is perceived to be threatened (Brehm, 1966), and when they believe they will not have the opportunity to return the help they receive in the future (Wills & DePaulo, 1991). Reactance was incorporated into the BHSS with items such as "I don't like other people telling me what to do" and "I like to be in charge of everything in my life." With regard to ego-centrality, theory suggests that people should report being less willing to seek help if they think that doing so would threaten a valued quality about themselves, such as stoicism. Similarly, the principle of normativeness suggests that people should report being less likely to seek help for a problem if the problem is thought to be uncommon, and the principle of reactance suggests that people should be less likely to seek help if they think that doing so would limit their autonomy or independence. Finally, the principle of reciprocity suggests that people should be less likely to seek help if there is no opportunity to return the help in the future.

In summary, we had two goals in developing the BHSS. First, we hoped to identify the extent to which GRC and the social psychological processes identified above contribute to barriers to men's help seeking for specific problems in living. Second, we wanted to create a measure that allowed for the study of variations in the context of help seeking, such as the particular problem, the type of help that might be sought, as well as individual differences in the particular masculinity norms to which different men adhere.

HYPOTHESES

We hypothesized that the BHSS would reveal a multifactor structure of barriers to help seeking corresponding to different masculinity norms and social psychological processes. Specifically, we predicted that four factors would emerge. We expected a factor related to the desire to appear in emotional control would emerge along with a factor related to the desire to appear autonomous and self-reliant. We also predicted that a factor related to concerns about privacy and physical touch would emerge because the BHSS asks participants to consider seeking help from a medical professional. Finally, we predicted that a factor related to concrete, nonmasculinity-related barriers to help seeking would emerge. With regard to validity, we predicted that barriers to help seeking would correlate with a measure of masculine GRC and with attitudes toward help seeking.

STUDY 1

The goal of this study was to develop an item pool and format for the BHSS, and to evaluate its factor structure, internal consistency, and convergent validity in an all-male sample of undergraduates.

Method

Measure Development

We began the process of developing items for the BHSS by reviewing the literature on gender role strain, GRC (e.g., O'Neil et al., 1986; O'Neil, Good, & Holmes, 1995; Pleck, 1981, 1995), and help seeking (e.g., Fischer & Turner, 1970; Leong & Zachar, 1999; Nadler, 1990; Nadler & Mayless, 1983; Robertson & Fitzgerald, 1992; Wills & DePaulo, 1991). Based on the literature review, we generated a list of potential barriers to help seeking and phrased each as a reason a person might choose not to seek help for a problem. We created between one and four items for each barrier. Some items were intended to tap male gender role norms, such as the idea that men should be self-reliant, emotionally controlled, and strong. Other items targeted social psychological processes related to help seeking, such as the need to maintain autonomy, and other items referred to more concrete barriers to seeking help, such as lack of time, money, or transportation. Finally, some items reflected the tendency to minimize problems and therefore avoid seeking help for them. The original item pool consisted of 54 statements, each worded as a potential reason why a person might choose not to seek help for a persistent, but not disabling, pain in his body.

The directions for the BHSS read as follows:

> Imagine that you begin to experience some pain in your body. The pain is not so overwhelming that you can't function. However, it continues for more than a few days and you notice it regularly. You consider seeking help from a medical doctor or other clinician at the student health center. Below are several reasons why you might choose NOT to seek help. Please read each reason and decide how important it would be in keeping you from seeking help.

The BHSS uses a 5-point Likert-type scale to rate each item, with lower numbers indicating that the item is less of a barrier to seeking help.

Participants

Participants were 537 undergraduate men at a private all-men's college in the Midwest; 30.2% were first-year students, 27.2% were sophomores, 19.0% were juniors, and 21.0% were seniors. Of the sample, 91.6% identified themselves as European American, 0.7% as Hispanic/Latino, 0.4% as African American, 1.1% as Native American, and 1.1% as Asian. In addition, 1.1% of participants identified their race or ethnic identity as Other, and 2.2% chose not to provide any information for this item. The mean age of participants was 19.9 years ($SD = 1.16$).

Measures

The Barriers to Help Seeking Scale   The original version of the BHSS consisted of 54 items, each of which identified a reason someone might choose not to seek help for a persistent pain in his or her body. Forty-four of the items were aimed at general help seeking, and eight additional items targeted barriers specific to medical intervention (e.g., "I don't want some stranger touching me in ways that I'm not comfortable with" or "It's difficult for me to talk with doctors and health professionals"). The scale asks participants to use a Likert-type scale ranging from 0 to 4 (0 = *not at all*, 4 = *very much*) to rate how much of a reason each item would be to not seek help for the problem described above.

The Gender Role Conflict Scale   The Gender Role Conflict Scale (GRCS; O'Neil et al., 1986) assesses *male gender role conflict*, which is defined as a "psychological state in which socialized gender roles have negative consequences on the person and others" (O'Neil et al., 1995, p. 167). More specifically, O'Neil et al. (1995) explain that GRC occurs when adherence to rigid or restrictive gender norms results in damage to the self or others. The GRCS consists of 37 statements that target the extent to which respondents endorse statements such as "Moving up the career ladder is important to me," "Expressing feelings makes me feel vulnerable to attack by other people," "I often feel that I need to be in charge of those around me," or "Men who touch other men make me uncomfortable." Participants are asked to rate the degree to which they agree with each statement on a scale of 1 (*disagree*) to 6 (*agree*). The GRCS comprises four subscales, including Success, Power, and Competition; Restrictive Emotionality; Restrictive Sexual and Affectionate Behavior Between Men; and Conflicts Between Work and Family Relations. Responses are summed with higher scores reflecting an expression of greater GRC. The subscales are summed to yield a total score. The internal consistency of the measure is good (Cronbach's alpha ranges from .75 to .85), as is test–retest reliability (.72 to .86) (O'Neil et al., 1986). The GRCS has demonstrated discriminant validity with the Personal Attributes Questionnaire (Sharpe & Heppner, 1991; Sharpe, Heppner, & Dixon, 1995) and convergent validity with the Brannon Masculinity Scale (Good et al., 1995).

Procedure

The BHSS and GRCS were administered as part of a larger survey of an array of health-related behaviors among the student body. Students received an e-mail providing a link to an online questionnaire. Participation was anonymous, and data collection lasted for 2 weeks. Students who participated had their names entered into a lottery for a chance to win prizes.

Results

Exploratory Factor Analysis

Our intent was to develop a multidimensional measure of barriers to help seeking. We began by conducting a series of principal components factor analyses to determine the underlying structure of the BHSS. In the initial analysis, all 54 items were included. The analysis yielded nine factors with eigenvalues greater than 1 and accounted for 66% of the variance. Because the last four of the nine factors accounted for only 9.3% of the variance and were difficult to interpret, we considered a 5-factor solution to be a good estimate of the factor structure. We conducted a second principal components analysis with a specified 5-factor solution and rotated the matrix to an oblique solution. An oblique rotation was chosen because we did not expect the factors to be uncorrelated with each other; men who endorsed some barriers to help seeking were also likely to endorse others. These five factors accounted for 57% of the variance and made sense conceptually. We also ran a principal components analysis with a specified 3-factor solution, but the factors were less interpretable than those in the 5-factor solution. Therefore, we chose to use the 5-factor solution for interpretation. Items were retained if they loaded at least .4 on a factor, did not load higher than .3 on more than one factor, and were related conceptually. There was a spread of at least .18 on all cross-loaded items. Thirty-one items met the criteria for inclusion. Factor 1 accounted for 40% of the variance and reflected a theme of a need for control and self-reliance (e.g., "Asking for help is like surrendering authority over my life"). Factor 2 accounted for 6% of the variance and related to tendencies to minimize the problem or to be resigned to it (e.g., "I wouldn't want to overreact to a problem that wasn't serious," or "Problems like this are part of life; they're just something you have to deal with"). Factor 3 accounted for 4% of the variance and concerned concrete barriers to help seeking, including distrust of doctors and financial obstacles. Factor 4 accounted for 4% of the variance and reflected concerns about privacy (e.g., "I don't like taking off my clothes in front of other people"), and Factor 5 accounted for 3% of the variance and related to concerns with emotional control (e.g., "I'd rather not show people what I'm feeling").

Items and factor loadings are presented in Table 10.1. Subscales were computed by summing the scores on the items within each factor. Subscale scores were then summed to compute a total score, with higher scores indicating more barriers to help seeking. The number of items per subscale ranged from 4 to 10, with a mean of 6.2. Table 10.2 lists the number of items, means, and standard deviations for each subscale.

Reliability

Table 10.1 lists the internal consistency coefficients for the BHSS. The subscales demonstrated good to excellent internal consistency;

TABLE 10.1 BHSS Factors, Items, Percentage of Variance, and Internal Consistency Coefficients

Items	Factor Loadings
Factor 1: Need for Control and Self-Reliance (α = .93, accounts for 40% of variance)	
I would think less of myself for needing help.	.67
I don't like other people telling me what to do.	.85
Nobody knows more about my problems than I do.	.63
I'd feel better about myself knowing I didn't need help from others.	.75
I don't like feeling controlled by other people.	.88
It would seem weak to ask for help.	.61
I like to make my own decisions and not be too influenced by others.	.67
I like to be in charge of everything in my life.	.45
Asking for help is like surrendering authority over my life.	.52
I do not want to appear weaker than my peers.	.48
Factor 2: Minimizing Problem and Resignation (α = .89, accounts for 6.4% of variance)	
The problem wouldn't seem worth getting help for.	.77
The problem wouldn't be a big deal; it would go away in time.	.87
I wouldn't want to overreact to a problem that wasn't serious.	.81
Problems like this are part of life; they're just something you have to deal with.	.55
I'd prefer just to suck it up rather than dwell on my problems.	.60
I would prefer to wait until I'm sure the health problem is a serious one.	.65
Factor 3: Concrete Barriers and Distrust of Caregivers (α = .79, accounts for 4.3% of variance)	
People typically expect something in return when they provide help.	.50
I would have real difficulty finding transportation to a place where I can get help.	.69
I wouldn't know what sort of help was available.	.44
Financial difficulties would be an obstacle to getting help.	.80
I don't trust doctors and other health professionals.	.45

TABLE 10.1   BHSS Factors, Items, Percentage of Variance, and Internal Consistency Coefficients (Continued)

Items	Factor Loadings
A lack of health insurance would prevent me from asking for help.	.76
Factor 4: Privacy (α = .83, accounts for 3.5% of variance)	
Privacy is important to me, and I don't want other people to know about my problems.	.53
This problem is embarrassing.	.73
I don't want some stranger touching me in ways I'm not comfortable with.	.69
I don't like taking off my clothes in front of other people.	.64
I wouldn't want someone of the same sex touching my body.	.44
Factor 5: Emotional Control (α = .89, accounts for 3.0% of variance)	
I don't like to get emotional about things.	.64
I don't like to talk about feelings.	.69
I'd rather not show people what I'm feeling.	.41
I wouldn't want to look stupid for not knowing how to figure this problem out.	.66

TABLE 10.2   Descriptive Statistics for BHSS and GRCS Subscales in a Midwestern All-Male Undergraduate Sample

BHSS Subscale	Number of Items	M	SD
Need for Control and Self-Reliance	10	16.50	7.82
Minimizing Problem and Resignation	6	17.49	5.00
Concrete Barriers and Distrust of Caregivers	6	9.75	4.23
Privacy	5	9.15	4.17
Emotional Control	4	7.03	3.74
Total	31	59.37	19.76
GRCS Subscale			
Success, Power, and Competition	13	46.64	11.77
Restrictive Emotionality	10	29.38	10.16
Restrictive Affectionate Behavior Between Men	8	23.84	8.55
Conflicts Between Work and Family	6	20.84	6.51
Total	37	120.39	28.02

TABLE 10.3. Correlations Between BHSS Subscales in a Midwestern All-Male Undergraduate Sample

BHSS Scales	Need for Control and Self-Reliance	Minimizing Problem and Resignation	Concrete Barriers and Distrust of Caregivers	Privacy	Emotional Control	BHSS Total
Need for Control and Self-Reliance	—					
Minimizing Problem and Resignation	.45**	—				
Concrete Barriers and Distrust of Caregivers	.58**	.37**	—			
Privacy	.63**	.44**	.54**	—		
Emotional Control	.72**	.48**	.53**	.67**	—	
BHSS total	.89**	.68**	.73**	.80**	.84**	—

Note: **$p < .01$.

coefficient alphas ranged from .79 to .93, and the internal consistency coefficient for the entire scale was .95. Table 10.3 presents correlations between BHSS subscales. As mentioned earlier, we predicted that BHSS subscales would correlate with each other, and the data were consistent with this hypothesis. The moderate correlations suggest that the subscales tap related but distinct clusters of reasons for choosing not to seek help for a physical problem.

Validity

Table 10.4 lists correlations between BHSS and GRCS subscales. As expected, the BHSS total score was correlated with the GRCS total score, $r = .58$, $p < .01$. Table 10.4 shows that each of the BHSS subscales showed small to moderate correlations with each of the GRCS subscales. The one exception was the minimizing and resignation subscale of the BHSS, which revealed consistently large correlations with each of the GRCS subscales.

We predicted that the restrictive emotionality subscale of the GRCS would correlate with the emotional control subscale of the BHSS. The restrictive emotionality scale of the GRCS targets the degree to which men believe it is important to restrict their emotions in general, whereas the emotional control subscale of the BHSS appears to tap the

TABLE 10.4.   Correlations Between BHSS Subscales and GRCS Subscales in a Midwestern All-Male Undergraduate Sample

Scales	Need for Control and Self-Reliance	Minimizing Problem and Resignation	Concrete Barriers and Distrust of Caregivers	Privacy	Emotional Control	BHSS Total
Success, Power, and Competition	.31**	.57**	.14**	.25**	.25**	.39**
Restrictive Emotionality	.31**	.75**	.26**	.33**	.47**	.51**
Restrictive Affectionate Behavior Between Men	.29**	.76**	.27**	.37**	.40**	.50**
Conflicts Between Work and Family	.08	.52**	.21**	.14**	.08	.25**
GRCS total	.36**	.87**	.28**	.38**	.43**	.58**

Note: **p < .01.

degree to which men believe it is important to keep their emotions under control in the context of dealing with a physical problem. As predicted, this correlation was significant, $r = .47$, $p < .01$. In addition, we predicted that the success, power, and competition subscale of the GRCS would correlate with the control and self-reliance subscale of the BHSS because the items in the self-reliance and general control subscale of the BHSS assess the extent to which men feel the need to safeguard their personal power and status in the context of seeking help for a physical problem. For men to retain social power and status, they often deny their own needs, including their needs for medical care (Courtenay, 2000b; Kaufman, 1994). Consistent with this prediction, the correlation between the Success, Power, and Competition subscale of the GRCS and the Control and Self-Reliance subscale of the BHSS was significant, $r = .31$, $p < .01$.

STUDY 2

The goal of Study 2 was to evaluate whether findings regarding the reliability and validity of the BHSS would replicate in a separate sample of undergraduate males. In addition, we further evaluated the construct validity of the BHSS by correlating it with scores on a measure of attitudes toward seeking professional psychological help, the Attitudes Toward Seeking Professional Psychological Help Scale (ASPPH). We included the ASPPH to test the construct validity of the BHSS because the ASPPH is the most widely used measure of attitudes toward professional help seeking. Although the ASPPH assesses attitudes toward psychological rather than medical help, it seemed reasonable to assume that attitudes toward seeking help from mental and physical health professionals would be related. We hypothesized that the BHSS would correlate positively with the GRCS and negatively with the ASPPH.

Method

Participants

Participants were 58 undergraduate males at a small liberal arts university in New England. Of the sample, 53% were first-year students, 29% were sophomores, 9% were juniors, and 9% were seniors. The mean age of participants was 19.3 years ($SD = 1.17$). Ninety percent of the sample identified themselves as White, 3% as Latino, 2% as Asian, and 5% as other ethnicities.

Measures

The Barriers to Help Seeking Scale and Gender Role Conflict Scale The BHSS and GRCS are described in Study 1.

The Attitudes Toward Seeking Professional Psychological Help Scale The ASPPH (Fischer & Turner, 1970) was developed to explore attitudes toward seeking professional psychological help. The scale consists of 29 items, and each item is scored on a scale of 0 to 4. Items that express negative attitudes toward help seeking are reverse scored. After reverse scoring, items are summed to yield a total score, with higher scores indicating more positive attitudes toward help seeking. Although the ASPPH has four factors, the total score is usually used because the factor structure has not been shown to be robust (Good et al., 1989; Good & Mintz, 1990; Good & Wood, 1995). According to Fischer and Turner, the ASPPH has good internal consistency ($\alpha = .86$), and its test–retest reliability is acceptable as well ($r = .73$ to $.89$). The ASPPH has been used in several studies exploring the relationship between masculinity and help seeking (Good et al., 1989; Good & Mintz, 1990; Good & Wood, 1995; Robertson & Fitzgerald, 1992). According to Good and Wood (1995), it has demonstrated construct validity as evidenced by its ability to discriminate between college students who had sought professional psychological assistance from those who had not.

Procedure

Participation in this study was voluntary. The principal investigator and two undergraduate research assistants visited classes and dorm rooms at the university. They explained that the principal investigator was conducting a study about why people sometimes choose not to seek help for a physical problem. Students who chose to participate then completed the ASPPH, the GRCS, and the BHSS.

Results

Reliability

The reliability coefficients and descriptive statistics for all five factors of the BHSS are listed in Table 10.5. Internal consistency coefficients (Cronbach's alpha) for the BHSS subscales in this sample ranged from .75 to .89, and coefficient alpha for the entire measure was .93. Correlations between BHSS subscales are listed in Table 10.6. All correlations between BHSS subscales were significant, and the majority were in the moderate range.

Test–retest reliability was assessed using a separate sample of nine undergraduates who completed the BHSS twice, with 2 weeks between each administration. BHSS total scores were found to have acceptable

TABLE 10.5 Internal Consistency Coefficients for BHSS, Descriptive Statistics for BHSS and GRCS Subscales in a New England All-Male Undergraduate Sample

BHSS Subscale	Coefficient α	Number of Items	*M*	*SD*
Need for Control and Self-Reliance	.89	10	10.47	8.44
Minimizing Problem and Resignation	.75	6	11.12	5.89
Concrete Barriers and Distrust of Caregivers	.77	6	3.65	3.96
Privacy	.76	5	4.78	4.76
Emotional Control	.85	4	4.22	3.95
Total	.93	31	34.16	21.85
GRCS Subscale				
Success, Power, and Competition		13	45.43	10.84
Restrictive Emotionality		10	26.50	10.11
Restrictive Affectionate Behavior Between Men		8	22.30	7.40
Conflicts Between Work and Family		6	20.05	7.30
Total		37	115.92	19.68
ASPPH				
Total score		29	79.98	12.38

TABLE 10.6   Correlations Between BHSS Subscales in a New England All-Male Undergraduate Sample

BHSS Scales	Need for Control and Self-Reliance	Minimizing Problem and Resignation	Concrete Barriers and Distrust of Caregivers	Privacy	Emotional Control	BHSS Total
Need for Control and Self-Reliance	—					
Minimizing Problem and Resignation	.56**	—				
Concrete Barriers and Distrust of Caregivers	.52**	.53**	—			
Privacy	.54**	.40**	.54**	—		
Emotional Control	.63**	.67**	.59**	.54**	—	
BHSS total	.87**	.79**	.75**	.74**	.84**	—

Note: **$p < .01$.

test–retest reliability ($r = .73$, $p < .05$), and BHSS subscales demonstrated test–retest reliabilities ranging from $r = .35$ to $r = .94$, with a mean of .67. Specifically, the control and self-reliance subscale demonstrated a marginally acceptable test–retest reliability of .68, $p < .05$; the minimizing the problem and resignation scale demonstrated poor test–retest reliability, $r = .35$, $p > .05$; the concrete barriers and distrust of caregivers scale evidence excellent test–retest reliability, $r = .95$, $p < .01$; the privacy subscale evidenced acceptable test–retest reliability, $r = .79$, $p < .05$; and the emotional control subscale demonstrated excellent test–retest reliability, $r = .93$, $p < .05$.

Validity

Table 10.7 presents correlations between the BHSS, the GRCS, and the ASPPH. As expected, the BHSS total score was negatively correlated with the ASPPH, $r = -.55$, $p < .01$. All BHSS subscales were also negatively correlated with ASPPH. In addition, as expected, the BHSS total score was correlated with the GRCS total score, $r = .37$, $p < .01$. As in Study 1, the correlation between the emotional control and restrictive emotionality subscale was significant, $r = .31$, $p < .05$, as was the correlation between the Success, Power, and Competition subscale and Self-Reliance and Control subscale, $r = .33$, $p < .05$.

TABLE 10.7 Correlations Between BHSS Subscales, GRCS Subscales, and ASPPH Scores in a New England Sample of Undergraduate Males

Scales	Need for Control and Self-Reliance	Minimizing Problem and Resignation	Concrete Barriers and Distrust of Caregivers	Privacy	Emotional Control	BHSS Total
Success, Power, and Competition	.33*	.41**	.32*	.29*	.28*	.40**
Restrictive Emotionality	.09	.14	.06	−.07	.32*	.11
Restrictive Affectionate Behavior Between Men	.07	.12	.10	.18	.27*	.16
Conflicts Between Work and Family	.17	.22	.31*	.21	.10	.23
GRCS total	.31*	.45**	.38**	.25	.46**	.43**
ASPPH total	−.42**	−.51**	−.54**	−.36**	−.44**	−.56**

Note: $*p < .05$; $**p < .01$.

DISCUSSION

General Comments

The aim of these two studies was to develop and psychometrically evaluate a measure of barriers to men's help seeking. The results indicate that the BHSS holds promise as a measurement tool. The factor structure of the BHSS supported the creation of subscales, which may have clinical utility because they could yield information about which kinds of barriers are salient for particular individuals. Exploratory factor analyses from Study 1 suggested that the BHSS possesses a 5-factor structure. Four of the factors that we predicted would emerge did emerge, as did one other, unexpected factor. We expected a factor related to concerns about autonomy and self-reliance to emerge, and these concerns are evident in Factor 1. This factor reflects aspects of masculine gender role norms that demand men be strong, stoic, and in control. In addition, items such as "I don't like other people telling me what to do," "I don't like feeling controlled by other people," "I like to make my own decisions and not be too influenced by others," and "Asking for help is like surrendering authority over my life" can be interpreted as indicating reactance, a social psychological process in which people seek to preserve and reestablish autonomy when they sense autonomy is threatened (Brehm, 1966). Some of these items also reflect the ego-centrality of help seeking itself: a concern with being perceived as strong and not in need of help. Thus, the very condition of needing help is ego-central. As discussed earlier, ego-centrality is a key social psychological process that mediates help seeking, and exploratory factor analysis of the BHSS suggests that it is related to perceived barriers to help seeking. Thus, the need for control and self-reliance factor on the BHSS appears to include two gender-relevant social psychological processes related to help seeking. This factor by far accounted for the largest percentage of variance compared with the other factors and may, therefore, best be able to capture important individual differences in men's perceived barriers to help seeking.

We expected a factor to emerge that reflected concerns with privacy, vulnerability, and, in a related vein, homophobia (e.g., apparent in the item "I wouldn't want someone of the same sex touching my body"), and these concerns are evident in Factor 4. Concerns about being or appearing vulnerable are consistent with masculine gender socialization messages that demand fortitude and abhor weakness (Brannon & Juni, 1984; Pollack, 1998). We expected a factor to emerge related to the need to restrict expression of one's emotions, and Factor 5 reflects these concerns. Finally, we expected that a factor related to concrete barriers to help seeking would emerge. We were surprised to see that a general distrust of caregivers also figured into this factor, but on reflection, it seems that such distrust contributes to general avoidance of professional help. Thus, this factor seems to reflect general reasons why a person would not choose to seek help for a problem, such as lack of money, transportation, or insurance, or distrust of medical personnel.

Interestingly, one factor emerged that we did not predict: minimizing the problem and resignation. This factor reflects a desire not to overreact to a physical problem. Although we did not expect this factor to emerge, its presence seems to be related to masculine gender socialization. Maintaining social power and status as a man often comes at the cost of self-care (Courtenay, 2000b; Kaufman, 1994). By extension, because asking for help might be perceived as threatening to one's power and status, men might be especially invested in not overreacting to physical problems. Alternatively, masculine gender norms such as emotional stoicism may make it more difficult for some men to recognize the severity of problems.

Interpretation of BHSS Subscales

To interpret scores on BHSS subscales, it is important to identify what each subscale means with regard to seeking help for the problem identified by the stem question of the BHSS. Subscale 1, Need for Control and Self-Reliance, reflects concerns with self-reliance and autonomy. High scores on this subscale suggest that a man believes that seeking help for the problem in question would threaten his autonomy or ability to function independently. Subscale 2, Minimizing the Problem and Resignation, concerns a cluster of barriers that keep people from seeking help because they do not believe that the problem they are experiencing is serious enough. For example, a man might choose not to seek help for chronic headaches because he does not believe they are indicative of a serious problem, and worries that the health care provider might think less of him for asking about such a minor problem. Thus, he might simply resign himself to living with the problem. Subscale 3, Concrete Barriers and Distrust of Caregivers, reflects the fact that concrete barriers such as finances, lack of insurance, lack of transportation, lack of knowledge about the sorts of help available, and lack of trust in care providers can prevent people from seeking help. High scores on this subscale indicate that the person is unlikely to seek help because he perceives numerous concrete barriers to doing so, or he does not trust particular health care providers. Subscale 4, Privacy, has to do with concerns about emotional and physical vulnerability. High scores on this subscale suggest that the person is unlikely to seek help because he perceives that doing so could leave him physically or emotionally vulnerable. Finally, Subscale 5, Emotional Control, is defined by barriers that revolve around concerns with keeping one's emotions under control and out of public view. High scores on this subscale indicate that the person is unlikely to seek help because he thinks that his ability to control his emotions might be threatened by doing so.

The BHSS consists of five clusters of barriers to help seeking that are intended to provide an assessment of the obstacles that men themselves identify. It is important to note, however, that the BHSS measures perceptions of barriers. Whether the barriers respondents identify actually prevent help seeking is an empirical question. Practically, it would be difficult to know independent of self-report exactly what the barriers are for particular men. However, it should be possible in future research to determine whether directly addressing the barriers identified by men is associated with an increased probability of help seeking.

Reliability and Validity

With regard to reliability, the BHSS demonstrated good internal consistency, with overall alphas of .95 and .94 for the two studies, and average subscale alphas ranging from .75 to .93, with an average of .84. BHSS total scores also demonstrated acceptable test–retest reliability, although future studies should replicate this finding. In addition, the BHSS demonstrated convergent validity with the GRCS, lending support to the idea that the specific barriers contained in the BHSS are related to GRC. We predicted that the Emotional Control scale of the BHSS would correlate with the Restrictive Emotionality scale of the

GRCS. Interestingly, the Emotional Control scale of the BHSS also correlated with the Success, Power, and Competitions scale of the GRCS, as well as with the Restrictive Affectionate Behavior Between Men scale of the GRCS. Perhaps all three subscales of the GRCS require controlled expression of one's emotions. We were surprised to find that unlike other BHSS scales, which demonstrated small to moderate correlations with the GRCS, the Minimizing scale of the BHSS demonstrated large correlations with all GRCS scales. It may be that the tendency to minimize problems is particularly influenced by GRC.

The Midwestern sample evidenced both more and stronger correlations between the BHSS and the GRCS than did the New England sample. The Midwestern sample was drawn from a conservative religious men's college, whereas the New England sample was drawn from a secular and politically liberal one. Perhaps the situation invoked in the BHSS, considering seeking help for pain in one's body, presents more of a threat to masculinity for conservative populations than for liberal ones. More study is needed to determine whether correlations between the BHSS and the GRCS vary by variables such as race, class, religious affiliation, or political conservatism.

Support of the criterion validity of the BHSS is indicated by the significant correlation between it and the ASPPH. This suggests that there is probably some overlap between attitudes toward seeking psychological help and barriers to seeking medical help.

Given the promising reliability and validity findings from these two studies, we believe that the BHSS holds promise as a context-specific measure of barriers to help seeking. Future research might explore different sorts of contexts for help seeking. In fact, we designed the measure for use with a variety of different mental and physical health problems so that barriers might be compared between problems. Although in the current study we assessed barriers to help seeking for a physical health problem, the structure of the measure could be restructured to allow the user to ask about other problems, such as depression, anxiety, or vocational uncertainty. Future research might target different sorts of help seeking contexts and examine whether the factor structure of the BHSS is consistent across different types of problems targeted. If such modifications are carried out, the psychometric properties of the BHSS will need to be reconsidered in light of them. Specifically, future studies would need to assess whether there are different factor structures for different types of problems targeted by the BHSS.

Limitations

Although the findings of these two studies show promise for the BHSS as a reliable and valid measure of barriers to help seeking, there are some limitations to them. First, both samples were drawn from a pool of largely White undergraduate students, which is not representative of the population of the United States. This limits the external validity of these findings and demands further study in the future. Subsequent work with the BHSS should explore its psychometric properties when administered to more diverse samples. Factor analyses, means, and standard deviations should be calculated for more diverse samples. In addition, because the samples were drawn from college-age men, future studies must consider the possibility that the factor structure may differ when a sample of older men is used. Similarly, the barriers most salient for young men may be different from those most salient for middle age or older men. The test–retest reliability of the BHSS must be investigated in future studies because of the small sample size used to derive it here. Finally, it is important to note that the BHSS measures self-reported barriers to a hypothetical health problem; it does not measure actual retrospective help seeking, and our data did not explore whether it can make predictions about potential future help seeking.

CONCLUSION

Although there is much more work to be done, these two studies represent a step toward examining the psychometric properties of the BHSS. We hope that this research will help to direct the field toward developing clinical interventions aimed at reducing barriers to men's help seeking. Future studies using the BHSS should explore whether the factor structure and psychometric properties of the measure are robust when more diverse samples are used, and when the measure is changed to ask about barriers to help seeking for various mental health problems, such as anxiety, depression, or anger management difficulties. Separate factor analyses should be run for these various alternate problem stems for the BHSS because clusters of barriers may be specific to distinct types of problems. In addition, subsequent work should explore whether the psychometric properties of the BHSS differ for men and women. Replicating this study with a sample of women or a mixed-sex sample would be an important step toward clarifying barriers unique to men, and those influenced by masculinity norms that affect both men and women.

The Drive for Muscularity and Masculinity

*Testing the Associations Among Gender Role Traits, Behaviors, Attitudes, and Conflict**

DONALD R. McCREARY, DEBORAH
M. SAUCIER, AND WILL H. COURTENAY

Until the last decade, research exploring gender differences in body image concerns and their outcomes has been based solely on perceptions of adiposity (i.e., body fat). This research has led to the belief that, because men are less concerned or dissatisfied than women with their degree of adiposity, are less likely than women to be dieting to lose weight, and rarely experience clinical disorders associated with body image (e.g., anorexia and bulimia nervosa), they are relatively happy with their bodies (e.g., Feingold & Mazzella, 1998; Garner, Olmstead, & Polivy, 1983; Muth & Cash, 1997). This belief, however,

* An earlier version of this chapter appeared in *Psychology of Men and Masculinity*, 6(2), 2005, 83–94, and is used by permission in modified/revised form.

does not take into consideration the fact that adiposity is not equally important for men and women. That is, whereas the social standard of bodily attractiveness for women reflects being small and thin, the social standard for men reflects being big and muscular, what Mishkind, Rodin, Silberstein, and Striegel-Moore (1986) referred to as the *muscular mesomorphic* shape.

There is an increasing amount of research demonstrating the importance of being muscular in both adolescent males (e.g., Jones, 2001; McCreary & Sasse, 2000, 2002; O'Dea & Rawstorne, 2001) and adult men (e.g., Fisher, Dunn, & Thompson, 2002; Jacobi & Cash, 1994; Lavine, Sweeney, & Wagner, 1999; Phillips & Diaz, 1997). For example, research has shown that many adolescent boys are engaged in resistance training activities to gain muscle mass (Ricciardelli & McCabe, 2003). Among adolescent boys, a higher drive for muscularity is associated with poorer self-esteem and more symptoms of depression (McCreary & Sasse, 2000). Pope et al. (2000) have shown that, when comparing men's actual degree of muscularity with their perceived degree of muscularity, men significantly underestimate their percentage of muscle mass. Pope et al. also showed that men's ideal body size represents an average increase of 28 pounds of muscle, and that men believe women are most attracted to a body shape that is, on average, 30 pounds heavier in muscle than their actual size. When asked where they would like to be more muscular, men and boys typically want larger pectorals, biceps, and shoulders (Drewnowski & Yee, 1987; Huenemann, Shapiro, Hampton, & Mitchell, 1966; Moore, 1990).

Some researchers (e.g., Grogan & Richards, 2002; Klein, 1993; Weinke, 1998) have suggested that one of the main reasons muscularity is so important to men and boys is that it is linked to perceptions of their masculinity; in other words, the more muscular a man or boy is, the more masculine he believes he is. One might also suggest that boys and men who are not muscular (e.g., those who are endomorphic or those who are ectomorphic) may see themselves as more feminine. For example, Grogan and Richards (2002) have suggested that boys and men who diet run the risk for being perceived as feminine, in part because dieting is perceived to be a feminine-typed behavior.

One way to test these hypotheses is to explore the associations among masculinity, femininity, and the drive for muscularity. Based on findings from qualitative research, we would predict that masculinity would be positively associated with the drive for muscularity, whereas femininity would be negatively associated with the drive for muscularity. However, there is an important limitation inherent in this prediction: Masculinity and femininity are global, higher-order constructs and cannot be measured directly (Spence, 1984). Psychology has overcome this limitation by developing indices of specific dimensions of masculinity and femininity. Personality trait measures such as the Personal Attributes Questionnaire (PAQ; Spence & Helmreich,

1978), the Extended PAQ (EPAQ; Spence, Helmreich, & Holahan, 1979), and the Bem Sex Role Inventory (BSRI; Bem, 1974) are used to assess the degree to which men and women have internalized the gender stereotypic personality traits of agency/instrumentality (i.e., male stereotypic traits) and communion/expressivity (i.e., female stereotypic traits). Engaging in gender-typed behaviors is assessed using the Sex Role Behavior Scale (SRBS; Orlofsky, 1981) and its short form companion (Orlofsky & O'Heron, 1987). The degree to which people have adopted traditional versus contemporary or liberal views about men, women, and the relationships between men and women is assessed using measures such as the Attitudes Towards Women Scale (AWS; Spence & Helmreich, 1978) and the Male Role Norms Scale (Thompson & Pleck, 1986; Thompson, Pleck, & Ferrera, 1992). Other frequently used measures of gender role socialization include the Gender Role Conflict Scale (GRCS; O'Neil, Helms, Gable, David, & Wrightsman, 1986), the Masculine Gender Role Stress Scale (Eisler & Skidmore, 1987), and the Feminine Gender Role Stress Scale (Gillespie & Eisler, 1992; see Beere, 1990, for more examples of how gender role socialization can be measured). Thus, researchers examining the relationships between the drive for muscularity and perceptions of masculinity and femininity need to be very specific about the gender role dimensions they are measuring.

In addition to studying the associations among the drive for muscularity and both male- and female-typed aspects of gender role socialization, researchers also need to consider whether those associations vary as a function of gender. McCreary and his colleagues (McCreary, Newcomb, & Sadava, 1999; McCreary & Sasse, 2000) refer to this notion as *differential salience*, and have argued that the associations between gender-typed dimensions and various outcome variables (e.g., self-esteem, alcohol dependence) should be moderated by gender. They believe that, even though men and women internalize many gender-typed dimensions in the same way (i.e., factor analyses have shown that there are few, if any, gender differences in the factor structures of many gender role measures; e.g., McCreary, Newcomb, & Sadava, 1998), differential social pressures to conform to gender role expectations are stronger for men than for women (i.e., failure to conform to gender role norms or expectations tends to be punished more in men than in women; McCreary, 1994; see also Chapter 3). They have demonstrated this differential salience in two studies: McCreary et al. (1999) showed that the associations between various dimensions of the male gender role and both alcohol use and alcohol problems were different for men and women, and McCreary and Sasse (2000) revealed that the drive for muscularity was associated with lower self-esteem and more depressive symptoms in boys but not in girls (McCreary & Sasse, 2000). In the present context, the notion of differential salience would predict that the association between gender role constructs and the drive for muscularity should be stronger for men than for women.

The purpose of the two studies presented here is to test the associations between several dimensions of masculinity, femininity, and the drive for muscularity. In Study 1, a sample of college-aged men and women completed measures of both gender-typed traits and gender-typed behaviors, and in Study 2, a group of young men completed a measure of masculine gender role conflict (GRC), as well as a measure of traditional attitudes about men. In both instances, the degree to which those gender-typed dimensions predicted the drive for muscularity was examined, whereas in Study 1, the extent to which those relationships varied as a function of the participants' gender also was assessed.

STUDY 1

Method

Participants and Procedure

One hundred fifty-seven men and 343 women between 17 and 78 years of age ($M = 20$, with 95% of the sample between 17 and 24 years) participated in the current study. All were recruited during a mass testing session for an Introductory Psychology subject pool at a large midwestern Canadian university. Seventy-four percent of the men and 79% of the women were in their first year of college. Ten percent of the men and 28% of the women reported being on a diet to lose weight, and 17% of the men and 1% of the women reported being on a diet to gain weight. No other demographic or health-related information was collected.

Measures

All participants completed the Drive for Muscularity Scale (DMS; McCreary & Sasse, 2000) and two commonly used measures of gender role socialization: the EPAQ (Spence et al., 1979) and the short form SRBS (Orlofsky & O'Heron, 1987). Each of these is described below.

Drive for Muscularity Scale   The DMS is a 15-item measure of the extent to which people desire to have a more muscular body. Items on the DMS represent a combination of attitudes and behaviors and are scored on a 6-point scale ranging from *not at all like me* to *very much like me*. Examples of items include "I wish I were more muscular" and "I feel guilty if I miss a weight training session." McCreary and Sasse (2000, 2002) have shown that the DMS has good construct validity (in the form of face validity), convergent validity, and discriminant validity. Recent factor analytic work has shown that the DMS has a two-factor, lower-order structure for men, representing the attitudinal and behavioral items. For both men and women, however, a single higher-order

DMS factor emerged (McCreary, Sasse, Saucier, & Dorsch, 2004). Thus, when comparing men and women, researchers should average over the DMS items to create a single DMS score. The Cronbach alphas were .91 (men) and .83 (women) in the current sample.

Extended Personal Attributes Questionnaire   The EPAQ is a 40-item measure of gender-typed personality traits and represents an extension of the PAQ (Spence & Helmreich, 1978). Although the EPAQ is composed of six subscales, problems with internal consistency (Spence et al., 1979) have led to only three being used on a regular basis: *Agency* (mastery-oriented traits that are socially desirable for both men and women to possess, but are more stereotypically associated with men; 8 items), *Communion* (interpersonally oriented traits that are desirable for both men and women to possess, but are more stereotypically associated with women; 8 items), and *Unmitigated Agency* (being focused on the self to the exclusion of others; socially undesirable for both men and women to possess, but are more stereotypically associated with men; 8 items). The other three subscales (i.e., Masculinity-Femininity, Unmitigated Communion, and Verbal Aggressiveness) were not used in this study. Items on the EPAQ are scored on a 5-point Likert-type scale, with higher scores representing greater degrees of internalization of each trait. The alphas for the present study were .74, .80, and .71, respectively (men) and .73, .70, and .62, respectively (women). The low level of internal consistency of the Unmitigated Agency scale in women is problematic because it will reduce the power of that scale to detect significant associations with smaller effect sizes.

Short Form Sex Role Behavior Scale   The SRBS is the only available measure of the extent to which people act in gender-typed ways. The 96 items from the short form version of the SRBS are grouped into three higher-order factors of 32 items each: *Male-Typed Behaviors* (equally desirable for men and women, but more stereotypic of men), *Female-Typed Behaviors* (equally desirable for men and women, but more stereotypic of women), and *Sex-Specific Behaviors* (more desirable and stereotypic of men or women). All items are rated on a 5-point Likert-type scale. The items within each of the Male- and Female-Typed Behaviors subscales are averaged into their respective scores, with higher values indicative of engaging in greater degrees of behavior in those domains. Scoring of the Sex-Specific Behaviors dimension is somewhat different, however. This subscale is comprised of items that are either male (16 items) or female specific (16 items). The latter items are reverse coded, and the two sets of items are averaged together to create the overall subscale score, which is then interpreted in the male-typed direction. In the present study, the SRBS demonstrated lower than expected levels of reliability, with men's Cronbach alpha coefficients being .71, .76, and .56 for the three scales, respectively, whereas women's Cronbach alpha coefficients were .63, .68, and .56, respectively. As we noted earlier, these lower than expected alpha coefficients will decrease the power of the analyses to detect significant associations with smaller effect sizes.

Results

To explore the associations between the drive for muscularity and self-reported gender-typed traits and behaviors, as well as whether those associations varied as a function of the participant's gender, a series of moderating variable, hierarchical regression analyses were performed. The results of these analyses will be presented below, after an overview of the various scale descriptive statistics.

Descriptive Statistics

Table 11.1 reports the means and standard deviations for the DMS and all gender role measures, separately for men and women. Independent sample *t* tests were used to explore gender differences among the variables. To control for the increased probability of making a Type I error, a Bonferroni correction was applied to all *p* values (.05/7 tests = .007). As Table 11.1 shows, all mean differences were statistically significant. Men reported significantly higher levels of the drive for muscularity and both agentic and unmitigatedly agentic personality traits; they also acted in significantly more male-typed and sex-specific ways. Women, on the other hand, reported significantly higher levels of communal traits and acted in more female-typed ways.

TABLE 11.1   Means and Standard Deviations for Drive for Muscularity Scale and Six Indices of Gender Role Socialization, Separately for Men ($N = 159$) and Women ($N = 349$)

	Men		Women		
	M	*SD*	*M*	*SD*	*t*
DMS	2.69	0.95	1.99	0.61	10.01***
Agency	3.64	0.60	3.40	0.58	4.25***
Communion	3.68	0.59	4.10	0.46	−8.58***
UA	2.71	0.58	2.47	0.51	4.75***
MV	3.25	0.43	2.83	0.35	11.74***
FV	2.62	0.37	3.17	0.36	−15.86***
SS	3.51	0.26	2.66	0.28	32.46***

Note: DMS = Drive for Muscularity Scale; UA = EPAQ Unmitigated Agency Scale; MV = SRBS Male-Valued Behaviors; FV = SRBS Female-Valued Behaviors; SS = SRBS Sex-Specific Behaviors. The *df* for all *t* tests was 506.
***$p < .001$.

Regression Analyses

Because gender role traits and behaviors are conceptually different from one another, we performed two separate moderating variable, hierarchical regressions, one with the three trait variables as the main predictors and one with the three behavioral variables as the predictors. In both analyses, the main effects for the gender role dimensions and participant's gender (men = 1, women = 2) were entered into the equation in Step 1. In Step 2, the centered gender by gender role interactions were entered (see Cohen, Cohen, West, & Aiken, 2002, for a discussion of moderating variable regression analysis and the use of centering). If the addition of the centered interaction terms in Step 2 accounts for a significant increase in the amount of variance explained in the criterion, then there is a significant gender by gender role moderating effect.

Univariate t tests will explore which main effect and interaction beta values are significant. The dependent variable for each analysis was the respondent's score on the DMS.[*]

Gender Role Trait Analysis   When the four main effects (agency, communion, unmitigated agency, participant's gender) were entered in Step 1, they predicted a significant amount of variance in DMS scores, $\Delta F(4, 508) = 28.48$, $p < .0001$ (adjusted $R^2 = 17.8\%$). Univariate t tests revealed that two beta values were significantly different from zero. Participant's gender was negatively related to DMS scores ($\beta = -.38$, $t = -8.59$, $p < .0001$), meaning that men scored significantly higher than women, after partialling out the effects of the three gender role dimensions. Unmitigated agency (i.e., being more concerned with the self than with others) scores were associated with DMS scores ($\beta = .15$, $t = 3.19$, $p < .002$), after controlling for participant's gender and the other two gender role dimensions. The direction of the effect means that those who were higher in unmitigated agency had higher levels of the drive for muscularity. The addition of the centered interaction terms in Step 2 did not add a significant amount of variance to the prediction of the criterion, $\Delta F(3, 500) = 2.34$, $p > .05$ ($\Delta R^2 = 1.1\%$), suggesting that the relationships between these three gender-typed personality traits and DMS scores do not vary as a function of participant's gender.

Gender Role Behavior Analysis   The addition of the four main effects (male- and female-valued behaviors, sex-specific behaviors, participant's gender) in Step 1 explained a significant amount of variance in DMS

---

[*] McCreary et al. (2004) noted that item 10 in the DMS ("I think about taking anabolic steroids") did not load on any factor for either men or women and should not be included in the DMS calculation. We included the item in these analyses because the paper on which the recommendation was made had not yet been published. However, we ran the analyses with item 10 removed from the DMS score, and the results were almost identical.

scores, $\Delta F(4, 503) = 42.46$, $p < .0001$ (adjusted $R^2 = 25.2\%$). Univariate t tests revealed that three beta values were significantly different from zero. As with the first regression analysis, participant's gender was a significant predictor ($\beta = -.19$, $t = -2.75$, $p < .006$). The direction of the standardized coefficient means that men scored higher than women on the DMS, after partialling out the effects of the three gender-typed behavior domains. Both the SRBS male-valued and sex-specific behavior scales were significantly and positively associated with DMS scores ($\beta = .27$, $t = 4.99$, $p < .0001$ and $\beta = .16$, $t = 1.99$, $p < .05$, respectively) after partialling out the effects of the other variables. Thus, those who acted in more male-valued and male sex-specific ways tended to have higher DMS scores. The centered interaction terms did not add a significant amount of variance to the prediction of the criterion, $\Delta F(3, 500) = 0.89$, $p > .05$ ($\Delta R^2 = 0.4\%$), suggesting that the relationships between these gender-typed behaviors and DMS scores did not vary as a function of participants' gender.

Discussion

To determine the extent to which the drive for muscularity was predicted by gender-typed traits and behaviors, two separate hierarchical, moderating variable regression analyses were performed. In the first analysis, gender, gender-typed traits, and their interaction terms were the predictors, whereas in the second analysis, gender, gender-typed behaviors, and their interaction terms were the independent variables. In both analyses, the participants' drive for muscularity served as the criterion.

The results from these two analyses revealed four important findings. First, in both analyses, men scored higher than women on the DMS, after controlling for gender-typed traits or behaviors. This is important because it shows that the gender differences in DMS scores observed here (see Table 11.1) and in other research (e.g., McCreary et al., 2004; McCreary & Sasse, 2000) are fairly robust and are not mediated by these two aspects of gender role socialization. Second, the findings revealed that three of the four male-typed gender role dimensions (unmitigated agency, male-valued behaviors, and male sex-specific behaviors) all were positively associated with the drive for muscularity. Third, the lack of association between DMS scores and feminine-typed traits and behaviors indicates that low levels of the drive for muscularity are not associated with greater degrees of femininity (at least as measured by these two dimensions of feminine gender role socialization). These two points have theoretical significance because it shows that it is higher levels of the male gender role, and not lower levels of the female gender role, that are most closely associated with the desire to be more muscular. The fourth important finding was that the associations between the drive for muscularity and gender-typed traits and behaviors were similar for men and women. In other words, there was no differential salience in these relationships. The reasons for this are unclear at this point, especially after finding a gender by gender role interaction in other studies (i.e., McCreary et al., 1999; McCreary & Sasse, 2000).

Thus, it appears as though the association between self-perceptions of masculinity and muscularity that emerged from the earlier qualitative research (i.e., Grogan & Richards, 2002; Klein, 1993; Weinke, 1998) can be quantified. However, gender-typed traits and behaviors are not the only aspects of masculinity that can be measured. In Study 2, we explore the relationships between the drive for muscularity and two other masculine gender role constructs: GRC (O'Neil et al., 1986) and traditional attitudes about men. GRC is a construct that explores the cognitive, emotional, unconscious, and behavioral problems men experience as they attempt to conform to society's expectations of how men should be (O'Neil, Good, & Holmes, 1995). O'Neil et al. (1986) have identified four dimensions in which this gender-based conflict occurs: (1) success, power, and competition; (2) restrictive sexual and affectionate behavior between men; (3) restrictive emotionality; and (4) conflicts between work and family relations. Research has shown that men who experience conflict in one or more of these dimensions tend to have lower self-esteem, lower levels of intimacy, and higher levels of anxiety and depression (O'Neil et al., 1995). Men with high GRC also are less likely to seek help for problems with psychological well-being (O'Neil et al., 1995; see also Chapter 1), are more likely to engage in multiple health risk behaviors (McCreary & Courtenay, 2003; see also Chapter 1), and tend to conform more to male gender role norms (Mahalik et al., 2003).

The degree to which people have adopted traditional attitudes about men (also referred to as *male role norms* or *masculinity ideology*) also is a significant aspect of gender role socialization. Traditional male role norms emphasize men's power, success, and toughness, as well as the avoidance of anything deemed feminine. Adult and adolescent males who have adopted traditional attitudes about men have been shown to engage in a wide range of risky health behaviors for which incidence rates are higher for men (see Chapter 1); these include increased use of alcohol (McCreary et al., 1999), sedatives, and tranquilizers (Snell, Belk, & Hawkins, 1987); a greater likelihood of being sexually active; a greater likelihood of having tricked or forced someone to have sex with them; a greater likelihood of engaging in unprotected sex and having had more sexual partners; and a greater likelihood of having been arrested (Pleck, Sonenstein, & Ku, 1994a). Traditional beliefs about men also have been found to predict greater involvement in multiple, high-risk behaviors over time (Courtenay, 1998a).

Thus, Study 2 extends the findings from Study 1 to these two dimensions of male gender role socialization. It is predicted that DMS scores should be positively associated with GRC and traditional attitudes about men. However, because the GRC paradigm is appropriate only for men, gender role salience was not examined in Study 2, as it was in Study 1.

STUDY 2

Method

Participants and Procedure

Five hundred twenty-seven men (aged 17 to 54 years; $Mdn = 20$, with only 1.3% of the sample being older than 22 years) were recruited from an all-male college in the midwestern United States. The participants reported being of mostly White, European ethnicity (92%); heterosexual (97%); not married (84%); and living on campus (90%). Thirty percent were in their first year of college, 29% were in their sophomore year, 20% were juniors, and 21% were seniors.

Participants were recruited via an e-mail sent to all students by staff at the university health clinic. The e-mail invited the students to participate in an anonymous online survey of their health and health behaviors. The voluntary nature of the survey was emphasized, as was the student's right to withdraw participation at any time. After completing the survey, participants were given the option of filling in a separate web page with their name and contact information to win a prize for a store voucher. Participants were notified that the data from the survey and the identification information from the form they completed to register for the prize went to separate computer servers and would not be combined. Of the 1,850 students enrolled at the college at that time, 527 (29%) completed usable surveys.

Measures

In addition to the DMS, participants completed the GRCS (O'Neil et al., 1986) and a series of items that assessed traditional attitudes about men and men's role in society. Other questions on the survey assessed health and health risk behaviors but are not reported here.

Drive for Muscularity Scale   The DMS (McCreary & Sasse, 2000) was described thoroughly in Study 1. However, it should be noted that the DMS's degree of internal consistency was .89 in this sample.

Gender Role Conflict Scale   The GRCS is a commonly used questionnaire designed to assess the psychological conflict men experience when rigid, sexist, or restrictive gender roles result in personal restrictions, devaluation, or negative consequences, for one's self or for other men (O'Neil et al., 1986, 1995). The GRCS contains 37 items that are grouped into four subscales: (1) Success, Power, and Competition (13 items), which measures concern about personal achievement and gaining dominance and superiority over others; (2) Restrictive Emotionality (10 items), which assesses difficulty and fears about emotional self-disclosure and verbal expression of feelings; (3) Restrictive

Affectionate Behavior Between Men (8 items), which examines discomfort associated with verbal and physical expressions of caring toward other men; and (4) Conflicts Between Work and Family Relations (6 items), which measures difficulty and dissatisfaction with the balancing of school or work and family relations. Each item is rated on a 6-point scale, from *strongly disagree* to *strongly agree*. Scores for each of the subscales were created by averaging their respective items. Higher scores indicate a higher degree of conflict in each area. Previous psychometric analyses of the GRCS have shown it to be both reliable and valid (O'Neil et al., 1995). In the present study, the alpha reliability coefficients were .90, .90, .89, and .85, respectively.

Traditional Attitudes About Men   To assess traditional attitudes about men, the following five items were included in the survey: (1) Do you believe that taking risks that are sometimes dangerous is part of what it means to be a man and part of what distinguishes men from women? (2) As a man, how important is it for you to be self-sufficient and always to try to handle problems on your own? (3) As a man, how important is it for you to be physically strong and tough? (4) As a man, how important is it for you to control your emotions and never to reveal sadness or vulnerability? and (5) As a man, how important is it for you not to engage in activities that you think others might consider feminine? These items are similar to those used on preexisting, albeit larger, measures of masculinity ideology (e.g., the Male Role Norms Scale; Thompson & Pleck, 1986). Survey size restrictions precluded our using one of these larger measures. Each item was scored on a 4-point scale, from *not at all true* to *very true* (item 1) and from *not at all important* to *very important* (items 2 to 5). All items were averaged into a single index, and higher scores indicate a more traditional view of how men should be. The alpha reliability estimate for the masculine ideology measure was .75.

Results

Descriptive Statistics

Table 11.2 contains the means and standard deviations for the DMS, the four GRCS subscales, as well as the measure of traditional male attitudes.

Regression Analysis

To determine the extent to which the four GRCS subscales and the measure of traditional attitudes about men are predictive of young men's desire to be more muscular than they are currently, a standard multiple regression analysis was performed. Because there were no hypotheses about order of entry, all five predictors were entered at the same time. The predictors explained a significant amount of variability in DMS

TABLE 11.2   Means and Standard Deviations for the Drive for Muscularity
Scale, Four Dimensions of the Gender Role Conflict Scale (GRCS), and a
Measure of Traditional Masculine Ideology in a Sample of Young Men
($N = 527$)

Scale	*M*	*SD*
Drive for Muscularity Scale	2.42	0.79
GRCS Success, Power, and Competition	3.59	0.88
GRCS Restrictive Emotionality	2.97	0.97
GRCS Restrictive Affectionate Behavior	2.99	1.04
GRCS Work and Leisure Conflict	3.47	1.05
Masculine Ideology	2.28	0.57

scores, $F(5, 501) = 27.87$, $p < .0001$ (adjusted $R^2 = 21.0\%$). An examination of the individual standardized coefficients revealed that three
betas were significantly different from zero: the GRCS Success, Power,
and Competition subscale ($\beta = .26$, $t = 5.28$, $p < .0001$), the GRCS
Work and Leisure Conflict subscale ($\beta = .15$, $t = 3.44$, $p < .001$), and
the Traditional Attitudes About Men scale ($\beta = .14$, $t = 2.98$, $p < .003$).
The direction of all three beta values was positive: As scores on the two
dimensions of the GRCS and the measure of traditional attitudes about
men increased, so did DMS scores.

General Discussion

Two studies revealed significant associations between the drive for muscularity and perceptions of several aspects of masculine gender role
socialization: unmitigatedly agentic personality traits, male-valued and
sex-specific behaviors, traditional attitudes about men, and GRC in the
areas of success, power, and competition, as well as work and leisure
conflict. In all cases, DMS scores were positively associated with the
indices of masculinity. Thus, in Study 1, both men and women associated male-typed traits and behaviors with a need to be more muscular, and in Study 2, men who endorsed more traditional, gender-typed
beliefs wanted to be more muscular. Finally, men in Study 2 who wanted
to be more muscular experienced greater levels of GRC with respect to
society's expectations that they be successful, powerful, and competitive, and the balancing of work and leisure.

These findings replicate and extend the limited, qualitative research
that explored men's perceptions that muscular men are more masculine
and that men will feel more masculine if they gain more muscularity. However, as noted earlier, the main limitation of this qualitative
research is that, although many people have an intuitive understanding of their degree of masculinity, this intuitive notion cannot be measured directly. Thus, the findings from these two studies extend the

existing literature by determining which aspects of masculinity are uniquely associated with the drive for muscularity. Future research might explore the associations between masculinity and muscularity even further. For example, whereas we chose to use a short, single measure of traditional attitudes about men, there are other, larger measures of this construct that assess various subdimensions of masculinity attitudes (e.g., toughness, violence or aggression, antifemininity, rejection of homosexuals, and attitudes toward scx). These more comprehensive scales include the Male Role Norms Scale (Thompson & Pleck, 1986), the Brannon Masculinity Scale (Brannon & Juni, 1984), and the Male Role Norms Inventory (Levant & Fischer, 1998). Other dimensions of masculinity that can be explored include dominance (McCreary & Rhodes, 2001; Sidanius, Liu, Shaw, & Pratto, 1994), hypermasculinity (Burk, Burkhart, & Sikorski, 2004; Mosher & Sirkin, 1984), and conformity to masculine norms (Mahalik et al., 2003). This latter aspect of masculinity is new and especially promising because it assesses the extent to which men feel compelled to conform to several aspects of the male gender role (e.g., winning, emotional control, risk taking, power over women, being a playboy, self-reliance, primacy of work, pursuit of status, disdain for homosexuals), as opposed to the stress and strain they experience as a result of acting in either stereotypically male-appropriate or male-inappropriate ways. Initial research suggests that both the Conformity to Masculine Norms Inventory's (CMNI) Winning subscale and the overall CMNI score are positively correlated with DMS scores (Mahalik et al., 2003). However, the overall sample size for the DMS portion of the CMNI study was small and precluded the use of multivariate analyses.

There are limitations to the present studies. First, both studies were correlational in nature, and only the presence and direction of significant relationships can be determined. Future research might explore the direction of causality in the associations between the drive for muscularity and perceptions of masculinity. For example, does an increase in muscularity cause an increase in perceived masculinity, and if so, which dimensions of masculinity are most strongly influenced by this potential causal relationship? Or could increases in perceived masculinity (e.g., from changes in other aspects of a person's life) cause an increased desire to become more muscular? Or could the association be cyclical? Experimental research is needed to address these questions.

A second limitation is the restricted nature of the samples, especially with regard to age and ethnicity. The samples used in these two studies were predominantly college-aged (18 to 22 years) and from a White, European ethnic background.[*] This leads to several possible questions that can be examined empirically in future research. First, are the associations between these dimensions of masculinity and the drive for

---

[*] While ethnicity was not assessed in Study 1, the student population at that university is mostly from a White, European background.

muscularity the same across all age groups, or could the associations be stronger or weaker at specific times in men's lives (or among specific age cohorts)? For example, do people perceive a stronger association between muscularity and masculinity in their earlier years than in their later years? Could the strength of these associations be linked to developmental tasks, in the same way that other researchers have linked developmental tasks with life span gender role development (e.g., Gutmann, 1975; McCreary, 1990b; Sinnott, 1986)? Second, do the associations between masculinity and muscularity vary across ethnic groups? One problem with testing this question is that it assumes that the various dimensions of masculinity and the drive for muscularity mean the same thing to all ethnic groups, which may not be the case (Doss & Hopkins, 1998). If they are valid, then multigroup comparisons across cultures should be conducted.

A third limitation stems from the low reliability coefficients of some of the measures used in Study 1. The alpha reliability coefficients for the women's responses to the Unmitigated Agency scale and all three dimensions of the SRBS, as well as men's responses to the Sex-Specific SRBS subscale were less than .70. The immediate impact of this reduction in internal consistency is to reduce the scales' power to detect significant associations. In other words, smaller effects that would have been found to be statistically significant if the scales' alphas were higher did not reach the threshold for statistical significance. This may have had implications for the predicted gender by gender role interactions in Study 1. These interactions were predicted based on the notion of differential salience but failed to emerge. Perhaps with more reliable measures, which would increase the power of the analyses, the interactions would have been observed. Developing new measures of these constructs may be required.

In summary, two studies demonstrated that the drive for muscularity is positively associated with several aspects of masculinity: unmitigated agency, male-valued and sex-specific behaviors, traditional attitudes about men, and two aspects of GRC (success, power, and competition; work and leisure conflict). These findings reinforce those from qualitative research in which men stated their belief that those with a greater degree of muscularity are more masculine, and that gaining muscularity increases one's masculinity.

Reaching Men

INTRODUCTION

Among other findings, research that I conducted with Donald R. McCreary provided a surprising and interesting finding: Men are more concerned about their own health than they think other men are concerned about their health. This may not seem like a particularly important finding, but it is. This is because social norms research shows that our perceptions of others' behavior influence our own behavior. These perceptions—and *mis*perceptions—of normative group behavior often influence our behavior by providing information about what is "normal"— for example, about how we should, and should not, act as a man. In the following brief article, "Making Health Manly," I discuss this kind of social norms research and its implications for men's health, as well as for interventions with men—which is the focus of this section of the book.

MAKING HEALTH MANLY: SOCIAL MARKETING AND MEN'S HEALTH[*]

"Health matters are women's matters." "Only women pamper their bodies." Rarely voiced, perhaps, these are commonly held assumptions. There is substantial evidence—at least in the United States—that asking for help and caring for one's health are widely considered to be the province of women (Courtenay, 2000c). Collective beliefs and assumptions such as these are what social scientists refer to as *social norms* (Berkowitz, 2003) or *subjective norms* (Ajzen, 2001).

Given the existence of these norms, it is not surprising that in most Western industrialized countries, women are the greatest consumers of health-related products and services. And their consumption benefits others besides themselves. Women are often first to take responsibility, not only for the health and well-being

---

[*] An earlier version of this article appeared in the *Journal of Men's Health & Gender*, 2004, vol. 1, nos. 2–3, pp. 275–276.

of themselves and their offspring, but also for the health of men. This helps to explain why single men have the greatest health risks—and why the benefits of marriage are consistently found to be greater for men than for women, who can suffer substantial stress in caring for their spouses (Courtenay, 2000a).

Ultimately, men need to take greater responsibility for their own health if they are to live as long and as healthily as women do. But here is the problem: Men receive strong social prohibitions against doing *anything* that women do (Courtenay, 2000c).

Men and boys who engage in behaviors that represent feminine social norms of gender risk being perceived as "wimps" or "sissies" (Courtenay, 2000b). Consequently, men often prove manhood by *actively rejecting* doing anything that women do—and this includes caring for their health. Men reject health-promoting beliefs and behaviors with varying degrees of force, depending on what other means they have for proving manhood. Not surprisingly, there is solid evidence that masculinity is associated with health behavior, and even predicts mortality (see Chapter 1).

Of course, many men *are* concerned about their health. But as long as men believe that their peers are unconcerned about *their* health, they will be less likely to attend to their own health needs. What this means is that for men to change, social norms will have to change.

According to social norms theory, unhealthy (and healthy) behavior is fostered by perceptions (which are often incorrect) of how one's peers behave (Berkowitz, 2003). For example, a man might overestimate his peers' involvement in unhealthy behavior, which would encourage him to engage in unhealthy behavior. Alternatively, he might underestimate his peers' adoption of healthy habits, which would discourage him from adopting healthy habits himself. Social norms theory focuses on peer groups because they have been found to have the greatest influence in shaping individual behavior.

One common intervention based on this theory is a marketing campaign that promotes accurate, healthy social norms. Research indicates that when people's perceived norm is challenged with evidence of the actual norm, the unhealthy behavior often decreases (Berkowitz, 2003). As discussed elsewhere (Mahalik, Burns, & Syzdek, 2007), social norms marketing campaigns hold promise for addressing a variety of health concerns relevant to men, including men's incorrect perception that most men are unconcerned about their health.

Results of a recent survey of more than 500 men on one U.S. college campus indicated that these men believed that most (55%) of their peers were either not at all concerned or only a little concerned about their health. Actually, only 35% of men were unconcerned about their health; most (65%) reported being either somewhat or very concerned (unpublished data). These findings are similar to those of Mahalik et al. (2007). These data could be used to create a social norms marketing campaign designed to promote the true norm that men at this particular college *are* in fact concerned about their health.

A similar, and similarly effective, way to change social norms is with the use of personal accounts by prominent members of a particular group. Research shows that people can be persuaded to behave in ways that they believe credible, influential colleagues or peers want them to behave (Petty, Wegener, & Fabrigar, 1997). Men's personal stories describing how they became involved in their health care will help influence men to become involved in their own health care. Personal accounts such as these will also help to change the perception that health matters are women's matters. Perhaps then men will begin to see health and well-being as *human* concerns, and see that following good health habits can be manly as well as lifesaving.

CHAPTER
12

Counseling Men About Their Health
An Evidence-Based Practice Guideline*

As I discussed in the preceding chapters, gender-based medicine and health care are receiving increasing attention among health professionals. In addition to having different reproductive health needs, women and men have different risks for specific diseases and disabilities. They also differ in their perceptions of health. Research consistently indicates, for example, that men are less likely than women to perceive themselves as being at risk for most health problems, even for problems that men are more likely than women to experience (see Chapter 1). Furthermore, as is evident from the preceding chapters, men's gender—not simply male biological sex—mediates men's health and preventive practices, and gender-specific interventions are often necessary to achieve positive clinical outcomes. For example, a substantial body of research has demonstrated that—based on their readiness to change health-related behaviors—women and men require different interventions, and that failure to tailor interventions to these specific needs significantly reduces the chance of behavioral change (see Chapter 1). Other studies have found that using such approaches as future awareness and imagining

---

* An earlier version of this chapter appeared in G. R. Brooks & G. E. Good (Eds.). (2001). *The new handbook of psychotherapy and counseling with men: A comprehensive guide to settings, problems, and treatment approaches* (pp. 59–91). San Francisco: Jossey-Bass, and is used by permission in modified/revised form.

289

symptoms to modify risk behaviors is more effective with men than with women (DePalma, McCall, & English, 1996; Rothspan & Read, 1996). This research consistently shows that it is necessary for medical and mental health professionals to address the influences of men's gender when working with men. This is particularly important when working with men who have traditional attitudes or beliefs about manhood and who—as I have demonstrated in the preceding chapters—are at greatest risk.

Any contact a health professional has with a man provides an important opportunity. As I explained in Chapter 2, more than twice as many men as women have not visited a physician in 2 to 5 years. Furthermore, men represent three of four people who have not seen a doctor in more than 5 years. Even among persons *with health problems*, men are significantly more likely than women to have had no recent physician contacts regardless of income or ethnicity. Therefore, any encounter a health professional has with a man—particularly a young or middle-aged man—may be the *only* opportunity for assessment and intervention that *any* health professional will have with that man for a long time. Furthermore, even one contact with a male patient can have significantly positive effects on both behavioral and clinical outcomes. One meta-analysis demonstrated that it is not the number of contacts or the amount of time spent with patients, but rather how the time is spent, that produces positive results (Mullen, Mains, & Velez, 1992).

Although a variety of counseling and psychological interventions with men have been recommended in the past several decades (Courtenay, 2000d), few psychosocial techniques have been developed for health professionals who work with men in health care settings (Courtenay, 1996b, 1998c; Sutkin & Good, 1987). Even more rarely are health interventions designed to address the unique needs of various populations of men, such as gay and bisexual men (Ramirez-Valles, 2007), men in prison (Courtenay & Sabo, 2001), Native American men (Joe, 2001), college men (Courtenay, 1998b), or men with cancer (Nicholas, 2000). Despite the fact that African American men die 6 years younger than European American men, the specific psychosocial health needs of African American men have only begun to be addressed (Davis, 1999; Rich, 2001). Given this lack of clinical guidance, it is not surprising that men receive significantly less physician time in their health visits than women do, and men generally receive fewer services and dispositions than women as well (see Chapter 1).

PRACTICE GUIDELINE FOR THE
TREATMENT OF MEN

The recommendations in this practice guideline are based on an extensive review of biopsychosocial research related to men's gender and health, located through keyword searches in Medline, PsychLit, and other similar online databases. This evidence-based guideline identifies behavioral and psychosocial factors that affect the onset, progression, and management of men's health problems; reviews evidence demonstrating the effectiveness of various interventions; and outlines specific recommendations for addressing these factors when working with men in clinical practice. This practice guideline focuses, in particular, on evidence related to men with traditional beliefs about masculinity, because of the greater health risks among men who hold these beliefs. Its findings and recommendations are summarized in this chapter.

Communication between clinicians and their patients—and the health education provided through this relationship—is emphasized here. Health professionals whose responsibility it is to counsel men in medical settings are in a unique position to assist men. An extensive review of scientific evidence reveals that patients are more likely to be helped to prevent future disease by clinicians who ask, educate, and counsel them about personal health behaviors than by those who perform physical examinations or tests (Agency for Healthcare Research and Quality [AHRQ], 2009; U.S. Preventive Services Task Force [USPSTF], 1996). Furthermore, patients' feelings and attitudes about their health are influenced both by the information they receive *and* by the way in which they receive it (Hall, Roter, & Katz, 1988; Horne, Vatmanidis, & Careri, 1994; Roter & Hall, 2004). These findings have led to the conclusions that "talking is more important than testing" (Woolf, Jonas, & Lawrence, 1996, p. xxxvii), and that offering prevention advice and communicating effectively with patients are the most important skills for clinicians to acquire (Koop, 1996; see Sidebar 12.1).

The American Medical Association (AMA) has referred to the lack of effective clinician–patient communication as a health "hazard" for men (AMA, 1991a, p. 1). Poor communication is associated with inaccurate diagnoses, poor compliance and outcomes, and low knowledge and knowledge retention (Davis & Fallowfield, 1991).[*] Conversely, effective patient and clinician communication has been found to be associated with improved compliance and better patient health status—as measured physiologically, behaviorally, and subjectively (Cramer, 1991; Cramer & Spilker, 1991; Hall et al., 1988; Kaplan, Greenfield, & Ware, 1989; Meichenbaum & Turk, 1987). Because the learning patterns and conversational styles of women and men in this society differ distinctively, and because women and men respond to and accept information differently (Golombok & Fivush, 1994; Tannen, 1990), it is imperative that health professionals incorporate what is currently understood about these gender differences into their interventions with men, if these interventions are to be effective.

This chapter consists of six sections. Each section represents one of six types of intervention discussed in the guideline. Together, the

---

[*] The terms *compliance* and *adherence* are used interchangeably throughout this chapter.

SIDEBAR 12.1   Why Effective Patient Communication Is Essential

Learning to communicate effectively with patients and offer prevention advice is the most important skill that health care providers can develop for this century, according to former Surgeon General Everett Koop.

In fact, research shows that health care providers who **ask, educate, and counsel** patients are more likely to help their patients to prevent disease than clinicians who perform physical examinations or tests.

Poor communication is linked with	→ Inaccurate diagnoses
	→ Poor compliance
	→ Poor outcomes
	→ Low patient knowledge
	→ Low knowledge retention
Effective communication is linked with	→ Better patient health status as measured:
	• Physiologically
	• Behaviorally
	• Subjectively
	→ Improved compliance

The American Medical Association (1991a) reported that a lack of effective clinician–patient communication is a health "hazard" (p. 1) for many men and emphasized the physician's responsibility in breaking through the barriers that men's embarrassment about health matters can create.

section titles form an acronym that spells HEALTH: Humanize, Educate, Assume the worst, Locate supports, Tailor plan, and Harness strengths.

HUMANIZE

The first step in working with a man is to humanize. This means validating, legitimizing, or normalizing his health problems and concerns. Conveying to patients that their feelings and experiences are understandable or legitimate—and that other people would probably feel the same way—is considered essential to effective communication with patients (Grüninger, 1995).

Humanizing is especially important with men. As I discussed in earlier chapters, attending to health matters has historically been socially sanctioned and encouraged among women, but not men. Consequently, many men associate health matters with womanly matters, and men receive strict social prohibitions against doing anything that women do. Because disease, disability, and behavioral responses to illness are antithetical to traditional meanings of manhood, men can experience shame when they have health problems. For example, one in five men have been found to report embarrassment as a reason for not discussing prostate, colon, or rectal cancers with a physician (AMA, 1991b). Humanizing is especially important with patients who have chronic or permanently disabling or life-threatening conditions, which can seriously undermine a man's identity as a man (Charmaz, 1995).

Permission to have physical problems or health concerns, and to discuss them openly, has been referred to as a primary health care need of men (DeHoff & Forrest, 1984). Clinicians can help men learn that asking for help, acknowledging pain, expressing fear, crying, or needing bed rest are normal, *human* experiences—they are *not unmanly*. Other authors reviewing research on masculinity have suggested that when male patients have difficulty expressing discouragement, fear, or concern about giving up control during physical or psychological examinations, clinicians should communicate that these experiences are both normal and appropriate (Copenhaver & Eisler, 1996). Humanizing is a form of validation, which some practitioners consider to be the most effective approach in beginning consultation with a man (Rappaport, 1984). Humanizing may also contribute to the development of trust, which is also considered to be a critical first step in helping men (May, 1990). Specific factors that should be humanized include help seeking, illness and vulnerability, pain, and sexuality.

Humanize Help Seeking

As I explained in Chapters 1 and 2, men are significantly less likely than women to seek health care, except perhaps when their condition is serious. This is because men have less *intention* to seek help from a variety of sources when they need it. In fact, men may be least likely to ask for help when they are most in need of it. Among people who are depressed, for example, men are more likely than women not to seek mental health services, to withdraw from others, and to try to manage their depression on their own. Men learn these behaviors early in their lives. As I discussed in Chapter 3, not only are boys actively discouraged from seeking the help of their parents or other adults, but also they are often punished when they do. Seeking help can undermine a man's sense of independence, which for some men is essential for self-respect (Tannen, 1990); this is believed to be true as well for African American (Lee, 1990) and Latino men (Marks, Garcia, & Solis, 1990). Needing help can be experienced by men as demeaning (Charmaz, 1995) and may lead to feelings of inadequacy (Heppner & Gonzales, 1987) and shame (Brooks, 1998). Consequently, men may undergo considerable inconvenience rather than ask for help (DePaulo, 1982).

Health care visits pose a variety of threats to the roles most familiar to men (Sutkin & Good, 1987). They necessarily mean surrendering some autonomy and relinquishing some control. Lying still in bed or on a consulting table is contrary to the action-oriented and problem-solving coping styles that are fostered in men. A clinician's reconceptualization of help seeking as positive behavior can disconfirm a man's anticipated response of disdain. Offer reinforcement by saying, "I'm glad you phoned me. It's an important first step." Or, "Contacting me when you did was the best thing you could have done." Reframing a man's help seeking as an act of strength, courage, and self-determination may decrease any embarrassment or self-doubt that he may experience in asking for help. Some clinicians consider this to be important when beginning work with a man (Allen & Gordon, 1990). You can say, for example, "I know it can be a real challenge to ask for help, but I'm glad to see that didn't stop you." Clinicians can also assess a man's intention of keeping follow-up appointments by saying, "You know, a lot of men have trouble keeping their follow-up appointments. Does that ever happen to you?" When asked nonjudgmentally, such questions help to predict future adherence and determine the need for treatment compliance techniques (Meichenbaum & Turk, 1987).

Humanize Illness and Vulnerability

Because illness and vulnerability threaten stereotypically masculine notions of competence, vitality, and strength (Charmaz, 1995), men may experience illness or vulnerability as personal flaws, or as failures to successfully demonstrate manhood (Courtenay, 2000c, 2006a). Simply saying, "You know, everybody gets sick sometimes" can bring relief to a man and help to establish rapport. A clinician can also directly label the influence of gender: "Getting sick doesn't mean you're less of a man." When they are ill, men are less likely than women to restrict their activities or stay in bed for both acute and chronic conditions. Some men consider staying in bed to rest or recover to be pampering, and by traditional standards, men should not pamper their bodies (Courtenay, 2000a). A man may think of himself as "lazy" if he misses work after an operation. Humanize the need for convalescence and bed rest by saying to a man, "Staying in bed and taking care of yourself when you're sick doesn't mean you're a bad employee or not a team player."

Humanize Pain and Fear

It is also important for clinicians to make human the experience of pain and fear, and to give men permission to acknowledge physical discomfort. Research consistently indicates that, compared with women, men report less pain for the same pathology, less severe pain, greater tolerance of pain and higher pain thresholds, and shorter duration of pain (Miaskowski, 1999; Unruh, 1996; Unruh, Ritchie, & Merskey, 1999). Men, and society in general, often view admitting or displaying fear and pain as unacceptable behaviors for men (Brooks, 1998; Courtenay, 2000c; Sutkin & Good, 1987). Not surprisingly, men are less likely than women to cry, and they report less fear than women do (see Chapter 1). Men are often uncomfortable in situations that require the expression of tender or painful emotions because they believe that to do so is a violation of traditionally masculine behavior (Copenhaver & Eisler, 1996). A man may need to experience literally intolerable pain before he can acknowledge to himself or to others that he is hurting. Failing to acknowledge or display physical pain can have far-reaching implications for men's health: It can influence the decision to seek help, delay intervention, and undermine diagnosis and treatment planning.

Clinicians should label conditions known to be painful as such: "Kidney stones can be very painful. I don't want you to hesitate for a moment if you think you might need to come back to the emergency room." Express surprise when a man denies that *his* kidney stones are painful. It may also be necessary to humanize the need for pain medication. Sutkin and Good (1987) suggest that a "tough guy" (p. 378) will characteristically wait 6 hours before requesting or taking a 4-hour-acting pain medication. You can compensate for this by saying, "There are no medals for enduring pain, so I want you to let me know if you experience even the *slightest bit* of discomfort." For a man who is refusing medication, a clinician can say, "It's routine for people to receive pain medication for this. Are you sure you don't want the doctor to write you a prescription?"

Humanize Sexuality

It is also important to humanize sexuality. Men's sexual performance is a measure of masculinity in this society (Fracher & Kimmel, 1992). Furthermore, masculinity is measured by *super*human standards that require men to be perpetually interested in and ready for sex (Zilbergeld, 1992). These cultural stereotypes, however, are inconsistent with many men's experience. At least one of four American men is unable to get or maintain an erection for sex (Goldberg, 1993), and this risk increases with age. In a survey of more than 3,000 health professionals, the frequency of erectile dysfunction was 4% in men under age 50, 26% in those aged 50 to 59 years, and 40% in those aged 60 to 69 years (Bacon et al., 2003). Erectile dysfunction is also a common side effect of prostate surgery and a variety of medications. Difficulty getting or maintaining an erection can threaten a patient's self-image as a man and undermine a fundamental aspect of his gender identity (Charmaz, 1995). Not surprisingly, at least three of four men with sexual concerns report not discussing those concerns with their physician, and report that they are deterred from doing so by embarrassment (AMA, 1991b; Metz & Seifert, 1990).

Humanizing sexuality gives men permission to discuss their concerns by normalizing sexual problems or fears among men (Fracher & Kimmel, 1992; Kaplan, 1974). A clinician can say, "Most men have concerns about sex; it's normal. And I hope you're comfortable telling me if you do." Or, "I'd be surprised if you *didn't* worry about that; most men do." In fact, one study found that most men with sexual concerns preferred that the clinician initiate the discussion (Metz & Seifert, 1990). Many men can also use help in identifying unrealistic and less-than-human perceptions of manhood that contribute to sexual anxiety, and help in learning how more *human* perceptions of sexuality can reduce stress and sexual dysfunction. A man with erectile dysfunction may benefit from being told that it is a common condition—that almost every man experiences occasional and transient erectile problems at some point in his life (Fracher & Kimmel, 1992; Zilbergeld, 1992). You can say, "Although the world often expects you to act like a machine, you aren't one. Your body can't really be expected to turn on and off at will. If you relax and don't expect so much out of yourself, you'll be surprised. Your anxiety will diminish and you'll feel a lot more pleasure."

Defining a Healthy Manhood

Although disease and disability are often unpleasant, they also provide men with the opportunity to redefine their lives and their manhood (Charmaz, 1995; Gordon, 1995). Indeed, many men may need to undergo this "reconstruction" of masculinity if they are to substantially improve their health (Levant & Kopecky, 1995). In a supportive manner, clinicians can challenge their patients concerning their preconceived beliefs about what a man should be or what a man must do, and discuss how these beliefs can damage them physically and psychologically (Brooks, 1998; Copenhaver & Eisler, 1996). This strategy is considered a consciousness-raising intervention (Copenhaver & Eisler, 1996), and research indicates that consciousness raising is an effective means of helping people to begin changing unhealthy behavior (Prochaska, Norcross, & DiClemente, 1994). For example, when humanizing help seeking, a clinician can ask, "How do you think being a man influences your ability to ask for help?" The clinician can then help male patients to see how their options are often limited not by their disability or illness, but rather by their beliefs about manhood and other gender-related factors, and help them explore more realistically human and healthy self-perceptions. Moderate self-disclosure on a clinician's part—particularly if the clinician is a man—may make a male patient feel safer in exploring these issues. Self-disclosure establishes a basis of similarity and promotes trust; it has also been found to increase treatment adherence and to increase the patient's sense of competence and self-efficacy (Copenhaver & Eisler, 1996; May, 1990; Meichenbaum & Turk, 1987). A clinician might say, "I know what you mean, I have a hard time admitting when I'm sick too." Or, "I often feel like I'm just supposed to handle things on my own."

EDUCATE

The next step is to educate men about their health. As noted previously, health education interventions are an essential aspect of disease and injury prevention (AHRQ, 2009; Council on Scientific Affairs, 1990; USPSTF, 1996; Woolf et al., 1996). Besides increasing patient and health practitioner satisfaction (Grüninger, 1995), reviews and meta-analyses offer strong evidence that health education improves compliance (Cramer, 1991; Cramer & Spilker, 1991; Hall et al., 1988; McCann & Blossom, 1990; Meichenbaum & Turk, 1987); reduces risk factors, disease, and death; and promotes healthy behaviors, such as exercise, healthy diet, and blood pressure control (Frank, Bouman, Cain, & Watts, 1992; Grüninger, 1995; Mullen et al., 1992; USPSTF, 1996). Similarly, psychoeducational interventions have been found to have a significantly positive effect on pain, psychological distress, and recovery, and to be cost-efficient as well (Byers et al., 1995; Devine, 1992; Horne et al., 1994). Education is also essential if patients are to become active participants in their own health care (Make, 1994).

Health Education and Men

There is strong evidence that men need to be educated about their health. If they are to maintain good health, it is critical that they be familiar with symptoms of life-threatening disease, know how the body should function, and know their family health histories (DeHoff & Forrest, 1984; Goldberg, 1993). However, as I have already explained in Chapter 1, research consistently indicates that men are less knowledgeable than women about health in general, and about specific diseases, such as heart disease, cancer, and sexually transmitted diseases (STDs). Men also ask fewer questions than women do when visiting a physician. Asking a question necessarily means admitting that there is something one does not know—which is often difficult for men to acknowledge (Tannen, 1990). Consequently, the AMA has concluded, based on two national surveys, that men are "surprisingly uninformed" (AMA, 1991a, para. 6) about basic health issues, and that health professionals have a responsibility to educate men (AMA, 1991a, 1991b; see also Chapter 1).

Too often, however, health professionals fail to provide the health education that could reduce men's risks. As I discussed in the preceding chapters, historically, health education generally and cancer education specifically have been directed primarily at women. Men also receive less information from physicians. In fact, no study has ever found that women receive less information from physicians than men do (Roter & Hall, 1997, 2004). This failure to educate men can result in a self-fulfilling prophecy and reinforce a damaging irresponsibility toward health matters among men. This need not be the case. Research indicates that health promotion and education can produce positive changes in knowledge, behavior, and health outcomes among men (Baer, 1993; Best, Davis, Vaz, & Kaiser, 1996; Danielson et al., 1990; Little, Stevens, Severson, & Lichtenstein, 1992; Murphy & Brubaker, 1990; Steffen, Sternberg, Teegarden, & Shepherd, 1994); indeed, these changes are sometimes even greater than those found among women

(Bjornson et al., 1995; Hornbrook et al., 1994; Oleckno & Blacconiere, 1990b). Studies designed to educate men about testicular cancer have reported increased knowledge, more positive attitudes toward testicular self-examination, stronger intentions to conduct self-examinations, and higher levels of actual practice of self-examination among men (Best et al., 1996; Murphy & Brubaker, 1990; Steffen et al., 1994). Furthermore, obtaining information from conversation appeals to many men (Tannen, 1990) and can also be reassuring. Hendricks (1999) cites evidence, for example, that learning about diabetes, its associated health-related problems, its treatment, what outcomes can be expected from treatment, and when patients can expect these outcomes reduces fear and anxiety among African American men with the disorder.

Specific educational interventions will vary depending on a man's current health, his presenting concern, and his future risks, as well as on the clinician's role and responsibilities. In general, a clinician can begin to educate a man by saying, "I don't know about you, but most men know very little about their bodies and their health, and that lack of knowledge actually increases their health risks." Or, "Most of the things that have the biggest impact on your health are completely within your control." Because they have had relatively little experience with the health care system, many men will need basic information, such as how to ask for help, whom to contact to schedule a follow-up appointment, whom to phone with questions after discharge, and what kinds of questions to ask their health care providers. When counseling men, word advice clearly, simply, and directly (Make, 1994; USPSTF, 1996). Because patients see health professionals as experts, a direct statement such as "I must insist that you do your rehabilitation exercises daily" can have a strong positive effect (USPSTF, 1996). To promote preventive care and behavioral change, it is considered essential to provide alternative behaviors (Frank et al., 1992). It is not enough simply to educate a man about the importance of taking medication as prescribed. Suggest strategies for adhering to his prescribed regimen, such as establishing a dosing schedule and checklist, and using a pillbox with daily compartments or an alarm (Cramer, 1991; Meichenbaum & Turk, 1987).

Clinicians should not be afraid to be enthusiastic in their interventions with men. Research indicates that men respond positively to active encouragement to engage in preventive health behavior (Myers et al., 1991). Because many men are less comfortable receiving information than giving it (Tannen, 1990), communicate to a male patient that the information he is being offered is provided routinely; he may be less likely to feel singled out because he believes the clinician thinks he's ignorant (Rappaport, 1984). You can say, "We tell all of our patients …," or, "You may already know this, but let me review it for the sake of good form." Then, supplement what you say with written materials. Although written materials alone may not help patients to change their behavior (Grüninger, 1995), they may be more helpful to men than to women (May, 1990). It is essential, however, to make sure that the patient can read and understand these materials (Meichenbaum & Turk, 1987).

Despite some inconsistent findings regarding the use of fear in motivating people to change unhealthy behaviors, health educators agree that some aspects of fear can be used effectively with some patients (Meichenbaum & Turk, 1987). In one study, fear of developing cancer was among the best predictors of testicular self-examination among young men (Katz, Meyers, & Walls, 1995). It is essential, however, that an intervention using fear also foster a man's sense of efficacy in remedying the problem (Meichenbaum & Turk, 1987). Offer information that induces a relatively low level of fear, provides positive reinforcement, and focuses on the immediate effects of modifying behavior, such as the reduction in high blood pressure and increased lung capacity that occurs when the patient stops smoking (Job, 1988): "Your diet is raising your risk of heart disease. But even the minor changes we've discussed will not only reduce this risk, but also lower your cholesterol and increase your vitality."

The Importance of Screening, Self-Examination, and Early Detection

Men need to be taught how to do self-examinations. They also need to be taught the importance of screenings and early detection. As I discussed in Chapter 2, screening tests are essential for preventing disease, detecting preclinical conditions, and identifying a variety of diseases at an early stage, when successful treatment is more likely. Men, however, are less likely than women to practice self-examination or to attend health screenings; African American men may be even less likely than European American men to do so (Pierce, 1999). Self-examinations are particularly important for men. Because they seldom visit physicians, self-examination is the *only* way most men will detect a variety of diseases when they are *still curable* (Goldberg, 1993). Self-examinations relevant to men include those for skin and testicular cancer, hypertension (for men at risk for heart disease or stroke), and STDs. Health professionals can do much to encourage men to practice self-examination. Expressions of concern and personal instruction by clinicians have been associated with the intention to conduct self-examinations (Brubaker & Wickersham, 1990; Neef, Scutchfield, Elder, & Bender, 1991).

Educating patients about their specific health risks is an essential aspect of disease and injury prevention (USPSTF, 1996). It is particularly important to do this with men. As I demonstrated in Chapter 2, males of all ages are more likely than females to engage in more than 30 behaviors that increase the risk of disease, injury, and death. Despite these findings, men receive less advice from physicians about changing risk factors for disease during checkups than women do (Friedman, Brownson, Peterson, & Wilkerson, 1994). Only 29% of physicians routinely provide age-appropriate instruction on performing self-examinations for testicular cancer, compared with 86% who provide age-appropriate instruction to women on performing breast self-examinations (Misener & Fuller, 1995). Clinicians need to assess the need for self-examination skills among all their male patients.

To determine a man's specific risks, a health risk assessment can be useful. I developed one such assessment specifically for men, and it includes items addressing both health behaviors and beliefs—including beliefs about manhood (Courtenay, 1996b). Once a man's risks are identified, a clinician can provide counseling as indicated. When counseling men about modifying unhealthy behaviors, emphasize the personal relevance of change and link it with a man's own circumstances (Meichenbaum & Turk, 1987), such as being healthy for his children. A man should also be invited to discuss what *he* believes he can do to reduce his health risks or modify his behaviors (May & Martin, 1993). In general, there is sufficient evidence regarding effective outcomes to strongly recommend counseling patients about avoiding tobacco, exercising regularly, limiting consumption of dietary fat, not driving while impaired by alcohol or other drugs, wearing bicycle helmets, and using condoms (USPSTF, 1996). There is also sufficient evidence to recommend counseling patients about avoiding excess sun exposure; consuming fiber, fruits, and vegetables; using safety belts; reducing alcohol consumption in problem drinkers; avoiding recreational activities while intoxicated; removing or safely storing firearms in the home to prevent youth violence; and caring for their teeth (USPSTF, 1996). Because men are at greater risk than women in relation to all these factors, which I demonstrate in Chapter 2, it is particularly important to provide counseling to men.

Make Sure Men Do Not Leave With Unanswered Questions

To foster compliance, it is important to make sure that a patient understands what he has been told (Meichenbaum & Turk, 1987). This is especially important in the case of men, who can have difficulty admitting that they do not understand (Moore, 1990a; Tannen, 1990). Simply asking the patient to restate the information he has been given, or to rehearse a regimen, is an effective technique (Meichenbaum & Turk, 1987). If you have explained to a patient how to perform a certain task—how to use a mechanical ventilatory support, for example—you should ask him to demonstrate the procedure (Kacmarek, 1994). You can further clarify whether the patient has understood the information he was given—and how he will implement that knowledge—by asking, "Given what we discussed about your diet, what changes do you think are realistic for you to make to lower your blood pressure?"

Similarly, it is important for clinicians to recognize that men may have questions that they will not ask. Admitting that there is something he does not know, or that he needs to learn from someone else, may be difficult for a man (Rappaport, 1984; Tannen, 1990). As I noted previously, women ask more questions—and more direct questions—than men do when visiting a physician. Consequently, clinicians should actively encourage men to ask questions by saying, for example, "I'll try to cover everything, but your questions will be very helpful." Regardless of what exactly one says, it is essential to issue a direct invitation; merely informing a patient that one is open to questions is not enough (Robinson & Whitfield, 1985). Conclude a consultation by saying, "I've explained a lot to you. I'd be surprised if you didn't have some questions." Or, "You know, people often leave here without talking about the things that they're most concerned about."

ASSUME THE WORST

As I demonstrated in Chapter 3, one of the most common and enduring cultural stereotypes about men is that they are healthier and more resistant to disease than women, despite a wealth of evidence to the contrary. Men who attempt to conform to these cultural stereotypes increase their health risks. They may try to appear strong and healthy, believe that they are invulnerable to risk, minimize pain and deny feelings that others may perceive as signs of weakness, and report their health inaccurately.

Men's Perceived Invulnerability to Risk

As I explain in Chapter 1, studies consistently indicate that men are less likely than women to perceive themselves as being at risk. This holds true for a variety of health problems, including problems associated with sun exposure; cigarette, alcohol, and other drug use; and physically dangerous activities. Men's perceived invulnerability can prevent them from practicing preventive care or changing unhealthy behavior, thus increasing their health risks. Perceived invulnerability has also been linked with poor compliance (Friedman & DiMatteo, 1989).

Men's Reported Health Needs

The AMA contends that clinicians need to more active than they are in inquiring about men's symptoms (AMA, 1991a). This is especially important because the information a man provides to a clinician does not always accurately reflect his needs. As I discussed in Chapter 1, research indicates that, except for anger, men express fewer emotions than do women, and disclose fewer fears and feelings of vulnerability. This is especially true of men who endorse traditional beliefs about masculinity (Copenhaver & Eisler, 1996; Saurer & Eisler, 1990; Thompson, Grisanti, & Pleck, 1985). These factors influence men's clinical consultations. Men provide less emotional and personal information in reporting their health (Corney, 1990; Verbrugge, 1985). Men may deny their physical or emotional distress, and conceal their illnesses or disabilities, in an effort to preserve their masculinity or in the hope that their doctor will admire their stoicism or courage (Charmaz, 1995; Sutkin & Good, 1987). Men may also deny that they engage in risk behavior. One large study of safety belt use that compared self-reports with actual use found that among drivers who had been *observed* not wearing safety belts— more than three of four of whom were men—one third had reported that they *always* wore safety belts (Preusser, Williams, & Lund, 1991).

Assessing Men's Health Needs

Taken together, the preceding research suggests that men fail to convey the information clinicians need to provide effective medical care, and that the clinician must therefore assume the worst. It is also essential to assume the worst to compensate for gender stereotypes, which influence the diagnostic decisions of—among others—mental health clinicians (see Chapter 1). One large study found that clinicians were less likely to identify the presence of depression in men than in women, and that they failed to diagnose nearly two thirds of the depressed men (Potts et al., 1991). Similarly, when patients are matched by symptoms or diagnoses, men are less likely than women to receive prescriptions for antidepressants and other psychotropic drugs (Hohmann, 1989; Taggart, McCammon, Allred, Horner, & May, 1993). Despite men's greater risk for uncontrolled hypertension, they are significantly less likely than women to receive prescriptions for medication to control high blood pressure (see Chapter 2).

Men's desire to appear strong and healthy, to believe that they are invulnerable to risk, to conceal physical and emotional distress, and to report their behaviors inaccurately are all factors that must be considered when working with men. First, these factors make it difficult to conduct an accurate assessment. Second, as a result of these factors, a man's physical and mental condition is often serious when he finally does seek help (Fabrega, Pilkonis, Mezzich, Ahn, & Shea, 1990; Gerber, Thompson, Thisted, & Chodak, 1993; Sawyer & Moss, 1993; Thomas & Kelman, 1990; Verbrugge, 1980, 1982). Assuming the worst compensates for these factors, and for the tendency among clinicians to underestimate men's vulnerability.

Getting the Information You Need

To diagnose a man's condition accurately and to plan his treatment, it is essential to elicit information about his symptoms and feeling states. Asking a man, "How do you feel?" is not recommended, however. It has been argued that this question is difficult for men to respond to (Rubin, 1983), and that it often elicits nothing more than a shrug of the shoulders or an unreflective "Fine" (Rappaport, 1984). Instead, you should inquire indirectly: "Tell me, how do you experience that?" Or,

"What is that like for you?" These questions are not as common and may be less likely to prompt an automatic response. Similarly, when assessing depression in men, it may be helpful to avoid the words *feel* and *depressed*, and instead ask, "Do you ever get a little down?" A man may find it easier to admit that he gets down than that he feels depressed.

A clinician who suspects that a man may be concealing his symptoms should question him further. If a 60-year-old African American man who has diabetes and a family history of stroke is not reporting any symptoms, the clinician should ask him if he has experienced any sudden weakness or numbness, any loss of vision or speech, and any dizziness or headaches. Individualized feedback on specific health risks can increase a man's accurate perception of his own susceptibility to these risks (Kreuter & Strecher, 1995). In response to perceptions of vulnerability that are inconsistent with a man's actual risks, a clinician can say, "I know it's important to you to think of yourself as strong and healthy. But that attitude can lead you to take unnecessary risks with your health."

LOCATE SUPPORTS

Men are taught to value independence, autonomy, and self-sufficiency in themselves (Courtenay, 2000c; Majors & Billson, 1992; Marks et al., 1990). Consequently, compared with women, men have significantly fewer and less intimate friendships, fewer lifetime ties, and smaller and less multifaceted social networks, and they receive less support from network members (see Chapter 2). Traditional beliefs about masculinity make a man even less likely to seek help from his friends, partner, and family.

Exaggerated self-sufficiency and lack of social support contribute to the shortening of men's lives. There is overwhelming evidence that a lack of social support constitutes a major risk factor for mortality— especially for men. As I explain in Chapter 2, men with the lowest levels of social support are 2 to 3 times more likely to die than those with the highest levels of support, even after controlling for health status and other possible confounding factors. In contrast, high levels of social support are associated with the maintenance of positive health practices, modification of unhealthy behavior, and compliance with treatment. Marriage also plays an important role in men's health; whether single, separated, widowed, or divorced, unmarried men have greater health risks than any other group.

Involving Friends and Family

Assessing social support is considered essential to promoting behavioral change and preventive behavior (Frank et al., 1992). Involving friends and family as sources of support can also be essential to improving clinician–patient relationships and clinical outcomes (Delbanco, 1992). Clinicians should recognize the importance of extended family for African American men specifically, and the need to involve family members collaboratively in these patients' care (Pierce, 1999). Because men have fewer social supports than women and are less likely to use the ones they do have, it is essential for clinicians to help men to identify the sources of support that are available to them. These may include significant others, friends, family, coworkers, classmates, and groups. You can ask a man, "Who are the people you are most comfortable asking to give you a hand?"

A clinician should assess—and help the patient to assess—whose involvement the patient finds helpful. Other people's involvement, in and of itself, is not necessarily supportive (Meichenbaum & Turk, 1987). A family member, friend, or health professional who has difficulty seeing vulnerability in men can undermine the patient's motivation to mobilize support. Once a man's supports are identified, encourage him to reach out to them. Otherwise, he may not. In a postoperative consultation, one man said, "You know, I was going into surgery and no one knew. It seemed like it would have been complaining to tell them." Assist men in recognizing that everyone needs help sometimes, reminding them that people really like to help, and that their friends are probably happy to be asked for a hand.

Using Familiar Concepts

In talking with male patients about social support, consider using concepts that are easily recognizable and familiar to many men (Gordon & Pasick, 1990), such as teamwork, networking, and strategic planning. Suggest that the man set regular times to meet with friends. It may be difficult for a man to contact other men to get together; he may think that doing so puts him in a one-down position (Tannen, 1990). The regular ball game, movie, or dinner out provides a man with regular contact and support without his having to ask for it or betray his need for it. Provide encouragement for any attempts—however small—men make to reach out to others (Gordon & Pasick, 1990). Clinicians should also consider referring men to support or educational groups that are available to, and appropriate for, male patients, and should encourage them to participate if a referral is made. It is also important not to overlook or underestimate contacts that men already have with others through activities such as work, church, or sports (Gordon & Pasick, 1990; Pasick, 1990).

Clinicians as Sources of Support

Health care providers are also an important source of support for men (Kaplan et al., 1989). For unmarried men, in particular, professionals may be one of the few sources of support that are available. Although a man may be reluctant at first to look to clinicians for support, research indicates that he will respond positively to efforts at follow-up contact.

Telephone follow-up, specifically, has been found to improve coun-seling effectiveness and behavioral change (USPSTF, 1996), reduce noncompliance, and improve appointment keeping (Meichenbaum & Turk, 1987).

TAILOR PLAN

The importance of developing and implementing realistic health mainte-nance plans with patients has been addressed elsewhere; a well-tailored plan fosters behavioral change and improves treatment adherence (e.g., Grueninger, Goldstein, & Duffy, 1990; Meichenbaum & Turk, 1987; Prochaska et al., 1994). Tailoring a plan is especially important with men, who are much less likely than women to persist in caring for a health problem (see Chapter 2). The type of plan, the extent of the plan, and its specific components will depend on each man's individual needs, as well as on the clinician's role and functions. The following discussion identifies aspects of a plan that warrant particular attention when working with men.

Planning a Healthy Future

Essentially, tailoring a plan means developing a health maintenance schedule, like the maintenance schedule for a car; this analogy may prove useful when introducing the concept to male patients. "Tailoring" the plan means individualizing it to the patient's needs, age, intellectual capacity, attitudes, cultural background, and circumstances; this is con-sidered essential both in establishing a plan and in fostering adherence (Meichenbaum & Turk, 1987). For the plan to be successful it must be realistic; it must be broken down into attainable steps; and the patient must have the skills necessary to carry it out (Meichenbaum & Turk, 1987; Prochaska et al., 1994; USPSTF, 1996). Discussing the pros and cons of various treatment possibilities with a patient, and inviting his suggestions and preferences, not only is useful in tailoring a plan but also can foster compliance (Meichenbaum & Turk, 1987). For example, suggest that men choose a day of the month to do self-examinations—a day with personal relevance that they can easily remember, such as a birth date.

Ideally, a man's comprehensive health maintenance plan includes periodic physicals, screenings, self-examinations, preventive behaviors, self-care techniques, and vitamin and medicine schedules. The plan should include a physical examination every few years for younger men and every year for men over 50 (Goldberg, 1993). Physical examinations provide the opportunity for screenings, further assessment, referrals, and the early detection of disease. Screenings should include periodic blood pressure measurement, periodic weight measurement, blood cho-lesterol screening every 5 years, periodic sigmoidoscopy, and annual fecal occult blood testing for colorectal cancer for men over 50; the plan should also include annual flu and pneumonia immunizations for men 65 and older (USPSTF, 1996).

Fostering Adherence

It is well known that patients do not always follow their doctor's advice. A man's beliefs about masculinity may undermine his compliance with the plan. Among men with heart disease, men with traditional beliefs have been found to be less likely to follow their physician's orders and to make fewer healthy lifestyle changes after hospital discharge than their less traditional peers (Helgeson, 1995). Therefore, in tailoring a plan with a patient it is important to assess his intention of complying with treatment recommendations, and to use adherence enhancement techniques as necessary (Meichenbaum & Turk, 1987). Ask your male patients to describe specifically how they intend to carry out their plans (USPSTF, 1996). For example, you can assess a man's intention to rest during recovery by asking, "What arrangements have you made at work to cover your absence?" The more specific a patient is in describing how he intends to carry out his regimen, the more likely he is to be compliant (USPSTF, 1996).

It is important to anticipate nonadherence. Inquiring into a patient's history of compliance can be effective in fostering adherence, if it is done in a nonjudgmental and nonthreatening manner (Meichenbaum & Turk, 1987; USPSTF, 1996). Several studies have found that clinicians who work with patients to overcome obstacles to adherence increase compliance (McCann & Blossom, 1990). A male patient can be asked, "Do you ever miss your medical appointments?" and, "Do you sometimes stop taking your medicine when you start to feel better?" Clinicians can also assess a patient's commitment to a proposed plan by asking directly, "Will you stick to this plan?" Or, "How are you going to carry out this plan?" (Grueninger et al., 1990; Hewson, 1993). Developing a written or verbal contract is also effective in fostering compliance in some patients (Meichenbaum & Turk, 1987).

HARNESS STRENGTHS

As I discussed in Chapter 1, masculinity, men's behavior, and men's coping styles are associated with both positive and negative health outcomes. Being aggressive, competitive, and achievement oriented, for example, increases a man's risk of heart disease (e.g., Strube, 1991). But these *same* characteristics can be turned to a health advantage. Being competitive and achievement oriented may be exactly what makes men more successful than women at quitting smoking, even though more women than men say they want to quit (see Chapter 2). Similarly, although traditional beliefs about manhood can increase men's risks, certain characteristics that are considered traditionally masculine ways of coping are highly adaptive for men (and women). These characteristics include having the ability to act independently, to be assertive, and to be decisive (Cook, 1985; Eisler, 1995; Nezu & Nezu, 1987; Sharpe & Heppner, 1991; Sharpe, Heppner, & Dixon, 1995). For example, reliance on traditionally masculine characteristics has been found to help to enable men to cope with cancer (Gordon, 1995) and chronic illness (Charmaz, 1995), to recover from spinal cord injuries (Schopp, Good, Mazurek, Barker, & Stucky, 2007), and to maintain good health (Wade, 2008a). Interpreting testicular cancer as a battleground for proving their courage gives some men greater self-confidence (Gordon, 1995).

Identifying a patient's strengths fosters motivation and compliance (Meichenbaum & Turk, 1987). It also conveys respect for his efforts and achievements—which is an important aspect of effective patient–clinician communication (Grüninger, 1995). Commenting on a man's strength before exploring his feeling states may reduce embarrassment and allow him to express his emotions more freely (Rappaport, 1984). An example is to say, "It's great that you took control of things the way you did and got yourself in here so quickly. Although sometimes even when we take decisive action, it doesn't always reduce our fears." Identifying men's strengths may also foster a clinician's sense of empathy and compassion, which some contend are essential factors in helping men to change (Brooks, 1998; Schinke, Cole, Williams, & Botvin, 1999). Harnessing men's strengths can also mean drawing from their cultural strengths. When discussing diet planning with African American men, for example, Hendricks (1999) suggests identifying high-fiber "soul foods" familiar to these patients and incorporating those foods into the plan.

The following sections discuss how to harness a man's strengths by reinforcing specific coping strategies.

Teamwork

The most fundamental way to begin harnessing men's strengths is to encourage them to become active participants in their own health care. The relationship between health professionals and patients is increasingly viewed as a partnership in which health care is the shared work of the patient and the clinician (Grüninger, 1995; Make, 1994; Meichenbaum & Turk, 1987; Woolf et al., 1996). Collaborative treatment that encourages the patient's active involvement is associated with treatment adherence and improved outcomes (Deber, 1994; McCann & Blossom, 1990; Meichenbaum & Turk, 1987; O'Brien, Petrie, & Raeburn, 1992). Men may tend to perceive health care as something that is done *to* them, not something that they participate in. The patient–clinician relationship, however, can be the ideal type of interaction for a man, provided it is approached as teamwork. Although men are taught to value independence and self-sufficiency, many men have also learned to value the camaraderie and partnership fostered among men through sports, the military, and fraternities (Heppner & Gonzales, 1987). Similarly, men's friendships often focus on working together on tasks or activities (Buhrke & Fuqua, 1987; Miller, 1983).

Asking, "Where do you want to start?" (Grüninger, 1995) enlists a man's involvement and reinforces his active participation. Convey to a male patient that he is an integral part of the clinical team, and that the success of his treatment depends on his cooperation. Ask, "How do you think *I* can best help you to follow this regimen?" or "What do you think is the best way for you to track your cholesterol levels?" Exploring a patient's expectations and previous experiences, answering his questions, inviting his opinions, inquiring into his priorities and preferences, avoiding jargon, and being friendly will all help to make him feel like part of the team (Grüninger, 1995; Meichenbaum & Turk, 1987).

Denial as a Positive Coping Strategy

The negative effects of men's tendency to deny or minimize risk were cited previously. Denial, however, can also help a man to cope with illness—particularly when denial is used not dismiss that one is ill but to minimize the severity of a problem (Helgeson, 1995). Denial is associated both with noncompliance *and* with positive consequences, such as resuming work and sex, better medical outcomes, and effective coping after surgery (Helgeson, 1995; Levine et al., 1987). This research suggests that clinicians need to recognize how a patient is using denial. Identifying how a man uses denial as a *positive* means of coping will also convey respect (Grüninger, 1995). You can say, for example, "I admire the positive perspective you have on your recovery."

Intellectual Coping

Being intellectual, logical, and rational are highly valued coping mechanisms among men (Eisler, 1995; Meth, 1990). Although these coping mechanisms can create problems for men in their interpersonal relationships, they are an asset when a man is learning about his health. For example, being unemotional has been found to be associated with recovery among men in rehabilitation for spinal cord injuries (Schopp et al., 2007). Because men's conversational styles tend to focus on conveying and exchanging factual information (Moore, 1990; Tannen, 1990), men may be particularly responsive to health education interventions (Helgeson, 1995). Similarly, effective decision making about changing unhealthy behavior requires that the individual patient assess the pros and cons of change (Grüninger, 1995; Prochaska et al., 1994). Clinicians should make positive use of a man's tendency to weigh his options rationally by discussing with him the costs and benefits of change, and emphasizing the intellectual aspects of health care.

Action-Oriented, Problem-Solving, and Goal-Setting Coping

Men engage in more action-oriented, problem-solving, and goal-setting coping than women do (Nezu & Nezu, 1987; Stone & Neale, 1984). This also holds true for men who are coping with health problems (Fifc, Kennedy, & Robinson, 1994; Gordon, 1995; Helgeson, 1995). Although an action-oriented, problem-solving coping style can hinder a man's recovery from illness, it can also help him to recover and reduce his future risk (Charmaz, 1995; Gordon, 1995; Helgeson, 1995). Help a patient conceptualize his task as conquering or outsmarting an illness. You can say, "I'm impressed by how determined you are to outsmart this disease. And if you keep up that approach, there's a good chance you will!" Men with traditional attitudes about masculinity may be particularly responsive to interventions that emphasize problem-solving skills (Robertson & Fitzgerald, 1992). Teaching problem-solving skills has also been found to be effective in reducing risks among young African American men (Schinke et al., 1999).

A goal-oriented approach to solving problems can be used to a man's health advantage. For example, setting dates for achieving specific health goals can contribute to positive outcomes and foster adherence (Artinian et al., 2010; Little et al., 1992; Meichenbaum & Turk, 1987). You can reconceptualize a patient's goal after surgery as recovery and reframe health goals as targets to shoot for. You can also capitalize on a man's interest in keeping score when monitoring cholesterol or blood pressure. Ask, "What are the odds that you can bring your cholesterol down by the next time I see you?"

Maintaining a Healthy Sense of Control

For many men, being in control is an essential part of being a man. As noted previously, illness can threaten a man's sense of being in control. Furthermore, men are more likely than women to believe that they have little or no control over their future health, a belief that can increase men's risks (Courtenay, 1998a). To maintain healthy behaviors and modify unhealthy ones, it is essential that patients have a sense of self-efficacy and believe that they can respond effectively to reduce a health threat (Grüninger, 1995; Schinke et al., 1999; Taylor, 1990). The traditionally masculine attitude of self-reliance has been found to be associated with men's belief that they can influence their health and well-being (Wade, 2008b). Patients are more likely to adhere to treatment when they believe that they have some control over their illnesses (O'Brien et al., 1992). College men who have a personal sense of control over cancer, for example, are significantly more likely to practice monthly testicular self-examination (Neef et al., 1991). These findings suggest that clinicians should attempt to foster men's sense of self-efficacy by focusing on the positive aspects of control. Suggest to a man that he take "personal responsibility" for his well-being and "take charge" of his health, for example.

CONCLUSION

This chapter summarizes the findings and recommendations of a practice guideline for working with men. Six general strategies were identified. These strategies are represented by the acronym HEALTH: Humanize, Educate, Assume the worst, Locate supports, Tailor plan, and Harness strengths. These interventions are critical because men have serious health risks, and because these risks are compounded by men's gendered health behaviors and beliefs. Sidebars 12.2 through 12.4 summarize this guideline. In Table 12.1, additional men's health and wellness strategies that health professionals can use are outlined.

SIDEBAR 12.2   The 6-Point Health Plan—and Why

HUMANIZE	Because men are taught to be self-reliant and to conceal weakness. When they *do* need help or feel pain, they often think they should not, that these things are *unmanly*.
EDUCATE	Because men are less knowledgeable than women about health in general and about their specific health risks. And because a lack of knowledge can increase men's risks.
ASSUME THE WORST	Because men deny and minimize their symptoms, making accurate assessment and effective treatment difficult. And because men think they are invulnerable to disease and injury—which increases their health risks.
LOCATE SUPPORTS	Because men have fewer friendships and smaller social networks than women do—factors linked with health and longevity—and because men often hesitate to use the social support they do have.
TAILOR PLAN	Because men are more likely to have maintenance plans for their cars than for their bodies. And because health plans improve men's chances of successfully living healthy lives.
HARNESS STRENGTHS	Because many of men's attitudes and behaviors can benefit their health.

SIDEBAR 12.3   What You Can Do

HUMANIZE	Communicate to men that asking for help, admitting pain, expressing concerns, crying, or getting bed rest are normal, *human* experiences—they are *not unmanly*.
EDUCATE	Give men the health education they have never been taught. Teach them that following good health habits can be manly and lifesaving. Include:

- Their specific health risks
- Screening and early detection
- Self-examinations
- Sensation sensitivity skills
- Anger management skills
- Diet and nutrition

ASSUME THE WORST	Health care providers need to compensate for the tendency among both men *and* clinicians to overlook health risks and illness in men.
LOCATE SUPPORTS	Help men to identify his sources of support and suggest ways for him to use them.
TAILOR PLAN	Help men devise a realistic health maintenance plan that he *will* follow. Include:

- Regular physicals
- Specific screenings
- Diet plan
- Health protective behavior plan
- Medicine and supplement use plan
- Self-care techniques

HARNESS STRENGTHS	Capitalize on the attitudes and behaviors of men that can improve their health. Harness the benefits of:

- An intellectual style
- Autonomy and control
- A problem-solving approach
- A teamwork approach

SIDEBAR 12.4   Communication Strategies

HUMANIZE

- *"I know it can be hard to ask for help, but I hope you'll feel free to call me any-time you want to."*
- *"There are no medals for enduring pain. So I want you to let me know if it bothers you the slightest bit."*

EDUCATE

- *"Most of the things that have the biggest impact on your health and longevity are completely within your control!"*
- *"Did you know that three of four men who get any kind of cancer smoke?"*

ASSUME THE WORST

- *"Your work schedule sounds busy. Does it ever seem a little stressful?"*
- *"Most people with this disorder experience pain. Isn't it bothering you at all?"*

LOCATE SUPPORTS

- *"Who might be available to help you get back home today?"*
- *"When we need help ourselves, we sometimes forget how good it feels to give someone a hand—that our friends are usually happy to help."*

TAILOR PLAN

- *"What do you think is a good way to remember to do testicular exams?"*
- *"What kinds of things can cause you to miss an appointment?"*

HARNESS STRENGTHS

- *"Let's look at the costs and benefits of this approach."*
- *"I'm impressed by your determination not to give up despite your pain."*

In conclusion, it is important to note that clinicians—particularly male clinicians—need to examine their own health behavior. Like male patients, male clinicians are more likely than their female counterparts to engage in behaviors that increase their health risks (Allen & Whatley, 1986; Council on Scientific Affairs, 1990; Frank & Harvey, 1996; Lewis, Clancy, Leake, & Schwartz, 1991; Norman & Rosvall, 1994), and this gender difference influences their work with male patients (see Sidebar 12.5). Physicians who themselves practice good health habits are more likely to counsel their patients about healthy behaviors, and those with poor health habits are especially unlikely to do so (Lewis et al., 1991; Wells, Lewis, Leake, & Ware, 1984). Similarly, mental health professionals who have difficulty accepting or expressing their own feelings may have difficulty assisting male patients with their emotions (Heppner & Gonzales, 1987).

SIDEBAR 12.5   Look at Yourself

The counseling that health professionals provide to their patients reflects their own personal health habits. Therefore, it is essential that you look at your own health behavior—particularly if you are a man.

Male physicians differ little in their health behaviors from men in general. They have less healthy habits than female physicians when compared for cancer screening, smoking, alcohol use, and safety belt use—to name just a few.

To maximize your effectiveness with male patients:

- *Assess your own health behavior.*
- *Evaluate how your own health behavior may influence your clinical work with patients.*
- *Question whether your own views about manhood influence your assessments and your work with men.*

ASK YOURSELF

- "How do I feel when I see a man who is not in control of his emotions?"
- "What's it like for me to see a grown man express fear or cry about his health?"
- "Am I likely to see a man's hostile and aggressive behavior and fail to see his pain and sadness?"
- "Do I typically assume that all men are heterosexual?"
- "Does my manner make male patients feel safe enough to talk openly?"
- "Do I subtly communicate to a man with minor complaints that he should 'act more like a man'?"

Clinicians should also be aware of their views about what it means to be a man, and of how these views influence their work with men. Health professionals may subtly, or even unconsciously, convey contempt for male patients who do not "act like a man" (Heppner & Gonzales, 1987). To assess their beliefs, clinicians should ask themselves, "How do *I* feel when I see man who is not in control of his emotions?" "Am I likely just to see a man's hostility and fail to see the pain and sadness underneath?" "Do I simply assume that all male athletes are heterosexual?" "Does my manner make men feel safe?" The clinician may need to find means of compensating for his or her own stereotypes—and means to validate, respect, and foster the unique ways each man becomes involved in his health care.

TABLE 12.1 Men's Health and Wellness Strategies

- Bring services and education to men (e.g., sports events, churches, fitness centers, union halls, golf courses, barber shops, truck stops, bars, senior centers, fraternal organizations, etc.).
- Identify men or workers who have experienced health problems (e.g., testicular cancer, auto accidents) as spokesmen for providing peer-based education.
- Use men's bathrooms and locker rooms for the distribution of health education materials and health campaigns.
- Provide free men's health kits or fanny packs with educational materials, such as self-examination instructions and health service information, along with promotional items, such as healthy protein bars and toiletries.
- Offer health information in varied formats (e.g., outreach presentations, entertainment-related events).
- Establish an e-mail–based education campaign or question/answer service.
- Provide Internet survey tools and games.
- Offer competitive contests with prizes for involvement in health promotion activities.
- Provide health events with a theme (e.g., pop culture, rock music, or sports).
- Provide a "sports and fitness expo" with health and wellness components, as well as sports events, competitions, sporting equipment, exhibitions, and car, truck, or boat shows.
- Use high-profile spokesmen to promote men's health through media campaigns or for special events (e.g., community leaders, athletes, actors, or media personalities).
- Address the needs of special populations of men (e.g., poor men, gay/bisexual men, men of color).
- Provide incentives (e.g., free promotional items, food, and tickets to sports events).
- Screen men for high blood pressure at the obstetrician's office when they go with their partners for prenatal checkups.
- Set up public panel discussions on men's health topics.
- Provide opportunities for men to talk about health issues in small groups.
- Make wellness workshops for men fun, and ensure the information presented is easily understood.
- Provide health promotion and education to men in hospital emergency rooms.
- Design activities around National Men's Health Week (the week including and ending on Father's Day), including lectures, forums, debates, media campaigns, displays, workshops, and presentations.

(Continued)

TABLE 12.1   Men's Health and Wellness Strategies (Continued)

- Piggyback onto other community programs and activities.
- Provide school-based lectures to adolescent boys about male anatomy and the functioning of their bodies, as well as mental health concerns.
- Provide incentives for men to generate a personal health history form.
- Offer cash, credits to medical savings accounts, or memberships to fitness centers to participate in worksite health promotion efforts.
- Provide farm safety information in rural barbershops and in presentations at county fairs.
- Offer supplementary health services to agencies or organizations currently serving large populations of men, such as fathering and parenting programs, substance abuse centers, and homeless shelters.
- Provide convenient and free or low-cost services, such as screenings and immunizations.
- Provide a confidential telephone health line.
- Hire male staff and clinicians, and make them available to men.
- Determine how employers and health plans can build in incentives for men.
- Partner with employers to create worksite programs and leave time for men to attend to health care needs.
- Devise and use better indices to measure the health of men (e.g., employer information on the number of days of work lost to illness and injury or measures of the years of life lost as a result of disability).
- Work with public health agencies to deliver health care services during nontraditional hours for working men.
- Expand family services to better accommodate men.
- Network and create linkages with other community groups and organizations.

Designing Effective Programs and Services for College Men

Applying the Six-Point HEALTH Plan and Other Evidence-Based Strategies[*]

In several of the preceding chapters, I discussed college men's increased risks relative to college women. I also explain how college men's health behaviors and beliefs—including their beliefs about manhood—influence their health and well-being. In this chapter, I provide evidence-based strategies for designing effective programs and services for college men. These strategies include the application of the Six-Point HEALTH Plan (see Chapter 12) to college men, as well as strategies for educational campaigns, marketing, and outreach with this population.

---

[*] An earlier version of this chapter appeared in G. E. Kellom (Ed.). (2004). *Developing effective programs and services for college men* (pp. 59–74). San Francisco: Jossey-Bass, and is used by permission in modified/revised form.

EVIDENCE-BASED STRATEGIES FOR COLLEGE
HEALTH PROFESSIONALS: APPLYING
THE SIX-POINT *HEALTH* PLAN

Any contact a health professional has with a college man represents an important opportunity. College men are less likely than college women to seek health care. Therefore, any encounter a health professional has with a college man may be the *only* opportunity for assessment and intervention that *any* health professional will have with that man for a long time; as I pointed out in the preceding chapter, even one contact with a male patient can have significantly positive effects on both behavioral and clinical outcomes. Furthermore, research indicates that students often need gender-specific interventions, such as safer-sex education specifically tailored for women and men (see Chapter 6).

In Chapter 12, I addressed communication between clinicians and their patients, which is associated with treatment compliance and patient health status. College health professionals whose responsibility it is to counsel men in any capacity are in a unique position to assist these men. Research indicates that people are more likely to be helped to prevent future disease by health professionals who ask, educate, and counsel them about personal health behaviors than by those who perform physical examinations or tests.

In Chapter 12, I outlined a practice guideline for health professionals who work with men. Whether a health professional is treating college men in a health service, developing gender-specific programming for men, conducting outreach, or designing health education materials, the same basic principles of the Six-Point Plan hold true. Each of the six subsections here briefly summarizes one of six types of intervention discussed in Chapter 12. Together, the titles of the six points form an acronym that spells HEALTH: Humanize, Educate, Assume the worst, Locate supports, Tailor a plan, and Harness strengths.

Humanize

Humanizing is a technique that validates or normalizes patients' health problems and concerns. Conveying to patients that their feelings and experiences are understandable or legitimate—and that other people would probably feel the same way—is considered essential to effective communication with patients. Because disease, disability, and health-promoting responses to illness are antithetical to masculinity, men can experience embarrassment and shame when they do have health problems that they must address. Clinicians can compensate for this and help men learn that asking for assistance, acknowledging pain, expressing fear, crying, or needing bed rest are normal, human experiences; they are not unmanly. Moderate self-disclosure on a clinician's part, particularly if the clinician is a man, may make a male patient feel safer and is associated with positive outcomes. A clinician might say, "I know what you mean; I have a hard time admitting when I'm sick too."

Humanize Help Seeking

Men have less intention to seek help from a variety of sources when they need it. Seeking help can undermine a man's sense of independence and be experienced as demeaning, which may lead to feelings of inadequacy and shame. Reconceptualize a student's help seeking as positive behavior, and offer reinforcement by saying, "Coming to see me when you did was the best thing you could have done." Reframing a man's seeking help as an act of strength, courage, and self-determination may decrease any embarrassment or self-doubt that he may experience in reaching out for help.

Humanize Illness and Convalescence

Because illness threatens masculine ideals of competence, vitality, and strength, men may experience illness as a personal flaw or a failure to successfully demonstrate manhood. Simply saying, "You know, everybody gets sick sometimes" can bring relief to a man and help to establish rapport. When they are ill, men are less likely than women to restrict activities or stay in bed for both acute and chronic conditions. Some men consider staying in bed to recover to be unnecessary "pampering." A college man may think of himself as "lazy" if he misses school or sports practice after an injury or operation. Humanize the need for convalescence by saying to a student, "Staying in bed and taking care of yourself when you're sick doesn't mean you're not a team player."

Humanize Pain and Fear

Admitting or displaying fear and pain is largely unacceptable for men in our society. Not surprisingly, compared with women, men report less pain for the same pathology, less severe pain, greater tolerance of pain, and a higher pain threshold. Although hormones may play some role in mediating the experience of pain, it is clear that psychosocial factors do, too. Men report less pain to female clinicians than to male clinicians. The reluctance to acknowledge or report physical or emotional distress can have far-reaching implications for college men's health; it can influence help-seeking decisions, delay intervention, and undermine diagnosis and treatment planning.

In humanizing pain, health professionals should label conditions known to be painful as such: "Kidney stones can be very painful. I don't want you to hesitate for a moment if you think you might need to come back to urgent care." Express surprise when a student denies that his kidney stones are painful. To more accurately assess a college man's level of pain, and to compensate for his potential minimization of pain, say,

"There are no medals for enduring pain, so I want you to let me know if you experience even the *slightest* bit of discomfort."

Humanize Sexual Concerns

At least one of four American men is unable to get or maintain an erection for sex, and almost all men—including college men—experience occasional and transient erectile problems. Erectile dysfunction is also a common side effect of a variety of medications. These facts are inconsistent with the stereotype that men are perpetually interested in and ready for sex. Consequently, sexual dysfunction can threaten a student's self-image as a man, and it can be threatening to acknowledge. Three of four men with sexual concerns report being too embarrassed to discuss those concerns with their physician. To humanize college men's sexual concerns, problems, and fears, say, "Most men have concerns about sex; it's normal. And I'd be surprised if you didn't." Help men identify unrealistic perceptions of manhood that contribute to sexual anxiety, and help them learn how human perceptions of sexuality can reduce stress and sexual dysfunction. You can say, "You're not a machine. Your body can't be expected to turn on and off at will."

Humanize Men's Body Image

Superhuman perceptions of manhood distort college men's perceptions of their bodies. During the past several decades, cultural standards of the ideal male body have grown increasingly large and bulky. Not surprisingly, men and boys have become increasingly dissatisfied with their bodies. Research indicates that 28 to 68% of normal-weight young men either try to or want to gain weight, and that the desire to be bigger and more muscular is linked with traditional masculinity (see Chapters 1 and 11). This desire in young men is also associated with psychological distress, impaired social functioning, and substance abuse, including abuse of anabolic steroids. College health professionals can teach this to college men and help them make human their superhuman perceptions of the male body.

Educate

Health education interventions are an essential aspect of disease and injury prevention and can reduce risks, improve compliance, facilitate change, and promote health. Furthermore, research consistently indicates that college men are less knowledgeable than college women about health in general, and about specific diseases (see Chapters 1 and 6). College men, for example, know significantly less than college women about self-examinations for cancer and risk factors for HIV.

Despite these findings, health professionals often fail to provide health education to men. As I explain in previous chapters, men are provided with fewer and briefer explanations—as well as less information overall—from clinicians during medical examinations. Although college men are in the highest risk group for testicular cancer, only 29% of physicians routinely provide age-appropriate instruction on performing testicular self-examination (TSE), compared with 86% providing age-appropriate instruction to women on performing breast self-examination. Additionally, although college men engage in more unhealthy behaviors, they are less likely than college women to be counseled by clinicians about changing those behaviors. For example, college men are less likely than college women to be questioned in medical visits about tobacco use (Foote, Harris, & Gilles, 1996).

Specific educational interventions vary depending on a college man's current health, his presenting concern, and his future risks. A good way to start educating men is by communicating, "Most of the things that have the biggest impact on your health are completely within your control." When educating college men, it is essential to include even basic knowledge (such as whom to call for an appointment) because many men have had relatively little experience with health care. Educators should keep the information simple, offer written materials, and make statements and written materials clear and direct. They should also provide alternative responses to unhealthy behaviors. It is also important to encourage questions because men ask clinicians fewer questions than women do. You can say, "I've explained a lot to you. I'd be surprised if you didn't have some questions."

College men also need to be taught the importance of early detection of disease. Screening tests and self-examinations are essential for preventing disease and identifying a variety of diseases at an early stage, which is when successful treatment is more likely. However, men in general and African American men in particular are less likely than women to practice self-examination or to attend health screenings. Self-examinations particularly relevant to college men include those for skin and testicular cancer, and sexually transmitted diseases.

Assume the Worst

One of the most common and enduring cultural stereotypes about men is that they are healthier and more resistant to disease or injury than women, despite a wealth of evidence to the contrary. Men who conform to these cultural stereotypes increase their health risks. They may try to appear strong and healthy, believe that they are invulnerable to risk, minimize pain and deny feelings that others may perceive as signs of weakness, and report their health inaccurately.

Among college students, men perceive less risk than women for a variety of health threats, among them risks associated with the use of cigarettes, alcohol, and other drugs; sun exposure; physically dangerous sports; and driving. For example, college men perceive less risk associated with not using a safety belt, drinking and driving, and not making a full stop at a stop sign. These beliefs are inconsistent with the finding that men are at fault in the vast majority of car crashes, including most crashes resulting in injury and death. They are also not consistent with the fact that, among 15- to 24-year-olds, 3 times more men than women die in car crashes, which are the leading cause of death in this age group. Furthermore, as I discussed in preceding chapters, college men's perceived invulnerability prevents them from changing unhealthy behaviors.

The desire to conceal vulnerability can influence college men's decision not to seek care and can affect assessment and diagnosis when they do get care. Compared with college women, men are less likely to confide in friends, express vulnerability, disclose their problems, or seek help or support from others when they need it. Among college students with depression, for example, men are more likely than women to rely on themselves, withdraw socially, or try to talk themselves out of it. These behavioral responses to depression contribute to explaining why young men represent five of six deaths from suicide, which is the third leading cause of death in this age group (see Chapter 6).

Taken together, these findings about men suggest that clinicians should assume the worst. An additional reason for assuming the worst is that health professionals can also be blinded by gender stereotypes and fooled by men's displays of invulnerability. As I discussed in preceding chapters, mental health clinicians are less likely to diagnose depression correctly in men than in women, which contributes to the high suicide rate among men. Making matters worse, because of delays in their help seeking, men's physical and mental conditions are often serious when they finally do seek help.

To diagnose a man's condition correctly and to plan his treatment, it is essential to elicit accurate information about his symptoms and emotional states. Asking a man, "How do you feel?" is not recommended. This question can be difficult for men to respond to, and it often elicits nothing more than a shrug of the shoulders or an unreflective "Fine." Instead, a health professional should inquire indirectly: "Tell me, how do you experience that?" Or, "What is that like for you?" These questions are not common and may be less likely to prompt an automatic response. In response to perceptions of vulnerability that are inconsistent with a man's actual risks, a clinician can say, "I know it's important to you to think of yourself as strong and healthy. But that attitude can lead you to take unnecessary risks with your health."

Locate Supports

Men are taught to value independence, autonomy, and self-sufficiency in themselves. It is not surprising, then, that college men have fewer friendships and smaller social networks than college women do, and that they tend not to use the support they do have. There is strong evidence that a lack of social support constitutes a risk factor for disease and death, especially for men. Men with the lowest level of social support are much more likely to die than men with the highest level.

In contrast, men with a higher level of social support maintain more positive health practices.

It is essential for college health professionals to help men identify the sources of support that are available to them: significant others, friends, family, coworkers, classmates, and so forth. You can ask, "Who are the people you're most comfortable asking to give you a hand?" It is important then to encourage men to reach out to these people because often they will not do so of their own accord. Health professionals can also help college men identify support or educational groups and social activities—such as church and organized sports—that can be valuable sources of social support. In talking with college men about social support, use concepts that are familiar to many men, such as teamwork and strategic planning. Suggest that the student set regular times to meet with friends. The routine ball game, movie, or dinner out gives a college man regular contact and support without his having to ask for it or betray his need for it.

Tailor Plan

Tailoring a plan means devising a health maintenance plan (like a maintenance schedule for a car). A man is more likely to have a maintenance plan for his car than for himself. Developing and implementing such a plan are associated with improved treatment follow-through and behavioral change. The type of plan, the extent of the plan, and its specific components depend on each man's individual needs, as well as on the clinician's role and functions. Ideally, a man's comprehensive health maintenance plan includes periodic physicals, screenings, self-examinations, preventive behaviors, self-care techniques, and vitamin and medicine schedules.

Tailoring the plan means individualizing it to the student's needs, age, intellectual capacity, attitudes, cultural background, and circumstances; this is considered essential both in establishing a plan and in fostering adherence. For the plan to be successful it must be realistic, it must be broken down into attainable steps, and the patient must have the skills necessary to carry it out. College health professionals should also invite the student's own input and suggestions, as well as help him identify potential obstacles. He may know, for example, that if he drinks he is not likely to use a condom. It is also beneficial to develop a verbal or written contract, with dates for achieving specific goals. As explained in previous chapters, all these factors are associated with improved outcomes.

Harness Strengths

Identifying and engaging—or harnessing—a patient's strengths fosters motivation and compliance. It also conveys respect for his efforts and achievements, which is an important aspect of effective patient–clinician communication. Although endorsement of traditional masculinity in general is associated with increased health risks among men, there are certain masculine-identified characteristics that are highly adaptive for men (and women). Among them are having the ability to act independently, be assertive, and be decisive. Reliance on some specific masculine characteristics such as these has been found to help enable men to cope with cancer and chronic illness. Some specific strengths that should be harnessed are intellectualized and goal-oriented coping, a need for control, and a teamwork approach.

Begin by commenting on a student's strength before exploring his physical symptoms or emotional states. An example is to say, "It's great that you took control of things the way you did and got yourself in here so quickly." Because being intellectual, logical, and rational are highly valued coping mechanisms among men, health professionals should emphasize the intellectual aspects of health education. Similarly, men engage in more action-oriented, problem-solving, and goal-setting coping than women do. Goal setting is also an effective way to modify behavior and improve health; therefore, college health professionals can frame health goals as targets to shoot for. Similarly, they can capitalize on a student's talent for keeping baseball scores when he is tracking cholesterol, blood pressure, or behavioral change.

To maintain healthy behaviors and modify unhealthy ones, it is essential that people have a sense of self-efficacy or control, and to believe that they can respond effectively to reduce a health threat. College men who have a personal sense of control over cancer, for example, are more likely to practice monthly TSE. Illness, however, can threaten a man's sense of being in control. Additionally, men are more likely than women to believe they have little or no control over their future health. College health professionals can foster a student's sense of self-efficacy by focusing on the positive aspects of control and suggesting that he take "personal responsibility" for his well-being and "take charge" of his health.

Emphasize teamwork, too. For most men, health care is something that is done *to* them; it is not something in which they see themselves as active participants. Clinicians need to invite a man's active involvement and emphasize teamwork, which can be ideal for a man; men are often most comfortable engaging in relationships through action and by doing things, such as projects, together. As I explained in Chapter 12, this kind of patient–clinician collaboration is associated with positive health outcomes. Asking, "Where do you want to start?" enlists a man's involvement and reinforces his active participation.

EVIDENCE-BASED STRATEGIES FOR DESIGNING GENDER-SPECIFIC EDUCATIONAL CAMPAIGNS, MARKETING, AND OUTREACH TO MEN

The Six-Point Plan can also be applied to educational campaigns and marketing to college men. For example, these interventions can humanize by addressing the contradiction between human health care needs and masculinity, and assume the worst by addressing college men's perceived invulnerability to risk. Additional evidence-based strategies should guide the development of gender-specific educational campaigns, marketing, and outreach to men.

One example is research related to TSE educational brochures provided at many colleges. These brochures typically diagram how to conduct a TSE. Based on previous success educating women with materials diagramming breast self-examinations, we might expect TSE brochures to be similarly effective. According to emerging research, TSE instruction in general is indeed effective. College men also prefer written materials, such as brochures, over video instruction; they also prefer brief, specific checklists on how to perform TSE rather than more detailed instructions. Most important, according to one study, college men prefer written materials with *no* diagrams of the male anatomy. These materials were also the most effective in promoting TSE (Morman, 2002).

As the preceding example illustrates, health education, marketing, and outreach efforts must take gender-based research into account if they are to be successful; what is effective with women is not necessarily effective with men. Additional findings from studies of college students provide further support for gender-specific interventions (Dekin, 1996; DePalma, McCall, & English, 1996; Patrick, Covin, Fulop, Calfas, & Lovato, 1997; Rothspan & Read, 1996). Researchers have reported, for example, that using such approaches as future awareness (Rothspan & Read, 1996) and imagining symptoms (DePalma et al., 1996) to decrease sexual health risks are more effective with college men than with college women. Because college men are particularly disinclined to seek help, it has also been suggested that college health professionals should provide outreach to campus locations where large numbers of men congregate—athletic departments, sports events, Reserve Officers' Training Corps, campus police, and academic departments, such as business and economics (Kafka, 1997). A gender-sensitive approach to health could address college men's reluctance to seek help and their tendency to conceal vulnerability by providing health-related telephone hot lines or electronic mail and chat lines.

"Stages of change" research provides yet another example that illustrates the importance of gender-specific interventions. The stages of change model, or transtheoretical model, identifies five stages of change that people move through in modifying their behavior. The stages are precontemplation, contemplation, preparation, action, and maintenance (Prochaska, Norcross, & DiClemente, 1994). Precontemplators typically deny their problems or unhealthy behaviors. Contemplators recognize their problems and begin to seriously think about solving them. As I discussed in Chapter 1, extensive research indicates that women are more likely than men to be contemplating changing unhealthy behavior or already maintaining healthy habits.

The transtheoretical model has also identified interventions that are effective in helping people adopt healthier behavior at each stage. What women contemplators need most is assistance in identifying the causes and consequences of their behaviors, help in considering the pros and cons of changing, and support in maintaining their healthy lifestyles. What men precontemplators need most is increased awareness of their problems and education to help them begin to consider change. These strategies can be applied to interventions with individuals, and to educational, marketing, and outreach interventions. In fact, interventions that neglect to apply stage-specific strategies, or neglect to take people's readiness to change into account, are likely to fail.

According to this model, public health campaigns are often unsuccessful because they are typically designed for the small minority of people who are ready to change unhealthy behavior. However, people who are not ready to change (people who are more likely to be men) actively resist these campaigns. Precontemplators in particular are the hardest people to reach because they typically deny that they have a problem. Health campaigns for men not ready to change—the men at greatest risk—are more likely to be effective when they are designed for precontemplators. For example, one newspaper ad for a smoking cessation self-help program was directed to "smokers who do not wish to change." This unusually worded advertisement drew 400 precontemplators, which the researchers considered a great success (Prochaska et al., 1994). Interventions like this that effectively help men to simply *begin* contemplating the possibility of changing unhealthy behavior (which is the primary objective with precontemplators) double the probability that these men will ultimately change.

Another research-based approach that can be applied to gender-specific interventions with men is social norms marketing. According to social norms theory, unhealthy (and healthy) behavior is fostered by perceptions (often incorrect) of how one's peers behave (Berkowitz, 2003). For example, a college man might overestimate his peers' involvement in risky behavior, which would foster his own involvement in unhealthy behavior. Alternatively, he might underestimate his peers' adoption of healthy habits, which would discourage him from adopting healthy behavior. Social norms theory focuses on peers because they have been found to have the greatest influence in shaping individual behavior.

One common intervention based on this theory is a social norms marketing campaign, which promotes accurate, healthy norms. Research indicates that when college students' "perceived norm" is challenged with evidence of the "actual norm," the unhealthy behavior—such as heavy drinking—often decreases. Social norms marketing campaigns hold promise for addressing a variety of health concerns relevant to men. They can be used, for example, to change incorrect perceptions about men's indifference to health matters.

More than 500 men at a small Midwestern liberal arts college were recently surveyed. Results of this survey indicated that these men misperceived that most other male students (55%) were either not at all concerned or only a little concerned about their health as men.

Actually, only 35% of students were unconcerned; most (65%) reported being either somewhat or very concerned about their health as men (Courtenay, 2004b). Based on these data, a social norms marketing campaign could be designed to promote the true norm that men on this campus *are* interested in their health as men. Although it has yet to be developed, we can hypothesize, from previous research, that interest in and concern about men's health would increase among men on this campus if such a campaign were implemented.

Unfortunately, social marketing campaigns do not always work (Keeling, 2000). For example, students sometimes *underestimate*, rather than overestimate, their peers' unhealthy behavior. Social marketing is particularly ineffective with specific groups within a larger campus— groups such as fraternity men, for whom norms are riskier than they are for other groups on campus. It has been argued that new, alternative intervention methods are needed for these high-risk men (Carter & Kahnweiler, 2000). One new, innovative, evidence-based approach is based on "sensation-seeking" research.

Sensation seekers are disinhibited people who seek thrills and adventure, lust for new experiences, and are easily bored (Zuckerman, 1994). The instrument measuring this trait determines whether a person is a high or low sensation seeker. Thirty years of research consistently indicates that men are more likely than women to be high sensation seekers. It also shows that high sensation seekers are more likely than low sensation seekers to engage in a variety of risky behaviors such as heavy alcohol use, drug use, cigarette smoking, dangerous driving, high-risk sexual activity, high-risk sports, and criminal activity. For example, adolescent high sensation seekers are twice as likely as low sensation seekers to report using beer and liquor, and 2 to 7 times more likely to report drug use.

Researchers at the University of Kentucky have been studying intervention strategies based on these findings (e.g., Palmgreen & Donohew, 2006; Palmgreen, Donohew, Lorch, Hoyle, & Stephenson, 2001; Palmgreen et al., 1995). They hypothesized that because people who engage in unhealthy, high-risk behavior are more likely to be high sensation seekers who seek novel and stimulating experiences, health campaigns targeting this population would also need to be novel and stimulating. Findings from a growing body of research indicate that high sensation seekers do in fact prefer media and health campaigns that are novel, creative, or unusual (e.g., Palmgreen & Donohew, 2006; Palmgreen et al., 1995, 2001). Additionally, campaigns are most effective when they are intense, exciting, and stimulating; are graphic and explicit; are complex and unconventional; are fast-paced; are suspenseful and dramatic; use close-ups; and have strong audio and visual effects. Although not all of these features need be included in a single message, the most effective messages have multiple features from this list. Research shows that high sensation seekers pay greater attention to antidrug public service announcements (PSAs) that incorporate these

TABLE 13.1   Health Promotion Strategies for College Men

- Offer convenient and free or low-cost services, such as screenings and immunizations.
- Provide a confidential telephone health line.
- Bring services and education to men (e.g., classes, sports events, fraternities, and fitness centers).
- Furnish incentives (e.g., free promotional items, food, tickets to sports events, academic credit for attendance, or requiring attendance).
- Offer free men's health kits or fanny packs with educational materials such as self-examination instructions and health service information, along with promotional items, such as healthy protein bars and toiletries.
- Develop a health mentoring project with upperclassmen educating lowerclassmen.
- Address the needs of special populations of men (e.g., gay and bisexual men, men of color).
- Identify students who have experienced health problems (e.g., testicular cancer, auto accidents) as spokesmen and peer health educators.
- Use high-profile spokesmen to promote men's health through media campaigns or for special events (e.g., community leaders, athletes, actors, or media personalities).
- Offer competitive contests with prizes for involvement in health promotion activities.
- Attach men's health education information to prescriptions.
- Develop health events with a theme (e.g., related to pop culture, rock music, or sports).
- Make available health promotion and education to men in urgent care.
- Use concepts that appeal to men, especially high-risk men (like "health coaching" and "teamwork"), in marketing and education materials.
- Make use of men's bathrooms and locker rooms for distribution of health education materials and for health campaigns.
- Provide e-mail–based education and Internet survey tools or games.
- Offer a "sports and fitness expo" with health and wellness components, as well as sports events, competitions, sporting equipment, and exhibitions.
- Design activities around National Men's Health Week (the week including and ending on Father's Day), featuring lectures, forums, debates, media campaigns, displays, workshops, and presentations.
- Hire male staff and clinicians and make them available to men.
- Create opportunities for men to talk about health issues in small discussion groups (e.g., after peer educators speak to larger groups).
- Require entering freshmen to attend a workshop that addresses the health effects of masculinity and includes healthy strategies for adjusting to college life.

features than to PSAs that do not; they are also more likely to recall PSA content, phone a drug hotline, report a more negative attitude toward drug use, and report less intention to use. (Interestingly, high sensation seekers also prefer messages that do not preach, which is consistent with the transtheoretical model; preaching to, or nagging, a "precontemplator" about changing will make him more *resistant* to change. See also Helgeson, Novak, Lepore, & Eton, 2004; Tucker & Anders, 2001; Tucker & Mueller, 2000.)

These findings are relevant to college health professionals (particularly those concerned about men's health) because sensation seekers are primarily men and because they include those students who engage in the riskiest behaviors. These are the men who, historically, have been the most difficult to reach and for whom traditional health campaigns are ineffective. Sensation-seeking intervention strategies can be applied to college radio PSAs and to flyers and posters. They can also be adopted when marketing to and conducting health fairs for men, which should be designed differently than health fairs for women. Another application of this evidence is to provide safe, high sensation-seeking alternatives to risky activities. For example, at an all-male, liberal arts college in the Midwest, a climbing wall was set up and made available on the most popular midweek drinking night. Although the effectiveness of this specific intervention has yet to be tested empirically, research suggests that this high sensation-seeking alternative would effectively reduce drinking on this campus. The overwhelmingly enthusiastic response from students certainly suggests that it has been effective.

In conclusion, this chapter has identified evidence-based strategies for addressing psychosocial and behavioral factors that influence college men's health. Additional health promotion strategies for college health professionals to use on campuses are outlined in Table 13.1. If college health professionals adopt these strategies, research suggests that college men will live longer, healthier, and happier lives.

VI

Looking Forward

INTRODUCTION

In this final section of the book, I look to the future of men's health. In doing so, I begin by taking a step back. In 1999, the Philadelphia Department of Public Health sponsored the first national conference on men's health, and I was invited to give an opening address. That address provides the introduction to Section VI, which explores the health concerns of two men viewed from diverse professional and disciplinary perspectives.

How men's health is understood depends on the lens through which it is examined. Although it has historically been viewed from biomedical perspectives, social scientists such as myself have also identified countless cultural, psychosocial, and behavioral factors that influence men's health. I highlight the strengths and limitations of various disciplinary perspective as I examine the complexity of these men's lives and well-being. I conclude by proposing an interdisciplinary biopsychosocial and behavioral approach to the study of men's health that unites these complementary perspectives.

TEAMING UP FOR THE NEW MEN'S HEALTH MOVEMENT*

When I began speaking publicly about men's health in the early 1990s, I felt like a lone voice screaming in the wilderness. Nothing could evoke such an expression of complete and utter bewilderment on the part of an audience as the two simple words *men's health*. Finally, we have arrived at the first major men's health conference in this country. But where are we headed next with men's health? And how will we get there?

The structure of this conference reveals a lot about the current status of men's health. The first day focuses on diseases and

---

* An earlier version of this article appeared in the *Journal of Men's Studies*, 8(3), 2000, 387–392, and is used by permission.

their treatment; the second day, on psychological and social risks. We make this distinction because these are the individual lenses through which we view men's health. From a biomedical perspective, this conference format makes perfect sense. Through *that* lens, diseases have the same symptoms and outcomes regardless of psychological or social factors. Through *that* lens, medicine is a socially neutral science. But medicine is not a socially neutral science. And the problem is, we start thinking that we actually *can* separate men's diseases from the men who experience them. But the moment we put the word *men* into men's health, we are talking about health as *men* demonstrate health—as biological, psychological, and social beings. Men's health is by definition biopsychosocial.

During the past several decades, our knowledge of health has grown by leaps and bounds. But from a men's health perspective, what we have learned is limited. And it is largely genderless. Although male bodies are often used to study disease and its treatment, men are rarely studied as patients, or as men. Even in research that offers enormous potential for learning about differences between women and men, most researchers treat gender as a "nuisance variable"—a factor we have to control for to discover the really important information. As a result, we know a lot less than we might about health differences between women and men. But there are other reasons why we seem to know so little about men's health.

It has been nearly 30 years now since researchers published the first important papers on men's health. They had provocative titles like "The Hazards of Being Male" and "Socialized to Die Younger." These authors stirred up interest in men's health, but not much came of it. About the same time, the Boston Women's Health Collective wrote *Our Bodies, Ourselves*. That book launched a women's health movement that is still going strong. What happened to the *men's* health movement?

There are several reasons why the men's health movement has made comparatively little progress. The women's health movement was successful, in part, because it was linked with a larger social movement—one that addressed the many inequalities that women experience in this country. But there is another reason why progress has been slower for the men's health movement. The reason is because most of us men have been working in relative isolation from one another. Meanwhile, women have been networking and organizing grassroots movements that address the unique health concerns of women. This is why I used to think I was alone in the wilderness. But the truth is, I was not alone. And you are not alone. You have plenty of colleagues at your side. Teammates.

There are a lot of disciplines represented here today. This audience is made up of physicians, nurses, public health officials, health administrators, social workers, and psychologists—to name just a few. These are your teammates. The problem is, we tend not to rely on our teammates. Often, we do not even know what they do.

Let me tell you about John. He died last month of a heart attack, at the age of 65. He was a retired shopkeeper—an African American man who learned 2 years ago that he was at risk for heart disease. Why did John die? Partly because the people who were helping him did not talk to their teammates. If they had, they could have learned a lot about John—and what he, and others, could have done to prevent his death.

To begin with, John insisted that his health was "just fine." As survey researchers could have told the team, this perception is typical. Most American men think their health is "excellent"— and rate their health as better than women's. But epidemiologists could have set the team straight. Epidemiologists know that men have higher death rates than women for heart disease—and for the other 10 leading causes of death.

But John was unconcerned about that when he would sit down to breakfast. His favorite start of the day was two eggs sunny-side up, pancakes, and three strips of bacon. John had plenty of bad cholesterol in his system. And—had anyone asked them—the biologists could have explained that John's lack of estrogen might be lowering his level of good cholesterol as well. The psychophysiological researchers could have also pointed out that his problem was more than hormones. John's physiological response to stress was less effective than a woman's would be—and this too increased his risk.

And if geneticists had been on the team, they would have learned something more. John had inherited his father's hypertension, which also increased his risk. But these same teammates would also have raised some troubling questions, because geneticists are quickly eroding the myth of race—the myth that John was somehow fundamentally different because his skin color was black. If the answer is not race, how do we explain the compelling fact that—like most African American men—John died years younger than the average European American man?

One reason could be that John lived in a neighborhood filled with pollution and crime. Had colleagues in environmental justice been on the team, they would have pointed out that this is typical— African Americans are more likely than European Americans to live in these neighborhoods. The social workers would have reminded John's team about some other cultural factors. They would have told them that John's risk of heart disease was also influenced by whether he went to church, by where he worked, and by how he played.

Then there is John's doctor. She could have told the rest of the team a lot about the progression and management of his heart disease. But she complained that John rarely came to her office—just like most of her male patients. In fact, three of four people who have not seen a doctor in more than 5 years are men. That is where those who study health communication could have helped. Doctors, they would have said, spend less time talking with men than they do with women—and less time educating men, which may help to explain why men are less likely to seek care.

The child development researchers would have had something to say, too. They would have pointed out that when John was a boy, his parents probably discouraged him from seeking help, and may even have punished him when he did. If sociologists had been on the team, they would have added that it was not just his parents—that boys punish each other. When John wanted to see the school nurse when he got hit by a baseball in sixth grade, it was his friends who mocked him for being a crybaby.

So why did John die? That simple question is not so simple to answer. A physician alone could not answer it. An epidemiologist alone could not answer it. And a psychologist alone could not answer it. But together, we can answer it. Each one of us, in our various disciplines, has vital information and knowledge that can keep men like John alive—and improve their quality of life. But each of our fields, alone, leaves us with troubling and unanswered questions—like missing pieces of a puzzle.

Fortunately for Tony, the future holds promise. Tony was just seen in the emergency room for a knife wound he got in a fight. This was not his first trip to the emergency room. At age 24, Tony already has a long history of involvement in dangerous activities—as well as drinking and smoking. What do your teammates know about men like Tony? How can they help him—and help us—so his story ends differently than John's?

The child development researchers on our team can tell us how Tony first learned risky habits at home, and how, if his parents were like most, they were less concerned about his safety than about his sister's. Then our teammates who study cultural communication can help us to see that it was not just his parents who taught Tony unhealthy behaviors. He also learned them from television, movies, and magazines, and learned that on television, men and boys are the ones who usually drink and smoke—and the ones who commit violence and get away with it.

But with psychobiologists on our team, we know that it is not just the media that are to blame; there is another piece to the puzzle. The hormone testosterone contributes to Tony's involvement in dangerous activities. And a neurobiologist would add that low serotonin levels in Tony's brain may also contribute to his aggression.

But if you think Tony is just hardwired for violence, talk to the psychologists on our team. They will tell you that it is not just being biologically male that is increasing Tony's risks. It is also his gender. His "male gender role" and his beliefs about manhood can predict his high-risk behaviors. They will also tell you that Tony's perception that he has no control over his life increases his health risks, too. But what these teammates cannot tell you is how poverty influences Tony's perception of the control he has over his life.

That is why there are sociologists on our team. They can answer that question. They will tell you that when Tony endangers his health, it is often in pursuit of power—and in trying to maintain his social status and privilege relative to his sister and other women. Sociologists also caution us when we start talking about how Tony "is" as a man. They remind us that there is not just one "male sex role." There is not one masculinity, but rather many masculinities. And there are often bigger differences between men than there are between men and women.

Did I mention that Tony is gay? Well, he is gay, and he is Latino. The anthropologists on our team tell us that those are important pieces of the puzzle. They remind us to listen to the different voices of men. When we really listen to Tony, we can learn from him what interferes with safe sex. How for him and other gay Latino men, condoms conjure up images of death—which, not surprisingly, can ruin any passion in Tony's sex life.

But Tony does not like to talk about this—or to talk about feelings very much. The neurobiologists on our team say that this is because his brain is soaking in hormones. They tell us sex hormones promote divisions in brain functioning that make Tony less expressive than his sister. Putting words to emotions is more difficult for Tony because he does not move as quickly as she does between the left and right sides of the brain.

The social psychologists would say that this still leaves some missing pieces. They would point out that Tony is not inexpressive all the time. Like many men, he may not talk about his feelings with his peers, but he does talk about them with his mother and sister. They might add that what many of us call "risky" behaviors are often the very same behaviors that Tony is *expected* to demonstrate to prove that he is a man.

Finally, the researchers who study behavioral change can offer the rest of us powerful knowledge to inform our work with Tony and with other men. They tell us that the first step we need to take is to recognize that—if Tony is like most men—he is less ready than his sister to change his behavior. And that—because of that—he is going to need more health education than she does, if he is going to change. They also tell us that if we take the time to educate Tony—and he starts to think about change—he will double his chances of actually changing.

Tony and John. Life and death. In the last half hour, approximately 60 American men have died. How many of these men would still be alive if we were working together as a team? What if we developed an interdisciplinary approach to the study of men and men's health? If we pieced together our knowledge like the pieces of a puzzle? I think we would begin to find answers to the many perplexing questions that face us. Questions like why men—who supposedly do not get depressed—have suicide rates that are as much as 18 times higher than women's.

The goal of understanding men's health is not simply to understand male bodies. The goal of understanding men's health is to improve men's well-being. To reach that goal, we cannot isolate men's health from all the other aspects of men's lives. We cannot separate men's health from the boys who are taught the very behaviors that kill them. We cannot separate men's health from women, who are often the first to take responsibility for men's health care. We cannot separate men's health from the dangerous jobs that men perform, or from the poverty they experience in the inner cities, or from the rural towns they live in. We cannot separate men's health from what makes men men. Men's health is by definition biopsychosocial. And it is up to you and me to put the men into men's health.

We are on the brink of something tremendous here. The 21st century holds the promise of healthier lives for the men of this country. But the only way we are going to realize that promise is through interdisciplinary collaboration. We need to begin by integrating our specialized knowledge into a new discipline of men's health. I challenge you to begin the new men's health movement today. Here are five ways to start.

First, collect the business cards, phone numbers, and e-mail addresses of people who are interested in men's health at the conferences you attend. When you return to your work, keep the dialogue going with these people. When a man comes into your office—or you are writing a grant proposal—pick up the phone or e-mail these people, and collaborate with them.

Second, actively introduce your work to colleagues in other fields. If you are a clinician, provide training on men's health to professionals in another discipline. If you are a researcher, contribute to a journal that you might not normally consider. This will begin to expand our network.

Third, begin introducing new methods of practice into your work—whether you are a researcher or a practitioner. When you are at conferences like this, attend at least one session offered by colleagues in a completely different discipline than yours. When we combine our methods, we not only enrich our work, but also strengthen the inferences that we can make about men and men's health.

Fourth, use the Internet as a bridge builder. For example, the next time you log onto the Internet, join the Australian-based men's health listserv or the listserv offered by the American Psychological Association's Society for the Psychological Study of Men and Masculinity.

And fifth, we need to reach out to our allies in the women's health movement. These colleagues have been doing this work for decades, and they can help us to jump-start our efforts. We have come as far as we have, in large part, because of the trail blazed for us by these pioneers. Furthermore, much of what is learned about women's health has implications for men's health. And much of what we discover about men can inform our work with women.

Until all of us in our various disciplines work together as a whole, we are not going to see men as whole. We are going to see men as the fragmented pieces of humanity we see through our individual lenses. So know who your teammates are. These are the people who are going to help us better understand men and men's health. These are the people who will bring a greater richness and complexity to your work. These are the people who will help you to help men live longer and healthier lives.

A Global Perspective on Men's Health and Future Directions in Research*

Gender-specific approaches to health and health care recognize the different experiences of women and men, and of various populations of women and men. As yet, relatively little is known about men's gender-specific health care needs. This chapter outlines precepts for developing new theoretical paradigms and research models, and offers direction for social scientists and practitioners in the nascent field of men's health. In it, I advocate interdisciplinary approaches that explore how environmental, biological, sociocultural, psychological, and behavioral factors interact to mediate the physical and mental health of men and boys. I recommend that these approaches apply social structural analyses, examine geographic and cultural contexts, integrate recent theory and research on masculinity, and develop relational paradigms that recognize dynamic intersections of various social factors. I further suggest that the multinational nature of the health of men requires new global community health models for addressing the convergence of micro, meso, and macro health determinants at international, national, community, and individual levels.

---

* An earlier version of this chapter appeared in the *International Journal of Men's Health*, *1*(1), 2002, 1–13, and is used by permission in modified/revised form.

GENDER-SPECIFIC APPROACHES
TO HEALTH SCIENCE

Although it is often met with resistance (see Risberg, Hamberg, & Johansson, 2006), gender-specific health is receiving increasing attention among researchers, academic scholars, and health professionals (see Legato, 2004, 2009; Lent & Bishop, 1998). Gender-based approaches to health recognize that in addition to having different reproductive health needs, women and men have different risks for specific diseases and disabilities, and that they differ in their health-related beliefs and behaviors. Research conducted in the European Union and the United States indicates, for example, that men are less likely than women to perceive themselves as being at risk for most health problems, even for problems that they are more likely than women to experience (see Chapter 1). Gender-specific approaches take into account how factors such as this and various other health determinants differentially influence the health of women and men, as well as the health of different populations of men.

The concept of gender-specific health is not new. Thirty years ago, feminist theorists and researchers first challenged the medical establishments of Western nations to recognize that being a woman means more than being female, that gender—or womanhood—is relevant to women's health for reasons unrelated to biological sex (Boston Women's Health Book Collective, 1973; Ruzek, 1978; Ruzek & Becker, 1999). Yet even today, researchers in many countries do not take into account male and female sex, let alone gender. When reporting results, they provide aggregate results for women and men or hold constant the effects of male and female sex as researchers have done historically. Even in studies where there is enormous potential for learning about gender similarities and differences, sex is often treated as a "nuisance" variable that is statistically controlled.

The distinction between the term *gender*—which refers to the social and cultural meanings assigned to being a woman or a man at a given time in history—and *sex*—which refers to biological differences between human males and females—is more than semantic. It can be argued that most of what we know about health *is* about men's health, that most medical research of the past century was conducted on men (Auerbach & Figert, 1995; Mastroianni, Faden, & Federman, 1994). But in fact, it was conducted on male bodies. What we have learned from this research is, for example, the effects of a particular medicine on male physiological functioning. Until recently, men were rarely studied as men or as patients. Even the male-specific clinical specialties of urology and andrology have remained largely biomedically based and disease focused, and their scope has generally been limited to male reproductive health concerns, such as prostate cancer and erectile dysfunction (e.g., Macfarlane, 2006; Nieschlag, Nieschlag, & Behre, 2009).

Gender-specific health approaches go beyond physiology to explore how sociocultural, environmental, psychological, and behavioral factors influence the physical and mental health of men and boys—as well as how these factors interact with and mediate men's biological and genetic risks. In exploring these factors, they attempt to explain exactly *why* they occur, and to develop appropriate intervention strategies. For example, gender-specific interventions might take into account recent research in the United States indicating that traditional or dominant societal beliefs about what a man should be—and should *not* be—can predict high-risk behavior and the likelihood of death among men and boys (see Chapters 1, 3, and 4).

The past decade has witnessed a dramatic increase in the level of interest in men's health among scholars and health scientists internationally. But as the field develops, what theoretical paradigms and research models might provide direction for the future study of men and health? The existing ones appear to be less than adequate for examining the multitude of factors that influence men's physical and mental health. What precepts might guide the development of new paradigms and models and the work of theorists, researchers, and practitioners? In this chapter, I provide some preliminary answers to these questions.

INTERDISCIPLINARY THEORY AND RESEARCH

Most of what we currently understand about men's health is fragmented and diffuse. It is fragmented by the individual disciplinary lenses through which we view men's health as epidemiologists, health educators, medical anthropologists, nurses and physicians, psychiatrists, ethnographers, psychologists, public health workers, social workers, and sociologists. These individual lenses enable us to deeply understand specific aspects of men's health. However, they also often limit the ways in which we conceptualize and understand men's experiences more broadly—and consequently limit how we think about and understand men's health. From a traditional, strictly biomedical perspective, for example, medicine is considered a socially neutral science: Diseases have the same symptoms and outcomes regardless of psychological, environmental, social, or behavioral factors. However, men's diseases cannot be separated from the men who experience them, or from the locations and contexts in which disease occurs, is identified, and is treated. There are considerable differences, for example, in the life expectancy of men around the world. They range from 31 years for men in Angola and 38 years for men in Burundi to 77 for men in Canada and 78 for men in Sweden, Iceland, and Japan (World Health Organization, 2002).

As we study men's health in each of our respective fields, we must take into account what our colleagues have learned in disciplines other than our own. Sociologists have much to teach us about the male body: the meanings ascribed to and engendered in male bodies, how the body is itself regulated by institutional forces, how various populations of men embody masculinity, and how the male body is used as a vehicle for negotiating the often perilous landscape of masculinity (e.g., see Connell, 2000; Ervø & Johansson, 2003; Nasir & Rosenthal, 2009; Robertson, 2007; Watson, 2000). The work of Nasir and Rosenthal illustrates this point. They quote a 24-year-old Indonesian man describing his life in the *lorong*—a term referring to the slums of large cities, such as Makassar: "Drinking ballo' [local palm wine], taking some koplo [benzodiazepine], sometimes involving in group brawls, smoking chiming [marijuana], or injecting putaw [street-grade heroin] are just part of daily life among many boys in the lorong, part of proving ourselves as real men" (p. 240).

Yet in considering these sociocultural perspectives, we cannot ignore or dismiss the biological and genetic determinants of physical and mental health in men and boys. Men in most parts of the world are more likely than women to use their bodies to engage in high-risk activities—such as physically dangerous sports and physical fighting (Arnett & Balle-Jensen, 1993; Carton, Jouvent, & Widlocher, 1992; Rossier et al., 2007; Wang et al., 2000). Decades of research have shown a strong link between high-risk behaviors such as these and low levels of monoamine oxidase (MAO)—an enzyme involved in the metabolic breakdown and regulation of neurotransmitters in the brain, which has a strong genetic determination (Zuckerman, 1994; Zuckerman & Kuhlman, 2000). Further understanding of the relative effects of this and other biopsychosocial and behavioral factors requires interdisciplinary research paradigms, such as those recently proposed by Chloe Bird and Patricia Rieker (Bird & Rieker, 2008; Rieker & Bird, 2005). Regarding MAO, for example, sophisticated research has also demonstrated that its genetic influence is mediated by the environment (Foley et al., 2004).

This is not an isolated example. In terms of brain functioning specifically, scientists are increasingly discovering a variety of differences between women and men. Some of these findings may help to explain long-reported gender differences in emotional expression; research suggests that women have greater facility than men in moving quickly between the left and right sides of the brain, which may enable them to better identify and articulate emotions (Dorion et al., 2000; Driesen & Raz, 1995; Gur et al., 2000). However, this research does *not* suggest that men's brains are simply hardwired to be inexpressive and that this gender difference is immutable (Fausto-Sterling, 2003). On the contrary, scientists are also increasingly discovering how environment shapes brain development (see Kolb & Whishaw, 2009; Wolfe & Brandt, 1998). Social relations also influence emotional expression. In many parts of the world, men and boys learn that they gain greater social and economic advantages when they remain stoic and inexpressive (e.g., Uchendu, 2007).

Social, environmental, psychological, behavioral, and biological factors do not occur in isolation; they are interrelated. Furthermore, these factors often compound one another. High levels of the androgen testosterone can be inherited (Meikle, Stringham, Bishop, & West, 1988) and associated with increased aggression (Archer, 2006); acts of aggression—even the anticipation of competition in sport—further increase levels of testosterone in the body (Archer, 2006). Furthermore, in many societies, competition and physical aggression are more often encouraged among men and boys than among women and girls (Barry, Bacon, & Child, 1957; Geary, 1999; Low, 1989). This one example illustrates the complex interrelationships among the biological, environmental, genetic, social, and behavioral factors that influence men's health (see also Bird & Rieker, 2008; Rieker & Bird, 2005). Because these factors are interrelated, they are best addressed comprehensively from an interdisciplinary perspective (Bird & Rieker, 2008; Lohan, 2007; Rieker & Bird, 2005). This approach requires both basic and applied research, as well as interdisciplinary collaboration and investigation to develop interactive models and new perspectives on human behavior, health, and illness. This approach also makes it necessary to address a variety of methodological challenges, including the numerous and varied health determinants involved, and disciplinary differences in outcome measures, populations studied, methodologies applied, and rigor of intervention evaluations. As we meet these challenges— and combine our knowledge and research methods—not only will we improve our ability to understand the complex interplay among various health determinants, but we will also enrich our work and strengthen the inferences that we can make about men and the health of various populations of men.

STRUCTURAL APPROACHES

Health care industries, public policies, and health professionals alike increasingly hold individuals accountable for their health-related behaviors. In the United States, an estimated one half of men's deaths each year could be prevented through changes in personal health practices (see Chapter 2). And in the United States, as in many countries, men and boys are more likely than women and girls to adopt unhealthy beliefs and engage in risk-taking behavior, and are less likely to adopt health-promoting behaviors. However, although we have much to learn about the health beliefs and behaviors of men in many parts of the world, it is not enough for us simply to acquire this knowledge. We must also begin to learn, and to explain, how larger contexts—social systems—either foster or constrain the adoption of particular beliefs and behaviors that influence the health of men and boys.

The health-related beliefs and behaviors that men and boys adopt are influenced and often determined by a wide variety of social structures (see Chapter 4). Men and boys are always participating in social systems larger than themselves—such as families, schools, temples, and workplaces—where their lives are structured by a broad range of material, political, religious, institutional, ideological, and cultural factors. They live in dynamic relationship with these social systems. And these systems are powerful influences in shaping men's sense of who they are, their place in the world, their gender, and their health beliefs and behaviors.

Economic structures profoundly influence health and shape men's health and health behavior. Poverty in Eastern European countries, for example, has been found to be linked with a variety of risky health behaviors among young men (LaCava et al., 2006). The social and institutional structuring of health care also influences men's health. Public health care systems, managed care, investor-owned hospital chains, corporate health care mergers, and government health polices all contribute to the patterning and organization of men's health beliefs and behaviors—as do political systems and policy-making institutions. Men and boys in the few countries where state or national men's health policies have been adopted—such as Australia and the United Kingdom (Smith & Robertson, 2008)—may develop different health perceptions, beliefs, and practices than men in countries that lack such policies. We must analyze social systems such as these, as well as the structuring of social inequality and poverty, if we are to understand the broader context of men's health and learn how these factors contribute to shaping men's health and risks.

GEOGRAPHIC AND CULTURAL CONTEXTS

In this era of ever-expanding globalization, researchers and social scientists are increasingly studying the influences of micro contexts on health and illness. These analyses are critically important. There are often significant interregional differences in men's health within nations and states. To more fully comprehend these differences—as practitioners or researchers—we need to consider them within the geographic and cultural contexts in which they occur. For example, in studying various psychological influences on men's health—such as perceived susceptibility to risk, coping behavior, self-efficacy, perceptions of control, and social support—we must consider context when designing and implementing research studies, and when interpreting results, if we are to enhance traditional biomedical research and offer new insights.

In the United States, death rates for cardiovascular disease—which is the leading cause of death for men—are highest in the South (Barnett et al., 2001; Gillum, 1994; Mensah, Mokdad, Ford, Greenlund, & Croft, 2005; Pearson & Lewis, 1998). Similarly, death rates from stroke—the third leading cause of death for men—are also highest in the South (Glymour, Kosheleva, & Boden-Albala, 2009). One possible explanation for this disparity is a high-fat Southern diet, which may or may not be a geocultural marker reflecting factors such as climate or agricultural practices unique to the South. In fact, the prevalence of obesity is highest in the South (Centers for Disease Control and Prevention [CDC], 2008i, 2009e). Another possible explanation is Southern men's views about manhood. Research indicates that, among men in the United States, Southern men hold the most traditional beliefs about gender (Rice & Coates, 1995)—beliefs that have been found to be associated with greater cardiovascular reactivity (Lash, Eisler, & Schulman, 1990; see also Eisler, 1995). But the geography is even more specific: It is *rural* Southern men who hold the most traditional beliefs, and *rural* Southern men who also have the highest death rates for cardiovascular disease among U.S. men (Barnett et al., 2001; Gillum, 1994; Rice & Coates, 1995). We must examine such levels of specificity if we are to better understand regional differences and the complex interactions that mediate them. How else might we understand the unsafe sexual practices of working-class *mostaceros* or middle-class *entendidos* in Lima, Peru, who have sex with other men before returning home to their wives (Caceres, 1996; Caceres & Rosasco, 1999)? As local populations increasingly attempt to improve the health of men and boys in families, schools, and workplaces, communities will greatly benefit from the strong evaluation skills that researchers can offer.

DIFFERENCES AMONG MEN

There are enormous health disparities among various populations of men throughout the world (see Table 14.1). Whereas life expectancy is increasing in most Western European countries, it is decreasing in many newly independent states of Eastern Europe (Weidner & Cain, 2002). For example, Lithuanian men are 4 times more likely to die from heart disease than their Swedish counterparts (Kristenson et al., 1998), and the overall death rate for Russian men is 3 times higher than the European average (Powell, 1998). And although heart disease is the leading cause of death for men in Western industrialized nations, in Angola—and other countries in sub-Saharan Africa—it falls far behind malaria and diarrhea (Ratzan, Filerman, & LeSar, 2000). There are also enormous disparities among men *within* nations. Men are a heterogeneous group; their life experiences and health can vary dramatically based on their ethnic identity, marital status, parental status, social class or caste, education, income, participation in the labor force, sexual orientation, and religious or political affiliation. A man's age also influences his beliefs, behaviors, and health; it provides another important developmental or life span framework within which to understand health behavior, disease, and injury (Good, Sherrod, & Dillon, 2000).

In defining and operationalizing "men's" health, there is an ever-present risk for normalizing men's experiences and universalizing risk

TABLE 14.1   Life Expectancy for Women and Men in the
World's Ten Largest Population Countries

| Country | Life Expectancy in Years | | |
	Females	Males	Gender Difference in Years
Russia	72.3	58.9	13.4
Japan	84.7	77.9	6.8
Brazil	72.0	65.5	6.5
United States	79.5	74.3	5.2
Indonesia	67.4	64.4	3.0
China	72.7	69.8	2.9
Nigeria	52.6	50.6	2.0
India	61.7	60.0	1.7
Pakistan	61.5	61.0	0.5
Bangladesh	61.7	61.9	−0.2

Source: Annex Table 1 Basic Indicators for All Member States, World
   Health Organization, Geneva, Switzerland, 2002.

taking and poor physical or mental well-being as characteristic of all
men. However, the health and behavior of men who are economically,
socially, and politically disadvantaged—such as men in Russia during
the transition from communism—can differ greatly from the health
and behavior of other men (Bobak & Marmot, 1996; Waldron, 2008;
Whitfield, Weidner, Clark, & Anderson, 2002). The health needs,
coping styles, barriers to accessing care, and care accessed also vary
among diverse populations of men. Although economically disadvantaged men, men of color, and indigenous men are exposed to many
of the same underlying factors that contribute to poor health among
men in general, their risks are often compounded by additional social,
economic, and political factors. In the United States, the difference
between the life expectancies of African American men and European
American men exceeds the difference between the life expectancies
of women and men (Department of Health and Human Services,
2009a). The deaths of indigenous men and men of color around the
world account for much of the reported gender differences in mortality
(Bramley, Hebert, Jackson, & Chassin, 2004). Economic and ethnic
differences among men also contribute to risks associated with specific health behaviors (Whitfield et al., 2002). For example, whereas
nearly one in four U.S. men in general smoke cigarettes (CDC, 2009c),
the ratio among Laotian immigrants is nearly three in four (Lew &
Tanjasiri, 2003; Moeschberger et al., 1997).

Men also have very different experiences within various systems
of health care based on their ethnicity and socioeconomic background (e.g., Felix-Aaron et al., 2005). In the United States, African

American men are less likely than European American men to receive various treatments or clinical procedures for coronary heart disease (Canto et al., 2000; Giles et al., 1995; Vaccarino et al., 2005), to be prescribed a potentially life-saving medication for ischemic stroke (Johnston et al., 2001), to receive surgery for glaucoma (Devgan, Yu, Kim, & Coleman, 2000), or to have mental health conditions diagnosed (Borowsky et al., 2000); and they are more likely to be denied insurance authorization for emergency treatment than are European American men (Lowe et al., 2001). It is perhaps not surprising that African American men report less trust of doctors than other men do (Boulware, Cooper, Ratner, LaVeist, & Powe, 2003; Corbie-Smith, Thomas, & St. George, 2002; Gamble, 1997; Hall, Dugan, Zheng, & Mishra, 2001; LaVeist, Nickerson, & Bowie, 2000; Lillie-Blanton, Brodie, Rowland, Altman, & McIntosh, 2000; Musa, Schulz, Harris, Silverman, & Thomas, 2009; Petersen, 2002; Powell-Hammond, Matthews, & Corbie-Smith, 2010), rate their doctors and their doctors' decision-making styles as less participatory (Cooper-Patrick et al., 1999), and report more dissatisfaction with their care by doctors and in hospitals than European American men (Blendon, Aiken, Freeman, & Corey, 1989; Cooper-Patrick et al., 1999; LaVeist et al., 2000). However, little is known about the causes of these differences or about the relative health care experiences of men around the world. It remains unclear whether ethnic minority or indigenous men in other countries similarly distrust physicians, and whether indigenous men trust traditional healers more or less than they trust Western doctors, and more or less than nonindigenous men do. New research on men's health must examine questions of this kind. We must also examine similarities and differences among men in physical and mental health, in health care experiences, and in the mechanisms that mediate health status, health care utilization, and health behavior.

CONTEMPORARY STUDIES OF MEN AND MASCULINITY

A variety of relatively recent developments in the fields of gender studies, feminist theory, queer studies, and men's studies can provide much-needed direction for the field of men's health. Theorists, researchers, and practitioners developing new paradigms and methods for understanding and addressing men's health would be wise to incorporate the central conclusions about masculinity reached by researchers and scholars in these allied fields. These conclusions are summarized below.

Diversity of Masculinities

Men throughout the world are familiar with the celluloid masculinity embodied by Arnold Schwarzenegger, Jean-Claude van Damme, and the California lifeguards in the television series *Baywatch*—which *Guinness Book of World Records* reported in 2009 was watched by over 1 billion viewers in 142 countries and the most watched television show in the world (Guinness World Records, 2009). However, not all men embrace this dominant Western exemplar of manhood. In the United States, men with less education and lower family income are more likely to endorse traditional beliefs about masculinity; African American men are more likely to endorse them as well (see Chapter 4 and Section III Introduction). Yet even among African American men, there are differences; younger, less educated, nonprofessional men have been found to hold more traditional beliefs than do older, more educated, professional men.

These differences reflect not only diversity among men in their endorsement of traditional masculinity, but also diversity in masculinity. Theories of masculinity—or *"the* male gender role"—have historically presumed one universal masculinity (see Chapter 4). Contemporary theorists, however, recognize a variety of masculinities. But little is known about how various masculinities—such as those of bisexual and immigrant men or other marginalized populations— influence the health or health behavior of men and boys. Nor is it known how men's health is influenced by the diversity of masculinities that exists in any given setting, such as a school, workplace, or playing field. New theory and research must acknowledge the unique health problems associated with various definitions of manhood among diverse populations of men, including ethnic minorities, indigenous men, rural men, men who have sex with men, men in prison, single men, men with chronic or mental illnesses or other disabilities, and boys and older men.

Masculinities as Social Structures

Masculinity was long believed to reside solely in each man's individual psychology. Contemporary theories of masculinity recognize, however, that gender is not something that individuals possess. Although it is often experienced as something deeply personal, masculinity is also a social system or structure—or more specifically, multiple structures. Masculinities organize or pattern daily life and social relations. It is gender that shapes institutions, such as governments, corporations, and health care systems. It is gendered social structures that facilitate some men's access to positions of power and dominance (e.g., physicians) and that frequently relegate women to subordinated roles (e.g., nurses). Masculinity is also a way of structuring social practices. Many of these social practices have a significant influence on the health and well-being of men and boys, including the practices of sport, labor, health care, and military or paramilitary warfare (which increasingly enlists boys as *"child* soldiers"). (For further discussion of masculinities as social structures, see Chapter 4.)

Masculinities as Dynamic Structures

If we are to develop new comprehensive paradigms in this field, we must recognize that masculinity and men's health are not fixed or static. The same man is different in different contexts. He may believe that it is inappropriate to cry at work or in front of peers, but that it *is* appropriate to cry at home or with his wife. He may behave in one way when he is with drinking buddies and in another way when he is with his children. Gender is a dynamic process that is produced and reproduced daily through social interactions. Similarly, men's beliefs about manhood can and do change over time. Some men reinforce and reproduce traditional ways of being a man, whereas other men redefine and transform traditional masculinity. Still other men resist traditional masculinity completely and create their own standards of manhood, and some men simply reject the notion that masculinity is relevant at all (Emslie, Ridge, Ziebland, & Hunt, 2006; O'Brien, Hunt, & Hart, 2005; Robertson, 2007).

Broader cultural beliefs about masculinity also evolve historically. In the first half of the 19th century in Western Europe and the United States, men's physical prowess was considered relatively unimportant. It was not physical strength but strength of character that was valued and admired in men (Rotundo, 1993). In this respect, the past several decades have witnessed significant changes. The cultural standard for men's bodies in Western industrialized nations has become increasingly large and muscular (Pope et al., 2000; Pope, Phillips, & Olivardia, 2000). Today, the "ideal" male physique is represented by Arnold Schwarzenegger, not by John Wayne. The field of men's health must take such historical perspectives into account.

Men's Agency

Western theories of gender socialization have traditionally defined it as something that happens *to* people. Individuals are believed to acquire their various characteristics through a process of internalization; this process results in clusters of "traits" organized into an identifiable and enduring personality, and into one of two genders. Consequently, explanations of the damaging health effects of masculinity in Western countries have focused primarily on the hazardous influences of "*the* male gender role." But men and boys are not passive victims of a socially prescribed gender role, nor are they simply conditioned by their cultures. Rather, they are actors—or active agents—in their socialization and participate in generating a variety of male roles that variously influence their health. Men and masculinity contribute, for example, to shaping health care systems that ignore men's gendered health concerns. Indeed, they are often the very researchers and scientists who have ignored the subject. (For further discussion of men's agency, see Chapter 4.)

Men's poor health beliefs and behaviors were historically believed to reflect an underlying masculine personality. Contemporary theories, however, suggest that cognitions and behaviors are not an effect of people's personalities; rather, they are what personalities are made of (see Chapter 4). Women and men think and act in the gendered ways they do not because of their role identities or psychological traits, but because they are demonstrating cultural concepts of femininity and masculinity. The manner in which men carry out health-related activities contributes both to the defining of themselves as gendered and to social conventions of masculinity. Health beliefs and behaviors—such as dismissing the need for help or engaging in high-risk behavior—can thus be used by men and boys as means, or resources, to prove that they are "real" men.

Critical Analyses of Essentialist Assumptions About Gender

During most of the past century, Western theories of masculinity relied heavily on unfounded biological assumptions. It was considered natural and inevitable for men and women to differ; it was believed that there must be essential differences between women and men simply because male and female reproductive organs differ. To maintain this notion of gender *as difference* has required that we disregard decades of research indicating that—psychologically, at least—men and women are more similar than dissimilar (Hyde, 2005). New research on men's health must attempt to explore beyond this notion of gender as difference. As we do the important work of learning more about gender similarities and differences in those countries where we are only beginning to study them, it is important that we bear in mind that findings of gender difference often result from small statistical differences in a minority of the population (Schofield, Connell, Walker, Wood, & Butland, 2000), and that they rarely represent categorical differences between all men and all women.

We must also transcend this notion of gender as difference if we wish to further understand the contradictory nature of men's experiences, and hence to illuminate the mutability and inherent fragility of masculinity. These contradictions of manhood—such as frailty that often masquerades as strength—are frequently at the heart of men's health problems. Many men believe that they are "supposed" to be healthier and more resilient than women despite suffering more serious chronic conditions than women. (As I discussed in Chapter 1, men are more likely than women to believe that they *are* healthier.) Consequently, men often take risks or endanger their health in attempts to disprove this contradiction. Similarly, men in urban centers of industrialized countries might report being personally opposed to violence but report a willingness to use physical violence "if necessary," fearing that they will be victimized by other men if they appear weak or transgress masculinity, and believing that the display of some degree of violence—or, at least the threat of retaliation—will protect them from harm by other men (e.g., Rich & Stone, 1996). Until notions of gender as difference and their underlying essentialist assumptions are further questioned and addressed, it is likely that men will continue to struggle in their daily lives with such contradictions between their lived experiences of manhood and real or perceived social norms of masculinity.

RELATIONAL MODELS

Much of the preceding discussion suggests that relational models would be beneficial in conceptualizing and researching men's health (e.g., Connell, 2000; Sabo, 2000; Sabo & Hall, 2009; Schofield et al., 2000). These models would take into account the dynamic intersection of various health determinants, such as those among biological functioning, environmental pollution, psychological well-being, social and cultural norms, genetic predisposition, institutional policies, political climates, and economic disparities. Contemporary approaches to men's health must recognize the interrelationships among such factors, and must examine how they systematically foster or undermine the physical and mental health of men and boys.

Relationships Among Institutional Structures

Relationships among various institutionalized social structures—such as governments, military or paramilitary forces, corporations, technological industries, systems of health care, judicial systems, and the media—mediate the health of men (see Chapter 4). Furthermore, the dynamic interplay of these institutional structures results in different opportunities for, and constraints on, the realization of optimal health. Patterns of social relations related to class or caste systems and to the structure of economic markets expose working-class men performing manual labor to a range of occupational health and safety hazards. This is one reason why, in the United States, men constitute roughly half of the workforce, yet account for nearly all fatal injuries on the job (see Chapters 1 and 2). Working-class men labor in jobs that require the use of dangerous equipment—such as weapons and heavy machinery—and jobs that expose workers to hazardous chemicals: jobs in construction, agriculture, oil and gas extraction, water transportation, and forestry. These men's risks are compounded by the interaction of various structural factors, such as limited or poorly implemented occupational health and safety policies, lack of health insurance coverage, limited financial resources for health care, substandard living conditions, and limited geographic access to health services.

Health care systems and the allied health fields represent particularly important structural influences shaping gender and health. In the case of cardiovascular disease, for example, women in Western countries are less likely than men to be routinely tested or treated for symptoms (Hippisley-Cox, Pringle, Meal, & Wynn, 2001)—a fact that may foster unrealistic perceptions of risk among women. Little is understood, however, about the ways in which health care systems structure the health of men. As I discussed previously, research shows consistently that during medical examinations in the United Kingdom and the United States, men receive fewer explanations and less information than women do, and that despite their higher involvement in unhealthy behaviors, they are less likely than women to be counseled by clinicians about changing those behaviors. However, we have yet to understand this finding within the context of such interrelationships as those among masculinity (which is associated with desire for professional help), social power (e.g., the relative social power of clinicians and patients), and health care delivery systems (e.g., the time limitations of "managed care").

Gender Relations Between Women and Men

Relational approaches also recognize how gender relationships between women and men mediate health outcomes (Sabo, 2000; Sabo & Hall, 2009; Schofield et al., 2000). Gendered health care need not be a dialectic; indeed, men's and women's health are inextricably intertwined. In the United States, for example, men are at fault in most fatal automobile crashes in which women are killed (see Chapter 2), and female spouses foster health-promoting behavior in men (Umberson, 1992; see also Chapter 2). Relational models account for such health-relevant relationships between women and men, as well as for the interplay between gender relations and institutional structures. For example, they extend strictly biomedical and patient-focused models that medicalize reproductive health and enable researchers and theorists to address the relationships between social and economic power that underlie sexual relations and operate to undermine the health of both women and men. Although research indicates that heterosexual couples' communication about family planning increases contraceptive effectiveness in some countries (see DeRose, Dodoo, Ezeh, & Owuor, 2004), the negotiation of sexual practices is structured by social policies; in those countries where governments have endorsed national policies intended to protect the rights and ability of individuals to make informed choices about family planning and protection against sexually transmitted diseases or HIV—such as Malaysia, Mexico, Peru, and Zambia—(Seltzer, 2002), the negotiation of sexual practices is fostered. As all these examples illustrate, men's and women's health are reciprocal and interdependent. Studying and designing interventions that address these gender relations, therefore, may not only lead to improved health conditions for men and boys, but also contribute to building healthier families and communities.

Gender Relations Among Men

Relationships among men also influence their health, as in the case of male-on-male violence. Men and boys are most often both the perpetrators and the victims of physical violence (see Chapters 1 and 2). New and emerging paradigms offer the promise of understanding the pathways through which social relationships among men influence men's violence and men's health in general. To fully understand these pathways, however, requires acknowledging that ethnicity, sexuality, and economic status are intimately and systematically related to the social structuring of gender and power. Within hierarchies of manhood, some masculinities are exalted and rewarded, whereas others are devalued and punished (see Chapter 4). For example, the social privileging of heterosexuality in many cultures shapes the patterning of relationships among men and fosters the subordination of and physical violence against gay men.

Men's relative access to social power and resources, and their positioning relative to women and other men, contributes to shaping their health-related beliefs and behaviors. Disease and illness can alter relationships of social power between women and men and reduce men's status in hierarchies of masculinity. Some men are reluctant to address their health needs for fear that other men will perceive them as being unmanly or gay (Hong, 2000). New theoretical paradigms and research models can help us to better understand these relationships. They can also help us to understand how men can positively influence each other's health—as in the case of the intensive caregiving provided by gay men to other men with HIV disease (Altman, 1994), and the case of men's group discussions about health, which have been found to foster health-promoting behavior (Davies et al., 2000). Such understanding is necessary for developing resiliency- and strength-based interventions for improving men's health.

CONCLUSION: A GLOBAL AND RELATIONAL MODEL

The new field of men's health provides unique and exciting opportunities for the development of a robust international discipline. It offers an important prospect for the exchange of knowledge and health expertise with international partners, and for delivering analyses of state-of-the-art intervention strategies to parts of the world where the concept of men's health has only recently been recognized. The potential mutual benefits of such collaboration are many. This nascent field provides the opportunity for exploring and developing comprehensive and truly international models for addressing the health of men and boys—models that have yet to be formulated.

Comprehensive international and relational models of men's health would address micro (individual practice or context specific), meso (organizational), and macro (societal) health determinants at international, national, community, and individual levels (Annandale & Kuhlmann, 2010). They would identify interactions among these various levels of social relationships and explore the complex intersections among various personal, social, economic, cultural, and political health determinants. These models would recognize that men's health cannot be neatly separated from such factors as social justice, equality, political freedom, and sustainable development. A focus on the convergence of micro and macro social systems internationally—or what might be termed *global community health models*—will provide comprehensive frameworks within which to assess the physical and mental health of men and boys.

Globalization creates new challenges and opportunities for an international field of men's health. The globalization of trade can contribute both to the transnationalization of health risks such as HIV and to the availability of lifesaving medicines. The unprecedented globalization and economic power of transnational corporations can have enormous ramifications for men's health. International and relational models of men's health would provide the means for understanding how the health of men and boys in newly industrializing countries is influenced by multinational corporations—by alcohol and tobacco marketing strategies, by the opening and closing of plants for low-wage workers, and by the pricing of antiretroviral medications for HIV, for example. They would also provide the means for understanding how the globalization of Hollywood depictions of glorified, authoritative masculinities can influence the health attitudes and behaviors of men and boys worldwide.

The multinational nature of many threats to men's health requires us to recognize that the health of people in local communities is linked to global systems. The world economy and labor markets, for example, can have a powerful effect on men's health outcomes. As industrial production expands, workers face a range of occupational health and safety hazards, particularly in relatively economically disadvantaged countries where wage bills, health and safety legislation, and pollution controls are weaker than those established in the West. However, the social structural relationships that organize men's work life and their health are not simply imposed on men by global forces; these relationships are local, global, and reciprocal. Local labor politics and unionism mediate the influence of broader institutional structures. Similarly, the shifting of women's responsibilities from the home to employment in traditionally male jobs in some countries is also likely to influence men's health and coping. As these few examples suggest, a truly global and relational framework for exploring the interplay among structural, political, and cultural determinants of health is needed if we are to understand and respond comprehensively to the physical and mental health concerns of men and boys.

The 21st century holds the promise of healthier lives for the men and boys of the world, and for the communities in which they live. As we work together internationally to integrate our specialized knowledge into a new field of men's health, we *will* realize that promise. I look forward with great anticipation and hope as we embark on this exciting journey together.

REFERENCES

Abraham, I. L., & Krowchuk, H. V. (1986). Unemployment and health: Health promotion for the jobless male. *Nursing Clinics of North America, 21*(1), 37–47.

Abreu, J. M., Goodyear, R. K., Campos, A., & Newcomb, M. D. (2000). Ethnic belonging and traditional masculinity ideology among African Americans, European Americans, and Latinos. *Psychology of Men & Masculinity, 1*(2), 75–86.

Adams, J. (2006). Trends in physical activity and inactivity amongst U.S. 14–18 year olds by gender, school grade and race, 1993–2003: Evidence from the Youth Risk Behavior Survey. *BMC Public Health, 6*(57), 1–7.

Addis, M. E., & Mahalik, J. R. (2003). Men, masculinity, and the contexts of help seeking. *American Psychologist, 58*(1), 5–14.

Adimora, A. A., Schoenbach, V. J., & Doherty, I. A. (2007). Concurrent sexual partnerships among men in the United States. *American Journal of Public Health, 97*(12), 2230–2237.

Adler, D. A., Drake, R. E., & Teague, G. B. (1990). Clinicians' practices in personality assessment: Does gender influence the use of DSM-III axis II? *Comprehensive Psychiatry, 31*(2), 125–133.

Adler, N. E., Boyce, T., Chesney, M. A., Cohen, S., Folkman, S., Kahn, R. L., & Syme, S. L. (1994). Socioeconomic status and health: The challenge of the gradient. *American Psychologist, 49*(1), 15–24.

Adler, P. A., Kless, S. J., & Adler, P. (1992). Socialization to gender roles: Popularity among elementary school boys and girls. *Sociology of Education, 65*(3), 169–187.

Agency for Healthcare Research and Quality. (2004). *Preventing violence and related health-risking social behaviors in adolescents: Evidence report/ technology assessment no. 107* (AHRQ Publication No. 04-E032-2). Rockville, MD: Author.

Agency for Healthcare Research and Quality. (2009). *The guide to clinical preventive services, 2009: Recommendations of the U.S. Preventive Services Task Force.* Rockville, MD: Author.

Ahmed, N. U., Smith, G. L., Flores, A. M., Pamies, R. J., Mason, H. R., Woods, K. F., & Stain, S. C. (2005). Racial/ethnic disparity and predictors of leisure-time physical activity among U.S. men. *Ethnicity & Disease, 15*, 40–52.

Ainsworth, B. E. (2000) Challenges in measuring physical activity in women. *Exercise and Sport Sciences Reviews, 28*(2), 93–96.

Alexander, C. S., Somerfield, M. R., Ensminger, M. E., Kim, Y. J., & Johnson, K. E. (1995). Gender differences in injuries among rural youth. *Injury Prevention, 1*(1), 15–20.

Alfieri, T., Ruble, D. N., & Higgins, E. T. (1996). Gender stereotypes during adolescence: Developmental changes and the transition to junior high school. *Developmental Psychology, 32*(6), 1129–1137.

Allen, D. G., & Whatley, M. (1986). Nursing and men's health: Some critical considerations. *Nursing Clinics of North America, 21*(1), 3–13.

Allen, J. A., & Gordon, S. (1990). Creating a framework for change. In R. L. Meth & R. S. Pasick (Eds.), *Men in therapy: The challenge of change* (pp. 131–151). New York, NY: Guilford Press.

Allen, J. D., Fantasia, H. C., Fontenot, H., Flaherty, S., & Santana, J. (2009). College men's knowledge, attitudes, and beliefs about the human papillomavirus infection and vaccine. *Journal of Adolescent Health, 45*, 535–537.

Allen, M. T., Stoney, C. M., Owens, J. F., & Matthews, K. A. (1993). Hemodynamic adjustments to laboratory stress: The influence of sex and personality. *Psychosomatic Medicine, 55*(6), 505–517.

Allen-Burge, R., Storandt, M., Kinscherf, D. A., & Rubin, E. H. (1994). Sex differences in the sensitivity of two self-report depression scales in older depressed inpatients. *Psychology and Aging, 9*(3), 443–445.

Allison, D. B., Fontaine, K. R., Manson, J. E., Stevens, J., & VanItallie, T. B. (1999). Annual deaths attributable to obesity in the United States. *Journal of the American Medical Association, 282*, 1530–1538.

Allison, K. R., Adlaf, E. M., Dwyer, J. J., & Irving, H. M. (2007). The decline in physical activity among adolescent students. *Canadian Journal of Public Health, 98*(2), 97–100.

Altekruse, S. F., Cohen, M. L., & Swerdlow, D. L. (1997). Emerging foodborne diseases. *Emerging Infectious Diseases, 3*(3), 285–293.

Altman, D. (1994). *Power and community: Organizational and cultural responses to AIDS.* London, England: Taylor & Francis.

Alvos, L., Gregson, R. A., & Ross, M. W. (1993). Future time perspective in current and previous injecting drug users. *Drug and Alcohol Dependence, 31,* 193–197.

American Academy of Dermatology. (1997). *"It can't happen to me": Americans not as safe from the sun as they think they are.* Schaumburg, IL: Author.

American Academy of Dermatology. (2005, May 2). *New survey finds majority of women still associate a tan with beauty and health: Women better than men at protecting themselves from sun exposure, but both genders need to improve attitudes and behaviors* (press release). Schaumburg, IL: Author.

American Cancer Society. (1997). *Cancer facts and figures—1994.* Atlanta, GA: Author.

American Cancer Society. (2008). *Cancer facts and figures—2008.* Atlanta, GA: Author.

American Cancer Society. (2009). *Cancer prevention and early detection facts and figures—2009.* Atlanta, GA: Author.

American Cancer Society. (2010). *Cancer facts for gay and bisexual men.* Atlanta, GA: Author.

American College Health Association. (1995). *Integrated strategies for HPV, STD, and cancer prevention on campus.* Baltimore, MD: Author.

American College Health Association. (2006). *American College Health Association – National College Health Assessment (ACHA-NCHA) web summary*. Updated April 2006. Retrieved from http://www.acha.org/projects_programs/ncha_sampledata.cfm.

American College Health Association. (2008, Spring). *American College Health Association-National College Health Assessment (ACHA-NCHA): Reference group executive summary*. Baltimore, MD: Author.

American Dental Association. (2004a). *2003 public opinion survey: Oral health of the U.S. population*. Chicago, IL: Author.

American Dental Association. (2004b). *Survey results reveal oral hygiene habits of men lag behind women* (press release). Chicago, IL: Author.

American Dental Association. (2008). *The public speaks up on oral health care*. Chicago, IL: Author.

American Dental Association. (2009). *Men, women differ in oral health care habits* (press release). Chicago, IL: Author.

American Heart Association. (1994). *Heart and stroke facts: 1995 statistical supplement*. Dallas, TX: Author.

American Heart Association. (1995). *Heart and stroke facts: 1995 statistical supplement*. Dallas, TX: Author.

American Heart Association. (1996). *Heart and stroke facts*. Dallas, TX: Author.

American Heart Association. (2000). *Heart and stroke statistical update*. Dallas, TX: Author.

American Heart Association. (2006). Diet and lifestyle recommendations revision 2006. *Circulation, 114*, 82–96.

American Heart Association. (2009a). Heart disease and stroke statistics—2009 update: A report from the American Heart Association Statistics Committee and Stroke Statistics Subcommittee. *Circulation, 119*, 1–161.

American Heart Association. (2009b). *Heart disease and stroke statistics—2009 update: At-a-glance*. Dallas, TX: Author.

American Medical Association. (1991a, October). *Lack of doctor-patient communication hazard in older men* (News release). Chicago, IL: Author.

American Medical Association. (1991b, October). *Results of 9/91 Gallup survey on older men's health perceptions and behaviors* (News release). Chicago, IL: Author.

American Psychiatric Association. (1994). *Diagnostic and statistical manual of mental disorders* (4th ed). Washington, DC: Author.

American Psychiatric Association. (2000). *Diagnostic and statistical manual of mental disorders* (4th ed., text revision). Washington, DC: Author.

American School Health Association. (1989). *The National Adolescent Student Health Survey: A report on the health of America's youth*. Oakland, CA: Third Party Publishing.

Anaya, R. (1996). "I'm the king": The macho image. In R. Gonzales (Ed.), *Muy macho* (pp. 57–73). New York, NY: Doubleday.

Andersen, A. E. (1999). Eating disorders in gay males. *Psychiatric Annals, 29*(4), 206–212.

Anderson, C. A., & Bushman, B. J. (2002). The effects of media violence on society. *Science, 295*, 2377–2378.

Anderson, J. L., Cole, M., Reggie, I. L., Perez, E., Phillips, S., Warren, C. A., … Misra. (2006, November). *Is hand hygiene a social norm with a college population?* Paper presented at APHA 134th Annual Meeting and Exposition, Boston, MA.

Anderson, R. N. (2001). Deaths: Leading causes for 1999. *National Vital Statistics Reports, 49*(11), 1–88. Hyattsville, MD: National Center for Health Statistics.

Andres, R., Muller, D., & Sorkin, J. D. (1993). Long-term effects of change in body weight on all-cause mortality. *Annals of Internal Medicine, 119*(7, Pt. 2), 737–743.

Angell, M. (1993). Privilege and health—What is the connection? *New England Journal of Medicine, 329*(2), 126–127.

Ankney, R. N., Vizza, J., Coil, J. A., Kurek, S., DeFrehn, R., & Shomo, H. (1998). Cofactors of alcohol-related trauma at a rural trauma center. *American Journal of Emergency Medicine, 16*(3), 228–231.

Annandale, E., & Clark, J. (1996). What is gender? Feminist theory and the sociology of human reproduction. *Sociology of Health and Illness, 18*(1), 17–44.

Annandale, E., & Kuhlmann, E. (Eds.) (2010). Gender and healthcare: The future. In E. Kuhlmann & E. Annandale (Eds.), *The Palgrave handbook of gender and healthcare* (pp. 454–469). New York, NY: Palgrave Macmillan.

Annandale, E., & Riska, E. (2009). New connections: Towards a gender-inclusive approach to women's and men's health. *Current Sociology, 57*(2), 123–133.

Annest, J. L., Mercy, J. A., Gibson, D. R., & Ryan, G. W. (1995). National estimates of nonfatal firearm-related injuries: Beyond the tip of the iceberg. *Journal of the American Medical Association, 273*(22), 1749–1745.

Antoñanzas, F., Viscusi, W. K., Rovira, J., Braña, F. J., Portillo, F., & Carvalho, I. (2000a). Smoking risks in Spain: Part I—Perception of risks to the smoker. *Journal of Risk and Uncertainty, 21*(2), 161–186.

Antoñanzas, F., Viscusi, W. K., Rovira, J., Braña, F. J., Portillo, F., & Carvalho, I. (2000b). Smoking risks in Spain: Part III—Determinants of smoking behavior. *Journal of Risk and Uncertainty, 21*(3), 212–234.

Antonucci, T. C., & Akiyama, H. (1987). An examination of sex differences in social support among older men and women. *Sex Roles, 17*(11/12), 737–749.

Appelbaum, P. S. (2006). "Depressed? Get out!": Dealing with suicidal students on college campuses. *Psychiatric Services, 57*(7), 914–916.

Archer, J. (2004). Sex differences in aggression in real-world settings: A meta-analytic review. *Review of General Psychology, 8*(4), 291–322.

Archer, J. (2006). Testosterone and human aggression: An evaluation of the challenge hypothesis. *Neuroscience and Biobehavioral Reviews, 30*, 319–345.

Arciniega, G. M., Anderson, T. C., Tovar-Blank, Z. G., & Tracey, T. J. (2008). Toward a fuller conception of machismo: Development of a traditional machismo and caballerismo scale. *Journal of Counseling Psychology, 1*, 19–33.

Arday, D. R., Tomar, S. L., Nelson, D. E., Merritt, R. K., Schooley, M. W., & Mowery, P. (1997). State smoking prevalence estimates: A comparison of the Behavioral Risk Factor Surveillance System and Current Population Surveys. *American Journal of Public Health, 87*(10), 1665–1669.

Aries, E. J., & Olver, R. R. (1985). Sex differences in the development of a separate sense of self during infancy: Directions for future research. *Psychology of Women Quarterly, 9*, 515–532.

Armstrong, B. K. (2004). How sun exposure causes skin cancer: An epidemiological perspective. In D. Hill, J. M. Elwood, & D. R. English (Eds.), *Prevention of skin cancer* (pp. 89–116). Boston, MA: Kluwer Academic.

Arnett, J., & Balle-Jensen, L. (1993). Cultural bases of risk behavior: Danish adolescents. *Child Development, 64*(6), 1842–1855.

Aron, M., Nguyen, M. M., Stein, R. J., & Gill, I. S. (2008). Impact of gender in renal cell carcinoma: An analysis of the SEER database. *European Oncology, 54*(1), 1–240.

Artazcoz, L., Benach, J., Borrell, C., & Cortès, I. (2004). Unemployment and mental health: Understanding the interactions among gender, family roles, and social class. *American Journal of Public Health, 94*(1), 82–88.

Artinian, N. T., Fletcher, G. F., Mozaffarian, D., Kris-Etherton, P., Van Horn, L., Lichtenstein, A. H., … Burke, L. W. (2010). Interventions to promote physical activity and dietary lifestyle changes for cardiovascular risk factor reduction in adults: A scientific statement from the American Heart Association. *Circulation, 122*, 406–441.

Arvary, D., & Pope, H. G. (2000). Anabolic-androgenic steroids as a gateway to opioid dependence. *New England Journal of Medicine, 342*(20), 1532.

Arzt, M., Young, T., Finn, L., Skatrud, J. B., & Bradley, T. D. (2005). Association of sleep-disordered breathing and the occurrence of stroke. *American Journal of Respiratory and Critical Care Medicine, 172*(11), 1447–1451.

Ascherio, A. (2002). Epidemiologic studies on dietary fats and coronary heart disease. *American Journal of Medicine, 113*(Suppl. 9B), 9S–12S.

Ascherio, A., & Willett, W. C. (1995). New directions in dietary studies of coronary heart disease. *Journal of Nutrition, 125*(Suppl.), 647S–655S.

Ashton, W. A., & Fuehrer, A. (1993). Effects of gender and gender role identification of participant and type of social support resource on support seeking. *Sex Roles, 28*(7/8), 461–476.

Aslaksen, P. M., Myrbakk, I. N., Høifødt, R. S., & Flaten, M. A. (2007). The effect of experimenter gender on autonomic and subjective responses to pain stimuli. *Pain, 129*(3), 260–268.

Aten, M. J., Siegel, D. M., & Roghmann, K. J. (1996). Use of health services by urban youth: A school-based survey to assess differences by grade level, gender, and risk behavior. *Journal of Adolescent Health, 19*, 258–266.

Athlete dies young. (1995, October 1). *New York Times,* S1, S7.

Auerbach, J. D., & Figert, A. E. (1995). Women's health research: Public policy and sociology [Extra issue]. *Journal of Health and Social Behavior,* 115–131.

Augustson, E., & Marcus, S. (2004). Use of the Current Population Survey to characterize subpopulations of continued smokers: A national perspective on the "hardcore" smoker phenomenon. *Nicotine & Tobacco Research, 6*(4), 621–629.

Auld, G. W., Nitzke, S. A., McNulty, J., Bock, M. A., Bruhn, C. M., Gabel, K., … Sheehan, E. (1998). A stage-of-change classification system based on actions and beliefs regarding dietary fat and fiber. *American Journal of Health Promotion, 12*(3), 192–201.

Ajzen, I. (2001). Nature and operation of attitudes. *Annual Review of Psychology, 52*, 27–58.

Babey, S. H., Ponce, N. A., Etzioni, D. A., Spencer, B. A., Brown, E. R., & Chawla, N. (2003). *Cancer screening in California: Racial and ethnic disparities persist.* Los Angeles, CA: UCLA Center for Health Policy Research.

Babor, T. F., Caetano, R., Casswell, S., Edwards, G., Giesbrecht, N., Graham, K., … Rossow, I. (2003). *Alcohol and public policy: No ordinary commodity; Research and public policy.* Oxford, England: Oxford University Press.

Bach, P. B., Pham, H. H., Schrag, D., Tate, R. C., & Hargraves, J. L. (2004). Primary care physicians who treat blacks and whites. *New England Journal of Medicine, 351*(6), 575–584.

Bachman, R. (1992). Crime in non-metropolitan America: A national accounting of trends, incidence rates, and idiosyncratic vulnerabilities. *Rural Sociology, 57*(4), 546–560.

Bacon, C. G., Mittleman, M. A., Kawachi, I., Giovannucci, E., Glasser, D. B., & Rimm, E. B. (2003). Sexual function in men older than 50 years of age: Results from the Health Professionals Follow-Up Study. *Annals of Internal Medicine, 139,* 161–168.

Baer, J. T. (1993). Improved plasma cholesterol levels in men after nutrition education program at the worksite. *Journal of the American Dietetic Association, 93*(6), 658–663.

Baeseman, Z. J. (2009). Alcohol-related motor vehicle accident fatality: Wisconsin rural-urban trends and observations. *Wisconsin Medical Journal, 108*(7), 359–364.

Baffi, C. R., Redican, K. J., Sefchick, M. K., & Impara, J. C. (1991). Gender role identity, gender role stress, and health behaviors: An exploratory study of selected college males. *Health Values, 15,* 9–18.

Bagnardi, V., Zatonski, W., Scotti, L., La Vecchia, C., & Corrao, G. (2008). Does drinking pattern modify the effect of alcohol on the risk of coronary heart disease? Evidence from a meta-analysis. *Journal of Epidemiology and Community Health, 62*(7), 615–619.

Baker, A. H., & Wardle, J. (2003). Sex differences in fruit and vegetable intake in older adults. *Appetite, 40,* 269–275.

Baker, J. I., Griffin, R., Brauneis, P. F., Rue, L. W., & McGwin, G. (2010). A comparison of wakeboard-, water skiing-, and tubing-related injuries in the United States, 2000–2007. *Journal of Sports Science and Medicine, 9,* 92–97.

Baker, K., & Raney, A. A. (2007). Equally super? Gender-role stereotyping of superheroes in children's animated programs. *Mass Communication and Society, 10*(1), 25–41.

Balanda, K. P., Lowe, J. B., Stanton, W. R., & Gillespie, A. M. (1994). Enhancing the early detection of melanoma within current guidelines. *Australian Journal of Public Health, 18,* 420–423.

Baldwin, R. O. (1984). Stability of masculinity-femininity scores over an eleven-year period. *Sex Roles, 10*(3/4), 257–260.

Balluz, L. S., Kieszak, S. M., Philen, R. M., & Mulinare, J. (2000). Vitamin and mineral supplement use in the United States: Results from the third National Health and Nutrition Examination Survey. *Archives of Family Medicine, 9*(3), 258–262.

Balswick, J. O. (1982). Male inexpressiveness: Psychological and social aspects. In K. Solomon & N. B. Levy (Eds.), *Men in transition: Theory and therapy* (pp. 131–150). New York, NY: Plenum Press.

Bambra, C. (2010). Yesterday once more? Unemployment and health in the 21st century. *Journal of Epidemiology and Community Health, 64*(3), 213–215.

Banks, B. A., Silverman, R. A., Schwartz, R. H., & Tunnessen, W. W. (1992). Attitudes of teenagers toward sun exposure and sunscreen use. *Pediatrics, 89*(1), 40–42.

Barnett, E., Casper, M. L., Halverson, J. A., Elmes, G. A., Braham, V. E., Majeed, Z. A., ... Stanley, S. (2001). *Men and heart disease: An atlas of racial and ethnic disparities in mortality.* Atlanta, GA: Centers for Disease Control and Prevention.

Barone, B. B., Yeh, H. C., Snyder, C. F., Peairs, K. S., Stein, K. B., Derr, R. L., ... Brancati, F. L. (2010). Postoperative mortality in cancer patients with preexisting diabetes: Systematic review and meta-analysis. *Diabetes Care, 33*(4), 931–939.

Barr, E. L., Zimmet, P. Z., Welborn, T. A., Jolley, D., Magliano, D. J., Dunstan, D. W., ... Shaw, J. E. (2007). Risk of cardiovascular and all-cause mortality in individuals with diabetes mellitus, impaired fasting glucose, and impaired glucose tolerance: The Australian Diabetes, Obesity, and Lifestyle Study. *Circulation, 116*, 151–157.

Barrett-Connor, E. (1997). Sex differences in coronary heart disease: Why are women so superior? The 1995 Ancel Keys Lecture. *Circulation, 95*, 252–264.

Barry, H., Bacon, M. K., & Child, I. L. (1957). A cross-cultural survey of some sex differences in socialization. *Journal of Abnormal and Social Psychology, 55*, 327–332.

Bartecchi, C. E., MacKenzie, T. D., & Schrier, R. W. (1995, May). The global tobacco epidemic. *Scientific American,* 44–51.

Bartini, M. (2006). Gender role flexibility in early adolescence: Developmental change in attitudes, self-perceptions, and behaviors. *Sex Roles, 55*(3–4), 233–245.

Bastani, R., Erickson, P. A., Marcus, A. C., Maxwell, A. E., Capell, F. J., Freeman H., & Yan, K. X. (1996). AIDS-related attitudes and risk behaviors: A survey of a random sample of California heterosexuals. *Preventative Medicine, 25*, 105–117.

Bayne-Smith, M. (Ed.). (1996). *Race, gender, and health.* Thousand Oaks, CA: Sage.

Beaver, K. M., Vaughn, M. G., DeLisi, M., & Wright, J. P. (2008). Anabolic-androgenic steroid use and involvement in violent behavior in a nationally representative sample of young adult males in the United States. *American Journal of Public Health, 98*(12), 2185–2187.

Beck, L. F., Shults, R. A., Mack, K. A., & Ryan, G. W. (2007). Associations between sociodemographics and safety belt use in states with and without primary enforcement laws. *American Journal of Public Health, 97*(9), 1619–1624.

Beel, A., Maycock, B., & McLean, N. (1998). Current perspectives on anabolic steroids. *Drug and Alcohol Review, 17*(1), 87–103.

Beier, M. E., & Ackerman, P. L. (2003). Determinants of health knowledge: An investigation of age, gender, abilities, personality, and interests. *Journal of Personality and Social Psychology, 84*(2), 439–448.

Belle, D. (1987). Gender differences in the social moderators of stress. In R. C. Barnett, L. Biener, & G. K. Baruch (Eds.), *Gender and stress* (pp. 257–277). New York, NY: Free Press.

Belle, D., Burr, R., & Cooney, J. (1987). Boys and girls as social support theorists. *Sex Roles, 17*(11–12), 657–665.

Belloc, N. B. (1973). Relationship of health practices and mortality. *Preventive Medicine, 2*, 67–81.

Belloc, N. B., & Breslow, L. (1972). Relationship of physical health status and health practices. *Preventive Medicine, 1*, 409–421.

Belyea, M. J., & Lobao, L. M. (1990). Psychosocial consequences of agricultural transformation: The farm crisis and depression. *Rural Sociology, 55*(1), 58–75.

Benditt, L., Engel, E., Gavin, M., & Stransky, E. (2009). *Addressing health disparities affecting lesbian, gay, bisexual, and transgender (LGBT) youth and adults in Wisconsin*. Madison, WI: Publications Office, La Follette School of Public Affairs.

Benenson, J. F., Carder, H. P., & Geib Cole, S. J. (2008). The development of boys' preferential pleasure in physical aggression. *Aggressive Behavior, 34*, 154–166.

Ben-Shlomo, Y., Smith, G. D., Shipley, M., & Marmot, M. G. (1993). Magnitude and causes of mortality differences between married and unmarried men. *Journal of Epidemiology and Community Health, 47*(3), 200–205.

Bergen, D. J., & Williams, J. E. (1991). Sex stereotypes in the United States revisited: 1972–1988. *Sex Roles, 24*(7/8), 413–423.

Berger, J. M., Levant, R., McMillan, K. K., Kelleher, W., & Sellers, A. (2005). Impact of gender role conflict, traditional masculinity ideology, alexithymia, and age on men's attitudes toward psychological help seeking. *Psychology of Men & Masculinity, 6*(1), 73–78.

Berger, J. S., Bhatt, D. L., Steinhubl, S. R., Shao, M., Steg, G., Montalescot, G., … Berger, P. B. (2009). Smoking, clopidogrel, and mortality in patients with established cardiovascular disease. *Circulation, 120*(21), 109.866533.

Berger, K., Ajani, U. A., Kase, C. S., Gaziano, J. M., Buring, J. E., Glynn, R. J., & Hennekens, C. H. (1999). Light-to-moderate alcohol consumption and risk of stroke among U.S. male physicians. *New England Journal of Medicine, 341*(21), 1557–1564.

Berkman, L., & Epstein, A. M. (2008). Beyond health care: Socioeconomic status and health. *New England Journal of Medicine, 358*(23), 2509–2510.

Berkman, L. F. (1984). Assessing the physical health effects of social networks and social support. *Annual Review of Public Health, 5*, 413–432.

Berkman, L. F., & Breslow, L. (Eds.). (1983). *Health and ways of living: The Alameda County Study*. New York, NY: Oxford University Press.

Berkman, L. F., Breslow, L., & Wingard, D. (1983). Health practices and mortality risk. In L. F. Berkman & L. Breslow (Eds.), *Health and ways of living* (pp. 61–112). New York, NY: Oxford University Press.

Berkman, L. F., Leo-Summers, L., & Horwitz, R. I. (1992). Emotional support and survival after myocardial infarction: A prospective, population-based study of the elderly. *Annals of Internal Medicine, 117*, 1003–1009.

Berkowitz, A. D. (2003). Applications of social norms theory to other health and social justice issues. In H. W. Perkins (Ed.), *The social norms approach to preventing school and college-age substance abuse* (pp. 259–279). San Francisco, CA: Jossey-Bass.

Berlin, J. A., & Colditz, G. A. (1990). A meta-analysis of physical activity in the prevention of coronary heart disease. *American Journal of Epidemiology, 132*, 612–628.

Bertakis, K. D., & Azari, R. (2007). Patient gender and physician practice style. *Journal of Women's Health, 16*(6), 859–868.

Bertakis, K., Rahman-Azari, L., Helms, L. J., Callahan, E. J., & Robbins, J. A. (2000). Gender differences in the utilization of health care services. *Journal of Family Practice, 49*(2), 147–152.

Berwick, M., Armstrong, B. K., Ben-Porat, L., Fine, J., Kricker, A., Eberle, C., & Barnhill, R. (2005). Sun exposure and mortality from melanoma. *Journal of the National Cancer Institute, 97*(3), 195–199.

Berwick, M., Begg, C. B., Fine, J. A., Roush, G. C., & Barnhill, R. L. (1996). Screening for cutaneous melanoma by skin self-examination. *Journal of the National Cancer Institute, 88*(1), 17–23.

Berwick, M., Fine, J. A., & Bolognia, J. L. (1992). Sun exposure and sunscreen use following a community skin cancer screening. *Preventive Medicine, 21,* 302–310.

Best, D. L., Davis, S. W., Vaz, R. M., & Kaiser, M. (1996). Testicular cancer education: A comparison of teaching methods. *American Journal of Health Behavior, 20,* 229–241.

Bethel, J. W., & Waterman, S. H. (2009). Knowledge, attitudes and practices regarding influenza prevention and control measures among Hispanics in San Diego County—2006. *Ethnicity and Disease, 19*(4), 377–383.

Beyers, J. M., Bates, J. E., Pettit, G. S., & Dodge, K. A. (2003). Neighborhood structure, parenting processes, and the development of youths' externalizing behaviors: A multilevel analysis. *American Journal of Community Psychology, 31*(1/2), 35–53.

Bibbins-Domingo, K., Chertow, G. M., Coxson, P. G., Moran, A., Lightwood, J. M., Pletcher, M. J., & Goldman, L. (2010). Projected effect of dietary salt reductions on future cardiovascular disease. *New England Journal of Medicine, 362*(7), 590–599.

Biener, L. (1987). Gender differences in the use of substances for coping. In R. C. Barnett, L. Biener, & G. K. Baruch (Eds.), *Gender and stress* (pp. 330–349). New York, NY: Free Press.

Bild, D. E., Detrano, R., Peterson, D., Guerci, A., Liu, K., Shahar, E., … & Saad, M. F. (2005). Ethnic differences in coronary calcification: The Multi-Ethnic Study of Atherosclerosis (MESA). *Circulation, 111,* 1313–1320.

Bindman, A. B., Grumbach, K., Osmond, D., Vranizan, K., & Stewart, A. L. (1996). Primary care and receipt of preventive services. *Journal of General Internal Medicine, 11,* 269–276.

Binswanger, I. A., Stern, M. F., Deyo, R. A., Heagerty, P. J., Cheadle, A., Elmore, J. G., & Koepsell, T. D. (2007). Release from prison: A high risk of death for former inmates. *New England Journal of Medicine, 356*(2), 157–165.

Bird, C. E. (1999). Gender, household labor, and psychological distress: The impact of the amount and division of housework. *Journal of Health and Social Behavior, 40,* 32–45.

Bird, C. E., & Rieker, P. P. (1999). Gender matters: An integrated model for understanding men's and women's health. *Social Science & Medicine, 48*(6), 745–755.

Bird, C. E., & Rieker, P. P. (2008). *Gender and health: The effects of constrained choice and social policies.* New York, NY: Cambridge University Press.

Bish, C. L., Blanck, H. M., Serdula, M. K., Marcus, M., Kohl, H. W., & Khan, L. K. (2005). Diet and physical activity behaviors among Americans trying to lose weight: 2000 Behavioral Risk Factor Surveillance System. *Obesity Research, 13*(3), 596–607.

Bjornson, W., Rand, C., Connett, J. E., Lindgren, P., Nides, M., Pope, F., ... O'Hara, P. (1995). Gender differences in smoking cessation after 3 years in the Lung Health Study. *American Journal of Public Health, 85*(2), 223–230.

Black, H. S., Herd, A., Goldberg, L. H., Wolf, J. E., Thornby, J. I., Rosen, T., ... Andrews, K. (1994). Effect of a low-fat diet on the incidence of actinic keratosis. *New England Journal of Medicine, 330*(18), 1272–1275.

Blackmore, E. R., Stansfeld, S. A., Weller, I., Munce, S., Zagorski, B. M., & Stewart, D. E. (2007). Major depressive episodes and work stress: Results from a national population survey. *American Journal of Public Health, 97*(11), 2088–2093.

Blackwell, T. (2001). The Rural Men's Health Program. *Health Promotion Strategies, 2*(2), 3.

Blair, A., Blair, S., Howe, H., Pate, R., Rosenberg, M., Parker, G., & Pickle, L. (1980). Physical, psychological, and socio-demographic differences among smokers, ex-smokers, and nonsmokers in a working population. *Preventive Medicine, 9,* 747–759.

Blair, A., & Zahm, S. H. (1991). Cancer among farmers. *Occupational Medicine, 6*(3), 335–354.

Blair, E. H., Seo, D-C., & Torabi, M. R. (2004). Safety beliefs and safe behavior among midwestern college students. *Journal of Safety Research, 35*(2), 131–140.

Blair, S. N., Kohl, H. W., Paffenbarger, R. S., Clark, D. G., Cooper, K. H., & Gibbons, L. W. (1989). Physical fitness and all-cause mortality: A prospective study of healthy men and women. *Journal of the American Medical Association, 262*(17), 2395–2401.

Blake, S. M., Ledsky, R., Lehman, T., Goodenow, C., Sawyer, R., & Hack, T. (2001). Preventing sexual risk behaviors among gay, lesbian, and bisexual adolescents: The benefits of gay-sensitive HIV instruction in schools. *American Journal of Public Health, 91*(6), 940–946.

Blanchard, C. G., Ruckdeschel, J. C., Blanchard, E. B., Arena, J. G., Saunders, N. L., & Malloy, E. D. (1983). Interactions between oncologists and patients during rounds. *Annals of Internal Medicine, 99*(5), 694–699.

Blanco, C., Okuda, M., Wright, C., Hasin, D. S., Bridget, F., Grant, B. F., ... Olfson, M. (2008). Mental health of college students and their non-college-attending peers: Results from the National Epidemiologic Study on Alcohol and Related Conditions. *Archives of General Psychiatry, 65*(12), 1429–1437.

Blazer, D. G. (1982). Social support and mortality in an elderly community population. *American Journal of Epidemiology, 115*(5), 684–694.

Blazina, C., & Watkins, C. E. (1996). Masculine gender role conflict: Effects on college men's psychological well-being, chemical substance usage, and attitudes toward help-seeking. *Journal of Counseling Psychology, 43,* 461–465.

Blazina, C., & Watkins, C. E. (2000). Separation/individuation, parental attachment, and male gender role conflict: Attitudes toward the feminine and the fragile masculine self. *Psychology of Men and Masculinity, 1,* 126–132.

Bleeker, M. C., Heideman, D. A., Snijders, P. J., Horenblas, S., Dillner, J., & Meijer, C. J. (2009). Penile cancer: Epidemiology, pathogenesis and prevention. *World Journal of Urology, 27*(2), 141–150.

Blendon, R. J., Aiken, L. H., Freeman, H. E., & Corey, C. R. (1989). Access to medical care for black and white Americans: A matter of continuing concern. *Journal of the American Medical Association, 261*(2), 278–281.

Blesch, K. S. (1986). Health beliefs about testicular cancer and self-examination among professional men. *Oncology Nursing Forum, 13*(1), 29–33.

Block, G., Cox, C., Medars, G., Schreiber, G. B., Licitra, L., & Melia, N. (1988). Vitamin supplement use, by demographic characteristics. *American Journal of Epidemiology, 127*(2), 287–309.

Block, G., Patterson, B., & Subar, A. (1992). Fruit, vegetables, and cancer prevention: A review of the epidemiological evidence. *Nutrition and Cancer, 18*(1), 1–29.

Block, G., Rosenberger, W. F., & Patterson, B. H. (1988). Calories, fat and cholesterol: Intake patterns in the U.S. population by race, sex, and age. *American Journal of Public Health, 78*(9), 1150–1155.

Block, J. H. (1984). *Sex role identity and ego development.* San Francisco, CA: Jossey-Bass.

Bloom, J. R., Stewart, S. L., Oakley-Girvans, I., Banks, P. J., & Chang, S. (2006). Family history, perceived risk, and prostate cancer screening among African American men. *Cancer Epidemiology, Biomarkers & Prevention, 15*(11), 2167–2173.

Blot, W. J., & Fraumeni, J. F. (1992). Lung and pleura. In D. Schottenfeld & J. F. Fraumeni (Eds.), *Cancer epidemiology and prevention* (2nd ed., pp. 564–582). Philadelphia, PA: W. B. Saunders.

Bobak, M., & Marmot, M. G. (1996). East-west mortality divide and its potential explanations: Proposed research agenda. *British Medical Journal, 312,* 421–425.

Bocknek, E. R., Brophy-Herb, H. E., & Banerjee, M. (2009). Effects of parental supportiveness on toddlers' emotion regulation over the first three years of life in a low-income African American sample. *Infant Mental Health Journal, 30*(5), 452–476.

Boden, B., & Jarvis, C. (2009). Spinal injuries in sports. *Physical Medicine and Rehabilitation Clinics of North America, 20*(1), 55–68.

Boehm, S., Selves, E. J., Raleigh, E., Ronis, D., Butler, P. M., & Jacobs, M. (1993). College students' perception of vulnerability/susceptibility and desire for health information. *Patient Education and Counseling, 21*(1–2), 77–87.

Boehmer, U. (2002). Twenty years of public health research: Inclusion of lesbian, gay, bisexual, and transgender populations. *American Journal of Public Health, 92*(7), 1125–1130.

Bohan, J. S. (1993). Regarding gender: Essentialism, constructionism, and feminist psychology. *Psychology of Women Quarterly, 17,* 5–21.

Bolen, J. R., Kresnow, M., & Sacks, J. J. (1998). Reported bicycle helmet use among adults in the United States. *Archives of Family Medicine, 7*(1), 72–77.

Boman, E. K., & Walker, G. A. (2010). Barriers to men's health care utilization: The role of masculine norms and general self-efficacy. *Psychology of Men & Masculinity, 11*(2), 113–122.

Bonomo, Y., Coffey, C., Wolfe, R., Lynskey, M., Bowes, G., & Patton, G. (2001). Adverse outcomes of alcohol use in adolescents. *Addiction, 96*(10), 1485–1496.

Boor, M. (1980). Relationships between unemployment rates and suicide rates in eight countries, 1962–1976. *Psychological Reports, 47,* 1095–1101.

Booth-Kewley, S., & Friedman, H. S. (1987). Psychological predictors of heart disease: A quantitative review. *Psychological Bulletin, 101*(3), 343–362.

Borges, G., Walters, E., & Kessler, R. C. (2000). Associations of substance use, abuse, and dependence with subsequent suicidal behavior. *American Journal of Epidemiology, 151*(8), 781–789.

Borowsky, I. W., & Ireland, M. (2004). Predictors of future fight-related injury among adolescents. *Pediatrics, 113*(3), 530–536.

Borowsky, S. J., Rubenstein, L. V., Meredith, L. S., Camp, P., Jackson-Triche, M., & Wells, K. B. (2000). Who is at risk of nondetection of mental health problems in primary care? *Journal of General Internal Medicine, 15*(6), 381–388.

Bostick, R. M., Sprafka, J. M., Virnig, B. A., & Potter, J. D. (1993). Knowledge, attitudes, and personal practices regarding prevention and early detection of cancer. *Preventive Medicine, 22,* 65–85.

Boston Women's Health Book Collective. (1973). *Our bodies, ourselves.* New York, NY: Simon and Schuster.

Bottorff, J. L., Oliffe, J., Kalaw, C., Carey, J., & Mroz, L. (2006). Men's constructions of smoking in the context of women's tobacco reduction during pregnancy and postpartum. *Social Science & Medicine, 62*(12), 3096–3108.

Bouchard, C., Shephard, R. J., Stephens, T., Sutton, J. R., & McPherson, B. D. (Eds.). (1990). *Exercise, fitness, and health: A consensus of current knowledge.* Champaign, IL: Human Kinetics Books.

Boulding, K. E. (1990). *Three faces of power.* Newbury Park, CA: Sage.

Boulware, E. L., Cooper, L. A., Ratner, L. E., LaVeist, T. A., & Powe, N. R. (2003). Race and trust in the health care system. *Public Health Reports, 118,* 358–365.

Bovbjerg, V. E., McCann, B. S., Brief, D. J., Follette, W. C., Retzlaff, B. M., Dowdy, A. A., … Knopp, R. H. (1995). Spouse support and long-term adherence to lipid-lowering diets. *American Journal of Epidemiology, 141*(5), 451–460.

Brady, M. S., Oliveria, S. A., Christos, P. J., Berwick, M., Coit, D. G., Katz, J., & Halpern, A. C. (2000). Patterns of detection in patients with cutaneous melanoma. *Cancer, 89*(2), 342–347.

Bramley, D., Hebert, P., Jackson, R., & Chassin, M. (2004). Indigenous disparities in disease-specific mortality, a cross-country comparison: New Zealand, Australia, Canada, and the United States. *Journal of the New Zealand Medical Association, 117*(1207), 1215–1231.

Brannon, R., & David, D. (1976). The male sex role: Our culture's blueprint for manhood, and what it's done for us lately. In D. David & R. Brannon (Eds.), *The forty-nine percent majority: The male sex role* (pp. 1–48). Reading, MA: Addison-Wesley.

Brannon, R., & Juni, S. (1984). A scale for measuring attitudes toward masculinity. *JSAS Catalog of Selected Documents in Psychology, 14*(6), Ms. 2012.

Brehm, J. W. (1966). *A theory of psychological reactance.* Oxford, England: Academic Press.

Breier-Williford, S., & Bramlett, R. K. (1995). Time perspective of substance abuse patients: Comparison of the scales in Stanford Perspective Inventory, Beck Depression Inventory, and Beck Hopelessness Scale. *Psychological Reports, 77*(3), 899–905.

Brende, J. O., & Parson, E. R. (1985). *Vietnam veterans: The road to recovery.* New York, NY: Plenum Press.

Brener, N. D., & Collins, A. (1998). Co-occurrence of health-risk behaviors among adolescents in the United States. *Journal of Adolescent Health, 22*(3), 209–213.

Breslin, F. C., Koehoorn, M., Smith, P., & Manno, M. (2003). Age-related differences in work injuries and permanent impairment: A comparison of workers' compensation claims among adolescents, young adults, and adults. *Occupational and Environmental Medicine, 60*(9), 10e–16e.

Breslin, F. C., Smith, P., & Dunn, J. R. (2007). An ecological study of regional variation in work injuries among young workers. *BMC Public Health, 7*(91), 1–12.

Breslow, L., & Enstrom, J. E. (1980). Persistence of health habits and their relationship to mortality. *Preventive Medicine, 9,* 469–483.

Brewer, R. D., & Swahn, M. H. (2005). Binge drinking and violence. *Journal of the American Medical Association, 294*(5), 616–618.

Briefel, R. R., & Johnson, C. L. (2004). Secular trends in dietary intake in the United States. *Annual Review of Nutrition, 24,* 401–431.

Broadhead, W. E., Kaplan, B. H., James, S. A., Wagner, E. H., Schoenbach, V. J., Grimson, R., ... Gehlbach, S. H. (1983). The epidemiologic evidence for a relationship between social support and health. *American Journal of Epidemiology, 117*(5), 521–537.

Broadwell, S. D., & Light, K. C. (1999). Family support and cardiovascular responses in married couples during conflict and other interactions. *International Journal of Behavioral Medicine, 6,* 40–63.

Brody, L. R. (1999). *Gender, emotion, and the family.* Cambridge, MA: Harvard University Press.

Brooks, D. R., & Davis, L. K. (1996). Work-related injuries to Massachusetts teens, 1987–1990. *American Journal of Industrial Medicine, 29*(2), 153–160.

Brooks, G. R. (1998). *A new psychotherapy for traditional men.* San Francisco, CA: Jossey-Bass.

Broom, A. & Tovey, P. (Eds.). (2009). *Men's health: Body, identity and social context.* London, England: Wiley-Blackwell.

Brophy-Herb, H. E., Horodynski, M., Dupuis, S. B., Bocknek, E. L., Schiffman, R., Onaga, E., ... Thomas, S. (2009). Early emotional development in infants and toddlers: Perspectives of early Head Start staff and parents. *Infant Mental Health Journal, 30*(3), 203–222.

Brower, K. J. (1998). Anabolic steroids. *Psychiatric Clinics of North America, 16*(1), 97–103.

Brown, I. D. (1994). Driver fatigue. *Human Factors, 36*(2), 298–314.

Brown, J. S., & McCreedy, M. (1986). The hale elderly: Health behavior and its correlates. *Research in Nursing and Health, 9,* 317–329.

Brown, S. (2001). What makes men talk about health? *Journal of Gender Studies, 10*(2), 187–195.

Brown, S. A., & Tapert, S. F. (2004). Adolescence and the trajectory of alcohol use: Basic to clinical studies. *Annals of the New York Academy of Sciences, 1021,* 234–244.

Brown, S. A., Tapert, S. F., Granholm, E., & Delis, D. C. (2000). Neurocognitive functioning of adolescents: Effects of protracted alcohol use. *Alcoholism: Clinical and Experimental Research, 24*(2), 164–171.

Brown, S. L., & Cotton, A. (2003). Risk-mitigating beliefs, risk estimates, and self-reported speeding in a sample of Australian drivers. *Journal of Safety Research, 34*(2), 183–188.

Brownlee, K., Devins, G. M., Flanigan, M., Fleming, J. A. E., Morehouse, R., Moscovitch, A., … Shapiro, C. M. (2003). Are there gender differences in the prescribing of hypnotic medications for insomnia? *Human Psychopharmacology: Clinical and Experimental, 18*(1), 69–73.

Brownson, R. C., Boehmer, T. K., & Luke, D. A. (2004). Declining rates of physical activity in the United States: What are the contributors? *Annual Review of Public Health, 26*(1), 421–443.

Brubaker, R. G., & Wickersham, D. (1990). Encouraging the practice of testicular self-examination: An application of the theory of reasoned action. *Health Psychology, 9*(2), 154–163.

Bruns, J., & Hauser, W. A. (2003). The epidemiology of traumatic brain injury: A review. *Epilepsia, 44*(Suppl. 10), 2–10.

Buhrke, R. A., & Fuqua, D. R. (1987). Sex differences in same and cross-sex supportive relationships. *Sex Roles, 17*(5/6), 339–352.

Bunton, R., Crawshaw, P. & Green, E. E. (2004). Risk, gender and youthful bodies. In E. E. Green, W. A. Mitchell, & R. Bunton (Eds.), *Youth risk and leisure: Constructing identities in everyday life* (pp. 161–179). New York, NY: Palgrave Macmillan.

Burbach, A. D. (2003). Parenting among fathers of young children [Doctoral dissertation]. *Dissertation Abstracts International: Section B: Sciences and Engineering, 63*(7-B), 3512.

Burda, P. C., & Vaux, A. C. (1987). The social support process in men: Overcoming sex-role obstacles. *Human Relations, 40*, 31–44.

Burda, P. C., Vaux, A. C., & Schill, T. (1984). Social support resources: Variation across sex and sex role. *Personality and Social Psychology Bulletin, 10*, 119–126.

Bureau of Justice Statistics. (2005). *Special report: Suicide and homicide in state prisons and local jails (NCJ 210036)*. Washington, DC: Author.

Bureau of Labor Statistics. (1991). *Employment and earnings: January, 1991.* Washington, DC: Author.

Bureau of Labor Statistics. (1993). *National census of fatal occupational injuries, 1993.* [Brochure]. Washington, DC: Author.

Bureau of Labor Statistics. (2008). *Census of fatal occupational injuries charts, 2008: Fatal injury events by gender of worker.* Washington, DC: Author.

Bureau of Labor Statistics. (2010). *Labor force statistics from the Current Population Survey. Table 9: Employed persons by occupation, sex, and age.* Washington, DC: Author.

Burk, L. R., Burkhart, B. R., & Sikorski, J. F. (2004). Construction and preliminary validation of the Auburn Differential Masculinity Inventory. *Psychology of Men and Masculinity, 5*, 4–17.

Burns, D., Hoffman, D., Cummings, K. M., & Amacher, R. H. (Eds.). (1998). *Cigars: Health effects and trends* (Monograph No. 9, NIH Publication No. 98-4302). Bethesda, MD: National Institutes of Health.

Burt, C. W. (1995). Injury-related visits to hospital emergency departments: United States, 1992. *Advance Data from the Vital and Health Statistics, 261*, 1–20. DHHS Publication No. [PHS] 95-1250 5-0411. Hyattsville, MD: Department of Health and Human Services.

Burt, V. L., Whelton, P. Roccella, E. J., Brown, C., Cutler, J. A., Higgins, M., … Labarthe, D. (1995). Prevalence of hypertension in the U.S. adult population: Results from the third National Health and Nutrition Examination Survey, 1988–1991. *Hypertension, 25*, 305–313.

Bushman, B. J., & Anderson, C.A. (2001). Media violence and the American public: Scientific facts versus media misinformation. *American Psychologist, 56*, 477–489.

Butcher, K., Sallis, J. F., Mayer, J. A., & Woodruff, S. (2008). Correlates of physical activity guideline compliance for adolescents in 100 U.S. cities. *Journal of Adolescent Health, 42*(4), 360–368.

Butler, J. (1993). *Bodies that matter: On the discursive limits of "sex."* New York, NY: Routledge.

Butler, J. (1999). *Gender trouble: Feminism and the subversion of identity.* New York, NY: Routledge.

Byers, T., Mullis, R., Anderson, J., Dusenbury, L., Gorsky, R., Kimber, C., … Smith, C. A. (1995). The costs and effects of a nutritional education program following work-site cholesterol screening. *American Journal of Public Health, 85*(5), 650–655.

Byers, T., Nestle, M., McTiernan, A., Doyle, C., Currie-Williams, A., Gansler, T., … The American Cancer Society 2001 Nutrition and Physical Activity Guidelines Advisory Committee. (2002). American Cancer Society guidelines on nutrition and physical activity for cancer prevention: Reducing the risk of cancer with healthy food choices and physical activity. *CA Cancer Journal for Clinicians, 52*(2), 92–119.

Byrd-Bredbenner, C., Finckenor, M., & Grasso, D. (2003). Health related content in prime-time television programming. *Journal of Health Communication, 88*(4), 329–341.

Byrnes, J. P. (1999). Gender differences in risk taking: A meta-analysis. *Psychological Bulletin, 125*, 367–383.

Caceres, C. F. (1996). Male bisexuality in Peru and the prevention of AIDS. In P. Aggelton (Ed.), *Bisexualities and AIDS: International perspectives* (pp. 136–147). London, England: Taylor & Francis.

Caceres, C. F., & Rosasco, A. M. (1999). The margin has many sides: Diversity among gay and homosexually active men in Lima. *Culture, Health & Sexuality, 1*(3), 261–275.

Cafferata, G. L., Kasper, J., & Berstein, A. (1983). Family roles, structure, and stressors in relation to sex differences in obtaining psychotropic drugs. *Journal of Health and Social Behavior, 24*, 132–143.

Cafferata, G. L., & Meyers, S. M. (1990). Pathways to psychotropic drugs: Understanding the basis of gender differences. *Medical Care, 28*(4), 285–300.

California Highway Patrol. (1994). *1993 annual report of fatal and injury motor vehicle traffic accidents.* Sacramento, CA: Author.

California Highway Patrol. (1995). *Pedestrians killed and injured report: Collision dates January, 1994 through December, 1994 (Statewide Integrated Traffic Records System).* Sacramento, CA: Author.

California Postsecondary Education Commission. (n.d.a). *Total enrollment by segment by student level by ethnicity (undergraduates/graduates).* Retrieved from http://www.cpec.ca.gov/StudentData/StudentSnapshot.ASP?Data Report=2

California Postsecondary Education Commission. (n.d.b). *Total enroll-ment by segment by student level by gender (undergraduates/graduates)*. Retrieved from http://www.cpec.ca.gov/StudentData/StudentSnapshot. ASP?DataReport=2

Callahan, E. J., Bertakis, K. D., Azari, R., Helms, L. J., Robbins, J., & Miller, J. (1997). Depression in primary care: patient factors that influence recogni-tion. *Family Medicine, 29*(3), 172–176.

Calle, E. E., Rodriguez, C., Walker-Thurmond, K., & Thun, M. J. (2003). Overweight, obesity, and mortality from cancer in a prospectively studied cohort of U.S. adults. *New England Journal of Medicine, 348*(17), 1625–1638.

Camacho, T. C., Kaplan, G. A., & Cohen, R. D. (1987). Alcohol consumption mortality in Alameda County. *Journal of Chronic Disease, 40*, 229–236.

Camacho, T. C., & Wiley, J. (1983). Health practices, social networks, and changes in physical health. In L. F. Berkman & L. Breslow (Eds.), *Health and ways of living* (pp. 176–209). New York, NY: Oxford University Press.

Campbell, A., & Muncer, S. (2008). Intent to harm or injure? Gender and the expression of anger. *Aggressive Behavior, 34*(3), 282–293.

Campbell, H., & Bell, M. M. (2000). The question of rural masculinities. *Rural Sociology, 65*(4): 532–546.

Canaan, J. E. (1996). One thing leads to another: Drinking, fighting and working class masculinities. In M. Mac An Ghaill (Ed.), *Understanding masculinities: Social relations and cultural arenas* (pp. 114–125). Buckingham, England: Open University Press.

Canto, J. G., Allison, J. J., Kiefe, C. I., Fincher, C., Farmer, R., Sekar, P., … Weissman, N. W. (2000). Relation of race and sex to the use of reperfusion therapy in Medicare beneficiaries with acute myocardial infarction. *New England Journal of Medicine, 342*(15), 1094–1100.

Cappell, H., & Greeley, J. (1987). Alcohol and tension reduction: An update on research and theory. In H. T. Blane & K. Leonard (Eds.), *Psychological theories of drinking and alcoholism* (pp. 15–54). New York, NY: Guilford Press.

Cappuccio, F. P., & MacGregor, G. A. (1997). Dietary salt restriction: Benefits for cardiovascular disease and beyond. *Current Opinion in Nephrology and Hypertension, 6*(5), 477–482.

Capraro, R. L. (2000). Why college men drink: Alcohol, adventure and the para-dox of masculinity. *Journal of American College Health, 48*(6), 307–315.

Carli, L. L. (1997). Biology does not create gender differences in personality. In M. R. Walsh (Ed.), *Women, men, and gender* (pp. 44–53). New Haven, CT: Yale University Press.

Carlson, S. A., Densmore, D., Fulton, J. E., Yore, M. M., & Kohl, H. W. (2009). Differences in physical activity prevalence and trends from 3 U.S. surveil-lance systems: NHIS, NHANES, and BRFSS. *Journal of Physical Activity & Health, 6*(Suppl. 1), S18–S27.

Carlsson, S., Andersson, T., Lichtenstein, P., Michaelsson, K., & Ahlbom, A. (2007). Physical activity and mortality: Is the association explained by genetic selection? *American Journal of Epidemiology, 166*(3), 255–259.

Carmel, S. (1990). The health belief model in the research of AIDS related pre-ventive behavior. *Public Health Review, 18*, 73–85.

Carmont, M. R. (2008). Mountain biking injuries: A review. *British Medical Bulletin, 85*(1), 101–112.

Carroll, L. (1991). Gender, knowledge about AIDS, reported behavioral change, and the sexual behavior of college students. *Journal of American College Health, 40*(1), 5–12.

Carroll, M. D., Lacher, D. A., Sorlie, P. D., Cleeman, J. I., Gordon, D. J., Wolz, M., … Johnson, C. L. (2005). Trends in serum lipids and lipoproteins of adults, 1960–2002. *Journal of the American Medical Association, 294*(14), 1773–1781.

Carter, B. D., & McCloskey, L. A. (1984). Peers and the maintenance of sex-typed behavior: The development of children's conceptions of cross-gender behavior in their peers. *Social Cognition, 2*(4), 294–314.

Carter, C. A., & Kahnweiler, W. M. (2000). The efficacy of the social norms approach to substance abuse prevention applied to fraternity men. *Journal of American College Health, 49*(2), 66–70.

Carton, S., Jouvent, R., & Widlocher, D. (1992). Cross cultural validity of the sensation seeking scale: Development of a French abbreviated form. *European Psychiatry, 7*(5), 225–234.

Carver, C. S. (2007). Stress, coping, and health. In H. S. Friedman & R. C. Silver (Eds.), *Foundations of health psychology* (pp. 117–144). New York, NY: Oxford University Press.

Casey, R. J. (1993). Children's emotional experience: Relations among expression, self-report, and understanding. *Developmental Psychology, 29*(1), 119–129.

Caspersen, C., & Merritt, R. K. (1995). Physical activity trends among 26 states, 1986–1990. *Medicine and Science in Sports and Exercise, 27*(5), 713–720.

Cassano, M., Perry-Parrish, C., & Zeman, J. (2007). Influence of gender on parental socialization of children's sadness regulation. *Social Development, 16*(2), 210–231.

Catalano, R., Dooley, D., & Jackson, R. L. (1981). Economic predictors of admissions to mental health facilities in a nonmetropolitan community. *Journal of Health and Social Behavior, 22*, 284–297.

Celentano, D. D., Linet, M. S., & Stewart, W. F. (1990). Gender differences in the experience of headache. *Social Science and Medicine, 30*(12), 1289–1295.

Center for Nutrition Policy and Promotion. (2000). *Consumption of food group servings: People's perceptions vs. reality. Nutrition insights* (Insight 20). Washington, DC: United States Department of Agriculture.

Centers for Disease Control and Prevention. (1992a). Behaviors related to unintentional and intentional injuries among high school students—United States, 1991. *Morbidity and Mortality Weekly Report, 41*(41), 760–772.

Centers for Disease Control and Prevention. (1992b). Cigarette smoking among Southeast Asian immigrants—Washington State, 1989. *Morbidity and Mortality Weekly Report, 41*(45), 854–855.

Centers for Disease Control and Prevention. (1992c). Physical fighting among high school students—United States, 1990. *Morbidity and Mortality Weekly Report, 41*(6), 91–94.

Centers for Disease Control and Prevention. (1992d). Safety-belt and helmet use among high school students—United States, 1990. *Morbidity and Mortality Weekly Report, 41*(7), 111–114.

Centers for Disease Control and Prevention. (1992e). Selected behaviors that increase risk for HIV infection, other sexually transmitted diseases, and unintended pregnancy among high school students—United States, 1991. *Morbidity and Mortality Weekly Report, 41*(50), 945–950.

Centers for Disease Control and Prevention. (1992f). Sexual behavior among high school students—United States, 1990. *Morbidity and Mortality Weekly Report, 40*(51/52), 885–888.

Centers for Disease Control and Prevention. (1992g). Tuberculosis transmission in a state correctional institution—California, 1990–1991. *Morbidity and Mortality Weekly Report, 41*, 927–929.

Centers for Disease Control and Prevention. (1992h). Vigorous physical activity among high school students—United States, 1990. *Morbidity and Mortality Weekly Report, 41*(3), 33–35.

Centers for Disease Control and Prevention. (1993a). Alcohol use and aquatic activities—United States, 1991. *Morbidity and Mortality Weekly Report, 42*(36), 675–676, 681–682.

Centers for Disease Control and Prevention. (1993b). Office visits to cardiovascular disease specialists—United States, 1989–90. *Advance Data, 226*(March 4).

Centers for Disease Control and Prevention. (1993c). Public health focus: Impact of safety-belt use on motor-vehicle injuries and costs—Iowa, 1987–1988. *Morbidity and Mortality Weekly Report, 42*(36), 704–706.

Centers for Disease Control and Prevention. (1993d). Use of smokeless tobacco among adults—United States, 1991. *Morbidity and Mortality Weekly Report, 42*(14), 263–266.

Centers for Disease Control and Prevention. (1994a). Adults taking action to control their blood pressure—United States, 1990. *Morbidity and Mortality Weekly Report, 43*(28), 509–511, 517–518.

Centers for Disease Control and Prevention. (1994b). Deaths resulting from firearm- and motor-vehicle-related injuries—United States, 1968–1991. *Morbidity and Mortality Weekly Report, 43*(3), 38–42.

Centers for Disease Control and Prevention. (1994c). Drivers with repeat convictions or arrests for driving while impaired—United States. *Morbidity and Mortality Weekly Report, 43*(4), 759–762.

Centers for Disease Control and Prevention. (1994d). Firearm-related years of potential life lost before age 65 years—United States, 1980–1991. *Morbidity and Mortality Weekly Report, 43*(33), 609–611.

Centers for Disease Control and Prevention. (1994e). Homicides among 15–19-year-old-males—United States, 1963–1991. *Morbidity and Mortality Weekly Report, 43*(40), 725–727.

Centers for Disease Control and Prevention. (1994f). Motor-vehicle-related deaths involving intoxicated pedestrians—United States, 1982–1992. *Morbidity and Mortality Weekly Report, 43*(14), 249–253.

Centers for Disease Control and Prevention. (1994g). Risky driving behaviors among teenagers—Gwinnett County, Georgia, 1993. *Morbidity and Mortality Weekly Report, 43*(22), 405–409.

Centers for Disease Control and Prevention. (1994h). Surveillance for smoking-attributable mortality and years of potential life lost, by state—United States, 1990. *Morbidity and Mortality Weekly Report, 43*(SS–1), 1–3, 6–7.

Centers for Disease Control and Prevention. (1994i). Update: Alcohol-related traffic fatalities—United States, 1982–1993. *Morbidity and Mortality Weekly Report, 43*(47), 861–863.

Centers for Disease Control and Prevention. (1995a). Deaths from melanoma—United States, 1973–1992. *Morbidity and Mortality Weekly Report, 44*(44), 337, 343–347.

Centers for Disease Control and Prevention. (1995b). *Hepatitis surveillance* (Report No. 56). Atlanta, GA: Author.

Centers for Disease Control and Prevention. (1995c). Injury-control recommendations: Bicycle helmets. *Morbidity and Mortality Weekly Report, 44*(RR-1), 1–11.

Centers for Disease Control and Prevention. (1995d). *Skin cancer prevention and early detection: At-a-glance.* Atlanta, GA: Author.

Centers for Disease Control and Prevention. (1995e). Youth risk behavior surveillance—United States, 1993. *Morbidity and Mortality Weekly Report, 44*(SS-1), 1–56.

Centers for Disease Control and Prevention. (1996). Prevalence of physical inactivity during leisure time among overweight persons—Behavioral Risk Factor Surveillance System, 1994. *Morbidity and Mortality Weekly Report, 45*(9), 185–188.

Centers for Disease Control and Prevention. (1997a). Demographic differences in notifiable infectious disease morbidity—United States, 1992–1994. *Morbidity and Mortality Weekly Report, 46*(28), 637–641.

Centers for Disease Control and Prevention. (1997b). Smoking attributable mortality and years of potential life lost—United States, 1984. *Morbidity and Mortality Weekly Report, 46*(20), 445–451.

Centers for Disease Control and Prevention. (1997c). Youth risk behavior surveillance: National College Health Risk Behavior Survey—United States, 1995. *Morbidity and Mortality Weekly Report, 46*(SS-6), 1–54.

Centers for Disease Control and Prevention. (1998a). Demographic characteristics of persons without a regular source of medical care—Selected states, 1995. *Morbidity and Mortality Weekly Report, 47*(14), 277–279.

Centers for Disease Control and Prevention. (1998b). Fatal occupational injuries—United States, 1980-1994. *Morbidity and Mortality Weekly Report, 47*(15), 297–302.

Centers for Disease Control and Prevention. (1998c). Selected cigarette smoking initiation and quitting behaviors among high school students—United States, 1997. *Morbidity and Mortality Weekly Report, 47*(19), 386–389.

Centers for Disease Control and Prevention. (1998d). State-specific prevalence among adults of current cigarette smoking and smokeless tobacco use and per capita tax-paid sales of cigarettes —United States, 1997. *Morbidity and Mortality Weekly Report, 47*(43), 922–926.

Centers for Disease Control and Prevention. (1998e). Tobacco use among high school students—United States, 1997. *Morbidity and Mortality Weekly Report, 47*(12), 229–233.

Centers for Disease Control and Prevention. (1998f). *Unintentional injury prevention fact sheet: Bicycle-related head injury.* Atlanta, GA: National Center for Injury Prevention and Control.

Centers for Disease Control and Prevention. (1998g). Youth risk behavior surveillance—United States, 1997. *Morbidity and Mortality Weekly Report, 47*(SS 3), 1–87.

Centers for Disease Control and Prevention. (1999). Surveillance for use of preventive health-care services by older adults, 1995–1997. *Morbidity and Mortality Weekly Report, 48*(SS08), 51–88.

Centers for Disease Control and Prevention. (2000a). Tobacco use among middle and high school students—United States, 1999. *Morbidity and Mortality Weekly Report, 49*(3), 49–53.

Centers for Disease Control and Prevention. (2000b). *Tracking the hidden epidemics: Trends in STDs in the United, 2000.* Atlanta, GA: Author.

Centers for Disease Control and Prevention. (2001). Fatal occupational injuries—United States, 1980–1997. *Morbidity and Mortality Weekly Report, 50*(16), 317–320.

Centers for Disease Control and Prevention. (2002a). Cigarette smoking among adults—United States, 2000. *Morbidity and Mortality Weekly Report, 51*(29), 642–645.

Centers for Disease Control and Prevention. (2002b). Non-fatal sports- and recreation-related injuries treated in emergency departments—United States, July 2000–June 2001. *Morbidity and Mortality Weekly Report, 51*(33), 736–740.

Centers for Disease Control and Prevention. (2003a). Physical activity levels among children aged 9–13 years—United States, 2002. *Morbidity and Mortality Weekly Report, 52*(33), 785–788.

Centers for Disease Control and Prevention. (2003b). Preventing skin cancer: Findings of the Task Force on Community Preventive Services on Reducing Exposure to Ultraviolet Light. *Morbidity and Mortality Weekly Report, 52*(RR15), 1–12.

Centers for Disease Control and Prevention. (2003c). State-specific prevalence of selected chronic disease-related characteristics—Behavioral Risk Factor Surveillance System, 2001. *Morbidity and Mortality Weekly Report, 52*(SS08), 1–80.

Centers for Disease Control and Prevention. (2003d). Traumatic brain injury-related hospital discharges: Results from a 14-state surveillance system, 1997. *Morbidity and Mortality Weekly Report, 52*(SS04), 1–18.

Centers for Disease Control and Prevention. (2004a). Access to health-care and preventive services among Hispanics and non-Hispanics—United States, 2001–2002. *Morbidity and Mortality Weekly Report, 53*(40), 937–941.

Centers for Disease Control and Prevention. (2004b). Alcohol-attributable deaths and years of potential life lost—United States, 2001. *Morbidity and Mortality Weekly Report, 53*(37), 866–870.

Centers for Disease Control and Prevention. (2004c). Declining prevalence of no known major risk factors for heart disease and stroke among adults: United States, 1991–2001. *Morbidity and Mortality Weekly Report, 53*(1), 4–7.

Centers for Disease Control and Prevention. (2004d). Diagnosis and management of foodborne illnesses. *Morbidity and Mortality Weekly Report, 53*(RR04), 1–33.

Centers for Disease Control and Prevention. (2004e). Surveillance for fatal and nonfatal injuries—United States, 2001–2002. *Morbidity and Mortality Weekly Report, 53*(SS07), 1–57.

Centers for Disease Control and Prevention. (2005a). Notice to readers: "You Drink & Drive. You Lose" Program, August 19–September 5, 2005. *Morbidity and Mortality Weekly Report, 54*(32), 801.

Centers for Disease Control and Prevention. (2005b). QuickStats: Percentage of adults aged >18 years who used complementary and alternative medicine (CAM) during the preceding 12 months, by sex—United States, 2002. *Morbidity and Mortality Weekly Report, 54*(11), 283.

Centers for Disease Control and Prevention. (2005c). Racial/ethnic disparities in prevalence, treatment, and control of hypertension—United States, 1999-2002. *Morbidity and Mortality Weekly Report, 54*(01), 7–9.

Centers for Disease Control and Prevention. (2005d). State-specific trends in self-reported blood pressure screening and high blood pressure—United States, 1991-1999. *Morbidity and Mortality Weekly Report, 51*(21), 456–460.

Centers for Disease Control and Prevention. (2005e). The role of public health in mental health promotion. *Morbidity and Mortality Weekly Report, 54*(34), 841–842.

Centers for Disease Control and Prevention. (2005f). Trends in cholesterol screening and awareness of high blood cholesterol—United States, 1991–2003. *Morbidity and Mortality Weekly Report, 54*(35), 865–870.

Centers for Disease Control and Prevention. (2006a). *Deaths, percent of total deaths, and death rates for the 15 leading causes of death in 10-year age groups, by race and sex: United States, 2003* (National Vital Statistics System). Hyattsville, MD: National Center for Health Statistics.

Centers for Disease Control and Prevention. (2006b). *Final FoodNet surveillance report*. Atlanta, GA: Author.

Centers for Disease Control and Prevention. (2006c). Revised recommendations for HIV testing of adults, adolescents, and pregnant women in health-care settings. *Morbidity and Mortality Weekly Report, 55*(RR14), 1–17.

Centers for Disease Control and Prevention. (2006d). Sports-related injuries among high school athletes—United States, 2005–2006 school year. *Morbidity and Mortality Weekly Report, 55*(38), 1037–1040.

Centers for Disease Control and Prevention. (2006e). *Traumatic brain injury in the United States: Emergency department visits, hospitalizations, and deaths.* Atlanta, GA: Department of Health and Human Services.

Centers for Disease Control and Prevention. (2006f). Trends in strength training—United States, 1998–2004. *Morbidity and Mortality Weekly Report, 55*(28), 769–772.

Centers for Disease Control and Prevention. (2007a). Erratum: Vol. 56, no. 10. *Morbidity and Mortality Weekly Report, 56*(12), 282.

Centers for Disease Control and Prevention. (2007b). Fatal occupational injuries—United States, 2005. *Morbidity and Mortality Weekly Report, 56*(13), 297–301.

Centers for Disease Control and Prevention. (2007c). Fruit and vegetable consumption among adults—United States, 2005. *Morbidity and Mortality Weekly Report, 56*(10), 213–217.

Centers for Disease Control and Prevention. (2007d). Nonfatal traumatic brain injuries from sports and recreation activities—United States, 2001–2005. *Morbidity and Mortality Weekly Report, 56*(29), 733–737.

Centers for Disease Control and Prevention. (2007e). Prevalence of actions to control high blood pressure—20 states, 2005. *Morbidity and Mortality Weekly Report, 56*(17), 420–423.

Centers for Disease Control and Prevention. (2007f). Prevalence of self-reported cardiovascular disease among persons aged >35 years with diabetes—United States, 1997–2005. *Morbidity and Mortality Weekly Report, 56*(43), 1129–1132.

Centers for Disease Control and Prevention. (2007g). Suicide trends among youths and young adults aged 10–24 years—United States, 1990–2004. *Morbidity and Mortality Weekly Report, 56*(35), 905–908.

Centers for Disease Control and Prevention. (2007h). Sunburn prevalence among adults—United States, 1999, 2003, and 2004. *Morbidity and Mortality Weekly Report, 56*(21), 524–528.

Centers for Disease Control and Prevention. (2008a). Awareness of stroke warning symptoms—13 states and the District of Columbia, 2005. *Morbidity and Mortality Weekly Report, 57*(18), 481–485.

Centers for Disease Control and Prevention. (2008b). *Health risk behaviors by sex: National YRBS, 2007.* Atlanta, GA: Author.

Centers for Disease Control and Prevention. (2008c). *National diabetes fact sheet: General information and national estimates on diabetes in the United States, 2007.* Atlanta, GA: U.S. Department of Health and Human Services.

Centers for Disease Control and Prevention. (2008d). Persons tested for HIV—United States, 2006. *Morbidity and Mortality Weekly Report, 57*(31), 845–849.

Centers for Disease Control and Prevention. (2008e). Prevalence of regular physical activity among adults—United States, 2001 and 2005. *Journal of the American Medical Association, 299*(1), 30–32.

Centers for Disease Control and Prevention. (2008f). Prevalence of self-reported physically active adults—United States, 2007. *Morbidity and Mortality Weekly Report, 57*(48), 1297–1300.

Centers for Disease Control and Prevention. (2008g). QuickStats: Percentage of adults aged >18 years who reported an average of <6 hours of sleep per 24-hour period, by sex and age group—National Health Interview Survey, United States, 1985 and 2006. *Morbidity and Mortality Weekly Report, 57*(08), 209.

Centers for Disease Control and Prevention. (2008h). QuickStats: Percentage of adults aged >65 years who ever received a pneumococcal vaccination, by sex, age group, and race/ethnicity—National Health Interview Survey, United States, 2007. *Morbidity and Mortality Weekly Report, 57*(26), 723.

Centers for Disease Control and Prevention. (2008i). State-specific prevalence of obesity among adults—United States, 2007. *Morbidity and Mortality Weekly Report, 57*(28), 765–768.

Centers for Disease Control and Prevention. (2008j). Trends in HIV- and STD-related risk behaviors among high school students—United States, 1991–2007. *Morbidity and Mortality Weekly Report, 57*(30), 817–822.

Centers for Disease Control and Prevention. (2008k). Use of colorectal cancer tests—United States, 2002, 2004, and 2006. *Morbidity and Mortality Weekly Report, 57*(10), 253–258.

Centers for Disease Control and Prevention. (2008l). Youth Risk Behavior Surveillance—United States, 2007. *Morbidity and Mortality Weekly Report, 57*(SS-4), 1–131.

Centers for Disease Control and Prevention. (2009a). Announcement: Drowsy Driving Prevention Week—November 2–8, 2009. *Morbidity and Mortality Weekly Report, 58*(42), 1184.

Centers for Disease Control and Prevention. (2009b). Application of lower sodium intake recommendations to adults—United States, 1999–2006. *Morbidity and Mortality Weekly Report, 58*(11), 281–283.

Centers for Disease Control and Prevention. (2009c). Cigarette smoking among adults and trends in smoking cessation—United States, 2008. *Morbidity and Mortality Weekly Report, 58*(44), 1227–1232.

Centers for Disease Control and Prevention. (2009d). Differences in prevalence of obesity among Black, White, and Hispanic adults—United States, 2006–2008. *Morbidity and Mortality Weekly Report, 58*(27), 740–744.

Centers for Disease Control and Prevention. (2009e). Estimated county-level prevalence of diabetes and obesity—United States, 2007. *Morbidity and Mortality Weekly Report, 58*(45), 1259–1263.

Centers for Disease Control and Prevention. (2009f). High school students who tried to quit smoking cigarettes—United States, 2007. *Morbidity and Mortality Weekly Report, 58*(16), 428–431.

Centers for Disease Control and Prevention. (2009g). *HIV/AIDS Surveillance Report, 2007* (Vol. 19). Atlanta, GA: Department of Health and Human Services.

Centers for Disease Control and Prevention. (2009h). HIV testing among high school students—United States, 2007. *Morbidity and Mortality Weekly Report, 58*(24), 665–668.

Centers for Disease Control and Prevention. (2009i). Motor vehicle-related death rates—United States, 1999–2005. *Morbidity and Mortality Weekly Report, 58*(7), 162–165.

Centers for Disease Control and Prevention. (2009j). *National Center for HIV/ AIDS, Viral Hepatitis, STD, and TB Prevention: 2007 disease profile.* Atlanta, GA: Author.

Centers for Disease Control and Prevention. (2009k). Prevalence of autism spectrum disorders—Autism and Developmental Disabilities Monitoring Network, United States, 2006. *Morbidity and Mortality Weekly Report, 58*(SS-10), 1–20.

Centers for Disease Control and Prevention. (2009l). QuickStats percentage of adults aged >18 years who had ever been tested for Human Immunodeficiency Virus (HIV), by age group and sex—National Health Interview Survey, United States, 2007. *Morbidity and Mortality Weekly Report, 58*(03), 62.

Centers for Disease Control and Prevention. (2009m). Sexual and reproductive health of persons aged 10–24 Years—United States, 2002–2007. *Morbidity and Mortality Weekly Report, 58*(SS06), 1–58.

Centers for Disease Control and Prevention. (2009n). Sociodemographic differences in binge drinking among adults—14 states, 2004. *Morbidity and Mortality Weekly Report, 58*(12), 301–304.

Centers for Disease Control and Prevention. (2009o). State-specific prevalence and trends in adult cigarette smoking—United States, 1998–2007. *Morbidity and Mortality Weekly Report, 58*(09), 221–226.

Centers for Disease Control and Prevention. (2009p). State-specific smoking-attributable mortality and years of potential life lost—United States, 2000–2004. *Morbidity and Mortality Weekly Report, 58*(02), 29–33.

Centers for Disease Control and Prevention. (2009q). Surveillance for violent deaths—National Violent Death Reporting System, 16 states, 2006. *Morbidity and Mortality Weekly Report, 58*(SS-01), 1–44.

Centers for Disease Control and Prevention. (2010a). Any tobacco use in 13 states—Behavioral Risk Factor Surveillance System, 2008. *Morbidity and Mortality Weekly Report, 59*(30), 946–950.

Centers for Disease Control and Prevention. (2010b). Commercial fishing deaths—United States, 2000–2009. *Morbidity and Mortality Weekly Report, 59*(27), 842–845.

Centers for Disease Control and Prevention. (2010c). Prevalence of abnormal lipid levels among youths—United States, 1999–2006. *Morbidity and Mortality Weekly Report, 59*(02), 29–33.

Centers for Disease Control and Prevention. (2010d). *Web-based Injury Statistics Query and Reporting System (WISQUARS)* [Database]. Retrieved from http://www.cdc.gov/injury/wisqars/nvdrs.html

Centers for Disease Control and Prevention. (2010e). *Web-based Injury Statistics Query and Reporting System (WISQUARS)* [Database]. Retrieved from http://webappa.cdc.gov/sasweb/ncipc/ypll10.html

Cepeda, O. A., & Gammack, J. K. (2006). Cancer in older men: A gender-based review. *The Aging Male, 9*(3), 149–158.

Cerhan, J. R., Torner, J. C., Lynch, C. F., Rubenstein, L. M., Lemke, J. H., Cohen, M. B., … Wallace, R. B. (1997). Association of smoking, body mass, and physical activity with risk of prostate cancer in the Iowa 65+ Rural Health Study (United States). *Cancer Causes and Control, 8*(2), 329–338.

Cervantes, C. A., & Callanan, M. A. (1998). Labels and explanations in mother-child emotion talk: Age and gender differentiation. *Developmental Psychology, 34*(1), 88–98.

Chae, D. H., Gavin, A. R., & Takeuchi, D. T. (2006). Smoking prevalence among Asian Americans: Findings from the National Latino and Asian American Study (NLAAS). *Public Health Reports, 121*(6), 755–763.

Chan, K., Neighbors, C., Gilson, M., Larimer, M. E., & Marlatt, G. A. (2007). Epidemiological trends in drinking by age and gender: Providing normative feedback to adults. *Addictive Behaviors, 32*(5), 967–976.

Chandra, A., & Minkovitz, C. S. (2006). Stigma starts early: Gender differences in teen willingness to use mental health services. *Journal of Adolescent Health, 38*(6), 754e1–754e8.

Chang, V. W., & Christakis, N. A. (2003). Self-perception of weight appropriateness in the United States. *American Journal of Preventive Medicine, 24*(4), 332–339.

Chang-Claude, J., Raedsch, R., Waldherr, R., von Wulffen, H., Crespi, M., Yang, G. R., … Wahrendorf, J. (1995). Prevalence of Helicobacter pylori infection and gastritis among young adults in China. *European Journal of Cancer Prevention, 4*(1), 73–79.

Chao, A., Thun, M. J., Connell, C. J., McCullough, M. L., Jacobs, E. J., Flanders, W. D., … Calle, E. E. (2005). Meat consumption and risk of colorectal cancer. *Journal of the American Medical Association, 293*(2), 172–182.

Chaplin, T. M., Hong, K., Bergquist, K., & Sinha, R. (2008). Gender differences in response to emotional stress: An assessment across subjective, behavioral, and physiological domains and relations to alcohol craving. *Alcoholism: Clinical and Experimental Research, 32*(7), 1242–1250.

Chapple, A., Ziebland, S., & McPherson, A. (2004). Qualitative study of men's perceptions of why treatment delays occur in the U.K. for those with testicular cancer. *British Journal of General Practice, 54*, 25–32.

Charmaz, K. (1995). Identity dilemmas of chronically ill men. In D. Sabo & D. F. Gordon (Eds.), *Men's health and illness: Gender, power and the body* (pp. 266–291). Thousand Oaks, CA: Sage.

Chen, M. S. (1993). Cardiovascular health among Asian Americans/Pacific Islanders: An examination of health status and intervention approaches. *American Journal of Health Promotion, 7*(3), 199–207.

Chen, M. S., & Hawks, B. L. (1995). A debunking of the myth of the healthy Asian American and Pacific Islander. *American Journal of Health Promotion, 9*, 261–268.

Cherpitel, C. J. (2007). Alcohol and injuries: A review of international emergency room studies since 1995. *Drug and Alcohol Review, 26*(2), 201–214.

Chida, Y., & Hamer, M. (2008). Chronic psychosocial factors and acute physiological responses to laboratory-induced stress in healthy populations: A quantitative review of 30 years of investigations. *Psychological Bulletin, 134*(6), 829–885.

Chida, Y., & Steptoe, A. (2009). The association of anger and hostility with future coronary heart disease: Meta-analytic review of prospective evidence. *Journal of the American College of Cardiology, 53*(11), 936–946.

Chino, A. F., & Funabiki, D. (1984). A cross-validation of sex differences in the expression of depression. *Sex Roles, 11*, 175–187.

Chobanian, A. V., Bakris, G. L., Black, H. R., Cushman, W. C., Green, L. A., Izzo, J. L., … the National High Blood Pressure Education Program Coordinating Committee. (2003). Seventh report of the Joint National Committee on Prevention, Detection, Evaluation, and Treatment of High Blood Pressure. *Hypertension, 42*, 1206–1252.

Chobanian, A. V., & Hill, M. (2000). National Heart, Lung, and Blood Institute workshop on sodium and blood pressure. A critical review of current scientific evidence. *Hypertension, 35*, 858–863.

Chou, S. P., Dawson, D. A., Stinson, F. S., Huang, B., Pickering, R. P., Zhou, Y., & Grant, B. F. (2006). The prevalence of drinking and driving in the United States, 2001–2002: Results from the national epidemiological survey on alcohol and related conditions. *Drug and Alcohol Dependence, 83*(2), 137–146.

Chou, S. P., Grant, B. F., Dawson, D. A., Stinson, F. S., Saha, R., & Pickering, R. P. (2005). Twelve-month prevalence and changes in driving after drinking: United States, 1991-1992 and 2001-2002. *Drug and Alcohol Dependence, 80*(2), 223–230.

Chua, P., & Fujino, D. C. (1999). Negotiating new Asian-American masculinities: Attitudes and gender expectations. *Journal of Men's Studies, 7*(3), 391–413.

Chung, L. W., Isaacs, W. B., & Simons, J. W. (2007). *Prostate cancer: Biology, genetics, and the new therapeutics*. Totowa, NJ: Humana Press.

Clark, M. J. (1993). Seat belt use on a university campus. *Journal of American College Health, 41*(4), 169–171.

Clarke, G., & Whittemore, A. S. (2000). Prostate cancer risk in relation to anthropometry and physical activity: The National Health and Nutrition Examination Survey I Epidemiological Follow-Up Study. *Cancer Epidemiology, Biomarkers & Prevention, 9*, 875–881.

Clarke, J. N. (2004). A comparison of breast, testicular and prostate cancer in mass print media (1996–2001). *Social Science & Medicine, 59*, 541–551.

Clatterbaugh, K. (1997). *Contemporary perspectives on masculinity: Men, women, and politics in modern society* (2nd ed.). Boulder, CO: Westview Press.

Cochran, S. D. (2001). Emerging issues in research on lesbians' and gay men's mental health: Does sexual orientation really matter? *American Psychologist, 56*, 932–947.

Cohen, D., Nisbett, R. E., Bowdle, B. F., & Schwarz, N. (1996). Insult, aggression, and the southern culture of honor: An "experimental ethnography." *Journal of Personality & Social Psychology, 70*(5), 945–960.

Cohen, J., Cohen, P., West, S. G., & Aiken, L. S. (2002). *Applied multiple regression/correlation analysis for the behavioral sciences* (3rd ed.). Mahwah, NJ: Lawrence Erlbaum.

Cohen, J., Collins, R., Darkes, J., & Gwartney, D. (2007). A league of their own: Demographics, motivations and patterns of use of 1,955 male adult non-medical anabolic steroid users in the United States. *Journal of the International Society of Sports Nutrition, 4*(12), 1–14.

Cohen, R. Y., Sattler, J., Felix, M. R., & Brownell, K. D. (1987). Experimentation with smokeless tobacco and cigarettes by children and adolescents: Relationship to beliefs, peer use, and parental use. *American Journal of Public Health, 77*(11), 1454–1456.

Cohen, S., Frank, E., Doyle, W. J., Skoner, D. P., Rabin, B. S., & Gwaltney, J. M. (1998). Types of stressors that increase susceptibility to the common cold in healthy adults. *Health Psychology, 17*, 214–223.

Cohen, S., Janicki-Deverts, D., & Miller, G. E. (2007). Psychological stress and disease. *Journal of the American Medical Association, 298*(14), 1685–1687.

Cohn, L. D. (1991). Sex differences in the course of personality development: A meta-analysis. *Psychological Bulletin, 109*(2), 252–266.

Cohn, L. D., Macfarlane, S., Yanez, C., & Imai, W. K. (1995). Risk-perception: Differences between adolescents and adults. *Health Psychology, 14*(3), 217–222.

Colditz, G. A., Branch, L. G., Lipnick, R. J., Willett, W. C., Rosner, B., Posner, B., & Hennekens, C. H. (1985). Moderate alcohol and decreased cardiovascular mortality in an elderly cohort. *American Heart Journal, 109*, 886–889.

Collier, H. V. (1982). *Counseling women: A guide for therapists.* New York, NY: Macmillan.

Collins, K. S., Hall, A., & Neuhaus, C. (1999). *U.S. minority health: A chartbook.* New York, NY: The Commonwealth Fund.

Cominole, M, Siegel, P., Dudley, K., Roe, D., & Gilligan, T. (2004). *2004 National Postsecondary Student Aid Study (NPSAS:04) full-scale methodology report.* Retrieved from http://nces.ed.gov/pubsearch/pubsinfo. asp?pubid=2006180

Commonwealth Fund. (1995). *National comparative survey of minority health care.* New York, NY: Author.

Congressional Research Service. (2009). *United States military casualty statistics: Operation Iraqi Freedom and Operation Enduring Freedom.* Washington, DC: Government Printing Office.

Connell, R. W. (1992). Masculinity, violence, and war. In M. S. Kimmel & M. A. Messner (Eds.), *Men's lives* (2nd ed., pp. 176–183). New York, NY: Macmillan.

Connell, R. W. (1993). The big picture: Masculinities in recent world history. *Theory and Society, 22,* 597–623.

Connell, R. W. (1995). *Masculinities.* Berkeley: University of California Press.

Connell, R. W. (2000). *The men and the boys.* Berkeley: University of California Press.

Connell, R. W., & Messerschmidt, J. W. (2005). Hegemonic masculinity: Rethinking the concept. *Gender and Society, 19*(6), 829–859.

Connolly, G. N., Orleans, C. T., & Blum, A. (1992) Snuffing tobacco out of sport. *American Journal of Public Health, 82,* 351–353.

Consedine, N. S., Morgenstern, A. H., Kudadjie-Gyamfi, E., Magai, C., & Neugut, A. I. (2006). Prostate cancer screening behavior in men from seven ethnic groups: The fear factor. *Cancer Epidemiology, Biomarkers & Prevention, 15*(2), 228–237.

Constantine, M. G., Kindaichi, M., Okazaki, S., Gainor, K. A., & Baden, A. L. (2005). A qualitative investigation of the cultural adjustment experiences of Asian international college women. *Cultural Diversity and Ethnic Minority Psychology, 11*(2), 162–175.

Cook, E. P. (1985). *Psychological androgyny.* New York, NY: Pergamon Press.

Cook, J. R., & Tyler, J. D. (1989). Help-seeking attitudes of North Dakota farm couples. *Journal of Rural Community Psychology, 10,* 17–28.

Cook, L. J. (2007). Striving to help college students with mental health issues. *Journal of Psychosocial Nursing, 45*(4), 40–44.

Cook, S., Auinger, P., Li, C., & Ford, E. S. (2008). Metabolic syndrome rates in United States adolescents, from the National Health and Nutrition Examination Survey, 1999-2002. *Journal of Pediatrics, 152*(2), 165–170.

Cooper, M. L., & Orcutt, H. K. (1997). Drinking and sexual experience on first dates among adolescents. *Journal of Abnormal Psychology, 106*(2), 191–202.

Cooper, M. L., Pierce, R. S., & Huselid, R. F. (1994). Substance use and sexual risk taking among black adolescents and white adolescents. *Health Psychology, 13*(3), 251–262.

Cooper, R. S. (2003). Race, genes, and health: New wine in old bottles? *International Journal of Epidemiology, 32,* 23–25.

Cooper-Patrick, L., Gallo, J. J., Gonzales, J. J., Vu, H. T., Powe, N. R., Nelson, C.,& Ford, D. E. (1999). Race, gender, and partnership in the patient-physician relationship. *Journal of the American Medical Association, 282*(6), 583–589.

Cooperstock, R. (1978). Sex differences in psychotropic drug use. *Social Science & Medicine, 12*(3-B), 179–186.

Copenhaver, M. M., & Eisler, R. M. (1996). Masculine gender role stress: A perspective on men's health. In P. M. Kato & T. Mann (Eds.), *Handbook of diversity issues in health psychology* (pp. 219–235). New York, NY: Plenum.

Corbie-Smith, G., Thomas, S. B., & St. George, D. M. (2002). Distrust, race, and research. *Archives of Internal Medicine, 162,* 2458–2460.

Cordry, H. V. (2001). *Tobacco: A reference handbook.* Santa Barbara, CA: ABC-CLIO.

Corney, R. H. (1990). Sex differences in general practice attendance and help seeking for minor illness. *Journal of Psychosomatic Research, 34*(5), 525–534.

Corrao, G., Bagnardi, V., Zambon, A., & La Vecchia, C. (2004). A meta-analysis of alcohol consumption and the risk of 15 diseases. *Preventive Medicine, 38*(5), 613–619.

Correa, P., & Chen, V. W. (1994). Gastric cancer. *Cancer Surveys, 19-20,* 55–76.

Cosenzo, K. A., Franchina, J. J., Eisler, R. M., & Krebs, D. (2004). Effects of masculine gender-relevant task instructions on men's cardiovascular reactivity and mental arithmetic performance. *Psychology of Men and Masculinity, 5*, 103–111.

Costa, F. V. (1996). Compliance with antihypertensive treatment. *Clinical and Experimental Hypertension, 18*(3–4), 463–472.

Costa, F. V., D'Ausilio, A., Bianchi, C., Negrini, C., & Lopatriello, S. (2009). Adherence to antihypertensive medications: A review and update. *High Blood Pressure and Cardiovascular Prevention, 16*(3), 101–110.

Côté, S. M. (2007). Sex differences in physical and indirect aggression: A developmental perspective. *European Journal on Criminal Policy and Research, 13*(3–4), 183–200.

Council on Scientific Affairs. (1990). Education for health: A role for physicians and the efficacy of health education efforts. *Journal of the American Medical Association, 263*(13), 1816–1819.

Coups, E. J., Manne, S. L., & Heckman, C. J. (2008). Multiple skin cancer risk behaviors in the U.S. population. *American Journal of Preventive Medicine, 34*(2), 87–93.

Coups, E. J., Manne, S. L., Meropol, N. J., & Weinberg, D. S. (2007). Multiple behavioral risk factors for colorectal cancer and colorectal cancer screening status. *Cancer Epidemiology, Biomarkers & Prevention, 16*(3), 510–516.

Courtenay, W. H. (1996a). *Clinical practice guideline for the treatment of men: A biopsychosocial approach* (submitted in partial fulfillment of the doctoral degree). Berkeley: University of California.

Courtenay, W. H. (1996b). *Health mentor: Health risk assessment for men.* Berkeley, CA: Author.

Courtenay, W. H. (1998a). Better to die than cry? A longitudinal and constructionist study of masculinity and the health risk behavior of young American men. *Dissertation Abstracts International, 59*(08A), 9902042.

Courtenay, W. H. (1998b). College men's health: An overview and a call to action. *Journal of American College Health, 46*(6), 279–290.

Courtenay, W. H. (1998c). Communication strategies for improving men's health: The 6-Point HEALTH Plan. *Wellness Management, 14*(1), 1, 3–4.

Courtenay, W. H. (1999a). Situating men's health in the negotiation of masculinities. *The Society for the Psychological Study of Men and Masculinity Bulletin* (The American Psychological Association), *4*(2), 10–12.

Courtenay, W. H. (1999b). Youth violence? Let's call it what it is. *Journal of American College Health, 48*(3), 141–142.

Courtenay, W. H. (2000a). Behavioral factors associated with disease, injury, and death among men: Evidence and implications for prevention. *Journal of Men's Studies, 9*(1), 81–142.

Courtenay, W. H. (2000b). Constructions of masculinity and their influence on men's well-being: A theory of gender and health. *Social Science & Medicine, 50*(10), 1385–1401.

Courtenay, W. H. (2000c). Engendering health: A social constructionist examination of men's health beliefs and behaviors. *Psychology of Men and Masculinity, 1*(1), 4–15.

Courtenay, W. H. (2000d). Social work, counseling, and psychotherapeutic interventions with men and boys: A bibliography. *Men and Masculinities, 2*(3), 330–352.

Courtenay, W. H. (2000e). Teaming up for the new men's health movement. *Journal of Men's Studies, 8*(3), 387–392.

Courtenay, W. H. (2001a). Counseling men in medical settings. In G. R. Brooks & G. E. Good (Eds.), *The new handbook of psychotherapy and counseling with men: A comprehensive guide to settings, problems, and treatment approaches* (Vol. 1, pp. 59–91). San Francisco, CA: Jossey-Bass.

Courtenay, W. H. (2001b). Men's health: Ethnicity matters. *Social Work Today, 1*(8), 20–22.

Courtenay, W. H. (2002). A global perspective on the field of men's health. *International Journal of Men's Health, 1*, 1–13.

Courtenay, W. H. (2003). Key determinants of the health and well-being of men and boys. *International Journal of Men's Health, 2*(1), 1–30.

Courtenay, W. H. (2004a). Best practices for improving college men's health. In G. E. Kellom (Ed.), *Developing effective programs and services for college men* (pp. 59–74). San Francisco, CA: Jossey-Bass.

Courtenay, W. H. (2004b). Making health manly: Social marketing and men's health. *Journal of Men's Health & Gender, 1*, 275–276.

Courtenay, W. H. (2006a). Constructions of masculinity and their influence on men's well-being: A theory of gender and health. In S. Whitehead (Ed.), *Men and masculinities* (pp. 386–416). Andover, England: Routledge.

Courtenay, W. H. (2006b). Rural men's health: Situating men's risk in the negotiation of masculinity. In H. Campbell, M. Mayerfeld-Bell, & M. Finney (Eds.), *Country boys: Masculinity and rural life* (pp. 139–158). University Park: Pennsylvania State University Press.

Courtenay, W. H. (2007). Making health manly: Norms, peers, and men's health. In L. Cohen, V. Chávez, & S. Chehimi (Eds.), *Prevention is primary: Strategies for community wellbeing* (pp. 51–52). San Francisco, CA: Jossey-Bass.

Courtenay, W. H. (2009). Chapter 1: Theorizing masculinity and men's health. In A. Broom & P. Tovey (Eds.), *Men's health: Body, identity and social context* (pp. 9–32). London, England: Wiley-Blackwell.

Courtenay, W. H., & Keeling, R. P. (2000a). Men, gender, and health: Toward an interdisciplinary approach. *Journal of American College Health, 48*(6), 1–4.

Courtenay, W. H. (Guest Ed.), & Keeling, R. P. (Ed.) (2000b). Men's health: A theme issue. *Journal of American College Health, 48*(6).

Courtenay, W. H., McCreary, D. R., & Merighi, J. R. (2002). Gender and ethnic differences in health beliefs and behaviors. *Journal of Health Psychology, 7*(3), 219–231.

Courtenay, W. H., & Sabo, D. (2001). Preventive health strategies for men in prison. In D. Sabo, T. A. Kupers, & W. London (Eds.), *Prison masculinities* (pp. 157–172). Philadelphia, PA: Temple University Press.

Coward, R. (1984). *Female desire: Women's sexuality today*. London, England: Paladin Publishing.

Cowie, C. C., Rust, K. F., Byrd-Holt, D. D., Eberhardt, M. S., Flegal, K. M., Engelgau, M. M., ... Gregg, E. W. (2006). Prevalence of diabetes and impaired fasting glucose in adults in the U.S. population: National Health and Nutrition Examination Survey 1999–2002. *Diabetes Care, 29*(6), 1263–1268.

Coyne, J. C., & DeLongis, A. (1986). Going beyond social support: The role of social relationships in adaptation. *Journal of Consulting and Clinical Psychology, 54*, 454–460.

Cramer, C. (1998). A crash is not an accident [Editorial]. *International Journal of Trauma Nursing, 4*(1), 4.

Cramer, J. A. (1991). Overview of methods to measure and enhance patient compliance. In J. A. Cramer & B. Spilker (Eds.), *Patient compliance in medical practice and clinical trials* (pp. 3–10). New York, NY: Raven Press.

Cramer, J. A., & Spilker, B. (Eds.). (1991). *Patient compliance in medical practice and clinical trials*. New York, NY: Raven Press.

Crandall, C. S., Fullerton, L., Olson, L., Sklar, D. P., & Zumwalt, R. (1997). Farm-related injury mortality in New Mexico, 1980–91. *Accident Analysis & Prevention, 29*(2), 257–261.

Crawford, M. (1995). *Talking difference: On gender and language.* Thousand Oaks, CA: Sage.

Crawshaw, P. (2009). Critical perspectives on the health of men: Lessons from medical sociology. *Critical Public Health, 19*(3), 279–285.

Croake, J. W., Myers, K. M., & Singh, A. (1987). Demographic features of adult fears. *International Journal of Social Psychiatry, 33*(4), 285–293.

Cross, A. J., Leitzmann, M. F., Gail, M. H., Hollenbeck, A. R., Schatzkin, A., & Sinha, R. (2007). A prospective study of red and processed meat intake in relation to cancer risk. *PLoS Med, 4*(12), e325.

Cummings, P., Rivara, F. P., Olson, C. M., & Smith, K. M. (2006). Changes in traffic crash mortality rates attributed to use of alcohol, or lack of a seat belt, air bag, motorcycle helmet, or bicycle helmet, United States, 1982–2001. *Injury Prevention, 12*(3), 148–154.

Curry, P., & O'Brien, M. (2006). The male heart and the female mind: A study in the gendering of antidepressants and cardiovascular drugs in advertisements in Irish medical publication. *Social Science & Medicine, 62*(8), 1970–1977.

Cutler, J. A., Sorlie, P. D., Wolz, M., Thom, T., Fields, L. E., & Roccella, E. J. (2008). Trends in hypertension prevalence, awareness, treatment, and control rates in United States adults between 1988–1994 and 1999–2004. *Hypertension, 52*, 818–827.

Cutter, S. L., Tiefenbacher, J., & Solecki, W. D. (1992). En-gendered fears: Femininity and technological risk perception. *Industrial Crisis Quarterly, 6*, 5–22.

Cwikel, J. M., Dielman, T. E., Kirsch, J. P., & Israel, B. A. (1988). Mechanisms of psychosocial effects on health: The role of social integration, coping style, and health behavior. *Health Education Quarterly, 15*, 151–173.

Dadlani, C., & Orlow, S. J. (2008). Planning for a brighter future: A review of sun protection and barriers to behavioral change in children and adolescents. *Dermatology Online Journal, 14*(9), 1.

Dalton, M. A., Sargent, J. D., Beach, M. L., Titus-Ernstoff, L., Gibson, J. J., Aherns, M. B., … Heatherton, T. F. (2003). Effect of viewing smoking in movies on adolescent smoking initiation: A cohort study. *Lancet, 362*(9380), 281–285.

Daniell, H. W. (1995). A worse prognosis for smokers with prostate cancer. *Journal of Urology, 154*(1), 153–157.

Danielson, R., Marcy, S., Plunkett, A., Wiest, W., & Greenlick, M. R. (1990). Reproductive health counseling for young men: What does it do? *Family Planning Perspectives, 22*(3), 115–121.

Dansky, K. H., Brannon, D., Shea, D. G., Vasey, J., & Dirani, R. (1998). Profiles of hospital, physician, and home health service use by older persons in rural areas. *Gerontologist, 38*(3), 320–330.

Dariotis, J. K., Pleck, J. H., Sonenstein, F. L., Astone, N. M., & Sifakis, F. (2009). What are the consequences of relying upon self-reports of sexually transmitted diseases? Lessons learned about recanting in a longitudinal study. *Journal of Adolescent Health, 45*(2), 187–192.

Darrow, C. J., Collins, C. L., Yard, E. E., & Comstock, R. D. (2009). Epidemiology of severe injuries among United States high school athletes: 2005–2007. *American Journal of Sports Medicine, 37*(9), 1798–1805.

Dauchet, L., Amouyel, P., Hercberg, S., & Dallongeville, J. (2006). Fruit and vegetable consumption and risk of coronary heart disease: A meta-analysis of cohort studies. *Journal of Nutrition, 136*(10), 2588–2593.

Davidson, D. J., & Freudenberg, W. R. (1996). Gender and environmental risk concerns: A review and analysis of available research. *Environment and Behavior, 28*(3), 302–339.

Davidson, P. M., White, P. N., Smith, D. J., & Poppen, W. A. (1989). Content and intensity of fears in middle childhood among rural and urban boys and girls. *Journal of Genetic Psychology, 150*(1), 51–58.

Davies, J., McCrae, B. P., Frank, J., Dochnahl, A., Pickering, T., Harrison, B., … Wilson, K. (2000). Identifying male college students' perceived health needs, barriers to seeking help, and recommendations to help men adopt healthier lifestyles. *Journal of American College Health, 48*(6), 259–267.

Davis, H., & Fallowfield, L. (1991). Counseling and communication in health care: The current situation. In H. Davis & L. Fallowfield (Eds.), *Counseling and communication in health care* (pp. 3–22). New York, NY: Wiley.

Davis, L. E. (Ed.). (1999). *Working with African American males: A guide to practice*. Thousand Oaks, CA: Sage.

Davy, S. R., Benes, B. A., & Driskell, J. A. (2006). Sex differences in dieting trends, eating habits, and nutrition beliefs of a group of midwestern college students. *Journal of the American Dietetic Association, 106*(10), 1673–1677.

Dawson, K. A., Schneider, M. A., Fletcher, P. C., & Bryden, P. J. (2007). Examining gender differences in the health behaviors of Canadian university students. *Journal of the Royal Society for the Promotion of Health, 127*(1), 38–44.

Day, C., Stolz, U., Mehan, T. J., Smith, G. A., & McKenzie, L. B. (2008). Diving-related injuries in children < 20 years old treated in emergency departments in the United States: 1990–2006. *Pediatrics, 122*(2), 388–394.

Dean, L., Meyer, I. H., Robinson, K., Sell, R. L., Sember, R., Silenzio, V. M., … Dunn, P. (2000). *Lesbian, gay, bisexual, and transgender health: Findings and concerns*. San Francisco, CA: Gay and Lesbian Medical Association; and New York, NY: Columbia University, Mailman School of Public Health.

Deaux, K. (1984). From individual differences to social categories: An analysis of a decade's research on gender. *American Psychologist, 39*(2), 105–116.

Deber, R. B. (1994). Physicians in health care management: 7. The patient-physician partnership: Changing roles and the desire for information. *Canadian Medical Association Journal, 151*(2), 171–176.

DeHoff, J. B., & Forrest, K. A. (1984). Men's health. In J. M. Swanson & K. A. Forrest (Eds.), *Men's reproductive health* (pp. 3–10). New York, NY: Springer.

DeJoy, D. M. (1992). An examination of gender differences in traffic accident risk perception. *Accident Analysis and Prevention, 24*(3), 237–246.

Dekin, B. (1996). Gender differences in HIV-related self-reported knowledge, attitudes, and behaviors among college students. *American Journal of Preventive Medicine, 12*(Suppl. 1), 61–66.

Delbanco, T. L. (1992). Enriching the doctor-patient relationship by inviting the patient's perspective. *American College of Physicians, 116*(5), 414–418.

Del Mar, C. B., Stanton, W. R., Gillespie, A. M., Lowe, J. B., & Balanda, K. P. (1996). What use do people make of physicians in checking their skin for cancer? *Cancer Detection and Prevention, 20,* 325–331.

Delsohn, S. (1996). *The fire inside: Firefighters talk about their lives.* New York, NY: Harper Collins.

Demark-Wahnefried, W., Strigo, T., Catoe, K., Conaway, M., Brunetti, M., Rimer, B. K., & Robertson, C. N. (1995). Knowledge, beliefs, and prior screening behavior among blacks and whites reporting for prostate cancer screening. *Urology, 46*(3), 346–351.

Denham, S. A., Mitchell-Copeland, J., Strandberg, K., Auerbach, S., & Blair, K. (1997). Parental contributions to preschoolers' emotional competence: Direct and indirect effects. *Motivation and Emotion, 21,* 65–86.

Denke, M. A., Sempos, C. T., & Grundy, S. M. (1993). Excess body weight: An underrecognized contributor to high blood cholesterol levels in white American men. *Archives of Internal Medicine, 153,* 1093–1103.

Denny, C. H., Holtzman, D., Turner-Goins, R., & Croft, J. B. (2005). Disparities in chronic disease risk factors and health status between American Indian/ Alaska Native and White elders: Findings from a telephone survey, 2001 and 2002. *American Journal of Public Health, 95*(5), 825–827.

De Oliveira, C., Watt, R., & Hamer, M. (2010). Toothbrushing, inflammation, and risk of cardiovascular disease: Results from Scottish Health Survey. *British Medical Journal, 340,* c2451.

DePalma, M. T., McCall, M., & English, G. (1996). Increasing perceptions of disease vulnerability through imagery. *Journal of American College Health, 44*(5), 227–234.

Department of Agriculture. (2003). *Food and agricultural commodity consumption in the United States: Looking ahead to 2020* (Agricultural Economic Report No. 820). Washington, DC: Author.

Department of Agriculture. (2009). *What we eat in America, NHANES 2005– 2006: Usual nutrient intakes from food and water compared to 1997 dietary reference intakes for vitamin D, calcium, phosphorus, and magnesium.* Washington, DC: Author.

Department of Education. (2006). *2003–04 National Postsecondary Student Aid Study (NPSAS:04): Undergraduate financial aid estimates for 12 states: 2003–04* (Publication No. NCES 2006-158). Washington, DC: National Center for Education Statistics.

Department of Health and Human Services. (1990). *Health, United States, 1989* (DHHS Publication No. [PHS] 90-1232). Washington, DC: U.S. Government Printing Office.

Department of Health and Human Services. (1991). *Healthy people 2000: National health promotion and disease prevention objectives* (DHHS Publication No. [PHS] 91-50212). Washington, DC: U.S. Government Printing Office.

Department of Health and Human Services. (1993). *Vital and health statistics: Health promotion and disease prevention, United States, 1990* (DHHS Publication No. [PHS] 93-1513). Hyattsville, MD: Public Health Service.

Department of Health and Human Services. (1994). *Vital statistics of the United States, 1990 (Vol. II—Mortality, part A)*. Hyattsville, MD: Public Health Service.

Department of Health and Human Services. (1995). Advance report of final mortality statistics, 1991 (DHHS Publication No. [PHS] 95-1120) *Monthly Vital Statistics Report, 42*(Suppl.). Hyattsville, MD: Public Health Service.

Department of Health and Human Services. (1996a). *Health, United States, 1995* (DHHS Publication No. [PHS] 96-1232). Washington, DC: U.S. Government Printing Office.

Department of Health and Human Services. (1996b). *Physical activity and health: A report of the surgeon general*. Atlanta, GA: Author.

Department of Health and Human Services. (1996c). Report of final mortality statistics, 1994. *Monthly Vital Statistics Report, 45*(3, Suppl.). Hyattsville, MD: Public Health Service.

Department of Health and Human Services. (1997). *National household survey on drug abuse main findings 1995*. (DIIIIS Publication No. [SMA] 97-3127). Rockville, MD: Substance Abuse and Mental Health Services Administration, Office of Applied Studies.

Department of Health and Human Services. (1998a). *Health, United, States, 1998: Socioeconomic status and health chartbook* (DHHS Publication No. [PHS] 98-1232-1). Hyattsville, MD: National Center for Health Statistics.

Department of Health and Human Services. (1998b). *Vital and health statistics: Current estimates from the National Health Interview Survey, 1995* (DHHS Publication No. [PHS] 98-1527). Hyattsville, MD: Government Printing Office.

Department of Health and Human Services. (2000a). Deaths: Final data for 1998 (DHHS Publication No. [PHS] 2000-1120). *National Vital Statistics Reports, 48*(11). Hyattsville, MD: National Center for Health Statistics.

Department of Health and Human Services. (2000b). *Health, United States, 2000: With adolescent health chartbook* (DHHS Publication No. 00-1232). Hyattsville, MD: U.S. Government Printing Office.

Department of Health and Human Services. (2000c). *Healthy people 2010: Understanding and improving health* (DHHS Publication No. [PHS] 017-001-001-00-550-9). Washington, DC: U.S. Government Printing Office.

Department of Health and Human Services. (2000d). *10th special report to congress on alcohol and health*. Bethesda, MD: National Institute on Alcohol Abuse and Alcoholism.

Department of Health and Human Services. (2001). *The Surgeon General's call to action to prevent and decrease overweight and obesity*. Rockville, MD: Author.

Department of Health and Human Services. (2002a). *Dietary intake of macronutrients micronutrients and other dietary constituents: United States 1988–94* (DHHS Publication No. [PHS] 2002-1695). Hyattsville, MD: Author.

Department of Health and Human Services. (2002b). *Strategic research plan and budget to reduce and ultimately eliminate health disparities volume 1: Fiscal years 2002–2006*. Bethesda, MD: National Institutes of Health.

Department of Health and Human Services. (2003). *Women's health USA 2003.* Rockville, MD: Health Resources and Services Administration.

Department of Health and Human Services. (2004a). *Patterns of mental health service. Utilization and substance use among adults, 2000 and 2001* (DHHS Publication No. SMA 04-3901, Analytic Series A-22). Rockville, MD: Author.

Department of Health and Human Services. (2004b). *The health consequences of smoking: A report of the Surgeon General.* Atlanta, GA: Author.

Department of Health and Human Services. (2005). *Dietary guidelines for Americans 2005* (Publication No. HHS ODPHP-2005-01-DGA-A). Washington, DC: U.S. Government Printing Office.

Department of Health and Human Services. (2006a). *Fertility, contraception, and fatherhood: Data on men and women from Cycle 6 (2002) of the National Survey of Family Growth* (DHHS Publication No. PHS 2006-1978). Hyattsville, MD: Author.

Department of Health and Human Services. (2006b). *Health, United States, 2006* (DHHS Publication No. 2006-1232). Hyattsville, MD: U.S. Government Printing Office.

Department of Health and Human Services. (2006c). *Incidence and prevalence: 2006 chart book on cardiovascular and lung diseases.* Bethesda, MD: Author.

Department of Health and Human Services. (2006d). *Women's health USA 2006.* Rockville, MD: Health Resources and Services Administration.

Department of Health and Human Services. (2007a). *Deaths: Leading causes for 2004* (DHHS Publication No. [PHS] 2008-1120). Hyattsville, MD: National Center for Health Statistics.

Department of Health and Human Services. (2007b). *Physical activity among adults: United States, 2000 and 2005.* Hyattsville, MD: Author.

Department of Health and Human Services. (2007c). *The Surgeon General's call to action to prevent and decrease overweight and obesity: Overweight in children and adolescents.* Atlanta, GA: Author.

Department of Health and Human Services. (2007d). *Trends in oral health status—United States, 1988-1994 and 1999-2004: Data from the continuous National Health and Nutrition Examination Survey (NHANES)* (DHHS Publication No. [PHS] 2007-1698). Hyattsville, MD: Author.

Department of Health and Human Services. (2007e). *Women's health USA 2007.* Rockville, MD: Health Resources and Services Administration.

Department of Health and Human Services. (2008a). Deaths: Final data for 2005 (DHHS Publication No. [PHS] 2008-1120) *National Vital Statistics Reports, 56*(10). Hyattsville, MD: National Center for Health Statistics.

Department of Health and Human Services. (2008b). *Injury in the United States: 2007 chartbook* (DHHS Publication No. [PHS] 2008-1033). Hyattsville, MD: Author.

Department of Health and Human Services. (2008c). *Physical activity guidelines advisory committee report, 2008.* Washington, DC: Author.

Department of Health and Human Services. (2009a). Deaths: Final data for 2006 (DHHS Publication No. [PHS] 2009-1120). *National Vital Statistics Reports, 57*(14). Hyattsville, MD: National Center for Health Statistics.

Department of Health and Human Services. (2009b). Deaths: Leading causes for 2005 (DHHS Publication No. [PHS] 2010-1120). *National Vital Statistics Reports, 58*(8). Hyattsville, MD: National Center for Health Statistics.

Department of Health and Human Services. (2009c). *Functional difficulties among school-aged children: United States, 2001–2007.* (National Health Statistics Reports; DHHS Publication No. [PHS] 2010-1250). Hyattsville, MD: Author.

Department of Health and Human Services. (2009d). *Health, United States, 2008* (DHHS Publication No. 2009-1232). Hyattsville, MD: U.S. Government Printing Office.

Department of Health and Human Services. (2009e). *Summary health statistics for U.S. adults: National Health Interview Survey, 2007* (DHHS Publication No. [PHS] 2009-1568). Hyattsville, MD: Author.

Department of Health and Human Services. (2009f). *The NSDUH report: Perceptions of risk from substance use among adolescents.* Rockville, MD: Substance Abuse and Mental Health Services Administration.

Department of Health and Human Services. (2009g). *The NSDUH report: Smokeless tobacco use, initiation, and relationship to cigarette smoking: 2002 to 2007.* Rockville, MD: Substance Abuse and Mental Health Services Administration.

Department of Health and Human Services. (2009h). *The NSDUH report: The National Survey on Drug Use and Health: Cigar use among young adults aged 18 to 25.* Rockville, MD: Substance Abuse and Mental Health Services Administration.

Department of Health and Human Services. (2010a). *Access to and utilization of medical care for young adults aged 20–29 years: United States, 2008* (NCHS Data Brief, No. 29). Hyattsville, MD: Author.

Department of Health and Human Services. (2010b). *Health, United States, 2009: With special feature on medical technology.* Hyattsville, MD: U.S. Government Printing Office.

Department of Health and Human Services. (2010c). *Healthcare cost and utilization project.* Rockville, MD: Agency for Healthcare Research and Quality.

Department of Health and Human Services. (2010d). *Medical expenditure panel survey.* Rockville, MD: Agency for Healthcare Research and Quality.

Department of Justice. (1994). *Sourcebook of criminal justice statistics, 1993* (Publication No. NCJ-148211). Rockville, MD: The National Criminal Justice Reference Service.

Department of Justice. (1995). *National Crime Victimization Survey: Criminal victimization—1993* (Publication No. NCJ-151658). Washington, DC: U.S. Government Printing Office.

Department of Justice. (2004). Percent distribution of characteristics of felony offenders convicted in State courts, by offense, United States, 2004. In *Sourcebook of criminal justice statistics* (Table 5.45.2004). Washington, DC: Bureau of Justice Statistics.

Department of Justice. (2005). *Sourcebook of criminal justice statistic, 2003* (Publication No. NCJ-208756). Washington, DC: U.S. Government Printing Office.

Department of Justice. (2006). Attitudes toward whether a gun in the home makes it safer or more dangerous. In *Sourcebook of criminal justice statistics* (Table 2.0011.2006). Washington, DC: Bureau of Justice Statistics.

Department of Justice. (2007a). Estimated number and rate (per 1,000 persons age 12 and older) of personal victimization. In *Sourcebook of criminal justice statistics* (Table 3.5.2007). Washington, DC: Bureau of Justice Statistics.

Department of Justice. (2007b). Offenders sentenced in U.S. District Courts under the U.S. Sentencing Commission guidelines, by primary offense, sex, race, and ethnicity, fiscal year 2007. In *Sourcebook of criminal justice statistics* (Table 5.26.2007). Washington, DC: Bureau of Justice Statistics.

Department of Justice. (2007c). Respondents reporting whether they engaged in selected behaviors because of concern over crime. In *Sourcebook of criminal justice statistics* (Table 2.40.2007). Washington, DC: Bureau of Justice Statistics.

Department of Justice. (2008a). *Bureau of Justice statistics bulletin: Prisoners in 2007* (Publication No. NCJ-224280). Washington, DC: U.S. Government Printing Office.

Department of Justice. (2008b). Full-time law enforcement employees, by sex and population group, on Oct. 31, 2008. In *Sourcebook of criminal justice statistics* (Table 1.68.2008). Washington, DC: Bureau of Justice Statistics.

Department of Justice. (2008c). Prisoners under sentence of death, by demographic characteristics, prior felony conviction history, and legal status, United States, on Dec. 31, 1996–2008. In *Sourcebook of criminal justice statistics* (Table 6.81.2008). Washington, DC: Bureau of Justice Statistics.

Department of Justice. (2009a). *Bureau of Justice statistics bulletin: Prisoners in 2008* (Publication No. NCJ-224280). Washington, DC: U.S. Government Printing Office.

Department of Justice. (2009b). Respondents reporting concern about crime victimization. In *Sourcebook of criminal justice statistics* (Table 2.39.2009). Washington, DC: Bureau of Justice Statistics.

Department of Justice. (2009c). Respondents reporting having a gun in their home. In *Sourcebook of criminal justice statistics* (Table 2.60.2009). Washington, DC: Bureau of Justice Statistics.

Department of Labor. (1999). *National census of fatal occupational injuries, 1988.* Washington, DC: Bureau of Labor Statistics.

DePaulo, B. (1982). Social-psychological processes in informal help-seeking. In T. Wills (Ed.), *Basic processes in helping relationships* (pp. 255–280). New York, NY: Academic Press.

DeRose, L. F., Dodoo, F. N., Ezeh, A. C., & Owuor, T. O. (2004). Does discussion of family planning improve knowledge of partner's attitude toward contraceptives? *International Family Planning Perspectives, 30*(2), 87–93.

Desmond, R. A., & Soong, S. J. (2003). Epidemiology of malignant melanoma. *Surgical Clinics of North America, 83*, 1–29.

De Stafani, E., Deneo-Pellegrini, H., Ronco, A. L., Boffetta, P., & Barrios, E. (2006). Epidemiology of esophageal cancer. In H. K. Kinner (Ed.), *Esophageal cancer research developments* (pp. 99–112). New York, NY: Nova Science Publishers.

Devesa, S. S., Grauman, D. J., & Blot, W. J. (1994). Recent cancer patterns among men and women in the United States: Clues for occupational research. *Journal of Occupational Medicine, 36*(8), 832–841.

Devgan, U., Yu, F., Kim, E., & Coleman, A. L. (2000). Surgical undertreatment of glaucoma in Black beneficiaries of Medicare. *Archives of Ophthalmology, 118*, 253–256.

Devine, E. C. (1992). Effects of psychoeducational care for adult surgical patients: A meta-analysis of 191 studies. *Patient Education and Counseling, 19*(2), 129–142.

DeVivo, M. J., Rutt, R. D., Black, K. J., Go, B. K., & Stover, S. L. (1992). Trends in spinal cord injury demographics and treatment outcomes between 1973 and 1986. *Archives of Physical Medicine and Rehabilitation, 13*, 424–430.

DeVivo, M. J., & Sekar, P. (1997). Prevention of spinal cord injuries that occur in swimming pools. *Spinal Cord, 35*(8), 509–515.

Diaz, R. M. (1998). *Latino gay men and HIV: Culture, sexuality, and risk behavior.* New York, NY: Routledge.

Di Castelnuovo, A., Costanzo, S., Bagnardi, V., Donati, M. B., Iacoviello, L., & de Gaetano, G. (2006). Alcohol dosing and total mortality in men and women: An updated meta-analysis of 34 prospective studies. *Archives of Internal Medicine, 166*(22), 2437–2445.

Dick, P., Sherif, C., Sabeti, S., Amighi, J., Minar, E., & Schillinger, M. (2005). Gender differences in outcome of conservatively treated patients with asymptomatic high grade carotid stenosis. *Stroke, 36*(6), 1178–1183.

Dickinson, V. A., Block, G., & Russek-Cohen, E. (1994). Supplement use, other dietary and demographic variables, and serum vitamin C in NHANES II. *Journal of the American College of Nutrition, 13*(1), 22–32.

Diefenbach, M. A. (2000, August). Treatment decision-making preferences among patients with early stage prostate cancer. In R. Hetzel (Chair), *Men's health in the new millennium: Emerging research theory and practice.* Symposium conducted at the 108th Convention of the American Psychological Association, Washington, DC.

Diepgen, T. L., & Mahler, V. (2002). The epidemiology of skin cancer. *British Journal of Dermatology, 146*(Suppl. 61), 1–6.

Dietz, W. H. (1996). The role of lifestyle in health: The epidemiology and consequences of inactivity. *The Proceedings of the Nutrition Society, 55*(3), 829–840.

Dilorio, C., Parsons, M., Lehr, S., Adame, D., & Carlone, J. (1993). Factors associated with use of safer sex practices among college freshmen. *Research in Nursing Health, 16*, 343–350.

DiMatteo, M. R. (2004). Social support and patient adherence to medical treatment: A meta-analysis. *Health Psychology, 23*(2), 207–218.

Dinh-Zarr, T. B., Sleet, D. A., Shults, R. A., Zaza, S., Elder, R. W., Nichols, J. L., … the Task Force on Community Preventive Services. (2001). Reviews of evidence regarding interventions to increase the use of safety belts. *American Journal of Preventive Medicine, 21*(4S), 48–65.

Division of HIV Prevention. (2010). *HIV among gay, bisexual and other men who have sex with men (MSM).* Atlanta, GA: Centers for Disease Control.

Division of Viral Hepatitis. (2010). *Viral hepatitis: Information for gay/bisexual men.* Atlanta, GA: Centers for Disease Control.

Dixon, J. B. (2010). The effect of obesity on health outcomes. *Molecular and Cellular Endocrinology, 316*(2), 104–108.

Donnermeyer, J. J., & Park, D. S. (1995). Alcohol use among rural adolescents: predictive and situational factors. *International Journal of the Addictions, 30*(4), 459–479.

Donovan, J. E., Jessor, R., & Costa, F. M. (1993). Structure of health-enhancing behavior in adolescence: A latent-variable approach. *Journal of Health and Social Behavior, 34,* 346–362.

Dorion, A. A., Chantome, M., Hasboun, D., Zouaoui, A., Marsault, C., Capron, C., & Duyme, M. (2000). Hemispheric asymmetry and corpus callosum morphometry: A magnetic resonance imaging study. *Neuroscience Research, 36,* 9–13.

Dorn, L. D., Burgess, E. S., Susman, E. J., von Eye, A., DeBellis, M. D., Gold, P. W., & Chrousos, G. P. (1996). Response to oCRH in depressed and nondepressed adolescents: Does gender make a difference? *Journal of the American Academy of Child & Adolescent Psychiatry, 35,* 764–773.

Dosman, D. M., Adamowicz, W. L., & Hrudey, S. E. (2001). Socioeconomic determinants of health- and food safety-related risk perceptions. *Risk Analysis, 21*(2), 307–317.

Doss, B. D., & Hopkins, J. R. (1998). The Multicultural Masculinity Ideology Scale: Validation from three cultural perspectives. *Sex Roles, 38,* 719–741.

Douglas, K. A., Collins, J. L., Warren, C., Kann, L., Gold, R., Slayton, S., … Kolbe, L. J. (1997). Results from the 1995 National College Health Risk Behavior Survey. *Journal of American College Health, 46*(2), 55–66.

Doyal, L. (1995). *What makes women sick: Gender and the political economy of health.* New Brunswick, NJ: Rutgers University Press.

Doyal, L. (2000). Gender equity in health: Debates and dilemmas. *Social Science & Medicine, 51,* 931–939.

Drewnowski, A., & Yee, D. K. (1987). Men and body image: Are males satisfied with their body weight? *Psychosomatic Medicine, 49,* 626–634.

Driesen, N. R., & Raz, N. (1995). The influence of sex, age and handedness on corpus callosum morphology: A meta-analysis. *Psychobiology, 23,* 240–247.

Driscoll, T. R., Harrison, J. A., & Steenkamp, M. (2004). Review of the role of alcohol in drowning associated with recreational aquatic activity. *Injury Prevention, 10*(2), 107–113.

Dugan, S. A., & Prather, H. (2007). Gender specific medicine: The psychiatrist and women's health: An issue of physical medicine and rehabilitation clinics [Special issue of *Physical Medicine and Rehabilitation Clinics of North America, vol. 18*]. Philadelphia, PA: W. B. Saunders.

Duke, N. N., Pettingell, S. L., McMorris, B. J., & Borowsky, I. W. (2010). Adolescent violence perpetration: Associations with multiple types of adverse childhood experiences. *Pediatrics, 125,* 778–786.

Duncan, M. C., & Messner, M. A. (2005). *Gender in televised sports: News and highlights shows, 1989–2004.* Los Angeles, CA: Amateur Athletic Foundation of Los Angeles.

Dunlop, D. D., Manheim, L. M., Song, J., & Chang, R. W. (2002). Gender and ethnic/racial disparities in health care utilization among older adults. *Journals of Gerontology Series B: Psychological Sciences and Social Sciences, 57,* S221–S233.

Dunn, J., Bretherton, I., & Munn, P. (1987). Conversations about feeling states between mothers and their young children. *Developmental Psychology, 23,* 132–139.

Dunn, J., Brown, J., Slomkowski, C., & Tesla, C. (1991). Young children's understanding of other people's feelings and beliefs: Individual differences and their antecedents. *Child Development, 62*(6), 1352–1366.

Dunn, J. R. (2010). Health behavior vs. the stress of low socioeconomic status and health outcomes. *Journal of the American Medical Association, 303*(12), 1199–1200.

Dunn, K. A., Runyan, C. W., Cohen, L. R., & Schulman, M. D. (1998). Teens at work: A statewide study of jobs, hazards and injuries. *Journal of Adolescent Health, 22*(1), 19–25.

Dunne, E. F., Nielson, C. M., Stone, K. M., Markowitz, L. E., & Giuliano, A. R. (2006). Prevalence of HPV infection among men: A systematic review of the literature. *Journal of Infectious Diseases, 194*(8), 1044–1057.

Dupre, M. E., Beck, A. N., & Meadows, S. O. (2009). Marital trajectories and mortality among U.S. adults. *American Journal of Epidemiology, 170*(5), 546–555.

Dustan, H. P. (1996). Gender differences in hypertension. *Journal of Human Hypertension, 10*(6), 337–340.

Eagly, A. H. (1983). Gender and social influence: A social psychological analysis. *American Psychologist, 38*, 971–981.

Eagly, A. H., & Steffen, V. J. (1986). Gender and aggressive behavior: A meta-analytic review of the social psychological literature. *Psychological Bulletin, 100*(3), 309–330.

Earle, T. L., Linden, W., & Weinberg, J. (1999). Differential effects of harassment on cardiovascular and salivary cortisol stress reactivity and recovery in women and men. *Journal of Psychosomatic Research, 46*(2), 125–141.

Eaton, C. B., Nafziger, A. N., Strogatz, D. S., & Pearson, T. A. (1994). Self-reported physical activity in a rural county: A New York County health census. *American Journal of Public Health, 84*(1), 29–32.

Eber, G. B., Annest, J. L., Mercy, J. A., & Ryan, G. W. (2004). Nonfatal and fatal firearm-related injuries among children aged 14 years and younger: United States, 1993–2000. *Pediatrics, 113*(6), 1686–1692.

Eby, D. W., Molnar, L. J., & Olk, M. L. (2000). Trends in driver and front-right passenger safety belt use in Michigan: 1984 to 1998. *Accident Analysis & Prevention, 32*, 837–843.

EDK Associates. (1995, February). *The ABCs of STDs*. New York, NY: Author.

Edwards, B. (1994, October 7). Report says market economy killing off eastern Europeans. In R. Ferrante (Executive Producer), *Morning edition*. Washington, DC: National Public Radio.

Egan, B. M., Zhao, Y., & Axon, R. N. (2010). U.S. trends in prevalence, awareness, treatment, and control of hypertension, 1988–2008. *Journal of the American Medical Association, 303*(20), 2043–2050.

Eikelenboom, M. J., Killestein, J., Kragt, J. J., Uitdehaag, B. M. J., & Polman, C. H. (2009). Gender differences in multiple sclerosis: Cytokines and vitamin D. *Journal of the Neurological Sciences, 286*(1–2), 40–42.

Einhorn, L. H., Richie, J. P., & Shipley, W. U. (1993). Cancer of the testis. In V. T. DeVita, S. Hellman, & S. A. Rosenberg (Eds.), *Cancer: Principles and practice of oncology* (4th ed., pp. 1126–1151). Philadelphia, PA: J. B. Lippincott.

Eisler, R. M. (1995). The relationship between Masculine Gender Role Stress and men's health risk: The validation of a construct. In R. F. Levant & W. S. Pollack (Eds.), *A new psychology of men* (pp. 207–225). New York, NY: Basic Books.

Eisler, R. M., & Blalock, J. A. (1991). Masculine gender role stress: Implications for the assessment of men. *Clinical Psychology Review, 11*, 45–60.

Eisler, R. M., Franchina, J. J., Moore, T. M., Honeycutt, H., & Rhatigan, D. L. (2000). Masculine gender role stress and intimate abuse: Effects of gender relevance of the conflict situation on men's attributions and affective responses. *Psychology of Men and Masculinity, 1*, 30–36.

Eisler, R. M., & Hersen, M. (2000). *Handbook of gender, culture, and health.* Mahwah, NJ: Lawrence Erlbaum.

Eisler, R. M., & Skidmore, J. R. (1987). Masculine gender role stress: Scale development and component factors in the appraisal of stressful situations. *Behavior Modification, 11*, 123–136.

Eisler, R. M., Skidmore, J. R., & Ward, C. H. (1988). Masculine gender-role stress: Predictor of anger, anxiety, and health-risk behavior. *Journal of Personality Assessment, 52*, 133–141.

Ekman, P. (1999). Genetic and environmental factors in prostate cancer genesis: Identifying high-risk cohorts. *European Urology, 35*, 362–369.

Elder, G. H., & Liker, J. K. (1982). Hard times in women's lives: Historical influences across forty years. *American Journal of Sociology, 88*, 241–269.

Elia, J., & Devoto, M. (2007). ADHD genetics: 2007 update. *Current Psychiatry Reports, 9*(5), 434–439.

Emery, S., Gilpin, E. A., Ake, C., Farkas, A. J., & Pierce, J. P. (2000). Characterizing and identifying "hard-core" smokers: Implications for further reducing smoking prevalence. *American Journal of Public Health, 90*(3), 387–394.

Emmons, K. M., Marcus, B. H., Linnan, L., Rossi, J. S., & Abrams, D. B. (1994). Mechanisms in multiple risk factor interventions: Smoking, physical activity, and dietary fat intake among manufacturing workers. *Preventive Medicine, 23*, 481–489.

Emmons, K. M., McBride, C. M., Puleo, E., Pollak, K. I., Napolitano, M., Clipp, E., … Fletcher, R. (2005). Prevalence and predictors of multiple behavioral risk factors for colon cancer. *Preventive Medicine, 40*(5), 527–534.

Emslie, C., & Hunt, K. (2009). Men, masculinities and heart disease: A systematic review of the qualitative literature. *Current Sociology, 57*(2), 155–191.

Emslie, C., Ridge, D., Ziebland, S., & Hunt, K. (2006). Men's accounts of depression: Reconstructing or resisting hegemonic masculinity? *Social Science & Medicine, 62*(9), 2246–2257.

Engels, R. C. M. E., Hermans, R., van Baaren, R. B., Hollenstein, T., & Bot, S. M. (2009). Alcohol portrayal on television affects actual drinking behaviour. *Alcohol and Alcoholism, 44*(3), 244–249.

Enstrom, J. E., Kanim, L. E., & Breslow, L. (1986). The relationship between vitamin C intake, general health practices, and mortality in Alameda County, California. *American Journal of Public Health, 76*, 1124–1130.

Enstrom, J. E., Kanim, L. E., & Klein, M. A. (1992). Vitamin C intake and mortality among a sample of the United States population. *Epidemiology, 3*(3), 194–202.

Enzinger, P. C., & Mayer, R. J. (2003). Esophageal cancer. *New England Journal of Medicine, 349*(23), 2241–2252.

Epstein, A. M. (2004). Health care in America: Still too separate, not yet equal. *New England Journal of Medicine, 351*(6), 603–605.

Epstein, C. F. (1988). *Deceptive distinctions: Sex, gender, and the social order*. New Haven, CT: Yale University Press.

Ericksen, K. P., & Trocki, K. F. (1992). Behavioral risk factors for sexually transmitted diseases in American households. *Social Science and Medicine, 34*(8), 843–853.

Ericksen, K. P., & Trocki, K. F. (1994). Sex, alcohol and sexually transmitted diseases: A national survey. *Family Planning Perspectives, 26,* 257–263.

Ervø, S., & Johansson, T. (Eds.). (2003). *Moulding masculinities: Vol. 2. Bending bodies*. Burlington, VT: Ashgate.

Evans, R. E., Brotherstone, H., Miles, A., & Wardle, J. (2005). Gender differences in early detection of cancer. *Journal of Men's Health, 2*(2), 209–217.

Evatt, M. L., Terry, P. D., Ziegler, T. R., & Oakley, G. P. (2009). Association between vitamin B12-containing supplement consumption and prevalence of biochemically defined B12 deficiency in adults in NHANES III (Third National Health and Nutrition Examination Survey). *Public Health Nutrition, 13*(1), 25–31.

Ewart, C. K., Taylor, C. B., Kraemer, H. C., & Agras, W. S. (1991). High blood pressure and marital discord: Not being nasty matters more than being nice. *Health Psychology, 10,* 155–163.

Eyre, H., Kahn, R., Robertson, R. M., & the ACS/ADA/AHA Collaborative Writing Committee. (2004). Preventing cancer, cardiovascular disease, and diabetes: A common agenda for the American Cancer Society, the American Diabetes Association, and the American Heart Association. *Stroke, 35*(8), 1999–2010.

Fabes, R. A., & Martin, C. I. (1991). Gender and age stereotypes of emotionality. *Personality and Social Psychology Bulletin, 17,* 542–550.

Fabrega, H., Mezzich, J., Ulrich, R., & Benjamin, L. (1990). Females and males in an intake psychiatric setting. *Psychiatry, 53,* 1–16.

Fackelman, K. A. (1992). Genital-wart virus linked to penile cancer. *Science News, 141,* 342.

Fagerli, R. A., & Wandel, M. (1999). Gender differences in opinions and practices with regard to a "healthy diet." *Appetite, 32,* 171–190.

Fagot, B. I. (1984). Teacher and peer reactions to boys' and girls' play styles. *Sex Roles, 11*(7/8), 691–702.

Faigel, H. (1983). Gender preference toward providers of genital examinations and frequency of genital self-examination among college students. *Journal of American College Health, 31*(6), 240–242.

Farrow, J. A., & Brissing, P. (1990). Risk for DWI: A new look at gender differences in drinking and driving influences, experiences and attitudes among new adolescent drivers. *Health Education Quarterly, 17*(2), 213–221.

Faulkner, L. A., & Schauffler, H. H. (1997). The effect of health insurance coverage on the appropriate use of recommended clinical preventive services. *American Journal of Preventive Medicine, 13*(6), 453–458.

Fausto-Sterling, A. (2003). The problem with sex/gender and nature/nurture. In S. J. Williams, L. Birke, & G. A. Bendelow (Eds.), *Debating biology: Sociological reflections on health, medicine and society* (pp. 123–132). London, England: Routledge.

Federal Bureau of Investigation. (2009). *Law enforcement officers killed and assaulted, 2008* (Table 11—Race and sex of victim officer, 1999–2008). Washington, DC: Author.

Federiuk, C. S., Schlueter, J. L., & Adams, A. L. (2002). Skiing, snowboarding, and sledding injuries in a Northwestern state. *Wilderness & Environmental Medicine, 13*(4), 245–249.

Feingold, A., & Mazzella, R. (1998). Gender differences in body image are increasing. *Psychological Science, 9*, 190–195.

Felder, S. (2006). The gender longevity gap: Explaining the difference between singles and couples. *Journal of Population Economics, 19*(5), 543–557.

Feldman, M. B., & Meyer, I. H. (2007). Childhood abuse and eating disorders in gay and bisexual men. *International Journal of Eating Disorders, 40*, 418–423.

Felix-Aaron, K., Moy, E., Kang, M., Patel, M., Chesley, F., & Clancy, C. (2005). Variation in quality of men's health care by race/ethnicity and social class. *Medical Care, 43*(3), I-72–I-81.

Fellows, W. (1996). *Farm boys: Lives of gay men from the rural midwest.* Madison: University of Wisconsin Press.

Felton, G. M., Parsons, M. A., Pate, R. R., Ward, D., Saunders, R., Valois, R., … Trost, S. (1996). Predictors of alcohol use among rural adolescents. *Journal of Rural Health, 12*(5), 378–385.

Fernbach, B. E., Winstead, B. A., & Derlega, V. J. (1989). Sex differences in diagnosis and treatment recommendations for antisocial personality and somatization disorders. *Journal of Social and Clinical Psychology, 8*, 238–255.

Ferrence, R., Slade, J., Room, R., & Pope, M. (Eds.). (2000). *Nicotine and public health.* Washington, DC: American Public Health Association.

Ferrie, J. E., Shipley, M. J., Cappuccio, F. P., Brunner, E., Miller, M. A., Kumari, M., & Marmot, M. G. (2007). A prospective study of change in sleep duration: Associations with mortality in the Whitehall II cohort. *Sleep, 30*, 1659–1666.

Field, A. E., Coakley, E. H., Must, A., Spadano, J. L., Laird, N., Dietz, W. H., … Colditz, G. A. (2001). Impact of overweight on the risk of developing common chronic diseases during a 10-year period. *Archives of Internal Medicine, 16*(13), 1581–1586.

Fields, L. E., Burt, V. L., Cutler, J. A., Hughes, J., Roccella, E. J., & Sorlie, P. (2004). The burden of adult hypertension in the United States 1999 to 2000: A rising tide. *Hypertension, 44*(4), 398.

Fife, B. L., Kennedy, V. N., & Robinson, L. (1994). Gender and adjustment to cancer: Clinical implications. *Journal of Psychosocial Oncology, 12*(1), 1–21.

Findley, L. J., Levinson, M. P., & Bonnie, R. J. (1992). Driving performance and automobile accidents in patients with sleep apnea. *Clinics in Chest Medicine, 13*(3), 427–435.

Finley, L. L. (Ed.). (2007). *Encyclopedia of juvenile violence.* Westport, CT: Greenwood Press.

Finucane, M. L., Slovic, P., Mertz, C. K., Flynn, J., & Satterfield, T. A. (2000). Gender, race, and perceived risk: The "White male" effect. *Health, Risk & Society, 2*(2), 159–172.

Fiore, M. C., Jorenby, D. E., Wetter, D. W., Kenford S. L., Smith S. S., & Baker T. B. (1993). Prevalence of daily and experimental smoking among University of Wisconsin–Madison undergraduates, 1989–1993. *Wisconsin Medical Journal*, *92*(11), 605–608.

Fischer, C. S., & Oliker, S. J. (1983). A research note on friendship, gender, and life cycle. *Social Forces*, *62*(1), 124–133.

Fischer, E. H., & Turner, J. L. (1970). Orientations to seeking professional help: Development and research utility of an attitude scale. *Journal of Consulting and Clinical Psychology*, *35*(1), 79–90.

Fisher, A. R., & Good, G. E. (1998). Perceptions of parent-child relationships and masculine role conflicts of college men. *Journal of Counseling Psychology*, *45*, 346–352.

Fisher, E., Dunn, M., & Thompson, J. K. (2002). Social comparison and body image: An investigation of body comparison processes using multidimensional scaling. *Journal of Social and Clinical Psychology*, *21*, 566–579.

Fitzgerald, J. T., Anderson, R. M., & Davis, W. K. (1995). Gender differences in diabetes attitudes and adherence. *The Diabetes Educator*, *21*, 523–529.

Fitzpatrick, M. J., & McPherson, B. J. (2010). Coloring within the lines: Gender stereotypes in contemporary coloring books. *Sex Roles*, *62*(1–2), 127–137.

Fitzpatrick, S. G., & Katz, J. (2010). The association between periodontal disease and cancer: A review of the literature. *Journal of Dentistry*, *38*(2), 83–95.

Fivush, R., Brotman, M. A., Buckner, J. P., & Goodman, S. H. (2000). Gender differences in parent-child emotion narratives. *Sex Roles*, *42*(3–4), 233–253.

Flegal, K. M., & Cauley, J. A. (1985). Alcohol consumption and cardiovascular risk factors. *Recent Developments in Alcoholism*, *3*, 165–180.

Flegal, K. M., Graubard, B. I., Williamson, D. F., & Gail, M. H. (2005). Excess deaths associated with underweight, overweight, and obesity. *Journal of the American Medical Association*, *293*, 1861–1867.

Flegal, K. M., Graubard, B. I., Williamson, D. F., & Gail, M. H. (2007). Cause-specific excess deaths associated with underweight, overweight, and obesity. *Journal of the American Medical Association*, *298*, 2028–2037.

Fleming, R., Baum, A., Gisriel, M. M., & Gatchel, R. J. (1982). Mediating influences of social support on stress at Three Mile Island. *Journal of Human Stress*, *8*, 14–22.

Flores, A. H., Haileyesus, T., & Greenspan, A. I. (2008). National estimates of outdoor recreational injuries treated in emergency departments, United States, 2004-2005. *Wilderness and Environmental Medicine*, *19*(2), 91–98.

Florida Fish and Wildlife Conservation Commission. (2006). *2006 boating accidents statistical report*. Tallahassee, FL: Author.

Florida Fish and Wildlife Conservation Commission. (2007). *2006 boating accidents statistical report*. Tallahassee, FL: Author.

Flowers, N. T., Naimi, T. S., Brewer, R. D., Elder, R. W., Shults, R. A., & Jiles, R. (2008). Patterns of alcohol consumption and alcohol-impaired driving in the United States. *Alcoholism: Clinical and Experimental Research*, *32*(4), 639–644.

Flynn, J., Slovic, P., & Mertz, C. K. (1994). Gender, race, and perception of environmental health risks. *Risk Analysis*, *14*(6), 1101–1108.

Foerster, S. B., & Hudes, M. (1994). *California dietary practices survey: Focus on fruits and vegetables, trends among adults, 1989–1993*. Sacramento: California Department of Health Services.

Foley, D. L., Eaves, L. J., Wormley, B., Silberg, J. L., Maes, H. H., Kuhn, J., & Riley, B. (2004). Childhood adversity, monoamine oxidase A genotype, and risk for conduct disorder. *Archives of General Psychiatry, 61*(7), 738–744.

Foley, D. J., Wallace, R. B., & Eberhard, J. (1995). Risk factors for motor vehicle crashes among older drivers in a rural community. *Journal of the American Geriatrics Society, 43*(7), 776–781.

Foote, J. A., Harris, R. B., & Gilles, M. E. (1996). Physician advice and tobacco use: A survey of 1st-year college students. *Journal of American College Health, 45*(3), 129–132.

Ford, E. S. (1999). Body mass index and colon cancer in a national sample of adult U.S. men and women. *American Journal of Epidemiology, 150*(4), 390–398.

Ford, E. S. (2005). Prevalence of the metabolic syndrome defined by the International Diabetes Federation among adults in the U.S. *Diabetes Care, 28*(11), 2745–2749.

Ford, E. S., Ajani, U. A., Croft, J. B., Critchley, J. A., Labarthe, D. R., Kottke, T. E., … Capewell, S. (2007). Explaining the decrease in U.S. deaths from coronary disease, 1980–2000. *New England Journal of Medicine, 356,* 2388–2398.

Ford, E. S., & Jones, D. H. (1991). Cardiovascular health knowledge in the United States: Findings from the National Health Interview Survey, 1985. *Preventive Medicine, 20,* 725–736.

Ford, E. S., Kohl, H. W., Mokdad, A. H., & Ajani, U. A. (2005). Sedentary behavior, physical activity, and the metabolic syndrome among U.S. adults. *Obesity Research, 13*(3), 608–614.

Ford, E. S., Li, C., Zhao, G., Pearson, W. S., & Capewell, S. (2009). Trends in the prevalence of low risk factor burden for cardiovascular disease among United States adults. *Circulation, 120*(13), 1181–1188.

Ford, M. R., & Widiger, T. A. (1989). Sex bias in the diagnosis of histrionic and antisocial personality disorders. *Journal of Consulting and Clinical Psychology, 57*(2), 301–305.

Forrest, K. A. (2001). Men's reproductive and sexual health. *Journal of American College Health, 49*(6), 253–266.

Fortuna, R. J., Robbins, B. W., & Halterman, J. S. (2009). Ambulatory care among young adults in the United States. *Annals of Internal Medicine, 151*(6), 379–385.

Foss, R. D., Beirness, D. J., & Sprattler, K. (1994). Seat belt use among drinking drivers in Minnesota. *American Journal of Public Health, 84*(11), 1732–1737.

Fowke, J., Schlundt, D., Signorello, L., Ukoli, F., & Blot, W. (2005). Prostate cancer screening between low-income African-American and Caucasian men. *Urologic oncology: Seminars and original investigations, 23*(5), 333–340.

Fowler, P. J., Tompsett, C. J., Braciszewski, J. M., Jacques-Tiura, A. J., & Baltes, B. B. (2009). Community violence: A meta-analysis on the effect of exposure and mental health outcomes of children and adolescents. *Development and Psychopathology, 21,* 227–259.

Fox, J. A., & Swatt, M. L. (2008). The recent surge in homicides involving young black males and guns: Time to reinvest in prevention and crime control. Unpublished manuscript, Northeastern University, Boston, Massachusetts.

Fracher, J., & Kimmel, M. S. (1992). Hard issues and soft spots: Counseling men about sexuality. In M. S. Kimmel & M. A. Messner (Eds.), *Men's lives* (2nd ed., pp. 438–450). New York, NY: Macmillan.

Fragoso, J. M., & Kashubeck, S. (2000). Machismo, gender role conflict, and mental health in Mexican American men. *Psychology of Men & Masculinity, 1*(2), 87–97.

Frame, P. S. (1996). Developing a health maintenance schedule. In S. H. Woolf, S. Jonas, & R. S. Lawrence (Eds.), *Health promotion and disease prevention in clinical practice* (pp. 467–482). Baltimore, MD: Williams & Wilkins.

Franceschi, S. (1994). Fat and prostate cancer. *Epidemiology, 5*(3), 271–273.

Franchesci, S., Bidoli, E., LaVecchia, C., Talamini, R., D'Avanzo, B., & Negri, E. (1994). Tomatoes and risk of digestive tract cancer. *International Journal of Cancer, 59*(2), 181–184.

Franchina, J. J., Eisler, R. M., & Moore, T. M. (2001). Masculine gender role stress and intimate abuse: Effects of masculine gender relevance of dating situations and female threat on men's attributions and affective responses. *Psychology of Men and Masculinity, 2*, 34–41.

Frank, E., & Harvey, L. K. (1996). Prevention advice rates of women and men physicians. *Archives of Family Medicine, 5*(4), 215–219.

Frank, J. A. (1981). Economic change and mental health in an uncontaminated setting. *American Journal of Community Psychology, 9*, 395–410.

Frank, R. (2007). What to make of it? The (re)emergence of a biological conceptualization of race in health disparities research. *Social Science & Medicine, 64*(10), 1977–1983.

Frank, R. G., Bouman, D. E., Cain, K., & Watts, C. (1992). Primary prevention of catastrophic injury. *American Psychologist, 47*(8), 1045–1049.

Frankenhaeuser, M. (1996). Stress and gender. *European Review, 4*, 313–327.

Frankenhaeuser, M., Von Wright, M., Collins, A., Von Wright, J., Sedvall, G., & Swahn, C. (1978). Sex differences in psychoneuroendocrine reactions to examination stress. *Psychosomatic Medicine, 40*, 334–343.

Franklin, B. A., Bonzheim, K., Gordon, S., & Timmis, G. C. (1996). Snow shoveling: A trigger for acute myocardial infarction and sudden coronary death. *American Journal of Cardiology, 77*(10), 855–858.

Frattaroli, S., & Teret, S. P. (1998). Why firearm injury surveillance? *American Journal of Preventive Medicine, 15*(3, Suppl.), 2–5.

Friedman, C., Brownson, R. C., Peterson, D. E., & Wilkerson, J. C. (1994). Physician advice to reduce chronic disease risk factors. *American Journal of Preventive Medicine, 10*(6), 367–371.

Friedman, C. R., Hoekstra, R. M., Samuel, M., Marcus, R., Bender, J., Shiferaw, B., … Tauxe, R. V. (2004). Risk factors for sporadic campylobacter infection in the United States: A case-control study in FoodNet sites. *Clinical Infectious Diseases, 38*(Suppl. 3), S285–S296.

Friedman, H. S. (Ed.). (1991). *Hostility, coping, and health*. Washington, DC: American Psychological Association.

Friedman, H. S., & Booth-Kewley, S. (1987). Personality, Type A behavior, and coronary heart disease: The role of emotional expression. *Journal of Personality and Social Psychology, 53*(4), 783–792.

Friedman, H. S., & DiMatteo, M. R. (1989). Cooperation (adherence) and practitioner-patient relations. In H. S. Friedman & M. R. DiMatteo, *Health psychology* (pp. 68–100). Englewood Cliffs, NJ: Prentice Hall.

Friedman, L. A., & Kimball, A. W. (1986). Coronary heart disease mortality and alcohol consumption in Framingham. *American Journal of Epidemiology, 124*, 481–489.

Friedman, L. C., Bruce, S., Weinberg, A. D., Cooper, H. P., Yen, A. H., & Hill, M. (1994). Early detection of skin cancer: Racial/ethnic differences in behaviors and attitudes. *Journal of Cancer Education, 9*(2), 105–110.

Frimpong, N. A., & Lapp, J. A. (1989). Effects of moderate alcohol intake in fixed or variable amounts on concentration of serum lipids and liver enzymes in healthy young men. *American Journal of Clinical Nutrition, 50*, 987–991.

Frydenberg, E., & Lewis, R. (1991). Adolescent coping: The different ways in which boys and girls cope. *Journal of Adolescence, 14*, 119–133.

Fung, I. C-H., & Cairncross, S. (2007). How often do you wash your hands? A review of studies of hand-washing practices in the community during and after SARS outbreak in 2003. *International Journal of Environmental Health Research, 17*(3), 161–183.

Furman, R. (2010). *Social work practice with men at risk.* New York, NY: Columbia University Press.

Furnham, A., & Kirkcaldy, B. (1997). Age and sex differences in health beliefs and behaviors. *Psychological Reports, 80*, 63–66.

Gabory, A., Attig, J., & Junien, C. (2009). Sexual dimorphism in environmental epigenetic programming. *Molecular and Cellular Endocrinology, 304*, 8–18.

Gabrielsen, M. A., McElhaney, J., & O'Brien, R. F. (2001). *Diving injuries: Research findings and recommendations for reducing catastrophic injuries.* Boca Raton, FL: CRC Press.

Galdas, P., Cheater, F., & Marshall, P. (2005). Men and health help-seeking behaviour: Literature review. *Journal of Advanced Nursing, 49*(6), 616–623.

Galuska, D. A., Serdula, M., Pamuk, E., Siegel, P. Z., & Byers, T. (1996). Trends in overweight among U.S. adults from 1987 to 1993: A multistate telephone survey. *American Journal of Public Health, 86*(12), 1729–1735.

Gamble, V. (1997). Under the shadow of Tuskegee: African Americans and health care. *American Journal of Public Health, 87*, 1773–1778.

Gami, A. S., Howard, D. E., Olson, E. J., & Somers, V. K. (2005). Day-night pattern of sudden death in obstructive sleep apnea. *New England Journal of Medicine, 352*(12), 1206–1214.

Gamm, L., Hutchinson, L., Dabney, B., & Dorsey, A. (2003). *Rural healthy people 2010: A companion document to* Healthy People 2010. Rockville, MD: Department of Health and Human Services.

Gandini, S., Sera, F., Cattaruzza, M. S., Pasquini, P., Picconi, O., Boyle, P., & Melchi, C. F. (2005). Meta-analysis of risk factors for cutaneous melanoma: II. Sun exposure. *European Journal of Cancer, 41*(1), 45–60.

Gangwisch, J. E., Heymsfield, S. B., Boden-Albala, B., Buijs, R. M., Kreier, F., Pickering, T. G., … Malaspina, D. (2006). Short sleep duration as a risk factor for hypertension: Analyses of the first National Health and Nutrition Examination Survey. *Hypertension, 47*, 833–839.

Gangwisch, J. E., Heymsfield, S. B., Boden-Albala, B., Buijs, R. M., Kreier, F., Pickering, T. G., … Malaspina, D. (2007). Sleep duration as a risk factor for diabetes incidence in a large U.S. sample. *Sleep, 30*(12), 1667–1673.

Gann, P. H., Hennekens, C. H., Sacks, F. M., Grodstein, F., Giovannucci, E. L., & Stampfer, M. J. (1994). Prospective study of plasma fatty acids and risk of prostate cancer. *Journal of the National Cancer Institute, 86,* 281–286.

Ganong, L. H., & Coleman, M. (1991). Remarriage and health. *Research in Nursing and Health, 14,* 205–211.

Garber, C. E., Allsworth, J. E., Marcus, B. H., Hesser, J., & Lapane, K. L. (2008). Correlates of the stages of change for physical activity in a population survey. *American Journal of Public Health, 98*(5), 897–904.

Garcia, A. N., Kushang, B. A., Patel, V., & Guralnik, J. M. (2007). Seatbelt use among American Indians/Alaska Natives and non-Hispanic whites. *American Journal of Preventive Medicine, 33*(3), 200–206.

Garner, D. M., Olmstead, M. P., & Polivy, J. (1983). Development and validation of a multidimensional eating disorder inventory for anorexia nervosa and bulimia. *International Journal of Eating Disorders, 2,* 15–34.

Garrison, C. Z., McKeown, R. E., & Valois, R. F. (1993). Aggression, substance use, and suicidal behaviors in high school students. *American Journal of Public Health, 83*(2), 179–184.

Gasparro, F. P., Mitchnick, M., & Nash, J. F. (1998). A review of sunscreen safety and efficacy. *Photochemistry and Photobiology, 68*(3), 243–256.

Gay and Lesbian Medical Association. (2001). *Healthy people 2010: Companion document for lesbian, gay, bisexual, and transgender (LGBT) health.* San Francisco, CA: Author.

Gaziano, J. M., Buring, J. E., Breslow, J. L., Goldhaber, S. Z., Rosner, B., Vandenburgh, M., … Hennekens, C. H. (1993). Moderate alcohol intake, increased levels of high-density lipoprotein and its subfractions, and decreased risk of myocardial infarction. *New England Journal of Medicine, 329,* 1829–1834.

Gaziano, J. M., Gaziano, T. A., Glynn, R. J., Sesso, H. D., Ajani, U. A., Stampfer, M. J., … Buring, J. E. (2000). Light-to-moderate alcohol consumption and mortality in the Physicians' Health Study enrollment cohort. *Journal of the American College of Cardiology, 35*(1), 96–105.

Geary, D. C. (1999). Evolution and developmental sex differences. *Current Directions in Psychological Science, 8*(4), 115–120.

Geis, F. L. (1993). Self-fulfilling prophecies: A social psychological view of gender. In A. E. Beall & R. J. Sternberg (Eds.), *The psychology of gender* (pp. 9–54). New York, NY: Guilford Press.

Geisel-Marbaise, S., & Stummer, H. (2010). Diabetes adherence—Does gender matter? *Journal of Public Health, 18,* 219–226.

Geller, A. C., Koh, H. K., Miller, D. R., Mercer, M. B., & Lew, R. A. (1992). Death rates of malignant melanoma among white men—United States, 1973–1988. *Morbidity and Mortality Weekly Report, 41,* 20–21, 27.

Geller, A. C., Miller, D. R., Annas, G. D., Demierre, M. F., Gilchrest, B. A., & Koh, H. K. (2002). Melanoma incidence and mortality among U.S. whites, 1969–1999. *Journal of the American Medical Association, 288*(14), 1719–1720.

Geller, A. C., Zhang, Z., Sober, A. J., Halpern, A. C., Weinstock, M. A., Daniels, S., … Gilchrest, B. A. (2003). The first 15 years of the American Academy of Dermatology skin cancer screening programs: 1985–1999. *Journal of the American Academy of Dermatology, 48*(1), 34–41.

Gelles, R. J., & Straus, M. A. (1988). *Intimate violence.* New York, NY: Simon & Schuster.

George, A., & Fleming, P. (2004). Factors affecting men's help-seeking in the early detection of prostate cancer: Implications for health promotion. *Journal of Men's Health & Gender, 1*(4), 345–352.

Gerber, G. S., Thompson, I. M., Thisted, R., & Chodak, G. W. (1993). Disease-specific survival following routine prostate cancer screening by digital rectal examination. *Journal of the American Medical Association, 269*(1), 61–64.

Gerberich, S. G., Robertson, L. S., Gibson, R. W., & Renier, C. (1996). An epidemiological study of roadway fatalities related to farm vehicles: United States, 1988 to 1993. *Journal of Occupational and Environmental Medicine, 38*(11), 1135–1140.

Gerbner, G., Gross, L., Morgan, M., & Signorielli, N. (1981). Health and medicine on television. *New England Journal of Medicine, 305*(15), 901–904.

Gerson, J. M., & Peiss, K. (1985). Boundaries, negotiation, consciousness: Reconceptualizing gender relations. *Social Problems, 32*(4), 317–331.

Gfroerer, J. C., Larson, S. L., & Colliver, J. D. (2007). Drug use patterns and trends in rural communities. *Journal of Rural Health, 23*(Suppl. 1), 10–15.

Gibbons, S., Wylie, M. L., Echterling, L., & French, J. (1986). Patterns of alcohol use among rural and small-town adolescents. *Adolescence, 21*(84), 887–900.

Gibbs, J. T. (1988). Health and mental health of young black males. In J. T. Gibbs (Ed.), *Young, Black and male in America: An endangered species* (pp. 219–257). New York, NY: Auburn House.

Gijsbers van Wijk, C. M. T., van Vliet, K. P., Kolk, K. P., & Everaerd, W. T. (1991). Symptom sensitivity and sex differences in physical morbidity: A review of health surveys in the United States and the Netherlands. *Women and Health, 17*(1), 91–124.

Gilchrist, J., Saluja, G., & Marshall, S. W. (2007). Interventions to prevent sports and recreation-related injuries. In L. S. Doll, S. E. Bonzo, D. A. Sleet, J. A. Mercy, & E. N. Haas (Eds.), *Handbook of injury and violence prevention* (pp. 117–136). New York, NY: Springer.

Giles, W. H., Anda, R. F., Casper, M. L., Escobedo, L. G., & Taylor, H. A. (1995). Race and sex differences in rates of invasive cardiac procedures in U.S. hospitals: Data from the National Hospital Discharge Survey. *Archives of Internal Medicine, 155*(3), 318–324.

Gillespie, B. L., & Eisler, R. M. (1992). Development of the Feminine Gender Role Stress Scale: A cognitive-behavioral measure of stress, appraisal, and coping for women. *Behavior Modification, 16,* 426–438.

Gillies, C. L., Abrams, K. R., Lambert, P. C., Cooper, N. J., Sutton, A. J., Hsu, R. T., & Khunti, K. (2007). Pharmacological and lifestyle interventions to prevent or delay type 2 diabetes in people with impaired glucose tolerance: Systematic review and meta-analysis. *British Medical Journal, 334*(7588), 299.

Gilligan, T., Wang, P. S., Levin, R., Kantoff, P. W., & Avorn, J. (2004). Racial differences in screening for prostate cancer in the elderly. *Archives of Internal Medicine, 164,* 1858–1864.

Gillman, M. W., Cupples, L. A., Gagnon, D., Posner, B. M., Ellison, R. C., Castelli, W. P., & Wolf, P. A. (1995). Protective effect of fruits and vegetables on development of stroke in men. *Journal of the American Medical Association, 273*(14), 1113–1117.

Gillum, R. F. (1994). Prevalence of cardiovascular and pulmonary diseases and risk factors by region and urbanization in the United States. *Journal of the National Medical Association, 86*(2), 105–112.

Gilpin, E., Pierce, J. P., & Rosbrook, B. (1997). Are adolescents receptive to current sales promotion practices of the tobacco industry? *Preventive Medicine, 26,* 14–21.

Gini, G., & Pozzoli, T. (2006). The role of masculinity in children's bullying. *Behavioral Science, 54*(7–8), 585–588.

Giovannucci, E., Ascherio, A., Rimm, E. B., Colditz, G. A., Stampfer, M. J., & Willett, W. C. (1995). Physical activity, obesity, and risk for colon cancer and adenoma in men. *Annals of Internal Medicine, 122*(5), 327–334.

Giovannucci, E., Harlan, D. M., Archer, M. C., Bergenstal, R. M., Gapstur, S. M., Habel, L. A., ... Yee, E. (2010). Diabetes and cancer: A consensus report. *CA: A Cancer Journal for Clinicians, 60,* 207–221.

Giovannucci, E., Rimm, E. B., Colditz, G. A., Stampfer, M. J., Ascherio, A., Chute, C. C., & Willett, W. C. (1993). A prospective study of dietary fat and risk of prostate cancer. *Journal of the National Cancer Institute, 85,* 1571–1579.

Giovino, G. A., Henningfield, J. E., Tomar, S. L., Escobedo, L. G., & Slade, J. (1995). Epidemiology of tobacco use and dependence. *Epidemiologic Reviews, 17*(1), 48–65.

Girdler, S. S., Turner, J. R., Sherwood, A., & Light, K. C. (1990): Gender differences in blood pressure control during a variety of behavioral stressors. *Psychosomatic Medicine, 52*(5), 571–591.

Girgis, A., Campbell, E. M., Redman, S., & Sanson-Fisher, R. W. (1991). Screening for melanoma: A community survey of prevalence and predictors. *Medical Journal of Australia, 154,* 338–343.

Giri, S., Thompson, P. D., Kiernan, F. J., Clove, J., Fram, D. B., Mitchel, J. F., ... Waters, D. D. (1999). Clinical and angiographic characteristics of exertion-related acute myocardial infarction. *Journal of the American Medical Association, 282*(18), 1731–1736.

Glanz, K., Patterson, R. E., Kristal, A. R., DiClemente, C. C., Heimendinger, J., Linnan, L., & McLerran, D. F. (1994). Stages of change in adopting healthy diets: Fat, fiber, and correlates of nutrient intake. *Health Education Quarterly, 21,* 499–519.

Glascock, J. (2008). Direct and indirect aggression on prime-time network television. *Journal of Broadcasting & Electronic Media, 52*(2), 268–281.

Glass, J., & Fujimoto, T. (1994). Housework, paid work, and depression among husbands and wives. *Journal of Health and Social Behavior, 35,* 179–191.

Glassman, A. H., Helzer, J. E., Covey, L. S., Cottler, L. B., Stetner, F., Tipp, J. E., & Johnson, J. (1990). Smoking, smoking cessation, and major depression. *Journal of the American Medical Association, 264*(12), 1546–1549.

Glover, E. D., Laflin, M., Flannery, D., & Albritton, D. L. (1989). Smokeless tobacco use among American college students. *Journal of American College Health, 38,* 81–85.

Glymour, B., Glymour, C., & Glymour, M. (2008). Watching social science: The debate about the effects of exposure to televised violence on aggressive behavior. *American Behavioral Scientist, 51,* 1231–1259.

Glymour, M. M., Kosheleva, A., & Boden-Albala, B. (2009). Birth and adult residence in the Stroke Belt independently predict stroke mortality. *Neurology, 73*(22), 1858–1865.

Glynn, L. M., Christenfeld, N., & Gerin, W. (2002). The role of rumination in recovery from reactivity: Cardiovascular consequences of emotional states. *Psychosomatic Medicine, 64,* 714–726.

Goff, D. C., Bertoni, A. G., Kramer, H., Bonds, D., Blumenthal, R. S., Tsai, M. Y., & Psaty, B. M. (2006). Dyslipidemia prevalence, treatment, and control in the Multi-Ethnic Study of Atherosclerosis (MESA): Gender, ethnicity, and coronary artery calcium. *Circulation, 113,* 647–656.

Goffman, E. (1961). *Asylums: Essays on the social situation of mental patients and other inmates.* Garden City, NY: Anchor Books.

Goldberg, H. (1976). *The hazards of being male: Surviving the myth of masculine privilege.* Plainview, NY: Nash Publishing.

Goldberg, K. (1993). *How men can live as long as women: Seven steps to a longer and better life.* Fort Worth, TX: The Summit Group.

Goldberg, N. M. (2009). *Race and gender differentials in self-perceived health status among the middle-aged: An examination of a Modified Health Belief Model.* (Doctoral dissertation, Howard University; Publication No. AAT 3355463).

Goldman, J. A., & Harlow, L. L. (1993). Self-perception variables that mediate AIDS-preventive behavior in college students. *Health Psychology, 12*(6), 489–498.

Goldsmith, S. K., Pellmar, T. C., Kleinman, A. M., & Bunney, W. E. (Eds.). (2002). *Reducing suicide: A national imperative.* Washington, DC: National Academies Press.

Golomb, M., Fava, M., Abraham, M., & Rosenbaum, J. F. (1995). Gender differences in personality disorders. *American Journal of Psychiatry, 152,* 579–582.

Golombok, S., & Fivush, R. (1994). *Gender development.* Cambridge, MA: Cambridge University Press.

Gomez, J. (1991). *Psychological and psychiatric problems in men.* New York, NY: Routledge.

Gong, Z., Kristal, A. R., Schenk, J. M., Tangen, C. M., Goodman, P. J., & Thompson, I. M. (2009). Alcohol consumption, finasteride, and prostate cancer risk: Results from the prostate cancer prevention trial. *Cancer, 115*(16), 3661–3669.

Gonzalez, G. M. (1989). Early onset of drinking as a predictor of alcohol consumption and alcohol-related problems in college. *Journal of Drug Education, 19*(3), 225–230.

Good, G. E., Dell, D. M., & Mintz, L. B. (1989). Male role and gender role conflict: Relations to help seeking in men. *Journal of Counseling Psychology, 36*(3), 295–300.

Good, G. E., & Mintz, L. B. (1990). Gender role conflict and depression in college men: Evidence for compounded risk. *Journal of Counseling and Development, 69*(1), 17–21.

Good, G. E., Robertson, J. M., O'Neil, J. M., Fitzgerald, L. F., Stevens, M., DeBord, K., ... Braverman, D. G. (1995). Male gender role conflict: Psychometric issues and relations to psychological distress. *Journal of Counseling Psychology, 42,* 3–10.

Good, G. E., Sherrod, N. B., & Dillon, M. G. (2000). Masculine gender role stressors and men's health. In R. M. Eisler & M. Hersen (Eds.), *Handbook of gender, culture, and health* (pp. 63–81). Mahwah, NJ: Lawrence Erlbaum.

Good, G. E., & Wood, P. K. (1995). Male gender-role conflict, depression and help seeking: Do college men face double jeopardy? *Journal of Counseling and Development, 74*, 70–75.

Gordon, B., & Pasick, R. S. (1990). Changing the nature of friendships between men. In R. L. Meth & R. S. Pasick (Eds.), *Men in therapy: The challenge of change* (pp. 261–278). New York, NY: Guilford Press.

Gordon, D. F. (1995). Testicular cancer and masculinity. In D. Sabo & D. F. Gordon (Eds.), *Men's health and illness: Gender, power and the body* (pp. 246–265). Thousand Oaks, CA: Sage.

Gorelick, P. B., Sacco, R. L., Smith, D. B., Alberts, M., Mustone-Alexander, L., Rader, D., … Rhew, D. C. (1999). Prevention of a first stroke: A review of guidelines and a multidisciplinary consensus statement from the National Stroke Association. *Journal of the American Medical Association, 281*(12), 1112–1120.

Gornick, M. E. (2003). A decade of research on disparities in Medicare utilization: Lessons for the health and health care of vulnerable men. *American Journal of Public Health, 93*(5), 753–759.

Gortmaker, S. L., Dietz, W. H., & Cheung, L. W. (1990). Inactivity, diet, and the fattening of America. *Journal of the American Dietetic Association, 90*(9), 1247–1252, 1255.

Gossard, M. H., & York, R. (2003). Social structural influences on meat consumption. *Human Ecology Review, 10*(1), 1–9.

Gottlieb, D. J., Redline, S., Nieto, F. J., Baldwin, C. M., Newman, A. B., Resnick, H. E., & Punjabi, N. M. (2006). Association of usual sleep duration with hypertension: The Sleep Heart Health Study. *Sleep, 29*(8), 1009–1014.

Gough, B. (2007). "Real men don't diet": An analysis of contemporary newspaper representations of men, food and health. *Social Science & Medicine, 64*(2), 326–337.

Gouin, J. P., Hantsoo, L., & Kiecolt-Glaser, J. K. (2008). Immune dysregulation and chronic stress among older adults: A review. *Neuroimmunomodulation, 15*(4–6), 251–259.

Granié, M.-A. (2010). Gender stereotype conformity and age as determinants of preschoolers' injury-risk behaviors. *Accident Analysis and Prevention, 42*(2), 726–733.

Gray, L. A., & Saracino, M. (1989). AIDS on campus: A preliminary study of college students' knowledge and behaviors. *Journal of Counseling Development, 68*(2), 199–202.

Grayson, M. L., Melvani, S., Druce, J., Barr, I. G., Ballard, S. A., Johnson, P. D., … Birch, C. (2009). Efficacy of soap and water and alcohol-based hand-rub preparations against live H1N1 influenza virus on the hands of human volunteers. *Clinical Infectious Diseases, 48*(3), 285–291.

Green, J. (2000). Introduction to transgender issues. In P. Currah & S. Minter (Eds.), *Transgender equality: A handbook for activists and policymakers.* New York, NY: Policy Institute of the National Gay and Lesbian Task Force and National Center for Lesbian Rights.

Green, C. A., & Pope, C. R. (1999). Gender, psychosocial factors, and the use of medical services: A longitudinal analysis. *Social Science & Medicine, 48*(10), 1363–1372.

Greenberg, B. (1982). Television and role socialization: an overview. In D. Pearl, L. Bouthilet, & J. Lazar (Eds.), *Television and social behaviour: Ten years of scientific progress* (pp. 179–190). Washington, DC: U.S. Government Printing Office.

Greenberg, B. S., Eastin, M., Hofschire, L., Lachlan, K., & Brownell, K. D. (2003). Portrayals of overweight and obese individuals on commercial television. *American Journal of Public Health, 93*(8), 1342–1348.

Gridley, G., McLaughlin, J. K., Block, G., Blot, W. J., Gluch, M., & Fraumeni, J. F. (1992). Vitamin supplement use and reduced risk of oral and pharyngeal cancer. *American Journal of Epidemiology, 135*(10), 1083–1092.

Griffin, J. M., Burgess, D., Vernon, S. W., Friedemann-Sanchez, G., Powell, A. van Ryn, M., … Partin, M. (2009). Are gender differences in colorectal cancer screening rates due to differences in self-reporting? *Preventive Medicine, 49*(5), 436–441.

Grigsby, J. B., & Weatherley, D. (1983). Gender and sex-role differences in intimacy of self-disclosure. *Psychological Reports, 53*, 891–897.

Grogan, S., & Richards, H. (2002). Body image: Focus groups with boys and men. *Men and Masculinities, 4*, 219–232.

Grönberg, H. (2003). Prostate cancer epidemiology. *Lancet, 361*(9360), 859–864.

Grucza, R. A., Norberg, K. E., & Bierut, L. J. (2009). Binge drinking among youths and young adults in the United States: 1979–2006. *Journal of the American Academy of Child & Adolescent Psychiatry, 48*(7), 692–702.

Grueninger, U. J., Goldstein, M. G., & Duffy, F. D. (1990). A conceptual framework for interactive patient education in practice and clinic settings. *Journal of Human Hypertension, 4*(Suppl. 1), 21–31.

Grüninger, U. J. (1995). Patient education: An example of one-to-one communication. *Journal of Human Hypertension, 9*(1), 15–25.

Gruskin, E., Greenwood, G., Matevia, M., Pollack, L., & Bye, L. (2007). Disparities in smoking between the lesbian, gay, and bisexual population and the general population in California. *American Journal of Public Health, 97*(8), 1496–1502.

Guinness World Records. (2009). *Guinness world records, 2009*. New York, NY: Bantam Dell.

Gur, R. C., Alsop, D., Glahn, D., Petty, R., Swanson, C. L., Maldjian, J. A., … Gur, R. E. (2000). An fMRI study of sex differences in regional activation to a verbal and a spatial task. *Brain and Language, 74*, 157–170.

Gustafson, P. E. (1998). Gender differences in risk perception: Theoretical and methodological perspectives. *Risk Analysis, 18*(6), 805–811.

Guthrie, B. J., Loveland-Cherry, C., Frey, M. A., & Dielman, T. E. (1994). A theoretical approach to studying health behaviors in adolescents: An at-risk population. *Family and Community Health, 17*(3), 35–48.

Gutmann, D. (1975). Parenthood: A key to the comparative study of the life cycle. In N. Datan & L. Ginsberg (Eds.), *Life-span developmental psychology: Normative life crises* (pp. 167–187). New York, NY: Academic Press.

Hadley, J. (2003). Sicker and poorer—The consequences of being uninsured: A review of the research on the relationship between health insurance, medical care use, health, work, and income. *Medical Care Research and Review, 60(*2), 3S–75S.

Hagberg, J. M. (1990). Exercise, fitness, and hypertension. In C. Bouchard, R. J. Shephard, T. Stephens, J. R. Sutton, & B. D. McPherson (Eds.), *Exercise, fitness, and health: A consensus of current knowledge* (pp. 455–466). Champaign, IL: Human Kinetics.

Hagenau, T., Vest, R., Gissel, T. N., Poulsen, C. S., Erlandsen, M., Mosekilde, L., & Vestergaard, P. (2009). Global vitamin D levels in relation to age, gender, skin pigmentation and latitude: An ecologic meta-regression analysis. *Osteoporosis International, 20*(1), 133–140.

Halkitis, P. N., & Parsons, J. T. (2003). Intentional unsafe sex (barebacking) among gay men who seek sexual partners on the Internet. *AIDS Care, 15*(3), 367–378.

Halkitis, P. N., Parsons, J. T., & Wilton, L. (2003). Barebacking among gay and bisexual men in New York City: Explanations for the emergence of intentional unsafe behavior. *Archives of Sexual Behavior, 32*(4), 351–357.

Hall, H. I., May, D. S., Lew, R. A., Koh, H. K., & Nadel, M. (1997). Sun protection behaviors in the U.S. white population. *Preventive Medicine, 26*(4), 401–407.

Hall, H. I., Miller, D. R., Rogers, J. D., & Bewerse, B. (1999). Update on the incidence and mortality from melanoma in the United States. *Journal of the American Academy of Dermatology, 40*(1), 35–42.

Hall, H. I., & Rogers, J. D. (1999). Sun protection behaviors among African Americans. *Ethnicity and Disease, 9*(1), 126–131.

Hall, H. I., Saraiya, M., Thompson, T., Hartman, A., Glanz, K., & Rimer, B. (2003). Correlates of sunburn experiences among U.S. adults: Results of the 2000 National Health Interview Survey. *Public Health Reports, 118*, 540–549.

Hall, J. A., Roter, D. L., & Katz, N. R. (1988). Meta-analysis of correlates of provider behavior in medical encounters. *Medical Care, 26*(7), 657–675.

Hall, M. A., Dugan, E., Zheng, B., & Mishra, A. K. (2001). Trust in physicians and medical institutions: What is it, can it be measured, and does it matter? *Milbank Quarterly, 79*, 613–639.

Hall, M. S., Muldoon, M. F., Jennings, R., Buysse, D. J., Flory, J. D., & Manuck, S. B. (2008). Self-reported sleep duration is associated with the metabolic syndrome in midlife adults. *Sleep, 31*(5), 635–643.

Hallqvist, J., Moller, J., Ahlbom, A., Diderichsen, F., Reuterwall, C., & de Faire, U. (2000). Does heavy physical exertion trigger myocardial infarction? A case-crossover analysis nested in a population-based case-referent study. *American Journal of Epidemiology, 151*(5), 459–467.

Halpern, C. T., Hallfors, D., Bauer, D. J., Iritani, B., Waller, M. W., & Cho, H. (2004). Implications of racial and gender differences in patterns of adolescent risk behavior for HIV and other sexually transmitted diseases. *Perspectives on Sexual and Reproductive Health, 36*(6), 239–247.

Halpern, M. T., Ward, E. M., Pavluck, A. L., Schrag, N. M., Bian, J., & Chen, A. Y. (2008). Association of insurance status and ethnicity with cancer stage at diagnosis for 12 cancer sites: A retrospective analysis. *Lancet Oncology, 9*(3), 222–231.

Hamer, M., & Chida, Y. (2008). Walking and primary prevention: A meta-analysis of prospective cohort studies. *British Journal of Sports Medicine, 42*(4), 238–243.

Hamilton, C. J., & Mahalik, J. R. (2009). Minority stress, masculinity, and social norms predicting gay men's health risk behaviors. *Journal of Counseling Psychology, 56*(1), 132–141.

Hammarstrom, A. (1994). Health consequences of youth unemployment: Review from a gender perspective. *Social Science and Medicine, 38*(5), 699–709.

Hammett, T. M., Harrold, L., Gross, M., & Epstein, J. (1994). *1992 update: HIV/AIDS in correctional facilities—Issues and options*. Washington, DC: National Institute of Justice, Department of Justice.

Hansen, W. B., Hahn, G. L., & Wolkenstein, B. H. (1990). Perceived personal immunity: Beliefs about susceptibility to AIDS. *Journal of Sex Research, 27*(4), 622–628.

Harachi, T. W., Catalano, R. F., Kim, S., & Choi, Y. (2001). Etiology and prevention of substance use among Asian American youth. *Prevention Science, 2*(1), 57–65.

Hargarten, S. W., & Karlson, T. (1994). Motor vehicle crashes and seat belts: A study of emergency physician procedures, charges, and documentation. *Annals of Emergency Medicine, 24*(5), 857–859.

Harnack, L., Stang, J., & Story, M. (1999). Soft drink consumption among U.S. children and adolescents: Nutritional consequences. *Journal of the American Dietetic Association, 99*, 436–441.

Harrell, J. S., Bangdiwala, S. I., Deng, S., Webb, J. P., & Bradley, C. (1998). Smoking initiation in youth: The roles of gender, race, socioeconomics, and developmental status. *Journal of Adolescent Health, 23*(5), 271–279.

Harrell, W. A. (1986). Masculinity and farming-related accidents. *Sex Roles, 15*(9/10), 467–478.

Harrington, J. M. (1991). Work related disease and injuries. *British Medical Journal, 303*, 908–910.

Harrington, N. G., Lane D. R., Donohew L., Zimmerman R. S., Norling G. R., An J-H., … Bevins C. C. (2003). Persuasive strategies for effective anti-drug messages. *Communication Monographs, 70*(1), 16–38.

Harris, I., Torres, J. B., & Allender, D. (1994). The responses of African American men to dominant norms of masculinity within the United States. *Sex Roles, 31*, 703–719.

Harris, J. B., Schwartz, S. M., & Thompson, B. (2008). Characteristics associated with self-identification as a regular smoker and desire to quit among college students who smoke cigarettes. *Nicotine & Tobacco Research, 10*(1), 69–76.

Harrison, J. (1978). Warning: The male sex role may be dangerous to your health. *Journal of Social Issues, 34*(1), 65–86.

Harrison, J., Chin, J., & Ficarroto, T. (1992). Warning: The male sex role may be dangerous to your health. In M. S. Kimmel & M. A. Messner (Eds.), *Men's lives* (2nd ed., pp. 271–285). New York, NY: Macmillan.

Hasin, D. S., Grant, B. F., & Weinflash, J. (1988). Male/female differences in alcohol-related problems: Alcohol rehabilitation patients. *International Journal of the Addictions, 23*(5), 437–448.

Haskell, W. L., Lee, I. M., Pate, R. R., Powell, K. E., Blair, S. N., Franklin, B. A., ... Bauman, A. (2007). Physical activity and public health: Updated recommendation for adults from the American College of Sports Medicine and the American Heart Association. *Circulation, 116*(9), 1081–1093.

Hatsukami, D. K., Lemmonds, C., & Tomar, S. L. (2004). Smokeless tobacco use: Harm reduction or induction approach? *Preventive Medicine, 38*(3), 309–317.

Hatsukami, D. K., & Severson, H. H. (1999). Oral spit tobacco: Addiction, prevention and treatment. *Nicotine & Tobacco Research, 1*(1), 21–44.

Hausenblas, H. A., & Carron, A. V. (1999). Eating disorder indices and athletes: An integration. *Journal of Sport & Exercise Psychology, 21*(3), 230–258.

Hawkins, M. S., Storti, K. L., Richardson, C. R., King, W. C., Strath, S. J., Holleman, R. G., & Kriska, A. M. (2009). Objectively measured physical activity of U.S.A. adults by sex, age, and racial/ethnic groups: A cross-sectional study. *International Journal of Behavioral Nutrition and Physical Activity, 6*(1), 1–7.

Hayes, D., & Ross, C. E. (1987). Concern with appearance, health beliefs and eating habits. *Journal of Health and Social Behavior, 28*, 120–130.

Hayes, R. B., Ziegler, R. G., Gridley, G., Swanson, C., Greenberg, R. S., Swanson, G. M., ... Hoover, R. N. (1999). Dietary factors and risks for prostate cancer among blacks and whites in the United States. *Cancer Epidemiology Biomarkers Prevention, 8*(1), 25–34.

Hayward, M. D., Pienta, A. M., & McLaughlin, D. K. (1997). Inequality in men's mortality: The socioeconomic status gradient and geographic context. *Journal of Health and Social Behavior, 38*, 313–330.

Hazan, A. R., Lipton, H. L., & Glantz, S. A. (1994). Popular films do not reflect current tobacco use. *American Journal of Public Health, 84*, 998–1000.

Health bulletin. (1995, September). *Men's Health, 10*, 112.

Hecht, S. S. (2008). Progress and challenges in selected areas of tobacco carcinogenesis. *Chemical Research in Toxicology, 21*(1), 160–171.

Heijne, J. C., Teunis, P., Morroy, G., Wijkmans, C., Oostveen, S., Duizer, E., ... Wallinga, J. (2009). Enhanced hygiene measures and norovirus transmission during an outbreak. *Emerging Infectious Diseases, 15*(1), 24–30.

Heintz–Knowles, K. (1995). *The reflection on the screen: Television's image of children*. Washington, DC: Children Now.

Hekner, J. M. (1995, July). *Sex-stereotyping of mathematics and English at three developmental periods: Students' attitudes towards peers.* Paper presented at the Annual Meeting of the Mid-Western Educational Research Association, Chicago, IL.

Helakorpi, S., Uutela, A., Prättälä, R., & Puska, P. (2005). *Health behavior and health among Finnish adult population* (Publication of the National Health Institute). Helsinki, Finland: Hakapaino.

Helgeson, V. S. (1990). The role of masculinity in a prognostic predictor of heart attack severity. *Sex Roles, 22*(11/12), 755–774.

Helgeson, V. S. (1994). Relations of agency and communion to well-being: Evidence and potential explanations. *Psychological Bulletin, 116*, 412–428.

Helgeson, V. S. (1995). Masculinity, men's roles, and coronary heart disease. In D. Sabo & D. G. Gordon (Eds.), *Men's health and illness: Gender, power and the body* (pp. 1–21). Thousand Oaks, CA: Sage.

Helgeson, V. S., Novak, S. A., Lepore, S. J., & Eton, D. T. (2004). Spouse social control efforts: Relations to health behavior and well-being among men with prostate cancer. *Journal of Social and Personal Relationships, 21*(1), 53–68.

Hellerstedt, W. L., & Jeffery, R. W. (1997). The association of job strain and health behaviours in men and women. *International Journal of Epidemiology, 26*(3), 575–583.

Helling, D. K., Lemke, J. H., Semla, T. P., Wallace, R. B., Lipson, D. P., & Cornoni-Huntley, J. (1987). Medication use characteristics in the elderly: The Iowa 65+ Rural Health Study. *Journal of the American Geriatrics Society, 35*(1), 4–12.

Hemenway, D., & Richardson, E. (1997). Characteristics of automatic or semiautomatic firearm ownership in the United States. *American Journal of Public Health, 87*(2), 286–288.

Hendricks, L. E. (1999). Working with African American males with diabetes. In L. E. Davis (Ed.), *Working with African American males: A guide to practice* (pp. 91–102). Thousand Oaks, CA: Sage.

Heppner, P. P., & Gonzales, D. S. (1987). Men counseling men. In M. Scher, M. Stevens, G. Good, & G. A. Eichenfield (Eds.), *Handbook of counseling and psychotherapy with men* (pp. 30–38). Thousand Oaks, CA: Sage.

Herbert, T. B., & Cohen, S. (1993). Stress and immunity in humans: A meta-analytic review. *Psychosomatic Medicine, 55*, 364–379.

Hessler, R. M., Jia, S., Madsen, R., & Pazaki, H. (1995). Gender, social networks and survival time: A twenty year study of the rural elderly. *Archives of Gerontology & Geriatrics, 21*(3), 291–306.

Hewson, M. G. (1993). Patient education through teaching for conceptual change. *Journal of General Internal Medicine, 8*(7), 393–398.

Hiatt, R. A., Armstrong, M. A., Klatsky, A. L., & Sidney, S. (1994). Alcohol consumption, smoking, and other risk factor and prostate cancer in a large health plan cohort in California. *Cancer Causes and Control, 5*(1), 66–72.

Hibbard, J. H., & Pope, C. R. (1986). Another look at sex differences in the use of medical care: Illness orientation and the types of morbidities for which services are used. *Women and Health, 11*(2), 21–36.

Hibbard, J. H., & Pope, C. R. (1993). The quality of social roles as predictors of morbidity and mortality. *Social Science and Medicine, 36*, 217–225.

Hill, D., White, V., Borland, R., & Cockburn, J. (1991). Cancer-related beliefs and behaviors in Australia. *Australian Journal of Public Health, 15*, 14–23.

Hingson, R., Heeren, T., Winter, M., & Wechsler, H. (2005). Magnitude of alcohol-related mortality and morbidity among U.S. college students ages 18–24: Changes from 1998 to 2001. *Annual Review of Public Health, 26*, 259–279.

Hingson, R., Heeren, T., Zakocs, R. C., Kopstein, A., & Wechsler, H. (2002). Magnitude of alcohol-related mortality and morbidity among U.S. college students ages 18–24. *Journal of Studies on Alcohol, 63*, 136–144.

Hingson, R. W., Zha, W., & Weitzman, E. R. (2009). Magnitude of and trends in alcohol-related mortality and morbidity among U.S. college students ages 18–24, 1998–2005. *Journal of Studies on Alcohol and Drugs, 16*(Suppl.), 12–20.

Hippisley-Cox, J., Pringle, M., Meal, A., & Wynn, A. (2001). Sex inequalities in ischemic heart disease in general practice: Cross sectional survey. *British Medical Journal, 322,* 832–836.

Hla, K. M., Young, T. B., Bidwell, T., Palta, M., Skatrud, J. B., & Dempsey, J. (1994). Sleep apnea and hypertension: A population-based study. *Annals of Internal Medicine, 120,* 382–388.

Ho, S. C. (1991). Health and social predictors of mortality in an elderly Chinese cohort. *American Journal of Epidemiology, 133*(9), 907–921.

Hoffman, R. M., Gilliland, F. D., Eley, J. W., Harlan, L. C., Stephenson, R. A., Stanford, J. L., … Potosky, A. L. (2001). Racial and ethnic differences in advanced-stage prostate cancer: The prostate cancer outcomes study. *Journal of the National Cancer Institute, 93*(5), 388–395.

Hohmann A. A. (1989). Gender bias in psychotropic drug prescribing in primary care. *Medical Care, 27*(5), 478–490.

Holbrook, M. I. (1997). Anger management training in prison inmates. *Psychological Reports, 81*(2), 623–626.

Holcomb, C. A. (1992). Personal health practices of couples in rural Kansas. *Health Values, 16*(6), 36–46.

Holmila, M., & Raitasalo, K. (2005). Gender differences in drinking: Why do they still exist? *Addiction, 100*(12), 1763–1769.

Hong, L. (2000). Toward a transformed approach to prevention: Breaking the link between masculinity and violence. *Journal of American College Health, 48*(6), 269–279.

Hopkins, W. G., Wilson, N. C., & Russell, D. G. (1991). Validation of the physical activity instrument for the Life in New Zealand national survey. *American Journal of Epidemiology, 133*(1), 73–82.

Hornbrook, M. C., Stevens, V. J., Wingfield, D. J., Hollis, J. F., Greenlick, M. R., & Ory, M. G. (1994). Preventing falls among community-dwelling older persons: Results from a randomized trial. *Gerontologist, 34*(1), 16–23.

Horne, D. J., Vatmanidis, P., & Careri, A. (1994). Preparing patients for invasive medical and surgical procedures 1: Adding behavioral and cognitive interventions. *Behavioral Medicine, 20*(1), 5–13.

Horwitz, A. V. (1982). Sex-role expectations, power, and psychological distress. *Sex Roles, 8*(6), 607–623.

Horwitz, I. B., & McCall, B. P. (2005). Occupational injury among Rhode Island adolescents: An analysis of workers' compensation claims, 1998 to 2002. *Journal of Occupational and Environmental Medicine, 47*(5), 473–481.

Hosoda, M., & Stone, D. L. (2000). Current gender stereotypes and their evaluative content. *Perceptual and Motor Skills, 90,* 1283–1294.

House, J. S., Landis, K. R., & Umberson, D. (1988). Social relationships and health. *Science, 241,* 540–545.

House, J. S., Robbins, C., & Metzner, H. L. (1982). The association of social relationships and activities with mortality: Prospective evidence from the Tecumseh Community Health Study. *American Journal of Epidemiology, 116*(1), 123–140.

Howard-Pitney, B., & Winkleby, M.A. (2002). Chewing tobacco: Who uses and who quits? Findings from NHANES III, 1988–1994. *American Journal of Public Health, 92*(2), 250–256.

Howland, J., Hingson, R., Mangione, T. W., Bell, N., & Bak, S. (1996). Why are most drowning victims men? Sex differences in aquatic skills and behaviors. *American Journal of Public Health, 86*(1), 93–96.

Hoyt, D. R., Conger, R. D., Valde, J. G., & Weihs, K. (1997). Psychological distress and help seeking in rural America. *American Journal of Community Psychology, 25*(4), 449–470.

Hsing, A. W., Tsao, L., & Devesa, S. S. (2000). International trends and patterns of prostate cancer incidence and mortality. *International Journal of Cancer, 85*, 60–67.

Hu, F. B., Manson, J. E., & Willett, W. C. (2001). Types of dietary fat and risk of coronary heart disease: A critical review. *Journal of the American College of Nutrition, 20*(1), 5–19.

Hu, F. B., & Willett, W. C. (2002). Optimal diets for prevention of coronary heart disease. *Journal of the American Medical Association, 288*(20), 2569–2578.

Hu, P. S., & Young, J. R. (1999). *Summary of travel trends: 1995 nationwide personal transportation survey.* Washington, DC: Federal Highway Administration.

Huang, Y., Kotov, R., de Girolamo, G., Preti, A., Angermeyer, M., Benjet, C., … Kessler, R. C. (2009). DSM-IV personality disorders in the WHO world mental health surveys. *British Journal of Psychiatry, 195*(1), 46–53.

Huenemann, R. L., Shapiro, L. R., Hampton, M. C., & Mitchell, B. (1966). A longitudinal study of gross body composition and body confirmation and their association with food and activity in a teen-age population. *American Journal of Clinical Nutrition, 18*, 325–338.

Huerta, E. E. (2003). Cancer statistics for Hispanics, 2003: Good news, bad news, and the need for a health system paradigm change. *CA: A Cancer Journal for Clinicians, 53*(4), 205–207.

Hulka, B. S., & Wheat, J. R. (1985). Patterns of utilization: The patient perspective. *Medical Care, 23*(5), 438–460.

Hulley, S. B., & Gordon, S. (1981). Alcohol and high-density lipoprotein cholesterol: Causal inference from diverse case study designs. *Circulation, 62*(Suppl. III), 57–63.

Humphrey, L. L., Fu, R., Buckley, D. I., Freeman, M., & Helfand, M. (2008). Periodontal disease and coronary heart disease incidence: A systematic review and meta-analysis. *Journal of General Internal Medicine, 23*(12), 2079–2086.

Hung, J., Whitford, E. G., Parsons, R. W., & Hillman, D. R. (1990). Association of sleep apnea with myocardial infarction in men. *Lancet, 336*, 261–264.

Hunt, J., & Eisenberg, D. (2010). Mental health problems and help-seeking behavior among college students. *Journal of Adolescent Health, 46*, 3–10.

Hunt, K., Lewars, H., Emslie, C., & Batty, G. D. (2007). Decreased risk of death from coronary heart disease amongst men with higher "femininity" scores: A general population cohort study. *International Journal of Epidemiology, 36*(3), 612–620.

Hunter, A. G., & Davis, J. E. (1992). Constructing gender: An exploration of Afro-American men's conceptualization of manhood. *Gender and Society, 6*, 464–479.

Hunter, W. W., Stutts, J. C., Steward, J. R., & Rodgman, E. A. (1990). Characteristics of seat belt users and non-users in a state with a mandatory belt use law. *Health Education Research, 5*(2), 161–173.

Huselid, R. F., & Cooper, M. L. (1992). Gender roles as mediators of sex differences in adolescent alcohol use and abuse. *Journal of Health and Social Behavior, 33*, 348–362.

Hwang, H. C., Stallones, L., & Keefe, T. J. (1997). Childhood injury deaths: Rural and urban differences, Colorado 1980–1988. *Injury Prevention, 3*(1), 35–37.

Hyde, J. S. (1986). Gender differences in aggression. In J. S. Hyde & M. C. Linn (Eds.), *The psychology of gender.* Baltimore, MD: Johns Hopkins University Press.

Hyde, J. S. (2005). The gender similarities hypothesis. *American Psychologist, 60*(6), 581–592.

Iemolo, F., Martiniuk, A., Steinman, D. A., & Spence, J. D. (2004). Sex differences in carotid plaque and stenosis. *Stroke, 35*(2), 477–481.

Imeri, L., & Opp, M. R. (2009). How (and why) the immune system makes us sleep. *Nature Reviews Neuroscience, 10*, 199–210.

Ingall, T. (2004). Stroke: Incidence, mortality, morbidity and risk. *Journal of Insurance Medicine, 36*, 143–152.

Institute for Women's Policy Research. (2010). *Fact sheet: More men to benefit from expanded coverage under healthcare reform* (Publication No. IWPR A142). Washington, DC: Author.

Institute of Medicine. (2001). *Clearing the smoke: Assessing the science base for tobacco harm reduction.* Washington, DC: National Academy Press.

Institute of Medicine. (2004). *Dietary reference intakes for water, potassium, sodium chloride, and sulfate.* Washington, DC: National Academies Press.

Isaacs, W. B., & Xu, J. (2007). Linkage studies of prostate cancer families to identify susceptibility genes. In L. W. Chung, W. B. Isaacs, & J. W. Simons (Eds.), *Prostate cancer: Biology, genetics, and the new therapeutics* (pp. 285–299). Totowa, NJ: Humana Press.

Jacklin, C. N., DiPietro, J. A., & Maccoby, E. E. (1984). Sex-typing behavior and sex-typing pressure in child/parent interaction. *Archives of Sexual Behavior, 13*(5), 413–425.

Jackson, A., Dijkers, M., DeVivo, M., & Poczatek, R. (2004). A demographic profile of new traumatic spinal cord injuries: Change and stability over 30 years. *Archives of Physical Medicine and Rehabilitation, 85*(11), 1740–1748.

Jackson, J. E., Doescher, M. P., & Hart, L. G. (2006). Problem drinking: Rural and urban trends in America, 1995/1997 to 2003. *Preventive Medicine, 43*(2), 122–124.

Jackson, R., Chambless, L., Higgins, M., Kuulasmaa, K., Wijnberg, L., & Williams, D. (1997). Sex difference in ischemic heart disease mortality and risk factors in 46 communities: An ecologic analysis. *Cardiovascular Risk Factors, 7*, 43–54.

Jackson, R. W., Treiber, F. A., Turner, J. R., Davis, H., & Strong, W. B. (1999). Effects of race, sex, and socioeconomic status upon cardiovascular stress responsivity and recovery in youth. *International Journal of Psychophysiology, 31*, 111–119.

Jackson, T. K. (2008). *Examining evidence of reliability and validity of mental health indicators on a revised national survey measuring college student health.* (Doctoral dissertation; Publication No. AAT 3307948).

Jacobi, L., & Cash, T. F. (1994). In pursuit of the perfect appearance: Discrepancies among self-ideal perceptions of multiple physical attributes. *Journal of Applied Social Psychology, 24*, 379–396.

Jacobs, E. J., Thun, M. J., & Apicella, L. F. (1999). Cigar smoking and death from coronary heart disease in a prospective study of U.S. men. *Archives of Internal Medicine, 159*(20), 2413–2418.

Jadack, R. A., Hyde, J. S., & Keller, M. L. (1995). Gender and knowledge about HIV, risky sexual behavior, and safer sex practices. *Research in Nursing Health, 18*, 313–324.

Jaffe, H. (1997). Dying for dollars. *Men's Health, 12*, 132–137, 186–187.

Jalal, D. I., Smits, G., Johnson, R. J., & Chonchol, M. (in press). Increased fructose associates with elevated blood pressure. *Journal of the American Society of Nephrology.*

Janda, M., Youl, P. H., Lowe, J. B., Elwood, M., Ring, I. T., & Aitken, J. F. (2004). Attitudes and intentions in relation to skin checks for early signs of skin cancer. *Preventive Medicine, 39*, 11–18.

Janz, N., & Becker, M. (1984) The health belief model: A decade later. *Health Education Quarterly, 11*(1), 1–47.

Jemal, A., Siegel, R., Ward, E., Hao, Y., Xu, J., & Thun, M. J. (2009). Cancer statistics, 2009. *CA Cancer Journal for Clinicians, 59*(4), 225–249.

Jemal, A., Thun, M. J., Ries, L. A., Howe, H. L., Weir, H. K., Center, M. M., … Edwards, B. K. (2008). Annual report to the nation on the status of cancer, 1975–2005: Featuring trends in lung cancer, tobacco use, and tobacco control. *Journal of the National Cancer Institute, 100*(23), 1672–1694.

Jenkins, T. M. (2005). Prevalence of overweight, obesity, and comorbid conditions among U.S. and Kentucky adults, 2000-2002. *Preventing Chronic Disease, 2*(1), 1–8.

Jessor, R. (1987). Risky driving and adolescent problem behavior: An extension of problem behavior theory. *Alcohol, Drugs, and Driving, 3*, 1–13.

Jessor, R., Donovan, J. E., & Costa, F. M. (1991). *Beyond adolescence: Problem behavior and young adult development.* New York, NY: Cambridge University Press.

Job, R. F. (1988). Effective and ineffective use of fear in health promotion campaigns. *American Journal of Public Health, 78*, 163–167.

Joe Camel designed to lure teens. (1998, January 15). *San Francisco Chronicle,* pp. A1, A15.

Joe, J. R. (2001). Out of harmony: Health problems and young Native American men. *Journal of American College Health, 49*(5), 237–242.

Johnson, C., Mimiaga, M., & Bradford, J. (2008). Health care issues among lesbian, gay, bisexual, transgender and intersex (LGBTI) populations in the United States: Introduction. *Journal of Homosexuality, 54*(3), 213–224.

Johnson, E. H., Gant, L., Hinkle, Y. A., Gilbert, D., Willis, C., & Hoopwood, T. (1992). Do African-American men and women differ in their knowledge about AIDS, attitudes about condoms, and sexual behaviors? *Journal of the National Medical Association, 84*(1), 49–64.

Johnson, K., Anderson, N. B., Bastida, E., Kramer, B. J., Williams, D., & Wong, M. (1995). Panel II: Macrosocial and environmental influences on minority health. *Health Psychology, 14*(7), 601–612.

Johnson, M. E. (1988). Influences of gender and sex role orientation on help-seeking attitudes. *Journal of Psychology, 122*(3), 237–241.

Johnson, N. J., Backlund, E., Sorlie, P. D., & Loveless, C. A. (2000) Marital status and mortality: The National Longitudinal Mortality Study. *Annals of Epidemiology, 10,* 224–238.

Johnston, L. D., O'Malley, P. M., & Bachman, J. G. (1996). *National survey results on drug use from the Monitoring the Future study, 1975–1994. Vol. II: College students and young adults* (NIH Publication No. 96-4027). Rockville, MD: National Institute on Drug Abuse.

Johnston, L. D., O'Malley, P. M., & Bachman, J. G. (2002). *Monitoring the future—national survey results on drug use, 1975-2001. Vol. II: College students and adults ages 19-40* (NIH Publication No. 02-5107). Bethesda, MD: National Institute on Drug Abuse.

Johnston, L. D., O'Malley, P. M., Bachman, J. G., & Schulenberg, J. E. (2009). *Monitoring the future—national survey results on drug use, 1975–2008: Vol. II: College students and adults ages 19-50* (NIH Publication No. 09-7403). Bethesda, MD: National Institute on Drug Abuse.

Johnston, S. C., Fung, L. H., Gillum, L. A., Smith, W. S., Brass, L. M., Lichtman, J. H., & Brown, A. N. (2001). Utilization of intravenous tissue-type plasminogen activator for ischemic stroke at academic medical centers: The influence of ethnicity. *Stroke, 32,* 1061–1068.

Joly, B. M., McDermott, R. J., & Westhoff, W. W. (2000).Transportation practices of college students: Effects of gender and residential status on risk of injury. *The International Electronic Journal of Health Education, 3*(2), 117–125.

Jones, D. A., Ainsworth, B. E., Croft, J. B., Macera, C. A., Lloyd, E. E., & Yusuf, H. R. (1998). Moderate leisure-time physical activity: Who is meeting the public health recommendations? A national cross-sectional study. *Archives of Family Medicine, 7*(3), 285–289.

Jones, D. C. (2001). Social comparison and body image: Attractiveness comparisons to models and peers among adolescent boys and girls. *Sex Roles, 45,* 645–664.

Judah, G., Aunger, R., Schmidt, W. P., Michie, S., Granger, S., & Curtis, V. (2009). Experimental pretesting of hand-washing interventions in a natural setting. *American Journal of Public Health, 99*(S2), S405–S411.

Kachur, S. P., Stennies, G. M., Powell, K. E., Modzeleski, W., Stephens, R., Murphy. R., … Lowry, R. (1996). School-associated violent deaths in the United States, 1992–1994. *Journal of the American Medical Association, 275*(22), 1729–1733.

Kacmarek, R. M. (1994). Make discussion. *Respiratory Care, 39*(5), 579–583.

Kafka, E. (1997, November). *Men: An endangered species.* Paper presented at the Annual Meeting of the Association of University and College Counseling Center Directors, Williamsburg, VA.

Kahn, J. A., Huang, B., Gillman, M. W., Field, A. E., Austin, S. B., Colditz, G. A., & Frazier, A. L. (2008). Patterns and determinants of physical activity in U.S. adolescents. *Journal of Adolescent Health, 42*(4), 369–377.

Kajantie, E. (2008). Physiological stress response, estrogen, and the male-female mortality gap. *Current Directions in Psychological Science, 17*(5), 348–352.

Kallai, I., Barke, A., & Voss, U. (2004). The effects of experimenter characteristics on pain reports in women and men. *Pain, 112,* 142–147.

Kandrack, M., Grant, K. R., & Segall, A. (1991). Gender differences in health related behavior: Some unanswered questions. *Social Science and Medicine, 32*(5), 579–590.

Kane, E. W. (2006). "No way my boys are going to be like that!" Parents' responses to children's gender nonconformity. *Gender and Society, 20*(2), 149–176.

Kann, L., Kinchen, S. A., Williams, B. I., Ross, J. G., Lowry, R., Hill, C. V., … State and Local YRBSS Coordinators (1998). Youth risk behavior surveillance—United States, 1997. *Morbidity and Mortality Weekly Report, 47*(3), 1–97.

Kannel, W. B., & Ellison, R. C. (1996). Alcohol and coronary heart disease: The evidence for a protective effect. *Clinica Chimica Acta, 246*(1 2), 59 76.

Kaplan, G. A. (1985). Psychosocial aspects of chronic illness: Direct and indirect associations with ischemic heart disease mortality. In R. M. Kaplan & M. H. Criqui (Eds.), *Behavioral epidemiology and disease prevention* (pp. 237–269). New York, NY: Plenum.

Kaplan, G. A., Seeman, T. E., Cohen, R. D., Knudsen, L. P., & Guralnik, J. (1987). Mortality among the elderly in the Alameda County Study: Behavioral and demographic risk factors. *American Journal of Public Health, 77,* 307–312.

Kaplan, H. B. (1991). Social psychology of the immune system: A conceptual framework and review of the literature. *Social Science and Medicine, 33*(8), 909–923.

Kaplan, H. S. (1974). *The new sex therapy: Active treatment of sexual dysfunctions.* New York, NY: Brunner/Mazel.

Kaplan, M. S., & Geling, O. (1998). Firearm suicides and homicides in the United States: Regional variations and patterns of gun ownership. *Social Science and Medicine, 46*(9), 1227–1233.

Kaplan, M. S., & Marks, G. (1995). Appraisal of health risks: The roles of masculinity, femininity, and sex. *Sociology of Health & Illness, 17*(2), 206–221.

Kaplan, N. M. (1999). Salt and blood pressure. In J. L. Izzo & H. R. Black (Eds.), *Hypertension primer: The essentials of high blood pressure* (pp. 247–249). Baltimore, MD: Lippincott Williams & Wilkins.

Kaplan, N. M. (2000). The dietary guideline for sodium: Should we shake it up? *American Journal of Clinical Nutrition, 71*(5), 1020–1026.

Kaplan, R. M., & Kronick, R. G. (2006). Marital status and longevity in the United States population. *Journal of Epidemiology and Community Health, 60*(9), 760–765.

Kaplan, S. H., Gandek, B., Greenfield, S., Rogers, W., & Ware, J. E. (1995). Patient and visit characteristics related to physicians' participatory decision-making style: Results from the Medical Outcomes Study. *Medical Care, 33*(12), 1176–1187.

Kaplan, S. H., Greenfield, S., & Ware, J. F. (1989). Assessing the effects of physician-patient interactions on the outcomes of chronic disease. *Medical Care, 27*(Suppl.), S110–S127.

Karter, A. J. (2003). Commentary: Race, genetics, and disease: In search of a middle ground. *International Journal of Epidemiology, 32,* 26–28.

Kaschak, E. (1992). *Engendered lives: A new psychology of women's experience.* New York, NY: Basic Books.

Kasparian, N. A., McLoone, J. K., & Meiser, B. (2009). Skin cancer-related prevention and screening behaviors: A review of the literature. *Journal of Behavioral Medicine, 32*(5), 406–428.

Katz, P. A., & Boswell, S. (1986). Flexibility and traditionality in children's gender roles. *Genetic, Social, and General Psychology Monographs, 112*(1), 105–147.

Katz, P. A., & Ksansnak, K. R. (1994). Developmental aspects of gender role flexibility and traditionality in middle childhood and adolescence. *Developmental Psychology, 30*(2), 272–282.

Katz, R. C., Meyers, K., & Walls, J. (1995). Cancer awareness and self-examination practices in young men and women. *Journal of Behavioral Medicine, 18*(4), 377–384.

Kauffman, S. E., Silver, P., & Poulin, J. (1997). Gender differences in attitudes toward alcohol, tobacco, and other drugs. *Social Work, 42*(3), 231–241.

Kaufman, M. (1994). Men, feminism, and men's contradictory experiences of power. In H. Brod & M. Kaufman (Eds.), *Theorising masculinities* (pp. 142–163). Thousand Oaks, CA: Sage.

Keeling, R. P. (1999). Modest reassurance in a season of sadness: Guns in college. *Journal of American College Health, 48,* 3–6.

Keeling, R. P. (2000). Social norms research in college health. *Journal of American College Health, 49*(2), 53–56.

Keil, J. E., Sutherland, S. E., Knapp, R. G., Lackland, D. T., Gazes, P. C., & Tyroler, H. A. (1993). Mortality rates and risk factors for coronary disease in Black as compared with White men and women. *New England Journal of Medicine, 329*(2), 73–78.

Kellermann, A. L., Rivara, F. P., Rushforth, N. B., Banton, J. G., Reay, D. T., Francisco, J. T., … Somes, G. (1993). Gun ownership as a risk factor for homicide in the home. *New England Journal of Medicine, 329,* 1084–1091.

Kellermann, A. L., Rivara, F. P., Somes, G., Reay, D. T., Francisco, J. T., Banton, J. K., … Hackman, B. B. (1992). Suicide in the home in relation to gun ownership. *New England Journal of Medicine, 327,* 467–472.

Kendler, K. S., & Prescott, C. A. (1999). A population-based twin study of lifetime major depression in men and women. *Archive of General Psychiatry, 56,* 39–44.

Kerr, D. C., Lopez, N. L., Olson, S. L., & Sameroff, A. J. (2004). Parental discipline and externalizing behavior problems in early childhood: The roles of moral regulation and child gender. *Journal of Abnormal Child Psychology, 32*(4), 369–383.

Kerr, Z. Y., Collins, C. L., & Comstock, R. D. (2010). Epidemiology of weight training-related injuries presenting to United States emergency departments, 1990 to 2007. *American Journal of Sports Medicine, 38*(4), 765–771.

Kessler, R. C., Berglund, P., Demler, O., Jin, R., Merikangas, K. R., & Walters, E. E. (2005). Lifetime prevalence and age-of-onset distributions of DSM-IV disorders in the national comorbidity survey replication. *Archives of General Psychiatry, 62,* 593–602.

Kessler, R. C., Brown, R. L., & Boman, C. L. (1981). Sex differences in psychiatric help seeking: Evidence from four large scale surveys. *Journal of Health and Social Behavior, 22,* 49–64.

Kessler, R. C., McGonagle, K. A., Zhao, S., Nelson, C. B., Hughes, M., Eshleman, S., … Kendler, K. S. (1994). Lifetime and 12-month prevalence of DSM-III-R psychiatric disorders in the United States: Results from the National Comorbidity Survey. *Archives of General Psychiatry, 51,* 8–19.

Kevorkian, R. T., & Cepeda, O. A. (2007). The biologic basis for longevity differences between men and women. In B. Lunenfeld, L. J. Gooren, A. Morales, & J. E. Morley (Eds.), *Textbook of men's health and aging* (2nd ed., pp. 23–30). London, England: Informa Healthcare.

Khan, K., Wang, J., Hu, W., Bierman, A., Li, Y., & Gardam, M. (2008). Tuberculosis infection in the United States: National trends over three decades. *American Journal of Respiratory and Critical Care Medicine, 177,* 455–460.

Khaw, K.-T., Bingham, S., Welch, A., Luben, R., O'Brien, E., Wareham, N., & Day, N. (2004). Blood pressure and urinary sodium in men and women: The Norfolk Cohort of the European Prospective Investigation into Cancer (EPIC-Norfolk). *American Journal of Clinical Nutrition, 80*(5), 1397–1403.

Kidd, B. (1987). Sports and masculinity. In M. Kaufman (Ed.), *Beyond patriarchy: Essays by men on pleasure, power, and change* (pp. 250–265). New York, NY: Oxford University Press.

Kiecolt-Glaser, J. K., Glaser, R., Cacioppo, J. T., & Malarkey, W. B. (1998). Marital stress: Immunologic, neuroendocrine, and autonomic correlates. *Annals of the New York Academy of Sciences, 840,* 656–663.

Kiecolt-Glaser, J. K., & Newton, T. L. (2001). Marriage and health: His and hers. *Psychological Bulletin, 127*(4), 472–503.

Kiecolt-Glaser, J. K., Newton, T., Cacioppo, J. T., MacCallum, R. C., Glaser, R., & Malarkey, W. B. (1996). Marital conflict and endocrine function: Are men really more physiologically affected than women? *Journal of Consulting and Clinical Psychology, 64*(2), 324–332.

Kiel, E. J., & Buss, K. A. (2006). Maternal accuracy in predicting toddlers' behaviors and associations with toddler's fearful temperament. *Child Development, 77*(2), 355–370.

Kimmel, M. S. (1986). Introduction: Toward men's studies. *American Behavioral Scientist, 29*(5), 517–529.

Kimmel, M. S. (1995). *Manhood in America: A cultural history.* New York, NY: Free Press.

King, A. C., Haskell, W. L., Young, D. R., Oka, R. K., & Stefanick, M. L. (1995). Long-term effects of varying intensities and formats of physical activity on participation rates, fitness, and lipoproteins in men and women. *Circulation, 91*(10), 2596–2604.

King, K. M., & Chassin, L. (2007). A prospective study of the effects of age of initiation of alcohol and drug use on young adult substance dependence. *Journal of Studies on Alcohol and Drugs, 68*(2), 256–265.

Kinnison, A., Cottrell, R. R., & King, K. A. (2004). Proper hand-washing techniques in public restrooms: Differences in gender, race, signage, and time of day. *American Journal of Health Education, 35*(2), 86–89.

Kirschbaum, C., Klauer, T., Filipp, S-H., & Hellhammer, D. H. (1995). Sex-specific effects of social support on cortisol and subjective responses to acute psychological stress. *Psychosomatic Medicine, 57,* 23–31.

Kirschbaum, C., Wust, S., & Hellhammer, D. (1992). Consistent sex differences in cortisol responses to psychological stress. *Psychosomatic Medicine, 54*(6), 648–657.

Kiviat, N. B., & Koutsky, L. A. (2007). Genital human papillomavirus infection in men: Incidence and risk factors in a cohort of university students. *Journal of Infectious Diseases, 196*(8), 1128–1136.

Klag, M. J., Ford, D. E., Mead, L. A., He, J., Whelton, P. K., Liang, K. Y., & Levine, D. M. (1993). Serum cholesterol in young men and subsequent cardiovascular disease. *New England Journal of Medicine, 328*(5), 313–318.

Klein, A. M. (1993). *Little big men: Body building subculture and gender construction.* Albany: State University of New York Press.

Klein, J. D., Brown, J. D., Childers, K. W., Oliveri, J., Porter, C., & Dykers, C. (1993). Adolescents' risky behavior and mass media use. *Pediatrics, 92*(1), 24–31.

Klimes-Dougan, B., Brand, A. E., Zahn-Waxler, C., Usher, B., Hastings, P. D., Kendziora, K., & Garside, R. B. (2007). Parental emotion socialization in adolescence: Differences in sex, age, and problem status. *Social Development, 16*(2), 326–342.

Kloner, R. A. (2006). Natural and unnatural triggers of myocardial infarction. *Progress in Cardiovascular Diseases, 48*(4), 285–300.

Klungel, O. H., de Boer, A., Paes, A. H., Seidell, J. C., & Bakker, A. (1997). Sex differences in the pharmacological treatment of hypertension: A review of population-based studies. *Journal of Hypertension, 15*(6), 591–600.

Kneller, R. W., Guo, W. D., Hsing, A. W., Chen, J. S., Blot, W. J., Li, J. Y., … Fraumeni, J. F. (1992). Risk factors for stomach cancer in sixty-five Chinese counties. *Cancer Epidemiology, Biomarkers and Prevention, 1*(2), 113–118.

Knight, G. P., Guthrie, I. K., Page, M. C., & Fabes, R. A. (2002). Emotional arousal and gender differences in aggression: A meta-analysis. *Aggressive Behavior, 28*, 366–393.

Knoops, K. T., de Groot, L. C., Kromhout, D., Perrin, A. E., Moreiras-Varela, O., Menotti, A., & van Staveren, W. A. (2004). Mediterranean diet, lifestyle factors, and 10-year mortality in elderly European men and women: The HALE project. *Journal of the American Medical Association, 292*(12), 1433–1439.

Knox, S. S., Siegmund, K. D., Weidner, G., Ellison, R. C., Adelman, A., & Paton, C. (1998). Hostility, social support, and coronary heart disease in the National Heart, Lung, and Blood Institute Family Heart Study. *American Journal of Cardiology, 82*, 1192–1196.

Knutson, K. L., Spiegel, K., Penev, P., & Van Cauter, E. (2007). The metabolic consequences of sleep deprivation. *Sleep Medicine Reviews, 11*(3): 163–178.

Koebnick, C., Smith, N., Coleman, K. J., Getahun, D., Reynolds, K., Quinn, V. P., … Jacobsen, S. J. (2010). Prevalence of extreme obesity in a multiethnic cohort of children and adolescents. *Journal of Pediatrics, 157*(1), 26–31.

Koh, H. K., Bak, S. M., Geller, A. C., Mangione, T. W., Hingson, R. W., Levenson, S. M., … Howland, J. (1997). Sunbathing habits and sunscreen use among white adults: Results of a national survey. *American Journal of Public Health, 87*(7), 1214–1217.

Koh, H. K., Geller, A. C., Miller, D. R., Caruso, A., Gage, I., & Lew, R. (1991). Who is being screened for melanoma/skin cancer? Characteristics of persons screen in Massachusetts. *Journal of the American Academy of Dermatology, 24*(2), 271–277.

Koh, H. K., Geller, A. C., Miller, D. R., & Lew, R. A. (1995). The early detection of and screening for melanoma: International status. *Cancer, 75*(Suppl. 2), 674–683.

Koh, H. K., Miller, D. B., Geller, A. C., Clapp, R. W., Mercer, M. B., & Lew, R. A. (1992). Who discovers melanoma? Patterns from a population-based survey. *Journal of the American Academy of Dermatology, 26*(6), 914–919.

Koh, H. K., Norton, L. A., Geller, A. C., Sun, T., Rigel, D. S., Miller, D. R., … Lew, R. A. (1996). Evaluation of the American Academy of Dermatology's national skin cancer early detection and screening program. *Journal of the American Academy of Dermatology, 34*(6), 971–978.

Kolb, B., & Whishaw, I. Q. (2009). Fundamentals of human neuropsychology (6th ed.). New York, NY: Worth Publishers.

Kolodinsky, J., Labrecque, J., Doyon, M., Reynolds, T., Oble, F., Bellavance, F., & Marquis, M. (2008). Sex and cultural differences in the acceptance of functional foods: A comparison of American, Canadian, and French college students. *Journal of American College Health, 57*(2), 143–149.

Kontos, A. P. (2004). Perceived risk, risk taking, estimation of ability and injury among adolescent sport participants. *Journal of Pediatric Psychology, 29*(6), 447–455.

Koop, C. E. (1996). Foreword. In S. H. Woolf, S. Jonas, & R. S. Lawrence (Eds.), *Health promotion and disease prevention in clinical practice* (pp. vii–ix). Baltimore, MD: Williams & Wilkins.

Koopmans, G. T., & Lamers, L. M. (2007). Gender and health care utilization: The role of mental distress and help-seeking propensity. *Social Science & Medicine, 64*(6), 1216–1230.

Kopp, M. S., Skrabski, A., & Szedmak, S. (1998). Why do women suffer more and live longer? *Psychosomatic Medicine, 60*, 92–135.

Koppes, L. L., Dekker, J. M., Hendriks, H. F., Bouter, L. M., & Heine, R. J. (2006). Meta-analysis of the relationship between alcohol consumption and coronary heart disease and mortality in type 2 diabetic patients. *Diabetologia, 49*(4), 648–652.

Korbel, C. D. , Wiebe, D. J. , Berg, C. A., & Palmer, D. L. (2007). Gender differences in adherence to type 1 diabetes management across adolescence: The mediating role of depression. *Children's Health Care, 36*(1), 83–98.

Korcuska, J. S., & Thombs, D. L. (2003). Gender role conflict and sex-specific drinking norms: Relationships to alcohol use in undergraduate women and men. *Journal of College Student Development, 44*(2), 204–216.

Korda, M. (1996). *Man to man: Surviving prostate cancer.* New York, NY: Random House.

Koskinen, S., Martelin, T., & Rissanen, H. (1999). Differences and trends in mortality by marital status. *Journal of Social Medicine, 3*, 271–284.

Koster, A., Harris, T. B., Moore, S. C., Schatzkin, A., Hollenbeck, A. R., van Eijk, J. T., & Leitzmann, M. F. (2009). Joint associations of adiposity and physical activity with mortality: The National Institutes of Health-AARP Diet and Health Study. *American Journal of Epidemiology, 169*(11), 1344–1351.

Kostyniuk, L. P., Streff, F. M., & Zakrajsek, J. (2002). *Identifying unsafe driver actions that lead to fatal car-truck crashes.* Washington, DC: AAA Foundation for Traffic Safety.

Kotchen, T. A., Kotchen, J. M., & Boegehold, M. A. (1991). Nutrition and hypertension prevention. *Hypertension, 18*(Suppl. I), I/115–I/120.

Kotloff, K. L., Tacket, C. O., Clemens, J. D., Wasserman, S. S., Cowan, J. E., Bridwell, M. W., & Quinn, T. C. (1991). Assessment of the prevalence and risk factors for human immunodeficiency virus type 1 (HIV-1) infection among college students using three survey methods. *American Journal of Epidemiology, 133*(1), 2–8.

Kottke, T. E., Battista, R. N., DeFriese, G. H., & Brekke, M. L. (1988). Attributes of successful smoking cessation interventions in medical practice: A meta-analysis of 39 controlled trials. *Journal of the American Medical Association, 259*(19), 2883–2889.

Kozlowski, L. T. (2002). Harm reduction, public health, and human rights: Smokers have a right to be informed of significant harm reduction options. *Nicotine and Tobacco Research, 4*(Suppl. 2), S55–S60.

Kozlowski, L. T., Dollar, K. M., & Giovino, G. A. (2008). Cigar/cigarillo surveillance: Limitations of the U.S. Department of Agriculture system. *American Journal of Preventive Medicine, 34*(5), 424–426.

Kposowa, A. J., & Breault, K. D. (2009). Motor vehicle deaths among men: Marital status, gender and social integration. *International Journal of Men's Health, 8*(2), 129–142.

Kraemer, D. L., & Hastrup, J. L. (1986). Crying in natural settings: Global estimates, self monitored frequencies, depression and sex differences in an undergraduate population. *Behavior Research and Therapy, 24*(3), 371–373.

Kraemer, S. (2000). The fragile male. *British Medical Journal, 321*(7276), 1609–1612.

Krannich, R. S., Berry, E. H., & Greider, T. (1989). Fear of crime in rapidly changing rural communities: A longitudinal analysis. *Rural Sociology, 54*(2), 195–212.

Krantz, D. S., Grunberg, N. E., & Baum, A. (1985). Health psychology. *Annual Review of Psychology, 36*, 349–383.

Kraus, J. F., & Conroy, C. (1984). Mortality and morbidity from injuries in sports and recreation. *Annual Review of Public Health, 5*, 163–192.

Kraus, J. F., Franti, C. E., Riggins, R. S., Richards, D., & Borhani, N. O. (1975). Incidence of traumatic spinal cord lesions. *Journal of Chronic Diseases, 28*, 471–492.

Kreuter, M. W., & Strecher, V. J. (1995). Changing inaccurate perceptions of health risk: Results from a randomized trial. *Health Psychology, 14*(1), 56–63.

Kripke, D. F., Ancoli-Israel, S., Klauber, M. R., Wingard, D. L., Mason, W. J., & Mullaney, D. J. (1997). Prevalence of sleep-disordered breathing in ages 40-64 years: A population-based survey. *Sleep, 20*(1), 65–76.

Kripke, D. F., Garfinkel, L., Wingard, D. L., Klauber, M. R., & Marler, M. R. (2002). Mortality associated with sleep duration and insomnia. *Archives of General Psychiatry, 59*, 131–136.

Kristal, A. R., Stanford, J. L., Cohen, J. H., Wicklund, K., & Patterson, R. E. (1999). Vitamin and mineral supplement use is associated with reduced risk of prostate cancer. *Cancer Epidemiology, Biomarkers and Prevention, 8*(10), 887–892.

Kristenson, M., Kucinskiene, Z., Bergdahl, B., Calkauskas, H., Urmonas, V., & Orth-Gomer, K. (1998). Increased psychosocial strain in Lithuanian vs. Swedish men: The LiVicordia Study. *Psychosomatic Medicine, 60*, 277–282.

Krosnick, J. A. (1999). Survey research. *Annual Review of Psychology, 50,* 537–567.

Krug, E. G., Dahlberg, L. L., Mercy, J. A., Zwi, A. B., & Lozano, R. (Eds.). (2002). *World report on violence and health.* Geneva, Switzerland: World Health Organization.

Kruger, J., Galuska, D. A., Serdula, M. K., & Jones, D. A. (2004). Attempting to lose weight: Specific practices among U.S. adults. *American Journal of Preventive Medicine, 26*(5), 402–406.

Kruszon-Morin, D., & McQuillan, G. M. (2005). Seroprevalence of six infectious diseases among adults in the United States by race/ethnicity: Data from the third National Health and Nutrition Examination Survey, 1988–94. *Advance Data From Vital and Health Statistics, 352.* Hyattsville, MD: National Center for Health Statistics.

Kruzich, J. M., Levy, R. L., Ellis, J., & Olson, D. G. (1984). Assessing health education needs in a prison setting. *Journal of Prison & Jail Health, 4*(2), 107–116.

Kudielka, B. M., Hellhammer, D. H., & Kirschbaum, C. (2000). Sex differences in human stress response. In G. Fink, T. Cox, E. R. de Kloet, B. S. McEwen, N. R. Rose, N. J. Rothwell, … L. Swanson (Eds.), *Encyclopedia of stress* (Vol. 3, pp. 424–429). San Diego, CA: Academic Press.

Kudielka, B. M., Hellhammer, D. H., & Kirschbaum, C. (2007). Ten years of research with the Trier Social Stress Test—Revisited. In E. Harmon-Jones & P. Winkielman (Eds.), *Social neuroscience: Integrating biological and psychological explanations of social behavior* (pp. 56–83). New York, NY: Guilford Press.

Kudielka, B. M., & Kirschbaum, C. (2005). Sex differences in HPA axis responses to stress: A review. *Biological Psychology, 69*(1), 113–132.

Kujala, U. M., Kaprio, J., Sarna, S., & Koskenvuo, M. (1998). Relationship of leisure-time physical activity and mortality: The Finnish twin cohort. *Journal of the American Medical Association, 279*(6), 440–444.

Kukull, W. A., Larson, E. B., Bowen, J. D., McCormick, W. C., Teri, L., Pfanschmidt, M. L., … van Belle, G. (1995). Solvent exposure as a risk factor for Alzheimer's disease: A case control study. *American Journal of Epidemiology, 141*(11), 1059–1071.

Kuller, L. H. (2006). Nutrition, lipids, and cardiovascular disease. *Nutrition Reviews, 64*(2, Pt. 2), S15–S26.

Kunkel, S. R. (1996). Why gender matters: Being female is not the same as not being male. *American Journal of Preventive Medicine, 12*(5), 294–296.

Kunst, A. E., Feikje, G., Mackenbach, J. P., & EU Working Group on Socioeconomic Inequalities in Health. (1998). Occupational class and cause specific mortality in middle aged men in 11 European countries: Comparison of population based studies. *British Medical Journal, 316,* 1636–1642.

Kupers, T. (1999). *Prison madness.* San Francisco, CA: Jossey-Bass.

Kurszewski, L. S., Gerberich, S. G., Serfass, R. C., Ryan, A. D., Renier, C. M., Alexander, B. H., … Masten, A. S. (2006). Sports and recreational injuries: Regional rural injury study-II: Impact on agricultural households and operations. *British Journal of Sports Medicine, 40*(6), 527–535.

Kushi, L. H., Byers, T., Doyle, C., Bandera, E. V., McCullough, M., Gansler, T., … The American Cancer Society 2006 Nutrition and Physical Activity Guidelines Advisory Committee. (2006). American Cancer Society guidelines on nutrition and physical activity for cancer prevention: Reducing the risk of cancer with healthy food choices and physical activity. *CA Cancer Journal for Clinicians, 56*(5), 254–281.

LaCava, G., Lytle, P., Kolev, A., Ozbil, Z., Clert, C., & Marginean, D. (2006). *From risk to empowerment: Young people in south eastern Europe.* Washington, DC: The World Bank.

Laforge, R. G., Greene, G. W., & Prochaska, J. O. (1994). Psychosocial factors influencing low fruit and vegetable consumption. *Journal of Behavioral Medicine, 17*(4), 361–374.

Laforge, R. G., Velicer, W. F., Richmond, R. L., & Owen, N. (1999). Stage distributions for five health behaviors in the United States and Australia. *Preventive Medicine, 28,* 61–74.

Lakka, H. M., Laaksonen, D. E., Lakka, T. A., Niskanen, L. K., Kumpusalo, E., Tuomilehto, J., & Salonen, J. T. (2002). The metabolic syndrome and total and cardiovascular disease mortality in middle-aged men. *Journal of the American Medical Association, 288*(21), 2709–2716.

Lamb, L. M. (2009). *Sex-typing, contingent self-esteem, and peer relations among adolescent males* (Doctoral dissertation, University of Texas at Austin; Publication No. AAT 3368846).

Lambert, D., Gale, J. A., & Hartley, D. (2008). Substance abuse by youth and young adults in rural America. *Journal of Rural Health, 24*(3), 221–228.

Lambrew, J. M., DeFriese, G. H., Carey, T. S., Ricketts, T. C., & Biddle, A. K. (1996). The effects of having a regular doctor on access to primary care. *Medical Care, 34,* 138–151.

Landrigan, P. J., & Baker, D. B. (1991). The recognition and control of occupational disease. *Journal of the American Medical Association, 266*(5), 676–680.

Landsbergis, P. A., Schnall, P. L., Dietz, D. K., Warren, K., Pickering, T. G., & Schwartz, J. E. (1998). Job strain and health behaviors: Results of a prospective study. *American Journal of Health Promotion, 12*(4), 237–245.

Lane, J. M., & Addis, M. E. (2005). Male gender role conflict and patterns of help seeking in Costa Rica and the United States. *Psychology of Men & Masculinity, 6*(3), 155–168.

Larsen, E. R., Mosekilde, L., & Foldspang, A. (2001). Determinants of acceptance of a community-based program for the prevention of falls and fractures among the elderly. *Preventive Medicine, 33*(2), 115–119.

Larsson, S. C., & Wolk, A. (2006). Meat consumption and risk of colorectal cancer: A meta-analysis of prospective studies. *International Journal of Cancer, 119,* 2657–2664.

Lash, S. J., Eisler, R. M., & Schulman, R. S. (1990). Cardiovascular reactivity to stress in men: Effects of masculine gender role stress appraisal and masculine performance challenge. *Behavior Modification, 14,* 3–20.

Lash, S. J., Gillespie, B. L., Eisler, R. M., & Southard, D. R. (1991). Sex differences in cardiovascular reactivity: Effects of the gender relevance of the stressor. *Health Psychology, 10,* 392–398.

Lashley, F. (2003). A review of sleep in selected immune and autoimmune disorders. *Holistic Nursing Practice, 17*(2), 65–80.

Lassila, H. C., Stoehr, G. P., Ganguli, M., Seaberg, E. C., Gilby, J. E., Belle, S. H., & Echement, D. A. (1996). Use of prescription medications in an elderly rural population: The MoVIES Project. *Annals of Pharmacotherapy, 30*(6), 589–595.

Lauderdale, D. S., Knutson, K. L., Yan, L. L., Liu, K., & Rathouz, P. J. (2008). Self-reported and measured sleep duration: How similar are they? *Epidemiology, 19*(6), 838–845.

Laumann, E. O., Gagnon, J. H., Micheal, R. T., & Michaels, S. (1994). *The social organization of sexuality: Sexual practices in the United States.* Chicago, IL: The University of Chicago Press.

LaVeist, T. A. (1993). Segregation, poverty, and empowerment: Health consequences for African Americans. *Milbank Quarterly, 71*(1), 41–64.

LaVeist, T. A., Nickerson, K. J., & Bowie, J. V. (2000). Attitudes about racism, medical mistrust, and satisfaction with care among African American and white cardiac patients. *Medical Care Research and Review, 57*(Suppl. 1), 146–161.

Lavine, H., Sweeney, D., & Wagner, S. H. (1999). Depicting women as sex objects in television advertising: Effects on body dissatisfaction. *Personality and Social Psychology Bulletin, 25,* 1049–1058.

Lazur, R. F., & Majors, R. (1995). Men of color: Ethnocultural variations of male gender role strain. In R. F. Levant & W. S. Pollack (Eds.), *A new psychology of men* (pp. 337–358). New York, NY: Basic Books.

Lee, C., & Owens, R. G. (2002). Issues for a psychology of men's health [Special issue]. *Journal of Health Psychology, 7*(3), 209–217.

Lee, C. C. (1990). Black male development: Counseling the "native son." In D. Moore & F. Leafgren (Eds.), *Problem solving strategies and interventions for men in conflict* (pp. 125–137). Alexandria, VA: American Association for Counseling and Development.

Lee, I. M., Hsieh, C. C., & Paffenbarger, R. S. (1995). Exercise intensity and longevity in men: The Harvard Alumni Health Study. *Journal of the American Medical Association, 273*(15), 1179–1184.

Lee, I. M., Paffenbarger, R. S., & Hsieh, C. C. (1991). Physical activity and risk of developing colorectal cancer among college alumni. *Journal of the National Cancer Institute, 83,* 1324–1329.

Lee, I. M., Sesso, H. D., Oguma, Y., & Paffenbarger, R. S. (2004). The "weekend warrior" and risk of mortality. *American Journal of Epidemiology, 160*(7), 636–641.

Lee, J. Y., & Soong, S. J. (1990). Cancer mortality in the South, 1950 to 1980. *Southern Medical Journal, 83*(2), 185–190.

Lee, P. R. (1996). Foreword. In *U.S. Preventive Services Task Force Guide to Clinical Preventive Services* (2nd ed., p. 5). Baltimore, MD: Williams and Wilkins.

Legato, M. J. (2003). Beyond women's health: The new discipline of gender-specific medicine. *Medical Clinics of North America, 87,* 917–937.

Legato, M. J. (2004). Gender-specific medicine: The view from Salzburg. *Gender Medicine, 1*(2), 61–131.

Legato, M. J. (Ed.). (2009). *Principles of gender-specific medicine.* New York, NY: Elsevier Academic Press.

Leger, D. (1994). The cost of sleep related accidents: A report for the National Commission on Sleep Disorders Research. *Sleep, 17*(1), 84–93.

Leigh, B. C., Temple, M. T., & Trocki, K. F. (1993). The sexual behavior of U.S. adults: Results from a national survey. *American Journal of Public Health,* *83*(10), 1400–1408.

Leigh, J. P., & Fries, J. F. (1993). Associations among healthy habits, age, gender, and education in a sample of retirees. *International Journal of Aging and Human Development, 36*(2), 139–155.

Leino, E. V., & Kisch, J. (2005). Correlates and predictors of depression in college students: Results from the Spring 2000 National College Health Assessment. *American Journal of Health Education, 36*(2), 66–74.

Lejuez, C. W., Read, J. P., Kahler, C. W., Richards, J. B., Ramsey, S. E., Stuart, G. L., … Brown, R. A. (2002). Evaluation of a behavioral measure of risk taking: The Balloon Analogue Risk Task (BART). *Journal of Experimental Psychology: Applied, 8*(2), 75–84.

LeMarchand, L., Kolonel, L. N., Wilkens, L. R., Myers, B. C., & Hirohata, T. (1994). Animal fat consumption and prostate cancer: A prospective study in Hawaii. *Epidemiology, 5,* 276–282.

Lemle, R., & Mishkind, M. E. (1989). Alcohol and masculinity. *Journal of Substance Abuse Treatment, 6,* 213–222.

Lent, B., & Bishop, J. E. (1998). Sense and sensitivity: Developing a gender issues perspective in medical education. *Journal of Women's Health, 7*(3), 339–342.

Leong, F. T., & Zachar, P. (1999). Gender and opinions about mental illness as predictors of attitudes toward seeking professional help. *British Journal of Guidance and Counseling, 27,* 123–132.

Lepore, S. J., Allen, K. A., & Evans, G. W. (1993). Social support lowers cardiovascular reactivity to an acute stressor. *Psychosomatic Medicine, 55,* 518–524.

Lerner, J. S., Gonzales, R. M., Small, D. A., & Fischhoff, B. (2003). Effects of fear and anger on perceived risks of terrorism. *Psychological Science, 14*(2), 144–150.

Lester, D. (1990). Depression and suicide in college students and adolescents. *Personal and Individual Differences, 11*(7), 757–758.

Levant, R. F., Cuthbert, A., Richmond, K., Sellers, A., Matveev, A., Mitina, O., … Heesacker, M. (2003). Masculinity ideology among Russian and U.S. young men and women and its relationships to unhealthy lifestyle habits among young Russian men. *Psychology of Men & Masculinity, 4*(1), 26–36.

Levant, R. F., & Fischer, J. (1998). The Male Role Norms Inventory. In C. M. Davis, W. H. Yarber, R. Bauserman, G. Schreer, & S. L. Davis (Eds.), *Sexuality-related measures: A compendium* (2nd ed., pp. 469–472). Newbury Park, CA: Sage.

Levant, R. F., & Kopecky, G. (1995). *Masculinity reconstructed: Changing the rules of manhood—at work, in relationships, and in family life.* New York, NY: Dutton.

Levant, R. F., & Majors, R. G. (1998). Masculinity ideology among African American and European American college women and men. *Journal of Gender, Culture, and Health, 2*(1), 33–43.

Levant, R. F., Majors, R. G., & Kelley, M. L. (1998). Masculinity ideology among young African American and European American women and men in different regions of the United States. *Cultural Diversity and Ethnic Minority Psychology, 4*(3), 227–236.

Levant, R. F., Richmond, K., Majors, R. G., Inclan, J. E., Rossello, J. M., Heesacker, M., … Sellers, A. (2003). A multicultural investigation of masculinity ideology and alexithymia. *Psychology of Men & Masculinity, 4*(2), 91–99.

Levant, R. F., Wimer, D. J., Williams, C. M., Smalley, K. B., & Noronha, D. (2009). The relationships between masculinity variables, health risk behaviors and attitudes toward seeking psychological help. *International Journal of Men's Health, 8*(1), 3–21.

Levant, R. F., Wu, R., & Fisher, J. (1996). Masculinity ideology: A comparison between U.S. and Chinese young men and women. *Journal of Gender, Culture, and Health, 1,* 217–220.

Levenson-Gingiss, P., Morrow, J. R., & Dratt, L. M. (1989). Patterns of smokeless tobacco use among university athletes. *Journal of American College Health, 38,* 87–90.

Levi, A., Chan, K. K., & Pence, D. (2006). Real men do not read labels: The effects of masculinity and involvement on college students' food decisions. *Journal of American College Health, 55*(2), 91–98.

Levine, F. M., & DeSimone, L. L. (1991). The effects of experimenter gender on pain report in male and female patients. *Pain, 44,* 69–72.

Levine, J., Warrenburg, S., Kerns, R., Schwartz, G., Delaney, R., Fontana, A., … Cascione, R. (1987). The role of denial in recovery from coronary heart disease. *Psychosomatic Medicine, 49*(2), 109–117.

Levine, M. (1998). *Gay macho: The life and death of the homosexual clone.* New York, NY: New York University Press.

Levinson, D. (1978). *The seasons of a man's life.* New York, NY: Knopf.

Lew, R., & Tanjasiri, S. P. (2003). Slowing the epidemic of tobacco use among Asian Americans and Pacific Islanders. *American Journal of Public Health, 93*(5), 764–768.

Lewington, S., Whitlock, G., Clarke, R., Sherliker, P., Emberson, J., Halsey, J., … Collins, R. (2007). Blood cholesterol and vascular mortality by age, sex, and blood pressure: A meta-analysis of individual data from 61 prospective studies with 55,000 vascular deaths. *Lancet, 370*(9602), 1829–1839.

Lewis, C. E., Clancy, C., Leake, B., & Schwartz, J. S. (1991). The counseling practices of internists. *American College of Physicians, 114*(1), 54–58.

Lewis, C. E., & Lewis, M. A. (1977). The potential impact of sexual equality on health. *New Journal of Medicine, 297*(16), 863–869.

Lewis, D. F., Goodhart, F., & Burns, W. D. (1996). New Jersey college students' high-risk behavior: Will we meet the health objectives for the year 2000? *Journal of American College Health, 45*(3), 119–126.

Lex, B. W. (1991). Some gender differences in alcohol and polysubstance users. *Health Psychology, 10,* 121–132.

Li, C., Ford, E. S., Zhao, G., & Mokdad, A. H. (2009). Prevalence of pre-diabetes and its association with clustering of cardiometabolic risk factors and hyperinsulinemia among U.S. adolescents: National Health and Nutrition Examination Survey 2005-2006. *Diabetes Care, 32*(2), 342–347.

Lichtenstein, A. H., Appel, L. J., Brands, M., Carnethon, M., Daniels, S., Franch, H. A., … Wylie-Rosett, J. (2006). Diet and lifestyle recommendations revision 2006: A scientific statement from the American Heart Association Nutrition Committee. *Circulation, 114,* 82–96.

Liddell, A., Locker, D., & Burman, D. (1991). Self-reported fears (FSS-II) of subjects aged 50 years and over. *Behavior Research and Therapy*, *29*(2), 105–112.

Lieberman, J. M. (1994). Rotavirus and other viral causes of gastroenteritis. *Pediatric Annals*, *23*(10), 529–532, 534–535.

Liebman, B. (1995, January–February). Dodging cancer with diet. *Nutrition Action Healthletter*, 4–7.

Liepins, R. (2000). Making men: The construction and representation of agriculture-based masculinities in Australia and New Zealand. *Rural Sociology*, *65*(4), 605–620.

Lighthall, N. R., Mather, M., & Gorlick, M. A. (2009). Acute stress increases sex differences in risk seeking in the balloon analogue risk task. *PLoS One*, *4*, e6002.

Lillie-Blanton, M., Brodie, M., Rowland, D., Altman, D., & McIntosh, M. (2000). Race, ethnicity, and the health care system: Public perceptions and experiences. *Medical Care Research and Review*, *57*(Suppl. 1), 218–235.

Lindsey, M. A., Korr, W. S., Broitman, M., Bone, L., Green, A., & Leaf, P. J. (2006). Help-seeking behaviors and depression among African American adolescent boys. *Social Work*, *51*(1), 49–58.

Linn, J. G., & Husaini, B. A. (1987). Determinants of psychological depression and coping behaviors of Tennessee farm residents. *Journal of Community Psychology*, *15*, 503–512.

Linn, S., Carroll, M., Johnson, C., Fulwood, R., Kalsbeek, W., & Briefel, R. (1993). High-density lipoprotein cholesterol and alcohol consumption in U.S. White and Black adults: Data from NHANES II. *American Journal of Public Health*, *83*(6), 811–816.

Lippa, R. A., Martin, L. R., & Friedman, H. S. (2000). Gender-related individual differences and mortality in the Terman longitudinal study: Is masculinity hazardous to your health? *Personality and Social Psychology Bulletin*, *12*, 1560–1570.

Little, J., & Jones, O. (2000). Masculinity, gender and rural policy. *Rural Sociology*, *65*(4), 621–639.

Little, S. J., Stevens, V. J., Severson, H. H., & Lichtenstein, E. (1992). Effective smokeless tobacco intervention for dental hygiene patients. *Journal of Dental Hygiene*, *66*(4), 185–190.

Liu, J.-T., & Hsieh, C.-R. (1995). Risk perception and smoking behavior: Empirical evidence from Taiwan. *Journal of Risk and Uncertainty*, *11*(2), 139–157.

Liu, S., Siegel, P. Z., Brewer, R. D., Mokdad, A. H., Sleet, D. A., & Serdula, M. (1997). Prevalence of alcohol-impaired driving: Results from a national self-reported survey of health behaviors. *Journal of the American Medical Association*, *277*(2), 122–125.

Liu, W. M., & Iwamoto, D. K. (2006). Asian American men's gender role conflict: The role of Asian values, self-esteem, and psychological distress. *Psychology of Men & Masculinity*, *7*(3), 153–164.

Livengood, J. R., Caspersen, C. J., & Koplan, J. (1993). The health benefits of exercise. *New England Journal of Medicine*, *328*(25), 1852.

Livingstone, M. B., Robson, P. J., Wallace, J. M., & McKinley, M. S. (2003). How active are we? Levels of routine physical activity in children and adults. *Proceedings of the Nutrition Society*, *62*(3), 681–701.

Lloyd-Jones, D. M., Adams, R., Carnethon, M., De Simone, G., Ferguson, T. B., Flegal, K., … Hong Y. (2009). Heart disease and stroke statistics—2009 update: A report from the American Heart Association Statistics Committee and Stroke Statistics Subcommittee. *Circulation, 119*, e1–e161.

Lloyd-Jones, D. M., Berry, J. D., Ning, H., Cai, X., & Goldberger, J. J. (2009). Lifetime risk for sudden cardiac death at selected index ages and by risk factor strata and race: Cardiovascular Lifetime Risk Pooling Project. *Circulation, 120*, S416–S417.

Lloyd-Jones, D. M., Dyer, A. R., Wang, R., Daviglus, M. L., & Greenland, P. (2007). Risk factor burden in middle age and lifetime risks for cardiovascular and non-cardiovascular death (Chicago Heart Association Detection Project in Industry). *American Journal of Cardioliology, 99*, 535–540.

Lloyd-Jones, D. M., Leip, E. P., Larson, M. G., D'Agostino, R. B., Beiser, A., Wilson, P. W., … Levy, D. (2006). Prediction of lifetime risk for cardiovascular disease by risk factor burden at 50 years of age. *Circulation, 113*(6), 791–798.

Lloyd-Jones, D. M., Nam, B. H., D'Agostino, R. B., Levy, D., Murabito, J. M., Wang, T. J., … O'Donnell, C. J. (2004). Parental cardiovascular disease as a risk factor for cardiovascular disease in middle-aged adults: A prospective study of parents and offspring. *Journal of the American Medical Association, 291*, 2204–2211.

Locke, B. D., & Mahalik, J. R. (2005). Examining masculinity norms, problem drinking, and athletic involvement as predictors of sexual aggression in college men. *Journal of Counseling Psychology, 52*, 279–283.

Loeber, R., Pardini, D., Homish, D. L., Wei, E. H., Crawford, A. M., Farrington, D. P., … Rosenfeld, R. (2005). The prediction of violence and homicide in young men. *Journal of Consulting & Clinical Psychology, 73*(6), 1074–1088.

Lohan, M. (2007). How might we understand men's health better? Integrating explanations from critical studies on men and inequalities in health. *Social Science & Medicine, 65*(3), 493–504.

Lollis, C. M., Johnson, E. H., Antoni, M. H., & Hinkle, Y. (1996). Characteristics of African-Americans with multiple risk factors associated with HIV/AIDS. *Journal of Behavioral Medicine, 19*(1), 55–71.

Lombardo, W. K., Cretser, G. A., Lombardo, B., & Mathis, S. L. (1983). Fer cryin' out loud—there is a sex difference. *Sex Roles, 9*(9), 987–995.

Long, K. A. (1993). The concept of health: Rural perspectives. *Nursing Clinics of North America, 28*(1), 123–130.

Lonnquist, L. E., Weiss, G. L., & Larsen, D. L. (1992). Health value and gender in predicting health protective behavior. *Women and Health, 19*(2/3), 69–85.

Loria, C. M., Liu, K., Lewis, C. E., Hulley, S. B., Sidney, S., Schreiner, P. J., … Detrano, R. (2007). Early adult risk factor levels and subsequent coronary artery calcification: The CARDIA Study. *Journal of the American College of Cardiolology, 49*, 2013–2020.

Loria, C. M., Obarzanek, E., & Ernst, N. D. (2001). Choose and prepare foods with less salt: Dietary advice for all Americans. *Journal of Nutrition, 131*, 536S–551S.

Loscalzo, M. J., Hooker, C. M., Zabora, J. R., & Bucher, J. A. (2000, August). How men manage the ongoing challenges of cancer. In R. Hetzel (Chair), *Men's health in the new millennium: Emerging research theory and practice.* Symposium conducted at the 108th Convention of the American Psychological Association, Washington, DC.

Losonczy, K. G., Harris, T. B., & Havlik, R. J. (1996). Vitamin E and vitamin C supplement use and risk of all-cause and coronary heart disease mortality in older persons: The established populations for epidemiologic studies of the elderly. *American Journal of Clinical Nutrition, 64*(2), 190–196.

Love, N. (1991). Why patients delay seeking care for cancer symptoms: What you can do about it. *Postgraduate Medicine, 89*(4), 151–158.

Lovell, M. R., Collins, M. W., Maroon, J. C., Cantu, R., Hawn, M. A., Burke, C. J., & Fu, F. (2002). Inaccuracy of symptom reporting following concussion in athletes. *Medicine and Science in Sports and Exercise, 34*(5), 298.

Low, B. S. (1989). Cross-cultural patterns in the training of children: An evolutionary perspective. *Journal of Comparative Psychology, 103*, 311–319.

Lowe, R. A., Chhaya, S., Nasci, K., Gavin, L. J., Shaw, K., Zwanger, M. L., … Berlin, J. A. (2001). Effect of ethnicity on denial of authorization for emergency department care by managed care gatekeepers. *Academic Emergency Medicine, 8*(3), 259–266.

Lowry, R., Powell, K. E., Kann, L., Collins, J. L., & Kolbe, L. J. (1998). Weapon-carrying, physical fighting, and fight-related injury among U.S. adolescents. *American Journal of Preventive Medicine, 14*(2), 122–129.

Lueptow, L. B., Garovich, L., & Lueptow, M. B. (1995). The persistence of gender stereotypes in the face of changing sex roles: Evidence contrary to the sociocultural model. *Ethology and Sociobiology, 16*(6), 509–530.

Lueptow, L. B., Garovich-Szabo, L., & Lueptow, M. B. (2001). Social change and the persistence of sex typing: 1974–1997. *Social Forces, 80*, 1–35.

Lundborg, P., & Lindgren, B. (2002). Risk perception and alcohol consumption among young people. *Journal of Risk and Uncertainty, 25*(2), 165–183.

Lunn, R. M., Bell, D. A., Mohler, J. L., & Taylor, J. A. (1999). Prostate cancer risk and polymorphism in 17 hydroxylase (CYP17) and steroid reductase (SRD5A2). *Carcinogenesis, 20*(9), 1727–1731.

Lytton, H., & Romney, D. M. (1991). Parents' differential socialization of boys and girls: A meta-analysis. *Psychological Bulletin, 109*(2), 267–296.

Maccoby, E. E. (1988). Gender as a social category. *Developmental Psychology, 24*(6), 755–765.

Maccoby, E. E. (2002). Gender and group process: A developmental perspective. *Current Directions in Psychological Science, 11*(2), 54–58.

Maccoby, E. E., & Jacklin, C. N. (1974). *The psychology of sex differences*. Stanford, CA: Stanford University Press.

Macdonald, S., Anglin-Bodrug, K., Mann, R. E., Erickson, P., Hathaway, A., Chipman, M., & Rylett, M. (2003). Injury risk associated with cannabis and cocaine use. *Drug and Alcohol Dependence, 72*(2), 99–115.

Macfarlane, M. T. (2006). *Urology* (4th ed.). New York, NY: Lippincott, Williams, & Wilkins.

MacGregor, G. A. (1997). Salt—more adverse effects. *American Journal of Hypertension, 10*(5, Pt. 2), 37S–41S.

MacIntyre, C. R., Kendig, N., Kummer, L., Birago, S., & Graham, N. M. (1997). Impact of tuberculosis control measures and crowding on the incidence of tuberculous infection in Maryland prisons. *Clinical Infectious Diseases, 24*, 1060–1067.

Macintyre, S., Hunt, K., & Sweeting, H. (1996). Gender differences in health: Are things really as simple as they seem? *Social Science and Medicine, 42*, 617–624.

Mackenbach, J. P., Stirbu, I., Roskam, A. R., Schaap, M. M., Menvielle, G., Leinsalu, M., & Kunst, A. E. (2008). Socioeconomic inequalities in health in 22 European countries. *New England Journal of Medicine, 358*(23), 2468–2481.

Maclure, M. (1993). Demonstration of deductive meta-analysis: Ethanol intake and risk of myocardial infarction. *Epidemiologic Reviews, 15*(2), 328–351.

Maden, C., Sherman, K. J., Beckmann, A. M., Hislop, T. G., Teh, C. Z., Ashley, R. L., & Daling, J. R. (1995). History of circumcision, medical conditions, and sexual activity, and risk of penile cancer. *Journal of the National Cancer Institute, 85*(1), 19–24.

Mahalik, J. R., Burns, S. M., & Syzdek, M. (2007). Masculinity and perceived normative health behaviors as predictors of men's health behaviors. *Social Science & Medicine, 64*(11), 2201–2209.

Mahalik, J. R., Lagan, H. D., & Morrison, J. A. (2006). Health behaviors and masculinity in Kenyan and U.S. male college students. *Psychology of Men and Masculinity, 7*, 191–202.

Mahalik, J. R., Levi-Minzi, M., & Walker, G. (2007). Masculinity and health behaviors in Australian men. *Psychology of Men & Masculinity, 8*(4), 240–249.

Mahalik, J. R., Locke, B. D., Ludlow, L. H., Diemer, M. A., Scott, R. P. J., Gottfried, M., & Freitas, G. (2003). Development of the Conformity to Masculine Norms Inventory. *Psychology of Men and Masculinity, 4*(1), 3–25.

Mahalik, J. R., Walker, G., & Levi-Minzi, M. (2007). Masculinity and health behaviors in Australian men. *Psychology of Men and Masculinity, 8*(4), 240–249.

Mahon, N. E., & Yarcheski, T. J. (1994). Future time perspective and positive health practices in adolescents. *Perceptual and Motor Skills, 79*(1), 395–398.

Mahon, N. E., Yarcheski, T. J., & Yarcheski, A. (1997). Future time perspective and positive health practices in young adults: An extension. *Perceptual and Motor Skills, 84*(3), 1299–1304.

Maio, R. F., Green, P. E., Becker, M. P., Burney, R. E., & Compton, C. (1992). Rural motor vehicle crash mortality: The role of crash severity and medical resources. *Accident Analysis and Prevention, 24*(6), 631–642.

Majors, R., & Billson, J. M. (1992). *Cool pose: The dilemmas of Black manhood in America*. New York, NY: Simon & Schuster.

Make, B. (1994). Collaborative self-management strategies for patients with respiratory disease. *Respiratory Care, 39*(5), 566–579.

Makridakis, N. M., Ross, R. K., Pike, M. C., Crocitto, L. E., Kolonel, L. N., Pearce, C. L., … Reichardt, J. K. (1999). Association of mis-sense substitution in SRD5A2 gene with prostate cancer in African-American and Hispanic men in Los Angeles, U.S.A. *Lancet, 354*(9183), 975–978.

Mandel, J. S., Bond, J. H., Church, T. R., Snover, D. C., Bradley, G. M., Schuman, L. M., & Ederer, F. (1993). Reducing mortality from colorectal cancer by screening for fecal occult blood. *New England Journal of Medicine, 328*(19), 1365–1371.

Mansfield, A. K., Addis, M. E., & Courtenay, W. (2005). Measurement of men's help seeking: Development and evaluation of the Barriers to Help Seeking Scale. *Psychology of Men and Masculinity, 6*(2), 95–108.

Mansfield, A. K., Addis, M. E., & Mahalik, J. R. (2003). "Why won't he go to the doctor?": The psychology of men's help seeking. *International Journal of Men's Health, 2*(2), 93–109.

Marcell, A. V., Ford, C. A., Pleck, J. H., & Sonenstein, F. L. (2007). Masculine beliefs, parental communication, and male adolescents' health care use. *Pediatrics, 119*(4), 965–974.

Marcenes, W., & Sheiham, A. (1996). The relationship between marital quality and oral health status. *Psychology and Health, 11*, 357–369.

Marin, J. M., Carrizo, S. J., Vicente, E., & Agusti, A. G. (2005). Long-term cardiovascular outcomes in men with obstructive sleep apnoea-hypopnoea with or without treatment with continuous positive airway pressure: An observational study. *Lancet, 365*(9464), 1046–1053.

Marks, G., Crepaz, N., Senterfitt, J. W., & Janssen, R. S. (2005). Meta-analysis of high-risk sexual behavior in persons aware and unaware they are infected with HIV in the United States: Implications for HIV prevention programs. *Journal of Acquired Immune Deficiency Syndromes, 39*, 446–453.

Marks, G., Garcia, M., & Solis, J. M. (1990). Health risk behaviors of Hispanics in the United States: Findings from HHANES, 1982-84. *American Journal of Public Health, 80* (Suppl.), 20–26.

Marlenga, B. (1995). The health beliefs and skin cancer prevention practices of Wisconsin dairy farmers. *Oncology Nursing Forum, 22*(4), 681–686.

Marquart, J. W., Merianos, D. E., Cuvelier, S. J., & Carroll, L. (1996). Thinking about the relationship between health dynamics in the free community and the prison. *Crime and Delinquency, 42*(3), 331–360.

Marshall, J. R., & Funch, D. P. (1979). Mental illness and the economy: A critique and partial replication. *Journal of Health and Social Behavior, 29*, 282–289.

Marshall, N. S., Wong, K. K., Liu, P. Y., Cullen, S. R., Knuiman, M. W., & Grunstein, R. R. (2008). Sleep apnea as an independent risk factor for all-cause mortality: The Busselton Health Study. *Sleep, 31*(8), 1079–1085.

Marshall, S. J., Jones, D. A., Ainsworth, B. E., Reis, J. P., Levy, S. S., & Macera, C. A. (2007). Race/ethnicity, social class, and leisure-time physical inactivity. *Medicine and Science in Sports and Exercise, 39*(1), 44–51.

Martin, C. L. (1990). Attitudes and expectations about children with nontraditional and traditional gender roles. *Sex Roles, 22*, 151–165.

Martin, C. L. (1995). Stereotypes about children with traditional and nontraditional gender roles. *Sex Roles, 33*(11/12), 727–751.

Massie, D. L., Green, P. E., & Campbell, K. L. (1997). Crash involvement rates by driver gender and the role of average annual mileage. *Accident Analysis and Prevention, 29*(5), 675–685.

Mastroianni, A. C., Faden, R., & Federman, D. (1994). *Women and health research: Ethical and legal issues of including women in clinical studies.* Washington, DC: National Academy Press.

Mathers, C. D., & Schofield, D. J. (1998). The health consequences of unemployment: The evidence. *Medical Journal of Australia, 168*, 178–182.

Matthews, C. E., Chen, K. Y., Freedson, P. S., Buchowski, M. S., Beech, B. M., Pate, R. R., & Troiano, R. P. (2008). Amount of time spent in sedentary behaviors in the United States, 2003–2004. *American Journal of Epidemiology, 167*(7), 875–881.

Matthews, C. E., Freedson, P. S., Hebert, J. R., Stanek, E. J., Merriam, P. A., Rosal, M. C., … Ockene, I. S. (2001). Seasonal variation in household, occupational, and leisure time physical activity: Longitudinal analyses from the Seasonal Variation of Blood Cholesterol Study. *American Journal of Epidemiology, 153*(2), 172–183.

Matthews, K. A., Weiss, S. M., Detre, T., Dembroski, T. M., Falkner, B., Manuck, S. B., & Williams, R. B. (Eds.). (1986). *Handbook of stress, reactivity & cardiovascular disease*. New York, NY: Wiley.

May, J. P., & Martin, K. L. (1993). A role for the primary care physician in counseling young African-American men about homicide prevention. *Journal of General Internal Medicine, 8*, 380–382.

May, R. (1990). Finding ourselves: Self-esteem, self-disclosure and self-acceptance. In D. Moore & F. Leafgren (Eds.), *Problem solving strategies and interventions for men in conflict* (pp. 11–21). Alexandria, VA: American Association for Counseling and Development.

Mayhew, D., Ferguson, S. A., Desmond, K. J., & Simpson, H. M. (2003). Trends in fatal crashes involving female drivers, 1975–1998. *Accident Analysis & Prevention, 35*(3), 407–415.

Mayne, S. T., Risch, H. A., Dubrow, R., Chow, W. H., Gammon, M. D., Vaughan, T. L., … Fraumeni, J. F. (2001). Nutrient intake and risk of subtypes of esophageal and gastric cancer. *Cancer Epidemiology, Biomarkers & Prevention, 10*, 1055–1062.

Mayrose, J., & Jehle, D. V. (2002). An analysis of race and demographic factors among motor vehicle fatalities. *Journal of Trauma, Injury, Infection and Critical Care, 52*, 752–755.

McCabe, S. E., Brower, K. J., West, B. T., Nelson, T. F., & Wechsler, H. (2007). Trends in non-medical use of anabolic steroids by U.S. college students: Results from four national surveys. *Drug and Alcohol Dependence, 90*(2–3), 243–251.

McCabe, S. E., Teter, C. J., Boyd, C. J., Knight, J. R., & Wechsler, H. (2005). Nonmedical use of prescription opioids among U.S. college students: Prevalence and correlates from a national survey. *Addictive Behaviors, 30*(4), 789–805.

McCann, D. P., & Blossom, H. J. (1990). The physician as a patient educator: From theory to practice. *Western Journal of Medicine, 153*(1), 44–49.

McCarron, P., Smith, G. D., Okasha, M., & McEwen, J. (2000). Blood pressure in young adulthood and mortality from cardiovascular disease. *Lancet, 355*(9213), 1430–1431.

McClelland, J. W., Demark-Wahnefried, W., Mustian, R. D., Cowan, A. T., & Campbell, M. K. (1998). Fruit and vegetable consumption of rural African Americans: Baseline survey results of the Black Churches United for Better Health 5 A Day Project. *Nutrition and Cancer, 30*(2), 148–157.

McCormack, G. R., Friedenreich, C., Shiell, A., Giles-Corti, B., & Doyle-Baker, P. K. (in press). Gender and age-specific seasonal variations in physical activity among adults. *Journal of Epidemiology and Community Health*.

McCrea, M., Hammeke, T., Olsen, G., Leo, P., & Guskiewicz, K. (2004). Unreported concussion in high school football players: Implications for prevention. *Clinical Journal of Sports Medicine, 14*, 13–17.

McCreary, D. R. (1990a). Multidimensionality and the measurement of gender role attributes: A comment on Archer. *British Journal of Social Psychology, 29*, 265–272.

McCreary, D. R. (1990b). Self-perceptions of life-span gender role development. *International Journal of Aging and Human Development, 31*, 135–146.

McCreary, D. R. (1994). The male role and avoiding femininity. *Sex Roles, 31*, 517–531.

McCreary, D. R. (2002). Gender and age differences in the relationship between Body Mass Index and perceived weight: Exploring the paradox. *International Journal of Men's Health, 1*, 31–42.

McCreary, D. R. (2009). Men's body image. In R. Kirby, C. C. Carson, A. White, & M. Kirby (Eds.), *Men's health* (3rd ed.) (pp. 493–501). London, England: Informa Healthcare Press.

McCreary, D. R., & Courtenay, W. H. (2003, August). Gender role conflict predicts engaging in multiple health risk behaviors. In J. M. O'Neil & G. E. Good (Chairs), *Psychological and physical health correlates of gender role conflict: Five empirical studies.* Symposium presented at the annual meetings of the American Psychological Association, Toronto, Canada.

McCreary, D. R., Newcomb, M. D., & Sadava, S. W. (1998). Dimensions of the male gender role: A confirmatory analysis in men and women. *Sex Roles, 39*, 81–95.

McCreary, D. R., Newcomb, M. D., & Sadava, S. W. (1999). The male role, alcohol use, and alcohol problems: A structural modeling examination in adult women and men. *Journal of Counseling Psychology, 46*, 109–124.

McCreary, D. R., & Rhodes, N. D. (2001). On the gender-typed nature of dominant and submissive acts. *Sex Roles, 44*, 339–350.

McCreary, D. R., & Sadava, S. W. (2000, August). Gender differences in adult perceptions of body weight and their relationships to self-perceived attractiveness, life satisfaction, and health. In R. Hetzel (Chair), *Men's health in the new millennium: Emerging research theory and practice.* Symposium conducted at the 108th Convention of the American Psychological Association, Washington, DC.

McCreary, D. R., & Sadava, S. W. (2001). Gender differences in relationships among perceived attractiveness, life satisfaction, and health in adults as a function of Body Mass Index and perceived weight. *Psychology of Men and Masculinity, 2*, 108–116.

McCreary, D. R., & Sadava, S. W. (2009, August). Relationships among gender roles and risky health behaviors in men. In M. Epstein (Chair), *Masculinity in context: Examination of positive and negative effects.* Symposium presented at the annual meetings of the American Psychological Association, Toronto, Canada.

McCreary, D. R., & Sasse, D. K. (2000). An exploration of the drive for muscularity in adolescent boys and girls. *Journal of American College Health, 48*(6), 297–304.

McCreary, D. R., & Sasse, D. K. (2002). Gender differences in high school students' dieting behavior and their correlates. *International Journal of Men's Health, 1*, 195–213.

McCreary, D. R., Sasse, D. K., Saucier, D. M., & Dorsch, K. D. (2004). Measuring the drive for muscularity: Factorial validity of the Drive for Muscularity Scale in men and women. *Psychology of Men and Masculinity, 5*, 49–58.

McCreary, D. R., Saucier, D. M., & Courtenay, W. H. (2005). The drive for muscularity and masculinity: Testing the associations among gender role traits, behaviors, attitudes, and conflict. *Psychology of Men and Masculinity, 6*(2), 83–94.

McDonald, A. J., Wang, N., & Camargo, C. A. (2004). U.S. emergency department visits for alcohol-related diseases and injuries between 1992 and 2000. *Archives of Internal Medicine, 164*(5), 531–537.

McGhee, P. E., & Frueh, T. (1980). Television viewing and the learning of sex-role stereotypes. *Sex Roles, 6*(2), 179–188.

McGill, M. E. (1985). *The McGill report on male intimacy.* New York, NY: Holt, Rinehart and Winston.

McGinnis, J. M., & Foege, W. H. (1993). Actual causes of death in the United States. *Journal of the American Medical Association, 270*(18), 2207–2212.

McGinnis, J. M., & Foege, W. H. (2004). The immediate vs the important. *Journal of the American Medical Association, 291*(10), 1263–1264.

McGue, M., Iacono, W. G., Legrand, L. N., Malone, S., & Elkins, I. (2001). Origins and consequences of age at first drink. I. Associations with substance-use disorders, disinhibitory behavior and psychopathology, and P3 amplitude. *Alcoholism: Clinical and Experimental Research, 25*(8), 1156–1165.

McKay, J. R., Rutherford, M. J., Cacciola, J. S., & Kabaskalian-McKay, R. (1996). Gender differences in the relapse experiences of cocaine patients. *Journal of Nervous and Mental Disease, 184*(10), 616–622.

McKiernan, J. M., Goluboff, E. T., Liberson, G. L., Golden, R., & Fisch, H. (1999). Rising risk of testicular cancer by birth cohort in the United States from 1973 to 1995. *Journal of Urology, 162*(2), 361–363.

McKnight, R. H., Koetke, C. A., & Mays, J. R. (1995). Smokeless tobacco use among adults in Kentucky: 1994. *Journal of the Kentucky Medical Association, 93*(10), 459–464.

Mead, P. S., Slutsker, L., Dietz, V., McCaig, L. F., Bresee, J. S., Shapiro, C., … Tauxe, R. V. (1999). Food-related illness and death in the United States: Emerging infectious diseases. *Emerging Infectious Diseases, 5*(5), 607–625.

Mechanic, D., & Cleary, P. D. (1980). Factors associated with the maintenance of positive health behavior. *Preventive Medicine, 9,* 805–814.

Mehra, R., Stone, K., Blackwell, T., Israel, S. A., Dam, T. T., Stefanick, M. L., & Redline, S. (2007). Prevalence and correlates of sleep-disordered breathing in older men: Osteoporotic Fractures in Men Sleep Study. *Journal of the American Geriatrics Society, 55*(9), 1356–1364.

Meichenbaum, D., & Turk, D. C. (1987). *Facilitating treatment adherence: A practitioner's guidebook.* New York, NY: Plenum.

Meikle, A. W., Stringham, J. D., Bishop, D. T., & West, D. W. (1988). Quantitating genetic and nongenetic factors influencing androgen production and clearance rates in men. *Journal of Clinical Endocrinology & Metabolism, 67*(1), 104–109.

Meilman, P. W., Crace, R. K., Presley, C. A., & Lyerla, R. (1995). Beyond performance enhancement: Polypharmacy among collegiate users of steroids. *Journal of American College Health, 44*(3), 98–104.

Meilman, P. W., Yanofsky, N. N., Gaylor, M. S., & Turco, J. H. (1989). Visits to the college health service for alcohol-related injuries. *Journal of American College Health, 37,* 205–210.

Meinecke, C. E. (1981). Socialized to die younger? Hypermasculinity and men's health. *The Personnel and Guidance Journal, 60,* 241–245.

Melanson, K. J. (2008). Promoting nutrition for men's health. *American Journal of Lifestyle Medicine, 2*(6), 488–491.

Melman, A., & Gingell, J. C. (1999). The epidemiology and pathophysiology of erectile dysfunction. *Journal of Urology, 161,* 5–11.

Mendelson, M. E., & Karas, R. H. (1999). The protective effects of estrogen on the cardiovascular system. *New England Journal of Medicine, 340,* 1801–1811.

Mensah, G. A., & Brown, D. W. (2007). An overview of cardiovascular disease burden in the United States. *Health Affairs, 26*(1), 38–48.

Mensah, G. A., Brown, D. W., Croft, J. B., & Greenlund, K. J. (2005). Major coronary risk factors and death from coronary heart disease: Baseline and follow-up mortality data from the Second National Health and Nutrition Examination Survey (NHANES II). *American Journal of Preventive Medicine, 29*(Suppl. 1), 68–74.

Mensah, G. A., Mokdad, A. H., Ford, E. S., Greenlund, K. J., & Croft, J. B. (2005). State of disparities in cardiovascular health in the United States. *Circulation, 111,* 1233–1241.

Merighi, J., Courtenay, W. H., & McCreary, D. R. (2000, August). *College students' health beliefs and behaviors: Gender and ethnic differences.* Poster session presented at the annual meeting of the American Psychological Association, Washington, DC.

Mermelstein, R. J., & Riesenberg, L. A. (1992). Changing knowledge and attitudes about skin cancer risk factors in adolescents. *Health Psychology, 11*(6), 371–376.

Merzel, C. (2000). Gender differences in health care access indicators in an urban, low-income community. *American Journal of Public Health, 90*(6), 909–916.

Messerschmidt, J. W. (1993). *Masculinities and crime: Critique and reconceptualization of theory.* Lanham, MD: Rowman & Littlefield.

Messner, M., Hunt, D., Dunbar, M., Chen, P., Lapp, J., & Miller, P. (1999). *Boys to men: Sports media. Messages about masculinity: A national poll of children, focus groups, and content analysis of sports programs and commercials* (Report No. ED440775). Washington, DC: Education Resources Information Center.

Messner, M. A., & Sabo, D. F. (1994). *Sex, violence and power in sports: Rethinking masculinity.* Freedom, CA: The Crossing Press.

Meth, R. L. (1990). The road to masculinity. In R. L. Meth & R. S. Pasick (Eds.), *Men in therapy: The challenge of change* (pp. 3–34). New York, NY: Guilford Press.

Metz, M. E., & Seifert, M. H. (1990). Men's expectations of physicians in sexual health concerns. *Journal of Sexual and Marital Therapy, 16*(2), 79–88.

Metzger, J. S., Catellier, D. J., Evenson, K. R., Treuth, M. S., Rosamond, W. D., & Siega-Riz, A. M. (2008). Patterns of objectively measured physical activity in the United States. *Medicine and Science in Sports and Exercise, 40*(4), 630–638.

Meydani, S. N., Meydani, M., Blumberg, J. B., Leka, L. S., Siber, G., Loszewski, R., … Stollar, B. D. (1997). Vitamin E supplementation and in vivo immune response in healthy elderly subjects: A randomized controlled trial. *Journal of the American Medical Association, 277*(17), 1380–1386.

Meyer, F., Bairati, I., Shadmani, R., Fradet, Y., & Moore, L. (1999). Dietary fat and prostate cancer survival. *Cancer Causes and Control, 10*(4), 245–251.

Meyer, I. (2003). Prejudice, social stress, and mental health in lesbian, gay, and bisexual populations: Conceptual issues and research evidence. *Psychological Bulletin, 129*(5), 674–697.

Meyer, M. S., Joshipura, K., Giovannucci, E., & Michaud, D. S. (2008). A review of the relationship between tooth loss, periodontal disease, and cancer. *Cancer Causes and Control, 19*(9), 895–907.

Miaskowski, C. (1999). The role of sex and gender in pain perception and responses to treatment. In R. J. Gatchel & D. C. Turk (Eds.), *Psychosocial factors in pain: Critical perspectives* (pp. 401–411). New York, NY: Guilford Press.

Miaskowski, C. (2004). Gender differences in pain, fatigue, and depression in patients with cancer. *Journal of the National Cancer Institute Monographs, 32*, 139–143.

Miller, D. R., Geller, A. C., Wyatt, S. W., Halpern, A., Howell, J. B., Cockerell, C., ... Koh, H. K. (1996). Melanoma awareness and self-examination practices: Results of a United States survey. *Journal of the American Academy of Dermatology, 34*, 962–970.

Miller, E., & Wortman, C. B. (2002). Gender differences in mortality and morbidity following a major stressor: The case of conjugal bereavement. In G. Weidner, S. M. Kopp, & M. Kristenson (Eds.), *Heart disease: Environment, stress and gender* (NATO Science Series, Series I: Life and Behavioural Sciences, Vol. 327, pp. 251–266). Washington, DC: IOS Press.

Miller, K. E., Hoffman, J. H., Barnes, G. M., Sabo, D., Melnick, M. J., & Farrell, M. P. (2005). Adolescent anabolic steroid use, gender, physical activity, and other problem behaviors. *Substance Use & Misuse, 40*(11), 1637–1657.

Miller, M., Hemenway, D., & Wechsler, H. (1999). Guns at college. *Journal of American College Health, 48*, 7–12.

Miller, M. E., & Kaufman, J. D. (1998). Occupational injuries among adolescents in Washington State, 1988–1991. *American Journal of Industrial Medicine, 34*(2), 121–132.

Miller, S. (1983). *Men and friendship.* Boston, MA: Houghton Mifflin.

Millett, G. A., Peterson, J. L., Wolitski, R. J., & Stall, R. (2006). Greater risk for HIV infection of black men who have sex with men: A critical literature review. *American Journal of Public Health, 96*(6), 1007–1019.

Mills, D. S. (2000, August). Health knowledge of young males: Understanding and preventing negative health behaviors of men. In R. Hetzel (Chair), *Men's health in the new millennium: Emerging research theory and practice.* Symposium conducted at the 108th Convention of the American Psychological Association, Washington, DC.

Mirandé, A. (1997). *Hombres y machos: Masculinity and Latino culture.* Boulder, CO: Westview Press.

Misener, T. R., & Fuller, S. G. (1995). Testicular versus breast and colorectal cancer screen: Early detection practices of primary care physicians. *Cancer Practice, 3*(5), 310–316.

Mishkind, M. E., Rodin, J., Silberstein, L. R., & Striegel-Moore, R. H. (1986). The embodiment of masculinity: Cultural, psychological, and behavioral dimensions. *American Behavioral Scientist, 29*, 545–562.

Mittleman, M. A., Maclure, M., Tofler, G. H., Sherwood, J. B., Goldberg, R. J., & Muller, J. E. (1993). Triggering of acute myocardial infarction by heavy physical exertion: Protection against triggering by regular exertion. *New England Journal of Medicine, 329*(23), 1677–1683.

Modell, J. H. (1993). Drowning. *New England Journal of Medicine, 328*(4), 253–256.

Moeschberger, M. L., Anderson, J., Kuo, Y.-F., Chen, M. S., Wewers, M. E., & Guthrie, R. (1997). Multivariate profile of smoking in Southeast Asian men: A biochemically verified analysis. *Preventive Medicine, 26*(1), 53–58.

Mokdad, A. H., Ford, E. S., Bowman, B. A., Dietz, W. H., Vinicor, F., Bales, V. S., & Marks, J. S. (2003). Prevalence of obesity, diabetes, and obesity-related health risk factors, 2001. *Journal of the American Medical Association, 289*(1), 76–79.

Mokdad, A. H., Marks, J., Stroup, D., & Gerberding, J. (2004). Actual causes of death in the United States, 2000. *Journal of the American Medical Association, 291*(10), 1238–1245.

Mokdad, A. H., Serdula, M. K., Dietz, W. H., Bowman, B. A., Marks, J. S., & Koplan, J. P. (1999). The spread of the obesity epidemic in the United States, 1991–1998. *Journal of the American Medical Association, 282*, 1519–1522.

Moldofsky, H., Lue, F. A., Davidson, J. R., & Gorczynski, R. (1989). Effects of sleep deprivation on human immune function. *Federation of American Societies for Experimental Biology Journal, 3*, 1972–1977.

Moller-Leimkuhler, A. M. (2002). Barriers to help-seeking by men: A review of sociocultural and clinical literature with particular reference to depression. *Journal of Affective Disorders, 71*(1), 1–9.

Monk, D., & Ricciardelli, L. A. (2003). Three dimensions of the male gender role as correlates of alcohol and cannabis involvement in young Australian men. *Psychology of Men & Masculinity, 4*(1), 57–69.

Moore, D. (1990a). Helping men become more emotionally expressive: A ten-week program. In D. Moore & F. Leafgren (Eds.), *Problem solving strategies and interventions for men in conflict* (pp. 183–200). Alexandria, VA: American Association for Counseling and Development.

Moore, D. (1990b). Body image and eating behavior in adolescent boys. *American Journal of Diseases in Children, 144*, 475–479.

Moore, R. D., & Pearson, T. A. (1986). Moderate alcohol consumption and coronary artery disease: A review. *Medicine, 65*, 242–267.

Moore, T. M., & Stuart, G. L. (2004). Effects of masculine gender role stress on men's cognitive, affective, physiological, and aggressive responses to intimate conflict situations. *Psychology of Men and Masculinity, 5*(2), 132–142.

Mor, V., Masterson-Allen, S., Goldberg, R., Guadagnoli, E., & Wool, M. S. (1990). Pre-diagnostic symptom recognition and help seeking among cancer patients. *Journal of Community Health, 15*(4), 253–261.

Morman, M. T. (2000). The influence of fear appeals, message design, and masculinity on men's motivation to perform the testicular self-exam. *Journal of Applied Communication Research, 28*(2), 91–116.

Morman, M. T. (2002). Promoting the testicular self-exam as a preventative health care strategy: Do diagrams make a difference? *International Journal of Men's Health, 1*(1), 73–88.

Morrison, J. A., Friedman, L. A., Wang, P., & Glueck, C. J. (2008). Metabolic syndrome in childhood predicts adult metabolic syndrome and type 2 diabetes mellitus 25 to 30 years later. *Journal of Pediatrics, 152*(2), 201–206.

Morrongiello, B. A., & Dawber, T. (1998). Toddlers' and mothers' behaviors in an injury-risk situation: Implications for sex differences in childhood injuries. *Journal of Applied Developmental Psychology, 19*(4), 625–639.

Morrongiello, B. A., & Dawber, T. (2000). Mothers' responses to sons and daughters engaging in injury-risk behaviors on a playground: Implications for sex differences in injury rates. *Journal of Experimental Child Psychology, 76*(2), 89–103.

Morrongiello, B. A., & Dayler, L. (1996). A community-based study of parents' knowledge, attitudes and beliefs related to childhood injuries. *Canadian Journal of Public Health, 87*(6), 383–388.

Morrongiello, B. A., & Hogg, K. (2004). Mothers' reactions to children misbehaving in ways that can lead to injury: Implications for gender differences in children's risk taking and injuries. *Sex Roles, 50*(1–2), 103–118.

Morrongiello, B. A., & Lasenby-Lessard, J. (2007). Psychological determinants of risk taking by children: An integrative model and implications for interventions. *Injury Prevention, 13*(1), 20–25.

Morrongiello, B. A., & Rennie, H. (1998). Why do boys engage in more risk taking than girls? The role of attributions, beliefs, and risk appraisals. *Journal of Pediatric Psychology, 23*(1), 33–43.

Mortensen, P. B., Agerbo, E., Erikson, T., Qin, P., & Westergaard-Nielsen, N. O. (2000). Psychiatric illness and risk factors for suicide in Denmark. *Lancet, 355*(9197), 9–12.

Mosher, D. L. (1991). Macho men, machismo, and sexuality. *Annual Review of Sex Research, 2*, 199–247.

Mosher, D. L., & Sirkin, M. (1984). Measuring a macho personality constellation. *Journal of Research in Personality, 18*, 150–163.

Moyad, M. A., & Robinson, L. E. (2008). Lessons learned from the 2007-2008 cold and flu season: What worked and what was worthless. *Urologic Nursing, 28*(2), 146–148.

Mueller, K. J., Ortega, S. T., Parker, K., Patil, K., & Askenazi, A. (1999). Health status and access to care among rural minorities. *Journal of Health Care for the Poor and Underserved, 10*, 230–249.

Mueller, N. T., Odegaard, A., Anderson, K., Yuan, J. M., Gross, M., Koh, W. P., & Pereira, M. A. (2010). Soft drink and juice consumption and risk of pancreatic cancer: The Singapore Chinese Health Study. *Cancer Epidemiology, Biomarkers & Prevention, 19*(2), 447–455.

Muhlenkamp, A. F., & Sayles, J. A. (1986). Self-esteem, social support, and positive health practices. *Nursing Research, 35*(6), 334–338.

Mujumdar, U. J., Hay, J. L., Monroe-Hinds, Y. C., Hummer, A. J., Begg, C. B., Wilcox, H. B., … Berwick, M. (2009). Sun protection and skin self-examination in melanoma survivors. *Psychooncology, 18*(10), 1106–1115.

Muldoon, J. T., Schootman, M., & Morton, R. F. (1996). Utilization of cancer early detection services among farm and rural nonfarm adults in Iowa. *Journal of Rural Health, 12* (Suppl. 4), 321–331.

Mullen, P. D., Mains, D. A., & Velez, R. (1992). A meta-analysis of controlled trials of cardiac patient education. *Patient Education and Counseling, 19*(2), 143–162.

Mullenix, P. S., Martin, M. J., Steele, S. R., Lavenson, G. S., Starnes, B. W., Hadro, N. C., … Andersen, C. A. (2006). Rapid high-volume population screening for three major risk factors of future stroke: Phase I results. *Vascular and Endovascular Surgery, 40*(3), 177–187.

Mumford, E. A., Levy, D. T., Gitchell, J. G., & Blackman, K. O. (2006). Smokeless tobacco use 1992-2002: Trends and measurement in the Current Population Survey—Tobacco Use Supplements. *Tobacco Control, 15*(3), 166–171.

Mumola, C. J. (2005). *Suicide and homicide in state prisons and local jails* (Bureau of Justice Statistics Special Report No. NCJ 210036).Washington, DC: U.S. Department of Justice, Office of Justice Programs.

Munoz, R., Duran-Cantolla, J., Martínez-Vila, E., Gallego, J., Rubio, R., Aizpuru, F., & De La Torre, G. (2006). Severe sleep apnea and risk of ischemic stroke in the elderly. *Stroke, 37*(9), 2317–2321.

Murabito, J. M., Pencina, M. J., Nam, B. H., D'Agostino, R. B., Wang, T. J., Lloyd-Jones, D., … O'Donnell, C. J. (2005). Sibling cardiovascular disease as a risk factor for cardiovascular disease in middle-aged adults. *Journal of the American Medical Association, 294*, 3117–3123.

Murphy, J. K., Stoney, C. M., Alpert, B. S., & Walker, S. S. (1995). Gender and ethnicity in children's cardiovascular reactivity: Seven years of study. *Health Psychology, 14*, 48–55.

Murphy, S. P., Subar, A. F., & Block, G. (1990). Vitamin E intakes and sources in the United States. *American Journal of Clinical Nutrition, 52*(2), 361–367.

Murphy, W. G., & Brubaker, R. G. (1990). Effects of a brief theory-based intervention on the practice of testicular self-examination by high school males. *Journal of School Health, 60*(9), 459–462.

Musa, D., Schulz, R., Harris, R., Silverman, M., & Thomas, S. B. (2009). Trust in the health care system and the use of preventive health services by older black and white adults. *American Journal of Public Health, 99*(7), 1293–1299.

Mustapha, I. Z., Debrey, S., Oladubu, M., & Ugarte, R. (2007). Markers of systemic bacterial exposure in periodontal disease and cardiovascular disease risk: A systematic review and meta-analysis. *Journal of Periodontology, 78*(12), 2289–2302.

Muth, J. L., & Cash, T. F. (1997). Body-image attitudes: What difference does gender make? *Journal of Applied Social Psychology, 27*, 1438–1452.

Myers, H. F., Kagawa-Singer, M., Kumanyika, S. K., Lex, B. W., & Markides, K. S. (1995). Panel III: Behavioral risk factors related to chronic diseases in ethnic minorities. *Health Psychology, 14*(7), 613–621.

Myers, R. E., Ross, E. A., Wolf, T. A., Balshem, A., Jepson, C., & Millner, L. (1991). Behavioral interventions to increase adherence in colorectal cancer screening. *Medical Care, 29*(10), 1039–1050.

Nader, P. R., Bradley, R. H., Houts, R. M., McRitchie, S. L., & O'Brien, M. (2008). Moderate-to-vigorous physical activity from ages 9 to 15 years. *Journal of the American Medical Association, 300*(3), 295–305.

Nadler, A. (1990). Help-seeking behavior as a coping resource. In M. Rosenbaum (Ed.), *Learned resourcefulness: On coping skills, self-control, and adaptive behavior* (pp. 127–162). New York, NY: Springer.

Nadler, A., & Maysless, O. (1983). Recipient self-esteem and reactions to help. In J. D. Fisher, A. Nadler, & B. M. DePaulo (Eds.), *New directions in helping* (Vol. 1, pp. 167–188). New York, NY: Academic Press.

Naimi, T. S., Brewer, R. D., Mokdad, A., Denny, C., Serdula, M. K., & Marks, J. S. (2003). Binge drinking among U.S. adults. *Journal of the American Medical Association, 289*(1), 70–75.

Naimi, T. S., Nelson, D. E., & Brewer, R. D. (2009). Driving after binge drinking. *American Journal of Preventive Medicine, 37*(4), 314–320.

Naimi, T. S., Town, M., Mokdad, A., & Brewer, R. D. (2006). Health care access among U.S. adults who drink alcohol excessively: Missed opportunities for prevention. *Preventing Chronic Disease, 3*(2), 1–8.

Nasir, S., & Rosenthal, D. (2009). The social context of initiation into injecting drugs in the slums of Makassar, Indonesia. *International Journal of Drug Policy, 20*(3), 237–243.

Nathanson, C. (1977). Sex roles as variables in preventive health behavior. *Journal of Community Health, 3*(2), 142–155.

National Academies Press. (2005). Cholesterol. In *Food and Nutrition Board dietary reference intakes for energy, carbohydrate, fiber, fat, fatty acids, cholesterol, protein, and amino acids* (pp. 542–588). Washington, DC: Author.

National Cancer Institute. (1986). *The health consequences of using smokeless tobacco: A report of the Advisory Committee to the Surgeon General.* Atlanta, GA: Department of Health and Human Services.

National Cancer Institute. (1989). *Adult kidney cancer and Wilm's tumor: Research report.* (NIH Publication No. 90-2342). Bethesda, MD: Author.

National Cancer Institute. (1991). *Oral cancers: Research report* (Publication No. NIH 92-2876). Bethesda, MD: Author.

National Cancer Institute. (1992). *Smokeless tobacco or health: An international perspective.* Bethesda, MD: Author.

National Cancer Institute. (1996). *Cancer: Rates and risks* (4th ed.) (NIH Publication No. 96-691). Bethesda, MD: Author.

National Cancer Institute. (1997). *SEER cancer statistics review, 1973-1994.* Bethesda, MD: Author.

National Cancer Institute. (1998). *Cigars: Health effects and trends.* (NIH Publication No. 98-4302). Bethesda, MD: Author.

National Cancer Institute. (2003). *Fact sheet—smokeless tobacco and cancer: Questions and answers.* Bethesda, MD: Author.

National Cancer Institute. (2008). Themes and targets of tobacco advertising and promotion. In *Tobacco control monograph series, monograph 19: The role of the media in promoting and reducing tobacco use.* Rockville, MD: Author.

National Fire Protection Association. (2010). *Firefighting and fire prevention occupations by women and race* (from the U.S. Department of Labor, Bureau of Labor Statistics, Household Data Survey). Quincy, MA: Author.

National Highway Traffic Safety Administration. (1997). *Pedestrians: Traffic safety facts 1997.* Washington, DC: Author.

National Highway Traffic Safety Administration. (2001). Traffic safety facts 2001: Rural/urban comparison (Publication No. DOT HS 809 524). Washington, DC: Author.

National Highway Traffic Safety Administration. (2003a). *Pedestrian roadway fatalities* (Publication No. DOT HS 809 456). Washington, DC: Author.

National Highway Traffic Safety Administration. (2003b). *Traffic safety facts 2002: Alcohol* (Publication No. DOT HS 809 606). Washington, DC: Author.

National Highway Traffic Safety Administration. (2006). *Traffic safety facts, crash stats: Alcohol-related fatalities and alcohol involvement among drivers and motorcycle operators in 2005* (Publication No. DOT HS 810 644). Washington, DC: Author.

National Highway Traffic Safety Administration. (2007a). *Analysis of fatal motor vehicle traffic crashes and fatalities at intersections, 1997 to 2004* (Publication No. DOT HS 810 682; Table 58). Washington, DC: Author.

National Highway Traffic Safety Administration. (2007b). *Traffic safety facts, crash stats: Comparison of crash fatalities by gender and year from 1996 to 2005* (Publication No. DOT HS 810 780). Washington, DC: Author.

National Highway Traffic Safety Administration. (2007c). *Traffic safety facts 2007 data: Rural/urban comparison* (Publication No. DOT HS 810 996). Washington, DC: Author.

National Highway Traffic Safety Administration. (2008a). *National pedestrian crash report* (Publication No. DOT HS 810 968). Washington, DC: Author.

National Highway Traffic Safety Administration. (2008b). *Traffic safety facts, 2007: A compilation of motor vehicle crash data from the Fatality Analysis Reporting System and the General Estimates System* (Publication No. DOT HS 811 002). Washington, DC: Author.

National Highway Traffic Safety Administration. (2008c). *Traffic safety facts, 2007 data: Bicyclists and other cyclists* (Publication No. DOT HS 810 986). Washington, DC: Author.

National Highway Traffic Safety Administration. (2008d). *Traffic safety facts, 2007 data: Motorcycles* (Publication No. DOT HS 810 990). Washington, DC: Author.

National Highway Traffic Safety Administration. (2008e). *Traffic safety facts, 2007 data: Occupant protection.* (Publication No. DOT HS 810 991). Washington, DC: Author.

National Highway Traffic Safety Administration. (2008f). *Traffic safety facts, 2007 data: Older population* (Publication No. DOT HS 810 992; Table 2). Washington, DC: Author.

National Highway Traffic Safety Administration. (2008g). *Traffic safety facts, 2007 data: Speeding* (Publication No. DOT HS 810 998; Figure 2). Washington, DC: Author.

National Highway Traffic Safety Administration. (2009a). *Motor vehicle traffic crashes as a leading cause of death in the United States, 2006.* Washington, DC: Author.

National Highway Traffic Safety Administration. (2009b). *Traffic safety facts, 2008 data: Alcohol-impaired driving* (Publication No. DOT HS 811 155). Washington, DC: Author.

National Highway Traffic Safety Administration. (2009c). *Traffic safety facts, research note: Trends in fatal crashes among drivers with invalid licenses* (Publication No. DOT HS 811 229). Washington, DC: Author.

National Institute on Alcohol Abuse and Alcoholism. (2004/2005). The scope of the problem. *Alcohol Research & Health, 28*(3), 111–120.

National Institute on Drug Abuse. (2009a). *Info facts: Steroids (anabolic-androgenic).* Bethesda, MD: Author.

National Institute on Drug Abuse. (2009b). *Monitoring the future: National results on adolescent drug use—Overview of key findings, 2008* (NIH Publication No. 09-7401). Bethesda, MD: Author.

National Institute on Drug Abuse. (2009c). *Monitoring the future national survey results on drug use, 1975–2008: Vol. II, college students and adults ages 19-50* (NIH Publication No. 09-7403). Bethesda, MD: Author.

National Institute of Neurological Disorders and Stroke. (2004). *Brain basics: Preventing stroke* (National Institutes of Health [NIH] Publication No. 04-3440b). Bethesda, MD: National Institutes of Health.

National Institute for Occupational Safety and Health. (1993). *Fatal injuries to workers in the United States, 1980-1989: A decade of surveillance* (DHHS [NIOSH] No. 93-108). Cincinnati, OH: Author.

National Institute for Occupational Safety and Health. (1994a). *NIOSH: National Institute for Occupational Safety and Health* (DHHS [NIOSH] No. 94-108). Cincinnati, OH: Author.

National Institute for Occupational Safety and Health. (1994b). *Work-related lung disease surveillance report 1994* (DHHS [NIOSH] No. 94-120). Cincinnati, OH: Author.

National Institute for Occupational Safety and Health. (2004). *Worker health chartbook 2004* (DHHS [NIOSH] No. 2004-146). Cincinnati, OH: Author.

National Institute for Occupational Safety and Health. (2006). *NIOSH agriculture, forestry, and fishing safety and health program: National academies review*. Cincinnati, OH: Author.

National Institutes of Health. (1986). *Consensus development panel statement: Health implications of smokeless tobacco use*. Bethesda, MD: Author.

National Institutes of Health. (1992). *Cancer statistics review: 1973-1989* (NIH Publication No. 92-2789). Washington, DC: U.S. Government Printing Office.

National Institutes of Health. (1998). *Clinical guidelines on the identification, evaluation, and treatment of overweight and obesity in adults: The evidence report*. Rockville, MD: National Heart, Lung, and Blood Institute.

National Mental Health Association & The Jed Foundation. (2002). *Safeguarding your students against suicide: Expanding the safety network*. Alexandria, VA: Author.

National Safety Council. (1992). *Accident facts, 1992 edition*. Itasca, IL: Author.

National Safety Council. (1994). *Accident facts, 1994 edition*. Itasca, IL: Author.

National Safety Council. (1998). *Accident facts, 1998 edition*. Itasca, IL: Author.

National Safety Council. (2010). *Injury facts, 2010 edition*. Itasca, IL: Author.

National Sleep Foundation. (1995). *National Sleep Foundation* [Brochure]. Washington, DC: Author.

National Stroke Association. (1994). *The brain at risk: Understanding and preventing stroke* [Brochure]. Englewood, CO: Author.

National Stroke Association. (1995). *National health profile*. Englewood, CO: National Stroke Association.

Naylor, M. F., & Farmer, K. C. (1997). The case for sunscreens: A review of their use in preventing actinic damage and neoplasia. *Archives of Dermatology, 133,* 1146–1154.

Nebeling, L. C., Forman, M. R., Graubard, B. I., & Snyder, R. A. (1997). The impact of lifestyle characteristics on carotenoid intake in the United States: The 1987 National Health Interview Survey. *American Journal of Public Health, 87*(2), 268–271.

Neef, N., Scutchfield, F. D., Elder, J., & Bender, S. J. (1991). Testicular self-examination by young men: An analysis of characteristics associated with practice. *Journal of American College Health, 39*(4), 187–190.

Neel, J. V. (1990). Toward an explanation of the human sex ratio. In M. G. Ory & H. R. Warner (Eds.), *Gender, health, and longevity: Multidisciplinary perspectives* (pp. 57–72). New York, NY: Springer.

Neff, J. A., Prihoda, T. J., & Hoppe, S. K. (1991). "Machismo," self-esteem, education and high maximum drinking among Anglo, Black and Mexican-American male drinkers. *Journal of Studies on Alcohol, 52*, 458–463.

Neighbors, H. W., & Howard, C. S. (1987). Sex differences in professional help seeking among adult Black Americans. *American Journal of Community Psychology, 15*(4), 403–415.

Nelson, D., Naimi, T. S., Brewer, R. D., Bolen, J., & Wells, H. (2004). Binge drinking estimates for adults in U.S. metropolitan areas. *American Journal of Public Health, 94*(4), 663–671.

Nelson, D. E., Giovino, G. A., Shopland, D. R., Mowery, P. D., Mills, S. L., & Eriksen, M. P. (1995). Trends in cigarette smoking among U.S. adolescents, 1974 though 1991. *American Journal of Public Health, 85*(1), 34–40.

Nelson, D. E., Kirkendall, R. S., Lawton, R. L., Chrisman, J. H., Merritt, R. K., Arday, D. A., & Giovino, G. A. (1994). Surveillance for smoking-attributable mortality and years of potential life lost, by state—United States, 1990. *Morbidity and Mortality Weekly Report, 43*(1), 1–8.

Nelson, D. E., Mowery, P., Tomar, S., Marcus, S., Giovino, G., & Zhao, L. (2006). Trends in smokeless tobacco use among adults and adolescents in the United States. *American Journal of Public Health, 96*(5), 897–905.

Nelson, D. E., Thompson, B. L., Bland, S. D., & Rubinson, R. (1999). Trends in perceived cost as a barrier to medical care, 1991-1996. *American Journal of Public Health, 89*(9), 1410–1413.

Nelson, D. E., Tomar, S. L., Mowery, P., & Siegel, P. Z. (1996). Trends in smokeless tobacco use among men in four states, 1988 through 1993. *American Journal of Public Health, 86*(9), 1300–1303.

Ness, A. R., & Fowles, J. W. (1997). Fruit and vegetables, and cardiovascular disease: A review. *International Journal of Epidemiology, 26*, 1–13.

Newcomb, P. A., Norfleet, R. G., Storer, B. E., Surawicz, T. S., & Marcus, P. M. (1992). Screening sigmoidoscopy and colorectal cancer mortality. *Journal of the National Cancer Institute, 84*(20), 1572–1575.

Newman, L. S. (1995). Occupational illness. *New England Journal of Medicine, 333*, 1128–1134.

Newton, C. (1994). Gender theory and prison sociology: Using theories of masculinities to interpret the sociology of prisons for men. *The Howard Journal of Criminal Justice, 33*(3), 193–202.

Nezu, A. M., & Nezu, C. M. (1987). Psychological distress, problem solving, and coping reactions: Sex role differences. *Sex Roles, 16*(3/4), 206–214.

Ng, D. M., & Jeffery, R. W. (2003). Relationships between perceived stress and health behaviors in a sample of working adults. *Health Psychology, 22*, 638–642.

Nguyen, T. N., Cheem, T. H., Agarwal, B., Shah, R., Nguyen, J., and Viet, N. L. (2007). Acute coronary syndrome. In T. Nguyen, D. Hu, M. H. Kim, & C. Grincs (Eds.), *Management of complex cardiovascular problems: The evidence-based medicine approach* (pp. 1–18). Oxford, England: Blackwell.

Nicholas, D. (2000). Men, masculinity, and cancer: Risk-factor behaviors, early detection, and psychosocial adaptation. *Journal of American College Health, 49*(1), 27–33.

Nichter, M., Nichter, M., Lloyd-Richardson, E. E., Flaherty, B., Carkoglu, A., & Taylor, N. (2006). Gendered dimensions of smoking among college students. *Journal of Adolescent Research, 21*(3), 215–243.

Nickerson, A. B., & Slater, E. D. (2009). School and community violence and victimization as predictors of adolescent suicidal behavior. *School Psychology Review, 38*(2), 218–232.

Nielsen, J. M. (1990). Introduction. In J. M. Nielsen (Ed.), *Feminist research methods: Exemplary readings in the social sciences* (pp. 1–37). Boulder, CO: Westview Press.

Nieschlag, S. M. A., Nieschlag, E., & Behre, H. (Eds.). (2009). *Andrology: Male reproductive health and dysfunction* (3rd ed.). New York, NY: Springer-Verlag.

Nieto, F. J., Young, T. B., Lind, B. K., Shahar, E., Samet, J. M., Redline, S.,… Pickering, T. G. (2000). Association of sleep-disordered breathing, sleep apnea, and hypertension in a large community-based study. *Journal of the American Medical Association, 283*, 1829–1836.

Nijs, H. G., Essink-Bot, M. L., DeKoning, H. J., Kirkels, W. J., & Schroder, F. H. (2000). Why do men refuse or attend population-based screening for prostate cancer? *Journal of Public Health Medicine, 22*(3), 312–316.

Nisbett, R. E., & Cohen, D. (1996). *Culture of honor: The psychology of violence in the south.* Boulder, CO: Westview Press.

Nobis, R., & Sandén, I. (2008). Young men's health: A balance between self-reliance and vulnerability in the light of hegemonic masculinity. *Contemporary Nurse, 29*(2), 205–217.

Nocon, M., Hiemann, T., Müller-Riemenschneider, F., Thalau, F., Roll, S., & Willich, S. N. (2008). Association of physical activity with all-cause and cardiovascular mortality: A systematic review and meta-analysis. *European Journal of Cardiovascular Prevention & Rehabilitation, 15*(3), 239–246.

Nolen-Hoeksema, S. (1987). Sex differences in unipolar depression: Evidence and theory. *Psychological Bulletin, 101*(2), 259–282.

Norman, J., & Rosvall, S. B. (1994). Help-seeking behavior among mental health practitioners. *Clinical Social Work Journal, 22*(4), 449–460.

Nothwehr, F., Elmer, P., & Hannan, P. (1994). Prevalence of health behaviors related to hypertension in three blood pressure treatment groups: The Minnesota Heart Health Program. *Preventive Medicine, 23*, 362–368.

Oakley, A. (1994). Who cares for health? Social relations, gender, and the public health. *Journal of Epidemiology and Community Health, 48*, 427–434.

Obermeyer, C. M., Price, K., Schulein, M., Sievert, L. L., & Anderton, D. L. (2007). Medication use and gender in Massachusetts: Results of a household survey. *Health Care for Women International, 28*, 593–613.

O'Brien, K., Cokkinides, V., Jemal, A., Cardinez, C. J., Murray, T., Samuels, A., … Thun, M. J. (2003). Cancer statistics for Hispanics. *CA: A Cancer Journal for Clinicians, 53*(4), 208–226.

O'Brien, M. K., Petrie, K., & Raeburn, J. (1992). Adherence to medication regimens: Updating a complex medical issue. *Medical Care Review, 49*(4), 435–454.

O'Brien, R., Hunt, K., & Hart, G. (2005). "It's caveman stuff, but that is to a certain extent how guys still operate": Men's accounts of masculinity and help seeking. *Social Science & Medicine, 61,* 503–516.

O'Dea, J. A., & Rawstorne, P. R. (2001). Male adolescents identify their weight gain practices, reasons for desired weight gain, and sources of weight gain information. *Journal of the American Dietetic Association, 101,* 105–107.

Ogden, C. L., Carroll, M. D., Curtin, L. R., McDowell, M. A., Tabak, C. J., & Flegal, K. M. (2006). Prevalence of overweight and obesity in the United States, 1999-2004. *Journal of the American Medical Association, 295*(13), 1549–1555.

O'Leary, A., Goodhart, F., Jemmott, L. S., & Boccher-Lattimore, D. (1992). Predictors of safer sex on the college campus: A social cognitive theory analysis. *Journal of American College Health, 40,* 254–263.

Oleckno, W. A., & Blacconiere, M. J. (1990a). Risk-taking behaviors and other correlates of seat belt use among university students. *Public Health, 104,* 155–164.

Oleckno, W. A., & Blacconiere, M. J. (1990b). Wellness of college students and differences by gender, race, and class standing. *College Student Journal, 24*(4), 421–429.

Oliffe, J., & Mróz, L. (2005). Men interviewing men about health and illness: Ten lessons learned. *Journal of Men's Health & Gender, 2*(2), 257–260.

Oliver, M. B., & Hyde, J. S. (1993). Gender differences in sexuality: A meta-analysis. *Psychological Bulletin, 114*(1), 29–51.

Oliver, S. J., & Toner, B. B. (1990). The influence of gender role typing on the expression of depressive symptoms. *Sex Roles, 22*(11/12), 775–790.

Olsen, O., & Kristensen, T. S. (1991). Impact of work environment on cardiovascular diseases in Denmark. *Journal of Epidemiology and Community Health, 45,* 4–9.

O'Malley, P. M., & Johnston, L. D. (2002). Epidemiology of alcohol and other drug use among American college students. *Journal of Studies on Alcohol, 14,* 23–39.

O'Neil, J. M. (2008). Summarizing 25 years of research on men's gender role conflict using the Gender Role Conflict Scale. *The Counseling Psychologist, 36*(3), 358–445.

O'Neil, J. M., Good, G. E., & Holmes, S. (1995). Fifteen years of theory and research on men's gender role conflict: New paradigms for empirical research. In R. F. Levant & W. S. Pollack (Eds.), *A new psychology of men* (pp. 164–206). New York, NY: Basic Books.

O'Neil, J. M., Helms, B., Gable, R., David L., & Wrightsman, L. (1986). Gender-role conflict scale: College men's fear of femininity. *Sex Roles, 14,* 335–350.

O'Neil, M. K., Lancee, W. J., & Freeman, J. J. (1985). Sex differences in depressed university students. *Social Psychiatry, 20,* 186–190.

Ong, K. L., Cheung, B. M., Man, Y. B., Lau, C. P., & Lam, K. S. (2007). Prevalence, awareness, treatment, and control of hypertension among United States adults 1999-2004. *Hypertension, 49*(1), 69–75.

Oppenheim, M. (1994). *The man's health book.* Englewood Cliffs, NJ: Prentice Hall.

Orlofsky, J. L. (1981). Relationship between sex role attitudes and personality traits and the Sex Role Behavior Scale-1: A new measure of masculine and feminine role behaviors and interests. *Journal of Personality and Social Psychology, 40,* 927–940.

Orlofsky, J. L., & O'Heron, C. A. (1987). Development of a short-form Sex-Role Behavior Scale. *Journal of Personality Assessment, 51*, 267–277.

Orth-Gomer, K. (1994). International epidemiological evidence for a relationship between social support and cardiovascular disease. In S. A. Shumaker & S. M. Czajkowski (Eds.), *Social support and cardiovascular disease* (pp. 97–117). New York, NY: Plenum Press.

Orth-Gomer, K., & Chesney, M. A. (1997). Social stress/strain and heart disease in women. In D. G. Julian & N. K. Wenger (Eds.), *Women and heart disease* (pp. 407–420). London, England: Martin Dunitz.

Ory, M. G., & Warner, H. R. (Eds.). (1990). *Gender, health, and longevity: Multidisciplinary perspectives*. New York, NY: Springer.

Otte, C., Hart, S., Neylan, T. C., Marmar, C. R., Yaffe, K., & Mohr, D. C. (2005). A meta-analysis of cortisol response to challenge in human aging: Importance of gender. *Psychoneuroendocrinology, 30*(1), 80–91.

Otto, M. W., & Dougher, M. J. (1985). Sex differences and personality factors in responsivity to pain. *Perception and Motor Skills, 61*(2), 383–390.

Overfield, T. (1985). *Biologic variation in health and illness: Race, age, and sex differences*. Menlo Park, CA: Addison-Wesley.

Owen, N., Leslie, E., Salmon, J., & Fotheringham, M. J. (2000). Environmental determinants of physical activity and sedentary behavior. *Exercise and Sport Sciences Reviews, 28*(4), 153–158.

Oxman, T. E., Freeman, D. H., & Manheimer, E. D. (1995). Lack of social participation or religious strength and comfort as risk factors for death after cardiac surgery in the elderly. *Psychosomatic Medicine, 57*, 5–15.

Padesky, C. A., & Hammen, C. L. (1981). Sex differences in depressive symptom expression and help seeking among college students. *Sex Roles, 7*, 309–320.

Padron, J. M. (2006). Experience with post-secondary education for individuals with severe mental illness. *Psychiatric Rehabilitation Journal, 30*(2), 147–149.

Paffenbarger, R. S., Hyde, R. T., Wing, A. L., Lee, I. M., Jung, D. L., & Kampert, J. B. (1993). The association of changes in physical-activity level and other life-style characteristics with mortality among men. *New England Journal of Medicine, 328*, 538–545.

Palank, C. L. (1991). Determinants of health-promotive behavior. *Health Promotion, 26*(4), 815–832.

Palmgreen, P., & Donohew, L. (2006). Effective mass media strategies for drug abuse prevention campaigns. In Z. Sloboda & W.J. Bukoski (Eds.), *Handbook of drug abuse prevention: Theory, science and practice* (pp. 27–44). New York, NY: Springer.

Palmgreen, P., Donohew, L., Lorch, E. P., Hoyle, R. H., & Stephenson, M. T. (2001). Television campaigns and adolescent marijuana use: Tests of sensation seeking targeting. *American Journal of Public Health, 91*, 292–296.

Palmgreen, P., Lorch, E. P., Donohew, L., Harrington, N. G., D'Silva, M., & Helm, D. (1995). Reaching at-risk populations in a mass media drug abuse prevention campaign: Sensation seeking as a targeting variable. *Drugs and Society, 8*(3–4), 29–45.

Pan, Y., & Pratt, C. (2008). Metabolic syndrome and its association with diet and physical activity in U.S. adolescents. *Journal of the American Dietetic Association, 108*(2), 276–286.

Pappas, G., Queen, S., Hadden, W., & Fisher, G. (1993). The increasing disparity in mortality between socioeconomic groups in the United States, 1960-1986. *New England Journal of Medicine, 239*(2), 103–109.

Park, M. J., Mulye, T. P., Adams, S. H., Brindis, C. D., & Irwin, C. E. (2006). The health status of young adults in the United States. *Journal of Adolescent Health, 39*, 305–317.

Parker, D., Manstead, A. S. R., Stradling, S. G., & Reason, J. T. (1992). Intention to commit driving violations: An application of the theory of planned behaviour. *Journal of Applied Psychology, 77*, 94–101.

Parkinson, A. B., & Evans, N. A. (2006). Anabolic androgenic steroids: A survey of 500 users. *Medicine and Science in Sports and Exercise, 38*(4), 644–651.

Parrott, D. J. (2008). A theoretical framework for antigay aggression: Review of established and hypothesized effects within the context of the general aggression model. *Clinical Psychology Review, 28*(6), 933–951.

Pascale, P. J., & Evans, W. J. (1993). Gender differences and similarities in patterns of drug use and attitudes of high school students. *Journal of Drug Education, 23*(1), 105–116.

Pasick, R. (1990). Raised to work. In R. L. Meth & R. S. Pasick (Eds.), *Men in therapy: The challenge of change* (pp. 35–53). New York, NY: Guilford Press.

Pate, R. R., Pratt, M., Blair, S. N., Haskell, W. L., Macera, C. A., Bouchard, C., … Wilmore, J. H. (1995). Physical activity and public health: A recommendation from the Centers for Disease Control and prevention and the American College of Sports Medicine. *Journal of the American Medical Association, 273*(5), 402–407.

Patel, A. V., Rodriguez, C., Jacobs, E. J., Solomon, L., Thun, M. J., & Calle, E. E. (2005). Recreational physical activity and risk of prostate cancer in a large cohort of U.S. men. *Cancer Epidemiology, Biomarkers & Prevention, 14*(1), 275–279.

Patel, S. R., & Hu, F. B. (2008). Short sleep duration and weight gain: A systematic review. *Obesity, 16*(3), 643–653.

Patrick, M. S., Covin, J. R., Fulop, M., Calfas, K., & Lovato, C. (1997). Health risk behaviors among California college students. *Journal of American College Health, 45*(6), 265–272.

Patterson, F., Lerman, C., Kaufmann, V. G., Neuner, G. A., & Audrain-McGovern, J. (2004). Cigarette smoking practices among American college students: Review and future directions. *Journal of American College Health, 52*(5), 203–210.

Pearson, T. A., & Lewis, C. (1998). Rural epidemiology: Insights from a rural population laboratory. *American Journal of Epidemiology, 148*(1), 949–957.

Pecora, N. (1992). Superman/superboys/supermen: The comic book hero as socializing agent. In S. Craig (Ed.), *Men, masculinity, and the media* (pp. 61–77). Newbury Park, CA: Sage.

Pederson, E. L., & Vogel, D. L. (2007). Male gender role conflict and willingness to seek counseling: Testing a mediation model on college-aged men. *Journal of Counseling Psychology, 54*(4), 373–384.

Peele, S. (1993). The conflict between public health goals and the temperance mentality. *American Journal of Public Health, 83*(6), 805–810.

Peeters, A., Barendregt, J. J., Willekens, F., Mackenbach, J. P., Al Mamun, A., & Bonneux, L. (2003). Obesity in adulthood and its consequences for life expectancy: A life table analysis. *Annals of Internal Medicine, 138*, 24–32.

Peirce, K. (1989). Sex-role stereotyping of children and television: A content analysis of the roles and attributes of child characters. *Sociological Spectrum, 9*, 321–328.

Pelletier, A. R., Quinlan, K. P., Sacks, J. J., Van Gilder, T. J., Gilchrist, J. & Ahluwalia, H. K. (2000). Injury prevention practices as depicted in G-rated and PG-rated movies. *Archives of Pediatrics and Adolescent Medicine, 154*(3), 283–286.

Pender, N. J., Walker, S. N., Sechrist, K. R., & Frank-Stromborg, M. (1990). Predicting health-promoting lifestyles in the workplace. *Nursing Research, 39*(6), 326–332.

Pennebaker, J. W. (1997). *Opening up: The healing power of expressing emotions.* New York, NY: Guilford Press.

Pepler, D. J., Craig, W. M., Connolly, J. A., Yuilen, A., McMasters, L., & Jiang, D. (2006). A developmental perspective on bullying. *Aggressive Behavior, 32*, 376–384.

Peppard, P. E., Young, T., Palta, M., Dempsey, J., & Skatrud, J. (2000). Longitudinal study of moderate weight change and sleep-disordered breathing. *Journal of the American Medical Association, 284*(23), 3015–3021.

Perkins, H. W. (1992). Gender patterns in consequences of collegiate alcohol abuse: A 10-year study of trends in an undergraduate population. *Journal of Studies on Alcohol, 53*, 458–462.

Perrine, M. W., Mundt, J. C., & Weiner, R. I. (1994). When alcohol and water don't mix: Diving under the influence. *Journal of Studies on Alcohol, 55*, 517–524.

Perry, L. A., Turner, L. H., & Sterk, H. M. (Eds.). (1992). *Constructing and reconstructing gender: The links among communication, language, and gender.* Albany: State University of New York Press.

Petersen, L. (2002). Racial differences in trust: Reaping what we have sown? *Medical Care, 40*, 81–84.

Peterson, J. L., Folkman, S., & Bakeman, R. (1996). Stress, coping, HIV status, psychosocial resources, and depressive mood in African American gay, bisexual, and heterosexual men. *American Journal of Community Psychology, 24*(4), 461–487.

Petty, R. E., Wegener, D. T., & Fabrigar, L. R. (1997). Attitudes and attitude change. *Annual Review of Psychology, 48*, 609–647.

Pew Research Center. (2010). *Millennials: A portrait of generation next.* Washington, DC: Author.

Phelan, J. C., & Link, B. G. (2005). Controlling disease and creating disparities: A fundamental cause perspective. *Journals of Gerontology Series B: Psychological Sciences and Social Sciences, 60*, S27–S33.

Phillips, J. T., Giebaly, D., Gillham, T., Goring, J., Patil, S., Jeevan, D., ... Rajjayabun, P. (2010). Urological management of acute epididymo-orchitis in sexually active young men: Too great a public health risk? *Sexually Transmitted Infections, 86*(4), 328.

Phillips, K. A., & Diaz, S. F. (1997). Gender differences in body dysmorphic disorder. *Journal of Nervous and Mental Disease, 185*, 570–577.

Phillipson, E. A. (1993). Sleep apnea: A major public health problem. *New England Journal of Medicine, 328*(17), 1271–1273.

Pienta, K. J., & Esper, P. S. (1993). Editorial: Is dietary fat a risk factor for prostate cancer? *Journal of the National Cancer Institute, 85*, 1538–1541.

Pienta, K. J., & Esper, P. S. (1993). Risk factors for prostate cancer. *Annals of Internal Medicine, 118*, 793–803.

Pierce, R. (1999). Prostate cancer in African American men: Thoughts on psychosocial interventions. In L. E. Davis (Ed.), *Working with African American males: A guide to practice* (pp. 75–90). Thousand Oaks, CA: Sage.

Pietinen, P. (2006). Dietary habits and nutrition in health in Finland. In S. Koskinen, A. Aromaa, J. Huttunen, & J. Teperi (Eds.), *National Public Health Institute KTL* (pp. 30–31). Helsinki, Finland: Ministry of Social Affairs and Health, National Research and Development Centre for Welfare and Health.

Pignone, M., Rich, M., Teutsch, S. M., Berg, A. O., & Lohr, K. N. (2002). Screening for colorectal cancer in adults at average risk: A summary of the evidence for the U.S. Preventive Services Task Force. *Annals of Internal Medicine, 137*(2), 132–141.

Pinch, W. J., Heck, M., & Vinal, D. (1986). Health needs and concerns of male adolescents. *Adolescence, 21*(84), 961–969.

Pine, K. J. (2001). Children's perceptions of body shape: A thinness bias in preadolescent girls and associations with femininity. *Clinical Child Psychology and Psychiatry, 6*, 519–536.

Pi-Sunyer, F. X. (1993). Medical hazards of obesity. *Annals of Internal Medicine, 119*(7, Pt. 2), 655–660.

Pivarnik, J. M., Reeves, M. J., & Rafferty, A. P. (2003). Seasonal variation in adult leisure-time physical activity. *Medicine & Science in Sports & Exercise, 35*(6), 1004–1008.

Plant, E. A., Hyde, J. S., Keltner, D., & Devine, P. G. (2000). The gender stereotyping of emotions. *Psychology of Women Quarterly, 24*, 81–92.

Plasqui, G., & Westerterp, K. R. (2004). Seasonal variation in total energy expenditure and physical activity in Dutch young adults. *Obesity Research, 12*(4), 688–694.

Pleck, J. H. (1981). *The myth of masculinity*. Cambridge, MA: MIT Press.

Pleck, J. H. (1987). *The myth of masculinity* (3rd ed.). Cambridge, MA: MIT Press.

Pleck, J. H. (1995). The gender role strain paradigm: An update. In R.F. Levant & W.S. Pollack (Eds.), *A new psychology of men* (pp. 11–32). New York, NY: Basic Books.

Pleck, J. H., Sonenstein, F. L., & Ku, L. C. (1993). Masculinity ideology and its correlates. In S. Oskamp & M. Costanzo (Eds.), *Gender issues in contemporary society* (pp. 85–110). Newbury Park, CA: Sage.

Pleck, J. H., Sonenstein, F. L., & Ku, L. C. (1994a). Attitudes toward male roles among adolescent males: A discriminant validity analysis. *Sex Roles, 30*(7/8), 481–501.

Pleck, J. H., Sonenstein, F. L., & Ku, L. C. (1994b). Problem behaviors and masculinity ideology in adolescent males. In R. D. Ketterlinus & M. E. Lamb (Ed.), *Adolescent problem behaviors: Issues and research* (pp. 165–186). Hillsdale, NJ: Lawrence Erlbaum.

Poe-Yamagata, E. (1997). *Known juvenile homicide offenders by sex, 1980–1995*. Washington, DC: Office of Juvenile Justice and Delinquency Prevention.

Polednak, A. P. (1990). Knowledge of colorectal cancer and use of screening tests in persons 40–74 years of age. *Preventive Medicine, 19*, 213–226.

Polednak, A. P. (1997). Use of selected high-fat foods by Hispanic adults in the northeastern U.S. *Ethnicity and Health, 2*(1–2), 71–76.

Polefrone, J. M., & Manuck, S. B. (1987). Gender differences in cardiovascular and neuroendocrine response to stressors. In R. Barnett, L. Biener, & G. K. Baruch (Eds.), *Gender and stress* (pp. 13–38). New York, NY: Free Press.

Pollack, W. (1998). *Real boys: Rescuing our sons from the myths of boyhood.* New York, NY: Random House.

Polych, C., & Sabo, D. (1995). Gender politics, pain, and illness: The AIDS epidemic in North American prisons. In D. S. Sabo & D. F. Gordon (Eds.), *Men's health and illness: Gender, power, and the body* (pp. 139–157). Thousand Oaks, CA: Sage.

Polych, C., & Sabo, D. (2001). Sentence—Death by lethal infection: IV-drug use and infectious disease transmission in North American prisons. In D. Sabo, T. A. Kupers, & W. London (Eds.), *Prison masculinities* (pp. 173–183). Philadelphia, PA: Temple University Press.

Pomerantz, E. M., & Ruble, D. N. (1998). The role of maternal control in the development of sex differences in child self-evaluative factors. *Child Development, 2,* 458–478.

Poo-Hwu, W. J., Ariyan, S., Lamb, L., Papac, R., Zelterman, D., Hu, G. L., … Buzaid, A. C. (1999). Follow-up recommendations for patients with American Joint Committee on Cancer Stages I-III malignant melanoma. *Cancer, 86*(11), 2252–2258.

Pope, H. G., Gruber, A. J., Choi, P., Olivardia, R., & Phillips, K. A. (1997). Muscle dysmorphia: An underrecognized form of body dysmorphic disorder. *Psychosomatics, 38,* 548–557.

Pope, H. G., Gruber, A. J., Mangweth, B., Bureau, B., deCol, C., Jouvent, R., & Hudson, J. I. (2000). Body image perception among men in three countries. *American Journal of Psychiatry, 157,* 1297–1301.

Pope, H. G., & Kanayama, G. (2005). Can you tell if your patient is using steroids? *Current Psychiatry in Primary Care, 1*(2), 28–34.

Pope, H. G., Olivardia, R., Gruber, A., & Borowiecki, J. (1999). Evolving ideals of male body image as seen through action toys. *International Journal of Eating Disorders, 26*(1), 65–72.

Pope, H. G., Phillips, K. A., & Olivardia, R. (2000). *The Adonis complex: The secret crisis of male body obsession.* New York, NY: The Free Press.

Pope, S. K., Smith, P. D., Wayne, J. B., & Kelleher, K. J. (1994). Gender differences in rural adolescent drinking patterns. *Journal of Adolescent Health, 15*(5), 359–365.

Popkin, B. M., & Udry, R. (1998). Adolescent obesity increases significantly in second and third generation U.S. immigrants: The National Longitudinal Study of Adolescent Health. *Journal of Nutrition, 128*(4), 701–706.

Poppen, P. J. (1995). Gender and patterns of sexual risk taking in college students. *Sex Roles, 32*(7/8), 545–555.

Potts, M. K., Burnam, M. A., & Wells, K. B. (1991). Gender differences in depression detection: A comparison of clinician diagnosis and standardized assessment. *Psychological Assessment, 3,* 609–615.

Potts, R., Doppler, M., & Hernandez, M. (1994). Effects of television content on physical risk-taking in children. *Journal of Experimental Child Psychology, 58,* 321–331.

Potts, R., & Henderson, J. (1991). The dangerous world of television: A content analysis of physical injuries in children's television programming. *Children's Environments Quarterly, 8*, 7–14.

Potts, R., Runyan, D., Zerger, A., & Marchetti, K. (1996). A content analysis of safety behaviors of television characters: implications for children's safety and injury. *Journal of Pediatric Psychology, 21*(4), 517–528.

Potts, R., & Swisher, L. (1998). Effects of televised safety models on children's risk taking and hazard identification. *Journal of Pediatric Psychology, 23*, 157–163.

Posner, B. M., Jette, A., Smigelski, C., Miller, D., & Mitchell, P. (1994). Nutritional risk in New England elders. *Journal of Gerontology, 49*(3), 123–132.

Powell, D. E. (1998). The dismal state of health care in Russia. *Current History, 97*(621), 335–341.

Powell, K. E., Caspersen, C. J., Koplan, J. P., & Ford, E. S. (1989). Physical activity and chronic diseases. *American Journal of Clinical Nutrition, 49*, 999–1006.

Powell, K. E., Jacklin, B. C., Nelson, D. E., & Bland, S. (1998). State estimates of household exposure to firearms, loaded firearms, and handguns, 1991–1995. *American Journal of Public Health, 88*(6), 969–972.

Powell, K. E., Thompson, P. D., Caspersen, C. J., & Kendrick, J. S. (1987). Physical activity and the incidence of coronary heart disease. *Annual Review of Public Health, 8*, 253–287.

Powell, N. B., Riley, R. W., Schechtman, K. B., Blumen, M. B., Dinges, D. F., & Guilleminault, C. (1999). A comparative model: Reaction time performance in sleep-disordered breathing versus alcohol-impaired controls. *Laryngoscope, 109*(10), 1648–1654.

Powell, W. A. (2005). *Preventive health behavior among African American men: Historical barriers, psychosocial factors, and implications for patient-provider relationships* (Doctoral dissertation, University of Michigan). *Dissertation Abstracts International, 66*(2-B), Publication No. 3163913.

Powell-Griner, E., Anderson, J. E., & Murphy, W. (1997). State-and sex-specific prevalence of selected characteristics—Behavioral Risk Factor Surveillance System, 1994 and 1995. *Morbidity and Mortality Weekly Report, 46*(3), 1–31.

Powell-Hammond, W., Matthews, D., & Corbie-Smith, G. (2010). Psychosocial factors associated with routine health examination scheduling and receipt among African American men. *Journal of the National Medical Association, 102*(4), 276–289.

Powers, E. A., & Kivett, V. R. (1992). Kin expectations and kin support among rural older adults. *Rural Sociology, 57*(2), 194–215.

Prattala, R., Paalanen, L., Grinberga, D., Helasoja, V., Kasmel, A., & Petkeviciene, J. (2006). Gender differences in the consumption of meat, fruit and vegetables are similar in Finland and the Baltic countries. *European Journal of Public Health, 17*(5), 520–525.

Prendergast, M. L. (1994). Substance use and abuse among college students: A review of recent literature. *American College Health Association, 43*(3), 99–113.

Presley, C. A., Leichliter, M. A., & Meilman, P. W. (1998). *Alcohol and drugs on American college campuses: A report to college presidents: Third in a series, 1995, 1996, 1997.* Carbondale: Core Institute, Southern Illinois University.

Presley, C. A., Meilman, P. W., & Cashin, J. R. (1996). *Alcohol and drugs on American college campuses: Use, consequences, and perceptions of the campus environment. Vol. IV: 1992–94.* Carbondale: Core Institute, Southern Illinois University.

Presley, C. A., Meilman, P. W., & Cashin, J. R. (1997). Weapon carrying and substance abuse among college students. *Journal of American College Health, 46*(1), 3–8.

Preston, D. S., & Stern, R. S. (1992). Nonmelanoma cancers of the skin. *New England Journal of Medicine, 327*(23), 1649–1662.

Preusser, D. F., Williams, A. F., & Lund, A. K. (1991). Characteristics of belted and unbelted drivers. *Accident Analysis and Prevention, 23*(6), 475–482.

Preventive Services Task Force. (1996). *Guide to clinical preventive services* (2nd ed.). Baltimore, MD: Williams & Wilkins.

Prochaska, J., Norcross, J., & DiClemente, C. (1994). *Changing for good: The revolutionary program that explains the six stages of change and teaches you how to free yourself from bad habits.* New York, NY: William Morrow.

Prohaska, T. R., Leventhal, E. A., Leventhal, H., & Keller, M. L. (1985). Health practices and illness cognition in young, middle aged and elderly adults. *Journal of Gerontology, 40*, 569–578.

Prosser-Gelwick, B., & Garni, K. F. (1988, Summer). Counseling and psychotherapy with college men. *New Directions for Student Services, 42*, 67–77.

Prout, G., & Griffin, P. (1984). Testicular tumors: Delay in diagnosis and influence on survival. *American Family Practice, 29*, 205–209.

Punjabi, N. M. (2008). The epidemiology of adult obstructive sleep apnea. *Proceedings of the American Thoracic Society, 5*(2), 136–143.

Puntillo, K., & Weiss, S. J. (1994). Pain: Its mediators and associated morbidity in critically ill cardiovascular surgical patients. *Nursing Research, 43*, 31–36.

Pyke, K. D. (1996). Class-based masculinities: The interdependence of gender, class, and interpersonal power. *Gender and Society, 10*, 527–549.

Quan, L., Bennett, E., Cummings, P., Trusty, M. N., & Treser, C. D. (1998). Are life vests worn? A multiregional observational study of personal flotation device use in small boats. *Injury Prevention, 4*(3), 203–205.

Quinlan, K. P., Brewer, R. D., Siegel, P., Sleet, D. A., Mokdad, A. H., Shults, R. A., & Flowers, N. (2005). Alcohol-impaired driving among U.S. adults, 1993–2002. *American Journal of Preventive Medicine, 28*(4), 346–350.

Qureshi, A. I., Suri, M. F., Kirmani, J. F., & Divani, A. A. (2005). Prevalence and trends of prehypertension and hypertension in United States: National Health and Nutrition Examination Surveys 1976 to 2000. *Medical Science Monitor, 11*(9), 403–409.

Raag, T. (1999). Influences of social expectations of gender, gender stereotypes, and situational constraints on children's toy choices. *Sex Roles, 41*(11–12), 809–831.

Rager, E. L., Bridgeford, E. P., & Ollila, D. W. (2005). Cutaneous melanoma: Update on prevention, screening, diagnosis, and treatment. *American Family Physician, 72*(2), 269–276.

Rakowski, W. (1986). Personal health practices, health status, and expected control over future health. *Journal of Community Health, 11*(3), 189–203.

Ramachandran, S. V., Pencina, M. J., Cobain, M., Freiberg, M. S., & D'Agostino, R. B. (2005). Estimated risks for developing obesity in the Framingham Heart Study. *Annals of Internal Medicine, 143*(7), 473–480.

Ramirez-Valles, J. (2007). "I don't fit anywhere": How race and sexuality shape Latino gay and bisexual men's health. In I. H. Meyer & M. E. Northridge (Eds.), *The health of sexual minorities: Public health perspectives on lesbian, gay, bisexual and transgender populations* (pp. 301–319). New York, NY: Springer.

Randolph, M. W., Torres, H., Gore-Felton, C., Lloyd, B., & McGarvey, E. L. (2009). Alcohol use and sexual risk behavior among college students: Understanding gender and ethnic differences. *American Journal of Drug and Alcohol Abuse, 35*(2), 80–84.

Ransdell, L. B., Vener, J. M., & Sell, K. (2004). International perspectives: The influence of gender on lifetime physical activity participation. *Journal of the Royal Society for the Promotion of Health, 124*(12), 12–14.

Rappaport, B. M. (1984). Family planning: Helping men ask for help. In J. M. Swanson & K. A. Forrest (Eds.), *Men's reproductive health* (pp. 245–259). New York, NY: Springer.

Rasmussen, M., Krølner, R., Klepp, K. I., Lytle, L., Brug, J., Bere, E., & Due, P. (2006). Determinants of fruit and vegetable consumption among children and adolescents: a review of the literature—Part I: Quantitative studies. *International Journal of Behavioral Nutrition and Physical Activity, 3*(22), 1–19.

Ratner, P. A., Bottorff, J. L., Johnson, J. L., & Hayduk, L. A. (1994). The interaction effects of gender within the health promotion model. *Research in Nursing and Health, 17,* 341–350.

Ratzan, S. C., Filerman, G. L., & LeSar, J. W. (2000). Attaining global health: Challenges and opportunities. *Population Bulletin, 55*(1), 1–49.

Raudenbush, B., & Zellner, D. A. (1997). Nobody's satisfied: Effects of abnormal eating behaviors and actual and perceived weight status on body image satisfaction in males and females. *Journal of Social & Clinical Psychology, 16*(1), 95–110.

Rauste-von Wright, M., & Frankenhaeuser, M. (1989). Females' emotionality as reflected in the excretion of the dopamine metabolite HVA during mental stress. *Psychological Reports, 64,* 856–858.

Reagan, L. J. (1997). Engendering the dread disease: Women, men and cancer. *American Journal of Public Health, 87,* 1779–1787.

Rediahs, M. H., Reis, J. S., & Creason, N. S. (1990). Sleep in old age: Focus on gender differences. *Sleep, 13*(5), 410–424.

Redline, S., Kump, K., Tishler, P. V., Browner, I., & Ferrette, V. (1994). Gender differences in sleep disordered breathing in a community sample. *American Journal of Respiratory and Critical Care Medicine, 149*(3, Pt. 1), 722–726.

Redline, S., Yenokyan, G., Gottlieb, D. J., Shahar, E., O'Connor, G. T., Resnick, H. E., … Punjabi, N. M. (2010). Obstructive sleep apnea hypopnea and incident stroke: The Sleep Heart Health Study. *American Journal of Respiratory and Critical Care Medicine, 182*(2), 269–277.

Reis, S. E., Holubkov, R., Young, J. B., White, B. G., Cohn, J. N., & Feldman, A. M. (2000). Estrogen is associated with improved survival in aging women with congestive heart failure: Analysis of the vesnarinone studies. *Journal of the American College of Cardiology, 36,* 529–533.

Ren, X. S. (1997). Marital status and quality of relationships: The impact on health perception. *Social Science and Medicine, 44,* 241–249.

Renner, B., Kwon. S., Yang, B. -H., Paik, K. -C., Kim, S. H., Roh, S., ... Schwarzer, R. (2008). Social-cognitive predictors of eating a healthy diet in South Korean men and women. *International Journal of Behavioral Medicine, 15*, 4–13.

Reno, D. R. (1988). Men's knowledge and health beliefs about testicular cancer and testicular self-exam. *Cancer Nursing, 11*(2), 112–117.

Restif, O., & Amos, W. (in press). The evolution of sex-specific immune defences. *Proceedings of the Royal Society B: Biological Sciences, 277*(1691), 2247–2255.

Results of National Stress Survey. (1995, March). *Prevention*, 74–81.

Retting, R. A., Ulmer, R. G., & Williams, A. F. (1999). Prevalence and character- istics of red light running crashes in the United States. *Accident Analysis & Prevention, 31*(6), 687–694.

Retting, R. A., Williams, A. F., & Greene, M. A. (1998). *Red-light running and sen- sible countermeasures* (Transportation Research Record 1640, pp. 23–26). Washington, DC: Transportation Research Board.

Retting, R. A., Williams, A. F., Preusser, D. F., & Weinstein, H. B. (1995). Classifying urban crashes for countermeasure development. *Accident Analysis and Prevention, 27*(3), 283–294.

Reyner, A., & Horne, J. A. (1995). Gender- and age-related differences in sleep determined by home-recorded sleep logs and actimetry from 400 adults. *Sleep, 18*(2), 127–134.

Reynolds, C. F., Mesiano, D., Houck, P. R., & Kupfer, D. J. (1993). Patterns of sleep episodes in young and elderly adults during a 36-hour constant routine. *Sleep, 16*(7), 632–637.

Reynolds, K., Lewis, B., Nolen, J. D., Kinney, G. L., Sathya, B., & He, J. (2003). Alcohol consumption and risk of stroke: A meta-analysis. *Journal of the American Medical Association, 289*(5), 579–588.

Reynolds, P., & Kaplan, G. A. (1990). Social connections and risk for cancer: Prospective evidence from the Alameda County study. *Behavioral Medicine, 16*(3), 101–110.

Rhoades, E. R. (2003). The health status of American Indian and Alaska Native males. *American Journal of Public Health, 93*(5), 774–778.

Rhodes, A., & Goering, P. (1994). Gender differences in the use of outpatient mental health services. *Journal of Mental Health Administration, 21*(4), 338–346.

Riboli, E., & Norat, T. (2003). Epidemiologic evidence of the protective effect of fruit and vegetables on cancer risk. *American Journal of Clinical Nutrition, 78*(3), 559S–569S.

Ricciardelli, L. A., & McCabe, M. P. (2003). A longitudinal analysis of the role of biopsychosocial factors in predicting body change strategies among adoles- cent boys. *Sex Roles, 48*, 349–359.

Rice, T. W., & Coates, D. L. (1995). Gender role attitudes in the southern United States. *Gender and Society, 9*(6), 744–756.

Rich, J. A. (2001). Primary care for young African American men. *Journal of American College Health, 49*(4), 183–186.

Rich, J. A., & Ro, M. (2002). *A poor man's plight: Uncovering the disparity in men's health*. Battle Creek, MI: W. K. Kellogg Foundation.

Rich, J. A., & Stone, D. A. (1996). The experience of violent injury for young African-American men: The meaning of being a "sucker." *Journal of General Internal Medicine, 11*, 77–82.

Rideout, V. J., Foehr, U. G., & Roberts, D. F. (2010). *Generation m²: Media in the lives of 8- to 18-year-olds*. Menlo Park, CA: Henry J. Kaiser Family Foundation.

Rieker, P. P., & Bird, C. E. (2005). Rethinking gender differences in health: Why we need to integrate social and biological perspectives. *Journals of Gerontology, 60B*(special issue II), 40–47.

Rigotti, N. A., Lee, J. E., & Wechsler, H. (2000). U.S. college students' use of tobacco products: Results of a national survey. *Journal of the American Medical Association, 284*(6), 699–705.

Rimm, E. B., & Moats, C. (2007). Alcohol and coronary heart disease: Drinking patterns and mediators of effect. *Annals of Epidemiology, 17*(5, Suppl.), S3–S7.

Rimm, E. B., Stampfer, M. J., Ascherio, A., Giovannucci, E., Colditz, G. A., & Willett, W. C. (1993). Vitamin E consumption and the risk of coronary heart disease in men. *New England Journal of Medicine, 328*(20), 1450–1456.

Rimm, E. B., Stampfer, M. J., Giovannucci, E., Ascherio, A., Spiegelman, D., Colditz, G. A., & Willett, W. C. (1995). Body size and fat distribution as predictors of coronary heart disease among middle-aged and older U.S. men. *American Journal of Epidemiology, 141*(12), 1117–1127.

Risberg, G., Hamberg, K., & Johansson, E. E. (2006). Gender perspective in medicine: A vital part of medical scientific rationality. *BMC Medicine, 4*(20), 1–5.

Rivara, F. P., Bergman, A. B., LoGerfo, J. P., & Weiss, N. S. (1982). Epidemiology of childhood injuries. *American Journal of Diseases of Children, 136*, 502–506.

Ro, M. J., Casares, C., Treadwell, H. M., & Thomas, S. (2004). *A man's dilemma: Healthcare of men across America—A disparities report*. Atlanta, GA: Moorehouse School of Medicine National Center for Primary Care.

Robbins, C. (1989). Sex differences in psychosocial consequences of alcohol and drug abuse. *Journal of Health and Social Behavior, 30*, 117–130.

Robertson, J. M., & Fitzgerald, L. F. (1992). Overcoming the masculine mystique: Preferences for alternative form of assistance among men who avoid counseling. *Journal of Counseling Psychology, 39*(2), 240–246.

Robertson, S. (2007). *Understanding men and health: Masculinities, identity and well-being*. Berkshire, England: Open University Press.

Robins, L. N. (1978). Sturdy childhood predictors of adult antisocial behaviour: Replications from longitudinal studies. *Psychological Medicine, 8*(4), 611–622.

Robins, L. N., Helzer, J. E., Weissman, M. M., Orvaschel, H., Gruenberg, E., Burke, J. D., & Regier, D. A. (1984). Lifetime prevalence of specific psychiatric disorders in three sites. *Archives of General Psychiatry, 41*, 949–958.

Robins, L. N., Locke, B. Z., & Regier, D. A. (1991). An overview of psychiatric disorders in America. In R. N. Robins & D. A. Regier (Eds.), *Psychiatric disorders in America* (pp. 328–266). New York, NY: Collier Macmillan.

Robinson, E. J., & Whitfield, M. J. (1985). Improving the efficiency of patients' comprehension monitoring: A way of increasing patients' participation in general practice consultations. *Social Science and Medicine, 21*(8), 915–919.

Robinson, J., Rigel, J., & Amonette, R. (1998). What promotes skin self-examination? *Journal of the American Academy of Dermatology, 39*(5), 752–757.

Robinson, J. K., Rademaker, A. W., Sylvester, J. A., & Cook, B. (1997). Summer sun exposure: Knowledge, attitudes, and behaviors of Midwest adolescents. *Preventive Medicine, 26*(3), 364–372.

Robles, T. F., & Kiecolt-Glaser, J. K. (2003). The physiology of marriage: Pathways to health. *Physiology & Behavior, 79*, 409–416.

Robles, T. F., Shaffer, V. A., Malarkey, W. B., & Kiecolt-Glaser, J. K. (2006). Positive behaviors during marital conflict: Influences on stress hormones. *Journal of Social and Personal Relationship, 23*, 305–325.

Rodgers, G. B. (1995). Bicyclist deaths and fatality risk patterns. *Accident Analysis and Prevention, 27*(2), 215–223.

Rodgers, G. B. (2000). Bicycle and bicycle helmet use patterns in the United States in 1998. *Journal of Safety Research, 31*(3), 149–158.

Rodriguez, J., Jiang, R., Johnson, W. C., MacKenzie, B. A., Smith, L. J., & Barr, R. G. (2010). The association of pipe and cigar use with cotinine levels, lung function, and airflow obstruction: A cross-sectional study. *Annals of Internal Medicine, 152*(4), 201–210.

Rodu, B. (1994). An alternative approach to smoking control. *American Journal of the Medical Sciences, 308*(1), 32–34.

Rogler, L. H., & Cortes, D. E. (2008). Help-seeking pathways: A unifying concept in mental health care. In J. E. Mezzich & G. Caracci (Eds.), *Cultural formulation: A reader for psychiatric diagnosis* (pp. 51–67). Lanham, MD: Jason Aronson.

Ronis, D. L., Lang, W. P., Farghaly, M. M., & Passow, E. (1993). Tooth brushing, flossing, and preventive dental visits by Detroit-area residents in relation to demographic and socioeconomic factors. *Journal of Public Health Dentistry, 53*(3), 138–145.

Rosamond, W., Flegal, K., Friday, G., Furie, K., Go, A., Greenlund, K., ... Hong, Y. (2007). Heart disease and stroke statistics—2007 update: A report from the American Heart Association Statistics Committee and Stroke Statistics Subcommittee. *Circulation, 115*, e69–e171.

Rosano, G. M., & Panina, G. (1999). Oestrogens and the heart. *Therapie, 54*(3), 381–385.

Rose, B. (Ed.). (1997). *A radical fairy's seedbed: The collected series.* San Francisco, CA: Nomenus.

Rosenman, K. D., Gardiner, J., Swanson, G. M., Mullan, P., & Zhu, Z. (1995). Use of skin-cancer prevention strategies among farmers and their spouses. *American Journal of Preventive Medicine, 11*(5), 342–347.

Rosenstock, I. M. (1990). The Health Belief Model: Explaining health behavior through expectancies. In K. Glanz, F. M. Lewis, & B. K. Rimer (Eds.), *Health behavior and health education: Theory, research and practice* (pp. 39–62). San Francisco, CA: Jossey-Bass.

Ross, C. E., & Bird, C. E. (1994). Sex stratification and health lifestyle: Consequences of men's and women's perceived health. *Journal of Health and Social Behavior, 35*, 161–178.

Rossi, J. S. (1992, March). *Stages of change for 15 health risk behaviors in an HMO population.* Paper presented at the 13th annual scientific sessions of the Society of Behavioral Medicine, New York, NY.

Rossi, J. S., & Blais, L. M. (1992, March). *Stages of change for sun exposure.* Paper presented at the 13th annual scientific sessions of the Society of Behavioral Medicine, New York, NY.

Rossier, J., Angleitner, A., De Pascalis, V., Wang, W., Kuhlman, M., & Zuckerman, M. (2007). The cross-cultural generalizability of Zuckerman's alternative five-factor model of personality. *Journal of Personality Assessment, 89*(2), 188–196.

Rossitter, L. F. (1983). Prescribed medicines: Findings from the National Medical Care Expenditure Survey. *American Journal of Public Health, 73*(11), 1312–1315.

Rossouw, J. E. (1999). Hormone replacement therapy and cardiovascular disease. *Current Opinion in Lipidology, 10*(5), 429–434.

Rossow, I. (1996). Alcohol-related violence: The impact of drinking pattern and drinking context. *Addiction, 91*(11), 1651–1661.

Roter, D. L., & Hall, J. A. (1997). *Doctors talking with patients/patients talking with doctors: Improving communication in medical visits.* Westport, CT: Auburn House.

Roter, D. L., & Hall, J. A. (2004). Physician gender and patient-centered communication: A critical review of empirical research. *Annual Review of Public Health, 25*, 497–519.

Roth, B. J., Nichols, C. R., & Einhorn, L. H. (1993). Neoplasms of the testis. In J. F. Holland, E. Frei, & R. C. Basett (Eds.), *Cancer Medicine* (Vol. 2, 3rd ed., pp. 1592–1619). Philadelphia, PA: Lea & Febiger.

Roth, E. M., & Streicher-Lankin, S. L. (1995). *Good cholesterol, bad cholesterol.* Rockland, CA: Prima.

Rothspan, S., & Read, S. J. (1996). Present versus future time perspective and HIV risk among heterosexual college students. *Health Psychology, 15*(2), 131–134.

Rotundo, E. A. (1993). *American manhood: Transformations in masculinity from the revolution to the modern era.* New York, NY: BasicBooks.

Rouhani, P., Hu, S., & Kirsner, R. S. (2008). Melanoma in Hispanics. *Expert Review of Dermatology, 3*(3), 279–285.

Ruberman, W., Weinblatt, E., Goldberg, J. D., & Chaudhary, B. S. (1984). Psychosocial influences on mortality after myocardial infarction. *New England Journal of Medicine, 311*, 552–559.

Rubin, L. B. (1983). *Intimate strangers.* New York, NY: Harper & Row.

Rule, W. R., & Gandy, G. L. (1994). A thirteen-year comparison in patterns of attitudes toward counseling. *Adolescence, 29*(115), 575–589.

Russell, M., Light, J. M., & Gruenewald, P. J. (2004). Alcohol consumption and problems: The relevance of drinking patterns. *Alcoholism, Clinical and Experimental Research, 28*(6), 921–930.

Ruzek, S. B. (1978). *The women's health movement: Feminist alternatives to medical control.* New York, NY: Praeger.

Ruzek, S. B., & Becker, J. (1999). The women's health movement in the United States: From grass-roots activism to professional agendas. *Journal of American Medical Women's Association, 54*(1), 4–8.

Ryb, G. E., Dischinger, P. C., Kufera, J. A., & Read, K. M. (2006). Risk perception and impulsivity: Association with risky behaviours and substance abuse disorders. *Accident Analysis and Prevention, 38*, 567–573.

Sabo, D. (1995). Caring for men. In J. Cookfair (Ed.), *Nursing care in the community* (2nd ed., pp. 345–365). St. Louis, MO: Mosby.

Sabo, D. (2000). Men's health studies: Origins and trends. *Journal of American College Health, 49*(3), 133–142.

Sabo, D., & Gordon, D. F. (Eds.) (1995). *Men's health and illness: Gender, power and the body.* Thousand Oaks, CA: Sage.

Sabo, D., & Hall, J. (2009). Gender and psychosocial adaptation after a coronary event: A relational analysis. In A. Broom & P. Tovey (Eds.), *Men's health: Body, identity and social context* (pp. 83–106). London, England: Wiley-Blackwell.

Sabo, D., & London, W. (1992). Understanding men in prison: The relevance of gender studies. *Men's Studies Review, 9*(1), 4–9.

Sacco, R. L., Elkind, M., Boden-Albala, B., Lin, I. F., Kargman, D. E., Hauser, W. A., … Paik, M. C. (1999). The protective effect of moderate alcohol consumption on ischemic stroke. *Journal of the American Medical Association, 281*(1), 53–60.

Salehi, S. O., & Elder, N. C. (1995). Prevalence of cigarette and smokeless tobacco use among students in rural Oregon. *Family Medicine, 27*(2), 122–125.

Salive, M. E., Smith, G. E., & Brewer, F. (1989). Suicide mortality in the Maryland state prison system, 1979 to 1987. *Journal of the American Medical Association, 252,* 365–369.

Sallis, J., Prochaska, J., & Taylor, W. (2000). A review of correlates of physical activity of children and adolescents. *Medicine and Science in Sports and Exercise, 32*(5), 963–975.

Sallis, J. F., Haskell, W. L., Wood, P. D., Fortmann, S. P., Rogers, T., Blair, S. N., & Paffenbarger, R. S. (1985). Physical activity assessment methodology in the Five-City Project. *American Journal of Epidemiology, 121*(1), 91–106.

Salmon, J., Owen, N., Crawford, D., Bauman, A., & Sallis, J. F. (2003). Physical activity and sedentary behavior: A population-based study of barriers, enjoyment, and preference. *Health Psychology, 22*(2), 178–188.

Saltonstall, R. (1993). Healthy bodies, social bodies: Men's and women's concepts and practices of health in everyday life. *Social Science and Medicine, 36*(1), 7–14.

Samad, A. K., Taylor, R. S., Marshall, T., & Chapman, M. A. (2005). A meta-analysis of the association of physical activity with reduced risk of colorectal cancer. *Colorectal Disease, 7*(3), 204–213.

Sandman, D., Simantov, E., & An, C. (2000). *Out of touch: American men and the health care system: Commonwealth Fund Men's and Women's Health Survey Findings.* New York, NY: Commonwealth Fund.

Sansbury, L. B., Wanke, K., Albert, P. S., Kahle, L., Schatzkin, A., Lanza, W., & the Polyp Prevention Trial Study Group. (2009). The effect of strict adherence to a high-fiber, high-fruit and -vegetable, and low-fat eating pattern on adenoma recurrence. *American Journal of Epidemiology, 170*(5), 576–584.

Santelli, J. S., Kaiser, J., Hirsch, L., Radosh, A., Simkin, L., & Middlestadt, S. (2004). Initiation of sexual intercourse among middle school adolescents: The influence of psychosocial factors. *Journal of Adolescent Health, 34*(3), 200–208.

Santelli, J. S., Lowry, R., Brener, N. D., & Robin, L. (2000). The association of sexual behaviors with socioeconomic status, family structure, and race/ethnicity among U.S. adolescents. *American Journal of Public Health, 90*(10), 1582–1588.

Santmyire, B. R., Feldman, S. R., & Fleischer, A. B. (2001). Lifestyle high-risk behaviors and demographics may predict the level of participation in sun-protection behaviors and skin cancer primary prevention in the United States: Results of the 1998 National Health Interview Survey. *Cancer, 92*(5), 1315–1324.

Saraiya, M., Hall, H. I., & Uhler, R. J. (2002). Sunburn prevalence among adults in the United States, 1999. *American Journal of Preventive Medicine, 23*, 91–97.

Sargent, J. D., Beach, M. L., Adachi-Mejia, A. M., Gibson, J. J., Titus-Ernstoff, L. T., Carusi, C. P., ... Dalton, M. A. (2005). Exposure to movie smoking: Its relation to smoking initiation among US adolescents. *Pediatrics, 116*(5), 1183–1191.

Sartor, O., Zheng, Q., & Eastham, J. A. (1999). Androgen receptor gene CAG repeat length varies in a race-specific fashion on men without prostate cancer. *Urology, 53*(2), 378–380.

Sarvela, P. D., Cronk, C. E., & Isberner, F. R. (1997). A secondary analysis of smoking among rural and urban youth using the MTF data set. *Journal of School Health, 67*(9), 372–375.

Sarvela, P. D., & McClendon, E. J. (1988). Indicators of rural youth drug use. *Journal of Youth & Adolescence, 17*(4), 335–347.

Sattar, N., McConnachie, A., Shaper, A. G., Blauw, G. J., Buckley, B. M., de Craen, A. J., ... Wannamethee, S. G. (2008). Can metabolic syndrome usefully predict cardiovascular disease and diabetes? Outcome data from two prospective studies. *Lancet, 371*(9628), 1927–1935.

Sattin, R. W., & Corso, P. S. (2007). The epidemiology and costs of unintentional and violent injuries. In L. S. Doll, S. E. Bonzo, D. A. Sleet, J. A. Mercy, & E. N. Haas (Eds.), *Handbook of injury and violence prevention* (pp. 3–20). New York, NY: Springer.

Saurer, M. K., & Eisler, R. M. (1990). The role of masculine gender role stress in expressivity and social support network factors. *Sex Roles, 23*(5/6), 261–271.

Savage, I. (1993). Demographic influences on risk perceptions. *Risk Analysis, 13*, 413–420.

Sawyer, R. G., & Moss, D. J. (1993). Sexually transmitted diseases in college men: A preliminary clinical investigation. *Journal of American College Health, 42*(3), 111–115.

Sax, L. (1997). Health trends among college freshmen. *Journal of American College Health, 45*(6), 252–262.

Sayer, L. C. (2005). Gender, time and inequality: Trends in women's and men's paid work, unpaid work and free time. *Social Forces, 84*(1), 285–304.

Scarce, M. (1999). *Smearing the queer: Medical bias in the health care of gay men.* New York, NY: Haworth Press.

Scheidt, P. C., Harel, Y., Trumble, A. C., Jones, D. H., Overpeck, M. D., & Bijur, P. E. (1995). The epidemiology of nonfatal injuries among U.S. children and youth. *American Journal of Public Health, 85*(7), 932–938.

Schinke, S., Cole, K., Williams, C., & Botvin, G. (1999). Reducing risk taking among African American males. In L. E. Davis (Ed.), *Working with African American males: A guide to practice* (pp. 103–112). Thousand Oaks, CA: Sage.

Schleicher, R. L., Carroll, M. D., Ford, E. S., & Lacher, D. A. (2009). Serum vitamin C and the prevalence of vitamin C deficiency in the United States: 2003-2004 National Health and Nutrition Examination Survey (NHANES). *American Society for Clinical Nutrition, 90*(5), 1252–1263.

Schlundt, D. G., Warren, R. C., & Miller, S. (2004). Reducing unintentional injuries on the nation's highways: A literature review. *Journal of Health Care for the Poor and Underserved, 15*(1), 76–98.

Schneck, M. J., Carrano, D., Hartigan, P., Page, W. F., Fayad, P. B., & Brass, L. (1995). *Physical activity is an independent risk factor for stroke.* Paper presented at the American Heart Association's 20th International Joint Conference on Stroke and Cerebral Circulation, Charleston, SC.

Schoen, C., Davis, K., DesRoches, C., & Shekhdar, A. (1998). *The health of adolescent boys: Commonwealth Fund survey findings.* New York, NY: Commonwealth Fund.

Schoenbach, V. J., Kaplan, B. H., Fredman, L., & Kleinbaum, D. G. (1986). Social ties and mortality in Evans County, Georgia. *American Journal of Epidemiology, 123*(4), 577–591.

Schoenborn, C. A. (1986). Health habits of U.S. adults, 1985: The "Alameda 7" revisited. *Public Health Reports, 101*(6), 571–580.

Schoenborn, C. A. (1993). The Alameda study—25 years later. In S. Maes, H. Leventhal, & M. Johnston (Eds.), *International review of health psychology* (Vol. 2, pp. 81–116). New York, NY: Wiley.

Schoenborn, C. A., & Adams, P. F. (2008). *Sleep duration as a correlate of smoking, alcohol use, leisure-time physical inactivity, and obesity among adults: United States, 2004-2006.* Hyattsville, MD: National Center for Health Statistics.

Schoenborn, C. A., & Benson, V. (1988). Relationships between smoking and other unhealthy habits: United States, 1985. In *Advance data from vital and health statistics, 154* (DHHS Publication No. [PHS] 88-1250). Hyattsville, MD: National Center for Health Statistics.

Schofield, T., Connell, R. W., Walker, L., Wood, J., & Butland, D. (2000). Understanding men's health and illness: A gender-relations approach to policy, research, and practice. *Journal of American College Health, 48*(6), 247–256.

Schone, B. S., & Weinick, R. M. (1998). Health-related behaviors and the benefits of marriage for elderly persons. *Gerontologist, 38*(5), 618–627.

Schopp, L., Good, G., Mazurek, M., Barker, K., & Stucky, R. (2007). Masculine role variables and outcomes among men with spinal cord injury. *Disability and Rehabilitation, 29*(6), 625–633

Schootman, M., Fuortes, L. J., Zwerling, C., Albanese, M. A., & Watson, C. A. (1993). Safety behavior among Iowa junior high and high school students. *American Journal of Public Health, 83*(11), 1628–1630.

Schulman, C. C., Kirby, R., & Fitzpatrick, J. M. (2003). Awareness of prostate cancer among the general public: Findings of an independent international survey. *European Urology, 44*, 294–302.

Schulte, M. T., Ramo, D., & Brown, S. A. (2009). Gender differences in factors influencing alcohol use and drinking progression among adolescents. *Clinical Psychology Review, 29*(6), 535–547.

Schwartz, J. (2008). Gender differences in drunk driving prevalence rates and trends: A 20-year assessment using multiple sources of evidence. *Addictive Behaviors, 33*(9), 1217–1222.

Schwartz, J., & Rookey, B. D. (2008). The narrowing gender gap in arrests: Assessing competing explanations using self-report, traffic fatality, and official data on drunk driving, 1980-2004. *Criminology, 46*(3), 637–671.

Schwartz, S. J., Zamboanga, B. L., Ravert, R. D., Kim, S. Y., Weisskirch, R. S., Williams, M. K., … Finley, G. E. (2009). Perceived parental relationships and health-risk behaviors in college-attending emerging adults. *Journal of Marriage and Family, 71*, 727–740.

Scoggins, C. R., Ross, M. I., Reintgen, D. S., Noyes, R. D., Goydos, J. S., Beitsch, P. D.,... Sunbelt Melanoma Trial. (2006). Gender-related differences in outcome for melanoma patients. *Annals of Surgery, 243*(5), 693–700.

Scott-Sheldon, L. A. J., Carey, K. B., & Carey, M. P. (2007). Health behavior and college students: Does Greek affiliation matter? *Journal of Behavioral Medicine, 31*(1), 61–70.

Seage, G. R., Mayer, K. H., Lenderking, W. R., Wold, C., Gross, M., Goldstein, R., ... Homberg, S. (1997). HIV and hepatitis B infection and risk behavior in young gay and bisexual men. *Public Health Reports, 112*, 158–167.

Seal, D. W., & Agostinelli, G. (1994). Individual differences associated with high-risk sexual behavior: Implications for intervention program. *AIDS Care, 6*, 393–397.

Sears, H. A., Graham, J., & Campbell, A. (2009). Adolescent boys' intentions of seeking help from male friends and female friends. *Journal of Applied Developmental Psychology, 30*(6), 738–748.

Seeman, T. E., Kaplan, G. A., Knudsen, L., Cohen, R., & Guralnik, J. (1987). Social network ties and mortality among the elderly in the Alameda County Study. *American Journal of Epidemiology, 126*, 714–723.

Sege, R., & Dietz, W. (1994). Television viewing and violence in children: The pediatrician as agent for change. *Pediatrics, 94*(4), 600–607.

Seltzer, J. R. (2002). *The origins and evolution of family planning programs in developing countries*. Santa Monica, CA: Rand.

Sempos, C. T., Cleeman, J. I., Carroll, M. D., Johnson, C. L., Bachorik, P. S., Gordon, D. J., ... Rifkind, B. M. (1993). Prevalence of high blood cholesterol among U.S. adults: An update based on guidelines from the Second Report of the National Cholesterol Education Program Adult Treatment Panel. *Journal of the American Medical Association, 269*(23), 3009–3014.

Serdula, M. K., Brewer, R. D., Gillespie, C., Denny, C. H., & Mokdad, A. (2004). Trends in alcohol use and binge drinking, 1985-1999: Results of a multi-state survey. *American Journal of Preventive Medicine, 26*(4), 294–298.

Serdula, M. K., Coates, R. J., Byers, T., Simoes, E., Mokdad, A. H., & Subar, A. F. (1995). Fruit and vegetable intake among adults in 16 states: Results of a brief telephone survey. *American Journal of Public Health, 85*(2), 236–239.

Serdula, M. K., Collins, M. E., Williamson, D. F., Anda, R. F., Pamuk, E., & Byers, T. E. (1993). Weight control practices of U.S. adolescents and adults. *Annals of Internal Medicine, 119*(7, Pt. 2), 667–671.

Serdula, M. K., Gillespie, C., Kettel-Khan, L., Farris, R., Seymour, J., & Denny, C. (2004). Trends in fruit and vegetable consumption among adults in the United States: Behavioral Risk Factor Surveillance System, 1994–2000. *American Journal of Public Health, 94*(6), 1014–1018.

Shafer, M. A., Hilton, J. F., Ekstrand, M., Keogh, J., Gee, L., DiGiorgio-Haag, L., ... Schachter, J. (1993). Relationship between drug use and sexual behaviors and the occurrence of sexually transmitted diseases among high-risk male youth. *Sexually Transmitted Diseases, 20*(6), 307–313.

Shankar, P. R., Fields, S. K., Collins, C. L., Dick, R. W., & Comstock, D. (2007). Epidemiology of high school and collegiate football injuries in the United States, 2005-2006. *American Journal of Sports Medicine, 35*(8), 1295–1303.

Shankar, R., & Goldson, I. (2000, August). Sexual health of lower income African American and Latino adult males. In R. Hetzel (Chair), *Men's health in the new millennium: Emerging research theory and practice.* Symposium conducted at the 108th Convention of the American Psychological Association, Washington, DC.

Shapiro, J. A., Jacobs, E. J., & Thun, M. J. (2000). Cigar smoking in men and risk of death from tobacco-related cancers. *Journal of the National Cancer Institute, 92*(4), 333–337.

Sharpe, M. J., & Heppner, P. P. (1991). Gender role, gender role conflict and psychological well-being in men. *Journal of Counseling Psychology, 38,* 323–330.

Sharpe, M. J., Heppner, P. P., & Dixon, W. A. (1995). Gender role conflict, instrumentality, expressiveness, and well-being in adult men. *Sex Roles, 33*(1/2), 1–18.

Sher, L. (2006). Functional magnetic resonance imaging in studies of neurocognitive effects of alcohol use on adolescents and young adults. *International Journal of Adolescent Medicine and Health, 18*(1), 3–7.

Sherrill, D. L., Kotchou, K., & Quan, S. F. (1998). Association of physical activity and human sleep disorders. *Archives of Internal Medicine, 158*(17), 1894–1898.

Sherrod, D. (1987). The bonds of men: Problems and possibilities in close male relationships. In H. Brod (Ed.), *The making of masculinities: The new men's studies* (pp. 213–239). Winchester, MA: Allen and Unwin.

Shi, L. (1998). Sociodemographic characteristics and individual health behaviors. *Southern Medical Journal, 91*(10), 933–941.

Shifren, K., Bauserman, R., & Carter, D. B. (1993). Gender role orientation and physical health: A study among young adults. *Sex Roles, 29*(5–6), 421–432.

Shopland, D. R., Eyre, H. J., & Pechacek, T. F. (1991). Smoking-attributable cancer mortality in 1991: Is lung cancer now the leading cause of death among smokers in the United States? *Journal of the National Cancer Institute, 83*(16), 1142–1148.

Shye, D., Mullooly, J. P., Freeborn, D. K., & Pope, C. R. (1995). Gender differences in the relationship between social network support and mortality: A longitudinal study of an elderly cohort. *Social Science and Medicine, 41*(7), 935–947.

Sickmund, M., Snyder, H., & Poe-Yamagata, E. (1997). *Juvenile offenders and victims: 1997 update on violence—Statistics summary.* Washington, DC: Office of Juvenile Justice and Delinquency Prevention.

Sidanius, J., Liu, J. H., Shaw, J. S., & Pratto, F. (1994). Social dominance orientation, hierarchy attenuators, and hierarchy enhancers: Social dominance theory and the criminal justice system. *Journal of Applied Social Psychology, 24,* 338–366.

Signorielli, N. (1993). *Mass media images and impact on health: A sourcebook.* Westport, CT: Greenwood Press.

Sijtsema, J. J., Veenstra, R., Lindenberg, S., & Salmivalli, C. (2009). Empirical test of bullies' status goals: Assessing direct goals, aggression, and prestige. *Aggressive Behavior, 35,* 57–67.

Silagy, C., & Stead, L. F. (2001). Physician advice for smoking cessation. *Cochrane Database of Systematic Reviews, 18*(4), CD000165.

Silver, R. C., Holman, E. A., McIntosh, D. N., Poulin, M., & Gil-Rivas, V. (2002). Nationwide longitudinal study of psychological responses to September 11. *Journal of the American Medical Association, 288*(10), 1235–1244.

Silverman, J. G., Raj, A., Mucci, L. A., & Hathaway, J. E. (2001). Dating violence against adolescent girls and associated substance use, unhealthy weight control, sexual risk behavior, pregnancy, and suicidality. *Journal of the American Medical Association, 286*(5), 572–579.

Silverman, M. M., Meyer, P. M., Sloane, F., Raffel, M., & Pratt, D. M. (1997). The Big Ten student suicide study: A 10-year study of suicides on midwestern university campuses. *Suicidal and Life Theatening Behavior, 27*(3):285–303.

Silverstein, B., Peterson, B., & Kelley, E. (1986). The role of the mass media in promoting a thin standard of bodily attractiveness for women. *Sex Roles, 14*, 519–532.

Sim, J. (1994). Tougher than the rest? Men in prison. In T. Newburn & E. A. Stanko (Eds.), *Just boys doing business? Men, masculinities and crime* (pp. 100–117). New York, NY: Routledge.

Simoni-Wastila, L. (2000). The use of abusable prescription drugs: The role of gender. *Journal of Women's Health and Gender Based Medicine, 9*(3), 289–297.

Simoni-Wastila, L., Ritter, G., & Strickler, G. (2004). Gender and other factors associated with the nonmedical use of abusable prescription drugs. *Substance Use & Misuse, 39*(1), 1–23.

Simoyi, P., Islam, S., Haque, A., Meyer, J., Doyle, E., & Ducatman, A. (1998). Evaluation of occupational injuries among young workers in West Virginia. *Human and Ecological Risk Assessment, 4*(6), 1405–1415.

Simpson, M. E., Serdula, M., Galuska, D. A., Gillespie, C., Donehoo, R., Macera, C., & Mack, K. (2003). Walking trends among U.S. adults: The Behavioral Risk Factor Surveillance System, 1987-2000. *American Journal of Preventive Medicine, 25*(2), 95–100.

Singh, G. K., Kogan, M. D., Siahpush, M., & van Dyck, P. C. (2008). Independent and joint effects of socioeconomic, behavioral, and neighborhood characteristics on physical inactivity and activity levels among U.S. children and adolescents. *Journal of Community Health, 33*(4), 206–216.

Singh, G. K., & Siahpush, M. (2002). Increasing rural-urban gradients in U.S. suicide mortality, 1970–1997. *American Journal of Public Health, 92*, 1161–1167.

Singleton, A. (2008). It's because of the invincibility thing: Young men, masculinity, and testicular cancer. *International Journal of Men's Health, 7*(1), 40–58.

Sinnott, J. D. (1986). *Sex roles and aging: Theory and research from a systems perspective*. Basil, Switzerland: Karger.

Siscovick, D. S., Weiss, N. S., Fletcher, R. H., & Lasky, T. (1984). The incidence of primary cardiac arrest during vigorous exercise. *New England Journal of Medicine, 311*(14), 874–877.

Skinner, W. (1994). The prevalence and demographic predictors of illicit and licit drug use among lesbians and gay men. *American Journal of Public Health, 84*(8), 1307–1310.

Slap, G. B., Chaudhuri, S., & Vorters, D. F. (1991). Risk factors for injury during adolescence. *Journal of Adolescent Health, 12*, 263–268.

Slater, M. D., Rouner, D., Murphy, K., Beauvais, F., Van Leuven, J., & Rodriguez, M. D. (1996). Male adolescents' reactions to TV beer advertisements: The effects of sports content and programming content. *Journal of Studies on Alcohol, 57*(4), 425–433.

Sleep Foundation. (2002). *2002 "Sleep in America" poll.* Washington, DC: Author.

Sleep Foundation. (2005). *2005 "Sleep in America" poll.* Washington, DC: Author.

Sleep Foundation. (2009). *2009 "Sleep in America" poll: Health and safety.* Washington, DC: Author.

Slesinski, M. J., Subar, A. F., & Kahle, L. L. (1995). Trends in use of vitamin and mineral supplements in the United States: The 1987 and 1992 National Health Interview Surveys. *Journal of the American Dietetic Association, 85*(8), 921–923.

Slesinski, M. J., Subar, A. F., & Kahle, L. L. (1996). Dietary intake of fat, fiber and other nutrients is related to the use of vitamin and mineral supplements in the United States: The 1992 National Health Interview Survey. *Journal of Nutrition, 126*(12), 3001–3008.

Slovic, P. (1999). Trust, emotion, sex, politics, and science: Surveying the risk-assessment battlefield. *Risk Analysis, 19*, 689–701.

Smith, A. L. (2003). Health policy and the coloring of an American male crisis: A perspective on community-based health services. *American Journal of Public Health, 93*(5), 749–752.

Smith, G. S., Branas, C. C., & Miller, T. R. (1999). Fatal nontraffic injuries involving alcohol: A meta-analysis. *Annals of Emergency Medicine, 33*(6), 659–668.

Smith, G. S., Keyl, P. M., Hadley, J. A., Bartley, C. L., Foss, M. D., Tolbert, W. G., & McKnight, J. (2001). Drinking and recreational boating fatalities: A population-based case-control study. *Journal of the American Medical Association, 286*(23), 2974–2980.

Smith, J. A., Braunack-Mayer, A., & Warin, M. (2007). "I've been independent for so damn long!" Independence, masculinity and aging in a help seeking context. *Journal of Aging Studies, 21*(4), 325–335.

Smith, J. A., Braunack-Mayer, A., & Wittert, G. (2006). What do we know about men's help-seeking and health service use? *Medical Journal of Australia, 184*(2), 81–83.

Smith, J. A., & Robertson, S. (2008). Men's health promotion: A new frontier in Australia and the U.K.? *Health Promotion International, 23*(3), 283–289.

Smith, J. C., Mercy, J. A., & Conn, J. M. (1988). Marital status and the risk of suicide. *American Journal of Public Health, 78*(1), 78–80.

Smith, M. H., Anderson, R. T., Bradham, D. D., & Longino, C. F. (1995). Rural and urban differences in mortality among Americans 55 years and older: Analysis of the National Longitudinal Mortality Study. *Journal of Rural Health, 11*(4), 274–285.

Smith, R. A., Cokkinides, V., & Brawley, O. W. (2009). Cancer screening in the United States, 2009: A review of current American Cancer Society guidelines and issues in cancer screening. *CA: A Cancer Journal for Clinicians, 59*, 27–41.

Smith, S. L., & Donnerstein, E. (1998). Harmful effects of exposure to media violence: Learning of aggression, desensitization, and fear. In *Human aggression: Theories, research, and implications for social policy* (pp. 167–202). San Diego, CA: Academic Press.

Smith, T. W., & Ruiz, J. M. (2002). Psychosocial influences on the development and course of coronary heart disease: Current status and implications for research and practice. *Journal of Consulting and Clinical Psychology, 70,* 548– 68.

Smyer, T., Gragert, M. D., & LaMere, S. (1997). Stay safe! Stay healthy! Surviving old age in prison. *Journal of Psychosocial Nursing, 35*(9), 10–17.

Smyth, J. M. (1998). Written emotional expression: Effect sizes, outcome types, and moderating variables. *Journal of Consulting and Clinical Psychology, 66,* 174–184.

Snell, W. E. (1986). The Masculine Role Inventory: Components and correlates. *Sex Roles, 15,* 445–455.

Snell, W. E., Belk, S. S., & Hawkins, R. C. (1987). Alcohol and drug use in stressful times: The influence of the masculine role and sex-related personality attributes. *Sex Roles, 16,* 359–373.

Snope, T. (1994). Survey reveals importance of continuing education. *American College Health Association Action, 33*(4), 1, 5–6.

Sobieraj, S. (1998). Taking control: Toy commercials and the social construction of patriarchy. In L. Bowker (Ed.), *Masculinities and violence* (pp. 15–28). Thousand Oaks, CA: Sage.

Sobralske, M. (2006). Machismo sustains health and illness beliefs of Mexican American men. *Journal of the American Academy of Nurse Practitioners, 18*(8), 348–350.

Sokoloff, M. H., Joyce, G. F., & Wise, M. (2007). Testicular cancer. In M. S. Litwin & C. S. Saigal (Eds.), *Urologic diseases in America* (pp. 555–585) (NIH Publication No. 07-5512). Bethesda, MD: National Institutes of Health.

Sokolosky, M. C., Prescott, J. E., Collins, S. L., & Timberlake, G. A. (1993). Safety belt use and hospital charge differences among motor vehicle crash victims. *West Virginia Medical Journal, 89*(8), 328–330.

Solis, J. M., Marks, G., Garcia, M., & Shelton, D. (1990). Acculturation, access to care, and use of preventive services by Hispanics: Findings from HHANES 1982-84. *American Journal of Public Health, 80*(Suppl.), 11–19.

Solomon, S. D. (2002). Gender differences in response to disaster. In G. Weidner, S. M. Kopp, & M. Kristenson (Eds.), *Heart disease: Environment, stress and gender* (NATO Science Series, Series I: Life and Behavioural Sciences, Vol. 327, pp. 267–274). Washington, DC: IOS Press.

Sonenstein, F. L., Ku, L., Lindberg, L. D., Turner, C. F., & Pleck, J. H. (1998). Changes in sexual behavior and condom use among teenaged males: 1988 to 1995. *American Journal of Public Health, 86*(6), 956–959.

Sorensen, E. S. (1994). Daily stressors and coping responses: A comparison of rural and suburban children. *Public Health Nursing, 11*(1), 24–31.

Sorlie, P. D., Backlund, E., & Keller, J. (1995). U.S. mortality by economic, demographic, and social characteristics: The National Longitudinal Mortality Study. *American Journal of Public Health, 85,* 949–956.

Sorlie, P. D., Johnson, N. J., Backlund, E., & Bradham, D. D. (1994). Mortality in the uninsured compared with that in persons with public and private health insurance. *Archives of Internal Medicine, 154*(21), 2409–2416.

South Eastern Health Board. (2004). *Getting inside men's health* (Publication No. 10-04-0035). Kilkenny, Ireland: Author.

Sowers, J. R. (2003). Obesity as a cardiovascular risk factor. *American Journal of Medicine, 115*(Suppl 8A), 37S–41S.

Spatz, E. S., Canavan, M. E., Krumholz, H. M., & Desai, M. M. (2009, April). Missing the benchmark: The underuse of lipid-lowering medications in individuals at risk for cardiovascular events—Data from the National Health and Nutrition Examination Survey. Paper presented at the American Heart Association 10th Scientific Forum on Care and Outcomes Research in Cardiovascular Disease and Stroke, Washington, DC.

Spaulding, A., Greene, C., Davidson, K., Schneidermann, M., & Rich, J. (1999). Hepatitis C in state correctional facilities. *Preventive Medicine, 28*, 92–100.

Spence, J. T. (1984). Masculinity, femininity, and gender-related traits: A conceptual analysis and critique of current research. In B. A. Maher (Ed.), *Progress in experimental personality research* (Vol. 13, pp. 1–97). New York, NY: Academic.

Spence, J. T., & Helmreich, R. (1978). *Masculinity and femininity: Their psychological dimensions, correlates, and antecedents.* Austin: University of Texas Press.

Spence, J. T., Helmreich, R. L., & Holahan, C. K. (1979). Negative and positive components of psychological masculinity and femininity and their relationships to self-reports of neurotic and acting out behaviors. *Journal of Personality and Social Psychology, 37*, 1673–1682.

Spence, J. T., Helmreich, R., & Strapp, J. (1974). The personal attributes questionnaire: A measure of sex-role stereotypes and masculinity-femininity. *Catalogue of Selected Documents in Psychology, 4*, 43–44.

Spigner, C., Hawkins, W., & Loren, W. (1993). Gender differences in perception of risk associated with alcohol and drug use among college students. *Women and Health, 20*(1), 87–97.

Spilman, M. A. (1988). Gender differences in worksite health promotion activities. *Social Science and Medicine, 5*, 525–535.

Springer, K. W., & Mouzon, D. (2009, August). *Masculinity and healthcare seeking among midlife men: Variation by adult socioeconomic status.* Paper presented at the American Sociological Association Annual Meeting, San Francisco, CA.

Stables, G. J., Subar, A. F., Paterson, B. H., Dodd, K., Heimendinger, J., Van Duyn, M. A., & Nebeling, L. (2002). Changes in vegetable and fruit consumption and awareness among U.S. adults: Results of the 1991 and 1997 Five A Day for Better Health Program surveys. *Journal of the American Dietetic Association, 102*(6), 809–817.

Stamler, J., & Neaton, J. D. (2008). The Multiple Risk Factor Intervention Trial (MRFIT): Importance then and now. *Journal of the American Medical Association, 300*(11), 1343–1345.

Stamler, J., Neaton, J. D., Garside, D. B., & Daviglus, M. (2005). Current status: Six established major risk factors—And low risk. In M. Marmot & P. Elliott (Eds.), *Coronary heart disease epidemiology: From aetiology to public health* (2nd ed., pp. 32–70). London, England: Oxford University Press.

Stamler, J., Stamler, R., Neaton, J. D., Wentworth, D., Daviglus, M. L., Garside, D., ... Greenland, P. (1999). Low risk-factor profile and long-term cardiovascular and noncardiovascular mortality and life expectancy: Findings for 5 large cohorts of young adult and middle-aged men and women. *Journal of the American Medical Association, 282*, 2012–2018.

Stamler, J., Vaccaro, O., Neaton, J. D., & Wentworth, D. (1993). Diabetes, other risk factors, and 12-yr cardiovascular mortality for men screened in the Multiple Risk Factor Intervention Trial. *Diabetes Care, 16*(2), 434–444.

Stamm, B. H. (Ed). (2003). *Rural behavioral health care: An interdisciplinary guide.* Washington, DC: American Psychological Association.

Stanford, J. L., Stephenson, R. A., Coyle, L. M., Cerhan, J., Correa, R., Eley, J. W., ... West, D. (1999). *Prostate cancer trends 1973–1995: SEER Program, National Cancer Institute* (NIH Publication No. 99-4543). Bethesda, MD: National Cancer Institute.

Stangler, R. S., & Printz, A. M. (1980). *DSM-III:* Psychiatric diagnosis in a university population. *American Journal of Psychiatry, 137*(8), 937–940.

Stanley, D., & Freysinger, V. J. (1995). The impact of age, health, and sex on the frequency of older adults' leisure activity participation: A longitudinal study. *Activities, Adaptation & Aging, 19*(3), 31–42.

Stanton, A. L., & Courtenay, W. H. (2003). Gender, stress and health. In R. H. Rozensky, N. G. Johnson, C. D. Goodheart, & R. Hammond (Eds.), *Psychology builds a health world: Research and practice opportunities* (pp. 105–135). Washington, DC: American Psychological Association.

Stapley, J. C., & Haviland, J. M. (1989). Beyond depression: Gender differences in normal adolescents' emotional experiences. *Sex Roles, 20*(5–6), 295–308.

Stasson, M., & Fishbein, M. (1990). The relation between perceived risk and preventive action: A within-subject analysis of perceived driving risk and intentions to wear seat-belts. *Journal of Applied Social Psychology, 20,* 1541–1557.

Steele, C. B., Miller, D. S., Maylahn, C., Uhler, R. J. , & Baker, C. T. (2000). Knowledge, attitudes, and screening practices among older men regarding prostate cancer. *American Journal of Public Health, 90*(10), 1595–1600.

Steffen, V. J., Sternberg, L., Teegarden, L. A., & Shepherd, K. (1994). Practice and persuasive frame: Effects on beliefs, intention, and performance of a cancer self-examination. *Journal of Applied Social Psychology, 24*(10), 897–925.

Steinberg, D., Pearson, T. A., & Kuller, L. H. (1991). Alcohol and atherosclerosis. *Annals of Internal Medicine, 114*(11), 967–976.

Steingart, R. M., Packer, M., Hamm, P., Coglianese, M. E., Gersh, B., Geltman, E. M., ... Pfeffer, M. A. (1991). Sex differences in the management of coronary artery disease. *New England Journal of Medicine, 325*(4), 226–230.

Stensland-Bugge, E., Bonaa, K. H., & Joakimsen, O. (2001). Age and sex differences in the relationship between inherited and lifestyle factors and subclinical carotid atherosclerosis: The Tromsø study. *Atherosclerosis, 154*(2), 437–448.

Stephens, N. G., Parsons, A., Schofield, P. M., Kelly, F., Cheeseman, K., & Mitchinson, M. J. (1996). Randomized controlled trial of vitamin E in patients with coronary disease: Cambridge Heart Antioxidant Study (CHAOS). *Lancet, 347*(9004), 781–786.

Stern, M., & Karraker, K. H. (1989). Sex stereotyping of infants: A review of gender labeling studies. *Sex Roles, 20*(9/10), 501–522.

Stern, R. S., Weinstein, M. C., & Baker, S. G. (1986). Risk reduction for nonmelanoma skin cancer with childhood sunscreen use. *Archives of Dermatology, 122,* 537–545.

Stevens, T., Jacobs, D. R., & White, C. C. (1985). A descriptive epidemiology of leisure-time physical activity. *Public Health Report, 100,* 147–158.

Stewart, S. H., & Silverstein, M. D. (2002). Racial and ethnic disparity in blood pressure and cholesterol measurement. *Journal of General Internal Medicine, 17*(6), 405–411.

Stewart, S. T., Cutler, D. M., & Rosen, A. B. (2009). Forecasting the effects of obesity and smoking on U.S. life expectancy. *New England Journal of Medicine, 361*(34), 2252–2260.

Stillion, J. M. (1995). Premature death among males: Extending the bottom line of men's health. In D. Sabo & D. F. Gordon (Eds.), *Men's health and illness: Gender, power, and the body* (pp. 46–67). Thousand Oaks, CA: Sage.

Stockwell, D. H., Madhavan, S., Cohen, H., Gibson, G., & Alderman, M. H. (1994). The determinants of hypertension awareness, treatment, and control in an insured population. *American Journal of Public Health, 84*(11), 1768–1774.

Stone, A. A., & Neale, J. M. (1984). New measure of daily coping: Development and preliminary results. *Journal of Personality and Social Psychology, 46*(4), 892–906.

Stone, S. V., Dembroski, T. M., Costa, P. T., & MacDougall, J. M. (1990). Gender differences in cardiovascular reactivity. *Journal of Behavioral Medicine, 13*(2), 137–156.

Stoney, C. M., Davis, M. C., & Matthew, K. (1987). Sex differences in physiologic responses to stress and in coronary heart disease: A causal link? *Psychophysiology, 24*(2), 127–131.

Stoohs, R., Guilleminault, C., Itoi, A., & Dement, W. C. (1994). Traffic accidents in commercial long-haul truck drivers: The influence of sleep-disordered breathing and obesity. *Sleep, 17*(7), 619–623.

Stoppe, G., Sandholzer, H., Huppertz, C., Duwe, H., & Staedt, J. (1999). Gender differences in the recognition of depression in old age. *Maturitas, 32*(3), 205–212.

Strate, L. (1992) Beer commercials: A manual on masculinity. In S. Craig (Ed.), *Men, masculinity, and the media* (pp. 78–92). Newbury Park, CA: Sage.

Strazzullo, P., D'Elia, L., Kandala, N. B., & Cappuccio, F. P. (2009). Salt intake, stroke, and cardiovascular disease: Meta-analysis of prospective studies. *British Medical Journal, 339*, b4567.

Street, C., Antonio, J., & Cudlipp, D. (1996). Androgen use by athletes: A reevaluation of the health risks. *Canadian Journal of Applied Physiology, 21*(6), 421–440.

Street, S., Kimmel, E. B., & Kromrey, J. D. (1995). Revisiting university student gender role perceptions. *Sex Roles, 33*(3/4), 183–201.

Stringhini, S., Sabia, S., Shipley, M., Brunner, E., Nabi, H., Kivimaki, M., & Singh-Manoux, A. (2010). Association of socioeconomic position with health behaviors and mortality. *Journal of the American Medical Association, 303*(12), 1159–1166.

Stroebe, M., Stroebe, W., & Schut, H. (2001). Gender differences in adjustment to bereavement: An empirical and theoretical review. *Review of General Psychology, 5*, 62–83.

Strube, M. J. (Ed.). (1991). *Type A behavior*. Newbury Park, CA: Sage.

Struber, D., Luck, M., & Roth, G. (2008). Sex, aggression and impulse control: An integrative account. *Neurocase, 14*(1), 93–121.

Stuart, G. L., & Moore, T. M. (2004). Effects of masculine gender role stress on men's cognitive, affective, physiological, and aggressive responses to intimate conflict situations. *Psychology of Men and Masculinity, 5*(2), 132–142.

Student dies of gunshot wound. (1993, October 20). *The Red & Black, 101*(28), 1.

Student dies of self-inflicted gunshot wound. (1994, April 29). *The Red & Black,* *101*(125), 1.

Stueland, D., Mickel, S. H., Cleveland, D. A., Rothfusz, R. R., Zoch, T., & Stamas, P. (1995). The relationship of farm residency status to demographic and service characteristics of agricultural injury victims in central Wisconsin. *Journal of Rural Health, 11*(2), 98–105.

Suarez, R. (1995, March 7). Women in combat. In P. Michaels (Executive Producer), *Talk of the nation.* Washington, DC: National Public Radio.

Subar, A. F., & Block, G. (1990). Use of vitamin and mineral supplements: Demographics and amounts of nutrients consumed: The 1987 Health Interview Survey. *American Journal of Epidemiology, 132*(6), 1091–1101.

Subar, A. F., Heimendinger, J., Patterson, B. H., Krebs-Smith, S. M., Pivonka, E., & Kessler, R. (1995). Fruit and vegetable intake in the United States: The baseline survey of the Five a Day for Better Health Program. *American Journal of Health Promotion, 9*(5), 352–360.

Substance Abuse and Mental Health Services Administration. (1997). *National household survey on drug abuse: Main findings 1995* (DHHS Publication No. SMA 97-3127). Rockville, MD: Author.

Substance Abuse and Mental Health Services Administration. (1998). *Prevalence of substance use among racial and ethnic subgroups in the United States.* (DHHS Publication No. SMA 98-3202). Rockville, MD: Author.

Substance Abuse and Mental Health Services Administration. (2000). *National Household Survey on Drug Abuse: Main findings 1998* (DHHS Publication No. SMA 00-3381). Rockville, MD: Author.

Substance Abuse and Mental Health Services Administration. (2004). *Results from the 2003 National Survey on Drug Use and Health: National Findings* (Office of Applied Studies, NSDUH Series H-25, DHHS Publication No. SMA 04-3964). Rockville, MD: Author.

Substance Abuse and Mental Health Services Administration. (2006). *Anabolic steroids* (Substance Abuse Treatment Advisory, Vol. 5, no. 3, DHHS Publication No. [SMA] 06-4169). Columbia, MD: Author.

Substance Abuse and Mental Health Services Administration. (2008a). *Drug Abuse Warning Network, 2006: National estimates of drug-related emergency department visits* (DHHS Publication No. SMA 08-4339). Rockville, MD: Author.

Substance Abuse and Mental Health Services Administration. (2008b). *Results from the 2007 National Survey on Drug Use and Health: National findings* (Office of Applied Studies, NSDUH Series H-34, DHHS Publication No. SMA 08-4343). Rockville, MD: Author.

Substance Abuse and Mental Health Services Administration. (2009). *Results from the 2008 National Survey on Drug Use and Health: National findings* (Office of Applied Studies, NSDUH Series H-36, HHS Publication No. SMA 09-4434). Rockville, MD: Author.

Substance Abuse and Mental Health Services Administration. (2010, March 25). *New national survey shows that more than a quarter of youth aged 12 to 20 drank alcohol in the past month* (press release). Rockville, MD: Author.

Sue, D. W., & Sue, D. (2003). *Counseling the culturally diverse: Theory and practice* (4th ed.) Hoboken, NJ: Wiley.

Sui, X., LaMonte, M. J., Laditka, J. N., Hardin, J. W., Chase, N., Hooker, S. P., & Blair, S. N. (2007). Cardiorespiratory fitness and adiposity as mortality predictors in older adults. *Journal of the American Medical Association, 298*(21), 2507–2516.

Suicide Prevention Resource Center. (2004). *Promoting mental health and preventing suicide in college and university settings*. Newton, MA: Education Development Center.

Suk, S. H., Sacco, R. L., Boden-Albala, B., Cheun, J. F., Pittman, J. G., Elkind, M. S., & Paik, M. C. (2003). Abdominal obesity and risk of ischemic stroke: The Northern Manhattan Stroke Study. *Stroke, 34*, 1586–1592.

Summala, H., & Mikkola, T. (1994). Fatal accidents among car and truck drivers: Effects of fatigue, age, and alcohol consumption. *Human Factors, 36*(2), 315–326.

Sutkin, L., & Good, G. (1987). Therapy with men in health-care settings. In M. Scher, M. Stevens, G. Good, & G. A. Eichenfield (Eds.), *Handbook of counseling and psychotherapy with men* (pp. 372–387). Thousand Oaks, CA: Sage.

Suzukawa, M., Ayaori, M., Shige, H., Hisada, T., Ishikawa, T., & Nakamura, H. (1998). Effect of supplementation with vitamin E on LDL oxidizability and prevention of atherosclerosis. *Biofactors, 7*(1–2), 51–54.

Svenson, O., Fischnoff, B., & MacGregor, D. (1985). Perceived driving safety and seat belt usage. *Accident Analysis and Prevention, 17*, 119–133.

Swahn, M. H., & Donovan, J. E. (2006). Alcohol and violence: Comparison of the psychosocial correlates of adolescent involvement in alcohol-related physical fighting versus other physical fighting. *Addictive Behaviors, 31*(11), 2014–2029.

Swahn, M. H., Simon, T. R., Hammig, B. J., & Guerrero, J. L. (2004). Alcohol-consumption behaviors and risk for physical fighting and injuries among adolescent drinkers. *Addictive Behaviors, 29*(5), 959–963.

Swank, M. E., Vernon, S. W., & Lairson, D. R. (1986). Patterns of preventive dental behavior. *Public Health Reports, 101*(2), 175–184.

Swenson, R. (2009). Domestic divo? Televised treatments of masculinity, feminity, and food. *Critical Studies in Media Communication, 26*(1), 36–53.

Taggart, L. P., McCammon, S. L., Allred, L. J., Horner, R. D., & May, H. J. (1993) Effect of patient and physician gender on prescriptions for psychotropic drugs. *Journal of Women's Health, 2*, 353–357.

Tanfer, K., Cubbins, L. A., & Billy, J. O. (1995). Gender, race, class and self-reported sexually transmitted disease incidence. *Family Planning Perspective, 27*(5), 196–202.

Tannen, D. (1990). *You just don't understand: Women and men in conversation*. New York, NY: Ballantine.

Taylor, S. E. (1986). *Health psychology*. New York, NY: Random House.

Taylor, S. E. (1990). Health psychology: The science and the field. *American Psychologist, 45*(1), 40–50.

Taylor, S. E. (2007). Social support. In H. S. Friedman & R. C. Silver (Eds.), *Foundations of health psychology* (pp. 145–171). New York, NY: Oxford University Press.

Taylor, S. E., Dilorio, C., Stephens, T. T., & Soet, J. E. (1997). A comparison of AIDS-related sexual risk behaviors among African-American college students. *Journal of the National Medical Association, 89*, 397–403.

Terry, D. F., Pencina, M. J., Vasan, R. S., Murabito, J. M., Wolf, P. A., Hayes, M. K., ... Benjamin, E. J. (2005). Cardiovascular risk factors predictive for survival and morbidity-free survival in the oldest-old Framingham Heart Study participants. *Journal of the American Geriatric Society, 53*, 1944–1950.

Tewksbury, R., & Gagne, P. (1996). Transgenderists: Products of non-normative intersection of sex, gender, and sexuality. *Journal of Men's Studies, 5*, 105–129.

The Gallup Organization. (1995). *CNN and USA Today Gallup poll: Gun ownership.* Princeton, NJ: Author.

Thom, B. (1986). Sex differences in help seeking for alcohol problems: The barriers to help seeking. *British Journal of Addiction, 81*, 777–788.

Thomas, B. S. (1995). The effectiveness of selected risk factors in mediating gender differences in drinking and its problems. *Journal of Adolescent Health, 17*(2), 91–98.

Thomas, C., & Kelman, H. R. (1990). Gender and the use of health services among elderly persons. In M. G. Ory & H. R. Warner (Eds.), *Gender, health, and longevity: Multidisciplinary perspectives* (pp. 25–37). New York, NY: Springer.

Thomas, S. B., Gilliam, A. G., & Iwrey, C. G. (1989). Knowledge about AIDS and reported risk behaviors among Black college students. *Journal of American College Health, 38*, 61–65.

Thompson, B., Coronado, G., Chen, L., Thompson, L. A., Halperin, A., Jaffe, R., ... Zbikowski, S. M. (2007). Prevalence and characteristics of smokers at thirty Pacific Northwest colleges and universities. *Nicotine & Tobacco Research, 9*(3), 429–438.

Thompson, E. H., Grisanti, C., & Pleck, J. H. (1985). Attitudes toward the male role and their correlates. *Sex Roles, 13*(7/8), 413–427.

Thompson, E. H., & Pleck, J. H. (1986). The structure of male role norms. *American Behavioral Scientist, 29*, 531–543.

Thompson, E. H., & Pleck, J. H. (1995). Masculinity ideologies: A review of research instrumentation on men and masculinities. In R. F. Levant & W. S. Pollack (Eds.), *A new psychology of men* (pp. 129–163). New York, NY: Basic Books.

Thompson, E. H., Pleck, J. H., & Ferrera, D. L. (1992). Men and masculinities: Scales for masculinity ideology and masculinity-related constructs. *Sex Roles, 27*, 573–607.

Thompson, I. M., Tangen, C. M., Tolcher, A., Crawford, E. D., Eisenberger, M., & Moinpour, C. M. (2001). Association of African-American ethnic background with survival in men with metastatic prostate cancer. *Journal of the National Cancer Institute, 93*(3), 219–225.

Thompson, P. D., Franklin, B. A., Balady, G. J., Blair, S. N., Corrado, D., Estes, N. A., ... Costa, F. (2007). Exercise and acute cardiovascular events: Placing the risks into perspective—A scientific statement from the American Heart Association Council on Nutrition, Physical Activity, and Metabolism and the Council on Clinical Cardiology. *Circulation, 115*(17), 2358–2368.

Thomsen, D. G., & Gilbert, D. G. (1998). Factors characterizing marital conflict states and traits: Physiological, affective, behavioral and neurotic variable contributions to marital conflict and satisfaction. *Personality and Individual Differences, 25*, 833–855.

Thorne, B. (1993). *Gender play: Girls and boys in school.* New Brunswick, NJ: Rutgers University Press.

Thun, M. J., Henley, S. J., Burns, D., Jemal, A., Shanks, T. G., & Calle, E. E. (2006). Lung cancer death rates in lifelong nonsmokers. *Journal of the National Cancer Institute, 98*(10), 691–699.

Thune, I., & Furberg, A. S. (2001). Physical activity and cancer risk: Dose-response and cancer, all sites and site-specific. *Medicine and Science in Sports and Exercise, 33*(6), S530–S550.

Thurman, Q. C., & Franklin, K. M. (1990). AIDS and college health: Knowledge, threat, and prevention at a northeastern university. *Journal of American College Health, 38,* 179–184.

Titus-Ernstoff, L., Dalton, M. A., Adachi-Mejia, A. M., Longacre, M. R., & Beach, M. L. (2008). Longitudinal study of viewing smoking in movies and initiation of smoking by children. *Pediatrics, 121,* 15–21.

Tofler, G. H., & Muller, J. E. (2006). Triggering of acute cardiovascular disease and potential preventive strategies. *Circulation, 114*(17), 1863–1872.

Tomar, S. L. (2003). Is use of smokeless tobacco a risk factor for cigarette smoking? The U.S. experience. *Nicotine & Tobacco Research, 5*(4), 561–569.

Tomar, S. L., & Winn, D. M. (1999). Chewing tobacco use and dental caries among U.S. men. *Journal of the American Dental Association, 130*(11), 1601–1610.

Tomar, S. L., Winn, D. M., Swango, P. A., Giovino, G. A., & Kleinman, D. V. (1997). Oral mucosal smokeless tobacco lesions among adolescents in the United States. *Journal of Dental Research, 76*(6), 1277–1286.

Torres, J. B. (1998). Masculinity and gender roles among Puerto Rican men: Machismo on the U.S. mainland. *American Journal of Orthopsychiatry, 68*(1), 16–26.

Torres, J. B., Solberg, V., Scott, H., & Carlstrom, A. H. (2002). The myth of sameness among Latino men and their machismo. *American Journal of Orthopsychiatry, 72*(2), 163–181.

Torsheim, T., Ravens-Sieberer, U., Hetland, J., Valimaa, R., Danielson, M., & Overpeck, M. (2006). Cross-national variation of gender differences in adolescent subjective health in Europe and North America. *Social Science and Medicine, 62*(4), 815–827.

Town, M., Naimi, T. S., Mokdad, A. H., & Brewer, R. D. (2006). Health care access among U.S. adults who drink alcohol excessively: Missed opportunities for prevention. *Preventing Chronic Disease, 3*(2), A53.

Transportation Research Board. (2003). *Statistics on drugged driving and young drivers reported* [Press release]. Washington, DC: Author.

Traustadottir, T., Bosch, P. R., & Matt, K. S. (2003). Gender differences in cardiovascular and hypothalamic-pituitary-adrenal axis responses to psychological stress in healthy older adult men and women. *Stress, 6*(2), 133–140.

Treadwell, H. (2003). Poverty, race, and the invisible men. *American Journal of Public Health, 93*(5), 705–707.

Trevino, D. B., Young, E. H., Groff, J., & Jono, R. T. (1990). The association between marital adjustment and compliance with antihypertension regimens. *Journal of the American Board of Family Practice, 3,* 17–25.

Triplitt, C., & Alvarez, C. A. (2008). Best practices for lowering the risk of cardiovascular disease in diabetes. *Diabetes Spectrum, 21*(3), 177–189.

Troiano, R. P., Berrigan, D., Dodd, K. W., Mâsse, L. C., Tilert, T., & McDowell, M. (2008). Physical activity in the United States measured by accelerometer. *Medicine and Science in Sports and Exercise, 40*(1), 181–188.

Troiano, R. P., Briefel, R. R., Carroll, M. D., & Bialostosky, K. (2000). Energy and fat intakes of children and adolescents in the united states: data from the National Health and Nutrition Examination Surveys. *American Journal of Clinical Nutrition, 72,* 1343–1353S.

Tsugane, S., & Sasazuki, S. (2007). Diet and the risk of gastric cancer: Review of epidemiological evidence. *Gastric Cancer, 10*(2), 75–83.

Tucker, J. S., & Anders, S. L. (2001). Social control of health behaviors in marriage. *Journal of Applied Social Psychology, 31,* 467–485.

Tucker, J. S., & Mueller, J. S. (2000). Spouses' social control of health behaviors: Use and effectiveness of specific strategies. *Personality and Social Psychology Bulletin, 26*(9), 1120–1130.

Tudiver, F., & Talbot, Y. (1999). Why don't men seek help? Family physicians' perspectives on help-seeking behavior in men. *Journal of Family Practice, 48*(1), 47–52.

Tuomilehto, J., & Lindström, J. (2003). The major diabetes prevention trials. *Current Diabetes Reports, 3*(2), 115–122.

Uchendu, E. (2007). Masculinity and Nigerian youth. *Nordic Journal of African Studies, 16*(2), 279–297.

Uitenbroek, D. G. (1993). Seasonal variation in leisure time physical activity. *Medicine & Science in Sports & Exercise, 25*(6), 755–760.

Umberson, D. (1992). Gender, marital status and the social control of health behavior. *Social Science and Medicine, 34*(8), 907–917.

Umberson, D., Wortman, C. B., & Kessler, R. C. (1992). Widowhood and depression: Explaining long-term gender differences in vulnerability. *Journal of Health and Social Behavior, 33,* 10–24.

University of Michigan. (2009, December 14). Smoking continues gradual decline among U.S. teens, smokeless tobacco threatens a comeback [Press release]. Ann Arbor: University of Michigan News Service.

Unruh, A. M. (1996). Gender variations in clinical pain experience. *Pain, 65*(2–3), 123–167.

Unruh, A. M., Ritchie, J., & Merskey, H. (1999). Does gender affect appraisal of pain and pain coping strategies? *Clinical Journal of Pain, 15,* 31–40.

Urban Institute. (2009). Uninsured and dying because of it: Updating the Institute of Medicine Analysis on the impact of uninsurance on mortality. Washington, DC: Author.

U.S. Bureau of the Census. (2001). *The native Hawaiian and other Pacific Islander population: 2000.* Washington, DC: U.S. Department of Commerce.

U.S. Bureau of the Census. (2002). *The Asian population: 2000.* Washington, DC: U.S. Department of Commerce.

U.S. Coast Guard. (2003). *2002 national recreational boating survey report.* Columbus, OH: Strategic Research Group.

U.S. Coast Guard. (2006). *Recent research on recreational boating accidents and the contribution of boating under the influence: Summary of results.* Washington, DC: Author.

U.S. Coast Guard. (2008). *2007 national life jacket wear rate observation study final report: Featuring a decade of data—Comparison data from 1998 to 2006.* Washington, DC: Author.

U.S. Coast Guard. (2009). *Recreational boating statistics 2008* (Publication No. COMDT P16754.22). Washington, DC: Author.

U.S. Department of Agriculture. (1993). *Tobacco situation and outlook report* (Economic Research Service, Publication No. TBS-241). Washington, DC: Author.

U.S. Department of Agriculture. (2009). *Health status and health care access of farm and rural populations* (Economic Information Bulletin No. 57). Washington, DC: Economic Research Service.

U.S. Department of Health and Human Services. (2000a). Deaths: Final data for 1998 (DHHS Publication No. [PHS] 2000-1120) *National Vital Statistics Reports, 48*(11). Hyattsville, MD: National Center for Health Statistics.

U.S. Department of Health and Human Services. (2000b). *Health, United States, 2000* (DHHS Publication No. 00-1232). Hyattsville, MD: U.S. Government Printing Office.

U.S. Fire Administration. (2009). *Firefighter fatalities in the United States in 2008* (Table 1). Washington, DC: Federal Emergency Management Agency.

U.S. General Accounting Office. (1996). *Motor vehicle safety: Comprehensive state programs offer best opportunity for increasing use of safety belts* (GAO/RCED Publication No. 96-24). Washington, DC: U.S. General Accounting Office.

U.S. Preventive Services Task Force. (1996). *Guide to clinical preventive services* (2nd ed.). Baltimore, MD: Williams & Wilkins.

Uwe, M., & Sieverding, M. (2008). What makes men attend early detection cancer screenings? An investigation into the roles of cues to action. *International Journal of Men's Health, 7*(1), 3–20.

Vaccarino, V., Rathore, S. S., Wenger, N. K., Frederick, P. D., Abramson, J. L., Barron, H. V., … Krumholz, H. M. (2005). Sex and racial differences in the management of acute myocardial infarction, 1994 through 2002. *New England Journal of Medicine, 353*(7), 671–682.

Vail-Smith, K., & Felts, M. (1993). Sunbathing: College students' knowledge, attitudes, and perceptions of risks. *Journal of American College Health, 42,* 21–26.

Vance, C. S. (1995). Social construction theory and sexuality. In M. Berger, B. Wallis, & S. Watson (Eds.), *Constructing masculinity* (pp. 37–48). New York, NY: Routledge.

Van den Berg, J. F., Miedema, H. M., Tulen, J. H., Hofman, A., Neven, A. K., & Tiemeier, H. (2009). Sex differences in subjective and actigraphic sleep measures: A population-based study of elderly persons. *Sleep, 32*(10), 1367–1375.

Van Horn, L. V., Ballew, C., Liu, K., Ruth, K., McDonald, A., Hilner, J. E., … Sidney, S. (1991). Diet, body size, and plasma lipids-lipoproteins in young adults: Differences by race and sex. *American Journal of Epidemiology, 133*(1), 9–23.

Van Sluijs, E. M., Van Poppel, M. N., Twisk, J. W., & Van Mechelen, W. (2006). Physical activity measurements affected participants' behavior in a randomized controlled trial. *Journal of Clinical Epidemiology, 59*(4), 404–411.

Vargas, C. M., Burt, V. L., Gillum, R. F., & Pamuk, E. R. (1997). Validity of self-reported hypertension in the National Health and Nutrition Examination Survey III, 1988–1991. *Preventive Medicine, 26*(5, Pt. 1), 678–685.

Verbrugge, L. M. (1980). Sex differences in complaints and diagnoses. *Journal of Behavioral Medicine, 3*(4), 327–355.

Verbrugge, L. M. (1982). Sex differences in legal drug use. *Journal of Social Issues, 38*(2), 59–76.

Verbrugge, L. M. (1985). Gender and health: An update on hypotheses and evidence. *Journal of Health and Social Behavior, 26*(3), 156–182.

Verbrugge, L. M. (1988). Unveiling higher morbidity for men: The story. In M. W. Riley (Ed.), *Social structures and human lives* (pp. 138–160). Thousand Oaks, CA: Sage.

Verbrugge, L. M. (1989). The twain meet: Empirical explanations of sex differences in health and mortality. *Journal of Health and Social Behavior, 30,* 282–304.

Verbrugge, L. M. (1990). The twain meet: Empirical explanations of sex differences in health and mortality. In M. G. Ory & H. R. Warner (Eds.), *Gender, health, and longevity: Multidisciplinary perspectives* (pp. 159–194). New York, NY: Springer.

Verbrugge, L. M., & Steiner, R. P. (1985). Prescribing drugs to men and women. *Health Psychology, 4*(1), 79–98.

Verbrugge, L. M., & Wingard, D. L. (1987). Sex differentials in health and mortality. *Women and Health, 12*(2), 103–145.

Vertinsky, P. A. (1994). *The eternally wounded woman: Women, doctors, and exercise in the late nineteenth century.* Urbana: University of Illinois Press.

Vessey, J. T., & Howard, K. I. (1993). Who seeks psychotherapy? *Psychotherapy: Theory, research, practice, training, 30*(4), 546–553.

Vigderhous, G., & Fishman, G. (1978). The impact of unemployment and familial integration on changing suicide rates in the U.S.A., 1920–1969. *Social Psychiatry, 13,* 239–248.

Vineis, P., & Simonato, L. (1991). Proportion of lung and bladder cancers in males resulting from occupation: A systematic approach. *Archives of Environmental Health, 46*(1), 6–15.

Vineis, P., Thomas, T., Hayes, R. B., Blot, W. J., Mason, T. J., Williams-Pickle, L., … Schoenberg, J. (1988). Proportion of lung cancers in males, due to occupation, in different areas of the USA. *International Journal of Cancer, 42,* 851–856.

Viscusi, W. K. (1990). Do smokers underestimate risks? *The Journal of Political Economy, 98*(6), 1253–1269.

Viscusi, W. K. (1992). *Smoking: Making the risky decision.* Oxford, England: Oxford University Press.

Vogt, T. M., Mullooly, J. P., Ernst, D., Pope, C. R., & Hollis, J. F. (1992). Social networks as predictors of ischemic heart disease, cancer, stroke and hypertension: Incidence, survival and mortality. *Journal of Clinical Epidemiology, 45*(6), 659–666.

Volavka, J. (1999). The neurobiology of violence: An update. *Journal of Neuropsychiatry & Clinical Neurosciences, 11*(3), 307–314.

Vorona, R. D., & Ware, J. C. (2002). Sleep disordered breathing and driving risk. *Current Opinion in Pulmonary Medicine, 8*(6), 506–510.

Wade, J. C. (2008a). Masculinity ideology, male reference group identity dependence, and African American men's health related attitudes and behaviors. *Psychology of Men and Masculinity, 9*(1), 5–16.

Wade, J. C. (2008b). Traditional masculinity and African American men's health-related attitudes and behaviors. *American Journal of Men's Health*, 3(2), 165–172.

Waisberg, J., & Page, S. (1988). Gender role nonconformity and perception of mental illness. *Women and Health*, 14(1), 3–16.

Waitzkin, H. (1984). Doctor-patient communication: Clinical implications of social scientific research. *Journal of the American Medical Association*, 252(17), 2441–2446.

Waldron, I. (1976). Why do women live longer than men? Part I. *Journal of Human Stress*, 2(1), 2–13.

Waldron, I. (1983). Sex differences in illness, incidence, prognosis and mortality: Issues and evidence. *Social Science & Medicine*, 17(16), 1107–1123.

Waldron, I. (1986). The contribution of smoking to sex differences in mortality. *Public Health Reports*, 101(2), 163–173.

Waldron, I. (1988). Gender and health-related behavior. In D. S. Gochman (Ed.), *Health behavior: Emerging research perspectives* (pp. 193–208). New York, NY: Plenum.

Waldron, I. (1995). Contributions of changing gender differences in behavior and social roles to changing gender differences in mortality. In D. Sabo & D. F. Gordon (Eds.), *Men's health and illness: Gender, power, and the body* (pp. 22–45). Thousand Oaks, CA: Sage.

Waldron, I. (1997). Changing gender roles and gender differences in health behavior. In D. S. Gochman (Ed.), *Handbook of health behavior research I: Personal and social determinants* (pp. 303–328). New York, NY: Plenum Press.

Waldron, I. (2008). Gender differences in mortality: Causes and variation in different societies. In P. Conrad (Ed.), *The sociology of health and illness: Critical perspectives* (pp. 38–55). New York, NY: Worth.

Waldron, I., & Johnston, S. (1976). Why do women live longer than men? Part II. *Journal of Human Stress*, 2(2), 19–30.

Walker, S. N., Volkan, K., Sechrist, K. R., & Pender, N. J. (1988). Health promoting life-styles of older adults: Comparisons with young and middle-aged adults, correlates and patterns. *Advances in Nursing Science*, 11, 76–90.

Wallace, R. B., Lynch, C. F., Pomehn, P. R., Criqui, M. H., & Heiss, G. (1981). Alcohol and hypertension: Epidemiologic and experimental considerations. *Circulation*, 64(Suppl. III), 41–47.

Wallace, S., Klein-Saffran, J., Gaes, G., & Moritsugu, K. (1991). Health status of federal inmates: A comparison of admission and release medical records. *Journal of Prison & Jail Health*, 10(2), 133–151.

Wallack, L., Breed, W., & Cruz, J. (1987). Alcohol on prime-time television. *Journal of Studies on Alcohol*, 48(1), 33–38.

Wallen, J., Waitzkin, H., & Stoeckle, J. D. (1979). Physician stereotypes about female health and illness: A study of patients' sex and the information process during medical interviews. *Women and Health*, 4(2), 135–146.

Wallner, B., & Machatschke, I. H. (2009). The evolution of violence in men: The function of central cholesterol and serotonin. *Progress in neuro-psychopharmacology and biological psychiatry*, 33(3), 391–397.

Walsh, J. M., & Grady, D. (1995). Treatment of hyperlipidemia in women. *Journal of the American Medical Association*, 274(14), 1152–1158.

Walton, M. A., Chermack, S. T., Shope, J. T., Bingham, C. R., Zimmerman, M. A., Blow, F. C., & Cunningham, R. M. (2010). Effects of a brief intervention for reducing violence and alcohol misuse among adolescents: A randomized controlled trial. *Journal of the American Medical Association, 304*(5), 527–535.

Wang, X. Q., Terry, P. D., & Yan, H. (2009). Review of salt consumption and stomach cancer risk: Epidemiological and biological evidence. *World Journal of Gastroenterology, 15*(18), 2204–2213.

Wang, W., Wu, Y. X., Peng, Z. G., Lu, S. W., Yu, L., Wang, G. P., … Wang, Y. H. (2000). Test of sensation seeking in a Chinese sample. *Personality and Individual Differences, 28*(1), 168–169.

Warburton, D. E., Nicol, C. W., & Bredin, S. S. (2006). Health benefits of physical activity: The evidence. *Canadian Medical Association Journal, 174*(6), 801–809.

Ward, K. D., Vander Weg, M. W., Read, M. C., Sell, M. A., & Beech, B. M. (2005). Testicular cancer awareness and self-examination among adolescent males in a community-based youth organization. *Preventive Medicine, 41*(2), 386–398.

Wardle, J., Haase, A. M., Steptoe, A., Nillapun, M., Jonwutiwes, K., & Bellisie, F. (2004). Gender differences in food choice: The contribution of health beliefs and dieting. *Annals of Behavioral Medicine, 27*(2), 107–116.

Wareham, N. J., & Rennie, K. L. (1998). The assessment of physical activity in individuals and populations: Why try to be more precise about how physical activity is assessed? *International Journal of Obesity, 22*(Suppl. 2), S30–S38.

Warner, M., Smith, J. S., & Langley, J. D. (2008). Drowning and alcohol in New Zealand: What do the coroner's files tell us? *Australian and New Zealand Journal of Public Health, 24*(4), 387–390.

Warr, M. (1984). Fear of victimization: Why are women and the elderly more afraid? *Social Science Quarterly, 65*(3), 681–702.

Warr, P. B., & Parry, G. (1982). Paid employment and women's psychological well being. *Psychological Bulletin, 91*, 498–516.

Warren, L. W. (1983). Male intolerance of depression: A review with implications for psychotherapy. *Clinical Psychology Review, 3*, 147–156.

Warren, T. Y., Barry, V., Hooker, S. P., Sui, X., Church, T. S., & Blair, S. N. (2010). Sedentary behaviors increase risk of cardiovascular disease mortality in men. *Medicine and Science in Sports and Exercise, 42*(5), 879–885.

Watson, J. (2000). *Male bodies: Health, culture, and identity.* Buckingham, England: Open University Press.

Wauchope, B. A., & Straus, M. A. (1987, July). Age, gender, and class differences in physical punishment and physical abuse of American children. Paper presented at the Annual Meeting of the National Conference on Family Violence Research, Durham, NH.

Wauquier, A., Van Sweden, B., Lagaay, A. M., Kemp, B., & Kamphuisen, H. A. (1992). Ambulatory monitoring of sleep-wakefulness patterns in healthy elderly males and females (greater than 88 years): The "Senieur" protocol. *Journal of the American Geriatrics Society, 40*(2), 109–114.

Weber, E. U. (2002). A domain-specific risk-attitude scale: Measuring risk perceptions and risk behaviors. *Journal of Behavioral Decision Making, 15*, 263–290.

Wechsler, H., Davenport, A. E., Dowdall, G. W., Grossman, S. J., & Zanakos, S. I. (1997). Binge drinking, tobacco, and illicit drug use and involvement in college athletics: A survey of students at 140 American colleges. *Journal of American College Health, 45*, 195–200.

Wechsler, H., Davenport, A. E., Dowdall, G. W., Moyekens, B., & Castillo, S. (1994). Health and behavioral consequences of binge drinking in college: A national survey of students at 140 campuses. *Journal of the American Medical Association, 272*(21), 1672–1677.

Wechsler, H., Lee, J. E., Kuo, M., & Lee, H. (2000). College binge drinking in the 1990s: A continuing problem: Results of the Harvard School of Public Health 1999 College Alcohol Study. *Journal of American College Health, 48*(5), 199–210.

Wechsler, H., Lee, J. E., Kuo, M., Seibring, M., Nelson, T. F., & Lee, H. (2002). Trends in college binge drinking during a period of increased prevention efforts. Findings from 4 Harvard School of Public Health College Alcohol Study surveys: 1993–2001. *Journal of American College Health, 50*(5), 203–217.

Wechsler, H., Lee, J. E., Nelson, T. F., & Kuo, M. (2002). Underage college students' drinking behavior, access to alcohol, and the influence of deterrence policies: Findings from the Harvard School of Public Health College Alcohol Study. *Journal of American College Health, 50*(5), 223–236.

Wechsler, H., Lee, J. E., Nelson, T. F., & Lee, H. (2003). Drinking and driving among college students: The influence of alcohol-control policies. *American Journal of Preventive Medicine, 25*(3), 212–218.

Wechsler, H., Rigotti, N. A., Gledhill-Hoyt, J., & Lee, H. (1998). Increased levels of cigarette use among college students: A cause for national concern. *Journal of the American Medical Association, 280*(19), 1673–1678.

Weed, D. L. (2010). Meta-analysis and causal inference: A case study of benzene and non-Hodgkin lymphoma. *Annals of Epidemiology, 20*(5), 347–355.

Wei, M., Kampert, J. B., Barlow, C. E., Nichaman, M. Z., Gibbons, L. W., Paffenbarger, R. S., & Blair, S. N. (1999). Relationship between low cardiorespiratory fitness and mortality in normal-weight, overweight, and obese men. *Journal of the American Medical Association, 282*(16), 1547–1553.

Weidner, G. (2000). Why do men get more heart disease than women? An international perspective. *Journal of American College Health, 48*(6), 291–294.

Weidner, G., Boughal, T., Connor, S. L., Pieper, C., & Mendell, N. R. (1997). The relationship of job strain to standard coronary risk factors in women and men of the Family Heart Study. *Health Psychology, 16*, 239–247.

Weidner, G., & Cain, V. S. (2003). The gender gap in heart disease: Lessons from Eastern Europe. *American Journal of Public Health, 93*(5), 768–770.

Weidner, G., & Collins, R. L. (1993). Gender, coping, and health. In H. W. Krohne (Ed.), *Attention and avoidance* (pp. 241–265). Seattle, WA: Hogrefe and Huber.

Weidner, G., Kopp, M., & Kristenson, M. (Eds.). (2002). *Heart disease: Environment, stress, and gender* (NATO Science Series, Series I: Life and Behavioural Sciences, Vol. 327). Amsterdam, the Netherlands: IOS Press.

Weidner, G., & Messina, C. R. (1998). Cardiovascular reactivity to mental stress and cardiovascular disease. In K. Orth-Gomer, M. A. Chesney, & N. Wenger (Eds.), *Women, stress, and heart disease* (pp. 219–236). Hillsdale, NJ: Erlbaum.

Weiler, R. M. (1997). Adolescents' perceptions of health concerns: An exploratory study among rural Midwestern youth. *Health Education and Behavior, 24*(3), 287–299.

Weinke, C. (1998). Negotiating the male body: Men, masculinity, and cultural ideals. *Journal of Men's Studies, 6*, 255–282.

Weinstein, N. D. (1987). Unrealistic optimism about illness susceptibility: Conclusions from a community-wide sample. *Journal of Behavioral Medicine, 10*(5), 481–500.

Weinstock, M. A. (2006). Progress and prospects on melanoma: The way forward for early detection and reduced mortality. *Clinical Cancer Research, 12*(Suppl. 7), 2297–2300.

Weinstock, H., Berman, S., & Cates, W. (2004). Sexually transmitted diseases among American youth: Incidence and prevalence estimates, 2000. *Perspectives on Sexual and Reproductive Health, 36*(1), 6–10.

Weinstock, M. A., Martin, R. A., Risica, P. M., Berwick, M., Lasater, T., Rakowski, W., … Dube, C. E. (1999). Thorough skin examination for the early detection of melanoma. *American Journal of Preventive Medicine, 17*(3), 169–175.

Weinstock, M. A., Risica, P. M., Martin, R. A., Rakowski, W., Smith, K. J., Berwick, M., … Lasater, T. (2004). Reliability of assessment and circumstances of performance of thorough skin self-examination for the early detection of melanoma in the Check-It-Out Project. *Preventive Medicine, 38*(6), 761–765.

Weinstock, M. A., Rossi, J. S., Redding, C. A., Maddock, J. E., & Cottrill, S. D. (2000). Sun protection behaviors and stages of change for the primary prevention of skin cancers among beachgoers in Southeastern New England. *Annals of Behavioral Medicine, 22*(4), 286–293.

Weisbuch, J. B. (1991). The new responsibility for prison health: Working with the public health community. *Journal of Prison & Jail Health, 10*(1), 3–18.

Weisman, C. S., & Teitelbaum, M. A. (1989). Women and health care communication. *Patient Education and Counseling, 13*, 183–199.

Weiss, G. L., & Larson, D. L. (1990). Health value, health locus of control, and the prediction of health protective behaviors. *Social Behavior and Personality, 18*, 121–136.

Weiss, G. L., Larsen, D. L., & Baker, W. K. (1996). The development of health protective behaviors among college students. *Journal of Behavioral Medicine, 19*(2), 143–161.

Weissfeld, J. L., Kirscht, J. P., & Brock, B. M. (1990). Health beliefs in a population: The Michigan Blood Pressure Survey. *Health Education Quarterly, 17*(2), 141–155.

Weissman, M. M., & Klerman, G. L. (1977). Sex differences and the epidemiology of depression. *Archives of General Psychiatry, 34*, 98–111.

Wells, K. B., Lewis, C. E., Leake, B., & Ware, J. E. (1984). Do physicians preach what they practice? A study of physicians' health habits and counseling practices. *Journal of the American Medical Association, 252*(20), 2846–2848.

Wells, K. B., Manning, W. G., Duan, H., Newhouse, J. P., & Ware, J. E. (1986). Sociodemographic factors and the use of outpatient mental health services. *Medical Care, 24*(1), 75–85.

Wells, S., Graham, K., Speechley, M., & Koval, J. (2005). Drinking patterns, drinking contexts, and alcohol-related aggression among late adolescent and young adult drinkers. *Addiction, 100*(7), 933–944.

Wendel-Vos, G. C., Schuit, A. J., Feskens, E. J., Boshuizen, H. C., Verschuren, W. M., Saris, W. H., & Kromhout, D. (2004). Physical activity and stroke: A meta-analysis of observational data. *International Journal of Epidemiology, 33*, 787–798.

Wenger, N. K. (1994). Coronary heart disease in women: Gender differences in diagnostic evaluation. *Journal of the American Medical Women's Association, 49*, 181–185.

Wenner, L. A., & Jackson, S. J. (Eds.). (2009). *Sport, beer, and gender: Promotional culture and contemporary social life.* New York, NY: Peter Lang.

Wesley, P. H. (1992). Gender patterns in consequences of collegiate alcohol abuse: A 10-year study of trends in an undergraduate population. *Journal of Studies on Alcohol, 53*(5), 458–462.

West, C., & Zimmerman, D. H. (1987). Doing gender. *Gender and Society, 1*(2), 125–151.

Wetter, D. W., Kenford, S. L., Welsch, S. K., Smith, S. S., Fouladi, R. T., Fiore, M. C., & Baker, T. B. (2004). Prevalence and predictors of transitions in smoking behavior among college students. *Health Psychology, 23*(2), 168–177.

Whitaker, L. C. (1987). Macho and morbidity: The emotional need vs. fear dilemma in men. *Journal of College Student Psychotherapy, 1*(4), 33–47.

White, A., & Cash, K. (2003). *A report on the state of men's health across 17 European countries.* Brussels, Belgium: The European Men's Health Forum.

White, A. A., & Klimis-Tavantzis, D. J. (1992). Dietary risk assessment for cardiovascular disease among central Maine adolescents. *Journal of School Health, 62*(9), 428–432.

White, P. G., Young, K., & McTeer, W. G. (1995). Sport, masculinity, and the injured body. In D. Sabo & D. F. Gordon (Eds.), *Men's health and illness: Gender, power, and the body* (pp. 158–282). Thousand Oaks, CA: Sage.

Whitfield, K. E., Weidner, G., Clark, R., & Anderson, N. B. (2002). Sociodemographic diversity and behavioral medicine. *Journal of Consulting and Clinical Psychology, 70*(3), 463–481.

Whittemore, A. S., Kolonel, L. N., Wu, A. H., John, E. M., Gallagher, R. P., Howe, G. R., … Paffenbarger, R. S. (1995). Prostate cancer in relation to diet, physical activity, and body size in Blacks, Whites, and Asians in the United States and Canada. *Journal of the National Cancer Institute, 87*(9), 652–661.

Whitt-Glover, M. C., Taylor, W. C., Floyd, M. F., Yore, M. M., Yancey, A. K., & Matthews, C. E. (2009). Disparities in physical activity and sedentary behaviors among U.S. children and adolescents: Prevalence, correlates, and intervention implications. *Journal of Public Health Policy, 30*(Suppl. 1), S309–S334.

Wiesenfeld-Hallin, Z. (2005). Sex differences in pain perception. *Gender Medicine, 2*(3), 137–145.

Wiley, D. C., James, G., Jordan-Belver, G., Furney, S., Calsbeek, F., Benjamin, J., & Kathcart, T. (1996). Assessing the health behaviors of Texas college students. *Journal of American College Health, 44*(4), 167–172.

Wiley, J. A., & Camacho, T. C. (1980). Life-style and future health: Evidence from the Alameda County Study. *Preventive Medicine, 9*, 1–21.

Wilkins, C. H., Shelin, Y. I., Roe, C. M., Birge, S. J., & Morris, J. C. (2006). Vitamin D deficiency is associated with low mood and worse cognitive performance in older adults. *American Journal of Geriatric Psychiatry, 14*(12), 1032–1040.

Willcox, B. J., He, Q., Chen, R., Yano, K., Masaki, K. H., Grove, J. S., … Curb, J. D. (2006). Midlife risk factors and healthy survival in men. *Journal of the American Medical Association, 296*, 2343–2350.

Willems, J. P., Saunders, J. T., Hunt, D. E., & Schorling, J. B. (1997). Prevalence of coronary heart disease risk factors among rural Blacks: A community-based study. *Southern Medical Journal, 90*(8), 814–820.

Willi, C., Bodenmann, P., Ghali, W. A., Faris, P. D., & Cornuz, J. (2007). Active smoking and the risk of type 2 diabetes: A systematic review and meta-analysis. *Journal of the American Medical Association, 298*(22), 2654–2664.

Williams, D. E., Cadwell, B. L., Cheng, Y. J., Cowie, C. C., Gregg, E. W., Geiss, L. S., … Imperatore, G. (2005). Prevalence of impaired fasting glucose and its relationship with cardiovascular disease risk factors in US adolescents, 1999–2000. *Pediatrics, 116*(5), 1122–1126.

Williams, D. G. (1985). Gender, masculinity-femininity, and emotional intimacy in same-sex friendship. *Sex Roles, 12*(5/6), 587–600.

Williams, D. R. (1999). Race, socioeconomic status, and health: The added effects of racism and discrimination. *Annals of the New York Academy of Sciences, 896*, 173–188.

Williams, D. R. (2003). The health of men: Structured inequalities and opportunities. *American Journal of Public Health, 93*(5), 724–731.

Williams, E. L., Winkleby, M. A., & Fortmann, S. P. (1993). Changes in coronary heart disease risk factors in the 1980s: Evidence of a male-female crossover effect with age. *American Journal of Epidemiology, 137*(10), 1056–1067.

Williams, J. E., & Best, D. L. (1990). *Measuring sex stereotypes: A multination study.* Thousand Oaks, CA: Sage.

Williams, J. K., Adams, M. R., Herrington, D. M., & Clarkson, T. B. (1992). Short-term administration of estrogen and vascular responses of atherosclerotic coronary arteries. *Journal of the American College of Cardiology, 20*, 452–457.

Williams, J. K., Adams, M. R., & Klopfenstein, H. S. (1990). Estrogen modulates responses of atherosclerotic coronary arteries. *Circulation, 81*, 1680–1687.

Williams, R., Barefoot, J. C., Califf, R. M., Haney, T. L., Saunders, W. B., Pryor, D. B., … Mark, D. B. (1992). Prognostic importance of social and economic resources among medically treated patients with angiographically documented coronary artery disease. *Journal of the American Medical Association, 267*(4), 520–524.

Williamson, C. S., Foster, R. K., Stanner, S. A., & Buttriss, J. L. (2004). Red meat in the diet. *British Nutrition Foundation Nutrition Bulletin, 30*, 323–355.

Willich, S. N., Lewis, M., Lowed H., Rants H. R., Stubbier. F., & Schroder, R. (1993). Physical exertion as a trigger of acute myocardial infarction. *New England Journal of Medicine, 329*(23), 1684–1690.

Willits, F. K., Bealer, R. C., & Timbers, V. L. (1990). Popular images of 'rurality': Data from a Pennsylvania survey. *Rural Sociology, 55*(4), 559–578.

Wills, T. A., & DePaulo, B. M. (1991). Interpersonal analysis of the help seeking process. In C. R. Snyder & D. R. Forsyth (Eds.), *Handbook of social and clinical psychology* (pp. 350–375). Elmsford, NY: Pergamon.

Wilper, A. P., Woolhandler, S., Boyd, W., Lasser, K. E., McCormick, D., Bor, D. H., & Himmelstein, D. U. (2009). The health and health care of U.S. prisoners: Results of a nationwide survey. *American Journal of Public Health, 99*(4), 666–672.

Wilsnack, R., Kristjanson, A., Wilsnack, S., & Crosby, R. D. (2006). Are U.S. women drinking less (or more)? Historical and aging trends, 1981–2001. *Journal of Studies on Alcohol and Drugs, 67*(3), 341–348.

Wilson, R. W., & Elinson, J. (1981). National survey of personal health practices and consequences: Background, conceptual issues, and selected findings. *Public Health Reports, 96*(3), 218–225.

Winawer, S. J. (1993). Colorectal cancer screening comes of age. *Journal of the American Medical Association, 328*(19), 1416–1417.

Winawer, S. J., & Shike, M. (1995). *Cancer free: The comprehensive cancer prevention program.* New York, NY: Simon & Schuster.

Wingard, D. L. (1984). The sex differential in morbidity, mortality, and lifestyle. *Annual Review of Public Health, 5,* 433–458.

Wingard, D. L., Cohn, M. A., Kaplan, G. A., Cirillo, P. M., & Cohen, R. D. (1989). Sex differentials in morbidity and mortality risks examined by age and cause in the same cohort. *American Journal of Epidemiology, 1380*(3), 601–610.

Winslade, W. J. (1998). *Confronting traumatic brain injury: Devastation, hope, and healing.* New Haven, CT: Yale University Press.

Wintemute, G. J., Parham, C. A., Beaumont, J. J., Wright, M., & Drake, C. (1999). Mortality among recent purchasers of handguns. *New England Journal of Medicine, 341*(21), 1583–1589.

Wise, D. A., Crooks, C. V., Lee, V., McIntyre-Smith, A., & Jaffe, P. G. (2002). Gender role expectations of pain: Relationship to experimental pain perception. *Pain, 96*(3), 335–342.

Wise, E., Price, D., Myers, C., Heft, M., & Robinson, M. (2002). Gender role expectations of pain: Relationship to experimental pain perception. *Pain, 96,* 335–342.

Wolf, D. A., Crooks, C. V., Lee, V., McIntyre-Smith, A., & Jaffe, P. G. (2003). The effects of children's exposure to domestic violence: A meta-analysis and critique. *Clinical Child and Family Psychology Review, (6)*3, 171–187.

Wolf, P. A., Kannel, W. B., & Verter, J. (1983). Current status of risk factors for stroke. *Neurotic Clinics, 1,* 317–343.

Wolfe, D. A., Crooks, C. V., Lee, V., McIntyre-Smith, A., & Jaffe, P. G. (2003). The effects of children's exposure to domestic violence: A meta-analysis and critique. *Clinical Child and Family Psychology Review, 6*(3), 171–187.

Wolfe, P., & Brandt, R. (1998). What do we know from brain research? *Educational Leadership, 56*(3), 8–13.

Woloshin, S., Schwartz, L. M., & Welch, H. G. (2008). The risk of death by age, sex, and smoking status in the United States: Putting health risks in context. *Journal of the National Cancer Institute, 100*(12), 845–853.

Wong, M. D., Chung, A. K., Boscardin, J. W., Li, M., Hsieh, H., Ettner, S. L., & Shapiro, M. F. (2006). The contribution of specific causes of death to sex differences in mortality. *Public Health Reports, 121*(6), 746–754.

Woolf, S. H., Jonas, S., & Lawrence, R. S. (Eds.). (1996a). *Health promotion and disease prevention in clinical practice.* Baltimore, MD: Williams & Wilkins.

World Health Organization. (2001a). *Mental health: A call for action by world health ministers.* Geneva, Switzerland: Author.

World Health Organization. (2001b). *Small arms and global health: WHO contribution to the UN Conference on Illicit Trade in Small Arms and Light Weapons, July 9–20, 2001.* Geneva, Switzerland: Author.

World Health Organization. (2002). *The world health report 2002: Reducing risks, promoting healthy life.* Geneva, Switzerland: Author.

World Health Organization. (2006). *WHO policy briefing: Interpersonal violence and alcohol.* Geneva, Switzerland: Author.

Worth, K. A., Dal Cin, S., & Sargent, J. D. (2006). Prevalence of smoking among major movie characters: 1996-2004. *Tobacco Control: An International Journal, 15*(6), 442–446.

Wu, X. C., Chen, V. W., Steele, B., Ruiz, B., Fulton, J., Liu, L., … Greenlee, R. (2001). Sub-site specific incidence rate and stage of disease in colorectal cancer by race, gender, and age group in the United States, 1992–1997. *Cancer, 92*(10), 2547–2554.

Wu, P., Hoven, C. W., Bird, H. R., Cohen, P., Liu, X., Moore, R. E., … Bird, H. R. (2001). Factors associated with use of mental health services for depression by children and adolescents. *Psychiatric Services, 52*(2), 189–195.

Wyant, B. R., & Taylor, R. B. (2007). Size of household firearm collections: Implications for subcultures and gender. *Criminology, 45*(3), 519–544.

Wyke, S., Hunt, K., & Ford, G. (1998). Gender differences in consulting a general practitioner for common symptoms of minor illness. *Social Science & Medicine, 46*(7), 901–906.

Xiang, H., Kelleher, K., Shields, B., Brown, K. J., & Smith, G.A. (2005). Skiing- and snowboarding-related injuries treated in U.S. emergency departments, 2002. *Journal of Trauma: Injury, Infection, and Critical Care, 58*(1), 112–118.

Xu, F., Sternberg, M. R., Kottiri, B. J., McQuillan, G. M., Lee, F. K., Nahmias, A. J., … Markowitz, L. E. (2006). Trends in herpes simplex virus type 1 and type 2 seroprevalence in the United States. *Journal of the American Medical Association, 296*(8), 964–973.

Yaggi, H. K., Concato, J., Kernan, W. N., Lichtman, J. H., Brass, L. M., & Mohsenin, V. (2005). Obstructive sleep apnea as a risk factor for stroke and death. *New England Journal of Medicine, 353*(19), 2034–2041.

Yan, A. F., Zhang, G., Wang, M., Stoesen, C. A., & Harris, B. M. (2009). Weight perception and weight control practice in a multiethnic sample of US adolescents. *Southern Medical Journal, 102*(4), 354–360.

Yang, S., Leff, M. G., McTague, D., Horvath, K. A., Jackson-Thompson, J., Murayi, T., … Angulo, F. J. (1998). Multistate surveillance for food-handling, preparation, and consumption behaviors associated with foodborne diseases: 1995 and 1996 BRFSS food-safety questions. *Morbidity and Mortality Weekly Report, 47*(4), 33–57.

Yeazel, M. W., Oeffinger, K. C., Gurney, J. G., Mertens, A. C., Hudson, M. M., Emmons, K. M., … Robison, L. L. (2004). The cancer screening practices of adult survivors of childhood cancer: A report from the Childhood Cancer Survivor Study. *Cancer, 100*(3), 631–640.

Yesalis, C. E., & Bahrke, M. S. (2005). Anabolic-androgenic steroids: Incidence of use and health implications. In C. B. Corbin, R. P. Pangrazi, & D. Young (Eds.), *Research digest* (Vol. 5, no. 5, pp. 1–8). Washington, DC: President's Council on Physical Fitness and Sports.

Young, T., Finn, L., Peppard, P. E., Szklo-Coxe, M., Austin, D., Nieto, J., ... Hla, K. M. (2008). Sleep disordered breathing and mortality: Eighteen-year follow-up of the Wisconsin Sleep Cohort. *Sleep, 31*(8), 1071–1078.

Young, T., Palta, M., Dempsey, J., Skatrud, J., Weber, S., & Badr, S. (1993). The occurrence of sleep-disordered breathing among middle-aged adults. *New England Journal of Medicine, 328*(17), 1230–1235.

Youngstedt, S. D. (2005). Effects of exercise on sleep. *Clinical Sports Medicine, 24*(2), 355–365.

Yusuf, S., Dagenais, G., Pogue, J., Bosch, J., & Sleight, P. (2000). Vitamin E supplementation and cardiovascular events in high-risk patients. *New England Journal of Medicine, 342*(3):154–160.

Yusuf, S., Hawken, S., Ounpuu, S., Dans, T., Avezum, A., Lanas, F., ... Lisheng, L. (2004). Effect of potentially modifiable risk factors associated with myocardial infarction in 52 countries (the INTERHEART study): Case-control study. *Lancet, 364,* 937–952.

Zador, P., Krawchuk, S., & Voas, R. (2000). Alcohol-related relative risk of driver fatalities and driver involvement in fatal crashes in relation to driver age and gender. *Journal of Studies on Alcohol, 61*(3), 387–395.

Zautra, A. J., Burleson, M. H., Matt, K. S., Roth, S., & Burrows, L. (1994). Interpersonal stress, depression, and disease activity in rheumatoid arthritis and osteoarthritis patients. *Health Psychology, 13,* 139–148.

Zaza, S., Briss, P. A., Harris, K. W., & Task Force on Community Preventive Services. (2005). Motor vehicle occupant injury. *The guide to community preventive services: What works to promote health?* (pp. 329–384). New York, NY: Oxford University Press.

Zazove, P., Caruthers, B. S., & Reed, B. D. (1991). Genital human papillomavirus infection. *American Family Physician, 43*(4), 1279–1290.

Zhang, Y., Lee, E. T., Devereux, R. B., Yeh, J., Best, L. G., Fabsitz, R. R., & Howard, B. V. (2006). Prehypertension, diabetes, and cardiovascular disease risk in a population-based sample: The Strong Heart Study. *Hypertension, 47*(3), 410–414.

Zilbergeld, B. (1992). *The new male sexuality.* New York, NY: Bantam.

Zimmer-Gembeck, M. J., & Helfand, M. (2008). Ten years of longitudinal research on U.S. adolescent sexual behavior: Developmental correlates of sexual intercourse, and the importance of age, gender and ethnic background. *Developmental Review, 28*(2), 153–224.

Zito, J. M., Safer, D. J., dosReis, S., Gardner, J. F., Boles, M., & Lynch, F. (2000). Trends in the prescribing of psychotropic medications to preschoolers. *Journal of the American Medical Association, 283*(8), 1025–1030.

Zucker, K. J., Wilson-Smith, D. N., Kurita, J. A., & Stern, A. (1995). Children's appraisals of sex-typed behavior in their peers. *Sex Roles, 33*(11/12), 703–725.

Zuckerman, D. M., Singer, D. G., & Singer, J. L. (1980). Children's television viewing, racial and sex-role attitudes. *Journal of Applied Social Psychology, 10*(4), 281–294.

Zuckerman, M. (1983). Sensation seeking and sports. *Personality and Individual Differences, 4*(3), 285–293.

Zuckerman, M. (1984). Sensation seeking: A comparative approach to a human trait. *The Behavioral and Brain Sciences, 7,* 413–471.

Zuckerman, M. (1994). *Behavioral expressions and biosocial bases of sensation seeking.* New York, NY: Cambridge University Press.

Zuckerman, M., & Kuhlman, M. D. (2000). Personality and risk taking: Common biosocial factors. *Journal of Personality, 68*(6), 1000–1029.

Zwerling, C., Merchant, J. A., Nordstrom, D. L., Stromquist, A. M., Burmeister, L. F., Reynolds, S. J., & Kelly, K. M. (2001). Risk factors for injury in rural Iowa: Round one of the Keokuk County Rural Health Study. *American Journal of Preventive Medicine, 20*(3), 230–233.

INDEX